The Cold War Encyclopedia

ALSO BY THOMAS PARRISH

The American Flag

The Simon and Schuster Encyclopedia of World War II

The American Codebreakers

Roosevelt and Marshall: Partners in Politics and War

To Make a Difference

The Cold War Encyclopedia

Thomas Parrish

A HENRY HOLT REFERENCE BOOK

Henry Holt and Company   New York

A Henry Holt Reference Book
Henry Holt and Company, Inc.
Publishers since 1866
115 West 18th Street
New York, New York 10011

Library of Congress Cataloging-in-Publication Data
Parrish, Thomas (Thomas D.)
The Cold War encyclopedia / Thomas Parrish.—1st ed.
    p.   cm.—(A Henry Holt reference book)
Includes index.
1. Cold War—Encyclopedias.   2. World politics—1945–
    —Encyclopedias.   I. Title.   II. Series.
D840.P28   1995   95-14082
909.82′5′03—dc20   CIP

ISBN 0-8050-2778-5

Henry Holt books are available for special
promotions and premiums. For details contact:
Director, Special Markets.

First Edition—1996

DESIGNED BY PAULA R. SZAFRANSKI

Printed in the United States of America
All first editions are printed on acid-free paper. ∞

1 3 5 7 9 10 8 6 4 2

Contents

Author's Preface

This book is written not simply for persons with a special interest in the Cold War but for general readers and students. It is intended to provide enjoyment as well as enlightenment and to reward both the browser and the person who comes to it seeking the answer to a specific question. It does not aspire to trace the history of the world since 1945, though obviously the course of Cold War history during the period overlaps considerably with that of world history as a whole. Many prominent persons and events do not appear here, because they do not fit even a generous test of Cold War relevance. And in the discussions of those who do receive attention (U.S. presidents, British prime ministers, for example), foreign affairs have the emphasis, with other issues appearing when they are pertinent or sometimes simply when they are of special interest. Hence, with one or two exceptions, such undeniably interesting areas as domestic politics in various countries, social trends and fashions, and novels and movies are necessarily excluded.

The entries are built up from documents; from quotations from persons involved in the events described; from anecdotes; from histories, biographies, and memoirs; from magazine and newspaper accounts; and from all the other sources that can help bring into being a thorough and at the same time appealing work of history. The entries tell not only what and when but, as far as seems possible, why actions were taken and events took place.

As a book designed to be read, *The Cold War Encyclopedia* is written in normal prose with normal spellings; abbreviations appear only to a very limited degree. To avoid endless and pointless repetition, I have often spoken of eminent figures (President Eisenhower, Marshal Stalin) simply by surname. As in my *Encyclopedia of World War II*, Russian names appear in their standard English spelling, if they have acquired one (e.g., Kiev); in general, Webster has served as the authority for the spelling of Russian and other proper names. I have also followed the practice of Harold Shukman, translator of Dmitri Volkogonov's biography of Stalin, who comments that "it is virtually impossible to transliterate all Russian names consistently, except by means of a variety of specialized annotations which would require their own glossary. It seems pedantic to insist on Aleksandr and Trotskii (or Trockij or Trotskiy) when Alexander and Trotsky are readily recognizable." Or, as Edward Crankshaw puts it, "It seems to be impossible to devise an entirely consistent system of transliteration from the Cyrillic to the Roman alphabet without introducing tiresome awkwardnesses and pedantries."

Regarding the Chinese, one must acknowledge the fact (however much one may deplore it) that the People's Republic has for some time now used the Pinyin system for transliterating names. For most names I give both the Pinyin and the previously established Wade-Giles versions (Mao Zedong, Mao Tse-tung), with the Pinyin serving as the basic reference. Chiang Kai-shek, however, appears in the older version; I believe he had no hand in the change to Pinyin, and, besides, what nonspecialist reader would recognize Jiang Jieshi?

As a work of reference, *The Cold War Encyclopedia* seeks to achieve fairness and balance. As I had occasion to do previously in a similar context, I quote the perhaps impossible standard established by Lord Acton for the *Cambridge Modern History*: "Our Waterloo must satisfy French and English, Germans and Dutch alike." For the Cold War, in particular, this represents a challenge perhaps even greater than that posed by Lord Acton's Napoleonic concerns. Nothing about the Cold War was precise and convenient except its ending. Unlike the great hot wars of the 20th century, it did not begin at a given moment with a pictorial scene: 1914's period piece featuring Uhlans with upraised lances riding onto the roads of Luxembourg, the tanks and Stukas of 1939 violating the land and air of Poland, aircraft from Japanese carriers assaulting penned-up U.S. battleships with bombs and torpedoes. But it certainly reached its true end in one of the most vivid moments in modern history, as Germans danced on top of the graffiti-covered cement-block wall that had divided their old capital for 28 years.

If a given subject does not appear here as the title of an entry, that does not mean that it has been overlooked. The reader should consult the index beginning on page 469 to find discussion of an unlisted subject; indeed, the index knits together the entire book and thus constitutes a vital part of it. Topics that do in fact have their own entries appear in small capitals on first mention in another entry. Since one of the most common uses of the *Encyclopedia* will be as a companion to reading, I describe a number of individual entities (military aircraft, for example) that have special importance or are often referred to by writers on the Cold War, even though not all members of such a category appear. Because the book has been written on the assumption that most readers will be far more familiar with Western persons, entities, and concepts than with those relating to the Soviet Union and its associated countries, the latter receive special attention. As a reader might expect, espionage and intelligence assume a prominent place in the book, reflecting their prominence in both the actuality and the literature of the Cold War; though any prudent writer dealing with these inherently murky matters will carefully avoid claiming to possess final and unassailable truth, I can say that the information presented here is the most accurate available.

The discussion that follows this preface, "The Cold War: Writers and Readers," is offered not so much as an introduction to this book as an introduction to the great amount and variety of writing that scholars, journalists, and political and military leaders have through the years produced about the Cold War—writing to which this book can serve as a companion and guide.

As always, I wish to express my admiration for reference librarians and photo archivists as a group and my gratitude to a number of them for their assistance, and I take particular pleasure in pointing out that the public is well served by the staffs of the United Nations and of the United States National Archives and the various presidential and other governmental libraries. I am also grateful to Judith N. Pugh, director of the Winston Churchill Memorial and Library at Westminster College, Fulton, Missouri, and her staff for their cooperation. Embassy staffs and other representatives of a number of countries also offered courteous and effective help. I thank Colonel Richard L. Uppstrom (retired), director of the U.S. Air Force Museum, for his assistance with photographs. I am grateful for the help of the Cold War International History Project of the Woodrow Wilson International Center for Scholars, although, of course, neither the center nor its director, Jim Hershberg, has any responsibility for any statements that appear in this book. I am grateful also to Scott Breckinridge for the loan of his manuscript on the CIA and for his helpful counsel on a number of points. Special thanks to Gyula Pauer for creating maps for the book.

Once again, I owe a special debt of gratitude to Professor George Herring of the University of Kentucky for reading the manuscript and offering constructive comments. And once again, I thank my agent, Stuart Krichevsky, for his many and invaluable services. I also acknowledge, with thanks, the contributions of three persons who helped me with research in certain areas: Professor Robert Brigham, of Vassar College; Professor Kyle Longley, of The Citadel; and Professor Nancy Coleman Wolsk, of Transylvania University.

The Cold War: Writers and Readers

The 45-year confrontation between East and West has produced many thousands of histories, biographies, analyses, and other works. Certain guideposts can help readers approach this great mass of material.

On June 5, 1947, during graduation ceremonies at Harvard University, U.S. secretary of state George C. Marshall delivered one of the most momentous speeches of the 20th century. Speaking quietly and undramatically, Marshall described the state of economic chaos and collapse in which Europe found itself two years after the end of the war against Germany and declared that the United States stood ready to provide its help "as far as it may be practical for us to do so." Whatever program was created, he said, "should be a joint one, agreed to by a number of if not all European nations."

Few observers could argue with Marshall's picture. Beyond Europe's economic plight, in fact, loomed clear signs of accompanying political and social collapse. To those who had studied the question, the need appeared not only compelling but urgent. Marshall's proposal, and the activities that grew out of it—generally summed up as the Marshall Plan—nevertheless evoked a variety of responses, depending not simply on the nationality of the person offering the comment but on such factors as background and intellectual status. For anyone setting out to read about or study the Cold War, a look at some of these responses can prove enlightening, not simply about the plan itself but about the great variety of attitudes that have been held concerning the Cold War—the profound and protracted confrontation between East and West that constituted the greatest series of connected actions and reactions, and thus the greatest overall phenomenon, in all of history, lasting for some 45 years and taking in the whole world.

Most Americans saw General Marshall's offer to help the Europeans as a great, unselfish, and unprecedented gesture by their country. But they feared that if it became a concrete program, it would bring higher taxes. The U.S. Congress—where altruism traditionally attracts few votes —did not automatically endorse the plan (many Republicans expressed their weariness and their wariness of "liberal give-aways," and members of both parties were fearful of pouring money down European "ratholes"; they wanted to cut spending, not increase it); President Harry S. Truman, Marshall, Undersecretary of State Dean Acheson, and other administration figures waged an intensive selling campaign on Capitol Hill, aided by a citizens' lobbying group. The senators and representatives did not appear to have any notion of welcoming the idea as an opportunity for the United States to better itself and extend its power in the world, though administration representatives attempted to build up the appeal of Marshall's proposal by pointing out the potential advantages it offered the donor country as well as the beneficiaries.

Across the Atlantic, Ernest Bevin, the British Labour foreign secretary, did not tarry to weigh possible American motives but quickly arranged for the French foreign minister to invite V. M. Molotov, the Soviet foreign minister, to a joint meeting in Paris. How had the Soviets reacted to what doubtful Americans saw as a great altruistic gesture? Though Marshall had declared in his speech that his proposal was "directed not against any country or doctrine but against hunger, poverty, despotism, and chaos," what might these fine words mean in practice? On June 16, after Joseph Stalin, the Soviet premier and general secretary, and his associates had mulled over the implications of the speech for a week and a half, the Communist Party newspaper *Pravda* denounced Marshall's proposal as merely a variation on the Truman Doctrine, a method of "using dollars for political pressure" and interfering in the internal affairs of other countries. But less than a week later the Soviet government announced that Molotov would lead a delegation to Paris to meet with the British and French foreign ministers to study the U.S. proposal; French Communist newspapers halted what had been their vociferous criticism of the Marshall proposal. When Molotov arrived in Paris on June 26 (only three weeks after Marshall's speech), he brought with him a large and varied group of experts that even included nutritional specialists. So it appeared Stalin had decided that the Marshall initiative at least deserved a hearing. Molotov made it clear, however, that the Kremlin wanted not a concerted European approach—as Marshall, the U.S. Congress, and the British and French governments all favored—but simply bilateral dealings, with the Soviets listing their needs and the Americans supplying them. The Kremlin did not get its way.

Thus ended, even before it had begun, Soviet participation in the Marshall Plan, and soon thereafter ended the participation of the countries in the Soviet sphere, several of which had originally expressed eagerness to take part. Though not yet behind the Iron Curtain, the Czechs, for example, reversed themselves after Stalin gave them an ultimatum to choose between East and West. As Stalin saw it, U.S. aid would come at too high a price—independent activity by the Eastern and Central European countries, which would weaken Soviet control over them and lead (in the words of Stalin's chief ideologue, Andrei Zhdanov) to "the enslavement of Europe." (Unbeknownst at the time to Western politicians or scholars, Stalin told the Czech delegation that, as one of the delegates remembered it, "the aim of Soviet policy was to get the Americans out of Europe and Asia.")

Many observers, of course, characterized the Marshall Plan simply as an anti-Communist program. The State Department planners, led by George Kennan, did in fact believe that the Communists were exploiting Europe's chaos for their own purposes, but at the same time they regarded economic recovery as an absolute necessity in itself; they seemed to look on Communism as, in a sense, merely a complicating factor. (A year later, in 1948, after the Communists took power in Prague—a coup that hastened congressional passage of the enabling legislation for the Marshall Plan—matters had changed considerably. A radio newscaster could now characterize the program simply as a "plan to fight Communism with dollars" without evoking much comment.)

Thus, in its practical working, the Marshall Plan accelerated the move toward European unity, and at the same time it in effect confirmed the division of Europe between East and West. How much of this result was intentional? How much of the motivation behind it was economic and how much political? The testimony of participants and political leaders and the observations of scholars have tended at times to differ considerably. In their memoirs and other writings, direct participants have, not altogether unnaturally, emphasized the influence and deeds of statesmen —that is, of themselves. Compared with scholars, the political leaders have traditionally tended to pay much less attention to trends and currents and hence sometimes have seemed to give events and situations less than their proper measure of complexity. A characteristically terse comment came from President Truman in March 1947: "The whole world should adopt the American system." General James Gavin declared that he and all his colleagues in the Pentagon "tended to see the world in terms of good guys and bad guys," with no one doubting "who the good guys were." (Though such a simple vision held much truth "when we faced the byzantine greed of Stalinism," Gavin went on to say, it encouraged a fallacious belief in monolithic world Communism.) No example can sum up the difference in attitudes better than a story Winston Churchill told about an exchange in the early 1930s with an Oxford student from Germany. Did Churchill, the student wanted to know, hold Germany responsible for causing the First World War? Churchill spent no time in reflective chin-rubbing concerning orthodox history, revisionism, economic factors, or any other intellectual considerations. "Yes, of course," he answered immediately. Insulted, the young man left the room. (Concluding the anecdote, Churchill said approvingly, "I thought him a spirited boy.")

In contrast, scholars writing about the Cold War (like those who write about most other subjects) tend to emphasize "forces" as explanations of events. No reader will be surprised to discover that these scholarly opinions come in a variety of forms. With reference to the Marshall Plan, H. G. Nicholas of Oxford University expresses one point of view in his judgment that by initiating the plan the United States "accepted her role and responsibilities as a creditor nation at the same time as she provided the sine qua non for restoring a European economy which could be both a rival and a counterpart to her own." To Thomas McCormick of the University of Wisconsin, however, the Marshall Plan and related activities serve as reminders that "throughout its five centuries, capitalism has been an inherently expansionistic type of economy"; economically, the United States pursued "hegemonic goals, awesomely global and omnipresent in nature." To Michael Hogan of Ohio State University, the Marshall Plan represented the product of an American "corporatist" vision, stemming from the "associationalism" of President Herbert Hoover and the "neocapitalism" that characterized President Roosevelt's New Deal; the Marshall Plan, he declares, set out to create a new Europe in the American image, but the attempt met with only limited success. Alan Milward of the London School of Economics advances the view—an unusual one—that the Marshall Plan possessed far less importance than everybody—"Cold War historians and 'revisionists' alike"—has ascribed to it. For Daniel Yergin of Harvard, the Marshall Plan "had two basic aims, which commingled and cannot really be separated—to halt a feared communist advance into Western Europe, and to stabilize an international economic environment favorable to capitalism." Almost immediately after Marshall launched his proposal, the official Soviet economist Yevgeny Varga told his superiors that "the Marshall Plan was meant primarily to be instrumental in resolving the imminent economic crisis, the approach of which no one in the USA denies." A later writer, the British journalist and historian Martin Walker, summed up matters by saying that "the Cold War was the strategic rationale behind the Marshall Plan." One other opinion perhaps deserves mention —that of the Nobel Prize Committee, which recognized the European Recovery Program by awarding General Marshall its 1953 Peace Prize, thus making him the only soldier ever to be so honored.

In general, historians writing in the earlier years agreed with the view of Western governments that Stalin's rejection of the Marshall Plan indicated the need for a defensive step against Soviet expansionism. Some years later, when revisionist accounts became prominent, historians such as William Appleman Williams and Gabriel Kolko explained the Marshall Plan and related policies as little else but aggressive American efforts to enhance the place of capitalism and thus as threats to the Soviet Union, which had no choice but to react defensively. Altogether, when we take a close look at the work of historians, we find, as Nicholas puts it, "interpretations to suit every ideological taste." (As a corollary to this point, a reader should be prepared for the occasional necessity to recognize what Leonard Schapiro of the London School of Economics calls "the fanatical conviction that there is one complete answer to all questions, past and future, if only it can be found.")

Western historical treatments of the Cold War as a whole fell—broadly speaking—into three phases that, though sometimes overlapping in time, nevertheless basically spoke for the periods in which they were written. First was the orthodox school, which prevailed until about 1960 (though outstanding orthodox history was still appearing in the 1970s); then came the work of the revisionists, who would have arrived on the scene in any case (since every generation reinterprets history) but took on special life in the United States, at least, because the general and bitter intellectual opposition to the U.S. involvement in Vietnam led a number of writers to take harsh views toward previous American activities—not only in the Cold War but much earlier. These points, however, by no means suggest that revisionism was unnecessary; it was, indeed, demanded by the passage of time itself and by the development of fresh intellectual conditions, such as the recognition of the divergence between the Soviet Union and China and the more open atmosphere that arose in the United States with the fading of McCarthyism.

WHERE THE COLD WAR TURNED HOT

Later came, inevitably, a school of synthesis-seeking postrevisionists—John Lewis Gaddis of Ohio University is an outstanding example—with lowered voices and more careful weighing of the evidence than had characterized some of the works produced during the preceding period. There also appeared, in Britain, a movement to demonstrate the importance of the British role in the beginning of the Cold War, with some scholars (Anne Deighton of Oxford, as one persuasive voice) assigning primacy to British diplomacy in the 1945–46 period. Until 1990, all these scholars labored under a severe handicap—they could work only the Western side of the street, since they had no access to Soviet archives. After the Cold War ended and limited Russian personal and archival sources began to become available, each of these schools had the opportunity to reexamine its contentions and revise or buttress them with fresh evidence, along with a chance to meet and exchange views with Russian scholars.

While the memoirs of the political leaders may often suffer from a shortened perspective, the writings of historians sometimes seem to foster such ideas as the belief that in a specific situation a political leader acts from a single and consciously held motive; a belief in conspiracies; and an implied view that a statesman ought to know exactly how an individual action is going to turn out. But as the historian and philosopher R. G. Collingwood pointed out some years ago in a discussion of Tacitus as a historian, "The extent to which people act with a clear idea of their ends, knowing what they are aiming at, is easily exaggerated. . . . Looking back over our actions, or over any stretch of past history, we see that something has taken shape as the actions went on which certainly was not present to our minds or to the mind of any one, when the actions which brought it into existence began." History, Collingwood even goes on to tell us, "cannot be scientifically written unless the historian can re-enact in his own mind the experience of the people whose actions he is narrating." This was where Tacitus failed as a historian; he saw his characters from outside, as "mere spectacles of virtue or vice."

"Scholars of [both] the so-called orthodox and new left persuasions basically described the developments that led to the breakdown of relations between Washington and Moscow after World War II as inevitable outgrowths of a historically preordained drama," wrote Hugh De Santis. These scholars "tended to explain these developments monistically: events were culturally, ideologically, or economically determined." But, as a diplomatic historian and former diplomat himself, De Santis felt that, in spite of its considerable value, the systems approach overlooked one vitally important element: the human factor. Collingwood would surely agree with him.

Perhaps, amid all the clashing points of view, Collingwood's observation can serve as a useful intellectual memento for anyone who sets out to read about the beginning, the course, and the meaning of the Cold War and to seek answers to such questions as: Was the Cold War inevitable? If it was not, how did it come about? What was the relationship between Communism and Russian nationalism? Can we say who "caused" the Cold War? What alternative courses could have been followed? What did the amazing events of 1989 in Eastern and Central Europe tell us about the nature of the Soviet bloc in earlier years? What can we learn from the overall experience of the Cold War?

In looking for answers to questions of this kind, we must constantly remind ourselves that what we see in the past tends to be shaped by what we know of the present. We know how the Cold War turned out; not a single one of the participants had access to such knowledge.

The historian Arthur Schlesinger, Jr., commented that "after seventy years of trial, communism turned out—by the confession of its own leaders—to be an economic, political, and moral disaster." Thus the ideological debate was over. But as the world began to realize during 1990 that the Cold War had actually come to its end—this great confrontation that had existed as a permanent fact of life for persons now middle-aged—only the naive were surprised to see that all of the world's international tensions and problems had not vanished with it. A full measure of other debates and differences remained—national, ethnic, religious, or simply political and strategic. Developments that came afterward lie beyond the scope of this book, but it seemed apparent that a more traditional pattern of international relations had returned, with all its varied possibilities for cooperation and conflict. "One would think history might take a rest," said the protagonist of Ivan Goncharov's 19th-century novel *Oblomov,* "but no, clouds gathered again, the edifice crashed down, and again the people had to toil and labor. . . . Life flows on; one crisis follows upon another." Oblomov, of course, was a pessimist, but he had his insights as well.

A-1E In the 1960s the U.S. Air Force brought back into service various piston-engine aircraft with special qualities that would make them useful in the kind of insurgent war being waged in Southeast Asia. The catalog of such airplanes included the single-engine, single-seat Douglas Skyraider, which had made its original appearance in 1945 and, in various versions as the navy's AD, saw considerable action during the KOREAN WAR, when it sometimes carried bombloads of 10,500 pounds —more than a World War II B-17 could deliver on the target. In 1963 the air force wanted the aircraft for close-support work in the VIETNAM WAR, to take advantage of its bomb-carrying capacity and its ability to operate at low altitudes. For its new assignment the navy's AD-5 was modified and redesignated the A-1E. The A-1E attained a maximum speed of 325 mph and had a range of 1,500 miles.

A-26 During World War II, some 2,500 Douglas A-26 Invaders saw service with the U.S. Army Air Forces as attack bombers, with much emphasis on harrying the enemy by strafing and rocket fire. This twin-engine piston aircraft had a maximum speed of about 370 mph and cruised at about 280 mph. When U.S. forces in the KOREAN WAR sought to harass North Korean supply activities, the A-26 was called on again (and given the confusing designation B-26, a designation earlier held by the Martin Marauder). Some years later, realizing the advantages subsonic aircraft offered in operations against insurgent forces in complex terrain, the air force brought out the A-26 again, with modifications, calling it first the B-26K and then the

A-26A. It carried up to 8,000 pounds of bombs underwing and internally.

Abel case One of the most famous of all Soviet KGB agents, Rudolf Abel (1902–1971) acquired his unsought notoriety by being caught in espionage, publicly tried, and convicted. As an "illegal"—an agent living in a foreign country with a false, carefully built-up identity—Abel enjoyed no diplomatic immunity. At various times he used the names Martin Collins, William Fisher, and Emil K. Goldfus. After a disaffected KGB operative described him to the Federal Bureau of Investigation, he was arrested in a Manhattan hotel in June 1957. His cover in the United States had been his work as a photographer in Brooklyn, while he actually held the rank of colonel in the KGB and, as post–World War II reorganizer of the Soviet spy network in the United States, controlled a number of agents in the field. Despite his eminence and daring, he displayed "retiring and cautious behavior" that struck Allen DULLES, director of the U.S. CENTRAL INTELLIGENCE AGENCY, as bearing little resemblance to the spying style of Ian Fleming's flamboyant fictional James Bond.

In 1962, eager to recover this important officer, the USSR agreed to an arrangement whereby Abel was traded to the United States for Francis Gary Powers, the U-2 pilot who had been shot down over the Soviet Union in 1960, together with two lesser-known young men, Frederic L. Pryor, a student from Yale whom the East German government had charged with espionage, and Marvin Makinen, a University of Pennsylvania student whom the Soviets had imprisoned for alleged espionage. Abel spent the latter years of his career sharing his highly specialized expertise with young KGB agents in training for assignment to the United States.

ABM   *See* ANTIBALLISTIC MISSILE.

A-Bomb   *See* ATOMIC BOMB.

Abrams, Creighton Williams, Jr. (1914–1974) During the World War II Battle of the Bulge, in December 1944, Creighton Abrams, then a U.S. Army lieutenant colonel, led the tank column that smashed its way into the besieged town of Bastogne and thus relieved the 101st Airborne Division. General George S. Patton once said of the young commander: "I'm supposed to be the best tank commander in the army. But I have one peer —Abe Abrams. He's the world champion."

A native of Springfield, Mass., Abrams was an eager if not gifted football player at West Point, class of 1936, and also was given to practical jokes. In 1940 he drew an assignment to the First Armored Division (literally the army's first) and began to acquire experience as a tank-company commander. During the U.S. fighting in Western Europe, Abrams served with the Fourth Armored Division, of which his 37th Tank Battalion was a component.

After the war Abrams held a variety of staff and command positions at home and in Europe and Korea. In October 1960 he was appointed commanding general of the Third Armored Division in West Germany. Back home in 1962 he held General Staff posts, culminating, in 1964, in that of vice chief of staff, with the rank of general. In 1967 he went to Vietnam as second in command of U.S. forces to General William C. WESTMORE-LAND, whom he succeeded in command in 1968, when the latter was eased out of the Vietnam command and brought back to Washington as army chief of staff. Abrams, who believed that the South Vietnamese should bear more of the military burden than had been the case previously, is credited with coining the term *Vietnamization,* which was employed prominently by President NIXON. Described in the press as the kind of soldier who let the "god-damns fall where they may," Abrams was also a serious student of war who gave careful

General Creighton W. Abrams, Jr., U.S. Vietnam commander and army chief of staff

and respectful study to the tactics and techniques employed by his opponents.

Appointed chief of staff of the army in 1972, Abrams took a realistic approach to the array of problems resulting from the disastrous venture in Vietnam, developing reforms to deal with racism, the high level of drug addiction, and the near collapse of morale. Fatally stricken with lung cancer, the general, who was widely respected in the army, gave his service a final gift by inducing the administration to increase its size by three divisions and to develop a new battle tank, which was named for him.

Acheson, Dean Gooderham (1893–1971)   As U.S. undersecretary of state from 1945 to the middle of

1947 and secretary from 1949 to 1953, Dean Acheson was not only "present at the Creation," as he described his State Department years—during which basic American policy was established for the Cold War—but played one of the two or three leading roles. His thinking and planning were central to the development of the TRUMAN DOCTRINE, the MARSHALL PLAN, and the NORTH ATLANTIC TREATY ORGANIZATION. The British correspondent Henry Brandon characterized Acheson as "a statesman in the grand manner, a leader with a strong will and a sharp mind."

The son of a clergyman who became Episcopal bishop of Connecticut, Acheson was a product of Groton and Yale (1915). After practicing law in Washington with the well-known firm then called Covington, Burling and Rublee, he joined the ROOSEVELT administration in May 1933 as undersecretary of the treasury, but just six months later he resigned over a disagreement with the president about monetary policy.

As was to be his pattern, he returned to his law firm, in which he now held a partnership, coming back to government in 1941 as assistant secretary of state—the position he held throughout World War II. From August 1945 until July 1947 he served as undersecretary of state, the number two position in the department.

In the six months of 1947 during which he worked closely with the new secretary of state, General George C. MARSHALL, Acheson acted as the coordinator and frequent inspirer of department policy; he was one of the original advocates of the aid to Greece and Turkey that became the policy labeled the Truman Doctrine, and also one of the principal originators of the ideas that went into the Marshall Plan.

After leaving the State Department in 1947, Acheson rejoined his law firm, but only until January 1949, when President TRUMAN appointed him secretary of state. As secretary, Acheson was the West's most influential creator of policy and took the lead in the development of the North Atlantic alliance and the establishment of the North Atlantic Treaty Organization. Although both as undersecretary and as secretary Acheson devoted his mind and energies to countering the generally perceived threat of Soviet expansionism, he became the particular target of right-wing (mostly Middle

U.S. secretary of state Dean Acheson *(l.)* with President Harry S. Truman

Western) Republican senators who, not content with accusing General Marshall of treason, assaulted Acheson in such extreme and inelegant terms as the following employed by William Jenner of Indiana: "This government of ours has been turned into a military dictatorship, run by Communist-appeasing, Communist-protecting betrayer of America, Secretary of State Dean Acheson." Senator Joseph MCCARTHY developed the habit of delivering an almost daily vilification of Acheson, having recognized that when the secretary stated his refusal to abandon the convicted perjurer Alger HISS—Hiss was an acquaintance—Acheson, in the atmosphere of 1950, was opening himself up to uninhibited assault as a lover of Communists. (Acheson's actual statement, following the announcement of the verdict, was the gentlemanly "I do not intend to turn my back on Alger Hiss.") A continuing conflict raged between the elegant, tailored Acheson and senators having the attitudes, if not the ideas, of populists. With persons like Jenner and McCarthy, or even lesser figures, Acheson could not or did not choose to control his particular character flaw, a tendency to condescend; such behavior, it has been widely noted, is particularly unwelcome on Capitol Hill.

On leaving government along with Truman in January 1953, Acheson once again went back to his old law firm, now known as Covington and Burling, where he remained until his death. He frequently interrupted his practice, however, to serve as an adviser to presidents or to conduct special presidential missions (as when he flew to Paris to seek President de Gaulle's support during the CUBAN MISSILE CRISIS). President JOHNSON, it has been said, shrewdly noticed that when asked for advice, Acheson always produced the same thought: strengthen NATO at all costs. Hence, when that was what Johnson wanted to hear, he knew whom to ask.

In his later years Acheson wrote several books and thereby revealed himself to be a fine prose stylist and one of the best memoirists in the language—"surpassed in modern times only by Winston Churchill," said the British weekly the *Economist*. His popular *Present at the Creation*, an account of the development of U.S. foreign policy in the late 1940s, won the 1970 Pulitzer Prize for history; in his earlier book, *Sketches from Life of Men I Have Known* (1961), Acheson combined insight, humor, and a gift for anecdote to produce an engaging and revealing group of word portraits of world leaders.

West German chancellor Konrad Adenauer

Acheson-Lilienthal Plan   *See* BARUCH PLAN.

Adenauer, Konrad (1876–1967)   One of the most important European leaders of the post–World War II era, Konrad Adenauer was the first chancellor and the chief builder of the FEDERAL REPUBLIC OF GERMANY (West Germany) and, having taken office when he was 73, came to occupy a special place as the German national patriarch. Seemingly ageless, with his immobile countenance, his prominent cheekbones, and narrow eyes, he looked to some observers as stoic as the stereotypical American Indian.

A native of Cologne, Adenauer studied law and political science and in 1906 won election to the Cologne City Council; in 1917, in the midst of World War I, he was elected lord mayor of the city.

In 1933, after Adolf Hitler came to power in Germany, the strongly anti-Nazi Adenauer was driven from office and even from the city; during the next years Nazi police harassed him and finally confined him in a concentration camp (he barely missed being sent on to an extermination camp). After the end of World War II, U.S. occupation authorities returned him to the mayor's office, but when British forces succeeded the Americans in Cologne, they—remarkably—accused Adenauer of incompetence and replaced him with a mayor of their own choosing.

Though 69 years old, with four decades in public life behind him, Adenauer gave little thought to retiring. A member of the prewar Catholic Center Party, he took the lead in forming a new, ecumenical alliance, the Christian Democratic Union, whose chairman he became in 1946. As the Western Allies moved toward the creation of West Germany, Adenauer presided over the founding constitutional commission and, on September 15, 1949, became (by one vote in Parliament) the first chancellor of the new nation.

In filling his difficult role as the leader of this new state risen from the ashes of the Third Reich, Adenauer—a conservative and a believer in individualism—cooperated closely with the Western Allies and supported the involvement of West Germany in the NORTH ATLANTIC TREATY ORGANIZATION, pursued an unwaveringly anti-Communist line, and labored tirelessly to bring about reconciliation between Germany and France. He also ordered full restitution to the Jewish victims of Nazism. Called *der Alte* (the Old Man), he seemed the incarnation of strength and time-honored values.

The major issue during Adenauer's era had to do with the kind of Germany that should exist—a country close to and allied with the West or one neutralized, tied neither to West nor to East. Adenauer's answer to the continuing question always came with clarity; during his time in office he succeeded in binding West Germany to its Western European neighbors by a web of treaties and memberships. In 1951, when the country established its own diplomatic relations with other countries, Adenauer himself took the portfolio of foreign minister, keeping it until 1955. In that year West Germany won full recognition as a sovereign state and was admitted to NATO. A believer in European unity, Adenauer in 1957 committed the country to this goal when it joined with five others to create the EUROPEAN ECONOMIC COMMUNITY (the Common Market).

Reelected federal chancellor in 1953, 1957, and 1961, Adenauer, like many other long-serving national leaders, saw the end of his political ascendancy approach even while he held power. In 1963, by previous agreement with a constituent party in his governing coalition, he resigned the chancellorship, having crowned his labors by signing a treaty of cooperation with France.

During the last months of his life, Adenauer worked on his memoirs. One day, concerning them, he made a characteristic remark: "There is no ghost in the house, because I want this book to be written by myself, whether it is good or bad." Described by the historian Hans W. Gatzke as "an uncomplicated person, a devout Catholic and a devoted family man," he could also be a subtle politician (with maneuvers, said one reporter, "that verged on prestidigitation"). Having spent many years of his career dealing with local questions, said the *New York Times* correspondent C. L. Sulzberger, Adenauer "managed to filter immensely intricate problems into a simplified pattern on which he based decisions, much as a burgomaster might plan a park. He was strong-willed and made up his mind definitively on the basis of what he believed right—plus what he considered feasible." Adenauer summed up his own ironic view of life in a favorite observation: "God made a great mistake to limit the intelligence of man but not his stupidity."

After *der Alte* died, an old pensioner in Bonn summed it all up: "God knows if everything would be the way it is if we hadn't had him."

Afghanistan, 1979 Soviet invasion In December 1979 a Soviet invasion of Afghanistan extinguished whatever fire remained in the ashes of Soviet-American DÉTENTE. The incursion by Moscow followed a chain of events that had begun with an April 1978 Afghan coup, in which a pro-Soviet party, led by Noor Mohammed Taraki, had overthrown the government of the republic and murdered President Mohammed Daoud and his entire family. After signing a treaty of friendship with the new government, the Soviet Union found itself having to prop up an exceedingly unpopular regime. This regime was overthrown in September 1979 by dissidents in its own ranks, who proceeded, in turn, to kill Taraki and his closest colleagues. After some deliberation, Moscow responded in December with an airlift of Soviet troops into Kabul. These arrivals, who professed to have been invited to Afghanistan by the new regime, then belied their own words by joining in the assassination game with the murder of Hafizullah Amin, the dissident leader who had overthrown Taraki, and installing a regime of their own choosing. What followed was a continuing guerrilla resistance by the Afghans that won the admiration of people around the world and earned the entire operation the name "Russia's Vietnam."

Soviet and American leaders, predictably enough, took opposite views of the Afghan adventure. Representatives of the CARTER administration saw it as a probable effort by the Soviets to extend their direct influence and presence into the Persian Gulf area, and therefore to threaten the existing strategic balance. Leonid BREZHNEV, president of the Soviet Union, claimed on the other hand to see the danger of Afghanistan's "transformation into a military platform for imperialism on the southern border of our country." Though this could not realistically have been regarded as a danger, it might have seemed so when the situation was viewed from the Kremlin; a more direct concern perhaps came from the possibility that a resurgence of Islamic fundamentalism in Afghanistan could have repercussions across the border among the Islamic peoples of the Soviet Union.

How much influence the slowly dying Brezhnev exerted on Soviet decisions remains a question. Overall, what seemed to be an endeavor to guarantee the existence of a pro-Soviet regime in Afghanistan backfired badly. The USSR found itself mired for ten years in an unpopular war. The United States reacted with a grain embargo, an OLYMPIC BOYCOTT, increased arms expenditures, and a general wave of anti-Soviet feeling. For the foreseeable future, anything resembling great-power détente was truly dead. "The worst disappointment to me personally," wrote President Carter, "was the loss of any chance for early ratification of the SALT II [arms limitation] treaty." Mikhail GORBACHEV finally managed to extricate the Soviet Union from the war in Afghanistan in 1989. *See also* PEOPLE'S DEMOCRATIC PARTY OF AFGHANISTAN.

AGITPROP *See* TASS.

AGM-28 U.S. jet-propelled, nuclear-tipped air-to-ground missile designed for use by B-52s. With its 500-mile range, it could be employed against a variety of enemy targets. The missile was popularly called the Hound Dog.

Agoniya Soviet film produced, but not released, in the 1970s that took on symbolic importance when it made its public appearance in 1985 during Mikhail GORBACHEV's first months in power. A portrayal of the final days of Czar Nicholas II, *Agoniya* had been banned apparently because it displayed some sympathy with the czar. Its release under Gorbachev suggested that a fresh outlook might have come to the Kremlin.

AirLand Battle A U.S. Army tactical doctrine developed during the early 1980s whereby aircraft and missiles—nuclear, chemically tipped, and conventional—would carry out deep strikes into enemy territory.

AJAX Code name given by the U.S. CENTRAL INTELLIGENCE AGENCY to operations in Iran in 1953 that led to the fall of the government of Premier MOHAMMED MOSSADEGH.

ALCM *See* CRUISE MISSILE.

Allende, Salvador (in full, Salvador Allende Gossens) (1908–1973) Chilean political figure elected president in 1970, after several earlier unsuccessful campaigns, at the head of a leftist alliance (though with only a 36 percent plurality), thereby becoming the first Marxist to win a Latin American presidential election. Financing his activities as president through seizure of foreign and domestic capital, Allende adopted an intensively socialistic program, nationalizing corporations and breaking up estates. Such an approach, by a Communist or a non-Communist, could hardly fail to arouse intense opposition on the part of the wealthier classes and the military, and, for their part, the expropriated U.S. companies encouraged the NIXON administration to adopt a hard line toward the leftist president. This was a particularly interesting development since Chile, because of its democratic tradition, had earlier been picked by the KENNEDY administration to receive the highest per capita amounts of economic aid under the ALLIANCE FOR PROGRESS program.

Allende had a friend in Cuba's Fidel CASTRO, however. Declaring that "Cuba in the Caribbean and a socialist Chile in the Southern Cone will make the revolution in Latin America," the Chilean president made his country available to Cuban intelligence as a base from which to support revolutionary movements in other Latin American countries. Commenting that Allende's international reputation "owed a good deal to overreaction in Washington," Christopher Andrew and Oleg Gordievsky pointed out in their book *KGB* that the CENTRAL INTELLIGENCE AGENCY, on White House instructions, spent eight million dollars seeking to prevent Allende's taking office and then to destabilize his regime, which was overthrown in September 1973 in a bloody military coup the CIA appears to have known about though not to have staged. Allende died in the fighting, probably by suicide, as reported by his personal physician in 1973 and as suggested by a viewing of the body in 1990. This episode made Allende a hero to the Soviets, who previously had held him in low esteem, and it also demonstrated the CIA's ability to attract unfavorable publicity. Whether or not the agency caused Allende's death, the belief that it did so was widespread and was fostered around the world by Soviet propagandists and the KGB. In perhaps the worst irony of the whole situation, the Chilean army, which out of respect for the constitution had declined to prevent Allende's taking office in 1970 and had staged the coup in 1973 in the name of the same constitution, then proceeded to install a harsh military dictatorship, the government of Augusto Pinochet.

Alliance for Progress   On March 13, 1961, the KENNEDY administration announced that the United States would commit more than $20 billion in grants over a ten-year period to promote Latin-American economic and social development, the underlying idea being that this Western Hemisphere adaptation of the MARSHALL PLAN would help create political stability in the volatile area. The Alliance for Progress, as the new program was called, actually built on programs established by the EISENHOWER administration in response to Vice President Richard M. Nixon's riot-harassed trip to the region in 1958 and also to the CASTRO revolution in Cuba. After Nixon had returned to the United States, according to Edwin Martin, later ambassador to Argentina, Eisenhower dispatched his brother Milton to South America to analyze the situation, and Milton Eisenhower's reports actually formed the basis of the Alliance for Progress. *See also* NIXON TRIP TO SOUTH AMERICA.

Except for the Cubans, most Latin Americans greeted the Alliance for Progress with enthusiasm, gathering at Punta del Este, Uruguay, in August 1961 to work on details of the plan. They agreed to encourage investment and to make a series of economic and social reforms. But the program encountered problems from the beginning—disagreements about jurisdiction, the autocratic nature of many of the governments involved—and the sought-for stability did not develop. Though Kennedy especially wished to strengthen the democratic governments, he served too short a time to be able to make much progress, despite giving strong support to such democratic leaders as Rómulo Betancourt of Venezuela and José Rivera of El Salvador. During the JOHNSON and Nixon administrations, the VIETNAM WAR crowded out many other concerns, including most of the efforts under the Alliance for Progress.

The plan received the name Alliance for Progress rather than Alliance for Development, according to a former State Department official, because Kennedy, who spoke no foreign language, had a "wooden tongue" when trying to pronounce foreign words; hence staff members decided that the president would find *Progreso* much easier to deal with than *Desarrollo*.

Alma-Ata   In December 1986 anti-Russian rioting broke out in this city, the capital of Kazakhstan, a Central Asian Soviet republic. The violence followed the replacement of the local Communist Party secretary by an ethnic Russian. What amazed observers, however, was not so much the rioting as the fact that it was reported in the Soviet press, since no news of this kind had been allowed to appear for more than 60 years. As time passed, such instances of GLASNOST would become commonplace, but in its early days, openness came as a shock to almost everybody.

Alma-Ata also became the city in which the GORBACHEV era came to its formal end when, on December 21, 1991, 11 former member republics of the Soviet Union, meeting in the Kazakh capital, joined together to create the COMMONWEALTH OF INDEPENDENT STATES.

Alpha Unit   An elite KGB group trained to carry out special missions, such as high-level kidnappings.

Ames case   On February 21, 1994, U.S. officials arrested Aldrich Ames (1941–   ), a veteran of 31 years with the CENTRAL INTELLIGENCE AGENCY, charging him with espionage for the Soviet Union (and, more prosaically, with tax evasion for not having reported the income he received from his treasonable activities). Ames's wife, Rosario (1952–   ), an American citizen born in Colombia, was also charged.

The findings of the CIA's inspector general, together with the report of the Senate Select Committee on Intelligence, made it plain that the Ames affair represented the worst breach of security in the history of the agency, leading (in the committee's words) "to the loss of virtually all of CIA's intelligence assets targeted at the Soviet Union at the height of the Cold War." Beginning in 1985, Ames—who, like Kim PHILBY in Britain, made treasonable use of his assignment to counterintelligence duties concerning the Soviets—turned over to Soviet intelligence thousands of pages of sensitive documents, the most spectacular result being that at least ten Western agents (of Soviet or Eastern European origin) had been executed and more than 100 intelligence operations compromised. In 1985 and 1986, said the inspector general in his report, "a significant number of CIA Soviet sources began to be compromised, recalled to the Soviet Union and, in many cases, executed."

Ames said in court that he spied for the Soviets because he needed money to pay creditors. Later, however, his wife, describing him as "obviously troubled," ascribed his decision to work for the KGB not to financial or ideological motives but to a desire to demonstrate his intelligence to the world—to show that he could really do it. (Kim Philby, too, seemed to derive a similar pleasure from fooling his colleagues.) Nevertheless, during Ames's years on their payroll, the KGB and its Russian successor, the Foreign Intelligence Service, paid him some $1.5 million. Rosario Ames cooperated wholeheartedly in spending the money. Among her activities was the amassing of a 500-pair collection of shoes.

Money, indeed, became the focus of much of the criticism CIA officials attracted for having failed to detect Ames's treachery. The inspector general declared in his report that agency security personnel had failed to follow up on various pieces of information about Ames's lavish spending habits (which could hardly square with his top annual salary of $70,000); he drove a Jaguar and paid for the family home in Arlington, Va., with $540,000 in cash and then added $100,000 in improvements. ("It raised eyebrows," said a retired federal official who lived three houses away, "that he paid cash for the house and simultaneously bought two new cars, including a Jaguar.") In 1986 and 1991, it appeared, officials did not look further despite what seemed to be lies told by Ames on a polygraph examination in response to questions about his finances. Not noted as a model of efficiency, Ames also acquired a considerable reputation as a drinker, but, to be sure, he shared this characteristic not only with Kim Philby but with numerous other celebrated secret agents. Even so, as the inspector general noted, supervisors "aware of Ames's poor performance and behavioral problems" paid little heed to them, though his alcohol abuse "worsened to the point that he often was able to accomplish little work after long, liquid lunches"; in fact, he frequently failed to return to the office at all.

The revelation to CIA chieftains in May 1993 of Ames's activities as a Soviet mole apparently came not from agency security investigators but from information given to the FBI by a former Communist intelligence officer. In long-established bureaucratic tradition, the CIA had seemed more concerned with keeping its business to itself than with cooperating with the FBI's spy catchers, in part because of the deep hostility that had existed between the agencies since the establishment of the CIA. It is also true, however, that the FBI has domestic investigative authority (checking bank accounts, for example) forbidden the CIA.

The revelation of the scandal proved a post–Cold War public-relations disaster for the CIA, with one newspaper caustically questioning "the credibility of a spy agency that could not find a lazy, drunken mole in its midst for eight years." "In the end," said the inspector general, "the Ames case is about accountability, both individual and managerial." In April 1994 Ames received a sentence of life imprisonment without parole.

Although Ames began his treasonable activities four months before the couple's marriage, Rosario Ames claimed to have learned of them only in

1991. (She was not, however, a stranger to espionage, since Ames had employed her as a contract agent in Mexico City, where he was supposed to be a diplomat and she was cultural attaché at the Colombian embassy.) Described by an FBI agent as a "control freak" and a "survivor" who would readily sacrifice her husband in order to save herself, Rosario Ames at first denied any knowledge of her husband's treasonable activities before admitting that she had discovered a strange note in her husband's wallet: instructions for a meeting with Soviet agents. She maintained that she failed to report Ames to the authorities only because she feared that the Russians would kill her and her son. The evidence convinced the court, however, that she had urged her husband to press on in his spying and had delightedly helped spend the "millions earned off the deaths of others."

Unfortunately for her, she could not benefit from one provision of the law of her native Colombia, where wives cannot be prosecuted for failing to report criminal activity by their husbands. On the other hand, she was clearly responsible for her own actions, as distinguished from those of her husband. She received a sentence of 63 months in prison. *See also* KGB; WALKER SPY RING.

Andropov, Yuri Vladimirovich (1914–1984)
Longtime chairman of the KGB who in 1982 succeeded Leonid BREZHNEV as general secretary of the COMMUNIST PARTY OF THE SOVIET UNION and thus as leader of the nation. A native of the Caucasus region, Andropov had a boyhood that smacks of the early years of Mark Twain and Thomas Edison, working as a telegraph boy and as a hand on Volga riverboats. After receiving training as an engineer, he became an organizer for the Young Communist League, an activity that led him into full-time party work, which he continued as a civilian during World War II.

In 1954, at the relatively young age of 40, Andropov, who had developed a worldly style and an elegance of dress, became ambassador to Hungary, an appointment that in 1956 was to put him at the center of one of the most dramatic events of the Cold War, the HUNGARIAN REVOLUTION. On November 1, with Hungarians defying Moscow and Soviet tanks encircling Budapest, Imre NAGY, the prime minister, summoned Andropov to his office.

What did the arrival of these Soviet army reinforcements mean? the prime minister asked the ambassador. It had no significance, Andropov replied; the tanks were standing by simply to make sure that the regular Soviet occupying forces could leave the country without unpleasant incidents. This answer told Nagy what he did not want to hear. If Andropov had said that the tanks had come to put pressure on the Hungarians or to crush the revolution, some negotiations might have been possible. But this barefaced lie obviously meant that the Soviets had decided what they were going to do and felt no need to talk about it.

Having approved of Andropov's conduct during the Hungarian events that shook the world, East as well as West, Nikita KHRUSHCHEV chose him to direct what the first secretary clearly believed to be a necessary new CENTRAL COMMITTEE department devoted to relations between the Soviet Communist Party and the other parties of the Eastern Bloc. Andropov won a seat on the Central Committee of the Soviet Communist Party in 1962, and in 1967 he was named chairman of the KGB. This appointment came about for complex reasons, one important factor apparently being that Andropov had incurred the disapproval, on ideological grounds, of the chief Soviet ideologue, Mikhail SUSLOV, a man of seemingly unbounded influence who had taken the lead in dethroning Khrushchev in 1964. Secret police officers, however efficient they may be, do not easily win friends and political influence; thus Andropov, though intelligent and able, would have little chance of ever becoming head of the Soviet Communist Party. But Suslov's death in January 1982 enabled Andropov's political star to shine again; in fact, he succeeded Suslov as Central Committee secretary in charge of ideology. In November 1982, after Brezhnev's death, he won election as general secretary, defeating Brezhnev's anointed successor, Konstantin CHERNENKO. A determined foe of cronyism and corruption, Andropov may have helped his cause through the blow to Brezhnev's reputation delivered by the KGB—and hence by Andropov—in the revelation that Brezhnev's daughter had taken part in a smuggling racket.

Though secret police tend to be among the most conservative and least flexible of political officials,

Andropov came to power as something of a reformer—structural rather than ideological—but he had held office only a few months when he was stricken by the kidney ailment and other disorders that would kill him in February 1984. On September 1, 1983, the destruction of a Korean passenger flight, KAL 007, exacerbated strains between the United States and the USSR, which had already hit one of the lowest points in their shifting history. During this period Andropov appears to have developed a fear, perhaps an obsession, that the Americans were planning a first-strike attack on the Soviet Union. Part of this apprehension came from the ongoing contorted Communist theorizing about "capitalist contradictions," which fed on the bristling rhetoric that characterized the REAGAN administration. Domestically, in his attempt to reverse the drift that had characterized the latter Brezhnev years, Andropov brought a fresh group of officials from the provinces to Moscow. But what had seemed to many Soviet citizens and others as the beginning of a promising era ended almost before it had begun, and in choosing Chernenko as Andropov's successor, the USSR seemed to be taking a step backward—though Chernenko's own poor health meant his regime would last an even shorter time than had that of Andropov. In any case, whatever Andropov's accomplishments in office might or might not have been, he takes a lasting place in history because of his sponsorship and promotion of Mikhail GORBACHEV.

antiballistic missile (ABM)   Missile system (called also antimissile missile) intended to shoot down incoming enemy missiles. The SALT I agreement, signed in 1972, imposed strict limits on the deployment of ABMs, and two years later the agreement was revised to limit both the United States and the Soviet Union to a single site. In 1975 the United States unilaterally abandoned the ABM concept, though in 1983 it appeared in quite a different form as President REAGAN'S STRATEGIC DEFENSE INITIATIVE. *See also* STRATEGIC ARMS LIMITATION TALKS.

antiparty group   Term applied to Soviet Communist Party leaders who tried to remove Nikita KHRUSHCHEV as first secretary of the party in June 1957. The membership of the group, which had a distinctly old-Bolshevik cast, included Vyacheslav MOLOTOV, Georgí MALENKOV, Lazar KAGANOVICH, and others. After being outvoted in the party Presidium, Khrushchev won the support of the CENTRAL COMMITTEE, made up chiefly of party officials, many of them hastily flown to Moscow. With Stalinism in mind, the Central Committee chided Molotov and his confederates for stubbornly opposing "measures carried out to eliminate consequences of the cult of the individual leader." Khrushchev then proceeded to deal with the antiparty-group members in a fashion new to the USSR. Instead of having them shot—as had been Stalin's way of handling opponents real or fancied—or simply disgraced, Khrushchev dispatched them to distant parts of the country, far from the centers of power, as managers of power stations, factories, and the like.

antiwar protests   During the VIETNAM WAR, for the first time in the history of the country (aside, to be sure, from the Civil War era), the United States experienced widespread, intense, prolonged, and sometimes violent dissent with national policy. What seemed to many Americans, young and older, the purposeless nature of the war and to others its immorality as it escalated in the middle 1960s led to a variety of protests, which took differing forms: peaceful marches, "teach-ins," the burning of draft cards, assaults on speakers defending the war, violent clashes with police, the seizure of campus buildings, and, later, the burning of university ROTC facilities.

Though arising from the perceived folly of the war, the protests had other roots relating to the era and culture in which they occurred. As Roland Stromberg of the University of Wisconsin pointed out, the 1960s and early 1970s saw a worldwide youth revolt that left few countries unaffected, in the West or behind the IRON CURTAIN. Although U.S. involvement in the Vietnam War became the focus of the wave of militant American protests, the youth rebellion actually began before the escalation in Vietnam and affected not only the U.S. allies Britain and West Germany but also France, whose president, Charles DE GAULLE, did not support the war. Thus, to a considerable extent, the war offered a focal point for youth already inclined toward rebellion. Three philosophers—Bertrand RUSSELL, Herbert MARCUSE, and Jean-Paul SARTRE—provided much of the ideological underpinning for the antiwar movement.

Many—but by no means all—of the participants in the antiwar movement belonged to an amorphous group known as the New Left, which focused, in a general way, on the alienating nature of modern technological society with its dominant and unresponsive bureaucracies. "New Leftists," said David Cochran of the University of Missouri, "sought to define themselves through praxis and by doing so felt they could avoid the rigid dogmatism that had marked older radical movements." The New Leftists saw U.S. actions in Vietnam as imperialistic and immoral. Many other antiwar protesters, while not necessarily disagreeing with the charge of immorality, emphasized the dubious pedigree of the South Vietnamese government and the pointlessness of a war undertaken under the erroneous idea that world Communism was a single great entity controlled by Moscow, even though the USSR and the People's Republic of China had entered into schism during the preceding several years; the DOMINO THEORY held that if such a country as South Vietnam fell under the sway of Communism, its neighbors would soon follow, resulting in a geopolitical success for the Soviet Union and a setback for the West. U.S. president Lyndon JOHNSON, whose effectiveness in domestic affairs was almost destroyed by the unpopularity of the war, found a simple explanation for the protests, declaring one day that "two or three intellectuals started it all."

Protesters staged a number of the U.S. demonstrations, including burning their draft cards outside draft-board offices and army induction centers with the aim of hampering the operation of the Selective Service System—a form of dissent somewhat reminiscent of the New York draft riots a century earlier but not seen in either of the world wars. Many young men due to be called up fled to Canada; others, better informed or better connected, found shelter in ROTC and National Guard units.

How much of the violence that accompanied many of the demonstrations was imposed by the police and other authorities and how much was incited by the demonstrators themselves has remained a complex question. Circumstances varied, since many participants in mass action held pacifist views while others clearly sought to be provocative. It was true, however, said Stromberg, that "New Left ideologists had encouraged violence, which is a constant theme in their writings." Sartre, for one, "consistently invoked the need for a violent, purifying, total revolution to destroy bourgeois society."

Perhaps the most famous protest action in the United States came in October 1967, when an array of antiwar groups staged a mass demonstration in Washington, D.C., with the Pentagon Building as its center. At the Democratic convention in Chicago the following summer, demonstrators opposed to the nomination of Vice President Hubert Humphrey to succeed Johnson engaged in a running riot with Chicago police; the uproar and its televised effects probably tipped the November election to the Republican nominee, Richard NIXON. In May 1970 came what was in many ways the most striking tragedy associated with antiwar protests, when panicking National Guardsmen at Kent State University in Ohio killed four members of a student crowd protesting the U.S. invasion of Cambodia. This event, said Nixon's security adviser, Henry KISSINGER, produced "a shock wave that brought the nation and its leadership close to psychological exhaustion." Campus unrest and violence spread across the country, all of these actions emphasizing the need to extricate the United States from Southeast Asia.

Overall, the antiwar protests in the United States and other countries, and the events and cultural environment that produced the protests, exerted a lasting effect on politics. Governments, at least in the West, would no longer tend to enter lightly upon major courses of action and to believe they could easily withstand any opposition to their policies.

Anzus Pact   A mutual-defense agreement signed on September 1, 1951, among Australia, New Zealand, and the United States. By its exclusion of Britain, the treaty demonstrated the decline of British influence in the region and the rise of a new relationship between the two Commonwealth nations and the United States. Under the treaty, an armed attack on any one of the parties would be regarded as an opening of hostilities on all of them.

apparatchik A Communist Party bureaucrat; i.e., a person working in the party *apparat*. Through the years party membership steadily increased in the Soviet Union and, correspondingly, the number of apparatchiks rose as well. Since the party took part in—indeed, dominated—all aspects of Soviet life, the number was substantial, in the 1980s amounting to several million.

Apparatchiks were likewise necessary for the administration of the other European Communist states. The mind-set that characterized their narrow and controlled world is powerfully presented in the novel *Judge on Trial,* by the Czech writer Ivan Klima (first English translation, 1993).

Arbenz, Jacobo (in full, Jacobo Arbenz Guzmán) (1913–1971) President of Guatemala elected in November 1950 in succession to President Juan José Arevalo Bermej, who in 1944 had overthrown the dictator Jorge Ubico Casteñada and established the country's first modern democratic government. Arbenz continued his predecessor's reformist policies, including expansion of educational opportunities, improvement of health care, redistribution of wealth, and—more controversially—the expropriation in 1952 of fallow lands for distribution to the peasants. Although the government promised to compensate the owners, this action brought it into conflict with the powerful American-owned UNITED FRUIT COMPANY (UFCO), which, together with Guatemalan conservatives, launched a successful campaign to discredit the Arbenz administration with the new U.S. EISENHOWER administration.

Severe attacks on Arbenz in the U.S. Congress and the U.S. press were followed on June 18, 1954, by a CENTRAL INTELLIGENCE AGENCY–inspired incursion from Honduras into Guatemala of some 150 Guatemalan exiles, with supporting elements, relying largely on radio and on leaflets dropped from airplanes. President Arbenz fled and the rebel leader, Colonel Carlos Castillo Armas, established what became a dictatorial regime.

Defenders of U.S. actions in Guatemala have maintained that Arbenz was suspect as far back as 1949, when his chief political rival was assassinated, leaving Arbenz with no effective opposition, and that as president he surrounded himself with Communist advisers and appointed numerous Communists to government positions. The main U.S. concern, from this point of view, was Central America's strategic significance because of the Panama Canal; the nationalization of the United Fruit Company's lands, though no doubt unwelcome, was not in itself viewed as proof of Communist orientation—Eisenhower himself later said that "expropriation in itself does not, of course, prove Communism." Arbenz had also supported the baseless Communist charge that the Americans had used GERM WARFARE in Korea. After Arbenz's departure, American critics noted with some interest that he chose to go to Czechoslovakia, behind the IRON CURTAIN.

In any case, perhaps the most important question to be discussed was whether the United States had a right to intervene, even if the Arbenz government was guilty of the murders with which U.S. officials charged it.

Army of the Republic of Vietnam (ARVN) Tracing its origins to the Vietnamese National Army, established by the French in 1950, the ARVN came into being as such after the fall of DIEN BIEN PHU and the creation of the Republic of Vietnam in 1954. Receiving U.S. economic and technical support, the ARVN (pronounced "Arvin" by U.S. soldiers) had grown by the end of 1959 to 235,000 troops. As the Americans escalated the VIETNAM WAR during the middle 1960s, ARVN strength increased correspondingly—to an estimated 500,000 in 1964 and 800,000 by the end of 1966. When the peace accord was signed in 1973, ARVN numbers had soared to more than one million. The army suffered huge losses during the war: 250,000 killed and 500,000 wounded.

During the war the ARVN principally handled pacification duties, while U.S. forces engaged in search-and-destroy operations. Although frequently and severely criticized by U.S. officers (one of whom observed that more ARVN personnel were lost in car accidents than in battle), the ARVN included some outstanding units, particularly the Airborne Division and the First Infantry Division. ARVN leaders, such as Generals Nguyen

Khanh and NGUYEN VAN THIEU, held the most powerful positions in the SAIGON government and often became the targets of official U.S. criticism because of the government's corruption.

Aron, Raymond (1905–1983)   Leading French author, sociologist, and political commentator whose opinions on international affairs won wide quotation in the West during the Cold War period. Independent in outlook, Aron parted intellectual company (in *The Opium of the Intellectuals*, 1955; English translation, 1957) with his friend Jean-Paul SARTRE over Sartre's general support of Soviet statements and actions. Sartre and others who professed both Communism and EXISTENTIAL-ISM evoked from Aron this comment: "One cannot be at the same time the heir of Hegel-Marx and the heir of Kierkegaard." Aron also advocated French withdrawal from Algeria. He favored the Atlantic alliance, a view that brought him into collision with General DE GAULLE's pronounced nationalism in defense matters. American Democrats who attacked the Republican president NIXON for involvement in Vietnam even though the war had begun under a Democratic administration were dryly called by Aron "lawyers unleashed against those who are receiving their inheritance." Aron was an editorial writer for *Le Figaro* (1947–77) and a columnist for *L'Express* in the following years.

ARVN   *See* ARMY OF THE REPUBLIC OF VIETNAM.

Asian-Pacific Security Order   As the leader of a land power that sprawled across Eurasia from Central Europe to the Pacific, Mikhail GORBACHEV held substantial ambitions for his country, intending it to play a full part in Asian affairs—with the emphasis on diplomacy rather than on military strength. Calling the Soviet Union an "Asian-Pacific power," he declared in an important speech in Vladivostok on July 28, 1986, that the USSR would be fully involved in the "renaissance of world history" taking place around the Pacific rim. He moved to improve relations with both China and Japan, with a view to cutting Soviet military expenditures and to benefiting from Japanese technology, and he proposed the creation of an equiva-lent of the Helsinki conference on European security. Putting aside the quarter century of animosity between the USSR and China, he even proposed that the Chinese take part in Soviet exploration of space. *See also* HELSINKI FINAL ACT.

Aswan High Dam   Major hydroelectric and irrigation project mounted in the 1950s on the upper Nile River by Egypt under Gamal Abdel NASSER. Seeking to improve unsatisfactory relations with Egypt, the United States and Britain announced that they would provide funding for the dam. But in the spring of 1956 the United States agreed to allow France to divert weapons intended for NATO use to Israel; Nasser responded by withdrawing Egyptian recognition of Nationalist China, a gesture having no effect whatever on the actual situation in Asia and made only to signal the United States that Nasser could not be intimidated. The U.S. secretary of state, John Foster DULLES, responded in July with what former secretary of state Dean ACHESON later termed "Foster's silly and clumsy attempt to wound Nasser," announcing that the United States would withdraw its support of the Aswan Dam. Nasser, in turn, reacted to this embarrassment by nationalizing the Suez Canal, a move that foreshadowed the SUEZ CRISIS of 1956. From the point of view of U.S. interests, it could only be said that the whole Aswan matter had been ineptly handled. The dam, whose construction created the world's largest man-made lake and made it necessary to move the great temple of Abu Simbel beyond the reach of the impounded waters, went into commission in 1971.

asymmetrical response   If SYMMETRICAL RESPONSE could be described as the belief that the United States should act directly to counter on a literal 1:1 basis any Soviet challenge anywhere, asymmetrical response was the contrasting idea that, since symmetry would inevitably overstrain American resources, responsive actions should instead be taken in situations considered favorable for Western action and at places in which vital interests were at stake. Though theorists used the term *asymmetrical response* as a balance to *symmetrical response*, *selective response* perhaps conveys the essential idea more clearly.

atomic bomb The only nuclear weapons ever used in warfare were the two atomic bombs dropped on the Japanese cities of Hiroshima and Nagasaki in August 1945; within five days of the Nagasaki bombing, World War II in the Pacific had ended. These bombs (the only ones possessed by the United States at the time) had been conceived, designed, and produced by joint U.S.-British-Canadian teams and were based on the idea, which arose after the splitting of the atom in the late 1930s, that the energy produced by this nuclear fission could be harnessed to make an explosive of a power vastly greater than any ever before known; in fact, the Hiroshima bomb produced an awesome explosion equal to the force of 20,000 tons of TNT. From that time forward, views and opinions about war had to be rethought and rearranged. Writing shortly after the end of the war, David Dietz quoted scientists as visualizing "the combination of atomic bombs with many other types of offensive weapons, for example, rockets travelling in the stratosphere with supersonic speeds"—indeed, the missiles that were to come. Although, as was commonly said, the United States possessed a "nuclear monopoly" (but, for some time, very few bombs), this proved for a range of reasons to have little effect on the developing course of international events in the mid-1940s and the beginning of the Cold War, and in any case no one concerned with such matters foresaw a long-term American monopoly. Owing to the fruitful results yielded by Soviet espionage, the interval turned out to be even shorter than scientists had expected; in August 1949 the USSR exploded its first nuclear bomb. *See also* ATOMIC ENERGY COMMISSION; BARUCH PLAN; FUCHS, Klaus; HYDROGEN BOMB; INTERCONTINENTAL BALLISTIC MISSILE; MAY, Alan Nunn; OPPENHEIMER, J. Robert; ROSENBERG CASE; TRUMAN, Harry S.; VENONA.

Atomic Energy Commission On October 3, 1945, just two months after the two ATOMIC BOMBS dropped on Japan had brought World War II to an end and had also clearly inaugurated a new era in world science and political perspectives, U.S. president Harry S. TRUMAN in a message to Congress requested legislation to keep much of the information about the bomb secret and to establish a commission that would control all nuclear research and formulate security regulations governing information policies concerning it.

The president's request evoked immediate hostility from many of the scientists who had created the bomb. For the first time in American history, scientists entered political discussion as a group, responding to the proposed bill through ad hoc organizations like the Atomic Scientists of Chicago, whose publication, the *Bulletin of the Atomic Scientists*, became famous with its doomsday clock on the cover of each issue; the hands, always set disturbingly near 12:00, would be advanced or moved back depending on the editors' changing assessments of the world situation.

The opponents of the bill Truman had requested based their objections on several points: that scientists in many countries had possessed the basic knowledge required to create the bomb even before World War II began, that secrecy was incompatible with the progress of science, and that attempts to impose it would stimulate an international nuclear race. Instead, the scientists expressed their belief that the whole matter should be turned over to the new UNITED NATIONS. They advocated the establishment of an international inspection system to guarantee that no country would be able to make atomic bombs or accumulate significant amounts of fissionable material. The U.S. response to this proposal on the international level was ultimately the BARUCH PLAN, presented to the UN in June 1946; the Soviets countered with the GROMYKO PLAN.

With respect to domestic U.S. policy, Congress established a joint atomic energy committee, under the chairmanship of Senator Brien McMahon, that produced a bill that, as amended, became the Atomic Energy Act of 1946, usually called the McMahon Act, and essentially granted President Truman's request. The decision for secrecy applied even to the British, who had performed as partners in the development of the atomic bomb. Making this point in a conversation with McMahon, Winston CHURCHILL, the wartime prime minister, expressed strong objections. According to Churchill's account, McMahon declared that if he had realized the extent of the British contribution, there would have been no McMahon Act. Though the senator perhaps expressed such a thought, and the exclusion of the British clearly violated wartime agreements, the fact was that, regardless of the senator's individual opinion, a McMahon Act under somebody's name was probably inevitable, because the atomic bomb made its possessors nervous. The United States controlled the terrifying new weapon and handled questions concerning it with extreme caution, much like a person juggling a charge of nitroglycerin—a single mistake could produce total catastrophe.

The McMahon Act called for a five-member commission; a joint congressional committee that would sit permanently; and a body called the General Advisory Committee—a panel of nine scientific and technical advisers. The Atomic Energy Commission received a wide range of responsibilities, civil and military. It controls the production of nuclear materials, the manufacture of nuclear weapons, and the development of nuclear reactors (in the early years, greater expectations were held for nuclear power than came to be the case later). President Truman named David LILIENTHAL the first chairman of the AEC.

In 1953 security officials declared J. Robert OPPENHEIMER, the director of the Los Alamos laboratory, where the bomb was built, a security risk principally because of his opposition to development of the HYDROGEN BOMB. This decision meant that Oppenheimer could no longer serve as a consultant to the commission; previously he had chaired the General Advisory Committee. In 1954, after violent public as well as official controversy, a review board confirmed the 1953 decision.

Atoms for peace   In an address to the United Nations General Assembly on December 8, 1953, President Dwight D. EISENHOWER proposed that the nuclear powers take the lead in promoting peaceful uses of atomic energy by donating part of their stockpiles to an international "bank of fissionable materials." It was important, the president wrote in his diary, "to make a clear effort to get the Soviet Union working with us in some phase of this whole atomic field that would have only peace and the good of mankind as a goal." Enthusiastically received, the speech enhanced the image of the United States as a seeker of peace at a time when the Soviet Union was scoring propaganda victories, and the phrase "atoms for peace" entered the language. Though the Soviets met the proposal

with skepticism, the International Atomic Energy Authority came into being in 1957. Working with this body, the United States helped various countries throughout the world develop reactors for power generation.

Attlee, Clement Richard (1883–1967)   British statesman who in July 1945 led the Labour Party to a resounding defeat of Winston CHURCHILL's Conservatives and served as prime minister until October 1951. Thus Attlee presided over the British government during the crucial era from the last phase of World War II through the difficult postwar period of adjustment, the establishment of the welfare state, the granting of independence to colonies, and the coming of the Cold War.

After engaging in social work in London's poverty-ridden East End, Attlee, an Oxford graduate, joined the Fabian Society in 1907 and the Independent Labour Party in 1908. In 1913 he became a lecturer at the London School of Economics and during World War I served in the army in the Gallipoli campaign, in Mesopotamia, and in France, rising to the rank of major. He entered Parliament in 1922 and in 1935 was elected leader of the Labour Party. In the crisis of May 1940, when Churchill created his coalition cabinet, Attlee took the post of lord privy seal, becoming deputy prime minister in 1942, a position that left him in charge of daily operations while Churchill concentrated on war strategy. A point in Attlee's favor with Churchill was his good war record, which earned him "Major Attlee" as a frequent designation.

As the result of Labour's victory in the 1945 election, announced during the Allied POTSDAM CONFERENCE, Attlee replaced Churchill as head of the British delegation. During the ensuing years, Attlee tended to leave foreign affairs almost completely in the hands of his foreign secretary, Ernest BEVIN—on the principle, said the prime minister, that "you don't keep a good dog and bark yourself —and Ernie was a very good dog." Politically, the course of foreign affairs did not run smoothly, however, because the Attlee government's generally close relations with the United States and its support of American policy drew opposition from forceful members of the left wing of the prime minister's own party, notably the eloquent Aneurin BEVAN.

British prime minister Clement Attlee *(seated, r.)* talks in Washington with President Harry S. Truman *(l.)*, Secretary of State Dean Acheson, and Secretary of Defense George C. Marshall.

A quiet individual, Attlee is supposed to have been described by Churchill as "a modest man with a great deal to be modest about." But that was only political talk. Indeed, one of Attlee's limitations, according to a colleague, was that "he thought the English were far better than anybody else." Another observer, however, saw him as the kind of straightforward type later exemplified in America by Gerald FORD.

Attlee held the distinction of being the first Labour prime minister to enjoy an absolute majority in the House of Commons. But the election of February 1950 saw his majority shrink to five. Despite his accomplishments, the slow pace of British recovery from the war left many voters discontented, and, said one observer, the Labour government was "physically and creatively worn out." Attlee lost the next election, held in October 1951. His administration, however, was one of the longest and most important in modern British history.

Austin, Warren Robinson (1877–1962) Republican senator from Vermont (1931–46) who had a close friendship in the U.S. Senate with Harry TRUMAN and, having served on the military affairs and foreign relations committees, became, in 1946, President Truman's appointee as the first U.S. ambassador to the UNITED NATIONS. His most intensive activity came during the time when the United States was working to create the UN force to fight in the KOREAN WAR in 1950.

Austrian State Treaty One of the fruits of the mild thaw that existed between East and West during the middle 1950s, following the death of Soviet premier Joseph STALIN, was the negotiating and signing of a treaty between the World War II Allies and Austria. For ten years the country had existed under four-power occupation, but First Secretary Nikita KHRUSHCHEV, whose ascendancy in the USSR had become clear early in 1955, agreed to terms under which Austria was declared a neutral state. Called the "state treaty" because it was not properly a peace treaty—since Austria had not existed as an independent country during the World War II period—the treaty was signed on May 15, 1955.

Azerbaijan   In February 1988 a nationalist and ethnic dispute between Muslim Azerbaijanis and Christian Armenians in this Soviet republic led to the most violent civil disturbances seen in the Soviet Union since World War II. The conflict was centered in a heavily Armenian enclave inside the Azerbaijan republic called Nagorno-Karabakh ("mischievously given Azerbaijan years earlier" by General Secretary Joseph STALIN, said one scholar), with the Armenians wanting the area detached from Azerbaijan and transferred to Armenia and the Azerbaijanis refusing to accede to this appeal. A series of demonstrations led to the killing of two persons and the wounding of numerous others, all this violence acting as the prelude to an anti-Armenian pogrom in an Azerbaijani town in which 32 people were killed and 197 wounded. Though it announced various mollifying proposals, the central Soviet government rejected any change in the status of Nagorno-Karabakh. Moscow's handling of the situation aroused the anger of both parties against Mikhail GORBACHEV, who never during his time as head of the Soviet Union managed to find any successful method for dealing with ethnic disputes. Other riots broke out, floods of refugees poured in both directions, and the fighting thus begun turned into full-scale war after the collapse of the Soviet Union in 1991.

B

B-1   Some of the fiercest battles in which this U.S. aircraft took part occurred on the ground, with politicians rather than enemy fire as its foe. Planning for a "Subsonic Low Altitude Bomber" went back to the 1960s, when the U.S. Air Force began to look for a successor to the B-52 and the B-58. A development contract for a new bomber was awarded to Rockwell in 1970; the first swing-wing B-1A flew on December 23, 1974, and work on three other prototypes proceeded. The air force and the fledgling B-1 itself had powerful friends in and out of Congress ("the B-1 lobby was one of the most formidable ever evolved in the military-industrial community," said President Jimmy CARTER, looking back a few years later). Nevertheless, a series of negative factors—economic dislocations resulting from the Middle East crisis and the worldwide oil embargo, hopes for successful arms-reduction negotiations, an increase in the expected unit cost of the B-1, a widespread opinion that in any case the aircraft lacked a clearly defined mission, faith in the deterrent power of the CRUISE MISSILE—led Carter, early in his presidency, to cancel B-1 production. This decision took effect in July 1977, though Congress supplied funds for continuing developmental studies. The sustenance kept the project alive long enough for it to find itself in a leading position when the Department of Defense decided in 1980 to reassess the bomber situation. In October 1981, with Ronald REAGAN now in the White House, Rockwell received orders for 100 revamped B-1s; the new aircraft would be designated the B-1B.

Called the Lancer, the B-1B possesses enhanced radar-eluding capabilities and carries a payload of about 40 tons more than that of the B-1A (477,000 pounds total weight compared with 389,000) and twice that of the B-52, while able to use shorter runways than the latter required. Capable of carrying a variety of weapons, nuclear and conventional, the B-1B has found a special—and ironic—role as a carrier for the Boeing ALCM (cruise missile), the weapon that once threatened to take its place. Powered by four General Electric engines hung in pairs beneath the fixed part of the wing, the B-1 attains a top speed of about Mach 1.25 and has a maximum range (unrefueled) of about 7,500 miles.

B-36   With its huge wingspan—230 feet—and its length of 162 feet, this piston-engine U.S. aircraft was the largest warplane ever built. (By comparison, the World War II superbomber, the B-29, had a 141-foot span and a length of 99 feet.) The wingtips were almost as far apart as the distance the Wright brothers covered in the first powered flight in 1903. The B-36 first flew in August 1946 and went into operational service in June 1948. Driven by six Pratt & Whitney pusher engines, it had a maximum speed of 435 mph and a range of 10,000 miles. The centerpiece of American DETERRENCE during its service, this cornucopia of explosives could carry more than 40 tons of conventional bombs, if necessary, instead of the nuclear weapons that provided its chief reason for being. Because of its deterrent role, the air force nicknamed it Peacemaker. Politically, however, the B-36 promoted anything but peace, since it figured at the center of the great Defense Department bat-

U.S. Air Force B-36, the largest warplane ever built

tle over strategy and roles marked by the REVOLT OF THE ADMIRALS. In 1958 and 1959, B-36s yielded their place in U.S. strategy to the new B-52s.

B-47 Boeing-built medium bomber, called the Stratojet, in service with the U.S. STRATEGIC AIR COMMAND in the 1950s and 1960s, notable because it was the first swept-wing bomber to be put into service by any air force. Powered by six General Electric engines, it had a top speed of 610 mph and could carry nuclear bombs or 10,000 pounds in conventional bombs.

B-52 Named the Stratofortress, this long-lived heavy bomber built by Boeing first flew in April 1952, entered service with the U.S. STRATEGIC AIR COMMAND in 1955 and has been SAC's principal long-range bomber ever since. Early in its career it received the nickname BUFF, for Big Ugly Fat Fellow. One part of its body, the nose, grew larger than intended when the commanding general of SAC, General Curtis E. LEMAY, ordered the planned tandem seating of pilot and copilot changed to a side-by-side arrangement. Powered by eight Pratt & Whitney jet engines mounted in

U.S. Air Force B-47, world's first swept-wing bomber

U.S. Air Force B-52, long-lived Cold War strategic bomber

podded pairs, the Stratofortress attains a maximum speed of about 640 mph and has a cruising range, without refueling, of about 8,300 miles. Primarily intended to carry nuclear bombs, the B-52 acted as a conventional bomber during the VIETNAM WAR; it is able to deliver more than 20 tons of bombs. Later models, the B-52Ds, were modified to accommodate air-to-surface missiles and Quail decoy missiles. Though B-52s have continued to serve for decades, none have been built since 1963.

B-57   *See* CANBERRA.

B-58   On duty with the U.S. Air Force from 1960 to 1970, the Convair B-58 Hustler was the service's first operational supersonic bomber. A curious feature of this aircraft was that, although it was created as a strategic bomber with a range (unrefueled) of about 4,500 miles, its slender body did not afford room for bombs, which, nuclear or conventional, had to be carried in a pod slung below. The pod could also carry fuel and various gear and could be dropped when its contents had served their purpose. The B-58 reached a top speed of about Mach 2. Its crew included pilot, navigator-bombardier, and defense-systems operator. The B-58's heavy and thus costly fuel consumption played a part in shortening its active life.

Baghdad Pact   Treaty signed in February 1955 between Turkey and Iraq, aimed at countering the activities of militant left-wing elements in the two countries. Since Turkey and Pakistan already had

established a mutual-defense relationship, the new arrangement created a larger alliance, which came to be called the Baghdad Pact. Britain and Iran soon joined the group, Britain in many ways acting as the sponsor. In general, this arrangement suited the United States' desire to build up coalitions that would, in various regions, counteract Soviet influence. After a revolution in 1958, Iraq withdrew from the Baghdad Pact, which then became the CENTRAL TREATY ORGANIZATION (CENTO).

Balance of terror   A play on the standard diplomatic expression "balance of power," suggesting that in the thermonuclear age the superpowers would not go to war with each other because each possessed the power not merely to defeat but to obliterate its adversary. Like many other ideas prominent during the Cold War, the balance-of-terror concept contains a paradoxical element, since it implies that the possession of large hydrogen-bomb arsenals by both sides made for greater stability, or balance, than would have existed if only one side controlled such awesome power. One writer, Thomas C. Schelling of Harvard University, likened the United States and the Soviet Union to two enemies on opposite sides of a canyon, each within range of the other's poisoned arrows, each possessing poison so slow-acting that either person could shoot his adversary before dying himself. The key, Schelling commented, was not the fact of the balance, but its stability—which existed when neither party could destroy its adversary's power to retaliate by striking first. *See also* DETERRENCE; MUTUAL ASSURED DESTRUCTION.

B-58, first U.S. Air Force supersonic bomber

Ball, George Wildman (1909–1994) U.S. public official primarily identified with issues of foreign policy and having special importance as a "wise man"—a presidential adviser—even when holding no office. Ball served President KENNEDY as undersecretary of state, originally for economic affairs and then for policy planning. In the last months of the JOHNSON administration he represented the United States as ambassador to the UNITED NATIONS.

After receiving his law degree from Northwestern University, Ball, a native of Iowa, worked for the federal government and then practiced tax law in Chicago until returning to Washington in World War II as counsel for the Lend-Lease Administration, which handled military aid to U.S. allies. In 1944 Ball initiated activities that led to a new kind of war research, the U.S. Strategic Bombing Survey, which made a thorough analysis of the actual (as opposed to the claimed) effects of World War II bombing. From the end of the war until he entered the Kennedy administration, Ball practiced international law. He was an early and heavily involved supporter of Adlai STEVENSON's presidential candidacies.

In 1965 Ball, as undersecretary of state, opposed decisions to increase the American role in the VIETNAM WAR, declaring his belief that the United States could not win a long war against guerrillas in the jungles of Asia. Later he supported a pause in bombing operations against North Vietnam. A continuing disbeliever in the war, Ball was characterized by John Kenneth GALBRAITH as the Johnson administration's "inside opponent." In later years Ball, as a private citizen, served as a consultant to President CARTER on questions of policy, always speaking with a moderate voice, as when he advised the administration to urge the shah of Iran to broaden popular representation in his government. Unfortunately, Ball's views on this matter were not sought until November 1978, not long before the shah left the country.

Baltic Assembly On August 23, 1939, the Soviet Union and Nazi Germany signed their famous nonaggression pact, which freed Adolf Hitler to launch the conflict that became World War II. In exchange for promising its neutrality, the Soviet Union received an expanded "sphere of influence" that included Estonia and Latvia, two of the three Baltic republics; a few weeks later, a second Nazi-Soviet agreement added Lithuania to Joseph Stalin's sphere. In 1940 the USSR annexed all three republics.

On August 23, 1989—the 50th anniversary of the Nazi-Soviet pact—the people of the three republics displayed their continuing nationalism and their resentment of the central Soviet government by staging a gigantic demonstration (an unimaginable event in the era before GLASNOST) in which some three million people—about 40 percent of the total population of the Baltics—formed a human chain across the three states. This remarkable phenomenon was followed by the creation of the Baltic Assembly, which demanded that the Soviet government grant the republics independence within a framework of neutrality and demilitarization.

In January 1991, with nothing resolved, the Soviets used troops to reassert control in Latvia and Lithuania—an action profoundly shocking to President Mikhail GORBACHEV's admirers in his own country and around the world. His message accusing the Lithuanian government of seeking to "use the slogans of democracy as a cover for implementing a policy aimed at restoring a bourgeois system" smacked more of Stalinism than of PERESTROIKA. Four Latvians died in a fight for control of government buildings, and in Vilnius, in a pitched battle at the Lithuanian television center, 13 people were killed and 112 were wounded by tanks and rifle butts.

This tactical move to the right by Gorbachev did him little good. The elected governments of Latvia and Lithuania remained in place, and though the president no doubt regretted the violence, he came under bitter attack from former allies and supporters at home and abroad; his name quickly lost much of its luster. In any case, the Baltics were soon to receive full independence, which was granted in September 1991, shortly after the failure of the right-wing coup by the STATE COMMITTEE FOR THE STATE OF EMERGENCY IN THE USSR.

Bandung Conference   From April 18 to April 24, 1955, 29 nations, mostly Asian and African, met at Bandung, Java, to discuss and applaud neutralism and raise the banner of NONALIGNMENT. For many leaders of developing countries—such as the host at Bandung, President SUKARNO of Indonesia —the conference held great importance for its af-

firmation of nationalism in the THIRD WORLD. Not all of the countries represented at Bandung could be considered nonaligned, however; for example, China was a leader in the "socialist camp" (the SECOND WORLD), and Japan had ties with the West (the FIRST WORLD). The participants pledged their support for the new Soviet policy of PEACEFUL CO-EXISTENCE and condemned various Western actions, such as French repression in Algeria.

Bao Dai (1913–)   Born Prince Nguyen Vinh Thuy, Bao Dai was the last emperor of Annam (Vietnam), coming to the throne in 1925 at the age of 12. During the Japanese occupation of his country in World War II, he cooperated with the invaders, even agreeing in March 1945 to serve as the chief of a Japanese-proclaimed "independent" state of Vietnam. But later in 1945, after the Japanese defeat and the taking of Hanoi by the VIETMINH under HO CHI MINH, Bao Dai abdicated his throne, thus bringing to its end a monarchy that had lasted for a thousand years. In 1949 the French brought him back from exile in Europe, where he had led an extravagant playboy existence, to become head of the "Free State" of Vietnam (the southern half of the country) within the French Union. Following the French defeat at DIEN BIEN PHU and the partition of Vietnam, Bao Dai was outmaneuvered by NGO DINH DIEM and removed from his briefly held position as chief of state of South Vietnam. In 1955 a national referendum actively sponsored by the United States confirmed his dismissal; he resumed his exile in France.

During his active career Bao Dai seemed to be pulled between his desire to perform as an effective political leader in Vietnam and his fondness for the good life on the Riviera. Speaking of the emperor's habits, Donald Heath, a former U.S. ambassador to Vietnam, said that they were not "the things of which Churchills are made."

Baruch Plan   On June 15, 1946, as the U.S. representative on the ATOMIC ENERGY COMMISSION of the UNITED NATIONS, the financier Bernard Baruch (1870–1965) presented an American proposal under which the commission would supervise the manufacture of nuclear weapons in all countries. The plan had been produced by scientists and government officials, including David LILIENTHAL, former chairman of the Tennessee Valley Authority; J. Robert OPPENHEIMER, the physicist who had directed activities at the Los Alamos atomic-bomb installation; and Dean ACHESON, undersecretary of state. (An early version of the proposal was known as the Acheson–Lilienthal Plan.) To present the plan, President Harry S. TRUMAN selected the 75-year-old Baruch, who over a long career had built up a reputation as confidential adviser to presidents.

What the USSR would have to accept, under the Baruch Plan, would be UN inspection of Soviet nuclear facilities. What the United States would have to surrender would be its then-existing nuclear monopoly. Some Americans hoped this high price might be offset by a lessening of Soviet suspiciousness and possibly a beginning of real disarmament. But, refusing to play the part of a mere "messenger boy," Baruch insisted that the plan include a provision that all countries must give up the right to veto Security Council resolutions on nuclear matters. Rejecting the proposal, the Soviets countered with what was called the GROMYKO PLAN.

"Basic Principles" Agreement In a summit meeting in Moscow in May 1972, during the so-called era of DÉTENTE, U.S. president NIXON and Soviet general secretary BREZHNEV publicly affixed their signatures to a remarkable document, a sort of code of international conduct in which the two leaders promised their respective countries would behave in a civilized fashion and that neither would seek "to obtain unilateral advantage at the expense of the other." Such statements could hardly be said to have conformed to the existing realities of the time, and, in fact, U.S.-Soviet competition continued as before.

Bay of Pigs Operation In March 1960 U.S. president EISENHOWER authorized the CENTRAL INTELLIGENCE AGENCY to train Cuban exiles for use in a possible attack on Fidel CASTRO's Cuba. Dutifully carrying out these instructions, the CIA selected some 1,500 refugees, provided them with U.S. military equipment, and began training them at bases in Guatemala, where a CIA-sponsored coup had been a complete success in 1954. (That action,

however, was a much smaller-scale affair.) The presidential authorization covered training only. "I will reserve to myself," Eisenhower said, "whether they will actually be committed or not." When an aide commented that plans of this kind often develop a momentum of their own, the president retorted, "Not so long as I'm here."

When Eisenhower left office in January 1961, having made no decision concerning the carrying out of the proposed operation (code-named Zapata), the plans were inherited by President KENNEDY, who had been briefed on them twice in November and who allowed them to proceed after he took office. In March the new president approved the launching of the operation, though with modifications.

Originally designed as a large-scale operation with American support, to take place at Trinidad on the southern coast of Cuba, the landing was switched to a spot about 100 miles west, due south of the city of Matanzas, called the Bay of Pigs (Bahia de Cochinos). The reason for the change has remained a question. The Trinidad site had been chosen because if the landing should go badly, the exiles could slip into the nearby Escambray Mountains, where they might be able to conduct a guerrilla insurgency like the one that had brought Castro to power a few years earlier. From a military point of view, Trinidad offered an eminently suitable landing site. But, with Kennedy insisting that the effort must be made entirely by a Cuban brigade with no U.S. troops involved, the operation was redesigned to focus on the Bay of Pigs—to lower the "noise level," it was said. One proffered explanation declared that the very suitability of Trinidad would mark it as having been chosen by professional soldiers, and hence by the United States, rather than by a band of insurgent amateurs.

In any case, on April 17, 1961, the insurgents of the 2506 Brigade came ashore at the Bay of Pigs, only to find themselves outmanned and outgunned by Cuban defenders, who easily rounded them up. Whatever local support the invaders may have expected failed to materialize, and there were no nearby mountains to offer any kind of refuge. Certainly no anti-Castro uprising gave the least sign of taking place. A curious aspect of the operation concerned the question of air support. Refugee pilots flying U.S. B-26s bombed Cuban bases; they were proclaimed to the world to be defectors from Castro's air force, but two of them who landed in Florida could not make the story stand up. Hence Kennedy canceled a planned second strike, which was supposed to provide cover for the actual landing. Aircraft did overfly the beach, but to no effect. (Some former officials have asserted that the initial operation was designed to fail, on the idea that Kennedy would then feel compelled to put in U.S. forces and thus create a genuine invasion of Cuba. Another commentator, Scott Breckinridge, a former CIA official, has observed that even after the passage of many years, the changes remain inexplicable to those involved, who were "taken from a carefully chosen battle site to a vulnerable one, and deprived of protection from hostile air.") The Bay of Pigs fiasco proved to be a major embarrassment for the Kennedy administration and a propaganda nightmare for the United States, with Castro winning worldwide sympathy for his condemnation of Yankee "imperialism." It also had other consequences. Later that year, describing the president as "wishy-washy," the USSR's Nikita KHRUSHCHEV declared, "I know for certain that Kennedy doesn't have a strong backbone."

What led President Kennedy to authorize this ill-starred operation, which had almost no conceivable chance of achieving success? The reason most often given is simply Kennedy's lack of experience —his approval was sought almost as soon as he took office, and the plan had the endorsement of generals, admirals, and the revered former president of the country. Bobby Baker, a well-known Washington "fixer" of the day, later said, "He was totally ill equipped for that kind of crisis that early in his administration." As Breckinridge put it, "Kennedy inherited the plan, and seems to have had neither the will to stop it nor the experience to contribute usefully to it." Others suggested that if Kennedy had failed to adopt the plan, his political opponent Richard M. NIXON, who of course knew about it, would take advantage of it—that is, make Kennedy out to be weak and ineffectual. And what about all those Cubans who had been trained under Eisenhower? Turned out on their own, with Operation Zapata canceled, what would they say about the new president as compared with his predecessor? Certainly it was true that at the begin-

ning of his administration and in the climate of the day, Kennedy did not wish to appear soft on Communism. That point may explain, as well, why he and all the others who favored the operation believed that the idea of invading Cuba possessed any merit at all.

Later the U.S. administration negotiated the release of the 1,100 prisoners held by the Cubans, paying a ransom of farm equipment and other supplies. Thus the incident itself ended, but not the tensions between the United States and Cuba, which in fact worsened, with the Kennedy administration developing what seemed an almost pathological obsession with "getting even," as a favorite expression went, by overthrowing or otherwise disposing of Castro. In addition, this incident and subsequent U.S. harassment of Cuba played an important part in the development of what in 1962 became the CUBAN MISSILE CRISIS. *See also* MONGOOSE, OPERATION.

Bech, Joseph (1887–1975) Foreign minister of Luxembourg for the amazingly long stretch of 33 years (1926–59), Joseph Bech used the relatively small platform the size of his country offered him to become one of the leaders in the movement toward Western European unity. He was influential in the creation of the BENELUX union, the EUROPEAN DEFENSE COMMUNITY, and the EUROPEAN ECONOMIC COMMUNITY.

Begin, Menachem (1913–1992) Prime minister of Israel (1977–83), an extreme and intransigent right-winger who, with the very close involvement of U.S. president Jimmy CARTER, negotiated with Egypt the September 1978 "Framework for Peace in the Middle East," commonly known as the CAMP DAVID ACCORDS. Though the agreement failed to produce some of the hoped-for results—Israeli right-wingers thwarted the development of Palestinian autonomy on the West Bank (indeed, Begin himself promoted the building of new Israeli settlements in the area), Israel evacuated only the Sinai and not the Gaza Strip, the Golan Heights, or the West Bank itself, and the Palestine Liberation Organization opposed the accord—it influenced developments in the Cold War by confirming Egyptian president Anwar SADAT's orientation to the West and upsetting the Soviets. *Pravda* called the agreement a "sellout" favored by "Israel, America, imperialism, and the Arab reactionaries."

Belarus *See* BYELORUSSIA.

Benelux Name, formed by the first letters of its members' names, given to the customs union formed in 1947 (effective date January 1, 1948) by Belgium, the Netherlands, and Luxembourg.

Beneš, Eduard (1884–1948) President of Czechoslovakia both before World War II and after. As foreign minister (1918–35) and president (1935–38) during the interwar years, Beneš favored a close relationship with France and also maintained friendly contacts with the Soviet Union. Not a strong leader, he found himself unable to put up effective opposition to the schemes of Adolf Hitler against Czechoslovakia, nor could he win support from his supposed friends France and Britain. Having resigned the presidency in 1938, after the disastrous Munich conference—in which his friends abandoned him, and which left his country at the mercy of Nazi Germany—Beneš founded the Czech National Committee. This committee was headquartered in London during World War II and was recognized by the Allies as the provisional government of Czechoslovakia.

After returning to liberated Prague in May 1945, Beneš served as president until the Communists took control of the government in February 1948. He believed that he had won Soviet dictator Joseph STALIN's friendship and that he could lead Czechoslovakia into participation in the MARSHALL PLAN without arousing Stalin's hostility. This proved to be a severe misreading of Stalin and of Soviet aims in Eastern Europe. Though accused of vacillating at critical moments, Beneš had been one of the founding fathers of the Czechoslovak republic. He had the tragic misfortune of being driven from office, in one way or another, by both Nazis and Communists.

Bentley, Elizabeth (1908–1963) A Communist who spied for the Soviet Union during World War II and then renounced the faith, Elizabeth Bentley worked for the U.S. Federal Bureau of Investiga-

tion as a double agent. In her most prominent act, she provided testimony for the prosecution in the ROSENBERG CASE, in which Julius and Ethel Rosenberg were convicted in 1951 of supplying atomic secrets to the Soviet Union.

Beria, Lavrenty (1899–1953) A native of Georgia, like Joseph STALIN, Beria became head of the Soviet secret police during the latter phases of the Great Purge of 1936–38 and held the position until the end of his life. Joining the Bolshevik Party at the time of the October Revolution in 1917, he became, at the age of just 22, director of the secret police in Georgia. Short, stocky, bespectacled, and unprepossessing, he would bear in later life an eerie resemblance to his Nazi German secret-police counterpart, Heinrich Himmler. In 1931 Beria was appointed first secretary of the Communist Party in Georgia and the following year extended his control over the other republics of Transcaucasia. Highly regarded by Stalin, he came to Moscow in 1938 as people's commissar of internal affairs—in effect, director of the Soviet secret police. Known through the years by a bewildering variety of names, as its status and scope changed, this organization was called at the time the NKVD, the initials of "People's Commissariat of Internal Affairs" in Russian. In this position, Beria followed two of the most unsavory figures of modern history, Genrikh Yagoda and Nikolai Yezhov, each of whom had diligently conducted purges for Stalin (the peak period of purges was called the *Yezhovshchina),* and each of whom ended his life before a firing squad.

Taking his new responsibilities with appropriate seriousness, Beria made his own contributions to the purges and also thoroughly reorganized the forced-labor camps (the GULAG). During World War II he supervised armaments production. In 1946 he became a full member of the POLITBURO; he served also as first deputy premier and as chief of atomic-energy development. When Stalin died in March 1953, his successors had many points of disagreement among themselves, but all were united in fearing Beria and, apparently, in agreeing that he must be disposed of. Certainly Beria possessed formidable power—as minister of state security (as well as of internal affairs), he had his own armed force of some 1.5 million men, with artillery, tanks, and aircraft.

Though exactly what happened to Beria has never been made clear, various accounts have appeared. In one version of the story, Marshal Ivan KONEV presided over a secret court that found Beria guilty of a range of atrocities; another, more dramatic story holds that on June 26, 1953, at a meeting in the Kremlin of the Soviet Communist Party Presidium, Beria, when accused of crimes, produced a revolver, and politicians and generals, Konev among them, fell on him and either shot or strangled him. Beria's survivors published a statement declaring him a "foul provocateur and enemy of the Party" and an agent of imperialism. His condemnation was made public in December 1953. In his famous de-Stalinization speech of February 25, 1956, First Secretary Nikita KHRUSHCHEV declared that Beria had "climbed up the Government ladder over an untold number of corpses." *See also* KGB.

Berlin   Capital of Germany from the establishment of the empire in 1871 to the destruction of the Third Reich in 1945, Berlin played an enduring symbolic role throughout the Cold War. Occupied in 1945 by the Allied powers—the United States, Britain, the Soviet Union, and France—the city, like the country as a whole, was divided among the Allies for the purposes of military control. "The area of Greater Berlin," declared a joint statement of June 5, 1945, "will be occupied by forces of each of the four Powers. An inter-Allied governing authority [called by the Soviets the *Kommandatura*] consisting of four Commandants, appointed by their respective Commanders-in-Chief, will be established to direct jointly its administration."

Despite the optimism of 1945, Cold War pressures drove Berlin in 1948 to become two separate cities with two mayors—Ernst REUTER for the western sector and Friedrich Ebert, son of the first president of the post–World War I German republic,

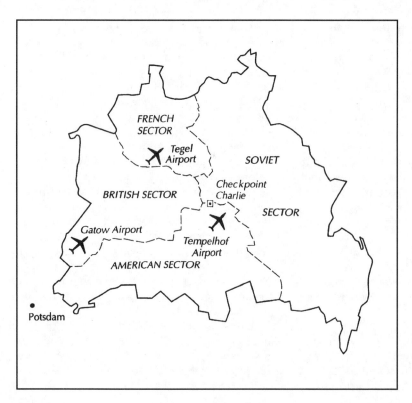

Divided Berlin

for the eastern sector. In 1949, when two German states came into being—the Federal Republic, or West Germany, and the Democratic Republic, or East Germany—the sectors of the city became parts of these states. For West Berlin and West Germany this situation posed obvious problems, since the city stood as an oasis 110 miles inside hostile East Germany. The East–West division of Berlin made it the almost preordained seat for high-level intelligence operations, exchanges of spies, and general international confrontation during the Cold War and won it a prominent place in drama and fiction as well as in reality.

In November 1958 a crisis over the state of Berlin flared up after Premier Nikita KHRUSHCHEV declared that the Soviet Union intended to turn all its responsibilities in Berlin over to the East German government. The Western powers, said *PRAVDA*, had constantly used their occupation of West Berlin "as a venomous weapon with which to poison the atmosphere in Europe. It is now high time for a radical solution of the Berlin problem." In spite of all the meetings and declarations that followed—including a U.S. mobilization in the summer of 1961—no fighting broke out. In August 1961 a fresh wave of tension, accompanied by a great increase in the number of East Germans fleeing to West Berlin, led to the building by the East German government of the BERLIN WALL. On October 27, 1961, U.S. and Soviet tanks faced each other down at CHECKPOINT CHARLIE in the center of Berlin. Though no one could know it at the time, of course, the 1958–62 collisions over Berlin marked the last U.S.-Soviet confrontation in Europe. A top-secret Allied planning group, Live Oak—established in April 1959 by the NATO supreme commander, General Lauris NORSTAD—continued, however, until October 1990, when the two German states were reunited.

One of Berlin's most striking Cold War moments came on June 26, 1963, two years after the building of the wall, when, after touring the city and inspecting the wall, U.S. president John F. KENNEDY declared to a huge throng: "Two thousand years ago the proudest boast in the world was *Civis Romanus sum*. Today, in the world of freedom, the proudest boast is *Ich bin ein Berliner!*" *See also* BERLIN BLOCKADE AND AIRLIFT; EAST BERLIN UPRISING.

Berlin Appeal   Antimilitarism document written in the early 1980s by East German peace activists and signed by more than 2,000 people. The appeal called for a public debate about the moral validity of such practices as producing "war toys" and conducting civil-defense exercises, and asked whether the schools should not consider teaching peace instead of providing military instruction. Such an appeal could hardly have been expected to exert any influence on the hard-line East German government, but, remarkably enough, after the 1989 revolution and the departure of the dictator Erich HONECKER, the principal author of the document, an East Berlin Lutheran minister, became the last defense minister of East Germany before its disappearance as a state.

Berlin blockade and airlift   Dramatic events in the former German capital played an important part in making 1948 a turning point in the development of the Cold War. In January the Soviets attacked Anglo-American moves toward the integration of the Western zones of Germany into the "Western Bloc," and in March the Soviet delegation walked out of the Allied Control Council, which was never to meet again. On March 31 the Soviet military government announced that for administrative reasons Soviet officials would henceforth inspect passengers and baggage on trains from the West bound for Berlin, and then went on to clamp restrictions on freight service and river traffic.

On June 18 matters took a new turn when, abandoning attempts to reach agreement with the Soviets on steps to combat the soaring German inflation, the Western powers introduced the new Deutschemark into their zones, while proposing to keep the previous currency in use in Berlin. Rejecting the offer, and fearing the impact of the D-mark on their Eastern-zone currency, the Soviets introduced their own new mark on June 23, and on the same day cut off electricity to the Western zones and stopped all deliveries of coal, food, milk, and other supplies. The next day all traffic, land and water, between West Berlin and the West had come to a stop—the blockade was now complete. The Soviets declared the Western powers no longer had any rights in the administration of Berlin.

During the Berlin airlift, Allied air-crews fly 4,000 tons of supplies a day into the city.

General Lucius D. CLAY, the U.S. commander in Germany, pressed Washington to allow him to send an armed highway convoy to Berlin. Fearing an outbreak of fighting, however, the U.S. administration decided to react to the Soviet pressure not by abandoning Berlin but by mounting an attempt to supply the city by air while negotiating to solve the overall problem. On June 28, the first day of the airlift, 150 aircraft brought in 400 tons of supplies, a total amounting to only a fraction of the normal daily requirements of the city. On June 30 the U.S. secretary of state, George C. MARSHALL, declared publicly that "the maximum use of air transport will be made to supply the civilian population." Apparently believing that such an airlift had no chance of succeeding, the Soviets at first made no attempt to interfere with it.

Although the crisis had developed amid a disagreement about currency, the Soviets said in early July that the blockade—"technical problems," as they described the situation—would last as long as the Western powers refused to renounce the idea of creating a German government in their occupation zones. By July 20, however, the airlift was bringing in about six times as much cargo daily as had been transported three weeks earlier, and the

people of the city, supporting the effort, were drawing their belts tight. Less publicized was an opposite stream of air traffic, which enabled West Berlin to make some contribution to its own support through exports. During July, the United States sent three strategic-bomber groups to British bases, but on the ground the Western powers in Germany were outweighed 5:1.

In the evening of August 2, in a Kremlin audience with Premier Joseph STALIN, the Western ambassadors heard the surprising statement that the Soviet dictator had no intention of forcing the West out of Berlin. "After all," said Stalin, "we are still allies." He went on to propose a compromise on the currency question, but, oddly, none of his subordinates seemed to have gotten this message. Instead, V. M. MOLOTOV, the Soviet foreign minister, proved unyielding in negotiations, and the Soviets in Berlin declared that aerial maneuvers would require the use of the air corridors by which the airlift was keeping Berlin supplied. Why was Stalin's proposed compromise being disavowed by his presumed subordinates? Naively, as the record would later show, Western experts wondered whether Stalin really had freedom of action. One high-level briefing on "bases, bombs, Moscow,

Leningrad," led U.S. president TRUMAN to note grimly, "I have a terrible feeling afterward that we are very close to war."

By November, General Clay could assure Truman that the airlift was an established success, bringing in 4,000 tons a day regardless of the weather. The airlift had also served to bring West Germans together in support of their kin in Berlin, which had become, not quite four years after the end of World War II, a symbol of liberty.

Early in 1949, the Soviets began to back-pedal. On April 26 TASS announced that the Soviet government had informed the United States of its willingness to lift the blockade if the Western powers would simultaneously abandon their countermeasures and would agree to convene a meeting of the Council of Foreign Ministers to discuss all issues relating to Germany. At 12:01 A.M. on May 12 the blockade came to its end, with U.S. and British trucks and other military vehicles crossing the boundary of the Soviet zone and heading for Berlin on the Helmstedt-Marienborn-Berlin autobahn. One important economic factor among the West's countermeasures had been the toll taken by the embargo on a range of exports from the East. The airlift continued for several months, however. It had been a spectacular achievement, delivering almost two and a half million tons of supplies. This success, made up of flight succeeding flight, seeming at times to be almost nose to tail, in all kinds of weather, had not come easily—some 60 American and British fliers lost their lives. The cost to all countries involved totaled more than $200 million (in 1949 dollars).

The status quo ante did not return to Berlin. From now until the end of the Cold War it would be two cities, with two governments. Twelve years later this separation would find brutal symbolization in the building of the BERLIN WALL.

Berlin Wall   During the night of August 12–13, 1961, the government of East Germany took an extraordinary action to deal with a situation that, existing since the late 1940s, had intensified in previous years. The city of West Berlin had served as a port of exit, an escape hatch, for some 2.5 million East Germans fleeing to the West; in the month of July 1961 alone more than 30,000 of them had left the East. Not only did this bleeding away of many

of the country's best and brightest weaken the state, it also served as a huge negative billboard for Communism. As Soviet premier Nikita KHRUSHCHEV saw it, looking back: "The question of whether this or that system is progressive ought to be decided in political terms. However, many people decide it in the pit of their stomach. They don't consider tomorrow's gains but only today's income." Even some of Khrushchev's subordinates joked that there would soon be nobody left in East Germany except Walter ULBRICHT, the Communist Party leader, and his mistress.

Though some Americans had speculated about the possibility of the East Germans' sealing off the border, no one seemed to expect what actually happened during the night in question. Workers suddenly began tearing up the streets and installing barbed wire and roadblocks. At 2:30 A.M. the border between East and West Berlin was closed; only 13 official crossing points were left open.

At first the purpose of the roadblocks and barbed wire was not completely clear. Contrary to a widespread later belief, the East Germans did not immediately confront the West with a finished and formidable concrete wall. Perhaps, it seemed, they and their Soviet overlords were setting up a valve to control the flow of refugees rather than a plug to stop it completely. On the other hand, perhaps this development portended some new threat to the status of West Berlin, always a concern of the Western powers.

Four days later the East Germans began to put up an ugly but effective wall of cinder blocks, augmented by barbed wire, which was designed to enclose West Berlin like a cage, sealing it off from East Berlin and neighboring parts of East Germany. It was, however, a paradoxical cage, intended to contain not those within it but those outside. As time went on, the first impromptu wall gave way to a permanent installation of concrete, barbed wire, and watchtowers, bordered by minefields; its total length reached slightly more than 100 miles. (The idea of putting up a barbed-wire barrier came from Ulbricht; after accepting the proposal as a way to maintain the status quo in Berlin, Khrushchev added his own touch, the elaboration of the fence into a concrete wall.)

As justification for this remarkable action, the East German government declared in its decree

From 1961 to 1989, the Berlin Wall stretched like a scar across the city.

that East Germans traveling to the West were subjected to "terroristic persecutions" and that West Germany was "carrying out a regular slave traffic," all with the aim of extending "the domination of the militarists" to the GERMAN DEMOCRATIC REPUBLIC. A few days before the appearance of the first barriers, U.S. president KENNEDY had commented to a colleague that Eastern Europe constituted a vital interest for Nikita Khrushchev; he could hardly stand by and let it trickle away. "I can get the alliance to move if he tries to do something about West Berlin," Kennedy said, "but not if he just does something about East Berlin." During all the clamor that followed the building of the wall, the United States and its NATO allies took no actions beyond those intended to stiffen the morale of the West Berliners and the West Germans. For all the shock it produced, the creation of the wall did not affect any vital Western interest. In September, Ulbricht wrote Khrushchev, "I must say that the adversary undertook fewer countermeasures than was expected." More graphically, Ulbricht told Khrushchev that the wall had brought the "cessation of the economic and cultural undermining of the capital of the GDR [East Germany] by the West Berlin swamp."

Documents becoming available in the 1990s have suggested that, in addition to their other motives for approving the building of the wall, the Soviets saw it as a way to restrain Ulbricht from adventurism involving West Berlin—perhaps even an attempt to seize it. More than a year earlier, in June 1960, a Soviet representative in Berlin had reported to his superiors that East German political activists were in a "fighting mood" and ready to storm West Berlin (with, of course, Soviet troops "in the vanguard"). Khrushchev later mildly referred to the building of the wall as "the establishment of border control."

During the first day of the existence of the barricade, a number of people—perhaps 1,500—were able to take advantage of its yet-unperfected state by fleeing East Germany through backyards, crawling over the rubble of bombed-out buildings, and swimming canals and the Havel River. On August 22 the GDR announced that nobody would be allowed to enter a 100-meter-wide strip on either side of the border. This proclamation applied not only to the regime's own citizens but also to West Berliners, who were admonished for their own safety to stay away. In addition, the East Germans cut the number of entry points to six.

Despite the existence of this formidable barrier, Germans from the East continued to try to make their way to the West during the ensuing years; some 5,000 of them succeeded, while another 5,000 were caught in the attempt to flee. Border guards, numbering about 15,000 at any one period, shot possibly as many as 600 people as they were trying to get over the wall or across the minefields. In January 1963, visiting Berlin for a Communist congress, Khrushchev declared the wall a success. Gone were the days when the border with West Berlin was an "open gate which subversive forces used without hindrance and with impunity, not only to squeeze the lifeblood out of you and rob the working people of the republic of billions of marks every year, but also to undermine the very foundations of Socialism."

Despite the talk of socialism, the wall created one strangely capitalistic enterprise involving the sale to West Germany of East German political prisoners, the total by the late 1980s reaching more than 30,000. This traffic in human beings, in which a central part was played by an East Berlin lawyer named Wolfgang Vogel, produced millions of hard-currency dollars for the regime. The East German government also established a "commercial coordination" agency that reunited families in exchange for West German cash; by 1989 some 250,000 of these "human alleviations" had brought in 3.5 billion marks.

During the collapse of the Eastern European Communist governments in 1989, the East German authorities made November 9 a perpetually memorable date by opening the wall to passage without exit visas. Crowds celebrated by dancing on top of this three-decade-old symbol of repression. The citizens who had lived beside it, East and West, hacked off pieces and took them for souvenirs.

In 1993 three former senior officials of East Germany were convicted on manslaughter charges for their role in the deaths of refugees killed trying to cross the wall. The trial, however, had something of an anticlimactic quality, since the three chief defendants—Erich HONECKER, the former Communist Party chief; Erich Mielke, the former head of the Stasi, the secret police; and Willi Stoph, a former premier—had been excused from undergoing punishment because of severe health problems

(Honecker, suffering from liver cancer, died the following year). In addition, the proceedings did not win universal approval in Germany. A former East German official serving in the Parliament in Bonn saw the trial as simply "an excuse to get even with East Germany and its leaders." To some extent, that was surely true. Speaking in no forgiving mood, the mother of the last person shot while trying to cross the Berlin Wall said that at least the sentences dealt out to the convicted officials offered "a little satisfaction."

Bevan, Aneurin (1897–1960)   Son of a Welsh coal miner, Bevan spent several of his early years working in a colliery before going off to London and entering politics as a Labourite; he won a seat in the House of Commons in 1929. Blessed with traditional Welsh eloquence, Bevan (who was known as "Nye") became a leading spokesman for the left wing of the Labour Party, his primary concern being social issues. A contemporary, Lord Swinton, described him as "a natural orator and a brilliant debater," adding that "the two qualities do not always go together." Once, delivering a lively attack on Winston CHURCHILL, Bevan made a point that seemed excessive, and Churchill, though on the receiving end of the rhetoric, sportingly said in a quiet way, "Now, now, don't spoil a first-class speech."

As minister of health in the Labour government elected in 1945, Bevan with his strong populist opinions generally opposed expenditures on arms and objected to the Cold War positions taken by the ATTLEE administration; his landmark achievement was the establishment of the National Health Service. To his disappointment, Attlee failed to offer him either the Foreign Office or the Treasury when these two posts became vacant in 1950. He resigned in 1951 as minister of labor after only a few months in that office, when the cabinet approved an increase in health-service charges to make up for money switched to the defense budget. The British government, Bevan declared, was allowing itself to be "dragged behind the wheels of American diplomacy." In 1955 he stood for the leadership of the party against Hugh Gaitskell, who had insisted on the higher health-service fees, and upon losing the contest underwent something of a transformation, his ideas becoming moderate enough so that he patched up his relationship with Gaitskell and won the post of foreign secretary in the shadow cabinet. Neither he nor Gaitskell, however, lived long enough to hold actual cabinet office again.

In conversation, Bevan, ever the social reformer, could express himself with marked directness. Once, speaking with Colonel NASSER, the Egyptian leader, Bevan pointedly asked why Nasser talked about revolution. "With all due respect," said Bevan, "what you have done is provide a revolutionary façade. You haven't changed Egyptian society." Nevertheless, when Britain, France, and Israel staged their 1956 invasion of Suez, Bevan took a leading part in public protests, declaring at a Trafalgar Square demonstration: "We are stronger than Egypt, but there are other countries stronger than us. Are we prepared to accept for ourselves the logic we are applying to Egypt?"

Bevin, Ernest (1881–1951) British trade-union leader who became one of the chief figures in the Labour Party and served as foreign secretary in the ATTLEE government from 1945 to 1951.

The child of a domestic servant and an un-

known father, Bevin began working at odd jobs at the age of 11, earning as little as sixpence a week. A dockworker in Bristol as a young man, he played the principal part in the creation of what became the largest union in the world, the Transport and General Workers' Union, which he served as general secretary from 1921 to 1940. In May 1940, having become one of Britain's most important labor leaders, he entered Winston CHURCHILL's wartime coalition government as minister of labor and national service; his political stature also gave him a seat in the inner council, the War Cabinet.

In July 1945, when the Labour Party led by Clement Attlee won a sweeping general-election victory over Churchill's Conservatives, the new prime minister as a matter of course chose Bevin for an important cabinet post. But although Bevin, with his deep knowledge of the economy, had wanted and expected to become chancellor of the exchequer—traditionally the number two position —Attlee made him foreign secretary. Discord with the Soviets was already looming; the change in ministerial assignments, said the British writer and broadcaster Michael Charlton, was "immediate evidence of the particular difficulty the Labour

British and American leaders developed close postwar relationships. Here is Foreign Secretary Ernest Bevin (r.), with Secretary of State George C. Marshall.

government and party would have" in adopting a policy that "would cast the Soviet Union in the role of potential aggressors rather than as allies."

Bevin in fact proved to be ahead of many Americans in concluding, from events at various postwar conferences, that the Soviet Union was not likely to collaborate in efforts to bring stability and prosperity to Europe. He also took the lead in welcoming the MARSHALL PLAN and organizing Europeans to create a framework for use of the forthcoming aid. He worked closely with the United States in the establishment of the NORTH ATLANTIC TREATY ORGANIZATION in 1949. Like the prime minister, Attlee, Bevin in his cooperation with the United States had to contend with the opposition of the left wing of his own party.

"Uncle Ernie," as Bevin was known to his subordinates, developed a particularly close friendship with a man of a very different type, the elegant U.S. secretary of state, Dean ACHESON, whom he called "me lad." Enormously fond of Bevin, Acheson said of him that "he seemed to have cornered the market for common sense." His mind, said Acheson, "was tough, and often stubborn, but always open to arguments strongly and honestly pushed."

Bidault, Georges (1899–1983) One of the most prominent French political figures during World War II and for some years in the postwar period, Bidault led an adventurous life. A leader in liberal Catholic politics as a professor of history and journalist before the war (he opposed the appeasement of Adolf Hitler at Munich), he spent a year as a war prisoner of the Germans and, after his release, served during the occupation as president of the National Council of the Resistance, an umbrella organization made up of groups of all political hues. In 1944 he narrowly escaped capture by the Gestapo, the German secret police. For several years after the liberation of France in 1944 he held the post of foreign minister, though for six months in 1946 he was president of the provisional government that preceded the establishment of the Fourth Republic. He worked for cooperation with the Soviet Union and favored the participation of Communist states in the MARSHALL PLAN, but the Communist takeover in Czechoslovakia in 1948 disillusioned him; he thereafter supported

French premier and foreign minister Georges Bidault

strong Western defense policies, including the establishment of the NORTH ATLANTIC TREATY ORGANIZATION.

Bidault founded the Mouvement Républicain Populaire, a Christian Democratic party, and served as premier (1949–50) in that era of fluctuating French cabinets, and again as foreign minister in 1952 and 1954. Dissenting violently from General Charles DE GAULLE's refusal to keep Algeria under French control by force, Bidault for the second time in his career became the head of a resistance organization, this time one opposing the legitimate government of France. (He titled his 1965 memoir *From One Resistance to the Other.*) After he fled a charge of treason for plotting against the security of the French state, he spent several years' exile in Brazil but returned home in

1968 under an amnesty granted as a result of the general upheavals of that year.

Bierut, Boleslaw (1892–1956)   Polish Communist politician, a strong Stalinist who became president of the Polish Committee of National Liberation (the Lublin Committee), which the Soviets created to serve as the provisional government of the country in the latter part of World War II. Like many other Eastern European Communists, Bierut in the interwar years had spent much time in prison for his political activities, and during the war he was in Russia. Introduced by Joseph STALIN to Winston CHURCHILL in a Moscow meeting in October 1944, Bierut and his fellow Lublin Committee members, said the British prime minister, demonstrated that they "had learned and rehearsed their part so carefully that even their masters evidently felt they were overdoing it" in following the Soviet line on postwar arrangements; Stalin, Churchill decided, was proud of his dutiful pupils. Later, at the POTSDAM CONFERENCE in July 1945, Bierut assured Churchill that Poland would "develop on the principles of Western democracy," suggesting (and apparently expecting to be believed) that this development might well be on the English model.

Supported by the presence of Soviet troops, Bierut's government took complete postwar control of Poland, and on August 31, 1948, he replaced Wladyslaw GOMULKA as secretary general of the Polish Workers' Party. This move came as part of Stalin's purge of Eastern European Communist leaders believed to be "Titoists"; that is, those who gave primary allegiance to their own countries and parties rather than to the USSR and the Soviet Communist Party. Called "the perfect Stalinist bureaucrat," Bierut merged leftist parties to create the Polish United Workers' Party. He resigned the presidency of Poland in 1952 to become premier, and retired from this position in 1954. Poignantly enough for so dedicated a Stalinist, he died in Moscow while attending the party congress that was to become famous because of Nikita KHRUSHCHEV's speech detailing Stalin's crimes.

Bissell, Richard (1909–1994)   A U.S. economist who studied at the London School of Economics and Yale University, Bissell served in various posts in Washington during World War II, taught for ten years at the Massachusetts Institute of Technology, and, after working with the MARSHALL PLAN and the Ford Foundation, came to the CENTRAL INTELLIGENCE AGENCY in 1954. Just before joining it, he produced a commissioned study showing clearly that the agency had little prospect, as some officials hoped, of mounting any successful clandestine operations in Eastern Europe. Serving as special assistant to the director, Allen DULLES, from 1954 to 1958, Bissell presided with great effectiveness over the creation, deployment, and operation of one of the CIA's most remarkable achievements, the U-2 spy aircraft, and led the way toward the development of reconnaissance satellites. In the autumn of 1958 Bissell succeeded Frank Wisner in the key CIA position of deputy director for plans. Here, in response to administration pressures for the overthrow of Cuban leader Fidel CASTRO, Bissell developed the plan that came to its bitter fruition as the BAY OF PIGS OPERATION in April 1961. Though Bissell continued in his position for almost a year, his resignation in 1962 resulted directly from the fiasco in Cuba. He then became president of the Institute for Defense Analyses.

Bizonia   Entity (also called the Bizone) that resulted from the U.S.-British agreement on December 2, 1946, to create an economic union from their occupation zones in Germany; the agreement took effect on January 1, 1947. The Allies declared that this union of the two zones "should be regarded as the first step towards the achievement of the economic unity of Germany as a whole" and stated their readiness to begin discussions with France and the Soviet Union (the other occupying powers) about extending the new arrangements to their zones. Taking quite a different view, the Soviets strongly objected to the creation of Bizonia, insisting that it was a move toward the establishment of a West German government and thus of a "military and industrial base of Anglo-American imperialism in Europe." More fearful of German resurgence than were the British and the Americans, the French waited until 1948 to join the project, which then became the "trizone." These developments laid the basis for the FEDERAL REPUBLIC OF GERMANY.

Blackett P(atrick) M. S. (1897–1974) British physicist who won the 1948 Nobel Prize for physics for his work on cosmic radiation. During World War II Blackett did important governmental work in operations research. He was also associated with the development of the ATOMIC BOMB, but his 1948 book *Military and Political Consequences of Atomic Energy* (published in the United States with the somewhat more inviting title *Fear, War and the Bomb*) created a considerable stir among Americans because of its criticism of U.S. nuclear policy, in particular Blackett's assertion that the United States had dropped atomic bombs on Hiroshima and Nagasaki not to defeat Japan but to overawe the Soviet Union. (In later years, of course, this argument was offered, in varying degrees, by many other writers.) A holder of strong left-wing views, Blackett was associated with the Labour government in the middle 1960s.

Blum, Léon (1872–1950) Although he had a law degree from the Sorbonne, Léon Blum entered politics from the unlikely profession of literary critic, becoming in 1936 the first Socialist (as well as the first Jew) to serve as French premier. Pulled between his desire to emphasize social programs and the inescapable military threat posed by Nazi Germany, Blum left office in 1937, returning briefly in 1938. He spent most of World War II as a prisoner of the Vichy government and the Germans, and in 1946, as an elder statesman, presided over a transitional government before the new Fourth Republic began its official existence.

In May 1946 Blum won much credit for negotiating a vitally needed loan agreement with the United States. The French historian Jean-Pierre Rioux acknowledges the "gracious" spirit with which the Americans conducted the negotiations but points out that the arrangement included a provision having long-term cultural consequences. Under the terms of this provision, the French agreed to accept an increased level of imports from the United States, including "massive" numbers of Hollywood movies.

Blunt, Anthony Frederick (1907–1983) The oldest member of the famous CAMBRIDGE FIVE Soviet espionage ring, Anthony Blunt also proved in his career as an art historian to be intellectually by far the most distinguished of the group. Long recognized as one of the world's leading authorities on the works of the French classic master Nicolas Poussin, Blunt for many years held the engaging title of Surveyor of the Queen's Pictures; he was summarily removed from this position in 1979 following his public unmasking as a Soviet spy—the "fourth man" (after Kim PHILBY, Guy BURGESS, and Donald MACLEAN) for whom the press and writers on espionage had been searching.

During the middle 1930s, Blunt, then a teaching fellow at Cambridge, had the assignment of recruiting undergraduates for the Communists. In addition to their shared political convictions, homosexuality bound Blunt and Burgess together; Burgess in his sexual dealings was later described by another friend, Goronwy Rees, as a "combination father confessor and pimp." (In this context, it is important to remember, however attitudes have changed since that time, that in the 1930s and 1940s committing a homosexual act was a criminal offense in Britain. Thus gay men and lesbians were vulnerable to blackmail, a fact that made their behavior a matter of concern for security services.)

In 1940, following service with the British army in France, Blunt joined MI5, the British counterespionage service. (As has frequently been observed, the British authorities in those days made only the sketchiest attempts to check up on recruits for sensitive positions, relying on personal relationships rather than on systematic investigations of background and associations. The Blunt case provides a striking instance, since as a Soviet spy he was acting in the service of a country that in 1940 was supporting Nazi Germany.) In the course of this remarkably convenient assignment, Blunt not only had access to a wide variety of secret information that he passed on, in copious quantities, to his Soviet controller, but also developed an important friendship with Philby, a fellow Cantabrigian. After World War II Blunt no longer held an intelligence post, but he remained available to the KGB for special jobs; a notable example was his hasty sanitizing of Burgess's flat after the latter's unexpected departure from England with Maclean in May 1951.

Blunt admitted his treason only in 1964, after it had been revealed to U.S. and British authorities by Michael STRAIGHT, an American upon whom Blunt had exercised his recruiting blandishments. Not only did Blunt receive immunity from prosecution, however, but he was allowed to continue his service to the queen until 1979, when, in answer to a question in the House of Commons, Prime Minister Margaret THATCHER publicly revealed his treachery. The revelation brought opprobrium not only to Blunt but to the authorities as well. Blunt received particular blame for having involved the royal family in an affair of espionage; in granting him immunity, the government, it was widely felt, had simply taken good care of a member of the establishment. Managing to administer her own specific punishment, the queen stripped Blunt of his knighthood.

Because of Blunt's intellectual prominence, his conduct of a double life aroused wide comment: How could he mix aesthetic honesty and pervasive falsehood on so grand a scale? What relation did his underground beliefs bear to his publicly stated critical principles? Perhaps he was able to practice what another spy, Klaus FUCHS, called "controlled schizophrenia." Perhaps also the rationality, the classical purity, and the mathematical precision that characterized the works of Poussin provided his twentieth-century admirer with a necessary counterpoint to a tangled underground life.

Bogotá Conference Building on the 1947 RIO TREATY at the ninth inter-American conference in Bogotá, Colombia, in March and April 1948, the United States led the way to the creation of the Organization of American States, which expanded existing agreements for consultation among nations of the hemisphere and reaffirmed the standing 1930s commitment to work together to prevent one American state from interfering in the affairs of another. The final document, signed on April 30, prohibited economic and political assistance to outside forces engaged in actions against elected governments.

The spectacular part of the conference, however, took place outside the meeting rooms. Even before the sessions opened, rumors had circulated that, as the U.S. ambassador, William Beaulac, expressed it, "Communists and left-wing liberals" intended to sabotage the conference "in order to embarrass the Colombian Government and create difficulties among American republics." Gangs egged cars and officials. On April 9, when the Liberal Party leader, Jorge Gaitán, was assassinated, angry crowds in the streets blamed the murder on the Colombian president, Mariano Ospiña Pérez. Mobs attacked public buildings, including those in which the conference sessions were being held. Antigovernment groups seized radio stations and called for assaults on government officials and other prominent persons.

That evening, U.S. secretary of state George C. MARSHALL and other members of the U.S. delegation returned to the house in which they were lodged for the conference. Despite the volatility of the Colombian situation—the government had changed hands shortly before the conference began —little advance thought had been given to security. At the U.S. residence, a hasty poll revealed only one weapon in the group, a pistol belonging to Marshall's orderly. This soldier, Sergeant (later Colonel) C. G. George, subsequently observed that Marshall under siege had the time of his life. Perhaps to compensate for having spent World War II in noncombat situations, the former U.S. chief of staff took great pleasure, when Colombian army reinforcements finally appeared, in instructing the young commander in the deployment of his force.

The riots in Bogotá reinforced American fears of Communist subversion in Latin America. Marshall expressed the view that the Communists had created the disorders to embarrass the United States on the eve of the crucial Italian elections, in which the West feared Communist gains. The Colombian Communist Party leader, Marshall declared, had called on the rioters to burn the presidential palace. As a result of all the disruption, representatives of several countries proposed that the conference be moved to another city. Marshall, however, insisted on staying. His presence, he believed, had served to diminish the importance of the uprising and to take the edge off Communist threats. In spite of all the tension and violence, it appears, he also had enjoyed himself.

Bohlen, Charles Eustis (1904–1974) U.S. Foreign Service officer who became one of the leading State Department specialists in SOVIETOLOGY and one of the most important modern American diplomats.

Born into a well-to-do family, Bohlen graduated

from Harvard in 1927 and two years later entered the U.S. Foreign Service, where he became a close friend of another young officer, George F. KENNAN. Having prepared himself for service in Russia, Bohlen (known universally as "Chip") went to Moscow after the United States and the USSR established diplomatic relations in 1933. After a period back in Washington, he returned to the Soviet Union in 1938, in time to attend the last of Joseph STALIN's Great Purge trials of alleged conspirators and traitors. In 1940 the diplomatic merry-go-round sent Bohlen on to Tokyo. The Japanese attack on Pearl Harbor brought a six-month internment for the staff of the American embassy before they were returned to Washington, where Bohlen became assistant chief of the Division of European Affairs, moving up to chief in 1944; in 1943 he had gone back to Moscow as first secretary of the embassy and served as President Franklin D. ROOSEVELT's Russian interpreter at the inter-Allied Tehran Conference.

In December 1944 Bohlen took on a unique and significant assignment as assistant to the secretary of state for White House liaison, a position that gave him fresh political insight to go along with his long professional diplomatic experience. He went to the 1945 YALTA CONFERENCE and POTSDAM CONFERENCE as a presidential adviser. Overall, Bohlen probably attended more high-level wartime and immediate postwar meetings than any other U.S. diplomat.

In the early years of the Cold War, Bohlen acted as adviser to U.S. delegations to various conferences and served as State Department counselor. In the spring of 1947 he wrote the first draft of the famous Harvard speech in which General George C. MARSHALL, then secretary of state, proposed the concept that developed into the MARSHALL PLAN for aid to Europe. In 1953 Bohlen came to public attention when his nomination by President Dwight D. EISENHOWER as ambassador to the Soviet Union brought an outcry from right-wing members of the president's own party, including Senator Joseph MCCARTHY. Though Bohlen was a professional, nonparty civil servant and no admirer of the Soviet government, the protesters objected to his having served as an adviser to President Roosevelt. Secretary of State John Foster DULLES supported the nomination (it would hardly have been made oth-

erwise) but went to considerable lengths to avoid even being photographed with the controversial nominee, who won confirmation by a 74-to-13 vote. In 1957, apparently not on the best of terms with Dulles, Bohlen was switched from Moscow to the Philippines as ambassador. In 1962 President John F. KENNEDY gave him a major assignment as ambassador to France, at a time when new relationships were being worked out between the U.S. government and General Charles DE GAULLE; Bohlen remained in Paris until 1968. He also served as special assistant to the secretary of state for Soviet affairs, 1959–61, and deputy undersecretary of state for political affairs, 1968–69.

Though a product of the Ivy League, Bohlen had an unusual style as a diplomat—casual, unpressed, spilling tobacco as he messed with his pipe. He once described the Soviet Union as resembling "the act of love. You can read and memorize every page of all the literature about it. But you can't possibly tell what it's really like until you've experienced it yourself."

Bosch, Juan (1909–) Leftist political leader in the Dominican Republic who returned from exile after the assassination of the dictator Rafael Trujillo in 1961 and in 1962 won the presidency in a free election. He served only ten months before rightists, with U.S. State Department approval, overthrew his government because of the perceived radicalism of his programs. In 1965, when the head of the ruling junta announced his intention to run for the presidency, pro-Bosch forces staged a rebellion. Convinced that a CASTRO-style revolution loomed ahead in the Dominican Republic, with the Communists plotting to extend their beachhead in Latin America, U.S. president Lyndon B. JOHNSON determined to thwart it and worked through the Organization of American States to create an "Inter-American Peace Force," which began landing troops on April 30. Bosch responded that "this was a democratic revolution smashed by the leading democracy of the world." The intervention drew widespread condemnation in Latin America, where observers accused the United States of once again relying on "gunboat diplomacy." The OAS force stayed in position until September 1966.

Boutros Boutros-Ghali, sixth United Nations secretary-general

Boutros-Ghali, Boutros (1922–) Taking office on January 1, 1992, succeeding Peru's Javier PÉREZ DE CUÉLLAR as secretary-general of the UNITED NATIONS, Boutros-Ghali became the first post–Cold War head of the organization. He likewise is the first Arab and first African to hold the position. A member of a prominent Coptic Christian family in Cairo, he holds degrees in law and international law from Cairo University; he also spent a year at Columbia University (1954–55) as a Fulbright scholar. As Egyptian foreign minister, he played an important part in the 1978 negotiation of the CAMP DAVID ACCORDS between Egypt and Israel, and his long-established advocacy of peaceful Arab-Israeli relations secured him election as secretary-general with no objections from Israel.

Brandt, Willy (1913–1992) Originally named Herbert Ernst Karl Frahm, this German political figure from Lübeck became one of the leading European statesmen of the Cold War era. He adopted his later name in 1933 when, as a Social Democratic student activist, he fled from Germany to Norway to escape arrest by the Nazi secret police, the Gestapo. His adventures continued in 1940, when the Germans landed in Norway and, this time, suc-

ceeded in imprisoning him; however, he managed to escape and flee to Sweden.

Returning to Germany after the end of World War II, Brandt resumed the German citizenship he had given up in Norway, entered the West German Parliament, and in 1957 won election to the challenging and highly visible post of mayor of West Berlin. During his administration the city not only lived with running tensions but underwent the 1958 crisis—when Soviet premier Nikita KHRUSHCHEV sought to demilitarize it and thus force out the Western powers—and the great 1961 shock caused by the East German government's building of the BERLIN WALL. In 1958 Brandt memorably declared: "We have no weapons, but we have a right to live and we have good nerves. Presumably there will be some further tests of our nerves, but that will neither confuse nor disconcert us." In the excitement following the erection of the Berlin Wall, Brandt told a throng of 300,000 citizens that they faced the most serious situation since the BERLIN BLOCKADE AND AIRLIFT of 1948–49. The Western Allies must take convincing countermeasures, he said in the Bundestag. These measures should be nonmilitary, but they must have substance; his constituents, he declared, would

West German chancellor Willy Brandt

"think nothing of countermeasures which would set off resounding laughter from the Potsdamerplatz to Vladivostok."

Brandt twice sought the federal chancellorship before becoming foreign minister in the 1966 "Grand Coalition" government under Kurt Kiesinger. In October 1969 he finally achieved his goal: the Social Democrats won the national election, and, as the head of the party, he became the first Social Democrat to hold the chancellorship.

Brandt quickly moved to launch the policy by which he is best remembered, his OSTPOLITIK (Eastern policy), which aimed at improving relations with the Soviet Union, East Germany, and the other Eastern Bloc nations. This policy had both admirers and detractors; notably, it involved a reversal of one of the key principles of West German

policy, the HALLSTEIN DOCTRINE, which called for the breaking of diplomatic relations with any country, aside from the Soviet Union, that gave diplomatic recognition to East Germany. Though the Eastern countries appeared to welcome Brandt's overtures, they by no means made his negotiating path easy, and he resisted many of their demands. Lengthy and complex wrangling was required before he could sign a nonaggression pact with the USSR and a treaty recognizing Poland's western boundary, both in 1970, and a treaty with East Germany in 1972. After a visit to Soviet leader Leonid BREZHNEV in 1971, Brandt sought to make one point clear. "We have not become friends of the Soviet Union or of its system," he said, "but rather have become partners in a businesslike contract, just like other Western states that are treaty partners of the Soviet Union." The treaty with Poland attracted strong criticism because, for many Germans, it represented the renunciation of land they felt ought to remain German, even if for the time being nothing could be done to repatriate it. Brandt energetically played the role of good European in the West as well, putting his influence behind the ultimately successful British attempt to join the EUROPEAN ECONOMIC COMMUNITY (the Common Market).

In recognition of his drive for conciliation in Eastern Europe, Brandt was awarded the 1971 Nobel Peace Prize. But three years later his notable career took a shocking turn: one of his closest colleagues, Günther Guillaume, was unmasked as an East German intelligence agent. This incident made a particularly poignant story. Guillaume's father was a doctor who had given Brandt medical treatment and helped him escape the clutches of the Gestapo almost four decades earlier. In 1956, at the father's request, Brandt had accepted the son as a political refugee from the East and, as chancellor, had innocently installed this East German mole as his confidential secretary and personal companion. Holding his post from 1970 to 1974, Guillaume had been able to keep the East Germans and the KGB thoroughly informed about Brandt's Ostpolitik ideas as well as about everything else that concerned the chancellor; such information unquestionably played a role in the negotiations between Brandt and Eastern Bloc representatives. After the tragic revelation of his trusted aide's true allegiance, Brandt had no choice but to resign the chancellorship, though he engaged in further public service in the late 1970s and early 1980s by serving as chairman of the BRANDT COMMISSION, an international economics study group.

Brandt Commission   In 1977, Willy BRANDT became chairman of a United Nations–sponsored, nongovernmental study group named the Independent Commission on International Development Issues and thenceforth popularly called the Brandt Commission. In 1980 the commission produced a report that discussed the continuing poverty in the THIRD WORLD, focusing on North-South divergences, and suggested measures that other nations could undertake to improve conditions. When no major actions followed, the group went to work to prepare another report, which declared that matters were becoming steadily worse. No more than the first report, however, did it seem to produce any significant reorientation in the thinking of the wealthier nations.

Braun, Wernher von (1912–1977)   A rocket enthusiast from his early years, this German engineer became at the age of 25 the technical director of the German army's rocketry research center at Peenemünde on the Baltic Sea. By 1938 he had developed the prototype of the V-2, the rocket with which the Germans began to attack southern England in 1944. In early 1945, as the Red Army advanced westward, the scientists fled Peenemünde; von Braun went into hiding until he could give himself up to Western troops. Sent to London for interrogation, he was later released and, in a remarkable turn of events, was given a contract with the U.S. government. A completely new chapter of his life now began in the United States.

Together with six colleagues, von Braun was to "undertake such research, design, development, and other tasks associated with jet propulsion and guided missiles" as he might be given. This arrangement resulted from what has often been called the race for German scientists. An original —and little-remembered—motive for the importation of scientists from Germany was the desire of the U.S. War Department to make use of their knowledge against Japan; however, the Pacific war ended about a month before the first group arrived in the United States. The project then focused totally on the Soviet Union.

After various vicissitudes in funding, von Braun became established at Huntsville, Ala., where he perfected the Redstone missile, a direct descendant of the V-2, and devised a project to put a satellite into orbit. His great moment came in December 1957, two months after the USSR had launched *SPUTNIK I.* Trying to catch up in this new space race, the United States called on a navy-sponsored satellite, the Vanguard, which blew up on launch. Within two months, the von Braun team had converted its Jupiter-C, a stretched Redstone, into a substitute satellite launcher, which on January 31, 1958, performed perfectly, to the massed cry from the watching crowd: "Go, baby, go!"

With Huntsville declaring itself the "space capital of the universe," von Braun continued to be a central figure in the development of U.S. rockets and missiles, leading to those that took the Apollo flights to the moon. Having become a U.S. citizen in 1955, von Braun was even seen at meetings of the local Rotary Club. He seems to have been a person who lived for his science, as artists are said to do for their art. In 1970 he became deputy associate administrator of the National Aeronautics and Space Administration (NASA).

Brezhnev, Leonid Ilyich (1906–1982)   Leading Soviet political figure from 1964 (as first secretary, then GENERAL SECRETARY, of the COMMUNIST PARTY OF THE SOVIET UNION) and 1977 (as chairman of the Presidium of the SUPREME SOVIET) until his death on November 10, 1982. By retaining his party post after 1977, Brezhnev became the first Soviet leader to serve as head of the party and chief of state simultaneously.

A farm and factory laborer as a young man in various parts of Russia and in his native Ukraine, Brezhnev later worked as a surveyor and graduated as an engineer. Edging his way up in party politics, in 1938 he began a quarter-century relationship in war and peace with his fellow Ukrainian politician, Nikita KHRUSHCHEV, and with others in the republic, some of whom would make up the "Dnieper Mafia" when Brezhnev reached the pinnacle of power. As a Red Army political officer during World War II, Brezhnev impressed Khrushchev with his work and developed a friendship with Andrei GRECHKO, who later, as a Soviet marshal, helped Brezhnev fabricate an image as a fighting World War II soldier.

As Khrushchev rose in national politics, he extended a helping hand to his protégé, putting him in a position to be elected to the party CENTRAL COMMITTEE in 1952 and, after the post-Stalin confusion had subsided, again in 1956. Brezhnev supported his mentor in the 1957 victory over the ANTIPARTY GROUP and served as a secretary of the Central Committee until he was for the first time elected chairman of the Presidium of the Supreme Soviet, a ceremonial position, apparently in an attempt by opponents of Khrushchev to weaken the leader by removing one of his allies from a position of line authority. However, Brezhnev kept his seat on the party Presidium, and he seems to have taken pleasure in his position as so-called president of the USSR. In 1963 he managed to work his way out of this sinecure and back into the inner circle as second secretary of the Communist Party.

Then, on October 15, 1964, Brezhnev demonstrated that his loyalty to Khrushchev had expired. A group of officials led by Mikhail SUSLOV, the party ideologist, and including Brezhnev, forced the flamboyant leader from power. With Suslov apparently declining the succession, Brezhnev took over as head of the party, and Alexei KOSYGIN was chosen head of the government as premier, but it soon became clear that Brezhnev had become first among equals. This was an interesting and perhaps surprising development, since Brezhnev's colleagues had looked on him as something of an equivocator, a man who tended to crumple up in the face of trouble. Khrushchev once commented that Brezhnev, in his early days, was known as "the ballerina," because anybody could turn him around.

As Soviet leader, Brezhnev left the supervision of most domestic matters to Kosygin while concentrating on foreign affairs and the strengthening of Soviet armed forces. Like Khrushchev, Brezhnev lacked the power Joseph STALIN had held, and at first he avoided any "cult of personality," but as time went on this modesty faded, to the extent that, having decided he wanted to be chief of state as well as head of the party and thus meet other

world leaders as an equal, he removed Nikolai PODGORNY from the chairmanship of the Presidium in 1977 and gave himself the job. He also would make a great show of his medals, wearing them on every important occasion. Moscow wags circulated the story that Brezhnev had undergone a unique kind of surgery—a chest enlargement to make room for the display of all of his decorations. In 1976 he became the only party leader besides Stalin to become a marshal of the Soviet Union.

Quiet in public, Brezhnev avoided the sensationalism and the sweeping declarations that had characterized Khrushchev. In private life, however, he was gregarious and talkative, fond of good food and drink and, notably, of fast cars. But for the last few years of his life he suffered visibly from deteriorating health, speaking haltingly, his face pale and bloated (the latter because of medication for heart trouble). Frequently walking like a robot, he sometimes had to be seized by the person nearest him and turned in the right direction.

During the PRAGUE SPRING of 1968, when Czechoslovakia appeared to be loosening the bonds of Soviet control, Brezhnev sent WARSAW PACT troops and tanks to crush the movement. He justified this invasion of Czechoslovakia by what the West came to call the BREZHNEV DOCTRINE, whereby "socialist" states must come to the aid of a fellow socialist state whose government was threatened by reactionary forces.

Domestically, the Brezhnev regime, marked by cronyism, spreading corruption, and failure to face the need for economic reform, created an era that would later be referred to by the people in code expressions such as the "period of stagnation"; Mikhail GORBACHEV would speak disapprovingly of the "administrative command system of government," under which all orders emanated from the Kremlin. Under Brezhnev, the Soviet economy suffered from inefficiency, shortages, and an increasing technology gap, and could ill support the defense expenditures with which the leadership burdened it.

In the 1970s an emphasis on DÉTENTE marked Soviet relations with the United States. Though never as thorough as its publicity often seemed to claim, détente was clearly preferable to confronta-

Soviet Communist Party general secretary Leonid Brezhnev *(l.)* and President Richard M. Nixon confer with the aid of Brezhnev's interpreter.

tion, but it had already faded by the time Soviet troops invaded AFGHANISTAN in 1979, and it died completely in 1981 following the imposition of martial law in rebellious Poland. Indeed, at the time of his death in the following year, Brezhnev left not only a stagnant economy but numerous contentious issues pending with the United States: Poland, arms control, trade relations, Afghanistan, Cambodia (where the USSR supported Vietnamese occupation), and human-rights and emigration questions. Relations between the superpowers had fallen to a low not seen for a number of years. Few could have dreamed that the era of PERESTROIKA and GLASNOST, with all its revolutionary consequences, lay only three years away. *See also* CARTER, Jimmy; KISSINGER, Henry Alfred; NIXON, Richard Milhous; REAGAN, Ronald Wilson.

Brezhnev Doctrine   The name given in the West to the justification put forward by the Soviet government for the invasion of Czechoslovakia in August 1968 to suppress the process of liberalization—the PRAGUE SPRING—taking place under the leadership of Alexander DUBČEK. Although the invasion resulted from a complex play of forces within the Kremlin and the EASTERN BLOC, Leonid BREZHNEV, the Soviet leader, declared several weeks later that the USSR had the duty to intervene, without regard to national boundaries, anywhere "social-

ism" was threatened by moves toward "the restoration of capitalism." In a meeting in the Kremlin, Brezhnev bluntly told Czech leaders that their country was linked with the Soviet Union "forever." So, by the same doctrine, were all the other Communist states of Eastern Europe. The intervention in Czechoslovakia aroused protests not only from Western governments but even from Western European Communist parties, especially those of France and Italy. These protests proved to be the beginnings of the 1970s movement called EUROCOMMUNISM.

Bricker Amendment   Proposed U.S. constitutional amendment, first offered in 1951 by Republican senator John W. Bricker of Ohio, to limit the ability of the president to make executive agreements with foreign countries. Bricker received support from other conservatives who believed that in the Tehran Conference and the YALTA CONFERENCE during World War II the United States (that is, President ROOSEVELT) had made damaging concessions to the Soviet Union. Under Bricker's amendment, all executive agreements would have been voted on by the full Senate, as is the case with treaties. In 1954 the amendment failed to pass the Senate by just one vote, for President EISENHOWER had put together an opposing coalition of liberal Democrats and moderate Republicans. Speaking of

Bricker's supporters, Ike said, "I wonder if they have lost all of their brains."

brinkmanship　Shortly after World War II, Stephen Potter, a British humorist, published a little book called *The Theory and Practice of Gamesmanship; or, The Art of Winning Games Without Actually Cheating.* This satirical tribute to poor sportsmanship became so popular that the suffix *-manship* was soon being used to create all kinds of new words. Hence it was hardly surprising that it was put to work anew when a sensational article in *Life* magazine (January 16, 1956) praised U.S. secretary of state John Foster DULLES by saying that "three times, new disclosures show, he brought the U.S. back from the brink"—that is, the brink of major war; "three times" referred to threats made by Dulles with respect to Communist actions in Korea, Indochina, and Formosa (Taiwan). Dulles's brand of DETERRENCE, *Life* observed, "has not only prevented the 'big' hydrogen war but the littler wars as well."

The article, based on an interview, contained lengthy quotes from the secretary. "You have to take chances for peace," Dulles told the reporter, "just as you must take chances in war. Some say that we were brought to the verge of war. Of course we were brought to the verge of war. The ability to get to the verge without getting into the war is the necessary art." Then, dropping *verge* in favor of the noun that was soon to become famous, he said, "If you try to run away from it, if you are scared to go to the brink, you are lost. . . . We walked to the brink and we looked it in the face."

Often his own worst enemy because of a tendency to grow overly expansive in a speech or an interview, Dulles this time succeeded in sending a shiver around the world, and for a number of years *brinkmanship* (sometimes *brinksmanship*) found wide usage as a synonym for reckless diplomacy. But the paradoxical fact was that Dulles's chief, President EISENHOWER, proved in many respects to be the most cautious of U.S. postwar presidents.

Brodsky, Joseph (1940–)　In 1964, at the age of 24, this promising Leningrad poet, whose early childhood was during the great German siege of

the city, found himself arrested for "social parasitism" and sentenced to five years at hard labor. This punishment caused such a stir in the Soviet literary world, more than two decades before GLASNOST, that the government released him the following year; in 1972 he was expelled from the country and settled in the United States, where he has taught at numerous universities and has spent much of his time as poet in residence at the University of Michigan. He became an American citizen in 1977.

Curiously, though perhaps not surprisingly, Brodsky did not begin to attract a wide Soviet audience until some 15 years after leaving the country, the operative factor being his receiving the Nobel Prize for literature in 1987. His personal, nonpolitical poetry clearly had greater appeal for the Nobel committee than such work had held for his political critics in the USSR in 1964.

Brown, Harold (1927–)　One of the "whiz kids" brought to Washington in the 1960s by U.S. defense secretary Robert MCNAMARA, Harold Brown served as secretary of the air force under President Lyndon JOHNSON (1965–69) and returned to serve as secretary of defense in the CARTER administration (1977–81). A physicist (with degrees from Columbia University), Brown held the directorship of the Lawrence Livermore Laboratory in California in 1961 when McNamara chose him to be director of research and engineering of the Defense Department. Between his tours in Washington, Brown served as president of the California Institute of Technology (1969–77); during this period he was a U.S. delegate to the STRATEGIC ARMS LIMITATION TALKS with the Soviet Union. In the latter phase of the Carter administration, Brown advocated what became known as Presidential Directive 59, which called for a broadening of the targets of U.S. missiles. During the Reagan era, commenting on the president's proposed STRATEGIC DEFENSE INITIATIVE, Brown made the interesting and paradox-laden point that such "Star Wars" weapons would be most effective not against attacking enemy missiles but against the opponent's own Star Wars weapons.

Bruce, David K. E. (1898–1977)　American political figure and diplomat, born in Baltimore, who became the first Foreign Service officer to hold the three major ambassadorial posts in Europe: France, 1949–52; West Germany, 1957–59; and Britain, 1961–69. Bruce also represented the United States with the Economic Cooperation Administration in Europe in the early days of the MARSHALL PLAN, chaired the U.S. delegation to the Paris peace talks on Vietnam (1970–71), directed the U.S. liaison office in China before the regime's formal recognition by the United States (1972–74), and rounded out his career as ambassador to the NORTH ATLANTIC TREATY ORGANIZATION (1974–75). During World War II Bruce had been a top official of the Office of Strategic Services in Europe. A highly trusted official, known for his sharp humor, Bruce in his European diplomatic duties not only carried out U.S. policy but had a hand in making it. He strongly supported plans for European unity, particularly with respect to Franco-German integration.

Brzezinski, Zbigniew (1928–) A Columbia University professor of international relations, Brzezinski served as U.S. president CARTER's national security adviser (1977–81). A native of Poland, Brzezinski graduated from McGill University in 1949 and received his master's degree from the same university in 1950; he earned his Ph.D. from Harvard in 1953 and became a U.S. citizen in 1958. He taught at Harvard before going to Columbia, and in 1989 he became a professor at Johns Hopkins University's Nitze School.

As national security adviser, Brzezinski advocated a policy of "architecture" to replace the "acrobatics" he ascribed to Henry KISSINGER. He consistently took a hard line toward the Soviet Union; his views brought him into continuing conflict with the secretary of state, Cyrus VANCE, who favored the policy of DÉTENTE. As Carter's term in office progressed, Brzezinski seemed increasingly to win the president's favor, though Vance was at the center of the successful negotiation of the 1978 CAMP DAVID ACCORDS between Egypt and Israel. With the support of President Carter, Brzezinski took a firm and probably influential stance in the crisis that erupted in Poland in 1979–80 with the emergence of the SOLIDARITY trade union, a public and political involvement that was continued in the REAGAN administration.

Bulganin, Nikolai (1895–1975) Soviet politician who served from 1955 to 1958 as premier, or chairman of the Council of Ministers, as the associate of First Secretary Nikita KHRUSHCHEV. Reported variously to have been the son of an office clerk or a factory worker in Nizhni Novgorod, Bulganin began his career in the secret police, then known as the Cheka, but moved into the public arena in 1931, when he was made chairman of the Moscow City Soviet. In this position he worked with Khrushchev, who was first secretary of the Moscow party committee—a relationship that paralleled on the local level the situation that was to occur on the national level in the mid-1950s, when Khrushchev held the political power as party first secretary and Bulganin was head of the government.

After serving as head of government of the Russian Federation in the late 1930s—an era when younger men moved up to take the positions left vacant by officeholders shot in the Great Purge of 1936–38—Bulganin spent the years of World War II as a political officer in the Red Army, reaching the rank of general in 1944. After the war, when Joseph STALIN decided to retire as minister of the armed forces, the post went to Bulganin, and with it came the rank of marshal. In 1948 Bulganin became a full member of the POLITBURO.

In 1953, after Stalin's death, Bulganin became Soviet defense minister. He came to worldwide notice in 1955 when, as Khrushchev's ally, he was named premier. The elegant Bulganin, goateed and well tailored, and the squat Khrushchev, who never managed to look at home in suit and tie, set off on a series of travels to capitals in Europe and Asia, while the press billed the pair as "B & K." Though outranked in appearance and style, Khrushchev left no doubt as to who wielded the power and who was simply the front man.

Identified with no program and viewed essentially as an amiable consensus politician, Bulganin made a serious misjudgment in the spring of 1957 by supporting the ANTIPARTY GROUP, which aimed at overthrowing Khrushchev. When Khrushchev emerged victorious from the struggle, Bulganin began to hold office on borrowed time. In March 1958 Khrushchev dismissed him from the premiership and took the post for himself. Like other persons removed from office by Khrushchev, the marshal found himself dispatched to a distant corner of the Soviet empire; his assignment called for him to become chairman of the economic council in Stavropol, in the North Caucasus. He retired in 1960.

Bunche, Ralph (1904–1971) Identified with the UNITED NATIONS for 25 years, Bunche, a native of Detroit, joined the UN Secretariat in 1946. He served on the peace commission in Palestine, and in 1948, after his chief, Count Bernadotte, was assassinated by a Jewish terrorist gang, Bunche handled the negotiations so ably that he won the 1950 Nobel Peace Prize for ending the Arab-Israeli war (the first black person to receive this prize). In 1954 he became undersecretary-general of the UN for political affairs, a position that saw him involved in a variety of peacekeeping activities. He remained with the UN until his retirement in 1971.

Valedictorian of his class at UCLA (1927), Bunche held master's and doctoral degrees from Harvard and taught at Howard and Northwestern Universities. In 1954 he was appointed a full professor at Harvard. UN secretary-general U Thant said of Bunche, "He was an international institution in his own right, transcending both nationality and race in a way achieved by so few."

Bundesrepublik Deutschland *See* FEDERAL REPUBLIC OF GERMANY.

Bundy, McGeorge (1919–) American educator (dean of arts and sciences at Harvard, 1953–61) who served Presidents John F. KENNEDY and Lyndon B. JOHNSON as national security adviser (1961–66), giving the position greater scope and authority than it had previously possessed (before his tenure, it was called "special assistant for national security affairs"). A 1940 Yale graduate, Bundy served in World War II as an intelligence officer. The son of a longtime associate of Henry L. Stimson, Bundy worked with that elder statesman in the preparation of his memoirs.

As national security adviser, Bundy participated in the planning of the BAY OF PIGS OPERATION in 1961, the handling of the CUBAN MISSILE CRISIS, the U.S. intervention in the Dominican Republic in 1965, and operations in other crises. But, as one of "the best and the brightest" (as David Halberstam

called certain U.S. military and foreign-policy planners in his 1972 book of that title), Bundy was especially identified with the heavy U.S. involvement in Vietnam. After resigning in 1966 to become president of the Ford Foundation, as protests mounted against the VIETNAM WAR, Bundy increasingly moderated his support of the war.

Bundy, William (1917–) Brother of McGeorge BUNDY, William Bundy (Yale, 1939) joined the CIA in the 1950s and in the 1960s served as assistant secretary of defense for international affairs and assistant secretary of state for Far Eastern affairs. In 1964 he played a leading part in the preparation of a draft congressional joint resolution that would authorize President JOHNSON to deploy military forces to defend any Southeast Asian country threatened by Communism. Though no action followed at the time, Johnson won such a resolution in August 1965 after the Gulf of Tonkin incident. William Bundy later (1972–84) edited the journal *Foreign Affairs. See also* GULF OF TONKIN RESOLUTION.

Bunker, Ellsworth (1894–1984) American corporate executive and Yale graduate (1916) who held several ambassadorial positions, culminating in his appointment in 1967 as ambassador to South Vietnam. Often spoken of as the U.S. proconsul in the country, Bunker held this controversial position under Presidents JOHNSON and NIXON, until a ceasefire between North Vietnam and South Vietnam took effect in 1973. Generally he took an optimistic view of events in Vietnam, holding, for instance, that the U.S. representatives would go to the talks opening in Paris in 1968 in a strong negotiating position. Several months earlier, in January 1968, the U.S. embassy compound in Saigon—a six-story building surrounded by a wall and nicknamed "Bunker's bunker"—had been invaded by VIETCONG guerrillas in the opening of the TET OFFENSIVE. Though military analysts argued that Tet had been a strategic defeat for the Vietcong, it had not looked like it on American television, and despite Bunker's sanguine outlook, objections to the VIETNAM WAR increased. By 1971, however, Bunker's disgust with the regime of South Vietnamese president NGUYEN VAN THIEU, who had forced his rivals out of the presidential election campaign, had become great enough for him to urge President Nixon to disavow Thieu.

After retiring from his ambassadorial post, Bunker—a tall, spare, dignified figure whom age did not seem to slow down—remained on call and later directed the negotiations between the United States and Panama that in 1978 produced a treaty providing for ultimate Panamanian control over the Panama Canal.

Burgess, Guy (1911–1963)   Member of the famous CAMBRIDGE FIVE Soviet espionage ring and one of the most widely admired undergraduates of his early-1930s generation, Burgess combined a personality that many persons found magnetic with a compulsive need to make a public display of his homosexuality and alcoholism. He took "an almost sensual pleasure" in the discussion of ideas, said his friend Michael STRAIGHT, and seemed to many admirers to embody the ideal of male beauty, but this was offset by his extreme personal slovenliness.

Burgess came up to Trinity College, Cambridge, from Eton in 1930. By 1932, under the influence of a don named Maurice Dobb, he had become a declared Communist, well ahead of his more famous Cambridge confrere, Kim PHILBY, who appears from KGB files, however, to have been recruited as an agent before rather than after (as has generally been believed) Burgess was approached. Instead of being the "first man" of the Cambridge Five, Burgess, as noted by the historian John Costello, appears to have ranked as number three, and, at that, his personal flamboyance made him only a marginal recruit. After leaving Cambridge he endured a spell of joblessness before having a piece of remarkable good fortune: he obtained the job of financial adviser to a member of the Rothschild family—Mrs. Charles Rothschild, mother of a friend from Trinity; the pay was £100 a month, an opulent sum at the time. In 1936 he was able to move into a more promising political arena when, through university friends, he acquired a job as a producer of current-affairs programs for the BBC.

After a visit to Moscow, Burgess had, for public purposes, undergone a change of political heart and joined the Anglo-German Fellowship, a disguise also adopted by Philby. In 1940 Burgess resigned from the BBC to join MI6 in a section concerned with propaganda and sabotage in enemy countries. Later in the war he returned to the BBC, but, everywhere he went, his flamboyant personal style and gossipy indiscretions served, however unintentionally, as a perfect screen for his espionage. Who could think of such an attention-attracting character as a Soviet agent? After the war he, rather remarkably, obtained a post as aide to a high official in the Foreign Office. His behavior there finally wore out his superiors, however, and he received one last chance to redeem himself—as second secretary at the British embassy in Washington. His habits continued unchanged, however, and after he had alienated various layers of British and U.S. officialdom, including the Virginia state police, he was sent back to England. With the net closing on his colleague Donald MACLEAN in May 1951, primarily as the result of information from the VENONA code-breaking operation, Burgess joined Maclean on his escape to Moscow. The story of the "missing diplomats" created a worldwide sensation.

In Moscow, said Philby years later, Burgess "was a bit of an embarrassment" who "never managed to fit in"; he "just kept going downhill."

Bush, George Herbert Walker (1924–)   George Bush, who took office in January 1989, possesses the inalienable distinction of having been president of the United States at the end of the Cold War. When he took the oath of office in January 1989, Communist regimes stood in place all across Eastern Europe; in December 1989, after an amazing year of revolutionary change in the Communist world, Bush and Soviet leader Mikhail GORBACHEV, meeting at Malta, issued a public declaration that the Cold War, the central fact of international life since the late 1940s, was over.

The son of an investment banker who was later a Republican senator from Connecticut, Bush grew up in such standard establishment surroundings as the Greenwich Country Day School and Andover. But on graduating from prep school in 1942, he went straight into the navy and after completing flight training was reputed to be its youngest pilot. After service as a torpedo-bomber pilot, including a submarine rescue after having ditched in the ocean, Bush was rotated back to the

George Bush *(r.),* then U.S. vice president, talks in the Oval Office with President Ronald Reagan

United States and spent the remainder of the war as a flying instructor. In January 1945 he married Barbara Pierce, the daughter of a magazine publisher *(McCall's, Redbook).*

On graduating from Yale in 1948, Bush declined an offer from the Wall Street firm with which his father was associated and went off to Texas, where he began a career in the oil business, first as a salesman of drilling equipment and later, helped by a loan from a relative, as cofounder of a firm dealing in oil and gas properties. Entering politics in the 1960s, Bush proved to be something of a Republican pioneer in Texas. In 1964, as a candidate for the U.S. Senate, he forced the first runoff in the annals of the Texas party, and in the general election, expressing strong support for Barry GOLD-WATER, he performed respectably even in the midst of Lyndon JOHNSON's landslide. Two years later he won election to the congressional seat of a silk-stocking Houston district.

After his reelection in 1968, Bush looked toward the Senate in 1970, but, despite heavy support from President NIXON, he lost that race to Lloyd Bentsen, and in the process also lost his seat in the House. Then began the phase of Bush's career that would later cause him to be nicknamed the Résumé Candidate. Politically jobless after his unsuccessful senatorial campaign, he received compensation from Nixon in the form of appointment as ambassador to the UNITED NATIONS, a post in which he performed ably despite his lack of experience in foreign affairs. In 1973 Bush moved into a true hot seat, becoming chairman of the Republican National Committee just as the facts about the WATERGATE AFFAIR began to emerge. After loyally supporting Nixon until telltale tapes revealed the president's attempts to block the FBI investigation of the burglary, Bush then played a leading part in convincing Nixon that he must resign.

The new president, Gerald FORD, then granted Bush's wish to become de facto ambassador to the People's Republic of China (not yet having established full diplomatic relations, the two countries had set up liaison offices in each other's capital). A year and a half later, however, Ford brought Bush back to Washington to head the CENTRAL INTELLIGENCE AGENCY, which had been the subject of Senate hearings creating headlines about attempted assassinations and other clandestine activities. In many ways the agency, which in this unprecedented situation had been ably defended by its director, William Colby, had become the victim of a struggle for power between Congress and the White House. Ford, dismissing Colby, apparently felt it necessary to appoint a political person as the new CIA director. Bush moved calmly into his new responsibilities, letting the dust of conflict settle while impressing one veteran agency official, Scott Breckinridge, as "a quick study, with the knack for early understanding of the agency's arcane intricacies." Contrary to the fears of some CIA veterans, the new director did not politicize the agency. As a politician, however, Bush resigned the directorship after the Republicans lost the White House in the 1976 election.

In 1980 Bush made his first run for the Republican presidential nomination. After a good showing in the Iowa party caucuses, he lost to Ronald

REAGAN in the New Hampshire primary and in May he conceded the contest to Reagan. As vice presidential candidate on the ticket, he shared in Reagan's impressive victory in the November election, with his relative moderateness somewhat offsetting Reagan's strongly proclaimed conservatism. For the next eight years, Bush performed with loyalty and circumspection, very much in the standard vice presidential pattern. His closest brush with possible trouble came with respect to the IRAN-CONTRA AFFAIR, in which he claimed to have taken no part—he was, he said, "out of the loop." Many political figures and journalists regarded this statement as somewhat disingenuous; if Bush was not fully in the loop, they believed, he certainly was not wholly outside it.

In 1988 Bush received the coveted reward for his vice presidential service as he became the Republican nominee for the presidency. After a campaign marked by unusual bitterness, he won the general election handily, defeating Democrat Michael Dukakis by seven million votes and an electoral count of 426 to 111. Though moving slowly to accept the reality of Gorbachev's expressed desire to cancel four decades of Cold War and start international relations anew, Bush ended his first year in office side by side, rhetorically and in fact, with the Soviet leader.

Bush's greatest prominence in world affairs came not in relation to the Soviet Union but in the Middle East, when he took the lead in opposing the Iraqi occupation of Kuwait in August 1990 and created a coalition that won the brief Gulf War in 1991.

Byelorussia   The unexpected declaration of independence from the Soviet Union by this republic on August 25, 1991 (following Ukraine by one day), signaled the unraveling of the USSR. On December 8, 1991, following a two-day meeting at a hunting lodge near Minsk, the president of Byelorussia joined with the presidents of Russia and Ukraine in proclaiming the new COMMONWEALTH OF INDEPENDENT STATES; Minsk, the capital of Byelorussia, would be the seat of the commonwealth's "coordinating bodies" for foreign affairs, defense, and economic matters. As an independent republic, Byelorussia adopted the name Belarus.

Byrnes, James Francis (1879–1972)   A native of South Carolina, which he represented both in the House of Representatives and in the Senate, Byrnes served as U.S. secretary of state during the pivotal years 1945–47, when East and West were moving from World War II into the Cold War. After giving early and influential support to President Franklin D. ROOSEVELT's New Deal, Byrnes in the later 1930s moved to the right on domestic issues but worked with FDR on foreign and defense matters. Although he was appointed to the Supreme Court in 1941, he gave up his seat in 1942, early in World War II, when Roosevelt appointed him director of economic stabilization. Named in 1943 director of the Office of War Mobilization, Byrnes exercised such broad authority that he acquired the popular nickname "assistant president."

In 1945, to Byrnes's astonishment—since he had devoted himself to the home front—Roosevelt included him in the U.S. delegation for the YALTA CONFERENCE with the USSR and Britain. In the president's view, Byrnes's standing on Capitol Hill would make him a valuable interpreter of the Yalta proceedings—including plans for the UNITED NATIONS organization—to members of Congress.

Later in 1945, Byrnes concerned himself with foreign affairs full-time when the new president, Harry S. TRUMAN, appointed him secretary of state. The relationship between these two men had an unusual complication: Byrnes had hoped and expected to receive the 1944 Democratic Party nomination for vice president; had this happened, he and not Truman would have become president in April 1945. Truman even had in his pocket a draft of a nominating speech he intended to make for Byrnes when he received the word that the place on the ticket was going to him and not to the South Carolinian. Though Truman had not sought this outcome, Byrnes, who had asked Truman to nominate him, suspected double-dealing.

As secretary of state, Byrnes—whose long legislative experience had trained him in the arts of negotiation and compromise—ultimately abandoned his hopes for accommodation with the Soviets. At the end of 1945, he declared his opposition to the use of the ATOMIC BOMB for "political purposes" and called for international control of atomic energy. Though beginning to harden toward the Soviets, in April 1946 he proposed to

U.S. secretary of state James F. Byrnes

the USSR a 25-year treaty that would keep Germany disarmed, the guiding idea being that both the British and the French, on the one hand, and the Soviets, on the other, would find reassurance in such an agreement. When the Soviets rejected this overture, many in Washington took the response as a sign of coming aggression, although the de facto division of Europe had not yet become widely recognized. In September, stiffening his position, Byrnes declared in a widely quoted speech delivered in Stuttgart that U.S. troops would stay in Germany as long as any other occupying forces remained, spoke in favor of a German national government, and suggested that the Polish absorption of East Prussia ought not necessarily to be regarded as final.

In January 1947, officially on the advice of his doctors, Byrnes resigned as secretary of state. His relations with Truman had worsened, and he later made speeches attacking Truman's domestic policies.

C

C-124 Behind the famous Sabres and Thunderjets and all the other combat aircraft of the U.S. Air Force stood support craft like the Douglas C-124 Globemaster II, which could carry personnel—200 soldiers with their equipment, or 127 patients with nurses—or cargo of all kinds, even bulldozers and tanks. The Globemaster II, which came into service in 1950, ferried supplies from the United States to American forces during the KOREAN and VIETNAM WARS and elsewhere overseas. It also helped move people and supplies in many civilian emergencies around the world, evacuating refugees from wars in the Congo and ferrying flood-relief supplies to Morocco, Chile, and other countries. Powered by four Pratt & Whitney 3,800-horsepower piston engines, it had a range of 2,175 miles.

Caffery, Jefferson (1886–1974) U.S. diplomat, a native of Lafayette, La., and graduate of Tulane University, who entered the Foreign Service in 1911 and, after serving in a variety of posts, became U.S. ambassador to General Charles DE GAULLE's French provisional authority in 1944. Later in 1944 Caffery became ambassador to France, holding the position through the early years of the Cold War, until 1949. He then moved to Egypt as ambassador (1949–55), retiring after his tenure there. He also represented the United States in a number of international conferences and negotiations. Caffery's arrival in Egypt in 1949, according to the Egyptian writer Mohamed Heikal, signaled American interest in establishing good relations with younger, educated elements of the local leadership. And, to the gratification of

this group, this "wealthy Southern aristocrat" and "very high-powered figure" staked out positions independent of those held by the British—to frequent British annoyance.

A strong conservative, Caffery as a prominent Catholic layman was named an honorary papal chamberlain by three popes. A British correspondent described him as "dryly taciturn and highly professional."

Cairncross, John (1913–) A Cambridge undergraduate recruited for the KGB by Anthony BLUNT and Guy BURGESS in 1935, thereby becoming a member of the ultimately famous CAMBRIDGE FIVE spy ring, Cairncross went on to serve in a remarkable variety of important positions and agencies: in the British Foreign Office; as secretary to the eminent Lord Hankey, longtime secretary of the Committee of Imperial Defence and minister responsible for supervision of the intelligence services; and with the Government Code and Cipher School at Bletchley Park. These activities gave Cairncross access to the Ultra code-breaking operation and to high-level scientific matters, including information about the ATOMIC BOMB. Thus he was involved with the two greatest secrets Britain possessed in World War II. A KGB official later told a colleague that during the war Cairncross handed over to his controllers "literally tons of documents." In the 1980s, after the other four members of the Cambridge Five had been identified, research established Cairncross as the eagerly sought FIFTH MAN.

Shortly after Burgess and Donald MACLEAN fled England in 1951, Cairncross quietly resigned his civil-service job and moved to Rome. Later he declared his ignorance of Burgess's espionage activities, but added, with impressive understatement, that he had been "fortunate not to be prosecuted."

calibration As early as 1950, U.S. planners sought ways to respond to the perceived Soviet threat without having to decide, as a policy statement put it, whether to "capitulate or precipitate a global war." What the United States needed to develop, planners said, was the ability to oppose aggression at any level without resorting to needless escalation. Instead of relying simply on the threat of nuclear weapons, the country must have forces that could be employed in a careful, deliberate, measured—that is, a calibrated—way. The possession of such forces did not necessarily mean that they would be put into action; their existence itself, and their installation in a particular theater (e.g., Vietnam), was regarded as a form of DETERRENCE. *See also* NSC-68.

Callaghan, (Leonard) James (1912–) British prime minister from 1976 to 1979, a Labour Party leader who worked his way up from his beginnings as a minor civil servant at the age of 17. In his middle 20s Callaghan entered a career as a full-time labor-union official, and, after service in naval intelligence in World War II, he won a seat in Parliament and received minor ministerial posts.

When Labour returned to power in 1964, Callaghan became chancellor of the exchequer and then (1967) home secretary. In 1974, when the Labourite Harold WILSON formed a new government, Callaghan became foreign secretary. When Wilson resigned in 1976, Callaghan, a moderate in an increasingly turbulent labor situation, succeeded him at No. 10 Downing Street. Widely respected for his fair-mindedness, Callaghan once summed up his methods of leadership by saying, "If the people are bullyable, I bully them. If they are persuadable, I persuade them. I use any technique that is appropriate. But I do not believe in using blackmail and fear to influence decisions." He maintained close relations with the United States. His calmness did not help him, however, when a wave of strikes in the late 1970s led in 1979 to a House of Commons vote of no confidence, followed by a general election in which Margaret THATCHER's Conservatives dealt the Labour Party a heavy defeat.

Cambodia Tiny Southeast Asian country lying between Thailand and Vietnam that gained unwanted international attention during the VIETNAM WAR. Prince Norodom SIHANOUK, who became head of state in 1954, sought to remain neutral in relation to the Cold War and, as the fighting developed next door in Vietnam, tried desperately to keep his country out of the conflict. He came under attack from his prime minister, LON NOL, however, after he allowed Vietnamese Communists to use Cambodia as a sanctuary. In early 1970, when Sihanouk was out of the country, Lon Nol staged a coup with U.S. support and then acquiesced in a U.S. bombing campaign intended to destroy Communist sanctuaries in his country. In October 1970 Lon Nol abolished the ancient Cambodian monarchy. But his support of the U.S. bombing and invasion undermined his position, leading to the coming to power in 1975 of the Communist KHMER ROUGE under POL POT.

Cambridge Five Probably the most famous group of spies in modern history, the five consisted of Kim PHILBY, Donald MACLEAN, Guy BURGESS, Anthony BLUNT, and John CAIRNCROSS, all of them recruited by the KGB during the 1930s. They occupied sensitive positions in diplomacy and intelligence during World War II, and later and otherwise, through their association with members of the British establishment, had access to a great deal of classified information. The American Michael STRAIGHT belonged to the group at Cambridge but later followed a different path. *See also* ORLOV, Alexander.

Campaign for Nuclear Disarmament U.K. peace movement founded in 1958 under the leadership of the British philosopher Bertrand RUSSELL. It aimed specifically at inducing the British government to give up its nuclear weapons. The group reflected a growing concern around the world, not only about the power of nuclear weapons, but also about the effect of nuclear testing, a concern that led in 1963 to the NUCLEAR TEST BAN TREATY. In the early 1980s, a decade after Russell's death, the CND organized demonstrations against the deployment in Britain of CRUISE MISSILES from the United States. Though the demonstrations did not sway Prime Minister Margaret THATCHER, they attracted considerable attention.

Camp David Accords   Properly the "Framework for Peace in the Middle East" and the "Framework for the Conclusion of a Peace Treaty Between Egypt and Israel," these accords were reached in September 1978 at Camp David, the U.S. presidential weekend retreat in Maryland, after intense negotiations between Egypt's President Anwar el-SADAT and Israel's Prime Minister Menachem BEGIN, with the intensive involvement of President Jimmy CARTER of the United States.

From the point of view of the Cold War, the Camp David Accords, by clearly aligning Egypt with the West and promoting peace with Israel, possessed considerable diplomatic and strategic importance. More immediately, however, they proved a disappointment, since, as Carter later wrote, Begin disavowed "the basic principles of the accords relating to Israel's withdrawal of its armed forces and military government from the West Bank, negotiations on an equal basis with the Palestinians and other Arabs, and the granting of full autonomy to the residents of the occupied areas"—matters that would, indeed, remain in contention for many years. As one problem after another cropped up between Carter and Begin, Carter and Sadat, Begin and other Israeli politicians, and Sadat and other Arab leaders after the accords were signed, Carter sadly confided to his diary that "it is obvious that the negotiations are going backwards."

Cam Ranh Bay   One of the finest deepwater ports in the world, located 185 miles northeast of Saigon, and the site during the VIETNAM WAR of one of the four U.S. central supply and maintenance depots, with a huge warehouse network and a 10,000-foot aircraft runway. After the American withdrawal from Vietnam, the Cam Ranh base became the subject of bitter controversy when it was turned over to the Soviets (who occupied it until 1989). This decision by the Vietnamese government is regarded as one of the chief reasons underlying the long U.S. diplomatic and economic boycott of Vietnam.

Camus, Albert (1913–1960)   Essayist, novelist, and playwright, this native of Algeria—son of a French agricultural laborer and a Spanish mother who worked as a cleaning woman—captured the moral climate of the post–World War II period and was often spoken of as the "conscience of a generation." Camus joined the Communist Party in 1936, the year of his graduation from the University of Algiers, but severed all ties with the party a year later. Having gone to Paris in March 1940 (only three months before the French surrender to the Germans) as a reporter for *Paris-Soir*, he joined the Resistance in 1942 and worked on the revolutionary journal *Combat*. His wartime books *L'Étranger* (*The Stranger*, 1942) and *Le Mythe de Sisyphe* (*The Myth of Sisyphus*, 1942) focused on

The "conscience of a generation"—the Algerian-born French writer Albert Camus

the irrational and the absurd, and the famous *La Peste* (*The Plague*, begun during the war and published in 1947) drew from his wartime experiences to emphasize the limitations that life imposes on political action.

In *L'Homme révolté* (*The Rebel*, 1951), Camus analyzed the nature of revolution. Like many other left-leaning intellectuals, he drew his sentiments more from opposition to fascism than from support for Joseph STALIN. In the end Camus repudiated Marxism and said of EXISTENTIALISM, "To speak frankly, I think its conclusions are false." His rejection of Communism brought about a break with Jean-Paul SARTRE and produced what French writer Angelo Rinaldi called "the dispute which will for eternity continue to oppose Camus to Sartre." Rinaldi went on to say of Camus, "Rarely has a writer aroused such fraternal feelings in his reader."

Canberra   First flown in 1949, this two-seat twin-engine jet tactical bomber was built by English Electric for Britain's Royal Air Force. It attained a maximum speed of about 570 mph, with a range of 2,000 miles, and could deliver both nuclear and conventional bombs. During the KOREAN WAR the Glenn L. Martin Company, under a licensing agreement with English Electric, built some 400 Canberras for the U.S. Air Force, which designated the aircraft the B-57.

Carter, Jimmy (1924–)   The first U.S. president to be sworn into office using a nickname (James Earl Carter, Jr., is his proper name), Jimmy Carter won the 1976 election after a long and patient campaign that began in relative obscurity. Announcing his candidacy in 1974, Carter faced a number of potential handicaps—he was a southerner, he was not widely known, he lacked any important financial or organizational support. Indeed, many observers and ordinary voters did not pay serious attention to his early drive for the Democratic nomination, which he conducted almost on a house-to-house basis.

Born in the village of Plains in southwestern Georgia, Carter graduated from the U.S. Naval Academy at Annapolis in 1946 (59th in a class of 820). After serving at sea on surface craft and submarines, he was assigned to the fledgling nuclear-

submarine program directed by Captain Hyman RICKOVER, whose drive and high intellectual standards—as shown in his trademark question: Why not the best?—shaped many of Carter's subsequent attitudes. He borrowed the line as the title of his self-explanatory 1975 book, in which he sought to introduce himself to the American voting public. Later, during his presidency, Carter drew encouragement from Rickover's counsel to "stick to principle."

After the death of his father in 1953, Carter resigned from the navy to manage the family peanut farm, an enterprise to which he added a shelling plant, warehouses, and other facilities, building the operation into a flourishing business. He encountered political ugliness when, in the aftermath of the 1954 Supreme Court decision declaring school segregation illegal, he refused to join the newly founded White Citizens' Council and saw his business subjected to a boycott. Having previously served on the school board and in other such public-service roles, Carter then sought political office, winning a seat in the state Senate in 1963—a victory he could claim only after proving election fraud on the part of the local political establishment, which had opposed him.

Elected governor of Georgia on his second try, in 1970, Carter proved to be efficient, generally liberal, and environmentally oriented. He made his racial attitude plain in his inaugural address, when he declared that the era of discrimination had ended, and he went on to appoint numerous African Americans to state agencies. Though this outlook won him a measure of favorable attention across the country, he was still not well known when, as his term came to its end, he began to look toward the 1976 presidential election. Presenting a point of view that was later to be emulated by his successor, Ronald REAGAN, Carter ran against Washington and the capital insiders who were widely felt to have made a mess of things during the preceding decade (with the WATERGATE AFFAIR as Exhibit Number One). Needing the publicity and the votes that would accrue, he entered presidential primaries across the country and scored an important psychological triumph by winning the standard launching-pad New Hampshire primary. By convention time in 1976 he had acquired the votes to win the Democratic nomination on the

Inauguration day, 1977: U.S. president Jimmy Carter and his wife, Rosalynn, walk down Pennsylvania Avenue in Washington

first ballot. He took the general election in a close contest with Gerald FORD, who damaged himself in one of the two televised debates between the candidates by appearing uninformed on the political situation in Eastern Europe, when he seemed to deny that the Soviet Union exercised domination over Poland.

After the inaugural ceremony, Carter gave an indication of the kind of image he would project by walking with his wife Rosalynn down the mile-and-a-half route from the Capitol to the White House, trailed by the bullet-proof presidential limousine. The next day he issued a blanket pardon to some 10,000 men who had left the country to avoid the VIETNAM WAR–era draft. In his most prominent move in foreign affairs, he stressed the importance of human-rights considerations in the formulation of U.S. policy, discussing the subject in his brief inaugural speech and then in an ad-

dress to the UNITED NATIONS on March 17, 1977. Commenting later that his emphasis on human rights brought criticism both in the United States and from abroad, Carter drily observed that he "was never criticized by the people who were imprisoned or tortured or otherwise deprived of basic rights." One of his critics was Soviet president BREZHNEV, who objected to Carter's correspondence with the Soviet dissident Andrei SAKHAROV. Later Carter conceded that, although opposed to the Soviet campaign against dissidents, he did not have the power to intervene in the internal affairs of other countries.

In 1978 Carter secured the passage of treaties under which the United States would, in stages, turn control of the Panama Canal over to the Panamanian government. Although these agreements had been under discussion for some years and had the support of leading Republicans such as former president Ford and former secretary of state Henry KISSINGER, Carter, unfortunately from a political point of view, became identified with them in some minds, a point seized on by Reagan, his 1980 opponent. In 1978 the United States began formal diplomatic relations with the People's Republic of China. The year 1978 also saw the foreign-policy high point of Carter's administration when he brought together Egypt's President SADAT and Israel's Prime Minister BEGIN at Camp David and after almost two weeks of intensive negotiations reaped the reward of agreements—the CAMP DAVID ACCORDS—defining a structure of peace for the Middle East. Though subsequent results did not bear out the promise of Camp David, the meeting did succeed in producing peace between the two countries. On June 18, 1979, Carter and Brezhnev, meeting in Vienna, signed the SALT II treaty, the final result of the STRATEGIC ARMS LIMITATION TALKS; after the Soviet invasion of AFGHANISTAN, however, Carter ordered the treaty put on the shelf. The Cold War seemed reborn, as Carter's reaction to the invasion also included the placing of an embargo on technology sales to the Soviet Union, heavy cuts in grain sales, and the U.S. OLYMPIC BOYCOTT of the 1980 games, to be held in Moscow.

What proved to be a fatal bolt of lightning struck the Carter administration on November 4, 1979, when Iranian revolutionaries seized the U.S. embassy in Tehran, taking 66 Americans hostage in an endlessly murky political and governmental situation. The militants declared their intention to hold the hostages until the United States returned the former shah to Tehran to stand trial on various charges, but as time went on it became evident that many factors were involved in the seizure and that no one in Iran spoke with consistent authority. A rescue attempt mounted in April 1980 had to be aborted because of inadequate planning and equipment failure. Finally, however, a deal was worked out, and, with profoundly ironic timing, the hostages gained their freedom on January 20, 1981, just as President Reagan assumed office.

In the 1980 campaign, Carter not only had to carry the burden of the hostage crisis but faced an array of other problems, chief among them a level of inflation that had reached some 12 percent. In an election featuring an independent run for the presidency by Congressman John Anderson of Illinois, Reagan won a solid victory, receiving an absolute majority of the votes; Carter thus became the first elected president since Herbert Hoover to be voted out of office after one term. In later years Carter devoted himself to public causes and spent much of his time as an observer of international elections and an impartial peace negotiator, notably in North Korea and Haiti. He thus won new respect as a model ex-president.

Casey, William Joseph (1913–1987) New York lawyer, an intelligence veteran of World War II, and the director of central intelligence (1981–87), appointed by President REAGAN.

A native of the New York City borough of Queens, Casey graduated from Fordham, did graduate work at Catholic University, and obtained his law degree from St. John's in 1937. During World War II he served with the Office of Strategic Services, and for most of the next 25 years he practiced and taught law in New York. In 1971 President NIXON brought him to Washington as chairman of the Securities and Exchange Commission; he was undersecretary of state for economic affairs (1973–74) and president and chairman of the Import-Export Bank (1974–75).

After playing a principal role in engineering the Republicans' return to power as President Reagan's campaign manager, Casey—amid some debate over what seemed the overtly political nature

of the appointment, though he did in fact possess credentials in the field of intelligence—became director of central intelligence, a position whose centerpiece is direction of the CENTRAL INTELLIGENCE AGENCY itself. He appears to have won popularity at the CIA, succeeding in restoring morale that had been shaken under the economizing administration of his predecessor, Admiral Stansfield Turner.

In the mid-1980s, Casey's unrelenting attempts to rescue William Buckley, the CIA station chief in Beirut who had been kidnapped and held hostage (he was later tortured and then murdered), represented the first steps on the trail that led to supplying embargoed weapons to Iran in exchange for the release of hostages and thence to the full IRAN-CONTRA AFFAIR. To circumvent congressional oversight, Casey used officers of the NATIONAL SECURITY COUNCIL as his agents in negotiations with Iran. He died before the whole matter had been thoroughly investigated.

Castro, Fidel (in full, Fidel Alejandro Castro Ruz) (1926–) The Cuban revolutionary is one of the most famous of all Latin American political leaders. His father, Angel Castro, a Spaniard who fought in the Spanish-American War, stayed on in Cuba to become a relatively prosperous sugarcane grower, though remaining an outsider in the local culture. One of several illegitimate children Angel produced with a young servant, Lina Ruz, Fidel during his childhood would often say to his best friend, "I don't have a name." In later years, however, he would make highly effective moves to remedy that perceived deficiency.

In 1945, after attending a Jesuit boarding school in Havana (where he displayed a marked interest in the personalities and techniques of European dictators, one of his favorites being Benito Mussolini), Castro studied law at the University of Havana, which at the time, like other Latin American universities, served as a shelter for a variety of political types and a stage for ideological gang battles. In 1947, while a student, Castro took part in an amateurish attempt to invade the Dominican Republic and overthrow the government of Rafael Trujillo, and the following year saw him in Colombia during the riots that accompanied the BOGOTÁ CONFERENCE of the Organization of American States.

Two years after receiving his law degree, Castro ran for a seat in the Cuban House of Representatives, but during the campaign the government was overthrown by a former president, Fulgencio Batista, who then canceled the elections. Sixteen months later, on July 26, 1953, Castro led an attack on an army barracks in Santiago. Most of his followers were killed; Castro and his brother Raúl were sent to prison but were released under an amnesty in 1955. At his trial, Castro had defended himself in a speech that, in edited form, became a famous testament under the name "History Will Absolve Me," a line he had used in his peroration. A Castro biographer, Georgie Anne Geyer, pointed to the striking parallels between Castro in this phase and an earlier political figure whose career he had carefully studied: hopeless attacks on government installations, followed by memorable speeches of self-defense containing many similar phrases; in each speech, the defendant became the accuser, declaring the state to be the guilty party. The earlier figure was, of course, Adolf Hitler during and after his Munich putsch attempt in 1923.

Naming his tiny group the 26th of July Movement, Castro moved temporarily to Mexico, where he impressed a KGB official as a promising leader, partly because he seemed to be determined to keep complete personal control of his movement. Castro and his band returned to Cuba on December 2, 1956, aboard an old 38-foot wooden boat, the *Granma*, bought from an American. After the landing, Castro's force encountered government forces that almost wiped it out; the leader and the other survivors fled into the Sierra Maestra, where they joined allies, all part of the widespread opposition to Batista. In February 1957 Castro acquired an important admirer when Herbert Matthews of the *New York Times* visited his guerrilla band and, as Castro later explained, was hoodwinked into believing the 26th of July group far more formidable than it was. Matthews, an old Spanish Civil War hand, saw Castro with a romantic-revolutionary eye, and his articles won the Cuban revolutionary many friends in the United States.

With his regime collapsing around him, belatedly realizing that he had not taken Castro seriously enough, Batista fled Cuba in the wee hours of January 1, 1959, leaving the capital and the country to Castro and his movement. Acting at first simply as the *caudillo* without portfolio, Castro made himself premier on February 16. From that point on, his regime and his career abound in paradox and even mystery. Having originally presented himself as a sort of populist democrat, with promises of the standard democratic rights, Castro had won wide admiration in the United States as a reformer. He now contradicted these words and expectations by staging a show trial of 43 air force pilots implausibly accused of disloyalty and immediately sought a major part in THIRD WORLD politics. Though many commentators have believed that Castro sought U.S. favor, the opposite was more nearly true—his trip to the United States in April 1959 actually took on triumphal proportions. His appearances in Washington and New York were some of the hottest tickets in town, and the State Department and other agencies attempted to engage him in economic discussions; their approaches, however, were rejected. Castro was, as Geyer said, the "new rage in revolutionary chic." In a speech to the Overseas Press Club in New York, Castro, a powerful and engaging speaker, humorously described how he had systematically misled Matthews about the size of the revolutionary force: "When Mr. Matthew [sic] say 'Where is the rest of your army?' I say, 'Oh, they over there!' " Listening to this public denigration of his perceptiveness as a reporter, Matthews could do little but smile.

It quickly became evident that Castro was basing his regime on opposition to the *Yanquis,* and by midsummer 1959 the KGB had sent experts to overhaul the Cuban security system. In February 1960 the government took all business under state control, and later in the year it confiscated U.S.-owned property, without the compensation Castro had spoken of in earlier days. In August 1960 Castro declared that he would look to the Soviets for military support against the "imperialist United States." Liking neither these developments nor Castro's general authoritarianism, the EISENHOWER administration imposed an embargo on Cuban sugar and then, on January 3, 1961, just before Ike left office, broke diplomatic relations with Cuba. One of the legacies Eisenhower left to his successor, President KENNEDY, was a plan to stage a counter-Castro landing in Cuba. After this attack

—the BAY OF PIGS OPERATION—had been launched and had failed, Castro enjoyed his hour of public triumph, but he had also acquired implacable enemies, the Kennedy brothers, who developed an obsessive interest in exacting revenge—almost as if they believed that Castro should willingly have allowed the invasion to succeed. As revealed in later congressional hearings, the administration relentlessly pursued a variety of schemes to humble or even assassinate Castro and cripple Cuba. In October 1962, Castro was the disgruntled party when the Soviet premier, Nikita KHRUSHCHEV, agreed to withdraw offensive missiles as part of the settlement of the CUBAN MISSILE CRISIS.

Internationally, Castro took an active hand in Communist guerrilla activities not only in Latin America but in Africa, sending troops to Angola, Ethiopia, and Zaire. But as the world situation evolved in the 1980s and 1990s, Castro became increasingly an anachronism—a hard-line Communist leader persisting in his ways even after the raising of the IRON CURTAIN and the subsequent dissolution of the Soviet Union. The latter event, in fact, led to the collapse of the Cuban economy, since it had been supported by aid from Moscow that disappeared with the USSR.

Cazab   Top-secret organization (indeed, super top-secret) established by senior intelligence officers of Australia, Britain, Canada, New Zealand, and the United States to coordinate the counterespionage activities of the member countries.

Ceauşescu, Nicolae (1918–1989)   Chief Romanian political figure from the 1960s until his downfall and then execution, along with his wife, on Christmas Day, 1989. Ceauşescu, who had a proper proletarian background as a factory worker, joined the underground Union of Communist Youth when he was 15 and within three years was arrested for his political activities; he served two and a half years in prison, was released, and in less than a year received a fresh sentence, although the authorities did not manage to confine him until 1940. Unlike various other Balkan Communist leaders, who built up outstanding records as partisan fighters, Ceauşescu spent the war years behind bars. But after the Soviets overthrew the Romanian government in August 1944, Ceauşescu now belonged to the side that held power. Becoming a full member of the Romanian Communist Party in 1948, he also won a subcabinet appointment and within two years had achieved the rank of major general and acquired the job of deputy minister of the armed forces.

As dictator of Romania, Ceauşescu held the position of first secretary of the party from 1965 until he was toppled in 1989, and along with this office he held an array of other titles—party, political, and military. He took the title "president of Romania" in 1974. For some years his less-than-complete subservience to Moscow, sometimes even seeming to verge on independence, won him considerable respect in the West. He was actually a thorough Stalinist, however, and the collapse of his regime and the hatred shown it by the people made the earlier Western regard seem singularly ill judged.

Center Alliance   One of the two groups into which the Polish SOLIDARITY movement split in 1990. The other group, CITIZENS' MOVEMENT—DEMOCRATIC ACTION, opposed the Solidarity leader, Lech WAŁESA.

CENTO   *See* CENTRAL TREATY ORGANIZATION.

Central Committee   The body in the structure of the COMMUNIST PARTY OF THE SOVIET UNION that stood between the party congress and the POLITBURO, the latter being, with its Secretariat, the actual executive arm of the party. The Central Committee consisted of several hundred members, most of them veteran party officials. During most of Joseph STALIN's rule as GENERAL SECRETARY, the committee had little except ceremonial importance; it met from time to time to hear what the general secretary and the Politburo wished to tell it. Later, after Stalin's death, the Central Committee at times possessed actual power, because it could serve as the referee between Politburo members seeking the leadership of the party. In 1957 it awarded the prize to Nikita KHRUSHCHEV, and in the 1964 coup it transferred its favor to Leonid BREZHNEV.

The constitutional changes of 1990 removed effective governmental power from the Politburo and other party organs and transferred it to the

Soviet president, the ministers, and other state (rather than party) officials.

Central Intelligence Agency (CIA)   Established under the National Security Act of 1947, the CIA has since been the best-known (though not the largest) intelligence arm of the U.S. government. Indeed, for a supposedly secret agency, the CIA managed during the Cold War to attract great and continuing attention around the world, some of it resulting from revelations of various clandestine operations but some coming also from foreign propagandists who credited the agency with an all-pervasive quality and accused it of activities in which it actually had no involvement.

The creation of the CIA ended a two-year interim following the disbanding, at the conclusion of World War II, of the Office of Strategic Services, the first American effort at a centralized intelligence agency. During this interval a body called the Central Intelligence Group, established by an executive order of President TRUMAN, attempted with only limited success to coordinate the gathering of intelligence. In 1947, as the government advanced such initiatives as the TRUMAN DOCTRINE and the MARSHALL PLAN, the generally acknowledged need for a greater intelligence capability led to the inclusion of a provision for the CIA in the National Security Act, which established the Department of Defense and the NATIONAL SECURITY COUNCIL; the CIA was, in fact, placed under the National Security Council, thus establishing the White House as the controlling authority of the agency.

The CIA was unique, wrote Allen DULLES, the agency's director from 1953 to 1961, because "it combined under one leadership the overt task of intelligence analysis and coordination with the work of secret intelligence operations." Further, it was "given the mandate to develop its own secret collection arm" separate from the office assigned to the collection and evaluation of information from other parts of the government. As time went on, the CIA also evolved toward the linking of espionage, counterespionage, and political warfare, with the aim of coordinating these commonly compartmentalized activities. In addition to responsibilities as the head of the agency, the director of the CIA was given the position of director of

central intelligence, which included chairing the United States Intelligence Board, made up of the intelligence units of various departments and agencies in addition to the CIA. In this position, however, CIA directors experienced only limited success, seeming to encounter the standard difficulties that afflict anybody who tries to exercise command and coordination while lacking line authority.

Organizationally, the CIA consists of four directorates: intelligence, operations (spying and covert activities), science and technology, and administration. (Inside the agency, the heads of these directorates have been dubbed the Four Princes.) Throughout the years the agency has not only engaged in espionage and counterespionage but produced DISINFORMATION and other propaganda; created "proprietary," or front, organizations, such as airlines; and been involved in the running of other organizations and enterprises.

Of all the agency's activities, those that have attracted the most attention and caused the greatest stir have been the covert operations that, in one way or another, have come to light—among them, those in Cuba (the BAY OF PIGS OPERATION), in Central America (campaigns against the ARBENZ government of Guatemala and in favor of the rulers of El Salvador; the mining of harbors in Nicaragua), in Chile (the downfall of Salvador ALLENDE), in Iran (the overthrow of Mohammed MOSSADEGH). The CIA also saw itself dragged into the WATERGATE AFFAIR through the involvement of former employees and through the attempts of the White House to use it as a cloak for the activities of administration operatives. The agency had also supplied tools used by White House "plumbers" to break into the office of Daniel Ellsberg's psychiatrist in connection with the PENTAGON PAPERS affair. Most spectacular were revelations produced by the Senate hearings known as the Church Committee hearings, which took place in 1975, on activities relating to attempted assassinations of foreign officials, especially, during the KENNEDY administration, Fidel CASTRO. But the record strongly suggested that the agency was trying, however ineptly, to do the bidding of the White House. A notable CIA success was the acquisition of Soviet first secretary Nikita KHRUSHCHEV's "secret" 1956 speech, in which he discussed the crimes of Joseph

STALIN. Another was the development of the U-2 reconnaissance airplane, which, by keeping U.S. officials informed of the state of the Soviet military during the latter 1950s, served as a balancing factor in strategic calculations.

Despite the many intense controversies in which it became involved, the CIA as a provider of information appears to have served presidents quite effectively during the Cold War. One of its principal functions was the production of an annual report called the "Soviet Estimate," which assessed the existing status and the probable future direction of Soviet military programs and activities. Although there were certainly gaps in intelligence, no instance has been adduced of a major Soviet aim or development having gone undetected. However, many critics who accepted the agency's functioning as a supplier of information either objected to its also being the vehicle for clandestine operations or objected to the idea of conducting such operations at all, no matter who had charge of them.

A continuing problem for the CIA, as for all intelligence agencies, has been the question of penetration by hostile agents. "Counterintelligence," said a former Foreign Service officer, John D. Stempel, "has ranked lowest in importance among the functions of intelligence since the creation of the CIA." During the 1960s and 1970s, the head of CIA counterintelligence, James J. Angleton, continuingly disrupted the agency and actually discredited counterintelligence through an obsessive search for supposed Soviet moles. In addition, Stempel commented, "a procession of Soviet 'defectors,' some real, some false, kept American counterintelligence running in circles in the 1960s and '70s."

As the result of the 1975 hearings, the Senate established an oversight committee to keep an eye on the doings of the intelligence community. The continual debates about the role and activities of the CIA made plain the doubts with which Americans viewed a large and secret part of government and the general awareness that any bureaucracy, whatever its charter says, tends to develop a momentum of its own.

Directors of the CIA during the Cold War included Roscoe Hillenkoetter (1947–50), Walter Bedell SMITH (1950–53), Allen W. Dulles (1953–61), John A. McCone (1961–65), William F. Raborn, Jr. (1965–66), Richard Helms (1966–73), James SCHLESINGER (February–July 1973), William E. Colby (1973–76), George H. W. BUSH (1976–77), Stansfield Turner (1977–81), William J. CASEY (1981–87), and William H. Webster (1987–93). It fell to Colby to defend the agency in the unprecedented and difficult 1975 hearings, a task he performed with skill and sensitivity.

Central Treaty Organization (CENTO)   When the 1958 revolution in Iraq overthrew the monarchy, the members of the BAGHDAD PACT agreed to transfer its headquarters to Ankara and adopted the name Central Treaty Organization (August 1959); Iraq had withdrawn its membership in March 1959. Though it had been one of the sponsors of the Baghdad Pact, Britain had lost much of its influence in the Arab world after the 1956 SUEZ CRISIS. This slack was taken up by the United States, which did not formally join CENTO but, as an associate member, gave it heavy avuncular support. The concept of CENTO fitted in with the EISENHOWER administration's general approach, which favored the establishment of groupings (for example, NATO, SEATO) across Eurasia to exert a deterrent influence on any Soviet-bloc adventurism. In practice, however, CENTO and SEATO, which had heavy THIRD WORLD membership, proved only faint analogues of NATO, and, though not at all disavowing them, the KENNEDY administration placed less emphasis on them than had its predecessor. CENTO was disbanded in 1979.

CFE-I Treaty   *See* CONVENTIONAL FORCES IN EUROPE TREATY.

Chambers, Whittaker (1901–1961)   A writer and editor *(Time-Life)*, Chambers (originally named Jay Vivian Chambers) became famous in 1948 when he told the U.S. House of Representatives Un-American Activities Committee that Alger HISS, a former State Department official who had become president of the Carnegie Endowment for International Peace, had given him confidential department documents in the 1930s, when the two were fellow Communists. Hiss denied the charge but was later convicted of perjury. Perhaps the most remarkable aspect of the case was provided

Checkpoint Charlie, crossover point between zones in Berlin, figured in many Cold War real-life and fictional dramas.

by the "Pumpkin Papers," corroborative documents Chambers had hidden in a pumpkin on his Maryland farm. The case gave national prominence to a young Republican congressman, Richard M. NIXON, who had proved a tenacious investigator as head of the subcommittee that pursued Chambers's charges. Actually, Chambers had broken with the Soviets in 1938 and had told his story to various persons, but in those days neither Federal Bureau of Investigation chief J. Edgar HOOVER nor anybody else displayed much interest in such matters. Chambers had to wait ten years for an appreciative audience.

Chamoun, Camille   *See* EISENHOWER DOCTRINE.

Charlie   NATO designation for a class of Soviet nuclear-powered missile submarines first seen in 1968. The class consisted of nine Charlie I's (5,000 tons) and six Charlie II's (5,500 tons). Each carried eight missile tubes; the Charlie II carried the SS-N-7 cruise missile, which could be fitted with either a conventional or a nuclear warhead.

Charter 77   In 1977 a Czech human-rights coalition presented the government of the republic with a charter calling for adherence to the standards of freedom outlined in the widely adopted Universal Declaration of Human Rights. Despite the fact that the government of Czechoslovakia had signed these HELSINKI FINAL ACT agreements, it displayed no sympathy with the intellectuals and clerics who had drawn up the charter. In October the leaders of the group, including Václav HAVEL, received prison sentences. As a whole, the signatories of Charter 77 were able subsequently to find only menial jobs and were reviled in the press. *See also* VELVET REVOLUTION.

Checkpoint Charlie   Border crossover point in BERLIN, on Friedrichstrasse near the Brandenburg Gate, between the U.S.- and Soviet-dominated zones. Berlin was celebrated in novels and movies as a world capital of Cold War intrigue, and Checkpoint Charlie played a prominent role in many such stories.

On October 26, 1961, Checkpoint Charlie became the scene of a direct, real-life U.S.-Soviet confrontation when tanks of the two sides faced each other. On the basis of a mistaken Soviet intelligence report, Premier KHRUSHCHEV had decided that U.S. forces in West Berlin were preparing to storm the BERLIN WALL. On the 27th, after he contacted President KENNEDY, the two resolved the situation peacefully.

Cheney, Richard Bruce (1941–) A native of Nebraska, Cheney (usually called "Dick" even in formal situations) came to Washington in 1969 as a congressional aide and then worked in the White House, his last position being as a presidential assistant to Gerald FORD (1975–77). In 1978 he won election to the U.S. Congress from Wyoming; in 1987–88 he served as Republican whip in the House of Representatives. Just in time for the end of the Cold War, Cheney was chosen by President BUSH in 1989 to be secretary of defense. He became widely known during the 1991 Persian Gulf War.

Chen Yi (1901–1972) A veteran Communist who was one of the Chinese Communist Party's "ten marshals" during the revolution and commanded the Third Communist Army in 1949, Chen Yi served as foreign minister of the People's Republic of China (1958–67). In 1967 RED GUARDS occupied the Foreign Ministry and forced Chen to make public self-criticisms; his death five years later was due in part to the effects of torture he had undergone during the CULTURAL REVOLUTION. At his funeral MAO ZEDONG (Mao Tse-tung) described him as "a good man, a good comrade"; the leader apparently forgot that he had presided over the punishment of this good comrade. This funeral is also noteworthy because it was to be Mao's last public appearance.

Chernenko, Konstantin Ustinovich (1911–1985) Although neither of the two general secretaries of the Soviet Communist Party who served between the death of Leonid BREZHNEV in 1982 and the accession of Mikhail GORBACHEV in 1985 is distinctively remembered by most people, they were in fact quite different personalities. Yuri ANDROPOV, who succeeded Brezhnev, in all probability would have had a considerable impact on events had he not suffered from the kidney disease and other disorders that killed him in February 1984. Chernenko, Andropov's successor, presents an entirely different picture. Whereas Andropov in his brief tenure introduced innovations and showed promise of bringing about needed changes (though not

necessarily any kind of political liberalization), Chernenko was essentially a status-quo politician and functionary who owed his position in the Communist Party to his friendship with Brezhnev. He won the post of GENERAL SECRETARY through the support of other politicians and functionaries who feared what radical actions Gorbachev, the strongest candidate, might take if he should be chosen. His seniority may also have won him some support in a political society in which elders predominated.

A career-long party APPARATCHIK specializing in propaganda, Chernenko developed a friendship with Brezhnev in the early 1950s, and from 1956, when his mentor joined the Secretariat of the CENTRAL COMMITTEE, his career was shaped and promoted by the man who was to succeed Nikita KHRUSHCHEV as Soviet leader in 1964. By 1971 Brezhnev had installed Chernenko in the Central Committee, and in 1978 the younger man became a member of the POLITBURO. Just as important, he was Brezhnev's closest friend and constant companion. Clearly, he had been given the status of anointed successor, though as matters turned out in 1982, it was Andropov who received the votes.

Despite a declaration in his inaugural address to the Central Committee that "the system of economic management and our whole economic mechanism are in need of serious restructuring," Chernenko as general secretary conducted matters as though the Andropov interlude had not existed; in its turning away from reform, its tolerance for cronyism and bribery, his regime seemed an extension of the later Brezhnev era. Even so—probably under the influence of Andrei GROMYKO—Chernenko agreed to the reopening of the arms-control talks with the United States that had been suspended by Andropov. He also urged party planners to concern themselves with the complicated problems that faced them immediately rather than to talk about the idealized future.

Chernenko made his last appearance in public in late December 1984. Within months he would be dead.

Chernobyl In late April 1986 scientists in Sweden detected a puzzling increase in atmospheric radioactivity. The source was obviously the Soviet Union, but what was the cause? The story came out slowly during the next three weeks, as the new Soviet policy of GLASNOST collided with traditional governmental reticence concerning any kind of domestic problem. As a great cloud of radioactive debris drifted across Europe, leading the Swedish government to test milk and the Polish government to issue iodine pills to children, "it took some doing," said Serge Schmemann, a *New York Times* reporter in Moscow, "to learn that anything was happening at all."

But soon an appalling story emerged. On April 26 the worst nuclear disaster of peacetime had occurred at a power station at Chernobyl, 70 miles from Kiev; an explosion and fire that followed the overheating of a reactor had created the deadly menace causing the area around Chernobyl to be evacuated for a radius of about 20 miles (with 92,000 people involved, according to Soviet reports) and, in the West, had given rise to fresh fears about the safety of all nuclear power stations.

When the power plant caught fire, it sent tons of radioactive particles into the air over BYELORUSSIA (now Belarus), the neighboring area of Russia, and the Ukraine. In 1994 a Russian scientist declared that, contrary to previous accounts, the accident had actually caused a complete meltdown of the reactor core. The fallout permanently poisoned as much as one-fourth of the soil of Belarus, and numerous children born in ensuing years have suffered from birth defects associated with exposure to radioactivity and from disorders, like thyroid cancer, not normally found in children. Dr. Vladimir Lupandin, a Russian physician who studied the effects of Chernobyl, spoke of the danger that continues to threaten the area: "One can sit down on a patch of strontium, drink a glass of milk with cesium-137, eat potatoes with plutonium, and taste mushrooms whose levels of irradiation make them radioactive waste."

Chiang Kai-shek (Jian Jieshi) (1887–1975) Chinese statesman and soldier, president of the republic, and generalissimo of its military forces, who rose to power as head of the political coalition called the GUOMINDANG (Kuomintang). After the death of its founder, Sun Yat-sen, in 1925, Chiang took over the leadership of the party, which was battling regional warlords to create a unified Chinese government. Though the Communists formed part of the Guomindang, Chiang broke with them in 1927, and a permanent if sometimes interrupted struggle followed between the two groups. Fighting both the Communists and the invading Japanese during the 1930s and 1940s, Chiang succeeded in surviving until the Japanese surrender in August 1945 seemed to bring the possibility of a new day to China. Meanwhile his authoritarian tendencies grew, although his U.S. World War II allies liked to speak of him as a great democratic leader. In March 1945 Chiang called on the Communists to incorporate their army and civilian administrative officials into the Nationalist government and army—a proposal unlikely to receive acceptance; instead, the Communists denounced the generalissimo.

During World War II Chiang had come to be considered the symbol of a rising China, but the ensuing years revealed the weakness and corruption of his regime. In 1946 full-scale civil war began between Chiang's Nationalists and MAO ZEDONG's Communist forces. U.S. president Harry S. TRUMAN dispatched General George C. MARSHALL to China in the unpromising role of mediator; in January 1947 the general, despite having made remarkable efforts to carry out his assignment, returned home, his impossible mission having failed. The war continued until Chiang's defeat in 1949. Declaring itself still the government of China, the Guomindang established a regime on the island of TAIWAN and succeeded in winning the moral and political support of many U.S. politicians, particularly Republican members of Congress, and business executives, who became identified as the CHINA LOBBY. The publications of Henry R. LUCE *(Time, Life)* gave the Nationalists particularly strong support. U.S. refusal to extend diplomatic recognition to the Communist government caused considerable dissent between the United States and its European allies, for whom the concept of recognition did not imply approval of any particular government. Chiang's supporters in the United States, particularly after the Chinese intervened in the KOREAN WAR, maintained, however, that the "Red Chinese" should not be allowed to "shoot their way into the United Nations." Chiang's government continued to hold the Chinese seat in the UN until 1972, when President NIXON, overhauling U.S. policy toward the

People's Republic of China, dropped U.S. objections to seating the Beijing government.

A native of Chekiang Province, son of a merchant, Chiang was educated at the Chinese Imperial Military College and at a military staff college in Japan. In 1927 he married Mei-ling Soong, a member of perhaps China's most famous family; as Mme. Chiang, she became a familiar figure in the United States, where, with great effectiveness, she pleaded Nationalist China's cause in Washington and in the media.

China Lobby Variegated group of U.S. supporters of CHIANG KAI-SHEK's Nationalist Chinese government. Originally formed during World War II, the lobby took on fresh importance in the late 1940s as the Nationalist position on the mainland deteriorated and finally collapsed. Well financed by gold from Chiang's coffers, this loose but influential group grew in strength during the following years as U.S. anti-Communist sentiments increased. Wealthy conservatives lent the lobby their support; old missionary families with sentimental attachments to China supported it (Chiang's untiring American booster, Henry R. LUCE of *Time* and *Life,* had such a background). Republican congressional leaders such as Senators William F. KNOWLAND (nicknamed in the press the "senator from Formosa"), Kenneth Wherry, and Styles Bridges and House Majority Leader Joseph W. Martin castigated the TRUMAN administration for failing to save Chiang's government on the mainland—the often-cited "loss of China." Secretary of State Dean ACHESON became the special scapegoat of the China Lobby, and many veteran State Department professionals were accused of favoring Communism because they had offered accurate reports about the strength of the Chinese Communists and the corruption and incompetence of the Nationalists. For his part, Acheson commented that when Knowland talked about China, he took on a "wild, stare-y look." Wherry's fervor could become so intense as to lead him to speak of the glorious possibilities that could result from turning Shanghai into a replica of Kansas City. During a visit to Taiwan, Knowland and Bridges joined their Nationalist hosts to toast "Back to the Mainland."

The China Lobby produced a potent offshoot, the Committee of One Million, which, determined to prevent any improvement in U.S.-Chinese Communist relations, funded friends and attacked opponents. The charges and accusations made by members of the China Lobby provided considerable material during the early 1950s for the investigations and the rhetoric of Senator Joseph R. MCCARTHY. Finally, in the 1970s, however, President NIXON, a Republican (and perhaps only a Republican could have done it), made the historic approach to the Chinese Communist government that transformed the situation and ended in U.S. recognition of the mainland regime and withdrawal of recognition from the Nationalists of TAIWAN (though numerous diplomatic and business contacts continued).

Churchill, Winston (Leonard) Spencer (1874–1965) Prime minister of Britain from the grim days in 1940 until the victory over Germany in 1945, Winston Churchill in his lifetime won as much renown as can come to a human being. He was selected by *Time* magazine as "Man of the Half Century," and described by one of his closest associates, Lieutenant General Sir Hastings ISMAY, as a person who "could not be judged by ordinary standards; he was different from anyone we had ever met before, or were likely to meet again . . . indispensable and completely irreplaceable." The historian Sir Arthur Bryant gave him this remarkable tribute: "No statesman save Alfred has done England such service as Churchill."

After the war, it was Churchill, in March 1946, who issued the declaration of Cold War in his IRON CURTAIN speech in Fulton, Mo.; he also continued to call for the development of European unity, although, as prime minister again from 1951 to 1955, he followed his own personal tradition by emphasizing the "special relationship" he had long espoused with the United States. But in these latter years, older now and the victim of various illnesses, he lacked the force that had characterized him as Britain's war leader. Even in this phase, however, Churchill, by his constant calls for meetings of world leaders—those individuals at the "SUMMIT"—gave the world a concept and a phrase that have been in constant (and even debased) use ever since.

In spite of the almost legendary standing he acquired from his inspired defiance of Adolf Hitler in

British prime minister Winston S. Churchill

to reiterate the danger posed by Nazi Germany both in the House of Commons and in articles and speeches outside it.

Although Churchill during the war constantly hectored his commanders in the field and advocated unwise military ventures of various kinds, his associates generally regarded these sides of his character as a small price to pay for his leadership. "As a war leader," said General Ismay, the prime minister's personal chief of staff, "he was head and shoulders above anyone that the British or any other nation could produce." (Churchill's constant drive for action, in the view of many commentators, represented his need to combat depression, which he called the "black dog" and from which he chronically suffered.)

A foretaste of the coming conflict between the Soviet Union and the Western Allies presented itself in the autumn of 1944, when Churchill attempted with little success to reach an understanding with Soviet premier Joseph STALIN about the postwar status of Poland, the country whose invasion by Germany in 1939 had pushed Britain into war. At the YALTA CONFERENCE in February 1945, Churchill, together with U.S. president ROOSEVELT, attempted to deal with what was in reality an insoluble question. No possibility existed that a free and democratic Poland, the dream of Western statesmen, would also be friendly to the Soviet Union, or that Stalin would tolerate the creation of such a state—which, indeed, would come into existence only four and a half decades later, with the end of the Cold War. Churchill, however, made a gallant effort but won only a paper concession that proved to have no meaning in practice.

On May 12, 1945, just two days after the official ending of the war in Europe, Churchill telegraphed President TRUMAN (who had succeeded Roosevelt on April 12) to express his concern about the refusal of the Soviets to deal openly with the U.S. and British commanders about matters in their zone of Germany. Churchill made his last appearance at an inter-Allied meeting (the POTSDAM CONFERENCE) in July 1945; when the results of the British general election became known, he was replaced, in the middle of the conference, by the new prime minister, Clement ATTLEE. But the following March, at Westminster College in Missouri, though out of office, Churchill startled—and in

1940, when many observers concluded too quickly that Germany had won the war, Churchill had a political past that left him for years unpopular in his own party. Considered a clever, self-seeking adventurer (who had changed parties not once but twice), he had been driven from the cabinet during World War I because critics unjustly gave him all the blame for the failure of the Dardanelles operation, which had been intended to open up the deadlocked war and give aid to Russia. (First lord of the Admiralty at that time, Churchill later drew from this experience the lesson that one could not undertake such an important operation from a subordinate position. This was one of the reasons that caused him to feel relief, rather than apprehension, when he became prime minister in May 1940.) He served again in the cabinet in the 1920s, but his intense opposition to the granting of a liberal constitution to India kept him in the "wilderness" during the 1930s. Meanwhile, he continued

many quarters shocked—the world by declaring that an iron curtain now divided Europe. A phrasemaker all his life, he had provided a memorable symbol for the world's next great contest.

Churchill held a marked advantage over the other national leaders of World War II: not only did he survive the war, as Roosevelt did not, but he had the gifts and the experience to write what became the most important and influential historical account of the war. This six-volume work, *The Second World War* (1948–53), became the leading factor in his winning the Nobel Prize for literature in 1953.

Despite his eminence, his achievements, his larger-than-life status, Churchill always retained a puckish side, including a detestation of red tape. Short, fat, pink and white, with the countenance of a cherub, he once startled the doorman at the Admiralty by refusing to present the pass that had been issued to him; he had, in fact, torn it up. He explained himself to the doorman by saying, "My face is my fortune."

CIA   *See* CENTRAL INTELLIGENCE AGENCY.

Citizens' Movement—Democratic Action   One of the two groups (the other was called the CENTER ALLIANCE) into which the Polish SOLIDARITY movement split in 1990. Its members accused Lech WALESA of acting in an authoritarian fashion. Its acronym in Polish was ROAD.

Civic Forum   When antigovernment demonstrations erupted in Czechoslovakia in the autumn of 1989, Civic Forum, an organization composed largely of intellectuals and led by the playwright Václav HAVEL, played a principal part. In June 1990 Civic Forum became the most important political element of the new Czechoslovak government. *See also* PUBLIC AGAINST VIOLENCE; VELVET REVOLUTION.

Clark, Mark Wayne (1896–1984)   Tall, lean, and energetic, General Clark (called Wayne by his friends and once dubbed "the American Eagle" by Winston Churchill) fought in three wars, his last post being as supreme commander of UNITED NATIONS forces in Korea and U.S. commander in chief in the Far East. One of the best-known U.S. gener-

als, he succeeded General Matthew RIDGWAY in Korea in May 1952, serving for some 15 frustrating months before signing the truce ending the KOREAN WAR.

A West Point graduate, class of 1917, Clark went to England with General Dwight D. EISENHOWER in 1942 and served as Ike's deputy commander for the invasion of French Northwest Africa in November 1942, winning special fame by carrying out a secret mission by submarine to meet with local leaders who supposedly could deliver local French support to the arriving U.S. and British forces. Although these expectations proved not to be justified, Clark's adventure remained one of the best stories of the war, complete with trousers lost and refuge taken in a wine cellar. Clark commanded the Fifth Army in Italy, where he created controversy by making Rome instead of German forces his target. But if he hoped for glory from the capture of the Eternal City, he had somewhat misread fate. Little more than a day later the Allies launched the Normandy invasion, which thenceforth dominated the news.

After the end of the war, Clark commanded U.S. occupation forces in Austria, where he effectively handled a complex political situation. From 1947 until 1952 he served in the United States. In October 1953, 40 years after beginning his military career at West Point, Clark retired. He then served 12 years as president of The Citadel military college in Charleston, S.C.

Clark Kerr, Sir Archibald   *See* INVERCHAPEL.

Clay, Lucius DuBignon (1897–1978)   One of the most prominent and important U.S. representatives overseas in the early years of the Cold War, General Clay served as commander in chief of U.S. forces in Europe and military governor of the American Zone of Germany.

A native of Georgia, the son of a U.S. senator, Clay was the youngest of six children and the only one to escape destruction by alcoholism. After graduating from West Point in 1918, Clay served in a variety of posts as an engineer officer until his assignment to Washington during World War II for high-level duties on the General Staff. Having been called "bolshevistic" early in his career because of his tendency to nonconformity, Clay in his Corps

General Lucius D. Clay, U.S. commander in West Germany, inspects troops.

of Engineers service in Washington during the 1930s acquired considerable political experience as well as a reputation for strict honesty. Summoned overseas in 1944 for a special task by his close friend, General Dwight D. EISENHOWER, Clay cleared up the snarled shipping situation in the key port of Cherbourg, being credited with doubling the flow of supplies in a single day. Also in 1944 he became deputy director of the Office of War Mobilization and Reconversion, and in 1945, as a lieutenant general, he was named, under Eisenhower, deputy in charge of all civil affairs in the U.S. Occupation Zone in Germany.

Clay moved up to the top two positions in Germany in 1947 and, serving until 1949, became a central figure in one of the most confrontational eras of the Cold War. In March 1948, when Soviet-controlled newspapers in eastern Germany warned Germans in the west not to cooperate with the Americans in view of the imminent "unavoidable withdrawal of the Allies," Clay telegraphed a warning to Washington that "war may come with dramatic suddenness." What actually came were the BERLIN BLOCKADE AND AIRLIFT (Clay launched the airlift on his own authority) and the development of the FEDERAL REPUBLIC OF GERMANY. After the lifting of the blockade, the local people honored Clay by making him the first American to have a street in Berlin named after him, and when he died, 30 years after the airlift, a local citizen who remembered those days said of him, "He was the best of them all."

A leading advocate of creating the West German state and integrating it into the Western defense system, the lean-faced, decisive, strong-willed Clay incurred the ire of some observers who believed he had rebuffed all the attempts of German Social Democrats to play an important part in the German recovery that became the "economic miracle." Though he usually spoke softly and courteously, Clay could on occasion show temper. After a tough negotiating session, a British officer said of him, "He looks like a Roman emperor—and acts like one." Clay "did not welcome interference from Washington intruders," said John Kenneth GALBRAITH, a frequent government adviser, but "neither could he resist any idea that seemed worthwhile."

In 1952 Clay, who had become chairman of the Continental Can Company after retiring from the army (though he had no more than $3,000 in the bank, he had refused to join any company holding defense contracts), helped persuade Eisenhower to try for the Republican presidential nomination. During their presidencies, both Ike and John F. KENNEDY often sought Clay's advice on issues concerning Berlin. In 1961, facing an East-West crisis involving the status and future of the divided city, Kennedy sent Clay to Berlin as his personal representative. Clay remained there eight months, assuring Berliners that the United States had no intention of abandoning them.

In 1963 General Clay dashed the hopes of a group of 100 businessmen who had formed the "Committee to Draft Clay" by declining their request that he seek the 1964 Republican presidential nomination. The general nevertheless remained extremely active in civic affairs for the rest of his life.

Clay, said Galbraith, was "one of the most intelligent, adept and, as necessary, politically resourceful administrators of his time" and "one of the most skillful politicians ever to wear the uniform of the United States Army."

Clayton, William Lockhart (1880–1966) Native of Tupelo, Miss., who became a leading cotton broker in Houston and, having served with the War Industries Board in World War I, held business-related U.S. government posts in the World War II era, as deputy federal loan administrator, vice president of the Export-Import bank, assistant secretary of commerce, and administrator of the Surplus War Property Administration. In the last phases of the war and the early years of the Cold War, Clayton exerted strong influence on U.S. economic policy as assistant secretary of state (1944–

45), as undersecretary of state for economic affairs (1945–47), and as alternate governor of the World Bank (1946–49). In 1947 he chaired the American delegation to the UNITED NATIONS Conference on Trade and Employment, held in Havana. A staunch believer in free trade for both economic and political reasons, Clayton once said, in commenting on trade restrictions, "Nations which act as enemies in the market place cannot long be friends at the council table."

Early in 1946, considerably more than a year before the first MARSHALL PLAN ideas were launched, Clayton favored a generous response to French premier Léon BLUM's urgent request for coal and cash. In 1947 Clayton played an important part in the development of the State Department thinking that culminated in the creation of the Marshall Plan.

Clemenceau Class of French aircraft carriers *(Clemenceau* and *Foch)* laid down in the 1950s, completed in the early 1960s, and important through the next decades. Of 22,000 tons' standard displacement (32,700 tons fully loaded), each carried about 40 aircraft. Armament included eight 3.9-inch guns.

Clifford, Clark McAdams (1906–) Washington lawyer who served as President JOHNSON's secretary of defense (1968–69) but became best known as an adviser to presidents and longtime leading member of the Washington establishment. A native of Kansas, Clifford grew up in St. Louis and after receiving his law degree from Washington University practiced with a local firm until entering the U.S. Navy in 1944, during World War II. Clifford's Missouri background played its part in his selection to be acting naval aide in the White House in 1945, while President TRUMAN, a Missourian himself, and his regular naval aide were attending the POTSDAM CONFERENCE. Continuing in this position, Clifford supplemented these duties by assisting the president's general counsel, Judge Samuel H. Rosenman, whom he succeeded as counsel during the following year. Clifford held this post until 1950.

As general counsel, Clifford presided over the creation of two notable documents. One, delivered on September 24, 1946, was a long (26,000-word) top-secret memorandum, "American Relations with the Soviet Union," based on reports and analyses supplied by cabinet departments, military officers, and others, including George KENNAN and Charles BOHLEN, the leading State Department Soviet specialists. Something new for the United States—a peacetime interagency policy review, as Clifford later described it—this document served both as a discussion of past events and as a forecast of policies to come.

Coming before an open U.S.-Soviet break, the memorandum declared that the "primary objective of United States policy is to convince Soviet leaders that it is in the Soviet interest to participate in a system of world cooperation," and it argued for "cultural, intellectual, and economic interchange" to promote the "peaceable coexistence" of capitalism and Communism. It also said that the United States must "maintain sufficient military strength to restrain the Soviet Union." Though Clifford was the responsible official, the bulk of the report was drafted by a former intelligence officer, George M. Elsey, who went on to become a key adviser to Truman.

The other document Clifford had an important hand in shaping was the legislation that gave birth to the Department of Defense in 1947. Here his experience in the navy and his skill as a negotiator played a significant part as well.

On March 1, 1968, Clifford replaced Robert MCNAMARA as secretary of defense. In 1965, in the early days of the U.S. buildup in South Vietnam, Clifford had observed to President Johnson that the United States was not likely to win a war in Vietnam, although when the administration pursued the VIETNAM WAR, Clifford lent the effort his support. Now, in 1968, Johnson not only recruited him as defense secretary but asked him to chair a panel that would examine alternatives for U.S. policy toward Vietnam. Though his panel recommended the sending of U.S. reinforcements, Clifford characterized the purpose as for "caution and for protection," and during his time at the Defense Department promoted U.S. disengagement from the war. By March 4, in fact—after relentlessly interrogating officers throughout the Pentagon—Clifford had concluded that the war could not be won, and he attempted to move Johnson toward the same view.

An elegant figure with wavy hair and a velvet-soft voice, Clifford was often described as the ultimate Washington insider. But his involvement in an international banking scandal marred his later years, though he maintained his innocence and was not convicted of wrongdoing.

Club for the Support of Glasnost and Perestroika
A loose association of Bulgarians involved in the quest for democracy. It was founded in 1988, at a time when the regime of the Bulgarian Communist Party leader, Todor ZHIVKOV, appeared unlikely to be influenced by such activities. In November 1989, however, groups of activists led the way in a series of events (if not a full-scale revolution like the one that took place in Poland) that forced Zhivkov from power. *See also* SOLIDARITY.

Cohn, Roy Marcus (1927–1986)   Lawyer and chief counsel of the U.S. Senate Permanent Investigations Subcommittee (better known as the MCCARTHY Committee) from 1953 to 1954. Cohn later practiced law in New York and wrote several books, one of which preached the practical value of obnoxiousness. Cohn achieved considerable notoriety by making a tour, with his friend G. David Schine, of U.S. information libraries in Western Europe for the purpose of picking out allegedly pro-Communist books on their shelves and thus discrediting those in charge of the information program. But Cohn's greatest fame came in the so-called Army-McCarthy hearings of 1954, when television viewers saw him continually at the senator's right hand. The discrediting of McCarthy's and Cohn's case and the subsequent censure of the senator ended the Washington phase of Cohn's career. He remains an important symbol of a particular phase of the Cold War, when capricious allegation became so common that it won the designation "MCCARTHYISM."

Cold War   The general term for the post-1945 political, ideological, strategic, and military conflict between the Western Allies—led by the United States—and the Soviet Union and other Communist countries. This usage of the term was coined in 1947 by a well-known newspaper writer and editor of the time, Herbert Bayard Swope, who employed it in a speech written for Bernard Baruch to deliver to the legislature of South Carolina, Baruch's home state. The expression actually has a long though little-known history, however, going back to the 14th century, when Prince Juan Manuel, the regent of Castile and Leon, applied it to the struggle between the Spanish Christians and the Moors. The prince meant that, unlike "hot," or formally declared, wars, the "cold war" began without a declaration of war and ended without a peace treaty.

Collins, J(oseph) Lawton (1896–1987) U.S. general, chief of staff of the army (1949–53) during a period that included the KOREAN WAR. Born in New Orleans, Collins graduated from West Point in 1917. In 1942, commanding a division in the battle for Guadalcanal, he acquired the nickname Lightning Joe from the division's code name.

As a corps commander in 1944, in the fighting in Western Europe after the landings in Normandy, Collins became known as one of the ablest and most aggressive U.S. generals; Britain's Field Marshal Bernard MONTGOMERY made a special request for his services during the Battle of the Bulge, and the American ground commander, General Omar Bradley, called Collins "one of the most outstanding field commanders in Europe."

After the war, Collins drafted the army's plan for unification of the U.S. armed services. As chief of staff, Collins strongly supported the U.S. commitment of troops to the NORTH ATLANTIC TREATY ORGANIZATION, on one occasion telling senators that the loss of western Germany to the Soviet Union could lead to an all-out war that the United States might not win. As a member of the JOINT CHIEFS OF STAFF, Collins played an important part in the decision to relieve General Douglas MACARTHUR in Korea in April 1951. MacArthur, Collins told a Senate committee, had violated strategic principles in preparing to drive to the Yalu River (the border between North Korea and China) while ignoring the potent threat of Chinese intervention—which had, in fact, occurred. In the decisive April 6 JCS meeting, Collins, though regretting the necessity for the decision, declared that MacArthur could no longer carry out U.S. policies.

Following his term as chief of staff, Collins served as U.S. representative to NATO. He also spent time in Vietnam as President EISENHOWER's personal representative. In the debate among U.S. officials about the advisibility of giving support to NGO DINH DIEM as prime minister, Collins cast a negative vote; but when the decision for Diem was made, the general gave him strong public endorsement. Collins retired from the army in 1956.

Columbine III Built by Lockheed, the *Columbine III* was a C-121, the military version of the civilian Super Constellation; this particular airplane bore the designation VC-121E because it was a specially modified C-121 that served as U.S. president EISENHOWER's personal aircraft from 1954 until he left office in 1961. Mrs. Eisenhower gave it the name *Columbine III* after the official flower of Colorado, where her family had lived for many years. The C-121, a larger version of Lockheed's famous Constellation (military designation: C-69), had a top speed of about 330 mph and a range of 4,000 miles.

Columbine III, U.S. president Eisenhower's personal aircraft

Comecon   In its attempts to counter in its own sphere the success of the MARSHALL PLAN in Western Europe, the Soviet Union produced a series of ideas and organizations: the MOLOTOV PLAN, the COMINFORM, and, in January 1949, the Comecon (its full name, in English, the Council for Mutual Economic Assistance), which had the mission of boosting trade among the countries of the EASTERN BLOC. For a variety of reasons, none of these efforts in any way rivaled the Marshall Plan; the USSR did not offer the other countries aid comparable to that extended by the United States, and some of them resisted incorporation into the Comecon system. Nevertheless, other countries, including Cuba and Vietnam, became members in later years, and the organization lasted until the collapse of the Eastern European Communist regimes in 1989–90.

Cominform   The Soviet Union established this organization (the Communist Information Bureau, in English) in 1947 to impose a common political line on all of the Communist parties of Eastern Europe. The Cominform could claim descent from previous international socialist and Communist bodies dating back to the First International (London, 1864) and the Second International (Paris, 1889). The Third, or Communist, International was organized in Moscow by Vladimir Lenin in 1919, with the twin aims of gaining foreign support for the Bolshevik Revolution in Russia and promoting revolution in other countries. In fact, the delegates to this Comintern congress came almost entirely from within Russia, and few of them represented any organized political group. By promoting a revolutionary psychology, however, the organization served Lenin's purposes. (Even so, events in Eastern Europe did not go at all as Lenin expected—every Communist revolution outside Russia failed.)

The Comintern continued as an officially revolutionary organization until 1943, when Joseph STALIN dissolved it in a rhetorically counterrevolutionary gesture, intended to convince the United States and Britain that the USSR no longer sought world revolution. But in September 1947, two years after the end of World War II, the Cominform was established, said the Yugoslav observer Vladimir DEDIJER, when "the Soviet Union had finally decided to take under her direct control a number of East European states." At the initial meeting the keynote speaker, Andrei ZHDANOV, describing the Cominform as a response to the proposed U.S. MARSHALL PLAN, declared that since 1945 the world had become irrevocably divided into an imperialist camp led by the United States and a progressive socialist camp led by the Soviet Union.

In 1956, in the aftermath of his famous de-Stalinization speech to the 20th Congress of the COMMUNIST PARTY OF THE SOVIET UNION, First Secretary Nikita KHRUSHCHEV dissolved the Cominform, a move that eased relations with Yugoslavia (which had been expelled from the organization in 1948) and, like Stalin's disbanding of the Comintern during World War II, was intended to attract favorable comment in the West.

Committee on the Present Danger   Bipartisan group of conservative former government officials and retired service officers who came together in the mid-1970s to press for increased U.S. defense measures to counter the Soviet military buildup. Members included Admirals Thomas Moorer and Elmo Zumwalt, a former deputy secretary of defense, David Packard, and a veteran State Department and defense figure, Paul NITZE, who became one of the committee's most prominent spokesmen. The United States, Nitze said, was entering "a dangerous period of strategic disadvantage vis-à-vis the Soviet Union." Two members of the committee became prominent officials in the REAGAN administration—George SHULTZ as secretary of state and Jeane Kirkpatrick as ambassador to the UNITED NATIONS.

Common Market   *See* EUROPEAN ECONOMIC COMMUNITY.

Commonwealth of Independent States   Intended by its founders to be the successor to the Soviet Union, the commonwealth was proclaimed on December 8, 1991, in a meeting held at a hunting lodge near Minsk. Taking part were the president of Russia, Boris YELTSIN; the chairman of the Supreme Soviet of the Republic of BYELORUSSIA, Stanislav Shuskevich; and the president of the Ukraine, Leonid Kravchuk. The attempted coup in

August 1991 and its aftermath not only had taken power away from the COMMUNIST PARTY OF THE SOVIET UNION but had destroyed the authority of President Mikhail GORBACHEV and the Soviet government. In their statement, the founders declared the commonwealth "open for accession by all member-states of the former USSR" (and by other states as well), and in a second meeting held in Alma-Ata, Kazakhstan, two weeks later they were joined by the leaders of eight other former Soviet republics; this second meeting constituted the formal establishment of the commonwealth (December 21).

In practice, the commonwealth proved to be more an idea than any kind of functioning union. In the 1990s it made various limited attempts to establish a common market. *See also* STATE COMMITTEE FOR THE STATE OF EMERGENCY IN THE USSR.

Communist Party of the Soviet Union (CPSU)   The organization that held all political authority in the Soviet Union from the establishment of the Bolshevik regime in Russia in 1917 to the constitutional changes of March 1990, which stripped the CPSU of its monopoly of power. The party acquired the name "All-Union Communist Party (Bolshevik)" in 1919 and became simply the Communist Party in 1925. On August 24, 1991, following the failed coup attempt by the STATE COMMITTEE FOR THE STATE OF EMERGENCY IN THE USSR, Soviet president Mikhail GORBACHEV repudiated the party (albeit reluctantly), dismissed its leaders, and removed it from participation in the government; he also expropriated its buildings and other property.

Because it held a legal monopoly of power, the CPSU did not conform to the traditional definition of a political party, which (as is suggested by such terms as *partisan* and *ex parte)* normally represents one side of a two- or many-sided political situation and engages in debate and competition with other parties. In official language, the CPSU was supposed to play the "leading role" in the Soviet state. Its supremacy was demonstrated by the fact that its head (called, at various times, GENERAL SECRETARY and first secretary) was regarded everywhere as the chief of the government, whether or not he was also chairman of the Council of Ministers or president.

Party membership—possession of the coveted red card—was considered a privilege and was the key to economic, social, and political success. Membership was generally restricted: in the 1970s, for example, it amounted to about 5 percent of the population.

In a conversation at the YALTA CONFERENCE with Premier and General Secretary Joseph STALIN, Winston CHURCHILL remarked that he might well lose his position as prime minister in the forthcoming British general election because "we had two parties in Britain, and I belonged to only one of them." The Soviet leader responded to this observation from a different set of values. Churchill described it thus: " 'One party is much better,' said Stalin, with deep conviction."

compellent threat   A concept employed by strategists who applied game theory to questions of Cold War planning; it contrasts with the idea of DETERRENCE. As explained by a leading student of strategy and conflict, Thomas C. Schelling of Harvard University, deterrence is passive, intended to keep an adversary from beginning some action, whereas a compellent threat is intended to make an adversary *do* something or cease doing something. In this context, however, conflict behavior was viewed not as an occasion for the use of force but as an element in a bargaining situation, just as a labor strike is intended not to destroy a business but to win concessions from management. In reference to the Cold War, as can readily be seen, game theory could quickly develop sophistication and complexity.

Congress for Cultural Freedom   European organization of liberal and left-wing intellectuals, founded to counter organized Communist groups and publications. The congress supported the well-known magazine *Encounter*, published in London and edited by the poet Stephen Spender, together with other publications in Paris, Berlin, and Vienna. Along with the National Student Association in the United States, and a variety of other groups, the congress received considerable unwanted publicity in 1967, when the American magazine *Ramparts* revealed that, going back to the early 1950s, these organizations had received subsidies from the U.S. CENTRAL INTELLIGENCE AGENCY, not directly but through various foundations. The CIA did not intend to turn the recipients into spies but was it-self acting as an instrument of U.S. foreign policy. U.S. administrations wished to support non-Communist intellectual activities in Europe but felt, with ample reason in the MCCARTHY era of the early 1950s, that if such support were to be given it would have to be clandestine; the agency acted in accordance with a policy adopted by the NATIONAL SECURITY COUNCIL. The National Student Association declared that it had accepted the money because it had no other such support in its effort to oppose the international student organizations heavily subsidized by the Soviets. The hand of the U.S. government was generally said to be invisible; the editors of *Encounter* declared that they had not known the source of the money.

Congress of People's Deputies A Soviet representative body established in 1988 on the initiative of President Mikhail GORBACHEV. The members of this "supreme government body" would be elected by voters at large and by so-called social organizations: trade unions, Communist Party organizations, and special groups like the evocatively named Society of Inventors and Rationalizers. The Congress in turn would elect a Supreme Soviet, a smaller, full-time body. The elections for the Congress were held in March 1989. In 1990 the provision for electing representatives of the social organizations was abolished.

containment Though given somewhat varying definitions at different times and by different interest groups, the containment of Soviet expansionism formed the fundamental U.S. strategy throughout the Cold War. It was first presented to the public by its principal author, George F. KENNAN, in his article "The Sources of Soviet Conduct" in the quarterly *Foreign Affairs* (July 1947), which became famous as the "X ARTICLE." Though Kennan did not clearly define the scope of containment or the degree to which he saw it as political or military, as time went on he became concerned about what he saw as its overextension (as, for example, to Southeast Asia) and its concentration on military means of execution. *See also* NSC-68.

contras Coalition organized in 1981 by REAGAN administration officials to act against *(contra,* in

Spanish) the Marxist SANDINISTA government of Nicaragua. On taking office in January 1981, the administration, having decided that the Sandinistas represented a Communist threat in Central America and that they were a principal cause of the civil war in neighboring El Salvador, began working to combine former Sandinistas, former members of the previous Somoza government's National Guard, and members of the middle class into an effective opposing force, based in Honduras and Costa Rica. Some members of this coalition were legitimately independent factions—especially that represented by Edgar Chamorro, leader of the largest contra group. Control of contra activities was exercised on behalf of the U.S. NATIONAL SECURITY COUNCIL by a marine officer, Lieutenant Colonel Oliver North.

Although President Reagan likened the contras to the U.S. Founding Fathers, these dissidents encountered much hostility at home and abroad because of their reported human-rights abuses. As the war continued through the 1980s, these negative perceptions and a general disillusionment with their activities caused the U.S. Congress to put the contras on a thin diet consisting entirely of humanitarian rather than military aid. Searching for alternative sources of support for a project it had no intention of abandoning, the administration turned to private and non-U.S. sources of funds, while also hoping to change congressional opinions. These maneuvers led to the great crisis of the Reagan administration, the IRAN-CONTRA AFFAIR. Eventually the contras and the Sandinistas sought a settlement, which President Oscar Arias Sánchez of Costa Rica succeeded in negotiating in 1987. A peace agreement in January 1992 formally ended the civil war in El Salvador.

Conventional Forces in Europe Treaty (CFE-I Treaty) Part of a wave of arms-control negotiations taking place at the end of the 1980s and the beginning of the 1990s (such as the STRATEGIC ARMS REDUCTION TALKS), the Treaty on Conventional Forces in Europe was signed in Paris by 22 countries on November 19, 1990. It limited both military personnel and military equipment on the Continent; importantly, the Soviet Union agreed to accept deeply asymmetrical cuts compared with those required of the NORTH ATLANTIC TREATY OR-

GANIZATION. In any case, however, the CFE negotiations had run parallel with political events in Eastern Europe that would of themselves require Soviet withdrawal from its former satellites.

Cooper, John Sherman (1901–1991) U.S. senator from Kentucky who became a prominent diplomat as ambassador to India and East Germany. A Yale graduate (1923), Cooper attended the Harvard Law School and then practiced in Kentucky, serving as a county judge before going into the army during World War II. After the war he entered an unusual career in the Senate, filling out unexpired terms of other members three different times before winning election to full terms in 1960 and 1966.

A widely respected liberal Republican and one of the greatest vote getters in the history of Kentucky, Cooper served the TRUMAN administration as a delegate to the UNITED NATIONS and adviser to the State Department. In 1955 President EISENHOWER appointed him ambassador to India, and in 1974 he became the first U.S. ambassador to East Germany, where he served until 1977. This was not, however, his first duty in Germany; he had been assigned there in military government in 1946.

In a day when Washington still boasted important hostesses, Cooper's wife, Lorraine, achieved renown as one of the most elegant of them all. A quiet but congenial man, Cooper had a close friendship with John F. KENNEDY; as senators the two had jointly introduced a resolution calling for a U.S.-European effort to support India's five-year plan for industrial development. At President JOHNSON's request, Cooper served on the Warren Commission, which investigated the assassination of President Kennedy.

Council of Europe Organization established in 1949 by democratic countries of Western Europe to discuss questions of general political concern. One of its leading elements is an assembly that sits at Strasbourg; an early delegate and strong supporter was Winston CHURCHILL, then out of office. Though some proponents saw the council as the beginning stage of European integration, the real impetus for progress in this area came from the MARSHALL PLAN, the SCHUMAN PLAN, and the establishment of the EUROPEAN COAL AND STEEL COMMUNITY.

Couve de Murville, (Jacques) Maurice (1907–) Premier of France briefly (1968–69), Couve de Murville served as foreign minister for almost all of Charles DE GAULLE's presidency (1958–68). After being associated with de Gaulle's rival, General Henri Giraud, in North Africa in 1943, during World War II, Couve de Murville joined de Gaulle, who efficiently disposed of Giraud as a political factor and became the sole leader of Fighting France. After the war Couve de Murville had a varied diplomatic career that took him to Egypt (1950–54), the United States (1955–56), and West Germany (1956–58) as ambassador before he came to the Foreign Ministry. As foreign minister, said de Gaulle, Couve de Murville "displayed in his field an ability which few have equaled in the course of our arduous history."

CPSU *See* COMMUNIST PARTY OF THE SOVIET UNION.

Cripps, Sir (Richard) Stafford (1889–1952) British political figure who served in the post–World War II Labour government as president of the Board of Trade and then as chancellor of the exchequer (1947–50), becoming identified with the post–World War II policy of economic recovery through austerity. A distinguished lawyer, Cripps entered the House of Commons in 1931. In the summer of 1940, because of his background as a far-left Labourite who had actually been expelled from the party for advocating a coalition with the Communist Party, Prime Minister Winston CHURCHILL gave him the "bleak and unpromising task" of serving as ambassador to the Soviet Union, in which he did not enjoy great success. "We did not at that time realise sufficiently," Churchill later wrote, "that the nearer a man is to Communism in sentiment, the more obnoxious he is to the Soviets unless he joins the party." Cripps resigned his ambassadorial post in January 1942 and, after experiencing some disagreements with Churchill, took the position of minister of aircraft production in November 1942 and held it for the rest of the war.

After the war, Cripps with his personal austerity

A cruise missile carries computerized maps that enable it to guide itself. This photo shows a Boeing AGM-86B air-launched missile.

seemed a fitting symbol of an economic policy featuring high taxes and controls on wages.

cruise missile   Type of guided missile that is essentially a miniature jet airplane. The U.S. Air Force's air-launched cruise missile (ALCM), designed originally to be launched from a B-52, is 20 feet 9 inches long, with a 12-foot wingspan, and is driven by a turbofan engine giving 600 pounds of thrust; range is about 1,500 miles. The missile carries computerized maps against which it continuously checks the area it passes over—called terrain contour matching. If the missile begins to stray from its proper path, its course is automatically corrected. Ground-launched cruise missiles (GLCMs) stirred up controversy when installed in Europe in 1983 but played a part in bringing about the INTERMEDIATE-RANGE NUCLEAR FORCES (INF) TREATY—signed December 8, 1987—between the United States and the Soviet Union. Sea-launched nonnuclear Tomahawk cruise missiles won great renown during the Persian Gulf War. The Soviet air force employed a cruise missile designated AS-15.

Cuban Missile Crisis   In June 1962, after various discussions between the Soviet Union and Cuba, Fidel CASTRO's brother Raúl and Soviet premier KHRUSHCHEV reached an agreement much desired by the Cuban premier: the Soviets would put intermediate-range missiles into Cuba, to act as a deterrent to possible U.S. invasion and to pose a continuing threat to the Americans. On October 14 a U.S. U-2F aircraft flying high over western Cuba (the first such American reconnaissance mission for almost six weeks) photographed what analysts determined to be missile-launching sites; the analysts concluded that the long, canvas-covered objects in the photos were medium-range missiles. Actually (as revealed in material declassified in 1992), CENTRAL INTELLIGENCE AGENCY operatives in Cuba had earlier reported that huge, missilelike objects were being transported in convoys, but Washington officials—captives of their own expectations, which called for the Soviets to send the Cubans defensive missiles but not to dare to install offensive missiles—dismissed such reports.

During the morning of Tuesday, October 16, after being informed of the discovery made by the U-2, President KENNEDY and his advisers began an intensive and extensive debate about the proper response to this Soviet challenge. Some of the president's counselors, led by General Maxwell TAYLOR, called for a "surgical" air strike on the missile sites; others, George BALL prominent among them, argued for a blockade of Cuba, to prevent the delivery of nuclear warheads and other equipment that would be required to make the new facilities operational. Various figures suggested the possibility of U.S. agreement to remove JUPITER missiles from Turkey—a move that would involve no strategic loss for the United States, already planning to decommission those missiles because the development of submarine-launched missiles had made them obsolete. Throughout the crisis the president's brother, Attorney General Robert KENNEDY, played a key role as adviser and informal go-between with persons in contact with the Soviets. Information about Soviet missiles from a Soviet military-intelligence colonel, Oleg PENKOVSKY, proved especially valuable to the president.

In a television address on October 22, President Kennedy informed the American people of the preparation on Cuba of a "series of offensive missile sites" and declared that the administration would regard any attack from Cuba on any country in the Western Hemisphere as an attack by the Soviet Union on the United States; such an attack, he said, would be met by a "full retaliatory response upon the Soviet Union." For action, the president announced the imposition of a "quarantine" on shipping to Cuba. He used this term because establishment of an acknowledged blockade would constitute a violation of international law; Defense Secretary Robert S. MCNAMARA later said that the administration liked "quarantine" because it did not sound warlike. The next day the president authorized the mobilization of reserve units and individual reservists. He also dispatched former secretary of state Dean ACHESON to Europe to explain the situation to the other members of the NORTH ATLANTIC TREATY ORGANIZATION.

As nerves remained taut, U.S. ships intercepted Soviet freighters, some of which stopped and turned away rather than reveal their cargoes to the ships of the U.S. cordon. On October 26 the White House declared that fresh evidence showed continuing activity on the missile sites. In a long message received the same day, Khrushchev made a compromise offer: the Soviets would dismantle the missile sites if the Americans would commit themselves not to invade Cuba. But on Saturday the 27th another message complicated matters by adding the stipulation that the United States must promise to remove the Jupiter missiles from Turkey. Also on the 27th, the crisis sharpened when a U-2 was reported missing and presumed, correctly, to have been brought down by a Soviet rocket; the order to fire appears, however, not to have been the result of any high-level decision but simply to have been given by the missile-battery commander.

On the same Saturday, after issuing a statement declaring that the situation in the Western Hemi-

sphere must be resolved in itself (that is, without reference to Turkey), Kennedy, who performed with exemplary sangfroid during the entire crisis (he called it "the week I earn my salary"), adopted his brother's suggestion to disregard the message involving Turkey and focus on the promising October 26 message. He replied to Khrushchev agreeing in principle to lift the quarantine and to "give assurances against an invasion of Cuba" and stipulating that Cuba agree to commit no aggressive acts in the Western Hemisphere. The next day Khrushchev announced that the Soviets would stop work on the bases, and Kennedy gave the desired assurances about invasion of Cuba. The United States also let it be known that the Jupiter missiles would be removed from Turkey, but told the Soviets that this move could not be mentioned in any formal agreement.

From this point, tensions began to ease, though the crisis was not over and Castro's refusal to allow U.S. or other inspectors to enter Cuba caused lingering problems. Enraged at Khrushchev's retreat, Castro in a meeting with the editors of *Revolución* launched into a tirade in which he called the Soviet premier "Son of a bitch! Bastard! Asshole!" and then proceeded to smash a huge wall mirror. Not only had Khrushchev rebuffed his plea to launch missiles against the United States, but the Soviet premier was knuckling under completely and taking them away.

On November 7 the United States and the USSR reached an agreement under which U.S. naval vessels would be allowed to check Soviet homeward-bound ships to verify the removal of the missiles. U THANT, the acting UN secretary-general, played a significant part in the negotiations and, for his efforts, won election on November 30 to complete the unexpired term of Dag HAMMARSKJÖLD.

The missile crisis exerted a sobering effect on both the United States and the Soviet Union, although many years would elapse before they came to understand how thoroughly they had misread each other's motives. Nevertheless, 1963, the very next year, would see the establishment of a HOT LINE between the Kremlin and the White House to prevent some of the problems in communication that had hampered negotiations during the crisis, and the creation of the first superpower agreement concerning weapons, the NUCLEAR TEST BAN TREATY.

The Caribbean Area

The crisis also launched an unending debate about the outcome—who won and who lost. Apart from all the possible subtleties of interpretation, it was clear that the Americans would not have to face a strategic threat from Cuba and the Cubans would not have to face a U.S. invasion, which, in fact, had not been contemplated until the threat posed by the missiles arose; this, indeed, was one of the leading misperceptions underlying the entire affair. Some observers, in a natural search for geopolitical symmetry, have believed that Khrushchev installed the missiles in Cuba with the intention of using them as a threat to make the United States accede to his wishes concerning BERLIN, but the Soviet premier seems already to have decided to settle for the status quo in the former German capital. Evidence that became available in 1992 revealed that when the Soviet foreign minister, Vassily Kuznetsov, suggested during the crisis that the Soviets consider making a move against Berlin, Khrushchev called him down.

Khrushchev's deployment and then withdrawal of the missiles widened the rift between the Soviet Union and the Chinese Communists, who condemned his actions as cowardly. The whole maneuver likewise increased the disfavor in which Khrushchev was held by some of his colleagues in the Soviet Communist Party CENTRAL COMMITTEE

and thus contributed to his downfall in October 1964.

Although a similarly dangerous situation was to develop in 1973 during the Middle East Yom Kippur War, when the U.S. STRATEGIC AIR COMMAND went on full alert, the Cuban Missile Crisis holds the distinction of being the Cold War event that brought the superpowers closest to nuclear war.

Cultural Revolution   The beginning of the Cultural Revolution is often traced back to an article that appeared in Shanghai on November 10, 1965. It officially began in August 1966, when during the 11th plenary session of its eighth meeting, the Central Committee of the Chinese Communist Party adopted a resolution declaring that the party had as its objective to struggle against and crush persons in authority who accepted Soviet-style revisionism with its belief that the transition from capitalism to socialism could come about peacefully.

To carry out the resolution, the party established committees in colleges, factories, cities, and villages to seek out and criticize bourgeois elements. In late August the government organized the RED GUARDS, made up of middle-school students from the families of peasants and revolutionary cadres, which would perform the effective work of the drive for purity. The guards carried out persecutions on a grand scale, and their members physically attacked people it deemed bourgeois, finding numerous victims among teachers, artists, and educated persons of all kinds. Thousands of Chinese died. Red Guard members also destroyed works of "decadent" art and literature and even buildings created by "decadent" architects. The whole process of "cultural revolution" most likely arose from MAO ZEDONG's fear that, as matters looked in the 1960s, Communism faced a bleak future and needed to be invigorated through peasant action. According to official Communist Party histories, the Cultural Revolution (which had disrupted the economy) ended after the ninth party congress in April 1969, although many commentators observed that purges continued until Mao's death in 1976.

Curzon Line Of the various vexing problems that arose between the Western Allies and the Soviet Union as World War II neared its end, none created more conflict than the question of Poland's boundaries and the composition of its government. After much discussion, some of it heated (at one point, Soviet premier Joseph STALIN accused British prime minister Winston CHURCHILL of seeking to commit "an act of injustice and unfriendliness toward the Soviet Union" simply because Churchill had suggested that all territorial decisions be put off until the war was over), the Allies agreed that the eastern boundary of Poland (its boundary with the USSR) should be drawn essentially along what was called the Curzon Line, a line proposed in 1920 by the British foreign secretary, Lord Curzon, as an armistice line between the forces of the newly created Republic of Poland and the Red Army of the Bolsheviks. After rejecting Curzon's proposal, the Russians had found themselves losing to the Poles, and in a 1921 agreement they ceded to Poland a large tract east of the Curzon Line, including parts of White Russia and the Ukraine. Stalin's agreement with Adolf Hitler in 1939, which established a "Ribbentrop-Molotov Line" similar to the Curzon Line, returned this area to the USSR, and in 1944–45 the Soviet dictator had no intention of giving it back to the Poles. In 1945 this 1939 boundary, with its curious history, became recognized as the official frontier between the USSR and Poland. (The boundary gave more territory to the USSR than it would have received if the actual Curzon Line had been used.) Two points became increasingly clear to the Americans and the British: (1) Stalin wished to have such decisions made while the war was still being fought, to take advantage of his country's military position; (2) the question of the Polish boundary, though important to the Russians, nevertheless did not possess quite the significance attributed to it because, in any case, Stalin intended to install in Warsaw a government wholly subservient to the Soviet Union. *See also* YALTA CONFERENCE.

D

Daniel, Yuli Markovich (1925–1988) Although the removal from office in 1964 of Premier Nikita KHRUSHCHEV did not mean that Stalinism had returned, it clearly brought with it the end of the Soviet THAW. Political control of literary and other cultural activities, which had been somewhat relaxed under Khrushchev, returned with the accession to power of Leonid BREZHNEV. The regime made this change plain in February 1966, with the trial of two writers, Yuli Daniel and Andrei SINYAVSKY, which followed their arrest in September 1965. Using the pseudonym Nikolai Arzhak, Daniel had published satirical short stories in the West. His writing and that of Sinyavsky were said by *IZVESTIA* to "vilify and defame everything that is dear to Soviet man." The two men had possibly established a bad precedent for themselves by serving as pallbearers at the funeral of the out-of-favor writer Boris PASTERNAK in 1960. Daniel drew a sentence of five years' imprisonment. "The pages steeped in bile," *Izvestia* predicted, "will rot in the dump."

Daniloff, Nicholas (1934–) On August 30, 1986, KGB officers in Moscow arrested a *U.S. News & World Report* correspondent for espionage—possession of prohibited material. The envelope in question had been handed to the correspondent, Nicholas Daniloff, by a KGB agent; the reporter was simply a pawn in a game whose purpose was to obtain the release from U.S. custody of Gennadi Zakharov, a Soviet physicist working at the United Nations, who had been arrested for espionage by the U.S. Federal Bureau of Investigation. Though this fairly standard Cold War action seemed to suit the bureaucratic purposes of the KGB, it created a whirlwind both at home and abroad. Soviet leader Mikhail GORBACHEV, still in the very early days of GLASNOST, apparently was dismayed at this setback to his hopes for a meeting with U.S. president Ronald REAGAN—a setback made unmistakably clear by the angry reaction of the American public. Further, the arrest of Daniloff, taking place while Gorbachev was on vacation, seemed to constitute a conservative challenge to his far-from-solid political position. Although Secretary of State George SHULTZ declared that the United States would not make a trade, the contending parties reached a settlement under which Zakharov pleaded *nolo contendere* and was then released; the deal was garnished by a Soviet agreement to allow two dissidents, a married couple, to emigrate. The arrangement had as its backdrop the conclusion of an agreement to hold the Reagan-Gorbachev REYKJAVÍK SUMMIT.

Dedijer, Vladimir (1914–) Yugoslav politician, writer, and translator, Dedijer had a close relationship with Marshal TITO, who once in pre–World War II days hid him from a search by the royal police. Of Bosnian background, Dedijer studied law at Belgrade University and then became a journalist and translator, producing versions of novels by H. G. Wells, John Galsworthy, and Pearl Buck. During the war he served as an officer with Tito's partisan army, and after the Communist victory he went to the United States as Yugoslav representative to the UNITED NATIONS General Assembly, a post he held almost continuously until 1953. In

1952 he became a member of the Central Committee of the Yugoslav League of Communists, but he enjoyed only a short tenure. The committee expelled him in 1954 because he defended the eminent politician and writer Milovan DJILAS, who had declared that, now well established in power, the Yugoslav Communist Party needed to grant greater freedom of speech to the people. In addition to his expulsion, Dedijer received a six months' probated prison sentence.

Having taught modern history for a year at Belgrade University, Dedijer in later years lectured in England, at Manchester and Oxford, and in the United States, at Cornell, the Massachusetts Institute of Technology, and Brandeis. Playing no favorites, he served as president of Bertrand RUSSELL's anti-American War Crimes Tribunal in 1964 and as honorary chairman of the Stockholm anti-Soviet Afghanistan Tribunal in 1981.

De Gasperi, Alcide (1881–1954)   A major European figure as Italian premier during the early years of the Cold War (1945–53). Earlier in his career, de Gasperi, a lifelong foe of dictatorship, had been imprisoned by Benito Mussolini, and after Il Duce's fall in 1943 he began to create a new kind of Italian political party. His efforts resulted in the Christian Democratic Party, which provided a democratic political vehicle for Italian Catholics. As premier, de Gasperi led the country into the emerging postwar Western system. A strong anti-Communist, he expelled Communist ministers from the Italian government in May 1947. He supported the NORTH ATLANTIC TREATY ORGANIZATION and the move toward European integration begun by the EUROPEAN COAL AND STEEL COMMUNITY.

de Gaulle, Charles André Joseph Marie (1890–1970) So closely did General de Gaulle identify himself with his country that justice seemed to require that his passion be fully requited. When he died, on November 10, 1970, President Georges POMPIDOU declared: "France is a widow." Since the summer of 1940, when de Gaulle raised the standard of Free France after his superiors had surrendered to Germany, he had been one of the greatest patriots and one of the most determined and altogether remarkable statesmen of the 20th century.

A graduate of the École Spéciale Militaire at Saint-Cyr, de Gaulle served in World War I as an infantry officer; captured by the Germans at Verdun, he spent most of his 32 months of imprisonment thinking and writing. Later he developed into an important military theorist, arguing in his writings that the French army must turn away from its emphasis on defense and create a powerful new kind of striking force based on tanks. During the 1930s his ideas received little attention, however, though in the doomed 1940 campaign he experienced some personal success as commander of an armored division.

Flown to England by Sir Edward Spears, a British general, as French resistance to the Germans was collapsing, de Gaulle soon began a series of radio broadcasts denouncing the armistice with Germany and issuing his call for Frenchmen to rally to him. Since de Gaulle was a junior general (in fact, the youngest in the French army) and was disavowing the actions of his superiors, other high officers viewed him with resentment and only two colonial generals declared for him. Though condemned as a traitor by the new French government headed by Marshal Philippe Pétain, de Gaulle did not waver in the task he had given himself of preserving the honor and greatness of France. A striking figure, standing six feet four inches, with his features embellished by a nose that seemed designed for caricature, persistently haughty and arrogant even with the British, who were supplying his basic needs, the general declared: *"Je suis la France."* Prime Minister Winston CHURCHILL treated him with marked magnanimity.

In discussing the sources of the ideas that impel great political leaders, the historian William H. McNeill said of de Gaulle that he "combined Gallicanism, technocracy, and a personal sense of mission that perhaps derived as much from his name as from anything more tangible." Against all conceivable odds, the general succeeded in creating what became in 1944 the provisional government of France. After the war, however, with inflation soaring out of control and the black market flourishing, the general's attempt to create an effective central government failed, as older politicians resisted his wish for a strong executive. De Gaulle resigned as provisional president on January 20, 1946, hoping, wrongly, that his absence would en-

French president Charles de Gaulle

courage delegates to create the kind of constitution he believed necessary for effective government. He withdrew from political life in 1953 and was not to return to office until 1958, when France, worn out with the ineffectual Fourth Republic and facing revolt in Algeria, called on him to become premier. Taking charge, supervising the writing of a new constitution with a potent presidency drawn to his design, de Gaulle on January 8, 1959, took the oath as the first president of the Fifth Republic.

In the presidency de Gaulle pursued an independent course, advancing the "grandeur" of France and forever seeming to be insulting or thwarting allies. In 1963 he vetoed the admission of Britain to the EUROPEAN ECONOMIC COMMUNITY (Common Market), and he pulled France out of the military framework of the NORTH ATLANTIC TREATY ORGANI-

ZATION. Though the French had begun work on a nuclear capability before he came to office, the general emphasized the creation of an independent striking force, making it clear that he did not wish to see France continue subservient to the United States. He refused to attend the June 1964 ceremonies marking the 20th anniversary of the D-Day Anglo-American landings in Normandy, which had constituted the beginning of the liberation of France from German occupation. In a 1965 conversation with the West German statesman Willy BRANDT, de Gaulle denounced the American hegemony that was "suffocating Europe and preventing the Europeans from being themselves." He carried his public aloofness to the "Anglo-Saxons" to the point of banning whiskey from the buffets at Élysée Palace receptions. Seeking to offset U.S. influence in Europe, he tried, with little success, to reach an entente with the Soviet Union. In July 1967 he stirred up a storm across Canada when he declared in a speech in Quebec, *"Vive le Québec libre"*—the slogan of those who wished to see the province break away from Canada. From Ottawa, Prime Minister Lester PEARSON fired back a sharp rebuke, leading de Gaulle to cancel a planned trip to the Canadian capital and go home a day early.

In 1968, not an easy year for Western politicians generally, de Gaulle weathered a wave of student riots, but in April 1969 he decided to resign after receiving unsatisfactory support from the voters in a referendum on a minor detail of a new regional structure for France. He retired to his home in Colombey-les-Deux-Églises, in eastern France, where he died suddenly just two days short of his 80th birthday.

De Gaulle possessed an overwhelming presence, said Henry KISSINGER, who, as U.S. president NIXON's security adviser, met the general in 1968. "One had the sense," said Kissinger, "that if he moves to a window the center of gravity might shift and the whole room might tilt everybody into the garden."

Delta Classes of Soviet nuclear-powered submarines that began appearing in the early 1970s and eventually totaled 44 boats in the Delta I through Delta IV classes. All except the Delta I's displaced more than 13,000 tons and carried 16 ballistic missiles with ranges of 3,750 miles or more.

demilitarized zone (DMZ)   Buffer zone, much of it running along the Ben Hai River, established between North and South Vietnam by negotiators at the 1954 conference that produced the GENEVA ACCORDS. It was based approximately on the 17th parallel. A demilitarized zone also separated the opposing forces in Korea. *See also* KOREAN WAR; VIETNAM WAR.

Deng Xiaoping (Teng Hsiao-ping) (1904–)   Chinese statesman who in his long career experienced a remarkable series of falls from power and comebacks before finally assuming the leadership of the state in 1978.

A participant in the famous Long March of the Chinese Communists (1934–35), Deng during World War II and the subsequent war that resulted in the defeat of CHIANG KAI-SHEK served the Communist Party as a political commissar in the Eighth Route Army and then the People's Liberation Army. Later he was party boss in southwestern China. In 1956 he became general secretary of the Chinese Communist Party, at the time the party was experiencing an internal struggle of a classic kind—between those faithful to traditional revolutionary ideology, like MAO ZEDONG, and those, like Deng, who favored industrial modernization along Western lines, with its accompanying complexities and doctrinal impurities.

During Mao's CULTURAL REVOLUTION of the 1960s, Deng went into eclipse—the first of his downfalls—only to return in 1973, having spent time as a worker in a plant that repaired tractors. After the death of his great supporter ZHOU ENLAI in 1976, Deng fell from grace again. Then, following the routing of the GANG OF FOUR, he rose once more. From this period on, Deng led the way into the economic reforms that characterized China in the 1980s. A Rand Corporation history of U.S.-Chinese negotiations (written for the CIA and declassified in 1994) showed Deng, like other Chinese leaders, as a wily adversary in discussion, keeping his U.S. interlocutors edgy and off balance by such basic techniques as pretending not to hear what had just been said.

A resolute opponent of the cult of personality—he did not care about titles as long as he held the power—Deng kept so low a profile that he often seemed almost invisible; he used as his power base his position as chairman of the Central Military Commission. None of Deng's economic actions involved any step toward democratization; he remained committed to the monolithic role of the Communist Party, with even minor political reforms being aborted if they seemed to challenge rule by the party. Essentially, he devoted himself to deconstructing the Marxist state while maintaining the political system. The tragic outcome of the 1989 TIANANMEN SQUARE demonstrations, when the government staged a massacre, gave ample evidence of his unchanging stance. In a historical irony, it had been in Tiananmen Square in 1976 that crowds had cried for Deng's own release from Maoist detention.

détente   In commenting favorably, in its issue of Monday, August 17, 1908, on a current change in the European situation, the London *Times* declared that "the characteristic feature of this transformation may be called a *détente.*" Unfortunately for the hopes of the *Times*'s correspondent, this "easing of strained relations"—as *détente* is defined—proved short-lived; the relaxation gave way to renewed tension, and just six years later World War I began. But this *Times* article remains memorable because it contains the first recorded example of the use in English of the French noun *détente* (a "relaxing") to describe a diplomatic situation. During the Cold War, with its alternating freezes and thaws through more than four decades, various situations of détente arose, but the term especially belongs to the 1970s, to the era of negotiations between U.S. president Richard M. NIXON and Soviet general secretary Leonid BREZHNEV, particularly concerning the STRATEGIC ARMS LIMITATION TALKS and the "BASIC PRINCIPLES" AGREEMENT; Presidents Gerald FORD and Jimmy CARTER (in the first part of his term) followed Nixon's general course.

Détente gave the Soviets two major benefits: it allowed them to reduce defense costs and to focus their foreign concerns on China. One problem with détente in the United States was that some

Americans eagerly took it for more than it was, wanting to see in it not a relaxation of tensions for various reasons of policy but an end to them and perhaps to the Cold War itself. Meanwhile, in 1979, the Soviet invasion of AFGHANISTAN brought the decade-long period of U.S.-Soviet détente to a sort of official end, although it had already faded.

deterrence   Although the idea of deterrence—discouraging an action through inspiring in the potential actor fear of its consequences—can be applied to nonnuclear as well as nuclear situations, during the Cold War—particularly after the development and deployment of delivery systems with hydrogen warheads—the term carried a special meaning: the existence of such weapons would deter any country from launching a nuclear attack on another country because the first country would thereby expose itself to devastating retaliation. Thus the purpose of possessing H-bombs came to be the prevention of war, not the winning of it. This BALANCE OF TERROR posed new kinds of problems for political and military planners, who did not find it easy to formulate rules for the game, which had to be played without explicit, agreed-upon regulations and without referees.

U.S. planners worked throughout the 1950s to evolve a code of nuclear conduct (with emphases varying as administrations changed), and a similar evolution took place in the Soviet Union. A rather chilling 1955 editorial in the Soviet journal *Military Thought* declared that the power of nuclear weapons made the element of surprise more important than it had been in the past, but the editor went on to warn readers that surprise could not win a decisive advantage (it is also true that at the time the USSR was markedly inferior in strategic strength to the United States). In a speech to the Supreme Soviet, First Secretary Nikita KHRUSHCHEV asked whether an attacker, even if he succeeded in achieving surprise, could "put out of commission all the stockpiles of nuclear weapons and all the missile-launching equipment located in the territory of the power under attack." He then answered his own question: "Certainly not." Though the point of his comments was to show that it would take "foolhardiness" for an adversary to at-

tack the USSR, he was also expressing a general truth.

An unusually important 1962 Soviet book, *Military Strategy* (a collective work of 15 officers, edited by one of the country's leading soldiers, Marshal V. D. Sokolovskii, a former chief of the General Staff), maintained that nuclear war could be fought successfully, although "the enormous destructive powers of the new weapons, the unlimited spatial scope of war, and the inevitable involvement of the majority of the earth's population in the sphere of destruction means that a new world war, if the imperialists start it, will inflict incalculable deprivation and suffering on mankind. It is difficult even to imagine the magnitude of the destruction and the human losses in such a war." Such comments certainly suggested the possibility of only the most limited kind of success. What the Sokolovskii group really seems to have believed was that the Soviet Union should be strong enough to frighten off foes variously characterized as the "imperialist aggressors," the "capitalist military coalition," and, in general, "world reactionaries." Looking past the obligatory jargon with which the book is laden, one can hear Sokolovskii talking about something quite similar to deterrence, American-style. Even so, the Soviets did not describe their doctrine as deterrence *(ustrashenie;* literally, intimidation) but used the term *sderzhivanie* (restraint).

Despite the overarching influence of deterrence or its equivalent ideas, the world during the Cold War always had to face the possibility that "hot" war might result from miscalculation, panic, or confusion—from human error of one kind or another. Numerous books and movies of the era exploited this idea. No one could wholly forget the classic historical figure of a nervous sentry, finger resting on the trigger of his rifle, peering at shadows moving in the darkness. And during the CUBAN MISSILE CRISIS, when he learned that an unwanted and possibly provocative U.S. reconnaissance flight had taken place, President KENNEDY uttered a memorable dictum: "There's always one son of a bitch that doesn't get the word."

Nevertheless, although the Cold War featured confrontations, side wars, clashes of proxies, and other encounters, the fact remains that this era governed by deterrence constituted the longest period of great-power peace not only during the 20th century but for many years earlier as well. The effectiveness of deterrence depended on the ability of the leaders of the United States and the Soviet Union to make rational calculations of their respective interests. Fortunately, they proved able to do so; a world that had just emerged from a struggle with Adolf Hitler, however, could not have taken rationality for granted.

Deutsche Demokratische Republik (DDR)   *See* GERMAN DEMOCRATIC REPUBLIC.

Dien Bien Phu   Mountaintop village in Vietnam that became the scene of a decisive siege in the First Indochina War (between France and the Democratic Republic of Vietnam, 1946–54). In 1953, in a misguided attempt to lure the opposing VIETMINH into open battle, the French commander in Indochina, General Henri Navarre, ordered a fort built in the valley near Dien Bien Phu. The site was ill chosen; high hills surrounded the fort, and the airstrips that were built could be fired on from many overlooking positions. When the monsoon season arrived, the French had to depend for supplies entirely on air drops, most of which fell into Vietnamese hands. In the spring of 1954 the French found themselves entirely cut off from any support; a bid for U.S. air strikes was rebuffed by President EISENHOWER, who was strongly influenced by the opposition of the army chief of staff, General Matthew RIDGWAY, and of the British. On May 7, 1954, the French were forced to surrender. Some 2,300 of the original defenders had been killed and another 5,100 wounded. This battle led to the GENEVA ACCORDS on Vietnam and the end of the First Indochina War.

Dimitrov, Georgi (1882–1949)   Premier of Bulgaria from 1946 to 1949, Dimitrov worked in printing as a young man, joined the Social Democratic Party at the age of 20, and during World War I became a Communist. In 1923 he took part in a Bolshevik uprising and, after its collapse, fled to Moscow. He moved on to Berlin, where in 1933 he was accused of involvement in the great Reichstag fire; even though he was in the hands of the Nazis, however, he defended himself so ably that he won acquittal. Returning to Moscow, he became secretary-general of the Comintern, and in 1945, finally back home in Bulgaria, he was placed by the Soviets at the head of the provisional government of the country. In 1946 he became premier of the new Bulgarian People's Republic. Although he faithfully carried out his commission from Soviet premier Joseph STALIN to communize the country, he, along with other leaders of satellite countries, incurred considerable harsh criticism from Stalin in the next several years; the Soviet dictator feared the possible spread of Titoist contagion from Yugoslavia. Enough so, as one commentator saw it, that Dimitrov was quite fortunate to die a fine natural death in 1949. *See also* TITO, Josip Broz.

disinformation   Intelligence specialists speak of three types, or levels, of information and propaganda: white—the actual truth; gray—a blend of fact and half-truths; black—lies. Disinformation is a form of black activity that flourished during the Cold War, its particular identifying characteristic being that it usually consists of, or is supported by, forged documents. Governments and opposing intelligence agencies are often the targets of disinformation; sometimes an agency aims simply at discrediting its counterpart in order to weaken the latter in the esteem of its own political chiefs. At other times, however, the purpose may be to sway national or world opinion.

Disinformation was so highly valued by the Soviets that the KGB operated a special *deszinformatsiya* bureau. A typical case of disinformation occurred in India during the 1950s, when a local newspaper published two telegrams, furnished by Soviet sources, in which the U.S. ambassador in Taiwan supposedly reported to Washington on plans to do away with CHIANG KAI-SHEK; the Soviets claimed they had obtained the telegrams from members of a mob that had raided the U.S. embassy in Taipei. In the same era U.S. Army officers hired North Vietnamese astrologers to write forecasts predicting disaster for VIETMINH leaders and success for the South.

The presence of paper documents is by no means necessary for an exercise in disinformation. The KGB appears at one time to have considered the possibility of leaking radioactive waste into the waters around a U.S. Polaris submarine base, so that when the contamination was "discovered" the resulting outcry would lead to a demand to ban such vessels. Some years later (1983–86) the Soviets produced one of their most successful acts of disinformation: a series of stories claiming that the AIDS virus had been produced by American biological-warfare experts; even a leading British newspaper gave the claim some credence. Under GLASNOST, however, the GORBACHEV government repudiated the story.

Though all sides practiced disinformation during the Cold War, the Soviets gave it a particularly broad definition, including the commission of murder and other violent acts if the purpose was to produce a psychological effect on chosen parties. (Murder for nonpsychological purposes would thus be handled by a different bureau.) A 1962 Soviet statement, however, took a decidedly one-sided view of the matter. Imperialist intelligence agencies, it declared, "either exploit or organize internal political dissension and dissension among nationalities [and races in a particular state], conspiracies, and political assassinations. They blackmail and bribe statesmen, party leaders, prominent scientists, newspaper publishers and editors. . . . Such missions and techniques are alien to Soviet intelligence." Actually, in their practice of disinformation, the Russians drew great inspiration from Lenin, who wrote that "poisoned weapons" must be used "not to correct an opponent's mistake but to destroy him, to wipe his organization off the face of the earth."

Dixon, Sir Pierson (1904–1965)   A leading British diplomat, Dixon was his country's permanent representative to the UNITED NATIONS from 1954 to 1960. Having begun his career in the Foreign Service in 1929, he was ambassador to Czechoslovakia (1948–50) and deputy undersecretary of state for foreign affairs (1950–54). Dixon left the UN to become ambassador to France (1960–64). Possibly to divert himself from his diplomatic cares, Dixon produced two novels, *Catullus* (1953) and *The Glittering Horn* (1958).

Djilas, Milovan (1911–1995)   Yugoslav politician, confidant of Marshal TITO, and writer whose book *Conversations with Stalin* became one of the most important sources of insight into the mentality of the Soviet dictator. Beginning as a strong admirer of STALIN, whom he described in 1942 as "the only head of state who has a generous conscience," Djilas after various meetings with his hero became a disillusioned opponent. *Conversations with Stalin,* smuggled to New York and published in 1961, gave most Western observers their first clear and believable behind-the-scenes picture of Stalin in power. Describing a dinner in the Kremlin in 1948, Djilas said of Stalin that "there was something both tragic and ugly in his senility," and, overall, he was struck by "the confinement, the inanity and senselessness of the life these Soviet leaders were living."

A native of Montenegro, Djilas joined the underground Yugoslav Communist Party in 1932 and within a year had been caught, arrested, and sentenced to three years' hard labor. In 1937 he met Josip Broz (Tito), whom Stalin had sent to Yugoslavia as the new general secretary of the Communist Party, and the two quickly became close friends. Serving at Tito's partisan headquarters in World War II, Djilas achieved the rank of lieutenant general and for a time led partisan activities in his native Montenegro. In the postwar years, having become secretary-general of the party under Tito and head of propaganda, he developed a reputation as a relentless cultural dictator. In this post he also, after Tito's 1948 break with Stalin, became an equally relentless foe of Stalinism.

During the closing months of 1953 Djilas's career as a Yugoslav Communist leader reached almost simultaneously its zenith and nadir. Just as he was being named president of the National Assembly, he began publishing a series of articles in which he argued that the party, well established and successful, now needed to allow greater freedom of opinion. Unfortunately, Tito did not agree. Even though, by some accounts, he loved Djilas like a son and perhaps had thought of the younger man as his heir, he had Djilas tried in January 1954 and condemned for "deviations." This stricture seems simply to have inspired Djilas to further deviationism. He went on to criticize Tito's regime in a *New York Times* article, an act that ultimately won him three years' imprisonment. Just before the door clanged shut, however, he managed to smuggle out the manuscript of his famous book *The New Class,* which expressed his view that the Communist Party had created a new aristocracy of its own and had outlasted its usefulness. When the book appeared, its message won its author four more years in prison, though he was paroled in 1961. Not surprisingly, he was arrested once again when the smuggled *Conversations with Stalin* appeared, this time with five years added to his original sentence. Tito relented in 1966, and this time Djilas spent his freedom for some years in traveling and lecturing. But in 1982 he was arrested again for criticizing the state. The Communist Party rehabilitated him in 1989.

In 1969 Djilas received the American Freedom Award.

Dobrynin, Anatoly Fedorovich (1919–) Veteran Soviet diplomat who figured in the 1962 CUBAN MISSILE CRISIS as ambassador to the United States. A member of the Soviet diplomatic service beginning in 1946, Dobrynin worked in the Secretariat of the UNITED NATIONS (1957–60) and then for almost two years directed the American Department of the Foreign Ministry before going to Washington as ambassador. Although Dobrynin, just before the missile crisis erupted, declared that Premier KHRUSHCHEV would never make such a move as placing Soviet medium-range missiles in Cuba, his diplomatic usefulness survived this untruth because U.S. leaders believed that his own government had kept him in ignorance of the facts. He then played an important part in the crisis as a conduit (though not the only one) between the U.S. administration and the Kremlin. An affable and lively man, Dobrynin remained at his post in Washington for the extraordinarily long time of 24 years. Averell HARRIMAN once described the ambassador as the most "civilized Bolshevik" he had ever known. In 1986 Mikhail GORBACHEV summoned Dobrynin to Moscow to become head of the International Department of the CENTRAL COMMITTEE. He retired in 1988.

Doctors' Plot On January 13, 1953, readers of the Soviet newspapers *PRAVDA* and *IZVESTIA* were informed that government security forces had arrested a group of Kremlin doctors accused of "using improper techniques to murder their pa-

tients." Their list of victims was said to include Andrei ZHDANOV, once considered Joseph STALIN's likely successor, who had died in murky circumstances in 1948; and Alexander Shcherbakov, another leading member of the POLITBURO. The authorities also accused the doctors of having tried to use their lethally improper techniques on such prominent soldiers as Marshal A. M. Vasilevsky and General S. M. Shtemenko, both of them high-level officers in World War II. Of the nine doctors listed in the announcement, six were Jews.

Arising in part from increasing anti-Semitism on Stalin's part, the "doctors' plot" scenario began unfolding in the autumn of 1952, as a result of the dictator's anger at an unfavorable report from his physician, a much-decorated 71-year-old named Vladimir Vinogradov, later to be charged with heading the conspiracy. With the aim of pleasing Stalin, Lavrenty BERIA and his security officers created a detailed story of the plot, claiming, for instance, that the doctors had falsified Zhdanov's electrocardiogram to conceal evidence of a heart attack, and had thus allowed this patient to work himself to death. Stalin responded eagerly to Beria's charges, telling the chief of the secret police to inform the interrogator on the case that if he should fail to get full confessions, "we'll reduce his height by a head."

The plot was said to be the work of a "Jewish bourgeois-nationalist organization" with U.S. and British connections. Although Stalin's original pique with Vinogradov had arisen from the doctor's candid statement that the leader of the nation was in poor health and should reduce his workload, Vinogradov, fortunately for himself and most of his colleagues, proved to be an accurate diagnostician. Stalin's death from a stroke on March 5, 1953, saved the Kremlin doctors from the firing squad, though two of them had already died under torture.

domino theory This term became the standard shorthand for the view that if one country in a particular area of the world should fall to Communism, the conquest of its neighbors would soon follow. In his press conference of April 7, 1954, explaining the strategic importance of Southeast Asia, U.S. president EISENHOWER said, "You have a row of dominoes, and you knock over the first one, and what will happen to the last one is the certainty that it will go over very quickly." The domino theory underlay U.S. involvement in Vietnam in the ensuing years. President KENNEDY, a subscriber to the theory, commented in 1963 that if the United States were to withdraw from South Vietnam, this "would mean a collapse not only of South Vietnam but Southeast Asia." The strongest assertion of the domino idea probably came in the statement by Eisenhower's secretary of state, John Foster DULLES, that if the Chinese Communists should succeed in pushing the Chinese Nationalist forces off the two small islands of QUEMOY AND MATSU, they would be on their way to "driving us out of the western Pacific, right back to Hawaii, and even to the United States."

Though Eisenhower, in articulating the domino theory, probably did not have George III in mind, that beleaguered head of state had indeed given the central idea succinct expression almost two centuries earlier, at the time of the American Revolution. If the Americans won their independence, wrote the king, "the West Indies must follow them. . . . Ireland would soon follow the same plan. . . . Then this island would be reduced to itself and soon would be a poor island indeed." *See also* VIETNAM WAR.

Douglas, Lewis Williams (1894–1974) U.S. business executive and government official who became a leading figure of post–World War II diplomacy as ambassador to Britain. The son of a wealthy Arizona mining family and a graduate of Amherst College, Douglas involved himself in mining and other ventures and served in Washington as the state's lone congressman (1927–33). In 1933 President ROOSEVELT appointed him director of the budget, but during the following year Douglas, who professed the economic conventional wisdom of the time and thus viewed even tiny deficits with strong disapproval, split with the president over fiscal policy; "conceivably the immediate fate of Western civilization," Douglas apocalyptically wrote Roosevelt, hung on balancing the federal budget. Douglas then went into the business world (American Cyanamid Company, Mutual Life of New York) until the coming of World War II. During the war Douglas held posts concerned with

war shipping, and in 1945 he served as special financial adviser to General Lucius CLAY in Germany.

Eager to return to Mutual Life when the war was over, Douglas had nevertheless agreed to join Clay in dealing with the German economy, on a temporary basis, because he thought it important to avoid the kinds of major mistakes that had been made in the rehabilitation of Germany after World War I. With an eye to the future economic needs of Europe, Douglas realized, earlier than most observers, that, in spite of Germany's sins, it made "no sense to forbid the most skilled workers in Europe from working as much as they can for a continent which is desperately short of everything." After he met with Treasury Secretary Henry Morgenthau, who disagreed with him and favored turning Germany into a country of farmers and shepherds, Douglas was attacked by gossip columnists to whom the secretary's secret recording of the meeting had been leaked. Philosophically, Douglas wrote his father that "this is the kind of thing I suppose one must expect." In 1947 President TRUMAN appointed Douglas to the London embassy. In this position he played a significant role in the launching of the MARSHALL PLAN and the creation of the NORTH ATLANTIC TREATY ORGANIZATION. During this time, the ambassador's daughter Sharman played a prominent part in London social life as an intimate friend of Princess Margaret, the younger daughter of King George VI.

Although a Democrat and the appointee of a Democratic president, Douglas voted (by absentee ballot from London) for Republican Thomas E. Dewey in the 1948 election, and he later served as an informal adviser to President EISENHOWER. But many years afterward he had apparently done some radical rethinking, telling Truman in a 1969 letter that "you will be rated by objective historians as the finest President we have ever had."

Douglas-Home, Sir Alec (1903–) Previously the 14th earl of Home (pronounced "Hume"), Sir Alec gave up his title for a seat in the House of Commons in order to succeed his fellow Conservative, Harold MACMILLAN, as British prime minister in 1963. Educated at Eton and Christ Church, Oxford, Douglas-Home entered Parliament in 1931 and from 1937 to 1939 (the critical era of failed negotiations with Adolf Hitler's Germany) served as parliamentary private secretary to Prime Minister Neville Chamberlain. Losing his seat in the Labour sweep of 1945, Douglas-Home won election again in 1950 but, succeeding his father as earl of Home, moved to the House of Lords in 1951. In July 1960 Macmillan chose him to replace Selwyn LLOYD as foreign secretary. In 1963, when the PROFUMO AFFAIR forced the ailing Macmillan to resign, the unassuming but politically skillful Douglas-Home replaced him. Sir Alec held the office of prime minister, however, only until October 1964, when the Conservatives lost a close election to Labour, led by Harold WILSON. In 1970 a Conservative victory under Edward HEATH brought Douglas-Home back to the foreign office, where he served until 1974.

Dubček, Alexander (1921–1992) Identified since 1968 with the PRAGUE SPRING movement for Czech liberalization and autonomy, Dubček was born in Slovakia and spent his childhood years in the Soviet Union, returning to Czechoslovakia just before the dismemberment of the country by the Third Reich (1938–39). During World War II, with Slovakia a German puppet state, Dubček fought in the underground. After the war he began his career as a Czechoslovak Communist Party official, rising in 1968 to the position of first secretary. His career took a distinct turn when, instead of following the repressive political patterns that had held the country in check for 20 years, he began to advocate and work for freedom from Soviet control; somewhat as Mikhail GORBACHEV was to attempt to do in the USSR in the 1980s, Dubček sought to make Marxism-Leninism more effective by applying democratization to it. Czech intellectuals seized on Dubček's ideas and pushed him farther along the new path.

This reaching for "socialism with a human face" led to a complex and protracted dispute with Soviet general secretary Leonid BREZHNEV, who finally summoned Dubček and his closest colleagues to the Kremlin and in browbeating confrontations ordered them to recant their words and rescind their actions. Czechoslovakia, Brezhnev declared,

was bound to the USSR "forever." Brezhnev accompanied these words with an invasion by WARSAW PACT forces, which crushed the Prague Spring. Though Dubček remained in office for a time, new disturbances (staged by the KGB) in 1969 brought about his dismissal in April in favor of the careerist politician Gustav HUSÁK. In the following year Dubček was expelled from the Communist Party.

After spending two decades in political obscurity, Dubček emerged again in what could be called the Prague Autumn—the VELVET REVOLUTION—of 1989, in which Husák was forced to yield power to a non-Communist government. Earlier in the year Dubček—a modest man of goodwill but, for all his experience, remarkably guileless—had declared on Hungarian television that he had not known in 1968 that Brezhnev intended to intervene in Czechoslovakia; the Soviet general secretary, he said, had deceived him. Viewing such statements as an attempt by Dubček to stage a political comeback, Czech Communist media made light of him as a has-been who had once led the country "to the brink of catastrophe." But in November, Dubček appeared in an interview on Soviet television and was shown in a favorable light in a TV documentary film broadcast in Leningrad, thus receiving a sort of apology from the GORBACHEV regime for his earlier treatment by Brezhnev.

On December 28, 1989, with full regard for the importance of history and symbol, the Czechoslovak Federal Assembly elected Dubček its chairman. On September 1, 1992, Dubček received ultimately fatal injuries when his chauffeur-driven car skidded off a rain-slickened highway and plunged into a gorge. He once summed up his difficult and frustrating career: "It's been a hard life, but you cannot suppress an idea."

dubok Since intelligence operatives throughout history have put a great deal of effort into concealing the tools of their trade and the fruits of their labor, it is not surprising that hiding places have acquired special names. In Soviet intelligence parlance, *dubok* was the term for a hiding place for documents and other small objects; a dubok might be the hole under a tree root, the crack between stones in a wall, the underside of a park bench.

Equivalent Western terms are *drop* and *dead-letter box*.

Dulles, Allen Welsh (1893–1969) One of the most important of all U.S. intelligence specialists, Allen Dulles held the directorship of the CENTRAL INTELLIGENCE AGENCY during the EISENHOWER administration (1953–61). The younger brother of John Foster DULLES, Eisenhower's secretary of state, Dulles was born in Watertown, N.Y., into a family that included a secretary of state (under Benjamin Harrison). Dulles later commented that he "grew up in the atmosphere of family debates on what was going on in the world."

Dulles received bachelor's and master's degrees from Princeton and a law degree from George Washington University; before attending law school, he held diplomatic posts, including, in 1918, his first intelligence assignment, which called on him to acquire information about the situation behind the lines in Germany, Austria-Hungary, and the Balkans. At the Paris peace conference in 1919, he later recalled, "I helped draw the frontiers of the new Czechoslovakia, worked on the problems created for the West by the Bolshevik Revolution of 1917 and helped on the peace settlement in Central Europe." By this time the family had added another secretary of state (under Woodrow Wilson), Robert Lansing, who had married Dulles's aunt.

After practicing law with Sullivan & Cromwell, the eminent Wall Street firm of which his brother was senior partner, Allen Dulles joined the Office of Strategic Services in 1942, early in World War II. In October 1942 he returned to Bern, Switzerland, where he had been based during his World War I mission, and remained there until the end of the war in Europe as the chief U.S. intelligence officer on the Continent.

After helping draw up the law that created the CIA—the first U.S. peacetime endeavor of its kind—and then serving on a committee to study the agency's effectiveness, Dulles was appointed deputy director in 1951 and in 1953 succeeded General Walter Bedell SMITH as director. During the ensuing years the CIA became unusually famous for an enterprise that put much of its effort into secret operations; however, Dulles observed that he did not try "to make a mystery of what is a

matter of common knowledge or obvious to friend and foe alike." When he became director, one of his first acts was to replace the deliberately disinformational sign at the CIA gate—"Government Printing Office"—with one bearing the agency's real name. Since every Washington bus driver and cabbie knew the truth, Dulles said, putting up a proper sign took away the glamour and mystery and allowed the CIA to appear as just another government office.

In 1961 the incoming President KENNEDY kept Dulles in office, but the failure of the BAY OF PIGS OPERATION in April 1961 led, within a few months, to what was in effect Dulles's dismissal. During the 1950s, however, as the officials in charge of U.S. foreign relations and intelligence operations, the Dulles brothers had exerted strong influence on U.S. policy.

Dulles, John Foster (1888–1959) Grandson of a 19th-century U.S. secretary of state, John Foster Dulles held that office for six years during the 1950s and, with his outspoken and vigorous anti-Communism, became a prominent American symbol around the world.

Born in Washington, D.C., the son of the Reverend Allen Dulles and Edith Foster Dulles, whose father was shortly to become President Benjamin Harrison's secretary of state, John Dulles graduated from Princeton in 1908 and received a law degree from George Washington University in 1911. That same year he began practice with the firm of Sullivan & Cromwell in New York, with which he remained throughout his legal career, retiring in 1949; specializing in international law, he became senior partner in 1927.

Having decided early in life that he wanted to follow in his grandfather's footsteps as secretary of state, Dulles began acquiring appropriate experience both within and outside his law practice. Under the tutelage of his grandfather, he had served as a secretary at the 1907 Hague peace conference. He represented the State Department in Central American negotiations in 1917 and, after serving in the army, became the counsel to the U.S. delegation to the Versailles conference and a member of the Reparations Commission; by this time his uncle, Robert Lansing, had become the second member of Dulles's extended family to hold the office of secretary of state (under Woodrow Wilson).

Between the world wars Dulles represented various foreign governments in litigation, as well as U.S. firms overseas, and also served as an international financial adviser. Some of these associations would later be recalled by critics of his diplomatic activities, who would accuse him (as, for example, in Guatemala) of having an improper interest in particular situations. During the 1944 political campaign Dulles appeared in elective politics as the foreign-policy adviser to the Republican candidate, Thomas E. Dewey.

After World War II, Dulles, though an active Republican, worked with the TRUMAN administration as a U.S. representative in various conferences and assemblies. He served as a member of the U.S. delegation to the founding UNITED NATIONS conference in San Francisco in 1945 and of subsequent UN delegations, was an adviser to the secretary of state at various meetings of foreign ministers, directed the arduous negotiations that produced the Japanese peace treaty (1951), and arranged security treaties with Australia, New Zealand, the Philippines, and Japan (1950–51).

As President EISENHOWER's secretary of state from the beginning of the administration until April 1959, when the cancer that would soon be fatal forced him to resign, Dulles not only enunciated U.S. foreign policy but seemed to create it, to a far greater extent than had any previous secretary. Though later evidence has suggested that Eisenhower supervised Dulles's activities more closely than was believed at the time, the secretary nevertheless operated in considerable freedom (and he was sometimes unwise enough to say in private that he and not the president made foreign policy).

As an active layman in the Presbyterian church, Dulles exemplified to a marked degree what a French historian regarded as the characteristic U.S. tendency to political Manichaeanism—the belief that the world is divided between good and evil. Such beliefs can appear exotic in the give-and-take world of diplomacy, as when Dulles declared that since Communism is wicked, "neutralism is immoral," a view not shared by THIRD WORLD countries wishing to find their own way, or even by U.S. allies. Yet allies and others often found Dulles

John Foster Dulles, U.S. secretary of state

not straightforward but, they complained, unnecessarily devious. A veteran British correspondent in Washington, Henry Brandon, observed that Europeans found Dulles difficult because "it was hard to predict whether at any given moment the blunt politician, the Christian moralist, the bluffing psychological warrior, the clever lawyer, the nationalistic patriot, the scheming Machiavelli, or the mature statesman would dominate his words

and actions." *See also* BRINKMANSHIP; MASSIVE RE-
TALIATION.

dumbbell concept In Western discussions of defense problems in 1947 and 1948, two general
ideas stood out: the "Atlantic" and the "European." Under the latter, North American forces
would be integrated into European arrangements.
The former, though also calling for cooperation
between North America and Europe, would emphasize joint efforts of the United States and Canada on their side of the ocean, while the Europeans
worked together across the water. The parallel
that suggested itself was that of a set of dumbbells.
Though the dumbbell approach was favored at the
time by such U.S. figures as George KENNAN and
Charles BOHLEN, it did not go on to prevail. *See
also* NORTH ATLANTIC TREATY ORGANIZATION.

E

East Berlin uprising   In June 1953, a little more than three months after the death of Soviet dictator Joseph STALIN, workers in East Berlin rose in spontaneous riots against the East German government and the Soviet occupying forces. These outbreaks began on June 16 as protests against moves by the government to step up the output required of industrial workers; the next day they exploded into mass demonstrations against the regime. Taken by surprise by this powerful challenge to Communist control—unprecedented anywhere in Eastern and Central Europe—the Soviets rushed infantry regiments and two armored divisions into the city, and in the resulting fight (as reported by the local authorities) 25 demonstrators were killed and 378 injured. The authorities declared martial law and imposed a curfew on the population. The protests were not confined to Berlin but spread across East Germany. Crowds stormed police stations and tore down red flags, even from the Brandenburg Gate. Overall, perhaps as many as 25,000 people were arrested in the aftermath of the riots. In 1992 newly opened East German files revealed that of the 109 people killed across East Germany, 41 were Soviet soldiers executed evidently for refusing to fire on the protesting Germans. East German paramilitary police, said participants, actually did most of the shooting.

Although declaring that "fascist bandits and Western provocative elements" had touched off the explosion, the East German premier, Otto GROTEWOHL, conceded during the following week that serious food shortages and other economic problems had supplied the fuse. He promised to move rapidly to improve conditions. On July 10

the United States entered the picture when President EISENHOWER offered to help out with U.S. grain, sugar, and other commodities. This offer received immediate rejection from both Russians and East Germans: Soviet foreign minister V. M. MOLOTOV called it "behavior that would offend even the population of a colony." Nevertheless, the United States sent large stocks of food to West Berlin, where depots were set up to make it available to East Berliners. During the ensuing weeks more than three million East Germans took advantage of the opportunity to obtain food parcels.

Some members of the Soviet leadership blamed Lavrenty BERIA, head of the secret police (later the KGB; then called the MVD), for not anticipating the eruption and taking steps to stifle it. His reorganization of the security forces following Stalin's death, particularly those in East Germany, was said to have created a chaotic situation for the intelligence services. After returning from an on-site investigation of the situation, Beria (according to the later account of Andrei GROMYKO) gave Kremlin colleagues a definition of East Germany that would normally be found in the Western press, and, at that, only in its more conservative sectors. "What is the German Democratic Republic?" Beria asked rhetorically. "It's not even a real state. It's only kept in being by Soviet troops."

Eastern Bloc   The Communist, Soviet-dominated countries of Eastern Europe were often spoken of as the Eastern Bloc, on the idea that the Cold War had created an East-West split on the Continent. The countries constituting the Eastern Bloc were the Soviet Union, Poland, East Germany, Czecho-

British foreign secretary Anthony Eden *(r.)* and Soviet foreign minister Vyacheslav Molotov pose for an official photograph at the February 1945 Yalta Conference.

slovakia, Hungary, Romania, and Bulgaria. Yugoslavia, though Communist, followed its own course after breaking with the USSR in 1948; Albania had a Maoist orientation.

East European Mutual Assistance Treaty *See* WARSAW PACT.

East Germany *See* GERMAN DEMOCRATIC REPUBLIC.

Economic Cooperation Administration The organization established to administer U.S. aid to Europe under the MARSHALL PLAN.

EDC *See* EUROPEAN DEFENSE COMMUNITY.

Eden, Anthony (Earl of Avon) (1897–1977) A British veteran of World War I, in which he had an outstanding combat record, Eden spent almost

four decades in the House of Commons, entering in 1923 and leaving in 1961, when he moved to the House of Lords as Lord Avon. During this span he served three different times as foreign secretary: from 1935 to 1938, when he became known as a leading antifascist in facing the challenges posed by Italy's dictator, Benito Mussolini, and by the rising power of Germany's Adolf Hitler; during almost all of World War II (1940–45), under Winston CHURCHILL; and again when Churchill and the Conservatives returned to power from 1951 to 1955. After succeeding Churchill as prime minister on April 6, 1955, Eden, who had spent years waiting in the wings to hold power, had only a brief time on stage; in January 1957, in the aftermath of the SUEZ CRISIS, he was forced to resign.

During the 1950s Eden suffered chronic illness as the result of a bungled gallbladder operation.

Friends felt that his physical condition played a part in what can only be considered his severe lapse of judgment in believing that he, with allies, could plan and carry out an invasion of Egypt behind the back of the United States. Despite the problems caused with the EISENHOWER administration by the Suez fiasco, Eden all through his career had advocated and followed a policy of strong cooperation between Britain and the United States.

Ehrenburg, Ilya (1891–1967)   Soviet journalist and novelist who spent many years in the West and became widely known as a spokesman for the Soviet Union. Born into a middle-class Jewish family in Kiev, Ehrenburg became involved in revolutionary activities while still a teenager. After being arrested, he escaped and joined the stream of political emigrés that found a home in Paris. Though he began writing poetry at a young age, he turned to journalism as his primary pursuit. During World War I he covered the fighting in the West before returning to Russia in 1917—where he joined not the Bolsheviks but the Whites. After converting to Communism in the early 1920s, he moved back and forth between Russia and the West. In 1921 the French government expelled him as a suspected Communist agent; he came back to France in 1924, and in 1932 became Paris correspondent of *IZVESTIA*.

Though Ehrenburg supported the Soviet Communist regime, he chose as a novelist to wear the garment of socialist realism loosely, giving frequent expression to his bent for satire. He received the greatest attention for his stirring World War II attacks on the Germans in newspaper articles. His 1954 novel, *The Thaw,* which reflected some of the changes in the USSR following the death of Joseph STALIN, lent its name to the ensuing period, particularly the next few years after Nikita KHRUSHCHEV's famous 1956 speech in which he revealed Stalin's crimes. Essentially, Ehrenburg pulled off an adroit balancing act, writing with some degree of freedom but managing to avoid head-on collisions with the authorities. Thus he escaped unscathed from the purges of Stalin's later and most paranoiac years; his work as a propagandist kept him in Stalin's favor, even though as a writer and a Jew he could well have encountered trouble. A Stalin biographer, Robert Payne, spoke of Ehrenburg

as "almost the sole survivor of a generation of writers murdered by Stalin." On the day after Stalin died, however, Ehrenburg, as an establishment writer, produced an elegy for *Pravda* suffused with expressions of loss and grief—giving readers a bizarre description of the way citizens of New York were supposed to have received the news of Stalin's passing. According to Ehrenburg's account, "upright people, surrounded by police, informers and ruffians, spoke with sadness: 'The friend of peace has died.' " *See also* THAW, THE.

Eisenhower, Dwight David (1890–1969)   U.S. general who as supreme Allied commander in Europe in World War II won acclaim as perhaps history's most successful leader of an allied coalition and who from 1953 to 1961 served as 34th president of the United States.

A Kansan in origin—though born in Denison, Tex., because his father briefly worked there—Eisenhower belonged to a Mennonite Brethren family. In later years people marveled at such an eminent soldier's having come from a pacifist background, though Ike—as he was universally known—would maintain that, of his parents, it was only his mother who was truly a pacifist. The family was also poor, but, Eisenhower said many years later, "the glory of America is that we didn't know it then."

After winning admission to West Point (he was willing to go to either of the service academies), Ike graduated in 1915 in "the class the stars fell on," as it was later known, because the timing was right for a high proportion of its members to become generals in World War II. Eisenhower did not go overseas in World War I, and he filled a variety of posts during the following years until November 1929, when he was assigned to the office of the assistant secretary of war. The next year he began one of the most important associations of his career when General Douglas MACARTHUR became chief of staff; in February 1933 the general showed his appreciation of Ike's work ("this officer has no superior of his time in the army," the general wrote in an efficiency report) by choosing him as personal assistant. Two years later, when MacArthur went to the Philippines to attempt to create an army for the new commonwealth, he took Eisenhower along.

U.S. president Dwight D. Eisenhower

In the fall of 1939 Ike finally received the opportunity to lead troops when he was assigned to the 15th Division as a battalion commander. But the next year he became the chief of staff of a corps and, in 1941, of the Third Army. His effective performance of this job during important maneuvers shortly before U.S. entry into the war proved to be the pivotal point of his career, because it brought him to the attention of the chief of staff, General George MARSHALL, who summoned him to Washington after Pearl Harbor to head the War Plans Division (soon renamed the Operations Division). From this assignment Marshall moved Ike to England, first to discuss planned operations with the British and then to take command of U.S. forces in Europe. A lieutenant colonel a year earlier, Eisenhower was now a major general, and his remarkable rise continued; he commanded the Allied landings in Northwest Africa in November 1942 and, after the launching of the Italian campaign, was appointed supreme commander of the Allied invasion of Northwest Europe. His fair-mindedness and ability to downplay national sentiments stamped him as a remarkable military diplomat and contributed to the working of an alliance that, with all its strains, functioned with an integration never seen before. He was thus instrumental in the victory over Germany in May 1945.

After the war Eisenhower commanded U.S. occupation forces in Germany until coming back to Washington in November 1945 to succeed Marshall as chief of staff. He held the position during the incubating years of the Cold War, when he gave solid support to such administration programs as the MARSHALL PLAN and anticipated NATO before it was created. During this time a host of admirers pressed Ike to run for president— a group including even, apparently, President TRUMAN. Ike's achievements and his striking personality—far stronger in person than when filtered through the media—seemed to have made him a universal favorite. Democrat or Republican? Many people did not seem to care. But, steadfastly denying any political ambitions (and, indeed, he had a strong distaste for politics), Ike accepted the presidency of Columbia University in 1948. At the end of 1950, however, when the Atlantic allies had decided to put some military meat on NATO's bones, Truman chose Eisenhower to be the supreme commander of alliance forces.

Truman's surprise election victory in 1948 put Republicans in need of a new nominee for 1952 to replace the twice-defeated Thomas E. Dewey. Since many of the eastern and internationalist Republicans did not want to see their party choose Senator Robert A. Taft of Ohio, the courtship of Eisenhower took on a new life; this time Ike agreed. A new organization, Citizens for Eisenhower, popularized the irresistible slogan "I Like Ike" and played its part in pushing the general into elective politics. He resigned his command at the beginning of June 1952 and came home to campaign against Taft for the nomination and then against Adlai STEVENSON for the presidency itself, which he won decisively, carrying 39 states. In this era of often-hysterical anti-Communism, the campaign had its ugly side, with repeated Republican charges of Democratic disloyalty. One incident disillusioned some of Ike's supporters and disturbed the general himself in future years. To keep the favor of Senator Joseph R. MCCARTHY, the most vocal of the soi-disant Communist hunters, Eisenhower deleted from a speech a passage defending his great benefactor, General Marshall, against wild accusations of conspiracy and treason. Marshall never commented publicly on this tactical defection, and during his presidential years the remorseful Eisenhower took great care to issue White House invitations to Marshall and show him every favor.

In foreign and defense affairs, Ike as president put pressure on negotiators to conclude an armistice in Korea (aided by the death of Soviet dictator Joseph STALIN in March 1953), favored the concept of MASSIVE RETALIATION (with its corollary of reduced expenditures on conventional armaments), and, while preaching "rollback" and "liberation" in Eastern Europe, proved to be an extremely cautious wielder of power (having no thought at all, for example, of intervening in the 1956 HUNGARIAN REVOLUTION). In the SUEZ CRISIS, which occurred at the same time, he refused to support the British-French-Israeli attack on Egypt; his straightforward stand won commendation from a British Foreign Office official, Sir Anthony Nutting, who acknowledged Ike's "clear and simple" standards of international behavior and his belief in the UNITED NATIONS.

Although suffering a heart attack in September 1955 and undergoing an abdominal operation in June 1956, Ike swept to a larger victory in his second presidential campaign than he had won in 1952. His second term was marked, in October 1957, by the shock of *SPUTNIK I,* the Soviet earth-orbiting satellite. In response, the government quickly got the United States into the satellite game, established the National Aeronautics and Space Administration (NASA), and stepped up funding for science education.

In May 1960, just as the president seemed to be developing a working relationship with Soviet premier Nikita KHRUSHCHEV, an American U-2 reconnaissance aircraft was shot down over the USSR. Refusing to engage in the practice of plausible denial (that is, the claim that one is not involved in specific decisions and therefore cannot be held responsible for them), Ike admitted his knowledge of the U-2 flights and refused to offer an apology. Khrushchev responded by withdrawing from a summit conference in Paris. This incident was to have later repercussions on Khrushchev's own career.

Eisenhower left the KENNEDY administration what proved a sinister legacy when he broke diplomatic relations with Cuba and gave the green light to the CENTRAL INTELLIGENCE AGENCY to develop a plan to invade the island with the aim of stirring up a rebellion. Whether or not Ike, as president, would have put any version of the plan into effect could never be known, but after leaving office he urged strong action against Fidel CASTRO. The result was the great fiasco called the BAY OF PIGS OPERATION.

Eisenhower spent much of his time in his later years producing his memoirs and other writings. In January 1965 he carried out a special personal mission when, as an invited private citizen, he delivered farewell remarks at the funeral of his old associate and friend, Sir Winston CHURCHILL. *See also* BRAUN, Wernher von; EISENHOWER DOCTRINE; NORTH ATLANTIC TREATY ORGANIZATION.

Eisenhower Doctrine Principle proclaimed in 1957, following the SUEZ CRISIS of 1956, whereby the United States would defend the Middle East against "overt armed aggression from any nation controlled by International Communism." In presenting the doctrine to Congress on January 5, 1957, President EISENHOWER asked for funds for economic aid to countries in the region and for the authority to employ armed force, if necessary. The doctrine amounted not to an alliance of any kind but simply to a one-sided (and, indeed, unrequested) guarantee, which in many quarters appeared to be primarily a way of providing a framework for possible U.S. intervention. It also seemed to rest on the dubious idea that Arab nationalism had been created by the Soviet Union. In any case, direct armed attack by the Soviet Union did not number among the leading concerns of Middle Eastern leaders. One specific act taken under the doctrine was the dispatch to Lebanon, in 1958, of 10,000 marines, on the plea of President Camille Chamoun, who feared internal disruption of the state; the intervention succeeded in keeping Chamoun in office.

As one would expect, the Soviets quickly condemned the Eisenhower Doctrine; the involvement of Communist China in the protest suggested that the two countries were still firm allies.

Elizabeth II (1926–   )   Elder daughter of the Duke of York, who became King George VI in 1936 on the abdication of his brother, Edward VIII, Queen Elizabeth came to the throne of the United Kingdom on February 6, 1952; her coronation followed on June 2, 1953. As Princess Elizabeth, she had been just old enough in the last phases of World War II to serve as a truck driver and mechanic in the Auxiliary Territorial Service; earlier in the war she had made a memorable radio address to the children of the Commonwealth and Empire. In November 1947 she married her distant cousin Prince Philip of Greece, nephew of Lord Mountbatten, who had promoted the marriage.

Though the monarch is essentially consigned to ceremonial and public-relations functions, Queen Elizabeth, whose knowledge of state business won general respect, played an important part in political decision making in January 1957, when, acting on the advice of Winston CHURCHILL and other senior counselors, she chose Harold MACMILLAN over R. A. Butler to succeed Anthony EDEN as prime minister.

Enterprise   Named for a famous World War II aircraft carrier and commissioned in 1961, the U.S.S. *Enterprise,* displacing some 75,000 tons, was the first nuclear carrier and, at the time, the largest warship ever built. Its success in operation opened the way for the U.S. Navy's NIMITZ class of nuclear-powered carriers, though expense remained such a consideration that, by congressional decision, a sister ship, the *John F. Kennedy,* had to be driven by oil instead of nuclear power. *Enterprise* carried up to 100 aircraft.

Equal Aggregates   *See* FORD, Gerald Rudolph, Jr.

Erhard, Ludwig (1897–1977)   An economist whom the U.S. occupation authorities hired from the University of Munich to draw up a plan for currency reform, Erhard became minister of economics of West Germany in 1949, and during the ensuing years won great acclaim for presiding over the *Wirtschaftswunder*—the "economic miracle"

of his country's rapid rise to prosperity from its bleak condition after World War II. Though he objected to the terms on which Chancellor Konrad ADENAUER had taken West Germany into the EUROPEAN ECONOMIC COMMUNITY (the Common Market), the round-faced, cigar-smoking Erhard became vice chancellor in 1957. Relations between the two deteriorated, with Adenauer objecting to Erhard's succeeding him as chancellor. Erhard, Adenauer declared, lacked the political qualifications to lead the government. Nevertheless, when Adenauer resigned in 1963, Erhard succeeded him. But the "Old Man" remained chairman of the Christian Democratic Union and, though nearly 90, made several unsuccessful attempts to organize a party revolt against Erhard, whose coalition government collapsed in November 1966 after passing a law raising taxes.

Euratom   *See* EUROPEAN ATOMIC ENERGY COMMUNITY.

Eurocommunism   Largely as a reaction to the Soviet invasion of Czechoslovakia in 1968, Communist parties in Western Europe began during the 1970s to declare a measure of independence from Moscow and to attempt to play a more normal part than had previously been the case in the electoral politics of their respective countries. Increasingly, these "Eurocommunists," particularly in Italy and France, questioned the value of Soviet Communism for countries outside the USSR. The Soviet invasion of AFGHANISTAN in 1979 further weakened Moscow's international appeal, especially for Italian Communists. Thus the Western Communist parties had ceased to be reliable instruments of Soviet policy. *See also* BREZHNEV DOCTRINE.

European Atomic Energy Community (Euratom)   Established in 1957 and operative in 1958, this association was intended to create an analogue to a free-trade area in nuclear matters and to coordinate nuclear research and development. Along with the EUROPEAN ECONOMIC COMMUNITY and the EUROPEAN COAL AND STEEL COMMUNITY, Euratom became a component of the EUROPEAN COMMUNITY.

European Coal and Steel Community   Organization established in 1951 in consequence of the

West German chancellor Ludwig Erhard

SCHUMAN PLAN. It created a unified free market for the coal and steel industries of Belgium, France, Italy, Luxembourg, the Netherlands, and West Germany. The architect of the plan was Jean MONNET.

European Community Overall supranational organization created in 1967 through the merger of the EUROPEAN COAL AND STEEL COMMUNITY, the EUROPEAN ATOMIC ENERGY COMMUNITY, and the EUROPEAN ECONOMIC COMMUNITY (the Common Market). The combining of the three communities had as its purpose the political and economic integration of Western Europe. The original members of the community were Belgium, France, Italy, Luxembourg, the Netherlands, and West Germany; in 1973 Britain, Denmark, and Ireland joined. The executive functioning of the community is vested in a commission, which administers the various treaties under which the structure was built; the chief executives are the members of the Council of Ministers, representing the member countries. In 1979 the European Parliament, previously composed of members acting as delegates from the legislatures of their respective countries, for the first time received its members by direct election.

European Defense Community (EDC) On October 24, 1950, Premier René Pleven of France proposed the creation of an all-European army that would

97

involve participation by West Germany. From the American point of view, a significant German contribution to Western defense would lighten the burden on the United States; the establishment of an integrated army, strongly advocated by Jean MONNET, represented a French response to U.S. pressure. It would offer a way of drawing on German strength without producing the nightmare of a new Wehrmacht marching across the Continent, a prospect regarded with dread by many Western Europeans only five years after the end of World War II. Such a military integration, its sponsors believed, could be modeled on the new supranational economic developments, notably the EUROPEAN COAL AND STEEL COMMUNITY. Winston CHURCHILL, then out of office, praised the idea, but after returning to power in 1951 seemed to look with less favor on the restrictions it might impose on independent British action. Although the concerned powers signed a treaty to implement the PLEVEN PLAN, as the EDC concept was sometimes called, the French National Assembly rejected it in 1954. By this time, in any case, the focus of European defense efforts had switched to the NORTH ATLANTIC TREATY ORGANIZATION; in October 1954, France agreed to the admission of West Germany into NATO.

European Economic Community (EEC)   Usually called the Common Market, the EEC was established in 1957 by Belgium, France, Italy, Luxembourg, the Netherlands, and West Germany. After much internal debate, Britain sought membership in 1961, as did Denmark, Ireland, and Norway; all saw these applications rejected by the veto of the French president, General DE GAULLE. A decade later, however, with de Gaulle out of the picture, Britain, Denmark, and Ireland finally gained admission to the Common Market; Norwegian voters turned down the proposition. The Common Market and two important institutions that preceded it, the EUROPEAN COAL AND STEEL COMMUNITY and the EUROPEAN ATOMIC ENERGY COMMUNITY, grew out of the post–World War II perception by West European leaders—Jean MONNET, Robert SCHUMAN, and others—that the economic plight of Europe could only be overcome by a supranational organization, which would also provide a way to integrate the potentially troublesome German

economy (really, to tame a Germany that had shown its might in two world wars) into a larger context. The Common Market also represented a major move toward the EUROPEAN COMMUNITY, which was scheduled to become operative in 1992 but has continued to encounter political and economic problems.

European Recovery Program   *See* MARSHALL PLAN.

"evil empire"   The Soviet invasion of AFGHANISTAN in 1979, followed by the election in 1980 of the conservative Ronald REAGAN as president of the United States, marked the end of whatever degree of DÉTENTE had existed between the superpowers. If the Cold War had been a religious conflict (as, indeed, some partisans on both sides seemed to consider it), then Reagan would have been classed as a thorough fundamentalist—doctrinally speaking—as when he described the USSR as "the focus of evil in the modern world." Appropriately enough, Reagan chose a religious forum—a convention of evangelical Christians—to place his own distinctive brand on the USSR: the "evil empire" (March 8, 1983). The phrase is said to have been supplied by a speechwriter named Tom Dolan, but it clearly expressed the president's own strong feeling.

existentialism   Literary and philosophical movement, led by Jean-Paul SARTRE, that flourished in Paris in the early Cold War years and seemed to capture much of the post–World War II intellectual mood. Influenced by earlier philosophers—Søren Kierkegaard, Martin Heidegger, and Edmund Husserl—Sartre, in *Being and Nothingness* (1943), opened the way for a whole generation's preoccupation with human consciousness and the place of the individual person in the world. Human beings, for Sartre, exist not as exemplars of metaphysical systems but as individuals condemned to think and to make choices. Ultimately, human dignity comes from choice and the resultant action; a life spent in contemplation, apart from the world, represents a refusal to "choose" and thus constitutes an act of cowardice.

After 1946, when Sartre formally declared himself an "existentialist," his philosophy permeated the café culture of intellectuals, artists, and students and moved into popular consciousness through novels and the press. Although existentialism drew criticism both from Pope Pius XII and from hard-line Communists, its adherents often combined belief in Sartre's ideas with the practice of Christian or Marxist doctrines. Never itself clearly articulated as a political ideology, existentialism nonetheless fostered a left-wing intellectual climate that included anti-Americanism as a prominent feature.

Experience and the Future (Doswiadezenie i Przyszlosc) One of the many nongovernmental groups formed in Poland during the 1970s and 1980s, Experience and the Future was made up of intellectuals, both Communist and non-Communist, who accepted the leading role of the Communist (United Workers') Party and sought structural reform within the existing system.

Explorer I *See* SPUTNIK I.

F

F-4   Originally developed by McDonnell for the U.S. Navy for fleet defense as an interceptor, the F-4 Phantom II (the original Phantom was the first jet created for aircraft-carrier operations) also was used by the Marine Corps and the air force, the latter designating it the F-4C and employing it for close support and related purposes. The first Phantom II (then designated XF4H-1) flew in May 1958. In its air force incarnation as a bomber engaged in interdiction, the F-4 could carry twice the bombload of a World War II Flying Fortress. In 1965, when the United States became thoroughly engaged in the VIETNAM WAR, the first F-4Cs were sent to the theater. Armed with a variety of rockets and missiles, the twin-engine, two-seat Phantom II could also carry up to 16,000 pounds of nuclear or conventional bombs. More than 5,000 Phantom IIs were built, this total making the aircraft one of the leading fighters of the Cold War era.

F-8   U.S. Navy single-seat jet fighter, called the Crusader, first flown in 1955. Built by Ling-Temco-Vought, the F-8 reached speeds of Mach 2; its armament included four cannons and four Sidewinder missiles.

F-14   U.S. Navy two-place jet fighter, called the Tomcat, built by Grumman. Its speed exceeded Mach 2, and it carried a variety of missiles. Its armament also included 20-mm cannons.

F-16   Beginning life as a prototype lightweight fighter, the General Dynamics single-seat F-16 evolved into a fighter-bomber capable of undertaking various kinds of missions. Tested in the late 1970s, the F-16 entered service with the U.S. Air Force in October 1980 and went on to become widely popular with U.S. allies in NATO and the Middle East and with South Korea; some 2,500 have been produced. The F-16, nicknamed the Fighting Falcon, can attain a top speed of about 1,350 mph and, in addition to a 20-mm cannon, carries missiles and bombs in conformity with its specific mission.

In 1981, in the most famous mission in which they took part, M-16s of the Israeli Air Force attacked an Iraqi nuclear reactor. Notoriety of a different sort came to this aircraft through the large number of reported crashes in which it was involved.

F-80   Called the Shooting Star, this single-seat Lockheed fighter was the first U.S. Air Force aircraft to exceed 500 mph in level flight. In the KOREAN WAR it performed not only as an interceptor but as a fighter-bomber for attacks on ground targets. During this conflict, on November 8, 1950, an F-80C piloted by First Lieutenant Russell J. Brown shot down a Soviet-made MIG-15 in the first all-jet battle in history. The first U.S. production jet, the Shooting Star was designed and built in only four and a half months during World War II by Clarence "Kelly" Johnson's design team, which gained increasing fame during subsequent years. Originally the Shooting Star was to have been built around an American version of the de Havilland H-1 turbojet engine, but when work on this power plant fell far behind schedule, Lockheed substituted the General Electric J-33. Two P-80s, as they were then called, reached Italy in

U.S. Air Force F-80 Shooting Star, fighter workhorse in the Korean War

early 1945, but too late to see action in the war. On June 19, 1947, a P-80R (the designation of these aircraft was changed from *P* [for pursuit] to *F* [for fighter] in 1948) set a world speed record of 623.753 mph. The F-80C carried eight five-inch rockets or a 2,000-pound bombload. A two-place all-weather interceptor based on the F-80 design bore the designation F-94, or Starfire; it first flew in July 1949.

F-82 Called the Twin Mustang because that is exactly what it looked like—two Mustang (P-51) bodies, side by side, sharing a single wing—the F-82 became operational in 1946. Conceived during World War II, it was the last piston-engine fighter to go into service in the U.S. Air Force. It could attain a maximum speed of about 480 mph. It is of particular historical interest because, already on station in Japan in June 1950, F-82s scored the first three victories of the KOREAN WAR.

F-84 One of the workhorses of the KOREAN WAR, the F-84 Thunderjet, built by Republic Aviation, entered production in June 1947 as the U.S. Air Force's first post–World War II fighter. In Korea

F-84s concentrated on low-level missions, hitting targets like bridges and supply dumps as well as concentrations of enemy troops. Armed with six .50-caliber machine guns and eight five-inch rockets, the Thunderjet could carry 2,000 pounds of bombs or napalm tanks. It had a top speed of 620 mph. A swept-wing version, the F-84F, served with the Tactical Air Command as a fighter-bomber and also was supplied to the air forces of several NATO countries.

F-86 A single-seat fighter built by North American, the F-86 Sabre entered production in May 1948. Intended as a day fighter, it gave rise to the F-86D, an all-weather interceptor version, and the F-86H, a fighter-bomber. Fighter versions achieved fame in the KOREAN WAR as conquerors of the Soviet MIG-15, shooting down some 800 for a loss of about 60 (the figures show some variation). The Sabre was armed with six 50.-caliber machine guns and eight five-inch rockets and could carry 2,000 pounds of bombs. Maximum speed of the F-86A was 685 mph; an F-86D set a world speed record of 715.697 mph on July 16, 1953.

101

U.S. Air Force F-100 Supersabre, first American supersonic fighter

Together, the United States and Canada built more than 5,500 Sabres.

F-89 U.S. twin-engine jet interceptor, built by Northrop. Designed as an all-weather fighter-interceptor, this aircraft, named the Scorpion, could carry two air-to-air rockets with nuclear warheads and also four Falcon missiles. The F-89 carried a pilot in front and a radar operator in the rear. The aircraft entered service in July 1950. Top speed was about 630 mph.

F-94 *See* F-80.

F-100 Representing an advance over the F-86 Sabre, the North American F-100 Supersabre, first flown in 1953, was the first supersonic fighter to enter service with the U.S. Air Force. A later version, the F-100D, was supplied with a low-altitude bombing system so that it could perform as a fighter-bomber to attack barges, bridges, and similar targets, besides concentrations of troops. Widely used in the VIETNAM WAR, the Supersabre attained a top speed of Mach 1.3 and carried mis-

siles, rockets, and more than 7,000 pounds of bombs.

F-101 Two-seat, all-weather interceptor built by McDonnell and first flown in 1954. Called the Voodoo, the aircraft began its design life as an escort for long-range bombers but lost its purpose with the development of the self-sufficient B-52. The F-101 reached a top speed in excess of Mach 1.7; it carried rockets and guided missiles. One version of the Voodoo, the RF-101, the world's first supersonic photoreconnaissance aircraft, played an important part with its cameras during the CUBAN MISSILE CRISIS in 1962.

F-102 Built by Convair, the F-102 Delta Dagger, a single-seat all-weather interceptor, was the first delta-wing aircraft put into service by the U.S. Air Force. It was first flown in 1953 and went on operational duty in 1956. Advanced for its time, it featured an automatic fire-control system and carried six Falcon air-to-air missiles. It had a maximum speed of 810 mph. A later version, the F-106 Delta Dart, first flew in 1956 and entered service in 1959. Its top speed—more than 1,500 mph—

U.S. Air Force F-111 is a fighter-bomber designed for both the air force and the navy. But each service wants its own aircraft; the navy cancels its order.

represented a notable advance over that of the F-102.

F-104 Called the Starfighter, the Lockheed F-104 appeared in two principal versions: as a tactical fighter with a six-barrel 20-mm Vulcan cannon, and as a day-night interceptor, with two Sidewinder missiles added. First flown in 1954, the Starfighter set world speed and altitude records in the late 1950s; it had a maximum speed of 1,321 mph. A popular airplane, the Starfighter (in one- and two-place versions) served in the air forces of most NATO countries and in the Japanese Self-Defense Force, some 1,700 being built for this purpose in the United States and overseas.

F-105 Produced in single-seat and two-seat versions (the latter were designated F-105F), this single-engine Republic-built fighter-bomber, named the Thunderchief, could deliver 12,000 pounds of bombs, a heavier load than a World War II Flying Fortress could carry. The prototype F-105 first flew in 1955, and—replacing the F-84F—the F-105D version entered service in 1959 and became in the 1960s one of the busiest aircraft in the VIETNAM WAR, flying three-fourths of the strikes against North Vietnam for a four-year period. It served as the standard fighter-bomber for the Tac-

tical Air Command. It had a top speed of 1,390 mph and a cruising range of 778 miles. The Thunderchief was retired in 1980.

F-106 *See* F-102.

F-111 In the early 1960s General Dynamics won a competition to create a tactical fighter-bomber for use by both the U.S. Air Force and the U.S. Navy. The winning swing-wing design, called the TFX during its development days, became the F-111, nicknamed the Aardvark. The world's first production swing-wing aircraft, the F-111 went into service with the air force in 1967 as the F-111A; the navy canceled its order. A two-seat twin-jet airplane, the F-111 would sweep its wings rearward for speed while in flight and move them forward for slower flight or for takeoff and landing. The F-111 was powered by two Pratt & Whitney engines and could reach a speed of 1,450 mph, with a range of 3,600 miles. Like other tactical aircraft of its era, the F-111 saw service in the VIETNAM WAR. Though an old aircraft by 1991, the F-111 also performed a variety of roles in the Persian Gulf War.

F-117A Best known as the Stealth, and called a night reconnaissance attack aircraft, this famous

Helmut Kohl *(r.)*, chancellor of the Federal Republic of Germany, greets the head of state of the German Democratic Republic, Erich Honecker.

radar-deceiving airplane carries the *F* in its name to indicate that it is a fighter as well. Though it yields an almost indistinguishable radar picture during the day, it is truly invisible only at night; this achievement is due to the development in the 1970s of special materials and engineering techniques. Created at Lockheed's famous Skunk Works, the Stealth is powered by two General Electric nonafterburning turbofan jets that give it a high subsonic top speed (perhaps 700 mph). The aircraft is of delta-wing design, with no horizontal tail but instead a structure that resembles a TV rabbit-ears antenna. The first Stealth flew in June 1981, and the aircraft became operational in October 1983. It found public recognition not during the Cold War but afterward, in attacking targets in Baghdad during the Persian Gulf War in 1991.

Fechteler, William M. (1896–1967) U.S. admiral who served as chief of naval operations from 1951 to 1953 and then went to Europe as commander in chief of NORTH ATLANTIC TREATY ORGANIZATION forces in southern Europe, from 1953 to 1956.

Federal Bureau of Investigation (FBI) *See* HOOVER, J(ohn) Edgar.

Federal Republic of Germany The English translation of Bundesrepublik Deutschland, the proper name of West Germany. Often spoken of as "the Federal Republic," this state was established in 1949 and ceased to exist in 1990, when the two German states reunited. *See also* GERMAN DEMOCRATIC REPUBLIC.

ferret missions Throughout the 1950s and 1960s, the U.S. Air Force, Navy, and the CENTRAL INTELLIGENCE AGENCY conducted a secret campaign to ferret out the secrets of Soviet air defenses. Flying a variety of aircraft, mostly modified bombers, the missions attempted to detect and record Soviet and Chinese radar signals, with the aim of finding defensive weaknesses; airborne radar observers were dubbed Ravens. Cameras photographed harbors, military bases, and other strategic sites. During the 1960s, by some estimates, the worldwide total of such flights reached 3,000 a year. While the program was functioning, some 250 U.S. aircrew members were shot down. Details about the program began appearing in magazine articles only in the 1990s.

Fierlinger, Zdenek (1891–1976) Czechoslovak politician, diplomat, and party official who served as prime minister from April 1945 until July 1946. In what was probably a unique bit of background for a Communist politician in Central Europe, Fierlinger had once been a salesman for McCormick reapers, having represented the U.S. manufacturer in Russia just before the outbreak of World War I. After serving with Czech units in the czarist army, he traveled to the United States as a recruiter for the Czech Legion in France.

A left-wing Social Democrat, for the next 20 years Fierlinger represented his country as an ambassador. During 1941 and 1942 he served in London with the Czech government-in-exile, transferring in 1942 to Moscow as that government's ambassador. In this position he displayed such an uncritically pro-Soviet and anti-Western attitude that the Communists found him an ideal person to support for the premiership of postwar Czechoslovakia. Serving as prime minister (1945–46), he worked so closely with the Communists that Czech citizens nicknamed him Quislinger (an allusion to Vidkun Quisling, the Norwegian Nazi whose name provided a new synonym for *traitor*). After yielding the premiership to the Communist Klement GOTTWALD in 1946, Fierlinger held various other political and party offices, including the chairmanship of the National Assembly from 1953 to 1964.

Fifth Man Known variously as the CAMBRIDGE FIVE, the Ring of Five, and—inside the KGB—the Magnificent Five (following the release in 1960 of the movie *The Magnificent Seven*), the Soviet penetration agents, or moles, recruited at Cambridge in the 1930s progressively came to official and public notice, beginning with Guy BURGESS and Donald MACLEAN, who fled to Moscow in 1951. Kim

PHILBY became known as the Third Man following his flight from Beirut to hide behind the IRON CURTAIN in 1963, and Anthony BLUNT, the Fourth Man, was finally revealed to the public in 1979. Spy hunters of all types engaged in an energetic hunt for the Fifth Man, with much attention going (particularly on the part of a London reporter named Chapman Pincher) to Sir Roger Hollis, former director-general of MI5, the British counterespionage service; the 1987 book *Spycatcher*, by a former assistant director of MI5, Peter Wright, made the same charge. But authoritative research by a former KGB colonel, Oleg Gordievsky, later revealed that a known former Soviet agent, John CAIRNCROSS, was in actuality the sought-for Fifth Man.

First Chief Directorate The foreign-intelligence branch of the KGB. Although in numbers it constituted a relatively small part of the vast KGB apparatus (in 1985, some 12,000 out of 600,000 employees), its members had the most prestige; it was the glamorous arm of the intelligence service, and jobs in it were eagerly sought, particularly by the sons of the Soviet establishment. In 1972 the FCD, as it was often known, moved into splendid new quarters in Yasenovo, a southern suburb of Moscow just off the Moscow Ring Road; the move bore remarkable parallels with the Americans' quartering of the CENTRAL INTELLIGENCE AGENCY off the Capital Beltway in a Virginia suburb of Washington, D.C. In 1985, as Mikhail GORBACHEV was coming to power as GENERAL SECRETARY, the FCD, which for some time had been steadily expanding, saw its headquarters space greatly increased by the opening of two new buildings, one of them a bulky high-rise that resembled a building in an American office park. Not temperamentally inclined to favor Gorbachev's PERESTROIKA, the intelligence agencies put up strong resistance to it. *See also* KRYUCHKOV, Vladimir.

First World One of the three categories into which thought around the world divided the nations in the later Cold War years. *First World*, not itself a widely used term, drew its significance from the contrast it emphasized between the industrialized, more-or-less capitalist West and the less developed (sometimes undeveloped) countries of Asia, Africa (many of them former colonies of Western powers), and Latin America—the THIRD WORLD. SECOND WORLD refers to the Soviet Union, China, and other Communist countries.

Ford, Gerald Rudolph, Jr. (1913–) On August 9, 1974, Gerald Ford took the oath as 38th president of the United States, thereby becoming the only person to have attained the office without having been elected president or vice president. Appointed in 1973 by President NIXON to replace the disgraced Spiro Agnew as vice president, under the terms of the 25th amendment to the Constitution (adopted in 1967), Ford succeeded Nixon as president following the latter's resignation in the wake of the WATERGATE AFFAIR.

Born in Omaha, Nebr., Ford was originally named Leslie King, Jr. When he was two, his parents were divorced, and after his mother moved to Grand Rapids, Mich., and remarried, the boy took the name of his stepfather, who adopted him. Majoring in economics and political science, Ford was a star player on two Michigan national-champion football teams. In 1941 he graduated from law school at Yale, where he also was an assistant football coach. Ford's athletic prowess and his continuing devotion to sports belie his later reputation for clumsiness.

During World War II Ford spent four years in the navy, reaching the rank of lieutenant commander as an operations officer on aircraft carriers. Originally elected to the House of Representatives in 1948, he made the year even more memorable by marrying Elizabeth Bloomer, a former member of the Martha Graham dance troupe. She became an outstandingly popular first lady, taking a leading part in the fight against drug abuse with the establishment in California of the Betty Ford Clinic.

In 1963 Ford, though 50 years old, represented younger Republicans in the House of Representatives by winning election as chairman of the House Republican Conference, and, widely respected for his integrity, followed this victory two years later with election as House minority leader. A newspaper reporter said of Ford that though all politicians tell lies at times, you could see that it pained Ford to do so.

A generally faithful Capitol Hill agent of Repub-

lican presidents, conservative on domestic issues, Ford with his unblemished personal reputation won wide approval as Nixon's vice presidential nominee, though Congress did not accept him without a thorough examination of his past. On his accession to the presidency, he seemed with his calm, reassuring personal style and his pledge of openness the ideal person for this time of national trauma—British correspondent Henry Brandon called him "the very antithesis of the neurotic Nixon"—but he brought his political honeymoon to an end just a month later by issuing a blanket pardon to Nixon. In a surprise televised speech he explained the move as an effort to end "our long national nightmare." Though the issuing of the pardon drew widespread criticism, Clark CLIFFORD, a leading member of the Democratic Party establishment, later endorsed it. "The nation," said Clifford, "would not have benefited from having a former Chief Executive in the dock for years after his departure from office."

In April 1975 Ford had to face the consequences of the collapse of the South Vietnamese government and its occupation by the victors from the North as the VIETNAM WAR ended. As U.S. and South Vietnamese officials fled Saigon, Ford authorized an airlift that brought out more than 200,000 Vietnamese refugees, of whom perhaps 100,000 settled in the United States, with lasting demographic effects. That same year was marked by the capture of an American ship by Cambodian forces in the MAYAGUEZ INCIDENT; Ford dispatched U.S. Marines to recover the ship. Also in 1975, Ford found himself the intended victim of two deranged women who, on separate occasions, attempted to assassinate him. In the following year, Ford responded to Watergate-inspired criticism of federal intelligence agencies by proposing and putting into effect a number of reforms.

With respect to relations with the Soviet Union, the Ford administration generally continued the policy of DÉTENTE established by Nixon. In a November 1974 meeting at Vladivostok, Ford and Soviet general secretary Leonid BREZHNEV signed an arms-control agreement, negotiated by Secretary of State Henry KISSINGER, intended to lead to a new SALT treaty. Introducing the "equal aggregates" principle, it allowed the two sides to have the same number of "launchers"—whether bombers or various kinds of missiles—but the mix on the two sides would not have to be the same. Though a treaty itself did not result from the agreement, the meeting and the discussions for the time being kept the arms-limitation process in motion.

In 1976 Ford barely won nomination for the presidency in the face of a vigorous challenge from Ronald REAGAN. During the campaign itself, illustrating the danger of debating high policy on live television, Ford committed what became a notorious gaffe by seeming to declare that the Soviet Union did not exercise control over Poland, a satellite nation then firmly in the Kremlin's grip. In losing the election to Jimmy CARTER, Ford became the first president since Herbert Hoover to be voted out of the White House. In his short time in office, however, he had succeeded, despite the Nixon pardon, in moving the country beyond the trauma of Watergate.

Formosa   See TAIWAN.

Forrestal   Class of four U.S. Navy aircraft carriers built during the 1950s. Besides *Forrestal,* which was named for the navy's great advocate James V. FORRESTAL, the first secretary of defense, the class included *Saratoga, Ranger,* and *Independence,* all named for previous carriers. Differing in some details, the Forrestals displaced about 79,000 tons loaded and carried about 75 fixed-wing aircraft and six helicopters.

Forrestal, James V. (1892–1949)   One of the many U.S. foreign-affairs and defense leaders from the Ivy League and Wall Street, James Forrestal became the first U.S. secretary of defense in September 1947.

After attending Dartmouth and Princeton and serving as a navy flier in World War I, Forrestal had risen to the presidency of Dillon, Read & Co., when President ROOSEVELT, a fellow Dutchess County, N.Y., native, called him to Washington in 1940 as an administrative assistant. Within two months Forrestal joined the new secretary of the navy, Frank Knox, as undersecretary, concentrating on the enormous task of expanding and equipping the navy for World War II. When Knox died in May 1944, Forrestal succeeded him. In December

ber of that year, the new secretary issued a notably popular regulation, setting aside tradition by allowing naval ships to carry beer and wine provided that the crews consumed these particular supplies ashore.

After the war, during which the army and navy had frequently seemed as hostile to each other as to the nation's official enemies, the TRUMAN administration moved toward the radical and challenging goal of completely unifying the armed services. Fearing that the army would dominate the new defense establishment, the navy's top admirals fought the proposals, with Forrestal serving as their vigorous and tenacious spokesman—sometimes even seeming more intransigent than the uniformed officers. Indeed, his excessive intensity and rigidity—though not noted as such at the time—were the first evidence of a mental disturbance. But Forrestal's and the navy's obduracy, together with the support of influential pro-navy members of Congress, succeeded in watering down the structure that became the Department of Defense (originally it did not carry the designation "department" but was called the National Military Establishment). Within a year of his appointment, however, Forrestal had acknowledged the inadequacy of the arrangement he had advocated and called for modifications, some of which were made in 1949.

But the deterioration of the secretary's mental condition led him to resign his post in March 1949. Not wishing him to be treated by civilian psychiatrists, because of his possession of top-secret information, the navy won its argument to have him placed in Bethesda Naval Hospital, which lacked the proper staff to deal with his problems. In the early hours of May 22, 1949, after tying one end of his bathrobe belt to a radiator and knotting the other end around his neck, Forrestal leaped to his death from a 16th-floor window of the hospital.

Fortress America   The post–World War II equivalent of the isolationism of the 1930s, the Fortress America idea called for the United States to concentrate on its own defense rather than on maintaining forces overseas and guaranteeing foreign borders. The view was held mostly by conservative Republicans and was opposed generally by Democrats and liberal Republicans. John Foster DULLES, a Republican secretary of state, declared that the United States should not "simply write off our friends in Europe."

forward-based systems The overall term for U.S. weapons systems outside the United States—such as attack bombers based in Britain, Poseidon submarines, nuclear aircraft carriers—capable of launching nuclear strikes against the Soviet Union. In arms-control negotiations of the 1970s, these systems were not included as strategic weapons, a Soviet concession that in effect balanced the Soviet advantage in numbers of missile launchers.

Foster, William Z. (1881–1961) U.S. Communist Party chairman, elected in 1945. A member of the party since 1921, Foster ran for the U.S. presidency in 1924, 1928, and 1932. In 1948 Foster and 11 other party officials were indicted under the Smith Act, which forbade advocacy of the violent overthrow of the government. Foster's case did not come to trial, however, because he suffered a heart attack. He survived, however, until 1961, when he died in Moscow.

Framework for Peace in the Middle East *See* CAMP DAVID ACCORDS.

Framework for the Conclusion of a Peace Treaty Between Egypt and Israel *See* CAMP DAVID ACCORDS.

Franks, Sir Oliver (1905–1992) British teacher and scholar, professor of moral philosophy at the University of Glasgow, who became a leading diplomat in the years following World War II. After serving as an official of the Ministry of Supply during the war, Franks played an important part as a top British representative in European planning for the use of MARSHALL PLAN aid. From 1948 to 1952 he held Britain's most important diplomatic post as ambassador to the United States. He developed close working and private friendships with U.S. secretary of state Dean ACHESON and undersecretary Robert A. LOVETT (later secretary of defense), relationships that greatly eased the making of Allied policy during the era leading up to the creation of the NORTH ATLANTIC TREATY ORGANIZATION.

Freedom and Peace (Wolsnosc i Pokój) A Polish group formed in Kraków in 1985 to express opposition to the Polish army's adoption of an oath that called for support of the Soviet army.

Fuchs, (Emil Julius) Klaus (1911–1988) Characterized by the eminent nuclear physicist Hans Bethe as "the one scientist I know who changed history," Klaus Fuchs was the chief Soviet scientific spy inside Anglo-American atomic-bomb research. A Communist leader as a university undergraduate in Germany, Fuchs fled to England in 1933, received a Ph.D. in 1936, and five years later became involved in secret nuclear research. That same year (1941), his offer to pass atomic secrets to the USSR resulted in his becoming a GRU (Soviet military intelligence) agent; he later transferred to the control of the NKGB (one of the forerunners of the KGB).

In August 1944 Fuchs was assigned to the British mission at the Los Alamos, N.Mex., laboratory, where the first ATOMIC BOMBS were to be assembled and the first detonation carried out. Here his theoretical and technical espionage was supplemented by the work of a 22-year-old Soviet agent, David Greenglass, a U.S. soldier assigned to Los Alamos as a machinist working on the bomb. Greenglass had been recruited by his wife, Ruth, on the instigation of his brother-in-law, Julius Rosenberg. Together, but unknown to each other, Fuchs and Greenglass provided their courier, Harry Gold, with material of the highest importance to take back to his case officer in New York. (In June 1945, for example, Fuchs told Gold about the plans to test the bomb the following month.) The two would meet in Santa Fe, with Fuchs describing the laboratory's progress on the implosion bomb and sometimes producing written notes. At Los Alamos, according to the physicist Edward TELLER, Fuchs was a friendly fellow who showed marked interest in the activities of all his colleagues.

In 1946 Fuchs returned to England to work at the new nuclear-research laboratory at Harwell, where he became deputy scientific officer. In addition, remarkably, Fuchs, along with another KGB agent, Donald MACLEAN, served as a British delegate to a 1947 conference in Washington concerned with the declassification of nuclear secrets. Fuchs's days as a Soviet agent ended in 1949, when the authorities arrested him as the result of cryptological intelligence and effective detective work. Because the U.S. and British governments did not wish to disclose their successes with Soviet ciphers, Fuchs could not be convicted without a confession, which patient interrogation finally succeeded in eliciting. His activities were said to have saved the USSR some four years in the development of its own atomic bomb. (Gold was arrested in 1950 and given a 30-year prison sentence.)

On his release from prison in 1959, Fuchs went to East Germany, where he received a royal welcome, married an old friend, and went on to enjoy life as a much-honored scientist.

In describing the mental compartmentalization he imposed on himself in order to function in society and at the same time carry on his espionage activities, Fuchs uttered a phrase that would become famous; this intense discipline, he said, should be called "a controlled schizophrenia." *See also* MAY, Alan Nunn.

Fulbright, J(ames) William (1905–1995) Known around the world for his sponsorship of the international scholarship legislation bearing his name, Senator Fulbright during the latter 1960s became one of the most severe congressional critics of U.S. policy in Vietnam. A native of Missouri, Fulbright attended the University of Arkansas and was a Rhodes Scholar; he served briefly as president of the University of Arkansas (1939–41) and came to the U.S. Senate in 1945. After the spring of 1965, though a Democrat, he used his powerful position as chairman of the Foreign Relations Committee (1959–74) to keep up a continuing attack on President JOHNSON, advocating peace talks and suggesting the possible "neutralization" of Southeast Asia. (In August 1965, however, as committee chairman, he had cosponsored the GULF OF TONKIN RESOLUTION, which served as the enabling legislation for the VIETNAM WAR.)

In a much-quoted 1966 speech, the senator declared, "America is succumbing to that arrogance of power which has afflicted, weakened, and, in some cases, destroyed great nations in the past." Fulbright retired from the Senate in 1974. *See also* ROSENBERG CASE.

G

Gadhafi, Moammar al- (1942–)   Libyan army officer who led a 1969 coup that overthrew the monarchy and set up the Libyan Arab Republic in its place. This development, modeled on Colonel NASSER's 1952 Egyptian coup, created a Moscow-oriented state that attracted continuing U.S. attention. While the Americans in the Mediterranean repeatedly challenged Gadhafi in the Gulf of Sidra, which Libya somewhat questionably claimed as territorial waters, Gadhafi encouraged acts of terrorism and offered asylum to terrorist groups of all stripes. In 1986 U.S. aircraft raided Libya's principal cities, Tripoli and Benghazi. The attacks smacked of an assassination attempt, but the victim in the Gadhafi family was the dictator's adopted baby daughter, while his wife and two other children were injured. The raids remained controversial, but in any case they did not appear to have weakened Gadhafi in the esteem of his own people. Whether they caused a diminution of terrorism remained a question.

Gaither Committee Report   In partial response to the Soviet launching of *SPUTNIK I* in October 1957 —an event that shocked U.S. defense officials, scientists, and educators—a presidential commission (chaired by H. Rowan Gaither, chairman of the Ford Foundation) that had already been studying the U.S. defense posture proposed in its report, submitted in November, that the United States move to decrease its vulnerability to Soviet attack by taking several specific steps, including increasing missile production and deployment, dispersing launch sites and hardening silos, and building a national system of fallout shelters. The estimated cost of these measures, to be spread over a five-year period, was $44 billion. Less panicked than many of his associates, and genuinely concerned about excessive spending on defense, President EISENHOWER rejected these recommendations. One presumable reason for his lack of concern was the intelligence produced by U-2 flights over the Soviet Union; this information showed that estimates made on other bases of Soviet missile strength were greatly exaggerated. Thus the U-2 was performing exactly the kind of function it had been created for.

Galbraith, John Kenneth (1908–)   American economist and widely popular author who held various government posts during World War II and served as President KENNEDY's ambassador to India (1961–64). A native of Ontario, Canada, Galbraith held a degree in animal husbandry but, after coming to the United States, undertook more abstract studies at the University of California. Professor of economics at Harvard for a number of years, Galbraith was one of the founders of Americans for Democratic Action, a liberal political group. Perhaps best known as a phrasemaker, Galbraith popularized the idea of the "affluent society" (and in so doing helped call attention to the existence, by contrast, of continuing areas and strata of poverty), wrote about the "technostructure" that controls the operation of modern corporations and about "countervailing power" as a regulatory mechanism in the economy, and regularly inveighed against blind obeisance to the "conventional wisdom," which, he said in his customarily dry manner, "is not the property of any political group" but exists in both conservative and liberal forms.

Galbraith's dispatches from New Delhi, said White House chronicler Arthur Schlesinger, Jr., delighted President Kennedy with their "suave irony." Shortly after arriving in India, Galbraith reported to the president that, in supervising the embassy staff, he would "try to combine decorum and discipline with a reasonably relaxed attitude toward rank but, of course, without descending to the raffish informality of the White House." Because of the world influence of India's neutralist prime minister, Jawaharlal NEHRU, the United States considered the ambassadorial post in New Delhi of great importance, and Galbraith was one of a series of outstanding private citizens appointed to fill it.

Gandhi, Indira (1917–1984) Indian political leader who served as minister of information in the administration of Prime Minister Lal Bahadur Shastri and succeeded him as prime minister on his death in January 1966. Gandhi served three terms in the office, from 1966 to 1977, and after an interval out of office returned in 1980 for a fourth term. On October 31, 1984, she was shot and killed by two of her Sikh bodyguards, apparently sectarian extremists protesting an Indian army attack on the Golden Temple, the Sikh shrine at Amritsar, which was the citadel of those seeking autonomy for the Punjab region.

The daughter of Jawaharlal NEHRU, the first prime minister of independent India, Gandhi received schooling in India and Switzerland and attended Oxford University. In 1942, having returned home the previous year, she married Feroze Gandhi, a journalist she had long known. Later, like many other members of the Congress Party, she was imprisoned for working in the nationalist movement, which sought Indian independence from Britain. After the end of World War II, the entire Indian political picture changed, with Britain granting independence in 1947.

Active in Congress Party politics during the 1950s, Gandhi served as an aide to her father and was appointed to the working committee of the Congress Party—the dominant force in Indian politics—in 1955 and in 1959 won election as president of the party, a position offering prominence if

not real power. Feroze Gandhi died in 1960; he and his wife had long been estranged.

When her father died in 1964 and Shastri succeeded him, Gandhi entered the government in the information post. Her choice as Shastri's successor in 1966 apparently represented a compromise between party factions that seemed to view her primarily as Nehru's daughter and thus expected her not to show herself a force in her own right. This judgment proved misguided, however, and after a series of intraparty battles Gandhi organized her own faction, resulting in a landslide victory in the 1971 election. In December 1971 she presided over the ten-day war with Pakistan that ended in victory and the creation of the new republic of Bangladesh out of East Pakistan. This breakup of Pakistan assured India's supremacy on the subcontinent.

In 1975 the Indian High Court convicted Indira Gandhi of election-law violations, a judgment that carried with it suspension of all political activity for a six-year period. Instead of accepting the penalty, Gandhi took countermeasures widely considered unconstitutional—imprisoning thousands of her opponents, assuming emergency powers, and restricting press freedom and other civil liberties. She also stirred up considerable opposition by carrying out a coercive birth-control program. In 1977, when she allowed overdue elections, the voters turned her out of office. In 1978 she spent a brief time in prison on corruption charges. Her remarkable career took a new turn in January 1980, when, having built her political faction into an independent party, she won her second landslide election victory.

During her terms of office, Gandhi leaned toward rapprochement with the Soviet Union, and as a strong leader of the largest of all THIRD WORLD countries, she exerted a measure of influence worldwide. In July 1966, attempting to bring about an armistice in the VIETNAM WAR, she called for a reconvening of the Geneva Conference, which produced the 1954 GENEVA ACCORDS; HO CHI MINH's North Vietnamese government, however, rejected the proposal. In October 1966, at a meeting in New Delhi, Yugoslavia and the United Arab Republic joined the Indian government in calling for cessation of the U.S. bombing of North Vietnam, implementation of the Geneva Accords, and participation of the Vietnamese NATIONAL LIBERA-TION FRONT as a principal party in the peace settlement. This time the Chinese government in Beijing offered the sharpest rejection, accusing Gandhi and Yugoslavia's Marshal TITO of trying to "peddle the peace fraud" that had been "concocted by the United States and the Soviet Union."

Later, Gandhi lost considerable international favor when she declined to criticize the Soviet BREZHNEV government for its December 1979 invasion of Afghanistan.

Since the Nehru-Gandhi family had, at least unofficially, established something of a dynasty in India, Gandhi and most observers expected her son Sanjay to succeed her in power. Though the younger son, he was more politically involved than his brother Rajiv and considered more effective. Sanjay's death in 1980 in an airplane crash, however, caused his mother to conscript Rajiv into politics. Rajiv Gandhi succeeded his mother as prime minister and won a general election later in 1984, but in 1989 he resigned his post amid charges of incompetence and corruption. On May 21, 1991, during his campaign to regain office, Rajiv Gandhi was assassinated, thus putting a violent end to the three-generation Nehru-Gandhi ascendancy in India.

Gang of Four   The name given to a group of four leaders of the Chinese CULTURAL REVOLUTION who, after the death of MAO ZEDONG in 1976, were arrested by his successors and charged with the "persecution" of more than 700,000 people and the deaths of some 35,000. Significantly, Mao's legacy was represented in the "gang," since his widow, JIANG QING, was a member; in fact, she had been the head of the Central Revolution Group. The other members of the accused gang were Zhang Chunqiao, a party leader from Shanghai; Wang Hongwen, a trade unionist and leading political officer of the People's Liberation Army; and Yao Wenyuan, a party propagandist. Tried on national television in 1980, the defendants, not surprisingly, were all convicted. Jiang Qing and Zhang Chunqiao drew death sentences, later commuted to life imprisonment; Wang Hongwen was sentenced to life imprisonment, and Yao Wenyuan to 18 years in prison.

Gang of Four   Nickname, borrowed from that of the Chinese group, applied in the late 1980s to four Eastern European Communist leaders who opposed the reforms associated with President Mikhail GORBACHEV of the Soviet Union. They were Nicolae CEAUŞESCU of Romania, Miloš JAKEŠ of Czechoslovakia, Erich HONECKER of East Germany, and Todor ZHIVKOV of Bulgaria.

GATT   *See* GENERAL AGREEMENT ON TARIFFS AND TRADE.

Gdansk Accords   Beginning in the middle of August 1980 in the Lenin Shipyards in Gdansk, Poland (the former German city of Danzig), a wave of sit-down strikes swept along the Baltic coast, leading the government of Premier Edward GIEREK to offer the discontented workers sizable pay increases, but not what the strikers really wanted: recognition of the right to form unions independent of Communist control. Sticking together in a movement that became the national union SOLIDAR-ITY led by shipyard electrician Lech WAŁESA, the workers forced the government to grant a degree of freedom in the agreement signed on August 31, 1980. The shipbuilding industry held particular importance for Poland, because it was the chief source of export earnings. A decade earlier (December 1970), a wave of strikes originating in Gdansk had led not to any agreement but to demonstrations and violence in which hundreds of people were killed and thousands injured.

General Agreement on Tariffs and Trade (GATT)   Signed in Geneva on October 30, 1947, by 23 countries (the membership later grew to 96), this agreement, strongly pushed by the United States, had the goal of promoting international trade through the lowering of barriers to it. Continuing to exist through the decades as an arm of the UNITED NATIONS, GATT was essentially a league against protectionism, though it did not always enjoy success (as 1990s conflicts between the United States and Japan demonstrated). In 1994, more than 100 trading nations adopted a new agreement that called for the elimination or reduction of a long list of barriers to trade and for a successor to GATT, the World Trade Organization, to come into operation on January 1, 1995. After much dissent and debate, the U.S. Senate ratified the agreement in 1994, but controversy continued.

general secretary   The title customarily used by the head of the COMMUNIST PARTY OF THE SOVIET UNION. Technically, the holder of this position was chief of the Secretariat and thus of the national machinery of the party. Originally Lenin and his colleagues saw the secretary-general (as most literature of the time called him) as simply an agent of the CENTRAL COMMITTEE, but, beginning in 1922, Joseph STALIN transformed the secretary-generalship into the key party and therefore national post, patiently building a personal political machine. "While others were burdened with great affairs of state," one observer wrote with a touch of irony, "Stalin merely decided who should be designated as key man in this or that local committee, who should be put in charge of party affairs in Kharkov or Minsk, or even some third-rate town in Siberia or Central Asia." Already, in 1923, Trotsky was complaining that "the participation of the party rank-and-file in the actual formation of the party organization is becoming more and more illusory." (Though Stalin held the position for the rest of his life, he was rarely identified by it in the world press. "Stalin" usually seemed sufficient until the coming of the war in 1941.)

As secretary-general (or general secretary, as the office was better known in later years), Stalin by the early 1930s had come to be treated by foreigners as the real head of the Soviet government, a status made formally correct in May 1941, shortly before the German invasion, when he assumed the post of premier (literally, chairman of the Council of People's Commissars) and became known by it. On becoming head of the CPSU in 1953, Nikita KHRUSHCHEV assumed the title "first secretary"; in 1966 his successor, Leonid BREZHNEV, restored the earlier title.

Geneva Accords   Agreements reached in a meeting opening on April 26, 1954, attended by the U.S., British, French, and Soviet foreign ministers and by representatives of the People's Republic of China, North Korea, South Korea, and Indochinese governments and factions. Devoted to discussing peace settlements for both Korea and Indochina, the conference made no progress in the former area; the 1953 cease-fire remained the only agreed settlement for the peninsula.

Early in the conference, U.S. secretary of state John Foster DULLES sought to block the settlement of Indochinese questions. It was early in April that President EISENHOWER had made his famous observation about the likely consequences of Communist success in Vietnam; the other countries in the region, said the president, would fall "like a row of dominoes." But the French government felt great pressure to end its eight-year-old war in Southeast Asia, and in June Pierre MENDÈS-FRANCE replaced Joseph Laniel as French premier, instituting a self-imposed deadline: he would resign, he said, if the conference failed to produce agreements by July 20. Fudging by a few hours, the participants met this deadline. The Geneva Accords included agreement on the withdrawal of troops from Laos and Cambodia and, of the greatest general interest, the establishment of the 17th parallel as a cease-fire line in Vietnam. The country north of the parallel—the stronghold of the VIETMINH—came under the formal control of HO CHI MINH and the Vietnamese Communists. In non-Communist South Vietnam, Emperor BAO DAI ruled. These arrangements, however, were officially temporary; general elections, to unify the country, were supposed to be held within two years. They were never to take place, as the United States supported South Vietnam's refusal to participate in them, fearing Ho Chi Minh's election. *See also* DOMINO THEORY; VIETNAM WAR.

German Democratic Republic   The English translation of Deutsche Demokratische Republik, the proper name of East Germany. This state was established in 1949 and ceased to exist in 1990, when the two German states reunited. Several years later, amid the problems of adjusting to the strange world of capitalism and competition, youthful residents of the former East Germany experienced a wave of what they called *Ostalgie* (nostalgia for the East), supposed yearning for the good old days under Communism. They wore old German Youth Party uniforms to discos, ate goose-fat sandwiches, and sang Marxist-Leninist songs. *See also* FEDERAL REPUBLIC OF GERMANY.

germ warfare   A favorite DISINFORMATION theme of Communist propaganda organs, both Soviet and Chinese, was the charge that the United States used bacteriological—germ—warfare in operations in Asia. This accusation first appeared during the KOREAN WAR, when the Chinese circulated photographs of schoolchildren supposedly picking up and handling imperialist "germs." (On July 3, 1952, the USSR vetoed a U.S. Security Council proposal for an impartial investigation of the charges. Irritated to an unusual degree by the accusation, U.S. secretary of state Dean ACHESON called it a sad commentary on the inability of the Communists to maintain a level of public health in Korea.) In the 1960s a forged document produced by the KGB purported to reveal the existence of U.S. bacteriological weapons in Vietnam and Thailand; this story received credence not only in Asia but in London, where even the *Times* made it the subject of a report (March 7, 1968). In the 1980s a notable piece of such disinformation clashed head-on with GLASNOST, when Mikhail GORBACHEV's government disavowed an earlier, preglasnost charge that American scientists had created the AIDS virus in their test tubes. This story had also played in London (this time in the *Sunday Express,* like the *Times* not normally sympathetic to Communist causes) and, despite the later Soviet disclaimers, proved to have a long life around the world.

Gheorghiu-Dej, Gheorghe (1901–1965)   Romanian Communist Party official, president of the State Council (chief of state) from 1952 to 1955 and from 1961 until his death. Aside from a 1954–55 interim, Gheorghiu-Dej was also secretary of the Communist Party of Romania (which later changed its name to the Romanian Workers' Party) through the two decades beginning in 1945, having been handpicked for the job by his Soviet master, Joseph STALIN. A Romanian who had spent 11 years (1933–44) in prison under the royal government, Gheorghiu-Dej entered the coalition Romanian cabinet in November 1944, after the Germans pulled back from the country, and in 1947 exacted a measure of revenge by forcing the abdication of King Michael. In 1952, victorious in a power struggle, he succeeded Petru GROZA in the premiership. In the next year, in the new atmosphere created by the death of Stalin, he, like the USSR's Georgi MALENKOV, acknowledged his country's excessive concentration on heavy industry (at the expense of producing consumer goods) and proceeded to close forced-labor camps. He also succeeded in winning complete control of the party congress. He went on to establish a tradition of relative independence from Moscow (this had to do with nationalism, not democracy), which he bequeathed to his chosen successor, Nicolae CEAUŞESCU.

Gierek, Edward (1913–   )   Polish government and Communist (United Workers') Party official who succeeded Władysław GOMUŁKA in 1970 as first secretary (and thus head of the party). When Gierek was 10 years old his family emigrated to France, and from the age of 13 the boy worked as a coal miner in France and Belgium. A genuine proletarian, Gierek joined the French Communist Party at the age of 18 and the Belgian party six years later. During World War II, he organized Belgian resistance groups, and after the war he used his organizational talents to create Communist groups of Belgian Poles. Returning to Poland in 1948, he joined the new Polish United Workers' Party—the result of the merging of the Communist and Socialist parties. He became a member of the Central Committee staff the same year and won a seat on the committee in 1954. Harking back to his early days as a miner, he earned a degree in mining engineering from the University of Kraków in 1953.

With a reputation as a leading party technocrat, Gierek headed the party in Silesia, and in 1970, when waves of student discontent, price rises, and workers' demonstrations drove Gomułka from office, Gierek became his successor; Gomułka had sealed his own fate by ordering soldiers and police to shoot the demonstrators. On taking office, Gierek disavowed the violence and promised to maintain close ties with the workers. But a decade later, finding himself in a similar tight spot, Gierek ordered the police to fire on striking demonstrators in Gdansk. This time, repression was not to keep the government in power, and Gierek was swept away in the Polish upheaval. For his pains, he was expelled from the United Workers' Party in 1981. *See also* GDANSK ACCORDS.

French president Valéry Giscard d'Estaing

Giscard d'Estaing, Valéry (1926–) President of France from 1974 to 1981, Giscard was a specialist in finance who had been a Gaullist deputy and in 1959, after General DE GAULLE's return to power, had become finance secretary; in 1962 he entered the cabinet as finance minister. A fiscal conservative, Giscard fell out of favor with de Gaulle in 1965 but served again as finance minister under de Gaulle's successor, Georges POMPIDOU. When Pompidou's death brought on a presidential election in 1974, Giscard was the winner. In his try for reelection in 1981, he was defeated by François MITTERRAND.

More technocrat than politician, Giscard, said the French historian André Fontaine, wished to "govern in the center." Though he maintained amiable relations with the USSR, his diplomacy, said Fontaine, was "too Atlantic and too European" for any close diplomatic friendship to arise

between the two nations. His closest ally was West German chancellor Helmut SCHMIDT.

glasnost In a speech made in December 1984 and little noticed around the world, Mikhail GORBACHEV, not yet the leader of the Soviet Union, spoke of the country's need for *glasnost,* which he characterized as "an integral part of socialist democracy." This Russian word, often translated as "openness," also conveys the idea of using this openness by speaking out—from *glas,* "voice." Soon Gorbachev's calls for greater glasnost in Soviet life attracted worldwide attention, mixed with amazement and doubt. "The matter of broadening glasnost is a matter of principle for us," Gorbachev said at the February 1986 congress of the COMMUNIST PARTY OF THE SOVIET UNION. "And it is a political matter, too. Without it there is not, and there cannot be, democratism, the political creativity of the masses and their participation in management." Following this meeting the drive for glasnost developed rapidly. Publication was announced of Vladimir Nabokov's long-banned novel *Lolita.* An anti-STALIN film, *Repentance,* was shown. Accurate economic statistics, the kind once suppressed if deemed to reflect unfavorably on the Soviet system, were published (during the BREZHNEV years of corruption and drift, statistics had ceased to have much real meaning). Military information was more widely disseminated. Educational authorities canceled high school history examinations because the textbooks had taught the students lies about Stalin and other aspects of the past.

These remarkable developments attracted worldwide attention, compounded of approval and skepticism. Could the Soviet system really be experiencing genuine change? In any case, the policy of glasnost did not mean that a completely free flow of information had now arrived in the Soviet Union; it was not a matter of Western-style freedom of the press, for which no Russian tradition existed. The authorities at the top still held control, and publications and other institutions that remembered the 1960s, when the Brezhnev freeze followed the KHRUSHCHEV thaw, moved cautiously. A year after Gorbachev's speech to the party congress, a high government official, Yegor LIGACHEV, could still chastise a newspaper for not measuring up to good Communist standards. On another occasion Ligachev, an avowed conservative, quoted favorably the saying, "Before going into the room, make sure you can get out again." Yuri Bondarev, an official of the Russian writers' union, accused glasnost of producing "anarchistic twaddle, empty sensationalism, all sorts of alien fashions and cheap, demagogic flirtations."

Gorbachev himself had problems with free expression. After the 1990 May Day parade—the annual Communist ritual—the leader responded to heckling he had received by calling for a law forbidding criticism of the Soviet president (and, though liberals succeeded in watering it down, such a law was passed). In general, however, the country was transformed in such a way that open debate about public issues now became possible. Gorbachev himself often led the charge, revealing, for instance, that Soviet military expenditures had been far higher than had previously been admitted. News of political protests in faraway Soviet republics appeared in PRAVDA and IZVESTIA, and the media presented accurate and vivid reports from the war in AFGHANISTAN. Essentially, glasnost was the prerequisite for any kind of democratization. In this realm, as in much else, Gorbachev had to perform something of a continual balancing act between contending forces. But whatever happened, as events were to show, glasnost could not be reversed—there was indeed no way out of the room. *See also* PERESTROIKA.

Glasnost   In June 1987, taking advantage of the openness, or GLASNOST, promoted by Mikhail GORBACHEV, a group of Soviet private citizens began publishing a magazine called *Glasnost*. Such a private-enterprise publication—with or without such a daring name—could not, of course, have appeared before the policy of openness.

Glassboro Conference   During the weekend of June 23–25, 1967, U.S. president JOHNSON and Soviet premier Alexei KOSYGIN held a SUMMIT conference in Glassboro, N.J. The site of the discussions was "Hollybush," the stone colonial house that served as the residence of the president of Glassboro State College, Dr. Thomas E. Robinson, and his family. With the Soviet premier coming to New York for UNITED NATIONS meetings, Glassboro was

chosen for the conference because it was halfway between New York and Washington and close to the New Jersey Turnpike. Sitting quietly in Robinson's study, alone except for interpreters, the two men, Johnson later said, "discussed the state of the world and its major problems." But, though the meetings were friendly and much talk was heard of the "spirit of Glassboro," little of substance emerged from the discussions. Nuclear missiles, the Middle East, and the VIETNAM WAR divided the two sides. In the immediate aftermath of the Six-Day War in the Middle East, Kosygin wanted prewar armistice lines restored, and he later said in addition that U.S.-Soviet relations could not improve until the United States withdrew from Vietnam.

GLCM   *See* CRUISE MISSILE.

Glomar Explorer   In March 1968, while on patrol in the Pacific Ocean, a 320-foot-long Soviet submarine, the PL-722, exploded and sank, taking all hands with it. Having learned of the explosion, apparently from listening devices, the U.S. CENTRAL INTELLIGENCE AGENCY decided to attempt to recover the submarine from its three-mile depths. To carry out the project, the CIA commissioned the building of an innovatively equipped 618-foot ship, the *Glomar Explorer,* and sent it to sea in 1974, under the cover story that it was a mining ship operated by one of the enterprises of the famous eccentric industrialist Howard Hughes. But in 1975, as CIA director William Colby later put it, "the Glomar project blew sky high," when the media learned some details of this high-tech effort and told the world how the *Glomar Explorer* had attempted to salvage the sunken Soviet submarine, scooping it up with a giant robotic claw.

Publicity put an end to the operation, but the stories did not tell what had really happened. Some accounts declared that the great claw had broken, dropping the submarine and its secrets back into the depths. Actually, the *Glomar Explorer* had managed to recover and retain the forward part of the ship, and in 1993 Russian reports acknowledged that this remarkable U.S. mission had succeeded in recovering two torpedoes with nuclear warheads. This represented a true intelligence coup, since, as an American arms designer

At the June 1967 Glassboro Conference, U.S. president Lyndon Johnson *(r.)* talks with Soviet premier Alexei Kosygin.

said, "Bombs can be very different from one another. There's a good chance Soviet weaponry held big surprises for us."

Goldwater, Barry Morris (1909–) Probably the most prominent conservative representative in American politics during the Cold War era, aside from Ronald REAGAN, Goldwater met an overwhelming defeat in his 1964 campaign for the presidency but nevertheless succeeded in drawing attention to a body of opinion that had previously received little notice. As observers said, his popularity in the South opened up new possibilities for the Republican Party.

A native of Phoenix, Ariz., Goldwater was the grandson of a Polish Jewish immigrant who had become a leading merchant in the area, and after attending college for only one year he went into the family business. In World War II—despite his age,

his poor eyesight, and the lingering effects of two basketball knee injuries—he talked his way into the army and, already a licensed pilot, ferried aircraft to Europe and Asia. In 1952, in the EISENHOWER sweep, Goldwater won a very close election for a seat in the U.S. Senate; he was reelected in 1958. In 1954, declaring his belief that Senator Joseph MC-CARTHY was an outstanding foe of Communism, Goldwater joined 22 other senators in opposing the successful motion to censure McCarthy.

Sent back to the Senate in 1968 after an interim following his presidential campaign, Goldwater showed a new side by becoming one of President NIXON's most persistent critics in regard to the WATERGATE AFFAIR, and on August 7, 1974, he led a group of Republican congressional leaders to warn Nixon that he faced almost-certain impeachment; the next day the president announced his resignation.

Always one of the most consistent congressional supporters of the military, especially the air force (in which he held a reserve commission), Goldwater received a striking present from the Senate in 1986. Surprising the senator, his colleagues placed his name on the sweeping new military-reform law, in which he had been deeply involved. Afterward, Goldwater said, characteristically, "It's the only goddamned thing I've done in the Senate that's worth a damn." *See also* JOINT CHIEFS OF STAFF.

Golf, Operation A 1982 KGB operation intended to discredit the conservative Jeane Kirkpatrick, the U.S. ambassador to the UNITED NATIONS (appointed by President REAGAN) through a forged letter purporting to show that she maintained a close relationship with, and had accepted an unspecified gift from, the apartheid government of South Africa. The Washington KGB residency planted the fake document on the correspondent of the *New Statesman* of London, a weekly never known for its sympathy with U.S. policies. The article with the false information appeared in the publication's issue dated November 5; it included a careful analysis of the reasons supposed to underlie the "birthday gift." The *New Statesman* editors titled it "A girl's best friend." They refused to believe U.S. and South African denials.

Gomułka, Władysław (1905–1982) Leading Polish Communist politician whose career was marked by extreme ups and downs. Frequently arrested as a young man for his political activities, he worked underground in the Polish Resistance during World War II and joined the new postwar government as deputy premier. Within a few months he had also become minister for the western territories acquired from Germany, while serving, as well, as first secretary of the Polish Workers' (Communist) Party—only to be turned out of office in 1948 and later imprisoned as a "Titoist" in a wave of purges ordered in Eastern Europe by the USSR's Joseph STALIN. Accused of minimizing the danger of Titoism, of not acknowledging the leading role of the USSR in the socialist camp, and of protecting the kulaks (so-called wealthy peasants), he performed as a loyal Communist, bowing to discipline and delivering a speech of self-criticism.

(Indeed, in seeing him as a patriotic Polish nationalist, Stalin was not wrong.)

Gomułka was not only expelled from the party but later imprisoned for three years—1951 to 1954. (The frequent confusion about the dates of Gomułka's confinement in prison comes from the fact that he was released late in 1954 though no official announcement was made until April 7, 1956.) On his way back into influence, Gomułka was present at the Warsaw airport in October 1956 to take part in a memorable scene with Soviet leader Nikita KHRUSHCHEV. Having come to the country to reassert the primacy of the USSR after a wave of anti-Soviet protests that had begun in Poznan, Khrushchev declared, "We have spilled our blood for this country and now they want to sell it to the Americans." A voice replied, "We have spilled more blood than you and nobody is selling us anything at all." "Who's that, who's that?" demanded the Soviet first secretary. "I'm the former party secretary-general that you and Stalin threw into prison. My name is Gomułka." Despite Khrushchev's anger, which could have found violent expression had he ordered the Soviet tanks ringing Warsaw to move, the visit ended peacefully. In fact, Gomułka completed his remarkable comeback by taking charge of the Communist Party as first secretary. Though making no attempts to break free of the Soviet Union, he presided over a program of limited (and essentially tactical) political and economic liberalization. He held his post until 1970, when it became his turn to be the object of violent dissent as workers rioted against increases in food prices. *See also* GIEREK, Edward.

Gorbachev, Mikhail Sergeyevich (1931–) Born to a Russian peasant family near Stavropol in the North Caucasus, Mikhail Gorbachev rose to become one of the chief political figures of the 20th century. Introducing the world to the terms *GLASNOST* (openness) and *PERESTROIKA* (restructuring), he led reforms that not only changed the face of the Soviet Union but were followed by the incredible fact of its dissolution—a development Gorbachev clearly did not foresee. In a strong sense, he was a gambler who played for the highest stakes and lost, but, even so, his individual significance remains great.

As Gorbachev observed later, he did not enter on his career as any kind of democrat. "In high school," he said, "I wrote an essay for which I received top marks, called 'Stalin Is the Glory of Our Country, Stalin Is the Youth.'" A member of the Komsomol (the Communist Party youth organization) during his teenage years, Gorbachev worked on a collective farm; this beginning represented the first installment on his credentials as an expert in agriculture, which he enhanced 20 years later with a correspondence degree from an agricultural college. In 1952, as a young man fresh from the provinces, he entered law school at Moscow State University. At the university he met Raisa Titorenko, a young woman from a small town in Siberia, whom he married in 1953. Another important part in Gorbachev's life as a Moscow student was played by his roommate, a Czech, Western and cosmopolitan, who exposed Gorbachev to ideas and styles utterly new to him. On graduating in 1955, however, Gorbachev returned to Stavropol, where, as a full-time Komsomol and later party worker, he followed the orthodox path for advancement, his activity leading to his becoming first secretary of the regional committee in 1970. This major appointment placed him in the Soviet elite and made him the de facto ruler of the more than two million inhabitants of the Stavropol region.

The progress of Gorbachev's career on the national level owed much to the interest taken in him by two leading party members: Mikhail SUSLOV, the chief ideologist (who had been party secretary in Stavropol in the 1940s), and Yuri ANDROPOV, the director of the KGB. This interest rested, to some extent, on the odd fact that both Suslov and Andropov suffered from kidney ailments, for which they would seek relief in the spas of Gorbachev's fiefdom, the North Caucasus. In 1971 Gorbachev was appointed to the CENTRAL COMMITTEE of the COMMUNIST PARTY OF THE SOVIET UNION. In 1978 he succeeded another important patron, Fedor Kulakov, also from Stavropol, as party agricultural secretary; this key development brought him to Moscow. The next year he also became a candidate (nonvoting) member of the POLITBURO, with full membership coming in 1980. During his rise Gorbachev produced rhetoric indistinguishable from that of any good party member

moving up the ladder in the BREZHNEV era. In 1978, for instance, he could speak of the doddering leader's "titanic daily work" that was "raising the well-being of workers and strengthening the peace and security of nations."

After Andropov succeeded Leonid Brezhnev as general secretary and Soviet leader in 1982, Gorbachev exerted great influence on policy, particularly with respect to economic affairs. Though much younger than his peers in the leadership, he could conceivably have been chosen in 1984 as Andropov's successor. But the post went instead to the 73-year-old Konstantin CHERNENKO, who had been Brezhnev's closest friend and associate. The choice of the conservative Chernenko, however, represented not so much a rejection of Gorbachev as a postponement of his election. When the ailing Chernenko died after little more than a year in office, Gorbachev, who had performed as the leading figure in the government and had carefully built up support in the Politburo, won the election to succeed him (March 11, 1985).

The main challenge the new leader appeared to face came from the economy—the legacy of the "era of stagnation," as he and others openly called the 1970s under Brezhnev. As quickly became clear, Gorbachev saw himself not as any kind of revolutionary but as a reformer, a physician called to attend the ailing Soviet body politic and economic. Shaking up the bureaucracy and installing his own people in key government and party positions, candidly facing the technological lag in industry, promoting an unprecedented degree of open discussion of economic problems, he nevertheless acted more as a tinkerer than as a designer. "We at first thought of perestroika only as an economic reform," Gorbachev later wrote. A particular problem early in his administration came from an antialcohol campaign promoted by his close associate, Igor LIGACHEV. Profoundly unpopular, the campaign produced results very much like those of Prohibition in the United States in the 1920s, one of its worst consequences being the damage done to Gorbachev's image with the public.

Since the remedies he had proposed produced only limited results while leaving the Soviet system itself unchanged, Gorbachev plunged ahead toward greater liberalization, though, as later events would make plain, he still intended only to

Soviet leader Mikhail Gorbachev wins an enthusiastic welcome from Washington crowds during his 1987 visit. With him is President Ronald Reagan.

refurbish the Communist system, not to replace it with something else. Under glasnost, his most visible and widely acclaimed policy, the media and the people themselves enjoyed a freedom of discussion previously unknown in the Russia of any era; for instance, Soviet TV now presented dramatic pictures showing the horrors of the disastrous war in AFGHANISTAN. Gorbachev also moved to decentralize much of Soviet industry and agriculture, in the interest of efficiency, but he moved only reluctantly toward a market economy. Politically, he allowed a kind of discussion that had never before been heard in Communist Party conclaves and created a new government body, the CONGRESS OF PEOPLE'S DEPUTIES, that, through the use of the secret ballot, was elected by the free choice of the voters.

In foreign affairs, Gorbachev—well-spoken, undogmatic, with an agreeable personal style unmatched by any of his predecessors—quickly made an enormous impact on the world. When he visited England in December 1984, a few months before becoming general secretary, the hardheaded Conservative prime minister, Margaret THATCHER,

took his measure in a long conversation. The content of his remarks, she said, was "largely the standard Marxist line." But "his personality could not have been more different from the wooden ventriloquism of the average Soviet APPARATCHIK." The style, she decided, was far more important than the Marxist rhetoric, leading her to conclude that "we can do business together." Her judgment proved quite correct, though many observers expressed skepticism about the sincerity of a Soviet leader who advocated the reduction of weapons stocks and favored closer relations with the West.

Even U.S. president Ronald REAGAN, the West's leading anti-Soviet rhetorician, came to believe in Gorbachev's sincerity, whatever its complex of motives. Certainly economic constraints constituted an important factor; the Soviet defense budget consumed more than 20 percent of the gross national product. Indeed, Reagan and Gorbachev were to have four SUMMIT meetings, including sessions in Washington and Moscow; during the latter meeting the two were seen strolling arm in arm across Red Square. As the Swedish writer Geir

Lundestad later observed, "Gorbiemania swept across the United States." No even remotely comparable Soviet-U.S. phenomenon had ever before occurred. In 1987 the United States and the USSR agreed to destroy their stocks of intermediate-range missiles. In 1989 Gorbachev extricated Soviet forces from Afghanistan. In 1990 the two sides reached an agreement on the reduction of conventional military forces in Europe. Essentially, Gorbachev saw PEACEFUL COEXISTENCE as a permanent state between East and West, not as a phase in a battle that ultimately had to end in victory for one side or the other.

Having already become one of the most admired statesmen in the world—which had eagerly welcomed the new smiles of reason emanating from the Kremlin—Gorbachev assured himself a prominent place in history when, in 1989, he refused to interfere with the independence movements in Eastern Europe that brought the end of Soviet control of the region and of the IRON CURTAIN itself, symbolized by the demolition of the BERLIN WALL. Could Gorbachev have acted differently, moving to suppress the popular uprisings and movements that swept the satellite countries? Perhaps so, perhaps not—but the important fact is that Gorbachev signaled to the governments of the client states only that they were on their own.

In December 1989, meeting at Malta, Gorbachev and President George BUSH declared the Cold War over. In the same month, the Soviet government gave formal status to its new policies by denouncing the BREZHNEV DOCTRINE, the principle under which the USSR had sent troops into Czechoslovakia in 1968 to put an end to the PRAGUE SPRING.

For all his international success, Gorbachev never succeeded in winning comparable favor and support at home, though in March 1990 the Congress of People's Deputies elected him to the powerful new presidency he had designed. Communist Party conservatives opposed his liberalizing moves, many of them fearing the results—rightly, from their particular point of view, as matters turned out. In his attempts to win and keep support, Gorbachev veered this way and that, sometimes seeming to aim at being all things to all men. His attempts at reform did not go deep enough to have much chance of bringing about urgently

needed changes in the Soviet economy. In the short run (which was all the time Gorbachev was to be granted), they actually made matters worse, as is often the case with reforms before their benefits begin to make themselves felt. In an interview given several years after he left office, Gorbachev commented: "Just like reformers before me, I thought that we had a system that could be improved. Instead, I learned that we had a system that needed to be replaced."

In August 1991, hard-line Communists—members of Gorbachev's administration, chosen by him—staged a putsch that at first seemed likely to succeed but quickly collapsed when the plotters proved indecisive, the army refused any significant support, and citizens in Moscow stood with Russia's President Boris YELTSIN in his inspired resistance to the junta. When Gorbachev returned to the capital from his vacation house in the Crimea, in which, he said, KGB guards had kept him and his wife under house arrest, the world quickly saw that Yeltsin had supplanted him as the most powerful political figure in the USSR. (Considerable mystery surrounds the situation at Gorbachev's summer house; some observers have doubted his claim that his communications were cut off. Further, the Russian public prosecutor suggested that because the plotters were the president's close associates, they may well have expected him to come over to their side within a few days.) Only under Yeltsin's prodding did Gorbachev move against officials who had not resisted the attempted coup; the Soviet president's reluctance to act made it clear that he did not aim at any general housecleaning and that he remained a believer in Communist doctrine. He apparently was not yet ready to look toward replacement of the system. Nevertheless, later in the year Gorbachev had to yield to pressure to disestablish the Communist Party of the Soviet Union and to allow constituent republics of the union to secede. As the country slid into political collapse, he resigned the presidency on December 25, 1991, and the Soviet Union itself ceased to exist on January 1, 1992—an eventuality unimaginable even a year earlier. For decades the USSR had seemed a permanent and unassailable fact of international life, but within a year this gigantic state had simply disappeared, swept away by waves of political and popular dissent, yielding its place to an imprecisely defined confederation called the COMMONWEALTH OF INDEPENDENT STATES.

Though his time in power ended in failure and the disappearance of the state over which he had presided, Mikhail Gorbachev had faced problems not dealt with by previous Soviet leaders. His constructive diplomacy and promotion of freedom in his own country and in the former Soviet satellites won him lasting admiration around the world.

Gottwald, Klement (1896–1953)   Pioneer member of the Czech Communist Party in the early 1920s who became a member of its Central Committee in 1925 and secretary of the Comintern in 1935. Gottwald spent the World War II years in Moscow, having fled Czechoslovakia after the Munich Conference in 1938; returning in 1945, he became deputy premier in the government of President Eduard BENEŠ, then, in 1946, premier. At the same time, and more significantly, he became head of the Czech Communist Party. In the autumn of 1947, when he saw indications that Communist political strength was declining, Gottwald with a group of associates began planning a coup d'état, which took place in February 1948. Gottwald's success apparently came in part from the tendency of his opponents to underestimate him because of his alcoholism. He assumed the presidency of the country in June 1948 and in 1949, following orders from the Kremlin, instituted a STALIN-oriented regime that acted with marked harshness even by the Eastern European standards of the time. In 1951, as part of the purges favored by Stalin during his last years, Gottwald's government arrested a number of leading officials, including the Communist general secretary, Rudolf SLANSKY; executions followed in 1952. Stalin's wishes had been met, and Gottwald at the same time had disposed of a rival Communist faction.

Government Communications Headquarters (GCHQ)   British signal-intelligence headquarters, located in two groups of buildings in Cheltenham, Gloucestershire. These complexes are the successors to the famous mansion and huts of Bletchley Park, where during World War II Allied cryptological teams carried on the work later known to the world as the Ultra secret. Wartime signal-intelligence cooperation between the United

States and Britain reached a level unprecedented in relations between allies, and since 1947 GCHQ has been linked with its counterparts in the United States and the former British dominions of Canada, Australia, and New Zealand in a cryptological consortium, with standardized terminology and procedures.

In 1982 the breaking of the PRIME CASE, in which a former GCHQ employee was revealed as a KGB agent, caused an uproar concerning security procedures at Cheltenham. Alex Lawrie, a member of Parliament who earlier had worked at GCHQ, called security "lax and fossilized"; espionage there, he said, was "child's play." Americans assigned to Cheltenham agreed. One even said that packages containing secret material were often delivered by cabdrivers who had picked them up at the town railroad station. As the result of the whole affair, though the British do not discuss such matters, security procedures presumably were tightened.

Great Leap Forward   A large-scale effort (1958–61) by MAO ZEDONG to increase industrial production in China not by conventional means but through the decentralization of production and the radical collectivization of peasants into large "people's communes." Mao took the decentralization idea so far as to encourage the creation of "backyard" steel furnaces. Revolutionary zeal, real or imposed, proved to be an ineffective substitute for manufacturing expertise and production standards. Nevertheless, the Chinese Communist Party published glowing reports exaggerating the success of the program and covering up the actual results of this dislocation of workers and resources, which included massive famine.

Grechko, Andrei Antonovich (1903–1976)   Soviet marshal with a cavalry and then armored-force background who became commander in chief of occupation forces in Germany in 1953, just in time to have a leading hand in the suppression of the EAST BERLIN UPRISING in June. In 1957 he returned to the USSR as commander in chief of ground forces and first deputy minister of defense; three years later he was promoted to the overall command of WARSAW PACT forces.

During World War II Grechko had developed a

close friendship with a Red Army political commissar, Major General Leonid BREZHNEV, who for
a time served under him. Their close relationship
continued 20 years later, with Grechko providing
testimonials concerning Brezhnev's supposed wartime exploits when the secretary, in time-honored
political fashion, began to create his own military
legend—something of an innovation for political
commissars, like Brezhnev, who normally were
looked on by their comrades more as jackals than
as lions. In 1967 Brezhnev, now in command in
the USSR, chose his friend Grechko, a traditional
hard-bitten and hard-line soldier, for the top rung
of the Soviet military ladder—minister of defense.
Hence Grechko was in charge during the two-
phase 1968 PRAGUE SPRING crisis in Czechoslovakia, when Warsaw Pact forces throttled the reform
movement led by Alexander DUBČEK; at one point,
Grechko threatened to occupy all sizable Czech
cities.

In 1973 Brezhnev, strengthening his hand for his
dealings with the Western powers, secured the appointment of his good friend Grechko to the POLIT-
BURO. The marshal, though not in actuality a great
believer in DÉTENTE, thus became the first defense
minister to serve in the Politburo since First Secretary Nikita KHRUSHCHEV fired Marshal Georgi
ZHUKOV in 1957. He retired from the Ministry of
Defense in 1976.

Grenada   This small Caribbean island some 100
miles north of Trinidad became the stage of Cold
War action on October 25, 1983, when 1,900 U.S.
Marines arrived, officially to safeguard the lives of
American medical students; also, the governments
of neighboring islands were said to have asked for
U.S. intervention. The action followed a coup in
which Grenada's military had overthrown Prime
Minister Maurice Bishop, a self-declared Marxist-
Leninist who had allowed the Cuban government
to assist in the building of an airfield on the island
and had received Soviet aid. U.S. intelligence sus-
pected, however, that the new leader, General
Hudson Austin, was more of a Communist than
Bishop had been (and if CENTRAL INTELLIGENCE
AGENCY analysts had read the general's outgoing
correspondence they would have known that during the previous year he had thanked Soviet general secretary Yuri ANDROPOV for "the tremendous

assistance which our armed forces have received
from your Party and Government"). Believing the
action necessary to preempt a Cuban attempt to
take over the island, the REAGAN administration
sent in the marines. Whether or not CASTRO's Cuba
had any immediate designs on Grenada continued
to be a matter of debate. The marines left in December, and, in a general election, Herbert Blaize
was elected president. The United States gave the
new administration heavy financial support.

Gromyko, Andrei Andreyevich (1909–1989)   Veteran Soviet diplomat and politician who not only
served the USSR as foreign minister far longer than
any other person but during his 28-year tenure,
from 1957 to 1985, became one of the longest-
serving foreign ministers of any country in modern
times. Through the years it became increasingly
clear that a truly candid memoir by Gromyko
would be one of the most valuable books of the
20th century.

A native of what is now Belarus, Gromyko came
from a peasant family and, after studying in institutes of economics and agronomy, entered the diplomatic service just about the time Maxim
Litvinov was giving way to V. M. MOLOTOV, who
was far more suitable as foreign commissar to conduct the 1939 negotiations with Germany. Having
caught Molotov's eye, Gromyko went to Washington as counselor of the embassy; in 1943, at quite
a young age, he became ambassador. In 1946 he
moved from Washington to New York as permanent representative of the USSR to the UNITED NA-
TIONS, a post he held until 1949, when he was
recalled to Moscow to become deputy minister of
foreign affairs. Then, in 1952, apparently out of
favor with General Secretary Joseph STALIN (as was
Molotov), he went to Britain as ambassador (not
by any means an unimportant assignment) but returned to the Foreign Ministry shortly after Stalin's death in March 1953.

In June 1957, when the ANTIPARTY GROUP, as it
was called, made its unsuccessful attempt to overthrow Nikita KHRUSHCHEV, Molotov, as one of the
group, was dismissed from the Foreign Ministry
(and, rather than undergoing disgrace, was dispatched to Outer Mongolia as ambassador). Gromyko became his successor, apparently not
suffering any guilt by association in Khrushchev's

Soviet foreign minister Andrei Gromyko *(l.)* talks with U.S. president Lyndon B. Johnson.

eyes. Khrushchev, indeed, developed high respect for Gromyko's professionalism; Khrushchev's son Sergei later described the new foreign minister as "a meticulous man, sensitive to the slightest nuances in international relations." Not nearly so sensitive himself, Khrushchev involved his foreign minister in a markedly unprofessional display at the United Nations in September 1960, when, to make a point, the Soviet premier banged on the table with both fists, then looked at Gromyko as if ordering him to follow suit—which Gromyko did. Another time, Khrushchev took off a shoe and whacked the table with it; Gromyko managed to keep his own shoes on.

Although not heavily identified with specific initiatives or policies, Gromyko reigned in the Foreign Ministry through the BREZHNEV era (being seated in the Politburo in 1973) and the succeeding short spans of ANDROPOV and CHERNENKO and, de-

spite his established conservatism, welcomed and supported the rise of Mikhail GORBACHEV, for whom he made a ringing nominating speech before the CENTRAL COMMITTEE following Chernenko's death. "Mikhail Sergeyevich," said Gromyko, was "a man of strong convictions," of "broad erudition, both by education and from his experience at work." During the general secretaryship of Chernenko, Gromyko said, Gorbachev had served ably as the number-two official of the COMMUNIST PARTY OF THE SOVIET UNION and had been "brilliant" when required to take over in Chernenko's absence. Since Gorbachev's election was by no means assured in advance, Gromyko's advocacy played an important part in his victory. But later that year Gorbachev saw to Gromyko's election as chairman of the Presidium of the Supreme Soviet—Soviet president—a post conferring status but not power on its possessor. Nor did Gromyko's effective political support win him immunity from criticism; a 1988 party document declared that in the past Soviet foreign policy had been marked by excessive "dogmatism" and "subjectivism." Gromyko retired from the Soviet presidency in 1988, when Gorbachev took the position for himself.

When Gromyko's volume of memoirs did appear, shortly before his death, it did not contain the hoped-for information and insights. Though he had supported the election of Gorbachev, the old statesman could not apply GLASNOST to his own experience.

Gromyko Plan During the early summer of 1946 the U.S.-Soviet rivalry found expression in two widely differing proposals for the international control of nuclear energy. On June 15 Bernard Baruch, the U.S. representative, presented to the UNITED NATIONS Atomic Energy Commission what became known as the BARUCH PLAN. Rejecting this proposal, which included among its features a key provision for international inspection of Soviet facilities, the Soviet representative, Andrei GROMYKO, countered four days later with a proposal calling for the destruction of all existing nuclear weapons; only after this had been accomplished would a system of control be established. Since the United States was at the time the world's only nuclear power (though not yet as much of one as was often believed), the Gromyko Plan, not unnaturally, found little favor with U.S. negotiators. In fact, so great a mistrust reigned between the two powers that no potentially workable plan could have been imagined; certainly it is difficult to conceive of any possible circumstances at that time in which the Americans would have surrendered their nuclear monopoly, particularly since the United States had hastened to dismantle the great bulk of its conventional military forces after the end of World War II.

Grósz, Károly (1930–) Hungarian Socialist Workers' (Communist) Party official and prime minister. A printer in his teenage years just after World War II, Grósz joined the Socialist Workers' Party in 1945 and went on to a career in propaganda as a regional director, a magazine editor, and a radio/TV official. He served as head of the

Agitation and Propaganda Committee of the party (1974–79) and was made a member of the Politburo in 1985. A major change came to Hungarian politics in 1988 when a party conference forced the resignation of the veteran general secretary, János KÁDÁR, who was replaced by a four-member Presidium, with Grósz named general secretary in charge of party operations.

Though considered a hard worker, Grósz was essentially a docile party bureaucrat characterized by one observer as a "colorless APPARATCHIK"—an interesting point when one realizes that Britain's Prime Minister Margaret THATCHER professed admiration for him (her favorable appraisal of Mikhail GORBACHEV was to prove rather more insightful). As general secretary, Grósz made some attempt to respond to demands for democratic pluralism, but his appointment proved inadequate to the revolutionary situation. In 1989 he was replaced by a figure less associated with conservative Communism, and the party itself dropped "Workers'" from its name, leaving it simply the Hungarian Socialist Party. Grósz refused to accept the change, with its concomitant rejection of Bolshevik principles, and took the lead of a minority right-of-center faction.

Grotewohl, Otto (1894–1964) First premier of the GERMAN DEMOCRATIC REPUBLIC (East Germany), taking office in 1949, Grotewohl retained the title during the last four years of his life, though actually not exercising the duties of the office, following a stroke suffered in 1960. A Social Democrat during his earlier political life, Grotewohl, unlike many of his fellows, neither fled Germany during the Hitler years nor spent time in prison; instead, he succeeded in keeping a safely low profile.

In 1946, as chairman of the Social Democratic Party in the Soviet zone of Germany, Grotewohl played a leading part in the merger of his party with the Communists to create the Socialist Unity Party—a move resented by many of his former comrades, since the Social Democrats greatly outnumbered the Communists and the latter were little trusted by the others. Social Democrats criticized Grotewohl as a turncoat who had sold out to the Communists not for power—which remained in Soviet hands—but simply for a handsome house in East Berlin. During Grotewohl's time as premier, the actual leader of the East German state was the general secretary of the Socialist Unity Party, Walter ULBRICHT.

When the EAST BERLIN UPRISING broke out in June 1953, Grotewohl at first declared that "fascist bandits and Western provocative elements" had touched off the explosion. During the following week, however, he was forced to concede that serious food shortages and other economic problems had supplied the fuse. The uprising provided dramatic evidence of the unpopularity of the East German regime.

A mild-mannered, bespectacled figure, Grotewohl was often likened to a professor in contrast to his Communist associates, many of whom were heartier figures who had risen to high places through rough-and-tumble politics.

Groza, Petru (1884–1958)   During World War II, Romania, controlled by a semi-Fascist dictator, Field Marshal Ion Antonescu, fought as an ally of Germany, but in August 1944 the country's young king, Michael, staged a coup against the dictator, removing him from power and turning the country into an ally of the Soviet Union. Nevertheless, on February 27, 1945, acting under the orders of Soviet foreign minister Andrei VYSHINSKY, a Soviet armored unit surrounded the royal palace. Banging on the king's desk, Vyshinsky demanded that he dismiss his premier and replace him with Dr. Petru Groza, who was said to be the leader of a political party called the Plowmen's Front and was, as one historian put it, "a willing instrument of the minute [Romanian] Communist Party." After holding out against Soviet force for a week, the king gave in.

A veteran politician, born in Transylvania, Groza took the lead in 1918 in transferring his native province from the collapsing Austro-Hungarian Empire to Romania; during the 1920s and 1930s he served in various cabinets. By giving Groza's government a face-lift through the addition of two non-Communist ministers, the Soviets succeeded in winning its recognition by the United States and Britain in February 1946. Combining the SALAMI TACTICS advocated by the Hungarian Communist leader, Mátyás RÁKOSI, with the rigging of a major election, Groza and his colleagues succeeded, by July 1947, in bringing about the dis-

solution of all opposition parties. The king finally abdicated on December 30, 1947. Groza served as premier until June 1952, when he was elected chairman of the Presidium of the National Assembly; he was reelected in March 1957.

GRU (Glavnoe Razvedyvatelnoe Upravlenie)   The Soviet military intelligence agency—in English, the Chief Intelligence Directorate of the General Staff (*razvedka* was the overall term for intelligence activities). Operating throughout the world, the GRU carried on strategic and technical espionage, with special attention given to obtaining industrial secrets; Soviet military attachés played key roles in its activities. These officers provided money, cipher equipment, and all the other impedimenta of espionage to GRU resident directors. In the field of signal intelligence, the GRU from the 1960s through the 1980s did much of the kind of work that in the United States was the responsibility of the NATIONAL SECURITY AGENCY. Among the most notable activities of the GRU that have come to light were the creation of the World War II nuclear spy ring in Canada in which Alan Nunn MAY played an important part, and the establishment in Japan of the German-Soviet double agent Richard Sorge, whose information about Japanese intentions proved of vital importance to the Soviet General Staff in the defense of Moscow in 1941. *See also* KGB.

Gruenther, Alfred Maximilian (1899–1983)   U.S. general who went from an outstanding career as a staff officer to become supreme Allied commander in Europe (1953–56). A native of Nebraska, Gruenther graduated from West Point in 1917 and later taught there for eight years. During World War II he served as deputy chief of staff at General EISENHOWER's Allied Force Headquarters, as chief of staff of the U.S. Fifth Army, and as chief of staff of the 15th Army Group. His work was especially admired by Eisenhower, whose chief of staff he became in Europe in 1951. Gruenther also had a considerable reputation as a bridge player and wrote a book on the subject.

Guevara de la Serna, Ernesto (1928–1967)   International revolutionist, known as Che Guevara. A native of Argentina who became one of Fidel CAS-

TRO's closest advisers, Guevara for a time served the Cuban government as minister of industries. A lean and in some eyes romantic figure, Guevara, who traveled the world looking to aid or incite revolution, exerted a kind of mystical appeal on members of the New Left in the United States and Europe. Last seen in public in Cuba in 1965, he reappeared the following year in Bolivia as leader of a guerrilla band. He was killed in a firefight between his force and a unit of the Bolivian army.

gulag   Official Soviet acronym for Glavnoye Upravlenye Lagerei (in English, Chief Administration of Camps; usually rendered, however, as Chief Administration of Corrective Labor Camps, since GULAG is an abbreviation of GUITLTP, the acronym for the full name). The term *gulag* became widely known in the West in the early 1970s from Alexander SOLZHENITSYN's epic account, *The Gulag Archipelago*, which presented the gulag as a microcosm of Soviet society. Solzhenitsyn gave a detailed picture of interrogation by torture, with prisoners having their skulls squeezed by iron rings, being immersed in acid baths, having heated ramrods shoved up their rectums, having their testicles crushed by jackboots. The luckiest prisoners, said Solzhenitsyn, were those who were merely "tortured by being kept from sleeping for a week, by thirst, and by being beaten to a bloody pulp."

Though the gulag had existed under Lavrenty BERIA's predecessors in the Commissariat for Internal Affairs—and in fact had grown to great size to make room for the millions of victims of the agriculture-collectivization campaign of the late 1920s and early 1930s and of the Great Purge of 1936–38—Beria gave it a thorough reorganization. He attended to its smallest details, such as the size of individual barracks and the amount of salt and margarine a prisoner ought to be given while in transit from jail to prison camp, and broadened its scope, making it not only a system of detention and punishment but an economically productive enterprise yielding timber, coal, and metals and supplying work gangs for railroads and highways. Some of the statistics produced by the gulag literally defy belief. For the 1935–40 period, a KGB report showed that some 19 million people were imprisoned overall, of whom at least 7 million were shot or died otherwise.

Gulf of Tonkin Resolution   On August 2, 1964, while engaged in secret electronic surveillance of North Vietnamese radar, the U.S. destroyer *Maddox* was attacked by three North Vietnamese patrol boats. Whether or not the *Maddox* was in international waters at the time was a murky question, partly because the United States and North Vietnam probably employed different definitions of territorial waters. Wishing neither to appear impetuous nor to reveal the purpose of the destroyer's mission (a form of surveillance unacknowledged but routinely practiced by both sides in the Cold War), U.S. president JOHNSON reacted calmly. "We concluded," the president said later, "that an over-eager North Vietnamese boat commander might have been at fault or that a shore station had miscalculated. So we decided against retaliation."

Two days later, in the dark hours of August 4—this time some 60 miles off the coast—the *Maddox* and an accompanying destroyer, the *C. Turner Joy*, became involved in a shooting incident with radar blips that may or may not have represented North Vietnamese boats. Partly influenced by the pressures of the presidential campaign, Johnson and Secretary of Defense Robert MCNAMARA reacted strongly to this supposed second attack, even though the captain of the *Maddox* reported his doubts about the incident. The United States retaliated with air strikes against North Vietnamese torpedo-boat bases and oil storage tanks. The president's request for authority to "repel any armed attacks against the forces of the United States" won quick approval from Congress; the measure was passed unanimously by the House of Representatives and with only two dissenting votes —Ernest Gruening (Democrat—Alaska) and Wayne Morse (ex-Republican, Democrat—Oregon)—in the Senate. This Gulf of Tonkin Resolution came to be used as the U.S. legislative basis for the VIETNAM WAR.

Guomindang (Kuomintang)   Political organization (in English, National People's Party) that controlled most of China from 1928 until 1949, when it was defeated by the Communists led by MAO ZEDONG and driven offshore to TAIWAN. Formed in 1912 from a number of small revolutionary groups, the party professed an ideology that in principle resembled Western political centrism; the "Three People's Principles"—nationalism, democracy, and people's livelihood—formed its basic tenets. As time passed, however, the constant battles in civil wars and then against the invading Japanese caused the party to take on a more nationalistic and authoritarian cast. It also emphasized traditional Chinese culture, unlike the Communists, who viewed it with the contempt they also directed against the bourgeoisie.

In its early years the Guomindang, with important Soviet help, extended its control over most of China. After the death of its founder, Sun Yat-sen, in 1925, CHIANG KAI-SHEK took over the leadership. Though the Communist Party had formed a part of the Guomindang, Chiang broke with it in 1927 and a struggle ensued that ended in 1934–35 in the famous Communist "Long March" to Yanan, in northwestern China.

During World War II the Guomindang's militaristic and nationalistic tendencies became greatly accentuated; Chiang Kai-shek developed into an essentially authoritarian ruler, though many in the United States liked to view him, almost sentimentally, as a great democrat. *See also* CHINA LOBBY.

Haig, Alexander Meigs, Jr. (1924–)   U.S. general who served as the first secretary of state in the REAGAN administration. Previously, as something of a new type of U.S. political general, Haig had moved back and forth between the military and the civilian worlds, having come from active military duty to the White House, where he began his association with National Security Adviser Henry KISSINGER as the latter's military assistant. Haig then went to the NATIONAL SECURITY COUNCIL, returned to regular service as vice chief of staff of the army (having been made a four-star general by President NIXON), and then came back to the civilian realm in the purely political role of chief of the White House staff under Nixon (1973–74); in this position he served as a steady center in the confusion of the WATERGATE AFFAIR. Haig then went to Europe as U.S. and supreme Allied commander (1974–79).

When President Reagan was shot by a would-be assassin in 1981, Secretary of State Haig attracted a great deal of negative comment with his televised statement, intended to be reassuring, that "I am in control here." His time as secretary of state was turbulent. Such Reagan stalwarts as James Baker, the president's chief of staff, and Richard Allen, the security adviser, saw the assertive Haig as eager to extend his power. Haig and Secretary of Defense Caspar WEINBERGER collided over Haig's desire to use force against Cuban ships ferrying supplies from Fidel CASTRO to the Nicaraguan SANDINISTAS. Finding himself in continuing disagreement with various administration policies, Haig resigned in June 1982. He had one more political aim, however, and for a time he made some gestures toward the 1988 Republican presidential nomination.

Born in Philadelphia, Haig graduated from the

General Alexander M. Haig, Jr., NATO commander, later U.S. secretary of state

U.S. Military Academy in 1947 and later acquired a master's degree from Georgetown University.

Hallstein Doctrine   Principle originally enunciated in September 1955 by Chancellor Konrad ADENAUER of West Germany and made official policy on December 9, 1955, whereby his country would break diplomatic relations with any country that granted recognition to East Germany and would refuse to maintain diplomatic relations with any Communist country except the Soviet Union. (Declaring that relations with the USSR were "not to be put on a level with a friendly treaty relationship," the chancellor reluctantly saw them as a practical necessity.) The policy became identified with Walter Hallstein (1901–1982), state secretary (senior permanent official) in the Foreign Ministry. The doctrine came into application several times, in relation to Syria, Yugoslavia, Cuba, Cambodia, and South Yemen. Some 14 years after its adoption, however, Chancellor Willy BRANDT abandoned the Hallstein Doctrine in favor of a new, conciliatory policy called OSTPOLITIK (May 1969).

Hammarskjöld, Dag (1905–1961)   Second secretary-general of the UNITED NATIONS—elected to succeed Trygve LIE on April 7, 1953, and reelected on September 26, 1957—Dag Hammarskjöld died in an air crash on September 18, 1961, while on a mission to negotiate a cease-fire in the Congo between UN forces and those of the rebel province of Katanga. A model of the contemporary civilized man, with an added touch of the mystic, Hammarskjöld was a student of literature, a writer *(Markings,* his posthumously published book of philosophical and personal meditations, won wide acclaim), and the translator into Swedish of the works of the French poet Saint-John Perse.

The son of a former Swedish prime minister, Hammarskjöld studied law and economics and for a number of years held nonpartisan posts in the national government, the last one being the chairmanship of the Swedish delegation to the UN General Assembly in 1952.

In many ways Hammarskjöld seemed ideally trained to become the world's chief international civil servant. This background, however, by no means led him to take a passive view of his duties

Dag Hammarskjöld, second United Nations secretary-general

as UN secretary-general. He proved to be an activist with great diplomatic talents and, pioneering in the use of UN emergency forces, took the lead in settling a variety of crises (notably the SUEZ CRISIS of 1956). His activity yielded successes and also—perhaps in confirmation of his fair-mindedness—brought attacks on him at different times from both East and West. His activism particularly perturbed Soviet premier Nikita KHRUSHCHEV, who proposed to replace him with a three-person team representing the Communist countries, the West, and the nonaligned nations. (In calling for such a *troika,* Khrushchev gave worldwide popularity to this previously little-known Russian word.) Rebuffing Khrushchev's proposal, Hammarskjöld refused to resign. UN mediation efforts in the Congo had brought particular conflict with the Soviets, who had begun to intervene directly in support of Prime Minister Patrice LUMUMBA, contrary to UN policy. It was after the presumed murder of Lumumba by the Katangans that the USSR announced it could not continue to recognize Hammarskjöld as secretary-general, but this declaration attracted little support.

After his death Hammarskjöld was awarded the Nobel Peace Prize for 1961. He was succeeded as UN secretary-general by U THANT of Burma.

Harrier A British "jump jet" (technically, V/STOL, or vertical short takeoff and landing) aircraft made by Hawker Siddeley (later British Aerospace); during its early developmental days it was nicknamed the Flying Bedstead. This single-engine reconnaissance and attack plane, which entered service with the Royal Air Force in 1966, flew slightly below Mach 1. Though extremely versatile and quite impressive to watch, the Harrier suffered from marked vulnerability to ground fire. Nevertheless, coming of age in Britain's Falklands war with Argentina in 1982, the Harrier in its Sea Harrier version made believers of those who had previously doubted its value.

Harriman, W(illiam) Averell (1891–1986) U.S. businessman, the son of the 19th-century financial and railroad tycoon E. H. Harriman, who enjoyed success in a variety of his own ventures and then, beginning during the New Deal, became an outstanding public servant and one of the leading U.S. diplomatic figures of the century

A graduate of Yale (1913), Harriman went to work for his late father's Union Pacific Railroad, becoming vice president in 1915. Later he founded the Wall Street brokerage firm that became Brown Brothers, Harriman & Company. He also engaged in complex and ultimately unprofitable mining deals in the Soviet Union, and in the 1930s he founded the Sun Valley resort and thus helped to create new groups of passengers for his railroad (of which he was chairman from 1932 to 1946) and to popularize the sport of skiing. A sportsman, Harriman also developed into one of the world's top polo players.

After holding positions as a businessman-Democrat in the New Deal during the 1930s, Harriman went to London in 1941 as expediter of Lend-Lease aid to Britain. He accompanied the close and confidential friendship he developed with Winston CHURCHILL by an equally close if different (and audacious) relationship with Churchill's daughter-in-law Pamela, who years later, in 1971, would become the third Mrs. Averell Harriman.

During 1941 and 1942 Harriman made trips to the USSR on Lend-Lease matters, where his former dealings with the Communist regime and his credentials as a front-rank capitalist stood him in useful stead. In 1943 President ROOSEVELT appointed him ambassador to the Soviet Union. In this post Harriman, though not hostile to the regime, proved to be a clear-eyed and cool diplomat, developing as effective a relationship with Premier Joseph STALIN as was possible, and as the war moved toward its conclusion, Harriman with his chief associate, George KENNAN, took a realistic view of Stalin's claims and intentions.

In 1946 Harriman served for six months as President TRUMAN's ambassador to Britain before receiving a stateside appointment as secretary of commerce. Back in Europe again in 1948, he coordinated the European recovery program (and in 1949 came close to being appointed secretary of state, losing out to Dean ACHESON). Next he worked directly for the president as a special assistant and from 1951 to 1953 was director of the Mutual Security Agency. In 1954, in a new departure, Harriman ran for and won the governorship of New York. Taking delight in calling himself "the guv," he proved to be an able political executive, though he lost his 1958 reelection campaign to Nelson Rockefeller.

Considered by many observers too old and too hard of hearing to fit into the youth-oriented KENNEDY administration, Harriman in 1961 willingly took the relatively minor post of assistant secretary of state for Far Eastern affairs and, as usual, demonstrated his skill, judgment, and patience in an important assignment—in this case, negotiating the neutralization of Laos; then, having become undersecretary for political affairs, he went to Moscow to negotiate the NUCLEAR TEST BAN TREATY. In 1968 President JOHNSON dispatched him to Paris as head of the U.S. delegation to the peace talks with North Vietnam. Harriman retired in 1969, though he still made his thoughts on international affairs available to the government of the day. George Kennan said of him, "The United States has never had a more faithful public servant."

Havel, Václav (1936–) Czechoslovak absurdist playwright and longtime democratic activist who as a result of the VELVET REVOLUTION of 1989 became the country's first non-Communist president since 1948.

Like many other writers everywhere, Havel in his youth had to hold various jobs unrelated to his literary interests, but in his case work as a laboratory technician and a taxi driver was necessary because his bourgeois background (his family was well off) kept him out of schooling reserved for members of the proletariat. He took evening classes at a gymnasium, studied business at the technical university in Prague, and in 1967 completed a course in stagecraft at a theatrical academy, where he not only learned professional techniques but wrote plays that did not please the authorities. During the same year he gave a strong indication of the future course of his career by attacking government censorship at a writers' conference, and in 1968 he became chairman of the Independent Writers' Union.

Heavily involved in the human-rights movement called CHARTER 77, Havel spent most of the first five months of 1977 in prison; the working class, Havel's interrogators ("various majors and colonels") absurdly told him, was "boiling with ha-

Averell Harriman, U.S. ambassador, governor, and diplomatic troubleshooter

tred" toward him. But it was true, the writer said in a 1993 speech, that some of his friends would avoid him on the street, because in talking with him "they would feel compelled to apologize for not openly defying the regime too." Havel was under arrest again for several months (1978–79) and then imprisoned as a subversive from May 1979 until February 1983. With his writings banned throughout the EASTERN BLOC, he and a colleague founded a SAMIZDAT publication called *Lidove Noviny,* the name taken from that of a famous Czech newspaper that had ceased publication in 1952. In 1975 Havel had written *Open Letter to Gustav HUSÁK,* in which he told the hard-line Czech president that the regime could not repress the people forever and there would come "the moment when something once more visibly begins to

President Václav Havel of Czechoslovakia, the central figure in the Velvet Revolution

happen." He bore consistent witness for his own creed, which held that "the intellectual should be provocative by being independent, should rebel against all hidden and open pressure and manipulations, should be the chief doubter of systems, of power and its incantations, should be a witness to their mendacity." Among his heroes, Havel said years later, figured the avant-garde rock musician Frank Zappa (who died in 1993); Zappa, Havel declared, was "one of the gods of the Czech underground during the 1970s and '80s."

At the beginning of 1989, the *annus mirabilis* in Eastern and Central Europe, the authorities arrested Havel during an outbreak of turbulence marked by demonstrations commemorating the death 20 years earlier of a student who had set himself on fire to protest the Soviet invasion. In New York members of the arts community pro-

tested the detention of Havel, whose wife declared with considerable prescience that the situation in 1989 differed from the circumstances of previous years because, in the wake of changes in the Soviet Union, the Czech government could no longer resist moves toward liberalization. The government did not concede the point, however, and instead, on February 21, sentenced Havel to nine months in prison for inciting illegal protests; the sentence aroused criticism across Europe. Released after serving just four months, Havel declared that he would speak out regardless of any danger of re-arrest.

In November, Havel took the lead in forming a democratic opposition coalition called CIVIC FORUM, and at the end of the year, in a development that in January would have seemed, appropriately, the climax of an absurdist fantasy, Parliament chose him as president of Czechoslovakia. In 1990 Havel won popular election to the office. "There have been few figures in European history quite like this man," the U.S. historian Gale Stokes said of Havel, "a writer by birth, a philosopher by inclination, a playwright by profession, and a moralist by conviction."

H-bomb   *See* HYDROGEN BOMB.

Healey, Denis Winston (1917–)   British Labour Party politician who served as minister of defense (1964–70) and chancellor of the exchequer (1974–79). A graduate of Balliol College, Oxford, Healey became secretary of the party's international department in 1945 and two years later drew the assignment of framing a report to define the approach the party should take to Europe and specifically to involvement in the MARSHALL PLAN. It was a particular challenge, Healey commented later, because many Labourites "found it very difficult to accept that the Soviet Union was as hostile to Britain as a social democratic country, as, in fact, she was"; to describe how the Soviets were "destroying the Socialist parties" in Eastern Europe, Healey produced a pamphlet called *The Curtain Falls*.

Healey entered the House of Commons in 1952, serving also as a British delegate to the Consultative Assembly of the COUNCIL OF EUROPE. He worked with the party leader, Hugh Gaitskell, to develop a proposed policy of British "disengagement" in Europe, which was presented in 1958. Commenting later on the British refusal in the 1950s to take part in the EUROPEAN COAL AND STEEL COMMUNITY, Healey said that the Labourites felt a federal structure involving Britain with conservative Christian Democrats on the Continent would interfere with the pursuit of Socialist goals in Britain. A member of the right wing of the Labour Party, Healey supported James CALLAGHAN in his losing contest with Harold WILSON for leadership of the party after Gaitskell's death in 1963. As minister of defense, Healey, like his counterpart Robert MCNAMARA in the United States, devoted great attention to cutting costs. After the Labour Party's defeat by Margaret THATCHER in 1979, Healey served as deputy leader of the party (1980–83).

Heath, Edward Richard George (1916–) British Conservative statesman, prime minister from 1970 to 1974.

As a student at Oxford, Heath took an extremely active part in both university and national politics, serving as president of Oxford's Conservative Association, president of the Oxford Union, and chairman of an association of Conservative groups. He won a seat in Parliament in the February 1950 election, though his party failed in its bid to turn the ATTLEE Labour government out of office. Heath began his parliamentary career with a striking speech in which he advocated that Britain renounce its insularity and take a major part in the fledgling SCHUMAN PLAN—the EUROPEAN COAL AND STEEL COMMUNITY.

In 1959 Heath entered Harold MACMILLAN's administration as minister of labor; the next year he became lord privy seal, a device to enable him to take part in foreign-policy matters. In this position, as the advocate of a "European" approach for Britain, he had charge of negotiations for British participation in the EUROPEAN ECONOMIC COMMUNITY (the Common Market); his efforts failed because they met the intransigent opposition of France's President Charles DE GAULLE.

In 1964 the Conservatives lost the general election to Harold WILSON's Labourites, and during the following year, when Sir Alec DOUGLAS-HOME resigned the party leadership, Heath became his suc-

Prime Minister Edward Heath of Great Britain

cessor. Losing the 1966 election, the party spent four more years in opposition before winning in 1970. Now, as prime minister, with de Gaulle gone from the scene, Heath succeeded in taking Britain into the Common Market. His time in office saw few other successes, however. The "troubles" in Northern Ireland, which had exploded into open violence in 1968, grew steadily worse, and the prime minister responded to rising inflation by imposing, contrary to Conservative doctrine, a series of price controls, which proved unpopular with the unions as well. He clashed head-on with the great bugbear of 1970s prime ministers, the miners' union, which staged a strike that threatened to bring economic chaos. In February 1974, seeking stronger public support, Heath called a general election, which resulted in neither party's winning a clear claim to power. Unable to build a coalition that could command majority support, however, Heath resigned; Wilson returned to office as his successor. Heath had no better luck in a second 1974 election, and in the following year he lost the party leadership to Margaret THATCHER.

Like other West European leaders, Heath looked with misgivings on U.S. involvement in the VIETNAM WAR, primarily because American failure might well make the country less able and willing to support its allies in Europe. In addition, President NIXON's security adviser, Henry KISSINGER, commented, leaders like Heath "traced some of the political unrest in their own countries to contagion from American universities and intellectual circles." However, Kissinger said, Heath and other leaders meeting Nixon early in his presidency registered no objections to the war.

Helsinki Final Act   On August 1, 1975, at the Conference on Security and Cooperation in Europe, 35 countries—including most of the major Western powers and the Soviet Union—agreed to accept the postwar Eastern European national boundaries as permanent (thus producing a kind of peace treaty to end World War II) and to respect and protect the human rights of citizens in this region. The agreement, which the Soviets had long sought and which followed a series of meetings that had begun in November 1972, seemed to many Western critics to legitimize Eastern European boundaries in exchange for nothing more than symbolic Soviet promises in the area of human rights; the accords contained no provision for any mechanism of enforcement. But in the following years history produced a surprise. Instead of confirming Soviet hegemony in Eastern Europe, as General Secretary Leonid BREZHNEV had expected, the Helsinki accords gave rise to "Helsinki watch" groups monitoring human rights, producing documents such as the Czech CHARTER 77 and leading at length to the creation of SOLIDARITY in Poland. Thus, while ending World War II, particularly by establishing the boundaries of Germany, the Helsinki accords could be said to have begun the dismantling of the Soviet empire in Eastern Europe.

Herter, Christian Archibald (1895–1966)   This Massachusetts political figure, editor, and former diplomat succeeded John Foster DULLES as secre-

tary of state in April 1959; previously, since 1957, he had served as undersecretary. Born in Paris of American parents, Herter graduated from Harvard in 1915; entering the Foreign Service, he saw duty at the Berlin embassy as an attaché in the midst of World War I and was secretary of the U.S. delegation to the Versailles conference. Later he worked for five years as assistant to Herbert Hoover before and during Hoover's service as secretary of commerce.

Herter went to Washington as a member of Congress in 1943, serving until 1953, when he took office as governor of Massachusetts. At the end of his gubernatorial term, he returned to the capital as undersecretary of state. Herter served at considerable personal sacrifice, since he was painfully crippled by arthritis. Probably the most memorable occurrence during his tenure as secretary of state was the shooting down of a U-2 reconnaissance aircraft over the Soviet Union, with the consequent refusal by President EISENHOWER to disguise the actual nature of the mission and Herter's declaration that the U-2s would continue their flights. This sequence of events led to Soviet premier KHRUSHCHEV's withdrawal from a summit conference in Paris.

Heuss, Theodor (1884–1963)   One of the founders of the German Free Democratic Party (originally called the Liberal Democratic Party), Theodor Heuss participated in the drafting of the constitution of the FEDERAL REPUBLIC OF GERMANY and served as the country's first president (1949–59). A historian and economist, Heuss wrote more than 40 books.

Hiss, Alger (1904–)   In 1948 a journalist named Whittaker CHAMBERS caused a sensation when he told the U.S. House of Representatives' Un-American Activities Committee that Alger Hiss, a former State Department official who had become a respected member of the establishment as president of the Carnegie Endowment for International Peace, had passed confidential department documents to him in the 1930s, when the two were fellow members of a Communist cell in Washington.

A native of Baltimore and graduate of Johns Hopkins University (1926) and the Harvard Law

School (1929), Hiss during his career had acquired important connections and influence. He served as law clerk to the eminent Supreme Court justice Oliver Wendell Holmes and during the ROOSEVELT administration worked in three of the executive departments, coming to State in 1936. As a specialist in international organization, he went to the 1945 YALTA CONFERENCE in the U.S. delegation—a fact Republicans were to make gleeful use of in the 1952 presidential campaign. In the spring of 1945 Hiss served as temporary secretary-general of the UNITED NATIONS during its founding meeting, held in San Francisco.

With this background, the Chambers-Hiss confrontation could hardly fail to stir up a political storm, particularly in view of Chambers's slovenly personal style and the establishment polish that characterized Hiss. Surely, liberals seemed to feel, Chambers was an adventurer, even a psychopath, trying to capitalize on the public's still-new but growing fear of Communism. The young Republican congressman from California, Richard NIXON, who chaired the operative subcommittee and had been unflagging in his investigation of Hiss, seemed to Democrats an opportunist trying to make a name by destroying an outstanding liberal. But thorough investigation made it plain to many observers that, whatever people might think of Chambers and Nixon, only an incredibly complex and detailed conspiracy could have fabricated the evidence Chambers presented; subsequent investigation established Hiss's guilt beyond ordinary reasonable doubt, though he never admitted to it. (The 1992 statement by the director of Russian military-intelligence archives, General Dmitri Volkogonov, that he had found no documentary evidence of Hiss's involvement with Soviet intelligence could not be regarded as definitive.) Charged with perjury (the statute of limitations having expired for the espionage itself), Hiss went through two trials. After the first ended in a hung jury, he was tried again and, on January 22, 1950, found guilty and sentenced to five years in prison (he was to serve three).

Three days later, Secretary of State Dean ACHESON, a former associate of Hiss though not a close friend, responded to a reporter's request for a comment with a gentlemanly—and fateful—statement: "I do not intend to turn my back on Alger Hiss." After hearing the report of these words and seeing the reaction they stirred up, in Congress and outside it, an obscure Republican senator from Wisconsin bided his time for just two weeks and then, on February 9, 1950, declared in a speech at Wheeling, W.Va., that he had a list of 57 or 208—or some number never pinned down—State Department employees who belonged to the Communist Party. The era of Joe MCCARTHY had begun.

Ho Chi Minh (1890–1969) Leading Asian revolutionary and president of the Democratic Republic of Vietnam (North Vietnam) from its founding on September 2, 1945, until his death, which supposedly occurred exactly 24 years later, on September 2, 1969. (Ho probably died in July, but it remains an article of faith in Vietnam that his death took place on the "glorious anniversary of our independence.") The continuing question about Ho has been his real name, since he adopted Ho Chi Minh (Bringer of Light) in 1941, when he was a revolutionary headquartered in the caves of Pac Bo in the northernmost reaches of Vietnam. Often said to have originally been named Nguyen Tat Thanh, he was actually born Nguyen Sinh Cung; he adopted Nguyen Tat Thanh as an alias in 1913, changing it during World War I to Nguyen Ai Quoc (Nguyen the Patriot).

Born in the village of Vinh in north-central Vietnam, Ho received his formal education at the Quoc Hoc School in Hue but spent much of his early life traveling the world. In 1911 he signed on as a galley boy on a French freighter and after two years at sea came to the United States, where he worked as a laborer in Boston, San Francisco, and Brooklyn. Two years later he moved on to London (now calling himself Nguyen Tat Thanh) and obtained work as a dishwasher at the Carlton Hotel, progressing from that menial job to the position of assistant pastry chef. During World War I, having gone to Paris to join fellow Vietnamese, he now patriotically became Nguyen Ai Quoc.

The early 1920s saw Ho in Moscow, where he attended the Fifth Congress of the Communist International, and from there he traveled to Canton, China, where he organized Vietnamese revolutionaries and, in 1929, founded the Indochina Communist Party (ICP) and began recruiting strategists and organizers as well as rank-and-file members.

Throughout the 1930s, in no-holds-barred repressions, the French, who ruled Vietnam as a colony, imprisoned and executed many of Ho's associates. In 1941 he moved his headquarters to Pac Bo, where he gave himself the symbolic name by which he would become known around the world. In Pac Bo he established a new revolutionary organization, the VIETMINH (the name is a contraction of Viet Nam Doc Lap Dong Minh, in English, League for the Independence of Vietnam).

In early 1945 the Americans trained some Vietminh contingents to prepare them to fight the Japanese occupiers in Indochina. Then in August, following the Japanese surrender to the Allies, the Vietminh moved into the power vacuum resulting from this capitulation and from the absence of French officials who during the war had been shot or jailed by the Japanese. But the French, having no intention of quietly disappearing, returned in force in the autumn of 1945 and launched what proved to be a nine-year war against Ho and his Vietminh. This, the first VIETNAM WAR, ended as a result of agreements signed at Geneva in 1954, but Ho then confronted a new chief opponent, the United States, and the South Vietnamese government it supported.

During this long struggle Ho faced the delicate task of dealing with the two great Communist powers, the USSR and China, without seeming to favor one ally over the other, though the Soviets saw him, probably correctly, as preferring Moscow. Like TITO, he was a Communist, but he, too, put his own country first. Though this second war ended in complete victory, Ho did not live to see the outcome. But he had inspired generations of Vietnamese with his dedication and determination —"Nothing," he said, "is more precious than freedom and independence"—and, to soften his image, party propagandists had created the picture of genial "Uncle Ho," who delighted in spending time with children. Taken to see Ho, British reporter Dennis Bloodworth likened him to "one of those electric heaters built to look like a pile of glowing coals—the friendly light is real enough but it has nothing to do with the true nature of the fire." In the West during the later 1960s, Ho's name was probably heard most often in the antiwar chant "Ho, Ho, Ho Chi Minh! NLF is going to win!"

Hodge, John R. (1893–1963) U.S. general, a native of Illinois who served as a divisional and corps commander in the Pacific in World War II and came to Korea in September 1945 as U.S. occupation commander for the southern part of the peninsula, which the United States and the Soviet Union had agreed to divide, for purposes of the occupation, at the 38th parallel. Since the United States had given little thought to the possibility that a Korean occupation might follow the war, the assignment went to Hodge literally because, commanding on Okinawa, he was the general closest to the scene. A military man cast in what is generally considered the standard mold—effective, decisive, direct in speech—Hodge was ill equipped for command in a politically ambiguous situation, with Soviets, Americans, and various Korean groups harboring clashing ideas about the proper future of the country. Nor did he receive enlightened and consistent support from the U.S. commander in the Far East, General MACARTHUR in Tokyo, or from his superiors in Washington.

Though Hodge did his best to build up a small South Korean defense force called the Constabulary—which was all Washington would permit—his task was complicated by his poor relationship with South Korea's President Syngman RHEE, whom he considered unreliable and corrupt. In September 1948, as the United States began to withdraw its occupation force, Hodge led the parade homeward. His time in Korea, he said later, had been the "worst job" he had ever had. He finished his career as chief of army field forces (1952–53).

Hoffman, Paul Gray (1891–1974) American automobile-company executive who came directly from the business world in 1948 to become administrator of the Economic Cooperation Administration, the agency set up to supervise the working of the MARSHALL PLAN. The kind of relationship Hoffman ought to aim for with the varying European governments was defined in a State Department briefing on U.S. policy toward France: "We should support any non-Communist French government by all reasonable means short of direct interference in the internal affairs of the country."

A native of Chicago, Hoffman briefly attended the University of Chicago and then began working as a salesman for the Studebaker Corporation in Los Angeles. By 1935, having seen the company through the Great Depression and bankruptcy, he had risen to its presidency, the position he held at the time the TRUMAN administration asked him to take charge of the Marshall Plan in Europe. Following these duties in public life, Hoffman served as president of the Ford Foundation (1951–53) and spent a number of years working in UNITED NATIONS development activities.

Hollywood Ten   Entertainment-industry notables, all members of the Writers' Guild and the Directors' Guild, who refused to testify before the U.S. House of Representatives' Un-American Activities Committee in October 1947 about Communist Party membership. Tried in 1948 for contempt, each went to federal prison. The Hollywood Ten were Alvah Bessie, Herbert Biberman, Lester Cole, Edward Dmytryk, Ring Lardner, Jr., John Howard Lawson, Albert Maltz, Samuel Ornitz, Adrian Scott, and Dalton Trumbo. *See also* LOYALTY AND SECURITY PROGRAM; NIXON, Richard Milhous.

Holt, Harold (1908–1967)   Australian Liberal Party politician who entered Parliament in 1936 and served in ministerial posts, including seven years as federal treasurer, under Sir Robert Menzies, whom he succeeded as prime minister in January 1966. Expressing strong support for U.S. policy in Vietnam—and thereby stirring up considerable opposition—Holt moved quickly to triple the size of the Australian forces serving in the VIETNAM WAR. On a June 1966 visit to Washington he made the memorable declaration that Australia would go "all the way with LBJ." In the following November he won a substantial victory in a general election, but a little more than a year later (December 16, 1967) he became the central figure in what many observers consider an unsolved mystery. While skin-diving near a reef off the state of Victoria, the prime minister disappeared. The logical—and official—presumption was that he had drowned. But, despite Holt's strong support for U.S. actions in Vietnam, a former Reuters correspondent, Anthony Grey, labeled him a Chinese spy, a long-serving mole, and claimed that, instead of having drowned, he was picked up by a submarine—his escape having been arranged because his

cover was about to be blown. However, no subsequent investigation has supported the assertion. In any case, Holt appears to have been the only democratically chosen head of any modern government to have vanished.

Honecker, Erich (1912–1994)   East German Communist Party leader who ruled the country from 1971 until he was overthrown in the turbulent events of 1989. A member of German Communist youth organizations in the 1920s, Honecker became an official in national youth groups in the 1930s. In 1935, with the Nazis in power, he was arrested and sentenced to ten years' imprisonment; he thus spent all of World War II in a concentration camp. Liberated by Soviet troops in 1945, he resumed his political work (the Communist Party now united with the Socialists to become the Socialist Unity Party) and was elected to the Central Committee in 1946. He won a seat in the East German Parliament in 1950 and became a member of the Politburo in 1958.

In May 1971, during the flowering of West German chancellor Willy BRANDT's OSTPOLITIK, the improving relations between West Germany and the Soviet Union led to the dismissal of General Secretary Walter ULBRICHT, an unreconstructed Stalinist who had held the post since 1950. As his successor (and head of state from 1976), however, Honecker turned into another hard-line dictator of East Germany. In 1980, disturbed at the rise of the SOLIDARITY labor union in Poland, Honecker (presumably remembering the WARSAW PACT invasion of Czechoslovakia) appealed to Soviet president Leonid BREZHNEV to stage an immediate invasion of Poland and choke off these "counterrevolutionary forces." In 1988 he spurned any suggestion that, like the Soviet Union, East Germany might need a dose of PERESTROIKA and GLASNOST. Though he might thus defy Mikhail GORBACHEV, he could not escape the fundamental fact that his regime depended on the support given it by the Soviet Union.

With the end of the Cold War, East Germany lost its raison d'être. The breaching of the BERLIN WALL on November 9 symbolized the end of the era of two Germanys. Honecker fled to Moscow, where he was said to be receiving medical treatment, but later returned to Berlin.

Erich Honecker, East German head of state and party secretary

In 1993 Honecker and two other former senior officials of East Germany were convicted on manslaughter charges for their role in the deaths of refugees killed trying to cross the wall. The trial, however, had something of an anticlimactic quality, since Honecker and the others had been excused from suffering the consequences because of severe health problems. Nor did his conviction seem to produce any regrets about his conduct while in power. "Look at what's happening now—the economic climate, the neo-Nazis in the streets," he said to the British writer Timothy Garton Ash. "I told you so."

Hoover, J(ohn) Edgar (1895–1972) One of the most complex and controversial of modern U.S.

public servants, as well as one of the longest-serving, J. Edgar Hoover created the Federal Bureau of Investigation from the remains of its scandal-ridden predecessor, called simply the Bureau of Investigation, and ruled it with a dictatorial hand from 1924 until his death.

Born in Washington, D.C., Hoover attended night law classes at George Washington University, graduating with an LL.B. in 1916 and receiving a master of laws degree in the following year. Having gone to work for the Department of Justice in 1917, he spent two years (1919–21) as a special assistant to Attorney General A. Mitchell Palmer, who in the aftermath of the Bolshevik Revolution in Russia presided over the famous American "Red scare" of the period. With the Justice Department and its Bureau of Investigation tainted by the scandals that characterized the Harding administration, the young Hoover was named director in 1924 and proceeded to establish his authority, freeing the renamed bureau—soon to become famous as the FBI—from party politics and making it a center of scientific crime detection. He also insisted on maintaining the bureau as an investigative agency instead of allowing it to grow into a kind of national police force.

In the 1930s Hoover's "G-men" became national heroes as they hunted down notorious criminals like the famous bank robber John Dillinger. Hoover displayed a blind spot, however—never fully explained—to the existence of organized crime, compared with which the colorful doings of Dillinger and his ilk were actually a minor affair. Some critics asserted that the director, realizing he could not put the Mafia out of business, decided simply to assert that it did not exist—though crime fighters at the Treasury Department, wielding weapons no more formidable than pencil and paper, succeeded in sending figures like Al Capone to prison for long terms.

In 1939, at the beginning of World War II, President ROOSEVELT—acting in the absence of any U.S. counterintelligence agency like Britain's MI5—charged Hoover and the FBI with exercising this function. The bureau continued to play the role during the Cold War and, benefiting from the director's masterly control of public relations and manipulation of the media, became for the public as much the scourge of spies and traitors as it had

J. Edgar Hoover, director of the FBI for almost half a century

earlier been of ordinary criminals. During this period Hoover drew increasing attacks for what were said to be his violations of civil liberties and the intransigent egotism that accepted no criticism. In a 1960 letter, former secretary of state Dean ACHESON called Hoover as trustworthy as "a rattlesnake with a silencer on its rattle." But the director, a remarkably skilled political infighter, proved invulnerable, and Washington politicians, especially those who had reason to fear the kinds of evidence said to be locked up in Hoover's files, dutifully supported his continuance in office long past retirement age. They seemed to share the point of view expressed by Lyndon JOHNSON: "It's better to have Hoover inside the tent pissing out than outside the tent pissing in."

Even in death, Hoover's idiosyncrasies persisted. In accordance with his directive, he was buried in a 1,000-pound, lead-lined coffin designed to survive a terrorist bomb and even a nuclear attack. The young FBI agents who served as pallbearers, however, endured casualties of their own. Two of them suffered ruptures and another collapsed from exhaustion.

For its part, the U.S. Congress, though praising Hoover's long and efficient service, moved to ensure that no future FBI director would be able to amass comparable power.

hot line   A link established in August 1963 between the White House and the Kremlin with the aim of simplifying communication between the U.S. president and the leader of the Soviet Union. During the 1962 CUBAN MISSILE CRISIS, a confusing variety of messages had passed between Washington and Moscow; the hot line—which was called Molink by the technicians and was a teletype, not a telephone—was intended to help the leaders deal directly with any subsequent crisis. In July 1984 the United States and the USSR agreed to update the hot line with a high-speed facsimile-transmission system that not only worked faster but could send maps, charts, and other graphic material.

In 1994, in a reflection of greatly changed times, the United States and Russia opened a so-called partnership line between the U.S. Department of Defense and the Russian Defense Ministry. Lacking such embellishments as red telephones and flashing lights, the new line used commercial telephone circuits; it would be, said Secretary of Defense Les Aspin, "more of a business line than a crisis line."

Hound Dog   *See* AGM-28.

Hoxha, Enver (1908–1985)   Albanian state and Communist Party leader, first secretary from 1948 to 1985. Born into a Muslim family, Hoxha went to France in 1930 to attend the University of Montpellier; he had hoped to study political science and history but won a scholarship in biology and physical science. After Montpellier, following a path trod by many another youthful revolutionary, he became a journalist, working in Paris. By 1936 he had returned to Albania, where he acquired a job as a teacher, only to lose it in 1939 for "anti-regime activity," the result of his membership in a leftist organization called Puna (in English, Work). But the regime itself did not have many days remaining. From April 1939, following invasion by Benito Mussolini's Italian forces, until September 1943, Albania existed under Italian occupation. Hoxha, who founded the Albanian

Communist Party on November 8, 1941, spent these years underground, and in 1943 and 1944, using arms supplied by the Allies and by Marshal TITO's Yugoslav forces, he led the liberation movement against the Germans in southern Albania (and fought Albanian nationalist groups as well) and became commander of the National Liberation Army. On November 28, 1944, he entered the capital, Tirana, as prime minister of a new Albanian government.

After 1948, profiting from the Soviet-Yugoslav split to free himself from Tito's tutelage, Hoxha clamped a rigid and reactionary dictatorship on his country. From then until his death he held all the high governmental portfolios for varying periods and remained for 37 years head of the Albanian Communist Party, to which he gave a strongly Maoist orientation, putting himself at odds not only with Yugoslavia but ultimately with the USSR. Tito once spoke of him as "this so-called Marxist who knows only the word Marxism-Leninism and nothing else." Seeking reconciliation with Tito in the 1950s after Joseph STALIN's expulsion of Yugoslavia from the Soviet camp, Nikita KHRUSHCHEV hurled rhetoric and economic sanctions at Hoxha and was said to have plotted a coup against him; Hoxha, a Stalinist like many of the other leaders of satellite Communist parties, declared that Khrushchev's de-Stalinization campaigns were destabilizing world Communism. The end result was the rupture of diplomatic relations between the USSR and Albania in 1961.

Hoxha was succeeded by Ramiz Alia, who allowed slightly increased contact between Albanians and Western Europeans.

Hukbalahap (Huks)   In 1943, when the Japanese occupying the Philippines proclaimed a so-called independent republic, this new puppet regime was defied by a resistance movement centered in Luzon and led by the Communist Hukbalahap (in English, People's Anti-Japanese Army) organization. After the war the Huks, as they were called, would not surrender their arms, as other guerrilla groups had done, and found a new foe in the national government of Manuel Roxas, which refused to allow the head of the Philippine Communist Party, Luis Taruc, to take the congressional seat he had

won; nor did talks between the government and the Communists create any kind of agreement. In 1948 the Huks began a major uprising featuring spectacular terrorist acts like the ambushing of the family of the late national hero and president, Manuel Quezon.

In the next few years the government succeeded in smashing this rebellion, largely through the effective tactics of the defense minister, Ramon Magsaysay, who not only fought the insurgents but responded to the need for land reform with programs to liberate peasants from the oppression of the landlords. In his war against the Huks, Magsaysay as a strong and effective anti-Communist received important help from the U.S. government (especially the CENTRAL INTELLIGENCE AGENCY), which regarded the Philippine situation as a serious security problem. Elected president in 1953, Magsaysay saw his anti-Huk campaign achieve success in the following year, with the surrender of Taruc, and he continued to push his reforms, which called for each peasant who rejected the Huks to receive land of his own, a carabao, tools, seeds, and money to buy basic provisions. The reforms ended, however, after Magsaysay died in an airplane crash in 1957. *See also* NEW PEOPLE'S ARMY.

"Hundred Flowers" campaign   A tactical move made by MAO ZEDONG in 1956 in opposition to Soviet-style industrial "modernizers," such as DENG XIAOPING, to decrease the influence of central Chinese planning authorities. Although the principal figure of the Chinese Communist Party, Mao found himself in various power struggles. At this time, looking to the peasants for support, Mao sought to keep control of the bureaucracy. The theme of the campaign was expressed in the saying of Confucius: "Let a hundred flowers bloom, let a hundred schools of thought contend." Mao launched the campaign in a speech delivered on May 2, 1956, to a planning conference. "Schools of thought" is said to have referred to scientists and their work, with "flowers" pertaining to writers and artists. The theme recurred in various forms during the next year until the supposed excesses of those who put it into practice led the government to crush the campaign.

Hungarian Revolution In the climate of de-Stalinization that followed Soviet first secretary Nikita KHRUSHCHEV's February 1956 speech to the 20th Congress of the COMMUNIST PARTY OF THE SOVIET UNION, the position of the Stalinist dictator of Hungary, Mátyás RÁKOSI—one of the most detested of all EASTERN BLOC leaders—became increasingly shaky. The following July, pressed by the Soviet government, Rákosi resigned, and various other officials confessed to violations of "socialist legality" and other offenses. Although Rákosi's successor, Ernó Geró, held Stalinist views similar to Rákosi's, political prisoners received amnesties; Imre NAGY, a former premier and a disgraced political foe of Rákosi, was readmitted to the Communist Party without being forced to recant his views; a former prisoner, János KÁDÁR, was appointed to the party Secretariat; and in a cold October rain a crowd of 200,000 people marched past the exhumed coffins of four party members whom the Rákosi regime had executed as traitors.

On October 21, as a wave of liberal hope spread across the country, speakers at a meeting in a provincial city called for the withdrawal of Soviet troops from Hungary. The next day came cries for Nagy to be given a high place in the party and the government. At the same time, the news from Poland, which had seen a summer of discontent and demonstrations, told of the Kremlin's acquiescence in the choice of a former political prisoner, Władysław GOMUŁKA, as party first secretary. On the 23rd, celebrating this development, participants in a student demonstration that grew to a crowd of more than 100,000, including workers and even soldiers, marched to Nagy's residence. Concerned about what might happen, especially since the demonstrators were waving flags from which the Communist red star had been ripped, Nagy greeted the crowd: "Comrades!" "We are not comrades!" they shouted back. Speaking carefully, Nagy then temporized, essentially advising his listeners not to act rashly. Several hours before this meeting, a demonstration in the eastern Hungarian city of Debrecen had erupted into a battle in front of the local secret-police building.

Despite Nagy's effort to calm the crowd, an unfortunate broadcast by Geró, in which he praised the Soviet Union for treating Hungary as an equal partner, inflamed the people on the streets, who moved on to the broadcasting center to demand air time for a rebuttal. At the same time, young men who had seized weapons at a police station engaged in a battle with a tank. At about nine o'clock, at the heavily guarded headquarters of Radio Budapest, a ferocious battle broke out. Soon a band of young people had toppled a huge statue of STALIN, which, to waves of cheering, a truck then dragged away. A particular focus of popular hatred was the AVO (State Protecting Special Group), the secret police. (For years commentators believed that revolutionary events were confined to Budapest—an impression desired by the government. Research in the 1990s demonstrated, however, that in most towns and villages the events of October 23 were followed by the removal of Stalinist symbols and the replacement of political and administrative leaders.)

Attempting to turn back the revolutionary wave, the Central Committee installed Nagy as premier, but Geró, still first secretary, asked the Soviets for help in restoring order; Soviet ambassador Yuri ANDROPOV also called for armed Soviet intervention. The Soviet troops played an odd double role —some of them fraternized with the Hungarians, but at the same time the presence on the street of these troops increased the anger of the people, leading to strikes and to the heavy involvement of factory workers in the resistance. On Soviet instructions, Geró resigned as party head, to be replaced by Kádár.

On October 28, Gomulka and other Polish leaders called on the Soviets to withdraw from Hungary. But Nagy, as premier, had become in effect only a passenger on a self-determining revolutionary train. Factory workers in various parts of the country were creating revolutionary councils, and even though Khrushchev had agreed to certain compromises in Poland, the Hungarian express was rushing farther ahead, toward territory the Kremlin would not allow it to explore. On October 29 Hungarians expressed dismay at the refusal of the UNITED NATIONS Security Council to take any action in support of the revolution. On the same day, Yugoslavia's Marshal TITO urged the Hungarians to end the uprising, before they wrecked "socialism" and imperiled world peace, and U.S. president EISENHOWER paid tribute to the Hungarians' "dedication to freedom"; having heard U.S. administration campaign rhetoric about "rollback" and "liberation" in Eastern Europe, Hungarian revolutionary leaders felt deep disappointment at this lack of all but rhetorical support.

On October 30, having unexpectedly become the symbol of revolution, Nagy announced that the government would abolish the one-party system and replace it with a coalition of democratic parties. Since the Soviets appeared to take this news calmly, Nagy declared that Hungary would remove itself from the WARSAW PACT, the year-old formal basis of Soviet control in Eastern Europe, and, like Austria, become a neutral state. Though Kádár had seemed to approve of these developments, he actually had gone across the Soviet border to Uzhgorod, and on November 4, when Soviet tanks rumbled into Budapest (Operation Whirlwind), Kádár returned with them, proclaiming a new government.

What followed were the dramatic, deadly scenes that defined the Hungarian Revolution as the world saw it on television and in films, with battles between Soviet tanks and citizens of Budapest with small arms and Molotov cocktails. "With a terror unparalleled in recent years," wrote the American novelist James A. Michener just a few weeks later, the Soviets "destroyed a city." Several thousand people were killed, thousands more wounded, and more than 200,000 Hungarians fled to the West. The Soviet victory was inevitable. Still, the fighting did not suddenly come to an end but trailed off over the ensuing weeks; the revolutionaries did not give up easily or quickly.

Nagy fled to the Yugoslav embassy, from which Kádár guaranteed him safe conduct. But the Yugoslavs, Kádár, and the Soviets all appear to have worked together to eliminate Nagy and his colleagues from Hungarian political life. The Soviets did not honor a promised safe-conduct pledge, and Nagy was seized. Two years later, he was tried for treason on the vote of the Hungarian Communist Party Central Committee and executed. *See also* POLISH UPRISING, 1956.

Husák, Gustáv (1913–1991) Slovak Communist leader who succeeded Alexander DUBČEK as first secretary of the Czechoslovak Communist Party in April 1969, as a somewhat delayed result of the Soviet suppression of Czechoslovakia's PRAGUE SPRING of 1968. Having at this point had what really amounted to a two-part career, Husák had demonstrated remarkable powers of survival. Born near Bratislava, he joined the Czech Communist Party when he was 21 and after receiving his law degree practiced in Bratislava. Following the turmoil of World War II he became a member of the Slovak Communist Party Central Committee, only to be arrested in 1951 for his advocacy of increased rights for Slovakia within Czechoslovakia and finally, in 1954, to be sentenced to life imprisonment as a "bourgeois nationalist." Released in 1960, he purged himself of his ideological sins by joining the proletariat as a construction worker. Deemed by the party hierarchy to be fully recovered, he won rehabilitation and readmission to the Czech Communist Party in 1963.

Five years later Husák had risen to be deputy prime minister and had also held high party positions and thus was waiting in the wings when, following new disturbances, Soviet pressure caused the removal of Dubček. Husák, whose earlier imprisonment for his opinions caused the Soviets to regard him as a leader who might appeal to a broad range of Czech opinion, gave the Kremlin one of its wishes by declaring that the 1968 invasion had been thoroughly justified (though in its earlier stages he had supported the Prague Spring). After taking power, Husák—a true hard-liner described by one observer as a "devious careerist"—purged the Czech Communist Party of more than a half-million members. In 1975 he became president of Czechoslovakia.

In December 1989, during the VELVET REVOLUTION, Husák resigned the presidency after swearing in the first cabinet since 1948 without a Communist majority. The Czech Parliament chose the playwright Václav HAVEL to succeed him.

Hydrogen bomb Developed first by the United States in the early 1950s, the hydrogen bomb draws its power from the nuclear fusion of isotopes of hydrogen—unlike the earlier ATOMIC BOMB, which works on the principle of nuclear fission. The creation in the hydrogen bomb of heavier elements from lighter ones to produce material that weighs less than its constituent elements releases energy on a vastly greater scale than that produced by nuclear fission.

The U.S. development of the hydrogen bomb, or H-bomb, proceeded only after an intense debate between two camps. The first group included many scientists who had worked on the original atomic bomb, notably J. Robert OPPENHEIMER, who saw that first bomb as sufficient evil for the world; the second consisted of those, such as Edward TELLER, who believed, particularly after the Soviets had exploded their own atomic bomb in 1949, that the United States dared not deprive itself of this newer and immensely more powerful weapon. The United States exploded its first H-bomb in 1952 at Eniwetok atoll in the Pacific; the Soviets followed with their own first H-bomb detonation in 1953.

In 1954, nuclear testing at Bikini atoll in the Marshall Islands (Operation Bravo) caused an uproar when fallout from the explosion contaminated the crew of a Japanese fishing boat, the *Lucky Dragon*. It later became clear that some natives in the Marshalls and U.S. service personnel had also experienced exposure. Although the Soviets conducted their nuclear tests *in camera* in the Soviet Union, with no foreign witnesses but with effects measurable in the atmosphere, worldwide concern about the effects of poisonous nuclear residues led to the adoption in 1963 of the NUCLEAR TEST BAN TREATY.

Though the Cold War saw no hydrogen bomb employed in fighting, this awesome weapon, when associated with the long-range missiles developed in the 1950s, became a doomsday symbol in the minds of people around the world. Long before, in 1910, the American historian Henry Adams had warned readers that ideas and forces already in motion might one day lead to the creation of "bombs of cosmic violence" that might destroy civilization itself. Now, during the Cold War, that terrible possibility had arrived, and people lived in what was termed a BALANCE OF TERROR—a phe-nomenon that became so familiar it tended to dwell far back in the consciousness rather than near the surface, except during crises—most notably, the CUBAN MISSILE CRISIS of 1962. To a profoundly disquieting extent, the survival of civilization seemed for decades to depend on the rational judgment of a few national leaders and their advisers. Fortunately, this inescapable gamble succeeded.

A curious and in some respects ironic fact came to light as information flowed more freely from Moscow after the dissolution of the Soviet Union. In 1993 Viktor Mikhailov, the Russian minister of atomic energy, declared that in the mid-1980s the Soviet nuclear arsenal had reached its peak with a total of 45,000 warheads—12,000 more than most U.S. experts had estimated and twice the number held by the United States. U.S. analysts immediately wondered whether this enormous inventory might offer evidence that Soviet planners had really believed in the possibility of a successful massive first-strike attack on the West. On the other hand, said Admiral Bobby Ray Inman, a former director of the National Security Agency, the vast size of the arsenal might simply indicate the working of a bureaucracy run amuck, with no connection to national strategy: "You just produce any number you can." *See also* SAKHAROV, Andrei.

Hyunh Tan Phat (1913–1989)   Native of southern Vietnam who in 1969 became president of the Provisional Revolutionary Government, the NATIONAL LIBERATION FRONT's governmental unit in South Vietnam, and held this position until Vietnam was officially reunified (1975–76). During the war with France he served as the editor of clandestine newspapers in Saigon. In 1960 he helped organize the National Liberation Front, and in 1964 became its secretary-general. He was a leader of the People's Revolutionary Party, the openly Communist organization of the 20 groups that comprised the National Liberation Front.

Ia Drang In November 1965, in the Ia Drang Valley of Vietnam, a U.S. battalion under the command of Major (later Lieutenant General) Harold G. Moore carried out a kind of operation that would soon become standard in the area— a search-and-destroy mission. It was, General Moore said later, "a dress rehearsal for the Vietnam War."

ICBM *See* INTERCONTINENTAL BALLISTIC MISSILE.

IL-28 Soviet tactical bomber, the USSR's first operational jet bomber. The IL-28 entered production in 1950 and during its long service took part in action across two continents, from Nigeria to Korea and Vietnam. Created by Sergei Ilyushin (hence the "IL" designation), this bomber received the NATO code name Beagle. Powered by two turbojet engines—based on the most powerful Rolls-Royce engine, which the British government chose to make available to the Soviets—it achieved a maximum speed of more than 550 mph, with a range of about 1,500 miles. It could carry more than 6,000 pounds of conventional bombs or mines; some versions had a nuclear configuration. As the H-5, this aircraft was manufactured in the People's Republic of China.

IMF *See* INTERNATIONAL MONETARY FUND.

Independence Douglas VC-118 Liftmaster four-engine transport named for U.S. president Harry S. TRUMAN's hometown in Missouri and used as the official presidential aircraft from July 4, 1947, to May 1953. (The *V* in the designation of the aircraft means that it was modified to provide special accommodations.) As a commercial airliner, the C-118 was known as the DC-6; the U.S. Air Force acquired one of the earliest production models to replace the *SACRED COW*, the C-54 that had been used by President ROOSEVELT and for two years by President Truman. The rear of the fuselage of the *Independence* was turned into a presidential stateroom; the main cabin held 24 persons, or 12 if the seats were made up into Pullman-style berths. The aircraft, said Truman, had "every gadget and safety device there is." The C-118 had a maximum speed of about 360 mph and a range of 4,400 miles.

In carrying President Truman to his famous meeting at Wake Island with General Douglas MACARTHUR in October 1950, the *Independence* figured in a scene of high-level protocol that would give rise to stories for years to come. Did MacArthur try to outlast Truman in the air so that the president's plane would have to land first, and thus the president would be forced to greet the arriving general? Truman is supposed to have said something of the kind in interviews conducted many years later by Merle Miller, and the story received wide circulation, but it was groundless. Though Truman did not see MacArthur's aircraft on the ground as the *Independence* came into Wake, the general actually was in the operations building awaiting the president's arrival. It might be noted, however, that MacArthur was not standing out on the tarmac, eagerly scanning the skies for the appearance of the *Independence*.

President Harry S. Truman's personal aircraft, the *Independence*

INF *See* INTERMEDIATE-RANGE NUCLEAR FORCES TREATY.

Intercontinental Ballistic Missile (ICBM) Ballistic missile with a range, as its name might suggest, beginning at about 3,000 miles and going up to 8,000 or more. An intermediate-range ballistic missile (IRBM) such as the Soviet SS-20 has a range from 1,500 to 3,000 miles. A ballistic missile is so named because it does not use aerodynamic surfaces (e.g., wings) for lift but follows a trajectory according to the laws of ballistics, like an artillery shell, when its thrust is terminated. Early ballistic missiles were "aimed," or set on their course, by radio direction. This method gave way to control by inertial guidance (automatic internal devices that keep the missile on track). U.S. ICBMs have included the MINUTEMAN and the POLARIS.

The development of ICBMs with nuclear warheads had a major effect on strategic thinking; spheres of influence clearly had much less significance than previously, now that countries could attack each other from the ends of the earth. *See also* MISSILE GAP.

Intermediate-Range Nuclear Forces (INF) Treaty December 1987 agreement between U.S. president REAGAN and Soviet general secretary GORBACHEV to eliminate stocks of intermediate-range missiles with nuclear warheads. This was the first treaty to call not simply for limiting the growth of nuclear weaponry but actually for reducing the size of existing nuclear arsenals.

International Bank for Reconstruction and Development *See* WORLD BANK.

International Monetary Fund (IMF) A product, as was the WORLD BANK, of the United Nations Monetary and Financial Conference, held at Bretton Woods, N.H., in July 1944. The IMF has as its principal purposes the promotion of international monetary cooperation, the encouragement of international trade, the promotion of stable currency-exchange rates, and the making available of international sources of currency to all members. It was intended to help member nations avoid currency devaluation as a way of correcting trade imbalances. Although the postwar years saw a variety of international economic problems arise, the IMF served as a powerful agent of stability. All members of the World Bank must also belong to the IMF.

Inverchapel, Archibald Clark Kerr, 1st Baron (1882–1951) Known through most of his career as Sir Archibald Clark Kerr, Inverchapel was a veteran diplomat by the time of World War II, having entered the British service in 1906. After serving as ambassador to China in the late 1930s, he went to the Soviet Union at the beginning of 1942, in succession to the prominent Labour Party figure Sir Stafford CRIPPS. Clark Kerr headed the embassy, first in Kuibyshev (to which many Soviet departments and offices had been evacuated when German forces approached Moscow in late 1941) and then in Moscow (1942–46), and took part in numerous meetings with Premier STALIN, both on his own and as the escort of visiting high-level persons such as Prime Minister CHURCHILL. Late in the war, together with the U.S. ambassador, Averell HARRIMAN, Clark Kerr had discussions with Stalin on the most vexed issue of the time, the future government and boundaries of Poland.

In 1946 Inverchapel came to Washington as ambassador, a move that persuaded his ex-wife to remarry him but that otherwise did not prove successful, as he failed to develop a close relationship with members of the State Department. Inverchapel once observed that he preferred dealing with Stalin, because the two could swap dirty stories and talk business at the same time; he seems to have held the odd belief that American officials did not like dirty jokes.

Invincible This class of British small (20,600-ton) aircraft carriers kept alive names from the Royal Navy's past, the members in addition to *Invincible* being *Illustrious* and *Ark Royal*. In the event of war, these ships, designed in the 1960s, would have played the same role in the eastern Atlantic as the Soviet MOSKVA "cruisers" would have performed in the Mediterranean, their quarry being enemy submarines. Invincibles carried a complement of jump jets and helicopters totaling about 20 aircraft.

Iowa The four battleships of this class *(Iowa, New Jersey, Missouri, Wisconsin),* which went into commission in 1943 and 1944, were the last U.S. battleships ever built. All fought in prominent operations during World War II in the Pacific, generally considered at the time to be the final arena for the battleship. But during the KOREAN WAR, these big ships (45,000 tons' standard displacement), with their powerful main batteries of nine 16-inch guns, came out of retirement and went to work bombarding enemy coastal positions, and in the late 1960s *New Jersey* saw service off Vietnam during the VIETNAM WAR. It then rejoined its sister ships in mothballs, but in the 1980s all four Iowas were recalled to duty and modernized, particularly with respect to electronics. In the Persian Gulf War of 1991, these ships, almost 50 years old, showed their value as platforms for the launching of Tomahawk CRUISE MISSILE.

Iran-contra affair On November 3, 1986, a Lebanese weekly magazine, *Al-Shiraa,* published a surprising account of secret dealings between the United States and Iran. The U.S. REAGAN administration, as the report accurately stated, had sent arms to Iran in exchange for the promise to release hostages held in Lebanon by groups under Iranian control. President Reagan, as much evidence later showed, was deeply concerned about the situation of the hostages, but the idea of the exchange contradicted public statements by the administration concerning its stance on dealing with terrorist states. A follow-up investigation revealed a strange complication within the arrangement: staff members of the NATIONAL SECURITY COUNCIL, led by the president's national security adviser himself, Admiral John Poindexter, and Marine Lieutenant Colonel Oliver North, had funneled the proceeds from the arms sales to the CONTRAS in Nicaragua, in direct contravention of congressional mandates. Reagan, Vice President George BUSH, and other high officials, not altogether convincingly, denied knowledge of these illegal activities.

In December 1985 and January 1986, when the idea first came up for discussion in the administration, Secretary of State George SHULTZ had been opposed to it, not only because the plan violated the established "no ransom" policy but also because of the hypocrisy that would be involved in delivering arms to the revolutionary Iranian government while, as Shultz later said, the United States "preached to and pressured" other governments to do nothing of this sort. Shultz distanced himself from the ensuing dealings while another opponent, Defense Secretary Caspar WEINBERGER,

The Iron Curtain—the two Germanys

dutifully followed the president's wishes despite his own doubts.

(The strangest aspect of the entire story was supplied by a cake that a group of Americans took to Tehran along with a load of military equipment. Shaped like a key—supposedly to represent the key to American-Iranian friendship—the cake did not survive to reach Iranian dignitaries; hungry Revolutionary Guards gobbled it up at the airport.)

The scandal, following earlier congressional action, weakened administration efforts to aid the contras against the SANDINISTAS, but within two years the ten-year war in Nicaragua had ended. As a sort of consolation for their discomfiture over the Iran-contra scandal (and not all of the partici-

pants were embarrassed by it; in fact, North made it the basis of his later political activities), officials who had supported the contras could celebrate a victory in 1990 when election defeats swept the Sandinistas from power.

Iron Curtain Following the German surrender to the Allies on May 8, 1945, which ended World War II in Europe, U.S. and British officers found themselves unable to learn the state of affairs in the Soviet-occupied zone of Germany. On May 12, much concerned over what seemed the reluctance of the Soviets to cooperate with their allies in matters of common concern, British prime minister CHURCHILL telegraphed to U.S. president TRUMAN that "an iron curtain is drawn down upon their

March 5, 1946: Winston Churchill delivers his landmark "Iron Curtain" speech.

front." Two months later, at the POTSDAM CONFER-ENCE of the United States, Britain, and the Soviet Union, Churchill employed a variation of his metaphor when he protested to Premier STALIN that the Soviets had surrounded the British mission in Romania with "an iron fence." On August 16, 1945, describing the situation in Eastern Europe, Churchill (now no longer prime minister, having been replaced by Clement ATTLEE) returned to his original phrase, telling the House of Commons that "it is not impossible that tragedy on a prodigious scale is unfolding itself behind the iron curtain."

But it was on March 5, 1946, at Westminster

College in Fulton, Missouri, that Churchill launched "iron curtain" on its public career, during which it would become the most famous and distinctive expression associated with the Cold War, while the Iron Curtain itself took on a geographical reality as definite as that possessed by any official international boundary. "From Stettin in the Baltic to Trieste in the Adriatic," Churchill declared, "an iron curtain has descended across the Continent. Behind that line lie all the capitals of the ancient states of central and eastern Europe. Warsaw, Berlin, Prague, Vienna, Budapest, Belgrade, Bucharest and Sofia, all these famous cities and the populations around them lie in what I might call the Soviet sphere and all are subject, in one form or another, not only to Soviet influence but to a very high and increasing measure of control from Moscow." These ideas, which later would not seem remarkable, did not receive general approval in a world that increasingly saw problems between East and West but for the most part was not, in early 1946, prepared for an open breach. Days later, wrote Dean ACHESON, then undersecretary of state, Washington "was still rocking" and "Congress was in an uproar." The British government of Prime Minister Attlee disavowed the speech, and State Department colleagues advised Acheson not to attend a New York dinner honoring the distinguished visitor.

Though Churchill could hardly have been aware of it, he was not the first political figure to relate the idea of an iron curtain to Soviet-controlled Eastern Europe. On February 25, 1945, the German publication *Das Reich* had predicted that if Germany should surrender, "an iron curtain would come down at once behind which the mass slaughter of the people would take place." This grim and unintentionally ironic forecast came from Dr. Joseph Goebbels, the Nazi minister of propaganda. *See also* BERLIN WALL.

Ismay, Hastings Lionel (Baron Ismay of Wormington) (1887–1965)   British general who became the first secretary-general of the NORTH ATLANTIC TREATY ORGANIZATION, serving from 1952 to 1957. Born in India, Ismay studied at Sandhurst and served in India and the Somaliland. For many years he was associated with the Committee of Imperial Defence, finally succeeding the renowned Lord Hankey as secretary (1938–39). "Pug," as he was known (and one look at his face made the reason clear), won wide admiration and popularity during World War II for the skill and tact with

which he managed the difficult task of serving as chief of staff to Prime Minister Winston CHURCHILL in the latter's capacity as minister of defense—a post that made Ismay the link between the prime minister, the heads of the services, and numerous other officials, British and Allied.

As he was ending his service to NATO, Ismay said in a speech, "Who would have believed that sovereign States would entrust their precious armed forces to the command of nationals other than their own in time of peace? But this is what has come to pass." The North Atlantic Alliance, he declared, was "the best, if not the only, hope of peace."

Izvestia   During the existence of the Soviet Union, two daily newspapers published in Moscow became known around the world—*PRAVDA* (Truth), the organ of the Communist Party, and *Izvestia* (News), the government newspaper; *Izvestia* had actually existed as a government publication prior to the Bolshevik Revolution. Once, trying to downplay the significance of a story in *Izvestia,* Foreign Commissar V. M. MOLOTOV described the publication as merely "the organ of the soviets of workers' deputies," but in fact no publication since the creation of the Communist state had possessed independence. The most distinguished of *Izvestia*'s editors was probably Nikolai Bukharin (1888–1938), a leading Bolshevik intellectual who held the position for a short time during 1934, though he had earlier lost out to Joseph STALIN in party controversies; he was executed during the Great Purge of 1936–38. During the KHRUSHCHEV era *Izvestia* was edited by the premier's son-in-law, Alexei Adzhubei (1924–1993), who lost the job as soon as his father-in-law was removed from power in October 1964.

J

Jackson-Vanik Amendment   From 1972 to 1974, the veteran U.S. senator Henry M. Jackson, a Democrat from Washington (1912–1983), known as one of Israel's most faithful supporters on Capitol Hill, succeeded in delaying the extending of most-favored-nation trading status to the Soviet Union (which was to be granted because the Soviets had agreed to pay World War II Lend-Lease debts), making the grant of this status, in the Jackson-Vanik Amendment to the Trade Reform Act, contingent on the liberalization of Soviet policy concerning the emigration of Jews. In true senatorial fashion, the wording of the amendment was not so explicit, though the point was clear; the USSR was termed a "nonmarket economy," and the emigration in question was that of "citizens." In fact, the Soviets since late 1971 had relaxed their emigration policy to the extent that the number of Jews departing from the country had doubled, and discreet diplomacy promised to produce even better results; Secretary of State Henry KISSINGER assured Jackson in October 1974 that the USSR had agreed to take the desired steps. But the "redoubtable" Jackson, as Kissinger called him, continually escalated his demands, and the Soviets, disinclined to accept what they deemed the open interference in their affairs represented by Jackson-Vanik, especially since DÉTENTE had not produced the food and other imports they had hoped for, decided to renounce the entire arrangement, which they did soon after Congress finally passed the act at the end of 1974. From a Soviet cost-benefit-analysis point of view, the drawbacks of the agreement outweighed the rewards. Indeed, as William G. Hyland, one of Kissinger's associates, put it:

"No Soviet leader could buckle to Jackson's demands and stay in power."

Besides, to many important Soviet officials, the WATERGATE AFFAIR, which came to a head in August 1974 with the resignation of U.S. president NIXON, seemed more a U.S. rejection of détente than simply a rejection of Nixon. Jackson-Vanik also had repercussions in South Vietnam, because the Soviets stepped up their aid to North Vietnam following the collapse of the trade arrangement; previously, in response to Kissinger's promise of most-favored-nation status, the Soviets had reduced their support of the North. Thus what was in good part a U.S. political issue made waves from Moscow to SAIGON. As for the Soviet Jews, thousands of them were now denied exit permits.

Jakeš, Miloš (1922–)   Czechoslovak Communist Party general secretary forced from power in 1989 by the VELVET REVOLUTION. An electrical engineer and designer who joined the Communist Party in 1945, Jakeš held positions in the Czech Union of Youth as he rose in the party structure. He won election to the Federal Assembly in 1971 and to the party Central Committee in 1977, becoming general secretary in 1987. Confronted by the great surge of dissidence in the autumn of 1989, Jakeš, a hard-line party official, showed himself unwilling or unable to develop any counterstrategy aside from issuing ritual denunciations of all rebels as antisocialist. On November 20, a crowd of some 200,000 demonstrators in Prague, many of them students on strike, called for free elections along with the dismissal of Jakeš. The next day Jakeš retorted that "there are boundaries that should not be overstepped," but within three days he had yielded to the overwhelming pressure and tendered his resignation. He was succeeded as general secretary of the Czech Communist Party by a little-known party official from Moravia, Karel Urbanek. Interestingly, even though the Communist regime had come almost to the end of its existence, citizens in Moravia expressed chauvinistic pride that one of their own had been chosen to head the party. In 1989, the playwright Václav HAVEL was named Czechoslovakia's first non-Communist president since 1948.

Jaruzelski, Wojciech (1923–) Polish soldier, Communist Party official, and government officeholder as prime minister and president. As a young army officer, Jaruzelski served with a Polish infantry division in the Red Army during the latter years of World War II, and after the war he fought in a brutal campaign to eliminate anti-Communist partisans in Poland. By 1965 he had become chief of the Polish General Staff, a position he held until being appointed minister of defense in April 1968. He received the latter appointment because the Polish first secretary, Władysław GOMUŁKA, and the Soviet authorities both wanted a capable and reliable officer in charge of the Polish defense establishment in case the Kremlin decided to crush the PRAGUE SPRING by an invasion of Czechoslovakia—as was done. Jaruzelski became a full member of the Politburo of the Polish Communist Party in 1971. In July 1983 he took the title commander in chief of Polish Armed Forces.

On February 11, 1981, this powerful but enigmatic and little-known professional soldier became the prime minister of Poland, which had undergone considerable turbulence since the general strikes and the creation of the SOLIDARITY trade union in 1980. Jaruzelski had the clear mission of establishing a stable government while keeping Solidarity in check in some sort of modus vivendi that would preserve the real power for the government. Jaruzelski himself declared on taking office that he saw "evil and hostile forces" opposed to socialism as the principal source of conflict in Poland. In October, Jaruzelski became first secretary of the United Workers' (Communist) Party, thus becoming head of both government and party. On December 13, 1981, after ten months of continu-

ing turbulence, Jaruzelski—acting partly under pressure from the Kremlin—brought in troops and tanks, instituted martial law, and rounded up and interned thousands of Solidarity members, thus for the time being putting an end to the Polish revolution. Jaruzelski's coup shocked Solidarity leaders, who had not believed he would use violence against them. Lech WAŁĘSA, Solidarity's spokesman, spent most of the following year in prison. (In later years Jaruzelski defended himself by saying that had he not declared martial law, Soviet troops would have marched into Poland.)

Unable to revive the Polish economy through the 1980s, Jaruzelski like other Eastern European leaders had to face the new situation brought about by the decision of the Soviet Union, under General Secretary Mikhail GORBACHEV, to allow political events in the EASTERN BLOC to take their own course. In 1989, in a compromise-flavored free election, Solidarity adherents took control of Parliament but Jaruzelski won the presidency. The combination of a Communist presidency and a free-market administration proved unworkable, however, and Jaruzelski resigned his office in 1990. Lech Wałesa defeated Tadeusz MAZOWIECKI in November for the presidency of Poland.

JCS *See* JOINT CHIEFS OF STAFF.

Jebb, Sir (Hubert Miles) Gladwyn (1st Baron Gladwyn) (1900–) British diplomat who achieved great television popularity in the United States as his country's permanent representative to the UNITED NATIONS from 1950 to 1954, a period covering the KOREAN WAR.

Having received his bachelor's degree at Oxford in 1922, Jebb entered the diplomatic service in 1924 and served in numerous posts. During World War II, as counselor of the Foreign Office, he attended all of the chief Allied conferences. In 1945 he served as executive secretary of the UN Preparatory Commission and in 1946, briefly, as acting secretary-general.

As British representative on the UN Security Council, the tall, handsome Jebb proved a skillful debating opponent of the Soviet ambassador, Yakov MALIK. Once, stopped on Long Island for speeding, the British newspaper correspondent Henry Brandon escaped a ticket because of the police officer's admiration for Jebb, whom he watched on TV. Since Brandon was an acquaintance of Jebb's, said the officer, "tell him that I think he's a great guy . . . and don't speed again."

Jiang Qing (1914–1991)   Daughter of a poor carpenter in China's Shandong province, Jian Qing attended Shandong University, where she married a fellow student, and then became a B-movie actress in Shanghai. Her own life quickly came to resemble such a movie, as, like many other radical young Chinese, she traveled to Yanan in 1937 to be near MAO ZEDONG and the spirit of revolution. Having enrolled in the Lu Xuan Arts and Literature College in Yanan, she happened to be sitting in the front row at a lecture given by the leader himself. Mao spotted her, and the two soon began an affair. The couple's respective spouses reacted promptly—Mao's wife (his second) left China for Moscow; Jiang Qing's husband simply divorced her—and the two lovers were married.

In 1966 Jiang led the CULTURAL REVOLUTION. Some observers maintain that, in an effort to purify her personal history, she attempted to have old acquaintances killed. After Mao's death in 1976, she was arrested as part of the GANG OF FOUR; in 1980 she was convicted of the "persecution" of some 700,000 people, with her death sentence being reduced to life imprisonment.

Mao once said of Jiang, "After I die, the people will kill her." In May 1991 she committed suicide in prison.

John Paul II (1920–   )   Born Karol Wojtyla, John Paul was elected pope on October 16, 1978, following the unexpected death of John Paul I, who reigned for only 34 days. Not only was John Paul II the first pope from a Slavic country and the first non-Italian pope since the 16th century, but he quickly proved to be a key political figure, playing a major part in developments in Poland and thus in the collapse of the Soviet system in Eastern Europe.

A student of literature and philosophy, Wojtyla spent much of World War II hiding in an archbishop's palace during the German occupation of Poland. After the war, having been ordained as a priest, he rose in the Catholic hierarchy, becoming

archbishop of Kraków in 1964 and a cardinal in 1967. In June 1979, not long after his election as pope, he made an epochal nine-day visit to his homeland, where his stature and his words heartened Polish Catholics and contributed to the rise of the labor movement SOLIDARITY and its leader, Lech WAŁĘSA. Occupying a unique international status, the pope gave the Poles the support of his authority and his personality, which far outweighed the influence of the government. A Polish political scientist called John Paul's pilgrimage a "psychological earthquake, an opportunity for mass political catharsis." The profound effect of the pope's activism has been strongly suspected as the reason behind an assassination attempt in St. Peter's Square on May 13, 1981, when a Turk named Mehmet Ali Ağca shot and seriously wounded him. Involvement of the KGB was suspected, but not proved, although strong evidence existed of ties between Ağca and the Bulgarian secret police.

In 1983 the pope paid another visit to Poland, which had entered a period of repression under General JARUZELSKI, the prime minister and head of the Communist Party. (John Paul appears to have let the Soviets know that if they invaded Poland, he would fly to the country and face their tanks. In all his actions he received strong and unpublicized support from the United States.) Urging his flock not to give in to demoralization, the pope prayed "help us to persevere in hope." During this trip John Paul met with Wałęsa and reaffirmed the right of the union to its own independent life—which meant there would be no papal concordat with the government at the expense of Solidarity. This trip so concerned the Soviets that they decided to create a campaign to discredit John Paul; the beginning of the campaign, as it happened, coincided with the election as GENERAL SECRETARY of Mikhail GORBACHEV. In a third pilgrimage, in June 1987, the pope supported Solidarity, which was continuing to suffer suppression, in a series of sermons concerned with the meaning of the word *solidarity* itself. In the triumph of Solidarity in 1989, the world could plainly see the great contribution of the pope.

Johnson, Louis Arthur (1891–1966)   U.S. secretary of defense who succeeded James V. FORRESTAL in the position in March 1949 and resigned under pressure from President TRUMAN in September 1950. A prominent Democratic Party politician and a leading figure in the American Legion, Johnson had earlier served the ROOSEVELT administration as assistant secretary of war (1937–40).

A West Virginia lawyer, Johnson rose to the rank of major in the army in World War I and in 1932 became national president of the American Legion. A glad-handing political type who gave FDR important political support, Johnson, after taking the post of assistant secretary of war in 1937, made it clear that he intended to force the secretary, Harry Woodring, out of office and take the top job for himself. The result was a bizarre feud that flamed between the two men until Roosevelt replaced Woodring with Henry L. Stimson in 1940. Johnson left the department at the same time, as Stimson brought in his own associates, a notable group from Wall Street that included such figures as Robert P. Patterson and Robert A. LOVETT. Despite his war of words with Woodring, however, Johnson has been given credit for some of the army's progress toward modernization in the late 1930s.

After serving as one of the few effective fundraisers for Truman in the 1948 presidential campaign (and making personal contributions said to have amounted to $250,000—in 1948 dollars), Johnson received an even bigger reward than he had hoped for under Roosevelt. The Department of Defense had been created in 1947, and when Forrestal resigned early in 1949, Truman appointed Johnson to take his place. But his tenure did not prove successful. In fact, Johnson's appointment was purely political; he proved to be a tireless self-promoter, this time apparently aiming at the presidency. In the process he alienated other members of the cabinet, particularly Secretary of State Dean ACHESON. Besides problems with his colleagues, Johnson received much of the blame for the malnourished state of U.S. defenses at the outbreak of the KOREAN WAR in June 1950, though the budget-cutting policies were those of Truman himself. In any case, as the historian Joseph G. Dawson III observed, Truman "needed better military advice than Johnson had offered," and in appointing General George C. MARSHALL to succeed

Johnson, Truman made a move that would reassure the nation. *See also* REVOLT OF THE ADMIRALS.

Johnson, Lyndon Baines (1908–1973)   In his extraordinary career, Lyndon Johnson knew great power, enjoyed great acclaim, and also experienced some of the worst times of any public figure in U.S. history. Suddenly becoming president after the assassination of John F. KENNEDY in November 1963, Johnson won impressive legislative victories —notably in the area of civil rights—swept on to an overwhelming triumph in the 1964 presidential election, launched what he called the Great Society, and then proceeded to see his successes turn to ashes as the nation became divided over the VIETNAM WAR. Marchers in the streets chanted, "Hey, hey, LBJ! How many kids did you kill today?"

Born in Stonewall, Tex., Johnson came from a farm family. Although his father had served in the Texas legislature, the elder Johnson was not wealthy and could not afford to send young Lyndon away to a university; the young man graduated from Southwest Texas State College in 1930. The next year Johnson made a connection vital for his future when he worked in the congressional campaign of Richard M. Kleberg; he then became the new representative's secretary in Washington, where he made contacts that led to his becoming the National Youth Administration's administrator for Texas. In 1937, as a strong supporter of ROOSEVELT's New Deal, Johnson won election to the U.S. House of Representatives. During the early months of U.S. involvement in World War II, he served in the navy, until FDR brought all congressmen on active duty back to Washington.

In 1948, in a controversial runoff senatorial primary election he won by just 87 votes, Johnson acquired the derisive nickname Landslide Lyndon. Despite debate about the validity of the results, this victory and an easy win in the general election put the hard-driving Johnson in the U.S. Senate and in a position to become Democratic floor leader in 1953, just four years after he joined the body. He held the position—with time out to recover from a heart attack, when his duties were ably handled by Senator Earle Clements of Kentucky—from 1953 until he became vice president in 1961. On November 22, 1963, after the death of President Kennedy had been announced from

U.S. president Lyndon B. Johnson *(l.)* in a pensive moment during the Vietnam War. With Johnson is General Earle Wheeler, chairman of the Joint Chiefs of Staff.

Parkland Hospital in Dallas, Johnson took the oath of office as president in an unforgettable scene aboard Air Force One, with Jacqueline Kennedy standing beside him in her blood-stained dress.

Although, like many other presidents, Johnson came to the office with great hopes and plans in the realm of domestic policy, within two years he found himself caught up in the situation in Vietnam, where a government created largely by the United States in the 1950s faced continuing war with the VIETCONG and the Communist forces of North Vietnam. Under the geopolitical DOMINO THEORY that had prevailed since the early days of General EISENHOWER's presidency, South Vietnam

was seen as a domino that could not be allowed to fall. In 1965 U.S. involvement in Southeast Asia took a quantum leap as Johnson presided over a buildup that turned a relative handful of U.S. "advisers" into a force, by the end of the year, of 180,000 troops, a number that was to keep climbing but without producing tangible results.

In 1967, as Johnson continued his grim pursuit of what seemed unattainable victory in the Vietnam War, young men, chanting "Hell no, we won't go," burned their draft cards and a wave of "Dump Johnson" feeling swept the country. That summer also saw cities explode in the worst riots in U.S. history, although a fresh round of urban violence would come in 1968, following the murder of Martin Luther King, Jr. Hoping desperately for a measure of international success, Johnson met in June 1967 in the GLASSBORO CONFERENCE with Soviet premier Alexei KOSYGIN, but the talks, though friendly, brought no concrete results. After a temporary boost provided by the conference, Johnson's national popularity rating fell to 39 percent.

In 1968 the United States maintained a force of half a million troops in Vietnam, but still suffered a damaging blow when the enemy unleashed the TET OFFENSIVE—which, though not the military victory it was originally trumpeted to be, produced huge psychological and propaganda dividends for the North Vietnamese, who seemed able to invade U.S.-held strongpoints with ease. On March 31, Johnson announced he would not run for reelection. By now his preoccupation with Vietnam had dashed his hopes and dreams of social progress at home.

Former secretary of state Dean ACHESON, who served Johnson as a foreign-policy adviser for several months in 1966, described the president as a person who was "not only devious but would rather be devious than straightforward." It was, Acheson said, "really too bad about LBJ. He could be so much better than he is. He creates distrust by being too smart. He is never quite candid." Though Johnson could be generous, Acheson said, he would allow meanness to predominate. Indeed, though Johnson possessed great abilities, an appetite for power, and an unrivaled mastery of the legislative process, he squandered these assets on a war that had little public support and, increasingly, little visible purpose.

Joint Chiefs of Staff (JCS) U.S. command, coordinating, and planning agency descended from the group of officers, also called the Joint Chiefs of Staff, that exercised these responsibilities during World War II. The modern structure of the JCS came into being under the National Security Act of 1947, which created the unified Department of Defense and established the JCS as the country's highest military agency and the chief military adviser to the president. The JCS included the chairman, the chief of staff of the army, the chief of naval operations, and the chief of staff of the air force; beginning in 1952, the commandant of the Marine

Corps sat as a member of the JCS for discussion of matters concerning the marines, and since 1969 the commandant has been a regular member. (A 1986 reorganization act also created the post of vice chairman.) In response to pressure from the navy and its supporters in Congress, the establishing legislation did not provide for a chairman of the JCS; in 1949, however, an amendment to the law remedied this obvious deficiency, though the navy still resisted the change. The first chairman was General Omar Bradley (1895–1981), one of the leading World War II commanders.

Though unceasing interservice rivalries—the endemic disease of the U.S. uniformed services—continually plagued the JCS, the most serious disturbance came in August 1967, when the entire group, dismayed at the management of the VIETNAM WAR by the civilian national leadership, threatened to resign; the underlying point was the chiefs' belief that U.S. forces were being put in harm's way without either the needed freedom of action or proper support. Further disillusionment came 16 years later in 1983 when a bomb killed 241 marines in exposed positions in Beirut, Lebanon. In essence, the chiefs called for more say in the use of the forces they represented in the high command.

Finally, under the Goldwater-Nichols Defense Reorganization Act, signed into law on September 20, 1986, the chairman of the JCS received a seat on the NATIONAL SECURITY COUNCIL and thus became a policy maker who could take part in debates with civilian officials. Under the act, the chairman moved up to a special position, replacing the collective JCS as the president's principal military adviser and receiving command authority over all the services, in the hope and expectation that JCS recommendations and actions would no longer consist of lowest-common-denominator stews, with equal army-navy-air force ingredients, but would rise above service parochialism. The first chairman to exercise this new authority—and the last chairman of the Cold War era—was Admiral William J. Crowe, Jr. *See also* REVOLT OF THE ADMIRALS.

Joint Declaration from Eastern Europe One of the early fruits of the Soviet policy of GLASNOST outside the USSR itself was a document, produced in October 1986 by 123 political activists, observing the 30th anniversary of the HUNGARIAN REVOLUTION. Taking a step that would have been inconceivable not long before, and that was notable also for bringing together dissidents in different Soviet bloc countries, the signatories—from Czechoslovakia, East Germany, Hungary, and Poland—pledged their "common determination to struggle for political democracy" and for independence, pluralism, self-government, the peaceful unification of Europe, and the rights of minorities. Since the satellite countries had not adopted policies of glasnost, however, the declaration did not receive an enthusiastic welcome from the various local authorities. The East German government, for example, reviled the signatories from the GERMAN DEMOCRATIC REPUBLIC, declaring that the Hungarian Revolution should be remembered as a fascist rebellion.

Juin, Alphonse (1888–1967)   French general, marshal of France, chosen in 1951 by General Dwight D. EISENHOWER to be the first commander of the NORTH ATLANTIC TREATY ORGANIZATION's Central Command. Like a number of other high French officers of his generation, General Juin had a complex military history, having fought the Germans in 1940 and then become Vichy French commander in North Africa. When the Anglo-American forces landed in November 1942, Juin felt it his duty to offer opposition; later, however, he commanded the Free French corps in Italy. A native of Algeria, he opposed General Charles DE GAULLE's self-determination policy for the country. He and de Gaulle, however, later renewed their friendship.

Jupiter   U.S. medium-range missile installed in Europe and Turkey in the 1950s; it had a range of about 1,500 miles. Jupiters became a matter of contention during the CUBAN MISSILE CRISIS when the Soviets asked that they be removed from Turkey. In fact, the United States had already decided to do so, because their role could be better performed by submarine-launched POLARIS missiles, but the KENNEDY administration did not wish to appear to be acceding to the Soviet demand and thus did not rush to acknowledge the change.

K

Kádár, János (1912–1989)   Hungarian Communist politician whose extraordinary career, with its challenges and peripeties, seemed to offer a dramatic summary of the Eastern European experience under Soviet hegemony.

Born László Csermanek, the illegitimate son of a Slovak woman, and becoming at the age of eight László Gyurko when a family adopted him, Kádár later took the name by which he became known as an underground alias. An active Communist during the 1930s, he was arrested many times by the Horthy regime, which had come to power in 1919 after the crushing of the brief Communist government of Béla Kun. During World War II, when Hungary fought as an ally of Germany, Kádár organized resistance activities. In 1944 he was arrested by the Gestapo, the German secret police.

Having become a member of the Communist Party Central Committee in 1942 and secretary in 1943, Kádár won a seat in Parliament in 1945. In 1948 he achieved both party and governmental offices, as deputy general secretary of the Hungarian Working People's Party (which represented a merging of the Communist Party and the Social Democratic Party), minister of internal affairs, and inspector general of the AVO, the secret police. In May 1949, as part of his official duties, he was called on to perform a singularly distasteful task involving one of his oldest friends, László Rajk, the foreign minister, who had been accused of TITOist connections by the Stalinist Hungarian dictator, Mátyás RÁKOSI. Besides his long friendship with Rajk, Kádár had another tie with the family: Rajk's wife had saved his life during the war. When Rajk refused to confess to the fabricated crimes of which he was accused, Rákosi ordered Kádár to promise the prisoner a safe-conduct out of the country in exchange for an admission of guilt. Kádár did as he was told; Rajk finally confessed. Rákosi sprang the trap, turning Rajk over to the hangman.

In 1951, however, Kádár's turn came to suffer at Rákosi's hands. The dictator flung him into prison as an "antistate conspirator," and he underwent some of the special kinds of torture often associated with the Nazis. But in 1953, with Soviet dictator Joseph STALIN dead and Rákosi's own stock down in Moscow, officials like Kádár and Imre NAGY were rehabilitated and given governmental responsibilities. In 1956 Kádár became a member of the Hungarian Politburo and general secretary of the party, with the discredited Rákosi having departed for Moscow in the wake of popular discontent. When the discontent exploded into the HUNGARIAN REVOLUTION, Prime Minister Nagy became identified with it, but Kádár took his own course. Believing that matters had gotten out of hand, Kádár left Budapest and crossed the border to Uzhgorod, only to return on November 4 accompanied by Soviet tanks. Nagy fled to the Yugoslav embassy, from which Kádár guaranteed him safe conduct. Once again, Kádár's word proved something less than pure gold. Nagy was seized in Romania, returned to Budapest, and executed.

After the crushing of the revolution, Kádár found himself firmly in power and remained as general secretary of the party until 1988. He also served as prime minister (1956–58 and 1961–68). In spite of some of Kádár's despicable deeds, it has been said, during the 1960s and 1970s he gave

Hungary a better government than those of other Eastern Bloc nations. The French writer André Fontaine, who interviewed Kádár at some length, felt that his eyes showed fleeting reflections of genuine misery. If so, perhaps Kádár was remembering what Rajk's widow had said when he had asked her whether she could forgive him. Yes, she said, but could he forgive himself?

Kaganovich, Lazar Moiseyevich (1893–1991) One of the pre–World War I group of "old Bolsheviks"—along with V. M. MOLOTOV and Anastas MIKOYAN—who survived the perils of close association with Joseph STALIN, Kaganovich was a native of the Ukraine from a working-class Jewish family and as a teenager worked in a tannery, where he learned to be a cobbler. During the 1920s he rose to high positions in the Ukrainian Communist Party, and in 1930 he was called to Moscow as first secretary of the party committee in the capital. In this position, which made him in effect a kind of city manager, Kaganovich presided over the creation of the famously baroque Moscow subway. At the same time, as a high party agricultural official, he had a major role in the collectivization of agriculture, with its liquidation of the kulaks (the so-called wealthy peasants) and all its other much-chronicled horrors.

One of Stalin's closest associates, Kaganovich was lavish with praise on such occasions as the dictator's 50th birthday, in 1929. "The role of Stalin," Kaganovich declared, "was already predetermined in the dawn of development of our party, when the foundation stones were being laid, when the first party circles were being organized." Thus, in other words, it was all ordained by history. In the Great Purge (1936–38), Kaganovich gave Stalin unquestioning assistance. At some point he took on a habit that no doubt contributed to his survival through his long career. Entering a discussion, sometimes without knowing the subject or having heard a word that had been said, he would quickly declare, "I agree with Comrade Stalin." At the time of the Nazi-Soviet pact in 1939, the German foreign minister, Joachim von Ribbentrop, could report that all Jews had been removed from positions of power in the Soviet Union except for Kaganovich. In the early 1950s, however, during Stalin's final surge of paranoia, Kaganovich like

other longtime allies faced the real danger of liquidation, from which the death of the dictator in March 1953 spared him. Prominent in the collective leadership that followed, Kaganovich took a leading role in the activities of the so-called ANTIPARTY GROUP that in 1957 attempted to remove his onetime Ukrainian protégé Nikita KHRUSHCHEV from his post as head of the Communist Party. After this challenge failed, Khrushchev demonstrated that, in at least one clear respect, the Stalinist era had ended. Displaying no desire to stand the defeated dissidents in front of a firing squad, the triumphant leader assigned them to minor positions in various parts of the Soviet empire. Kaganovich went to Sverdlovsk as manager of a cement factory.

KAL 007 By the 1970s the northwest Pacific region, the only area besides Europe in which Soviet and U.S. forces faced each other directly, had become one of the warmest areas of the Cold War. It was also in some respects an area of particular Soviet vulnerability, since it provided the bases for important elements of the country's naval nuclear deterrent force, while nearby, in South Korea and Japan, the United States had built up substantial forward air strength. As a continuing part of this picture of front-line rivalry, the two superpowers engaged in intensive mutual aerial surveillance.

Onto this stage of active rivalry, on September 1, 1983, came a civilian airliner, Korean Airlines Flight 007, which, wandering far off its course, flew over several Soviet military bases. The result was an appalling tragedy that shocked the world. At about 3:27 A.M. a Soviet interceptor fired two missiles into the Boeing 747. Immediately the pilot reported, "The target is destroyed." All 269 people aboard the aircraft were killed, including 10 Canadians and 61 Americans.

Something of this kind had occurred once before. In 1978 Soviet planes had forced down a KAL Paris-to-Seoul flight that had become lost near Murmansk; crippled by a missile, the aircraft managed to land on a frozen lake in Karelia. Even though a Soviet pilot identified the plane as a civilian airliner, it had flown over important military installations, as KAL 007 would do five years later. Had the Soviets now taken the opportunity 007 offered them to impress the world with their resolve and brutality, as some suggested, or did they genuinely believe the downed aircraft might have been a U.S. spy plane in disguise? Highly mistrustful in general of U.S. intelligence activities, various groups in the West declared that 007, even if it was a legitimate airliner, very likely was also engaged in espionage. The pilots, they maintained, could hardly have been so heedless or so inept as to allow themselves to stray so far from their proper course.

It soon became clear that the Americans, through signal intelligence, had more information than they wished to make public. Speaking like a true intelligence veteran, William J. CASEY, director of the CENTRAL INTELLIGENCE AGENCY, was later quoted by a reporter, Seymour Hersh, as declaring that "our SIGINT [signal intelligence] capabilities are more important than any charge we sent a spy plane"; that is, it was better to allow people to believe in the spy-plane theory, if they wished to do so, than to reveal what the United States had been able to learn from radio communications about what the Soviets had actually said.

For their part, the Soviets refused to allow U.S. or Japanese ships to search for black boxes—the flight data and cockpit voice recorders—inside Soviet territorial waters, and through harassing tactics they tried to disrupt the search in international waters.

In 1992 many of the questions were answered when Russian president Boris YELTSIN, calling the destruction of 007 "the most horrible catastrophe of the Cold War," released documents including transcripts of the flight-recorder tape and of part, at least, of the voice-recorder tape. The materials made it clear that the lost and frightened crew of the aircraft did not even realize they had been attacked and that 007's plunge toward the Sea of Japan had been caused by heat-seeking missiles that had slammed into it. Desperately the crew radioed for help from flight controllers in Tokyo.

The documents also revealed that the Soviet government made every effort to cover up evidence that did not support its claim that 007 was engaging in a spy mission. The materials showed how the defense minister and the chairman of the KGB, in time-honored bureaucratic fashion, had attempted to persuade the ailing general secretary, Yuri ANDROPOV, that the flight must have been

"premeditated," even though they found no direct evidence to support the claim.

One of the most effective summaries of U.S. and Soviet behavior in the days following the tragedy came later from Canada's Prime Minister Pierre TRUDEAU, who had access to information from signal intelligence: "The Americans knew that it was an accident, and the Soviets knew that the plane was not sent by the Americans. The two superpowers were talking past each other."

Kalinin, Mikhail Ivanovich (1875–1946) "Old Bolshevik" who became chairman of the Presidium of the SUPREME SOVIET (Soviet president) in 1938 but had no discernible effect on Soviet policies during his long career—a fact that may help account for the length of that career. Kalinin became chairman of the Central Executive Committee shortly after the end of World War I and held the position until becoming Soviet president. He was depicted in the latter role in a memorable scene in the World War II–era motion picture *Mission to Moscow* (based on a memoir by former U.S. ambassador Joseph E. Davies), one of the Hollywood films of the time intended to create American admiration for the USSR. Gazing thoughtfully at a slowly turning world globe in his Kremlin office, President Kalinin assures Ambassador Davies that the earth has ample room for a variety of doctrines and peoples. This propaganda effort, said the eminent critic James Agee, could almost be described as "the first Soviet production to come from a major American studio."

Katyn Forest Massacre In April 1943, in the midst of World War II, the Germans announced that in a forest near Smolensk, USSR, they had discovered mass graves containing the corpses of some 4,000 Polish officers and troops. These men, along with 11,000 others not accounted for, had surrendered to the Soviets in the autumn of 1939, when the Red Army, by agreement with Adolf Hitler, moved into Poland. The strong suspicion that the Soviets had committed the atrocity led the Polish government-in-exile in London to ask them to investigate the case. (The suspicion was thoroughly confirmed in 1992 with the release of POLITBURO and other documents showing that the Soviet dictator Joseph STALIN gave the direct order for the massacre.) Rebuffing the Polish request, the Soviets instead used the occasion to break relations with the Poles, accusing them of spreading German propaganda. Though the Polish premier, Stanislaw MIKOLAJ-CZYK, pleaded with Britain and the United States to press the Soviets, the Western Allies at this point in the war wished to avoid trouble with the Kremlin. Poland went on to become the subject of the most vexed issues between the West and the USSR, but in reality the discovery of 4,000 murdered non-Communist Poles who had been leading citizens—scientists, doctors, lawyers—called up in 1939 as reserve officers, together with the Soviet reaction, made it clear that Stalin intended for Poland to have the government of his choice; not even a friendly but Western-oriented regime (if such could exist) would do. In part, of course, security concerns lay behind the Soviet view. By presenting a painful incident of East-West doubt and conflict, muted though it was, the Katyn Forest Massacre represented a very early incident in what became the Cold War.

Revelations in the 1990s showed that the officers were shot in "gangland-execution style." In August 1993, in a cemetery in Warsaw, Russian president Boris YELTSIN, dressed in black, paid homage to the Poles who had been killed at Katyn and in three Soviet camps.

Kennan, George Frost (1904–)   One of the most influential diplomats of the 20th century, George Kennan played a leading part in shaping U.S. policy in the critical years following World War II. In particular, his concept of CONTAINMENT came to be, with all its accompanying variations, the basic U.S. strategy in the Cold War.

A Milwaukee native, Kennan had as a boyhood hero his grandfather's first cousin, after whom he was named. The elder George Kennan, an explorer and writer, won fame in the 1890s with his account of travels in Siberia and his indictment of the Russian system of justice. Saying that he felt connected to the older man "by bonds deeper than just our rather distant kinship," the younger Kennan later wrote, "I feel that I was in some strange way destined to carry forward as best I could the work of my distinguished and respected namesake."

In September 1926, a year after graduating from Princeton, where as a shy Midwesterner he often felt like an outsider, Kennan entered the U.S. Foreign Service. After serving in minor posts at various cities in Europe, he was given the chance to choose a language of specialization. With his elder relative in mind—and also in anticipation of the ultimate establishment of diplomatic relations between the United States and the Soviet Union—Kennan picked Russian and went off for two years of study in BERLIN. Afterward, he and several contemporaries, including Charles BOHLEN (who had engaged in comparable study in Paris), were assigned to duty in Baltic capitals. At the end of 1933, almost immediately after the establishment of U.S.-Soviet relations, Kennan went to Moscow, where, aside from several months in Vienna, he remained until 1937. After a time back in Washington, he was posted to Prague, arriving in the city on the day of the Munich Conference.

At the beginning of World War II, in September 1939, the State Department transferred Kennan to Berlin so that he could continue the kind of political reporting he had delivered from Prague. After the United States entered the war, Kennan and other Americans were interned for five months, during which time, to Kennan's disgust, the State Department made no effort to get in touch with them; later, they found that the government did not intend to pay their salaries for the period of their internment, on the grounds that they had not been working during this time. Such attitudes could only enhance Kennan's essentially dim view of politicians, with their habit of using questions of foreign affairs for domestic political advantage and their failure to appreciate the purposes and contributions of the Foreign Service.

After being sent to Lisbon in an exchange of interned personnel, Kennan was appointed counselor of the legation. He went to London in January 1944 to work as political adviser to Ambassador John G. Winant, who represented the United States on the newly created European Advisory Commission, which was supposed to plan for German surrender terms and a transition to peace at the end of the war. In 1944, after an absence of seven years, Kennan returned to Moscow, this time with the rank of minister, as counselor—a position that made him key adviser to Ambassador Averell HARRIMAN, for whom he developed great admiration. Together these two faced the increasing problems stemming from Soviet actions in Poland and the Balkans.

In February 1946, profoundly unhappy with what he saw as "the naïveté of our underlying ideas as to what it was we were hoping to achieve in our relations with the Soviet government," and also with "the methods and devices with which we went about achieving it," Kennan, then chargé d'affaires, turned a minor query from Washington into the occasion for a monumental reply, an 8,000-word disquisition on Soviet Russian attitudes and STALIN's foreign-policy aims. "All [was] neatly divided," Kennan said, "like an eighteenth-century Protestant sermon, into five separate parts," his idea being that the message thus split up would not appear so formidable to its recipients. The dispatch, with its analysis of Stalin's ideas and purposes, caused a quiet sensation in official Washington and ever since has been famous as the Long Telegram. Harriman, back in Washington, saw that it was read by Navy Secretary James FORRESTAL, who in turn distributed it widely in high places. Essentially, in a Washington that at the time lacked any consensus about U.S. relations with the Soviet Union, the telegram filled a vacuum. Though Kennan later tended to deprecate the document, speaking of rereading it "with horrified amusement," it transformed him into a leading expert on Soviet affairs. "My reputation was made," he said. "My voice now carried." (Despite Kennan's talk of horrified amusement, his outlook was not really idiosyncratic; during the same period, Frank Roberts, Kennan's counterpart at the British embassy, was expressing similar opinions in his dispatches to the Foreign Office.)

In July 1947 came a second famous document from Kennan's pen: the "X ARTICLE," "The Sources of Soviet Conduct," which appeared in the quarterly *Foreign Affairs* under the provocative byline "X." This article, though written unofficially, presented the world with the ideas for the containment policy, with which Kennan was associated forever after. The article appeared just as he assumed the new post—created by Secretary of State George MARSHALL—of chairman of the Policy Planning Staff. In 1949 and 1950 Kennan held a special position as long-range policy adviser to the secretary of state; by this time his views on con-

George F. Kennan, author of the influential "X article" on Soviet conduct

tainment were diverging from those of the TRUMAN administration, which had universalized and militarized Kennan's concepts—although, despite his marked talent as a writer of prose, Kennan's definitions had not always been sharp.

In the spring of 1952 Kennan went to Moscow as ambassador, but he stayed only until October, being declared persona non grata after making surprisingly indiscreet comments about Soviet treatment of diplomats. He was out of government service until 1961, when U.S. president John F. KENNEDY, wishing to make use of this eminent public servant, appointed him ambassador to Yugoslavia. Here again, however, Kennan did not have a happy experience, although he liked the country and the people and developed amicable relations with Marshal TITO. His ambassadorship came at a time when Tito seemed to be moving toward a rapprochement with Premier Nikita KHRUSHCHEV's Soviet government, and Yugoslavia's vaunted NONALIGNMENT seemed actually to be one-sided in favor of the Soviet Union. Though Kennan understood the complexities of Yugoslavia's situation and the advantages the United States could continue to draw from good relations with Tito, his unhappiness with congressional denunciations and trade sanctions—once again demonstrating to him the weakness of the U.S. way of diplomacy—led to Kennan's resignation in the summer of 1963.

After leaving Yugoslavia, Kennan returned to the Institute for Advanced Study at Princeton, with which he had first been associated in 1950, to continue his research and writing, which had won him acclaim as a leading historian of Russia and of diplomacy. During the 1960s, much sought after by interviewers and congressional committees, Kennan opposed the VIETNAM WAR as, succinctly, "not our business."

On reading Kennan's *Memoirs: 1925–1950,* published in 1967, the British scientist and writer C. P. Snow said, "We shan't see another Western diplomat like him for long enough."

Kennedy, John Fitzgerald (1917–1963)   The youngest person and first Roman Catholic to be elected president of the United States, John F. Kennedy served only 34 months in the office before being assassinated by a sniper as he rode in a motorcade in Dallas. Yet his brief administration saw both a historic U.S. low point in the Cold War—the BAY OF PIGS OPERATION in Cuba—and the successful resolution of the era's closest approach to nuclear war—the CUBAN MISSILE CRISIS. Kennedy's time as president also produced the first hopeful move in the field of arms control, the NUCLEAR TEST BAN TREATY of 1963. His administration was also strongly marked by a less tangible quality, a special tone and atmosphere that captivated press and people across the United States and around the world.

No family in American history has attracted more attention than the Kennedys, from "old Joe," JFK's multimillionaire father who was President ROOSEVELT's ambassador to Great Britain, to the president's brothers, to his beautiful and elegant wife, Jacqueline Bouvier Kennedy (1929–1994), who did much to set the tone of his admin-

istration, and to the president himself, with his good looks, charm, and sharp wit.

As a rich young man who thoroughly appreciated life's pleasures, John Kennedy showed no special interest in politics and clearly did not set out to become president of the United States. Though his hard-driving father expected all his children to be outstanding in some field or activity, the political role was assigned to the oldest Kennedy son, Joseph P. Kennedy, Jr.; Jack's thoughts were directed toward journalism or teaching. After graduating cum laude from Harvard in 1940, he worked as his father's secretary in the London embassy. Rejected by the army because of a chronic back problem, Kennedy managed to enlist in the navy in September 1941. In April 1943 he found himself taking command of an 80-foot torpedo boat, PT-109; in a Solomon Islands strait, a little more than three months later, a Japanese destroyer sliced through PT-109, sending the two halves to the bottom. For his courage and resourcefulness in directing the rescue and personally saving three men, Kennedy, whose injury had been aggravated in the collision, received the Navy and Marine Corps Medal. Asked later by a child how he had become a war hero, Kennedy declared: "It was involuntary. They sank my boat." (His World War II experience was to make possible another distinction: he would become the first U.S. president to have served in the navy.)

Discharged from the navy after an operation on his back for a problem that would cause him pain for the rest of his life (he also suffered from Addison's disease, a well-kept secret), Kennedy attended the founding UNITED NATIONS conference in San Francisco as a reporter. The next year, however, he moved from reporting into active politics, seeking and winning election to Congress from Boston's hard-core Democratic 11th district. Responsibility for this development has often been ascribed to Kennedy's father, who is said to have insisted that son Jack play the role originally assigned his brother Joe, killed late in World War II; the Kennedy administration's official chronicler, Arthur M. Schlesinger, Jr., has commented, however, that such a choice was natural for Jack and that no paternal coercion was required. After three unremarkable terms in the House of Representatives, Kennedy challenged Henry Cabot LODGE in the 1952 senatorial race and, in the face of an EISENHOWER victory in Massachusetts as well as in the country as a whole, defeated the incumbent by 70,000 votes.

Early in his first term in the Senate, Kennedy married Jacqueline Bouvier. For the next two years JFK, undergoing two more operations on his back, spent much of the time incapacitated. At one point his illness spared him the painful task of casting a vote to censure Senator Joseph MCCARTHY, who, though loathed by liberals, was not only his father's friend but had a large following among the Boston Irish. While Kennedy lay ill, he worked with the help of Ted Sorensen on his book *Profiles in Courage,* which won the 1957 Pulitzer Prize for biography. In 1956, at the Democratic National Convention, Kennedy came to the attention of the television audience when Adlai STEVENSON, the nominee for president, departed from tradition by leaving the choice of the vice presidential candidate to the delegates. Estes Kefauver's narrow win in this contest represented only a temporary setback for the telegenic young Massachusetts senator, whose impressive bid for the job seemed to demonstrate that the presidency itself did indeed lie within reach.

During the next four years JFK and his brothers spent much of their time, and of their father's wealth, driving toward his 1960 Democratic presidential nomination and to victory over Eisenhower's vice president, Richard NIXON, in the election, which was the closest since Grover Cleveland won the popular count but lost in the electoral college in 1888 (and the vote itself was the closest in percentage terms in U.S. history). The election, even if marred by allegations of vote fraud, put an end to the traditional belief that a Catholic could not become president of the United States. Continuing to capitalize on his charismatic appeal, Kennedy had shone to advantage during the campaign in the first series of televised debates between presidential candidates. Nixon, ill prepared for the cameras, underestimated the power of appearance. The face of campaigning would never be the same.

After professing in his widely praised inaugural address the faith of the true Cold Warrior "defending freedom in its hour of maximum danger," JFK authorized the mounting and the launch in April 1961 of a CENTRAL INTELLIGENCE AGENCY–supported landing in Fidel CASTRO's Cuba—the Bay of Pigs operation—which proved a resounding fiasco, one of the worst U.S. setbacks of the Cold War. Just a month and a half after this unpromising beginning, the new president met in Vienna with Soviet premier Nikita KHRUSHCHEV. The two men argued over ideology in general and over Laos, BERLIN, and other specific centers of conflict; Berlin, the most sensitive spot, sitting some 80 miles inside East Germany, had been called by Khrushchev the "testicles of the West," which he could squeeze any time he felt like it. Widely thought to have decided that Kennedy's failure to support the Bay of Pigs landings meant the president could be bullied (a belief confirmed by one of his aides in a 1993 interview conducted by Vladislav Zubok), Khrushchev yielded nothing in conversation and declared his intention to give Berlin a major squeeze in December by turning it over to East Germany.

Khrushchev's son later noted that his father returned from the Vienna meeting with "a very high opinion of Kennedy," seeing him as "a worthy partner and strong statesman, as well as a simple, charming man to whom he took a real liking." At the moment in Vienna, however, Khrushchev, disappointed at receiving no new proposals concerning Berlin, tended to dismiss the U.S. president as a young man still in "short pants," and overall, by his own statement, regarded JFK as in essence merely another EISENHOWER, the previous president with whom he had dealt, defending "the aggressive interests of monopolistic capital and the leading position of the United States in the world, without taking anyone else's interests into account." Khrushchev had the feeling, he said, that at their last meeting Kennedy was "not only anxious but deeply upset." But in July, after Khrushchev had proclaimed his intention to settle the Berlin question unilaterally, Kennedy activated the National Guard and called up army reserves. In September, Khrushchev and the East Germans presented the United States and the world with the BERLIN WALL. A year later came the potentially deadliest of all Cold War confrontations, the Cuban Missile Crisis.

In later years, as reporters probed more deeply into the private sides of public figures and recog-

U.S. president John F. Kennedy enjoys verbal sparring with reporters during a press conference.

nized few limits on what they might publish, two aspects of Kennedy's life received the kind of attention they escaped during his days as president—his sexual adventures and his medical condition. Various accounts and memoirs have disclosed the president's remarkable and frequent indiscretions extending even to a woman connected with figures in organized crime, and along with these stories have come revelations about the kinds of treatment Kennedy received—and was willing to accept —for his back and adrenal problems. Already the recipient of medication for his Addison's disease and procaine injections for his back pain, he welcomed the ministrations of the New York "feel good" doctor, Max Jacobson, who gave his patients injections of steroids and amphetamines mixed, at times, with bits of bone marrow, electric-eel tissue, and other unlikely substances.

Jacobson claimed that when Bobby Kennedy remonstrated with his brother for submitting himself to such injections, JFK simply brushed him off, saying "I don't care if it's horse piss. It works." In his study of the medical conditions of various world leaders, Dr. Bert Park concluded that the injections probably increased Kennedy's libido and, though not creating a tendency to take risks, very likely enhanced an already existing trait. But, of course, what relation these points might have borne to individual political decisions and actions could not be determined without specific knowledge of timing and dosage. In any case, in the Cuban Missile Crisis, the major test of his presidency, Kennedy by universal agreement conducted himself with admirable coolness and patience and an ability to see the situation from all sides.

The events of the fourth weekend in November

1963, from the assassination of Kennedy to his burial at Arlington National Cemetery, created a national television experience of unprecedented scope and intensity. The murder case itself, with its various supposed loose ends and questions not fully answered by the official commission of inquiry (the Warren Commission), has given rise to literally thousands of books and articles, and even to later congressional hearings. Kennedy's successor, Lyndon JOHNSON, established the high-level Warren Commission in large part to put an end to widespread rumors that Soviet or Cuban officials had plotted the assassination of the president as the third act in a back-and-forth drama that had opened with the Bay of Pigs attack and continued with the Cuban Missile Crisis; Johnson feared that the rumors might produce a new and worse crisis, even a nuclear war. Despite all the criticisms of the Warren Commission and all the subsequent theorizing, no proof has yet come to light to make an event of such magnitude anything more than the lone act of a psychotic misfit named Lee Harvey Oswald.

See also ALLIANCE FOR PROGRESS; NUCLEAR TEST BAN TREATY; PEACE CORPS.

Kennedy, Robert Francis (1925–1968) Younger brother of U.S. president John F. KENNEDY, Robert Kennedy became attorney general in the new administration in 1961 (with the president joking that his brother had to acquire experience somewhere) and served almost as JFK's alter ego through the 34 months of the Kennedy presidency. His presence at his brother's side and the utter trust between the two played an important part in the resolution of the CUBAN MISSILE CRISIS, when Robert Kennedy not only represented the president in negotiation with Soviet representatives but chaired meetings of the special group of advisers that came to be called ExComm (for executive committee of the National Security Council). After the assassination of the president on November 22, 1963, Robert stayed on as attorney general, despite a deep mutual detestation between himself and President JOHNSON, until September 1964, when he resigned to run for the U.S. Senate from New York.

A Harvard graduate, like his brother John, Robert Kennedy held a law degree from the University of Virginia (1951) and gained practical political experience by managing JFK's winning 1952 campaign for the Senate. He found himself at the center of political affairs in 1953 as assistant counsel to the Senate Permanent Subcommittee on Investigations, better known as the McCarthy Committee after its chairman, Joe MCCARTHY, a friend of Kennedy's father. After resigning from this position later in the year, Kennedy returned to the committee in February 1954 as minority (Democratic) counsel and was chief counsel from 1955 to 1957. In 1957, as chief counsel to a Senate committee looking into relations between labor and organized crime, Kennedy investigated the doings of the Teamsters Union president, Dave Beck, and began his celebrated running battle with Beck's right-hand man, Jimmy Hoffa. Continuing the fight as attorney general, he succeeded in getting Hoffa sent to prison. At the Justice Department he also took a strong personal interest in civil-rights questions, although he had not earlier professed any strong liberal convictions. Supreme Court Justice Thurgood Marshall (1908–1993) once offered an interesting comparison of the Kennedy brothers. Calling the late president "a very sweet man," Marshall described Robert as "like his father. He was a cold, calculating character."

Having won the 1964 senatorial election, Robert Kennedy became an influential critic of administration policy in Vietnam. He suggested in a February 1966 press conference, for example, that the NATIONAL LIBERATION FRONT—the political arm of the VIETCONG—be offered a share in the government of South Vietnam. In various political areas he positioned himself somewhat to the left of the Johnson administration, particularly in calling for more domestic spending for troubled cities, which experienced unprecedented racial rioting. A foretaste of the 1968 political picture came in Kennedy's 1966 campaign on behalf of Democratic congressional candidates, when it became clear that crowds were turning out to see the senator. He was no longer simply the brother of the late president but had established himself as an important public figure. Pollsters declared Kennedy more popular than President Johnson or Vice President Hubert Humphrey. By 1968, through his investigations of rural and urban poverty, Kennedy had come to be viewed by many as a sort of tribune of the poor. This outlook, together with his now-declared opposition to the VIETNAM WAR, made him a formidable contender for the Democratic presidential nomination. After his victory speech following the California primary, Robert Kennedy was cut down by an assassin's bullets. It seemed incredible, but there it was on television: a second Kennedy brother had been murdered.

KGB (Komitet Gosudarstvennoy Bezopasnosti) (in English, the Committee for State Security)   Although people in the West often spoke of the KGB as if it were simply the Soviet intelligence service—an organization analogous to the U.S. CENTRAL INTELLIGENCE AGENCY or British MI6—this idea gave only a very partial suggestion of the scope of the KGB's power and activities. Speaking in the CONGRESS OF PEOPLE'S DEPUTIES in 1989, a delegate, deploring the continuing power of the KGB, declared that it exercised "all-encompassing control over society and over each person individually" and called it "the most closed, the most clandestine of all state institutions."

Known through its history by a confusing series of titles, the KGB in its various forms held the chief responsibility for state security throughout the existence of the Communist state. Founded in 1917 as the Cheka, the organization included among its subsequent sets of initials OGPU, NKVD, MGB, and MVD. In addition to its espionage, political secret police, and counterintelligence functions, it controlled the regular police, the GULAG (concentration camp) system, fire departments, and even geological exploration. During Joseph STALIN's Great Terror in the 1930s, the NKVD (as the organization was called at that time) operated death camps with killing fields. A notable example, revealed in 1993, was the execution center at Butovo, now a woodsy village on the southern edge of Moscow; many of its approximately 25,000 victims were themselves purged NKVD employees. In the 1950s the KGB planted apple trees atop the mass graves and, in a benign gesture, distributed the fruit among local orphanages.

Internationally, the KGB controlled the links between the Comintern Executive Committee and foreign Communist parties. Overall, it served as the principal mechanism by which the leadership of the COMMUNIST PARTY OF THE SOVIET UNION exercised its control of the country and the people. In 1954, First Secretary Nikita KHRUSHCHEV moved to make the organization slightly less autonomous by causing the designation to be changed from MGB (for ministry) to KGB (for committee), but, whatever effect this alteration had on politics inside the Kremlin, it did not leave visible traces in the outside world.

The title of most famous KGB Western agent clearly belongs to the British intelligence officer Kim PHILBY. The most important Soviet penetration of Britain in later years was probably the PRIME CASE, involving the signal-intelligence officer Geoffrey Prime. In the United States the KGB scored its greatest success with the WALKER SPY RING (1968–85), which supplied the Soviets with a mass of naval ciphers and communications.

Criticizing the ideological limits within which KGB political officers had normally been forced to work, one of them declared in a 1991 interview in *IZVESTIA*: "In order to please our superiors, we sent in falsified and biased information, acting on the principle 'Blame everything on the Americans, and everything will be OK.' That's not intelligence, it's self-deception."

Khe Sanh   At the beginning of 1968, as part of the TET OFFENSIVE, combined forces of North Vietnam and the NATIONAL LIBERATION FRONT attacked the U.S. Marine base and an airfield located at Khe Sanh, in the western part of central Vietnam near the border with Laos and only 18 miles from the DEMILITARIZED ZONE (DMZ). Staged in an attempt to draw U.S. troops away from the real enemy targets—the major cities of South Vietnam—the attack achieved great success, causing U.S. commanders to become so preoccupied that they regarded evidence pointing to North Vietnamese plans to attack the cities as deliberate distractions; thus the priorities were exactly reversed.

At Khe Sanh, 40,000 North Vietnamese regulars surrounded the 3rd and 26th Marines; the siege lasted 75 days, until early April, when the North Vietnamese abandoned their positions after experiencing bombing attacks said to have been the most intense in the history of warfare. The reporting of the Khe Sanh battle has been controversial, with many commentators declaring that American reporters made the siege out to be a more severe affair than it was and thus, in effect, contributed to some disaffection of U.S. domestic public opinion. But this American DIEN BIEN PHU also increased U.S. determination to hold out.

Khmer Rouge Name for the Communist forces in Cambodia. Coined by Prince Norodom SIHANOUK, it means Red Khmer, Khmer being the name for a member of the largest Cambodian ethnic group. The origins of the Khmer Rouge go back to 1950 and the founding of a united revolutionary front by the Communists. Made up of several factions, it ultimately came under the control of Saloth Sar, later to be known to the world as POL POT. In 1975 the Khmer Rouge emerged victorious from the civil war in Cambodia.

Khrushchev, Nikita Sergeyevich (1894–1971) Soviet leader who came to power at the midpoint of the life of the Communist regime—roughly halfway between Lenin, the founding father, and Mikhail GORBACHEV, the reformer who unwillingly presided over the dissolution of the USSR in 1991. A longtime follower of Joseph STALIN and a believing Marxist-Leninist, Khrushchev displayed a colorful and often aggressive personal style and frequent lack of inhibition that tended to obscure his energetic (if limited) efforts to reform his country's economy and politics. A world that through the decades had grown accustomed to the granite-like public impassivity of Stalin, V. M. MOLOTOV, and other prominent Soviet figures had difficulty fathoming this mercurial and far more human-seeming politician with his blunt remarks and earthy peasant metaphors.

Certainly no shadow of undesirable middle-class connections darkened Khrushchev's background. The son of an itinerant miner and grandson of a serf, he was born in a village in southwest Russia, near the Ukrainian border, and received little schooling. At the age of 15 he began working as a pipe fitter in the mines of the Donets basin, a specialty that kept him from being drafted into the army in World War I. Though something of a labor activist, he did not join the Communist Party until 1918. In the following years, as a junior political commissar, he served in the Red Army in its struggles against the Whites and the Poles.

After these adventures, Khrushchev returned to the Donets basin, becoming assistant manager of a coal mine and then, to make up for his lack of earlier education, a student. Having lost his wife in the great famine of 1921, he married Nina Petrovna, known to the world many years later as the quiet and matronly wife of the ebullient Soviet leader. Khrushchev's performance as an executive and political worker won him the favor of the Ukrainian Communist Party boss, Lazar KAGANOVICH, who took him to the 1925 party congress in Moscow and, continuing to act as his mentor, back to the capital in 1929. Khrushchev moved into full-time party work, and by 1935, as first secretary of the local committee (in succession to Kaganovich), he had become in effect mayor of the Soviet capital. An unswerving follower of Stalin, he survived the Great Purge (1936–38), returning to the Ukraine in 1938 as party first secretary and, in 1939, becoming a full member of the Politburo. After serving as a Red Army political officer during World War II (including full participation in the battle for Stalingrad), he became party boss and head of government in the Ukraine, where his efforts to deal with the terrible famine of 1946 gave him a stern lesson in Soviet agricultural deficiencies. In 1949 he was back in Moscow as local party boss and member of the party Secretariat.

Stalin's death on March 5, 1953, created a vacancy at the top of the Soviet structure for the first time in three decades. Overlooking Khrushchev's persistence, his organizational talents, and his skill as a political infighter, most observers failed to foresee that, following an interregnum under the better-known Georgi MALENKOV, the dead dictator's seat of power would be claimed by the one-time peasant from the Kursk region. Acquiring the key post of party first secretary six months after Stalin's death, Khrushchev devoted special attention to increasing grain harvests through plowing up "virgin lands"—a program that ultimately proved a disappointment—and, in opposition to Malenkov, he advocated the development of heavy industry at the expense of consumer goods. Like Stalin in the 1920s, he made the most of his control of Communist Party machinery to win the battle for power; on February 8, 1955, the party Presidium voted to replace Malenkov as premier by Khrushchev's own nominee, Marshal Nikolai

BULGANIN, who would simply serve as a front for the first secretary. In March 1958 Khrushchev would take the post for himself, thus becoming head of both the party and the government.

In February 1956, at the 20th Congress of the COMMUNIST PARTY OF THE SOVIET UNION, Khrushchev produced the coup de théâtre for which history will always remember him. Speaking to the assembled party faithful, the first secretary astounded his listeners with a lengthy and detailed attack on the "cult of the person of Stalin," which had brought "a whole series of exceedingly serious and grave perversions of party principles, of party democracy, of revolutionary legality." Speaking of Stalin's "capricious and despotic character" and his use of "brutal violence," Khrushchev described the late dictator's paranoia, the "sickly suspicion" that caused Stalin to see around him nothing but " 'enemies,' 'two-facers' and 'spies.' " In particular, Khrushchev detailed the iniquities of the Great Purge; of 139 members elected to the Central Committee at the time, he said, 98—that is, 70 percent—were arrested and shot, the confessions being won by torture. Overall, Khrushchev declared, the Communist Party must rid itself of the cult of the individual and return to true Marxism-Leninism. By demonstrating how far astray the party had gone under Stalin, however, Khrushchev had also destroyed—presumably unintentionally—the idea of its infallibility.

The "de-Stalinization" speech, with its declaration of the end of Stalinist terror, and the consequent release of thousands of political prisoners introduced the period of relative relaxation in Soviet cultural life called the THAW. Frequently seeming in conflict with himself, however, Khrushchev veered this way and that in literary and artistic matters, forbidding Boris PASTERNAK, poet and author of the novel *Doctor Zhivago,* to accept the 1958 Nobel Prize for literature but allowing the publication in the USSR of Alexander SOLZHENITSYN's *One Day in the Life of Ivan Denisovich,* which dealt with life in Soviet prison camps. Part of this wavering came simply from the fact that Khrushchev did not hold unquestioned mastery of the scene, as Stalin had done, but had to deal with conflicting interest groups and with such influential figures as the veteran Communist Party ideologue Mikhail SUSLOV. "I'm truly sorry for the way I behaved toward Pasternak," Khrushchev said years later. "My only excuse is that I didn't read the book." Toward abstract art, however, Khrushchev showed no tolerance at all. In 1962, during a tour of an exhibition that included a few mild examples of nonrepresentational painting, the leader asked to speak with the artist. "What's the good of a picture like this?" he demanded. "To cover urinals with? We should take down your pants and set you down in a clump of nettles until you understand your mistakes."

To credit Khrushchev with important reforms, then, is not to characterize him as a reformer in the Western democratic sense, as if he were a more or less idealistic mayor or governor. By his own acknowledgment, he had grown up in a brutal political school; anyone who opposed the dictator simply put his own head on the chopping block. (Even socially, Stalin displayed cruelty. Years later, commenting on Stalin's habit of getting drunk at dinner and making his middle-aged, sedentary subordinates perform the strenuous folk dance called the gopak, Khrushchev said memorably, "When Stalin said dance, you danced!")

Khrushchev demonstrated the effects of his Stalinist training in October 1956 by his bloody repression of the HUNGARIAN REVOLUTION—although he appears to have resorted to force with some reluctance. Just a few days earlier he had resisted the temptation to use troops in a similar situation in Poland; unlike the Hungarians, however, the Poles had not gone further toward self-determination than the Kremlin of that era could tolerate. Khrushchev had definitely not intended de-Stalinization as a declaration of independence for the Soviet satellites, though in the following years he kept them on a far looser rein than they had previously known.

In June 1957 Khrushchev showed firm resolve and marked resourcefulness in resisting an attempt by a majority of the Presidium—including the old stalwarts Molotov and Kaganovich as well as Malenkov—to remove him from power. The dissidents objected to his agricultural policy and to what they regarded as his unsuccessful efforts to reach a kind of early-day DÉTENTE with the United States, particularly in regard to Germany. Refusing to accept the verdict of the Presidium, Khrushchev, with the vitally important help of Marshal Georgi

ZHUKOV (who provided the aircraft), summoned the CENTRAL COMMITTEE to Moscow. This body, many of whose members owed their jobs to First Secretary Khrushchev, overrode the decision of the Presidium, and thus it was the members of the ANTIPARTY GROUP, and not Khrushchev, who lost the battles, though they came to no personal harm. Molotov, in a nice non-Stalinist touch, found himself dispatched to Outer Mongolia as ambassador. Made to sound imbecilic in the laborious prose of the Central Committee resolution that condemned them, these veteran Communists stood accused of inability to understand a wide range of foreign and domestic questions, including the "new and vital tasks" of agriculture, notably the effort to "overtake the USA in per capita output of milk, butter and meat in the next few years." Khrushchev, apparently sincerely, would always hold to his dream of outproducing the United States both industrially and agriculturally, though the USSR would never even remotely approach this goal.

In foreign affairs, Khrushchev, for all his occasional violent rhetoric (often in relation to BERLIN), responded realistically to the awesome power of nuclear weapons. Rejecting Lenin's belief that war between capitalist and socialist states was inevitable, he emphasized the idea of PEACEFUL COEXISTENCE between East and West, though by this he did not mean the absence of conflict, which he appeared as a good Marxist-Leninist to regard as a permanent condition. His approach, combined with his discrediting of Stalin, earned him the hostility of the far more ideologically fervid Chinese Communist Party, which began to see in the Soviet leader another Marshal TITO. The Chinese became particularly upset when Khrushchev returned from a 1959 trip through the United States with affirmations of friendship for President Dwight D. EISENHOWER. During this visit, he declared that his famous "we will bury you" statement had been misconstrued. "I meant," he said, "that capitalism would be buried and Communism would come to replace it."

The benign effects of this "spirit of Camp David" lasted only until May 1960, when a Soviet missile brought down a high-flying U.S. U-2 reconnaissance aircraft over the USSR, shortly before the opening of a summit conference in Paris. Having offered Eisenhower the opportunity to issue the diplomatic denial of personal involvement standard in such cases, Khrushchev broke up the conference after the president admitted he had known that the particular flight was going to take place and declined to offer an apology. (The incident also offered Khrushchev the opportunity to demonstrate his toughness to Kremlin conservatives and to the Chinese.) From this point on, relations between the two countries declined, until October 1962 brought the threat of nuclear confrontation after Khrushchev had arranged for intermediate-range missiles to be placed in Cuba. The discovery by the KENNEDY administration of the missile sites, before the weapons could become operational, led to the CUBAN MISSILE CRISIS, by far the most serious great-power confrontation of the Cold War.

At home, Khrushchev's strength had begun to wane. The problems with China and the United States, economic difficulties, the failure of the virgin-lands program to yield the needed grain, discontent arising from a restructuring of the Communist Party, hostility of military officers who objected to the reduction in size of the army, weariness with Khrushchev's erratic behavior, indications that he might be moving toward a new German policy that could bring reunification and the consequent end of the East German government—all these factors, and perhaps others, led to the Central Committee meeting of October 14, 1964. Acting as chief prosecutor, Suslov, in standard fashion, accused the leader of a catalogue of offenses and omissions, ranging from his concentration of power into his own hands to his use of "dirty language" in sessions of the Presidium.

Retired as a "special pensioner" after his forced resignation, Khrushchev lived in Moscow and at his dacha, essentially under house arrest, until his death of a heart attack on September 11, 1971. The newspapers carried only a brief obituary notice—no article, only a few lines of small type, lacking even the usual expression of "deep regret." Certainly Khrushchev's conservative, neo-Stalinist successors would not have acknowledged that, for all his flaws, his swings to and fro, the premier had been the strongest reforming force the Soviet Union had known since the early days of Bolshevik power. Years later, in 1988, when GLASNOST brought prohibited subjects into public discussion, a writer gave a striking title to his profile of Khrushchev, calling his subject "The Last Romantic."

KI (Komitet Informatsii) Two Soviet foreign intelligence agencies bore this designation (in English, the Committee of Information). The first, made up of the combined foreign intelligence directorates of the MGB (predecessor of the KGB) and the GRU and known, for scholarly purposes, as the "large" KI, was created in the early autumn of 1947; Premier STALIN established it in response to the creation of the American CENTRAL INTELLIGENCE AGENCY. For a time the KI wielded considerable influence, particularly because it was headed by V. M. MOLOTOV, the Soviet foreign minister, but the agency became the victim of Stalin's increasing mistrust of Molotov (supposedly, the veteran foreign minister's wife participated in a "Zionist" plot) and also became embroiled in bureaucratic controversies. In November 1951 it was formally dissolved. But the central staff survived, immediately becoming the "small" KI and carrying on its work, officially as an affiliate of the Foreign Ministry but actually as an autonomous agency. Now, however, the MGB and the GRU saw it as a bureaucratic rival and tried to give KI as little information as possible. The great limitation of both KIs was that, to an extreme degree, their assessments and analyses reflected what they believed to be the views of their political masters. Thus, as one scholar, Vladislav Zubok, has pointed out, Stalinism (in which the agency staff had been nurtured and trained) tended, by a circular process between analysts and clients, to survive Stalin.

Kiev Class of Soviet aircraft carriers (called tactical aircraft-carrying cruisers) that appeared in the 1970s. The class included *Kiev, Minsk, Novorossisk,* and *Admiral Gorshov,* the last-named featuring a number of differences from the others in dimensions and armament. These were 43,000-ton ships (45,000 for *Admiral Gorshov)* that carried about 35 aircraft, fixed-wing and helicopter. Bristling with missile launchers, the Kievs were formidable warships as well as floating hangars.

Kim Il Sung (1912–1994) Chief of state of the Democratic People's Republic of Korea (North Korea) since its establishment in 1948—as premier (1948–72) and then as president (1972–94)—Kim Il Sung (born Kim Song-ju) became active in the early 1930s in an anti-Japanese guerrilla movement and, as other leaders were imprisoned or executed, rose in the resistance. He took the alias Kim Il Sung from a guerrilla leader of the previous generation. During World War II, according to most reports, he fought the Japanese in Manchuria.

After the end of World War II the Soviets, who controlled the northern part of Korea, treated Kim as a returning hero and supported him as the leader of the country. On December 19, 1945, he became head of the northern branch of the Communist Party (the North Korean Workers' Party). On September 9, 1948, after the North Koreans boycotted UNITED NATIONS–sponsored elections by which the Republic of Korea was established, Kim became premier of the new Soviet-style North Korean republic.

On June 25, 1950, Kim's North Korean People's Army moved south across the 38TH PARALLEL, the dividing line between North and South. The result was a major international conflict, the three-year KOREAN WAR, which ended not in a peace but in a continuing cease-fire.

Kim continued as North Korean head of state into the 1990s. Proclaimed president for life in 1972, he was said to be slowly giving up some of his dictatorial powers, but he seemed determined to keep them in the family; in 1984 he anointed his son, Kim Jong Il, as his chosen successor. After the father's death in 1994, the son appeared to have taken over the government, but the true extent of his authority remained unclear.

Kirkpatrick, Sir Ivone (1897–1964) British diplomat who served as high commissioner for Germany from 1950 to 1953, the period leading up to the integration of West German forces into the NORTH ATLANTIC TREATY ORGANIZATION. Earlier in his career Kirkpatrick had acquired extensive knowledge of the Germany of the Third Reich era as chargé d'affaires in Berlin (1933–38). After his time as high commissioner he returned to Britain as head of the Foreign Office, from which he retired in 1955.

Kirov Class of Soviet warships commissioned in the 1980s. These vessels, gigantic by postwar standards, heavily armed but not heavily armored, represented a sort of throwback to the battle-cruiser idea popular early in the century—particularly in the British navy—and also the battle cruiser's last hurrah. The Soviets called these ships missile cruisers, though at 28,000 tons they were of battleship size. Besides *Kirov,* the class included *Kalinin* and *Frunze.* The heavily armed Kirovs carried a variety of missiles, including the SS-N-19, which had a range of nearly 350 miles and could be fitted with either a conventional or a nuclear warhead.

Kissinger, Henry Alfred (1923–   )   As national security adviser (1969–75) and secretary of state (1973–77) under U.S. presidents NIXON and FORD, Henry Kissinger, a professor of political science at Harvard, had a remarkable opportunity to live out an academic's dream—to practice in the world of public affairs what he preached in the classroom, not merely as a consultant but as a prime shaper of national policy. Taking full advantage of the opportunity, Kissinger made himself perhaps the best-known diplomatic figure in the world during those years and, indeed, became something of an international pop celebrity.

A native of Germany, Kissinger came to the United States with his family in 1938 in their flight from the Nazis. After collecting his undergraduate and graduate degrees from Harvard, he began teaching there, and in 1957 caused a considerable stir in the still-new world of the defense intellectuals with his book *Nuclear Weapons and Foreign Policy,* in which he criticized the EISENHOWER administration's reliance on MASSIVE RETALIATION. Kissinger maintained that in many cases tactical (i.e., nonmassive) nuclear weapons might in fact serve as more effective instruments of DETERRENCE. Later, however, Kissinger moved toward the kinds of ideas that would be favored by the KENNEDY administration, featuring a buildup of conventional weaponry with strategic nuclear weapons standing in support.

A close adviser to Nelson Rockefeller, who lost to Nixon in the contest for the 1968 Republican presidential nomination, Kissinger nevertheless received his great chance when the victorious Nixon chose him as national security adviser. Sharing an outlook strongly based in realpolitik, the two worked well together, though not actually fond of each other. Their first objective, ending the VIETNAM WAR, took four years to accomplish (and then the agreement proved to have been a mere scrap of paper, for within two years North Vietnam took over the South). Kissinger and North Vietnam's LE DUC THO were jointly chosen for the 1973 Nobel Peace Prize (though Tho refused to accept his award, on the accurate grounds that the war had not really ended). Kissinger also encountered severe criticism in the United States when the public learned he had advocated devastating U.S. air raids on Vietnamese supply bases and trails inside Cambodia.

In 1971 the revelation that Kissinger had made a secret trip to China to prepare the way for relations between the Communist regime and the United States caused a sensation, both because it represented a reversal of a two-decades-old U.S. policy and also because the national security adviser appeared like an international superagent in a spy thriller. (A Rand Corporation study of U.S.-Chinese negotiations written for the CENTRAL INTELLIGENCE AGENCY and declassified in 1994 showed, however, how the Chinese used a range of tactics to influence and even overawe their U.S. counterparts. In a late-evening 1972 session, following a repast of Peking duck and mao tai liquor, Kissinger agreed to a communiqué in which TAIWAN was declared to be an integral part of China with the comment: "After a dinner of Peking duck, I'll sign anything." In general, according to the Rand study, the Chinese did their meticulous best to exploit U.S. personal insecurities and political rivalries.)

The opening to China, one of the triumphs of Nixon administration foreign policy, came in tandem with the careful development of DÉTENTE with the Soviet Union—a large-scale balancing act. Kissinger began a stance of détente in June 1969, when he proposed to the Soviet ambassador, Anatoly DOBRYNIN, that U.S. and Soviet leaders hold regular summit meetings, to avoid the exaggerated expectations created by occasional summits. He told Dobrynin that Nixon intended to make no move in relation to Eastern Europe that "would be assessed in Moscow as a 'challenge' to its position in this region." (In his report to the Politburo, Dobrynin observed of Kissinger that he was "an intelligent and erudite man" who was at the same

After the initialing of the Vietnam peace agreement—January 23, 1973—U.S. national security adviser Henry Kissinger *(r.)* talks with the chief North Vietnamese negotiator, Le Duc Tho, and an interpreter *(l.)*.

time "vain and prone in conversations with me . . . to brag of his influence.")

Kissinger also played a major part in Middle East diplomacy following the 1973 Yom Kippur war, when he made back-and-forth negotiating trips between Jerusalem and Cairo; his technique acquired the name "shuttle diplomacy." Somewhat surprisingly, Kissinger's Jewish background did not prove to be a disadvantage in this context; he succeeded in establishing sound relations with Egypt's President SADAT and, as a Jew, could op-

pose specific Israeli positions without having to concern himself overmuch about charges of anti-Semitism. He helped bring about a truce, but, unfortunately, he ultimately proved no more capable than anyone else of creating a genuine settlement in the Middle East.

In dealing with the USSR, Kissinger stressed the concept of "linkage," which he made famous. "To separate issues into distinct compartments," he declared, "would encourage the Soviet leaders to believe that they could use cooperation in one area as a safety valve while striving for unrelated advantages elsewhere." To Kissinger, diplomatic, military, and economic matters had to be seen as part of an "entire front."

In office, Kissinger attracted a group of associates and subordinates who played important parts in succeeding administrations—Alexander HAIG, Brent Scowcroft, and Lawrence Eagleburger among them. After leaving the government, Kissinger, through his international consulting firm, continued to exert considerable influence on world events.

Kitchen Debate   In Moscow, on July 24, 1959, Soviet premier KHRUSHCHEV and U.S. vice president NIXON met at an American exhibit at a trade fair, in front of a model kitchen, and engaged in a brief but brisk exchange about the comparative merits of life in the Soviet Union and in the United States. The discussion had little content, but it was caught by television cameras and gave Nixon and Republican publicists the opportunity, frequently capitalized on in subsequent campaigning, to make a point of the vice president's having "stood up to Khrushchev."

In a private meeting the previous evening, the two men had engaged in a much more heated exchange. A Soviet transcript made available in 1994 quotes Khrushchev as objecting to a just-passed congressional resolution criticizing current Soviet policies. The premier likened the resolution to "fresh manure," which, he said, "always smells more." Further, he told Nixon, "you laid it and the stench is spreading through the whole world." Nixon met this comment with the rather arcane observation that he, like Khrushchev, had grown up on a farm and "they used to say that pig manure is worse than horse." Khrushchev seemed to suspect that the U.S. government needed a reason for Nixon to be badly received in the Soviet Union. The vice president declared, however, that neither he nor President EISENHOWER was so stupid as to arrange such a congressional action before the Moscow trip.

Kleffens, Eelco Nicolaus van (1894–)   Dutch political leader, a native of the Frisian Islands, who worked for European unity through such arrangements as the BENELUX union and the EUROPEAN COAL AND STEEL COMMUNITY. Chief of the Netherlands delegation to the UNITED NATIONS (1946–47), van Kleffens then served as ambassador to the United States for the next three years. Later he was chief representative in Britain of the European Coal and Steel Community.

Van Kleffens spent the World War II years in London as foreign minister of his country's government-in-exile. In this capacity he responded to rumors that, late in the war, the Germans might open the dikes and flood the Netherlands. Van Kleffens let it be known that if the enemy took such a step, he would demand as reparation a sizable piece of German territory "minus Germans." He also showed himself tough concerning Indonesia, objecting to any attempts at UN involvement in the 1947 fighting between Dutch army troops and native forces.

Van Kleffens's first name struck everybody who met him as unique, but, an interviewer learned, the name *Eelco* was "as typical among Frisians as Robert is in America."

Knowland, William Fife (1908–1974)   Republican U.S. senator from California, appointed in 1945 to fill an unexpired term, who went on to serve through 1958, for the last five years acting as his party's floor leader. A newspaper publisher from Oakland *(Tribune)*, Knowland became so closely identified with the CHINA LOBBY and the cause of CHIANG KAI-SHEK that the press nicknamed him "the senator from Formosa." Along with other Republican senators such as Kenneth Wherry of Nebraska and Styles Bridges of New Hampshire, Knowland consistently accused the TRUMAN administration of allowing the Communists to defeat Chiang's government on the mainland—the often-cited "loss of China."

Kohl, Helmut (1930–)   After the BERLIN WALL began coming down in 1989 and the states of East and West Germany moved toward reunification, Helmut Kohl, as the West German chancellor, was the head of government who had to deal with the unprecedented political and economic problems presented by this long-dreamed-of situation that had finally and unexpectedly arrived.

A native of the Rhineland, Kohl began his political career as a teenager in the youth department of the Christian Democratic Union. Rising in state politics, he became minister-president of Rhineland-Palatinate in 1969, and in 1973 he was chosen as chairman of the national Christian Democratic Union. In 1976 he lost his first race against Helmut SCHMIDT for the chancellorship, but six years later the Bundestag elected him to the position after passing a no-confidence motion against Schmidt. His coalition then won the March 1983 general election.

In 1990, after the fall of the Berlin Wall, Kohl took a step unimaginable only months before and campaigned in East Germany against Communist candidates. With the victory of the opposition came the decision to reunify East and West Germany; the restored Germany came into official existence on October 3, 1990.

Konev, Ivan Stepanovich (1897–1973) One of the leading Soviet generals of World War II, commander of the First Ukrainian Front in the final battle for BERLIN, Konev was the son of a peasant family and as a young man saw service during World War I in the imperial Russian army. Joining the Bolshevik Party and the Red Army in 1918, he served as a political commissar during the civil war and the 1920s before receiving line commands. In World War II, in the Soviet counteroffensive before Moscow in December 1941, Konev commanded a front that drove the invading Germans back more than 100 miles. By the end of the war, as an offensive leader on a par with Georgi ZHUKOV, he had risen to marshal's rank.

In the years from 1946 to 1951 Konev served as commander in chief of Soviet ground forces, deputy minister of war, and inspector general of the Soviet army. In 1953 he appears to have played an important part—though its precise nature varies, depending on which account one wishes to believe—in the removal and execution of Lavrenty BERIA, the universally despised head of the secret police. In one version Konev presided over a secret court that found Beria guilty of a range of atrocities; another and more dramatic story has the climactic scene taking place on June 26, 1953, at a meeting in the Kremlin of the Soviet Communist Party Presidium, with Beria, accused of crimes, producing a revolver. Politicians and generals, Konev among

them, fell on Beria and either shot or strangled him.

In May 1955 Konev was called on to become commander in chief of the armies of the new WARSAW PACT (a position that made him something of an Eastern Bloc analogue to U.S. general Dwight D. EISENHOWER, the first commander of NORTH ATLANTIC TREATY ORGANIZATION forces). Konev also commanded Soviet ground forces in 1955 and 1956. In these positions he accompanied First Secretary Nikita KHRUSHCHEV from Moscow to Warsaw in October 1956, when it seemed that Polish riots might bring on Soviet military intervention. This situation did not develop, however, but Konev quickly found himself in overall command of forces engaged in suppressing the HUNGARIAN REVOLUTION. Although the state of his health caused him to resign as Warsaw Pact commander in 1960, he commanded the occupation army in East Germany (1961–62).

Korean War In the early morning of June 25, 1950, war erupted on the Korean peninsula when the government of North Korea sent troops in Soviet-made tanks rolling south across the 38TH PARALLEL against a position manned by 540 lightly equipped U.S. soldiers commanded by Lieutenant Colonel Charles "Brad" Smith.

The existence of two Koreas was an unanticipated consequence of World War II. At the YALTA CONFERENCE in 1945, the Allied leaders agreed to establish a temporary four-power trusteeship for the country, looking to the ultimate establishment of a free and independent Korea. Having given no discernible thought to any concrete action in the peninsula, the United States in late 1945 countered the movement of Soviet troops into northern Korea by hastily sending in Major General John R. HODGE with U.S. units from Okinawa. In the quick search for a line of demarcation between Soviet and U.S. forces, both powers accepted Lieutenant Colonel Dean RUSK's suggestion of the 38th parallel.

From that point on, matters followed a course not dissimilar to that in other parts of the world where the superpower client states faced each other across a line on a map. Two implacably opposed leaders, KIM IL SUNG in the North and Syngman RHEE in the South, presided over the

The two Koreas

State Dean ACHESON indicated that South Korea did not come within the U.S. strategic perimeter—although these statements, in themselves, did not necessarily mean the United States would stand aside if an attempt was made to unify Korea by force. By the beginning of 1950 the NKPA had grown into a well-trained force of some 135,000 men; the ROK army was not nearly as well equipped or trained. Tension continually ran high along the border between the two states.

Some Western historians suggest that Kim Il Sung launched the June 25 attack because of South Korean border raids during the preceding weeks; some have even maintained that the ROK started the war by invading North Korea. Others, more numerous, argue that by making war on South Korea, Kim was responding to increased U.S. aid given to Syngman Rhee's government: in February 1950 Congress authorized $60 million in economic aid, in March it granted $10 million in military assistance, and on June 5 it approved a further $100 million in economic aid.

A document made available from Russian archives in January 1993 has cleared up some of these points. This document, a report on the history of the Korean War prepared in 1966 for General Secretary Leonid BREZHNEV, details how, from the beginning of 1950, Kim bombarded Joseph STALIN with telegrams—some 50 in all—asking the Soviet dictator's support for a North Korean plan to unify Korea by the use of military force. Kim presented a three-phase plan; first, he would concentrate his forces north of the parallel, ready for attack; then he would call for "peaceful reunification" of the country; when the South Korean government had cooperated by issuing its expected rejection of the appeal, Kim would unleash his troops in a surprise attack. In meetings in Moscow in March and April 1950, Kim received Stalin's permission to implement the plan. Soviet officers helped draft the operational orders, and Stalin decreed that all of Kim's requests for weapons and equipment be given priority. Kim then moved on to China, where he obtained similar support from MAO ZEDONG. Stalin, it is clear, granted his approval on the assumption that the United States would not intervene in the war, and he did so in part to keep a step ahead of Mao. As an American scholar, Kathryn Weathersby, observed, "If he had

opposing states; in the Communist North all conservatives were driven from political life, and in the South leftists encountered similar fates; the North had the industry, the South the agriculture. Kim and Rhee each declared his intention to unite the nation under his own government.

The United States and the Soviet Union began withdrawing their respective forces in late 1948, with the Soviets devoting much attention to creating a potent North Korean People's Army (NKPA). Though leaving behind equipment for the Republic of Korea (ROK) Constabulary, the United States did not do so well by its client. Lacking much interest in Korea, the TRUMAN administration was also in a phase of severe military budget cutting; indeed, the Pentagon found much of its energy spent in interservice battles. At different times both General Douglas MACARTHUR, the U.S. commander in the Far East, and Secretary of

Fighting southward from the Chosin Reservoir area in northeastern North Korea in December 1950, outnumbered U.S. troops escape encirclement by Chinese Communist forces.

not approved Kim's plan, Kim would have turned to Mao for support. Stalin's claim to leadership of the Communist world would have diminished and Mao's would have risen." (This calculation is grimly reminiscent of the thinking of Kaiser Wilhelm II in 1914 in the weeks leading up to World War I.)

Initially supporting the South Koreans with naval and air units, the United States ultimately became fully involved in the war—the "police action," as Truman dubbed it—along with representatives from other countries, the troops together making up the first UNITED NATIONS peacekeeping force. Australia, Belgium, Britain, Canada, France, Greece, the Netherlands, New Zealand, the Philippines, and Turkey all sent con-

tingents, but the great bulk of those serving were U.S. soldiers (some 5.7 million served during the war). A total of 54,246 U.S. soldiers died, 33,629 of them in battle. Estimates of total dead, military and civilian, have varied widely; 2 million is a conservative figure. More than 7,000 Americans were taken prisoner, and the fate of some continued to be discussed into the 1990s.

In April 1951, amid great political and popular debate, General MacArthur was removed from his command for engaging in unauthorized statements about U.S. policy. In July, after a 13-month up-and-down course that had seen UN forces retreat to the Pusan perimeter in southeastern Korea and then fight their way back across the 38th parallel and into the northern area of North Korea, only to be driven south again by Chinese forces, the two sides began armistice talks that dragged on for two years. After Stalin's death, in March 1953, matters moved more rapidly; the two sides signed a cease-fire on July 27, 1953. But the peace has never been secure. Continually threatened by border problems, it suffered in the 1990s from the uncertainty surrounding North Korean nuclear activities.

In Korea, as in Czechoslovakia at the time of the coup in 1948, Communist actions produced important results directly contrary to Stalin's desires: fears of further Communist aggression led to an American military buildup and to the transformation of the NORTH ATLANTIC TREATY ORGANIZATION into a genuine alliance, and China emerged from the war as a strong challenger to Moscow's supremacy in the Communist world. *See also* CARTER, Jimmy; PRISONERS OF WAR; RIDGWAY, Matthew Bunker.

Korolev, Sergei Pavlovich (1907–1966) Longtime director of the Soviet space program who designed the first vehicles (the Vostok and Voskhod) used in manned space flight. Korolev began working in rocketry when in his 20s; in 1933 he became an official of the Soviet rocket research institute. Like many other Soviet scientists and engineers in the STALIN era, he spent time in prison (where he was used as a designer). Released in 1944, he headed the Soviet space effort for the last 20 years of his life. Described by Premier Nikita KHRUSHCHEV as "strong-willed and decisive," Korolev took part in the development of the first Soviet ballistic missile and *SPUTNIK I.*

Kosygin, Alexei Nikolayevich (1904–1980) Soviet statesman who took office as premier (chairman of the Council of Ministers) in October 1964, after the forced resignation of Premier Nikita KHRUSHCHEV, when Leonid BREZHNEV became first secretary of the Communist Party.

A graduate in engineering of the Leningrad Textile Institute, Kosygin worked in the textile industry until 1938, when he became chairman of the executive committee of the Leningrad Soviet (more or less equivalent to mayor of Leningrad, though the party boss had the ultimate say). During World War II he supervised much of the Soviet economy —food, textiles, light industry—and served as premier of the Russian Federation. He became a candidate (nonvoting) member of the POLITBURO in 1946 and attained full membership in 1952. A specialist in industry and planning, he was chosen deputy premier in 1953, after the death of Joseph STALIN; he later became minister of economic planning and then chairman of the State Economic and

At the Glassboro Conference, Soviet premier Alexei Kosygin (*l.*) has a serious conversation with U.S. president Lyndon B. Johnson.

Planning Committee. Considered primarily a technocrat who would devote the bulk of his attention to the economy and other domestic matters, Kosygin took office with Brezhnev in 1964. He made some beginning efforts, which met with only very limited success, to move the USSR in the direction of a market economy.

In June 1967, Kosygin and his family attracted great public attention in the United States when they came to Glassboro, N.J., for a summit conference with U.S. president Lyndon B. JOHNSON. Though the meetings were friendly and much talk was heard of the "spirit of Glassboro," little of substance emerged from the discussions. Kosygin later said that U.S.-Soviet relations could not improve until the United States withdrew from Vietnam. As time went on, Kosygin confined himself increasingly to economic matters, with Brezhnev taking full control of foreign policy.

Kosygin retired in 1980, two years before the death of his longtime colleague, Brezhnev. He died in December. Nicolai Tikhonov succeeded Kosygin as Soviet premier. *See also* GLASSBORO CONFERENCE.

Kozlov, Frol Romanovich (1908–1965) COMMUNIST PARTY OF THE SOVIET UNION organizer and political figure who rose by degrees through party machinery to become first secretary in Leningrad at age 45. In 1957 he was rewarded with a seat on the Presidium of the CENTRAL COMMITTEE. Kozlov served briefly as premier of the Russian Soviet Republic (1957–58); he left this post to become first deputy chairman of the Council of Ministers (deputy premier) of the Soviet Union. In 1960 he succeeded Alexei Kirichenko, a protégé of Premier Nikita KHRUSHCHEV, as second secretary of the Central Committee, with wide responsibilities, including defense and personnel.

Aside from hard work and perseverance, Kozlov's rise illustrates some of the complex forces with which an aspiring Soviet politician had to cope and the varying opinions he had to hold, or appear to hold. In January 1953, at the time Premier Joseph STALIN was pillorying his Kremlin doctors as murderers, Kozlov was the party figure under whose byline a magazine article appeared presenting the official view of this so-called DOCTORS' PLOT. When Stalin's death gave the doctors their miraculous reprieve, Kozlov and others in-

volved in creating the official story underwent setbacks in their careers. But by 1957, Kozlov, an ally though not a complete protégé of Khrushchev, had recovered enough to be useful to the older man on the Central Committee. Later, as second secretary, Kozlov took firm control of the party machinery, and, classed among the hard-liners, he pressed for toughness in relations with the West. The U-2 fiasco in 1960 not only caused an international sensation but weakened Khrushchev's standing with his own colleagues.

Kozlov's laborious climb through the levels of the party brought him to a position in which he came to be considered a likely rival of Khrushchev for supreme power. Generally more conservative than the mercurial Khrushchev, in both style and doctrine, Kozlov was regarded by many Western observers as a focal point of opposition to the colorful first secretary. Discounting such talk, Khrushchev's son Sergei—saying dryly "I don't want to argue with Sovietologists"—stated his belief that despite their disagreements his father came to trust Kozlov and saw him as his successor.

In any case, whether Khrushchev's rival or anointed successor, Kozlov lost his part in the Kremlin contest for power when he suffered a stroke in April 1963. Otherwise, he, instead of Leonid BREZHNEV, might well have become the next GENERAL SECRETARY. As it was, Kozlov kept his seat on the Presidium despite his complete incapacitation, partly, at least, because Khrushchev feared that the shock of losing this coveted position might kill him. The men who deposed Khrushchev in October 1964, led by Mikhail SUSLOV, did not display such charity. Dismissed in November, Koslov survived for only two months.

Kremlin The term for the citadel found in many Russian cities, *Kremlin* came to apply in particular to the fortress in Moscow, the seat of the medieval and Renaissance monarchy. Within its walls the 90-acre Moscow Kremlin includes an array of buildings, many of them outstanding palaces and churches. After 1918, when the Bolsheviks brought governmental functions back to Moscow a little more than two centuries after Czar Peter the Great had transferred the capital to St. Petersburg, the Kremlin, as the site of government offices, served as a standard symbol of the Communist regime.

Krishna Menon, V(engalil) K(rishnan) (1897–1974)
Indian delegate to the UNITED NATIONS during the 1950s who attracted considerable attention as a regular and stinging critic of U.S. policies. He was appointed to the UN in 1952 by Prime Minister NEHRU with the assignment of helping bring about an armistice during the KOREAN WAR, where negotiations were stalled on the question of repatriating prisoners of war who did not wish to return to their countries of origin—essentially, North Koreans. Krishna Menon developed a proposal that in fact supported U.S. opposition to forced repatriation and that, with modifications, was adopted by the General Assembly in December 1952.

A longtime opponent of colonialism and advocate of Indian independence, Krishna Menon had lived in Britain since 1924, where he practiced as a barrister and served as a founding editor of Pelican Books, a division of Penguin publishing nonfiction books.

Kruchkov, Vladimir Alexandrovich (1924–)
Official of the COMMUNIST PARTY OF THE SOVIET UNION who began his working life as a factory employee (an impeccable proletarian credential about which he later liked to boast) and who as a young diplomat served in Hungary under Yuri ANDROPOV and became his protégé. When Andropov moved from the embassy in Budapest to the CENTRAL COMMITTEE in Moscow, Kryuchkov accompanied him. In 1967 Andropov became chairman of the KGB, and it was in this agency that Kryuchkov was to spend the remainder of his Soviet career.

A hard-driving, single-minded official credited with no sense of humor, Kryuchkov served as deputy head of the FIRST CHIEF DIRECTORATE (the branch concerned with foreign intelligence) and in 1974 became head of the directorate, the position in which he remained until appointed chairman of the KGB by President Mikhail GORBACHEV in 1988.

This appointment marked the first time the head of foreign intelligence had ever won the top position. Though Kryuchkov had gone to the KGB as a politician rather than an intelligence professional, Gorbachev seemingly appreciated his achievements and his support of PERESTROIKA: Soviet adversaries, Kruychkov declared, "are recognizing the profound nature of our reforms and their beneficial effect on foreign policy." In 1989 Kryuchkov became a full member of the Politburo, and in the following year he was appointed to Gorbachev's Presidential Council.

As later events would show, however, Gorbachev, in spite of his many strong points, had limited talent as a personnel manager; he did not always choose his close associates wisely. Disturbed by what he later described as "the destruction of the country," Kruychkov took a leading part in the attempted 1991 coup against the president. Defending himself in his trial more than two years later, Kryuchkov declared that the real treason had been committed by Gorbachev when he allowed the Soviet republics to move toward independence. "The motherland we are accused of betraying," Kryuchkov declared, "no longer exists." It was "not our guilt but our tragedy that our efforts failed."

Kuomintang *See* GUOMINDANG.

Kuril Islands Lying in a chain stretching from Kamchatka to Hokkaido, these foggy, frigid islands have long constituted a point of contention between Russians and Japanese. An 1875 agreement awarded them to Japan, but in 1945, in accordance with a decision of the YALTA CONFERENCE, they were occupied by Soviet forces. Japan—no longer the prostrate defeated enemy of those days—has consistently demanded the return of the Kurils. The question continues as an irritant between the two countries, and failure to resolve it has stood in the way of Russia's receiving economic aid from Japan in the 1990s.

L

Laird, Melvin Robert (1922–) After nine terms in the U.S. House of Representatives, Melvin Laird became secretary of defense during the NIXON administration, serving from 1969 to 1973, when, as he had originally declared, he retired; a secretary of defense, he had said, should serve no longer than four years. During Nixon's last year in office (1973–74), Laird was White House adviser on domestic affairs.

Laird held the defense portfolio in a uniquely difficult time in American history—during the U.S. withdrawal from a theater of war on the other side of the world; the army, if not defeated, was nevertheless functioning at a low ebb emotionally. A historian of the JOINT CHIEFS OF STAFF, Mark Perry, declared that Laird "left a legacy of accomplishment clearly unequaled by any of his predecessors," not only presiding over the withdrawal from the VIETNAM WAR but using "his considerable political talents to begin closing the chasm of misunderstanding that had opened between military and civilian leaders during the eight years of the Vietnam conflict."

Laos—Geneva Agreement On July 23, 1962, after many months of negotiations, the West, the Soviet Union, and China signed an agreement neutralizing Laos. The principal U.S. negotiator was Averell HARRIMAN. The agreement, however, broke down within a year; Laos had the inescapable misfortune to be situated next to VIETNAM.

Lattimore case In March 1950, U.S. senator Joseph R. MCCARTHY publicly accused a scholar and sometime government adviser named Owen Lattimore (1900–1989) of serving the Soviet Union as an espionage agent. Having mentioned various figures for the number of Communists supposed to be serving in or involved with the State Department, McCarthy retreated from some of his totals but declared that he would "stand or fall" on the accuracy of his charges against Lattimore, whom he called the architect of U.S. policy in the Far East (though Lattimore was not in fact an official of the government).

Considered the West's leading authority on the peoples of the remote border country between Russia and China, Lattimore had enjoyed a remarkable and exotic career. His father, a teacher, had taken him to China when he was just a year old, and he had spent most of his childhood and youth there, becoming fluent in Chinese, Russian, and even Mongol. Never having gone to a university, Lattimore combined a business career in China with exploration on the frontier and engaged in anthropological research. In 1938, despite his lack of an academic degree, he became affiliated with Johns Hopkins University and its Walter Hines Page School of International Relations. In 1941, on the recommendation of U.S. president ROOSEVELT, Lattimore became an adviser to China's CHIANG KAI-SHEK. His writings during this period generally supported decolonization and self-determination for Asian countries. At one point in 1944, Lattimore, like many other Western visitors to Russia before him, was duped by a Potemkin village—in this case, a sanitized concentration camp in Siberia whose emaciated inmates were replaced, for the visit of Lattimore and Vice President Henry WALLACE, by KGB personnel. Lattimore's subsequent description, which spoke inaccurately of "hardy miners" working in a situation reminiscent of the Tennessee Valley Authority, had the tone of much blinkered U.S. reporting on the Soviet ally during World War II.

In July 1950 a Senate investigation cleared Lattimore of McCarthy's charges, but in 1952, pursued by Democratic senator Pat McCarran of Nevada, Lattimore had to undergo indictment for perjury supposedly committed before McCarran's Internal Security subcommittee. All charges were dropped in 1955. From 1963 to 1970 Lattimore was director of Chinese studies at the University of Leeds in England.

Leahy, William Daniel (1875–1959) U.S. admiral, onetime chief of naval operations (1937–39), who during World War II served President ROOSEVELT as personal chief of staff, a position that had never existed previously, and continued in this role for President TRUMAN until 1949. In 1946 Leahy also served briefly as director of the Central Intelligence Group, set up by President Truman after the abolition of the wartime Office of Strategic Services, and attempted, with little success, to plan and coordinate U.S. foreign-intelligence activities. Under 1947 legislation, these tasks were given to the new CENTRAL INTELLIGENCE AGENCY.

Le Duc Tho (1911–1990) A native of northern Vietnam and member of the Indochina Communist Party since his 20s, Le Duc Tho became known worldwide as the chief negotiator for North Vietnam in the peace talks with the United States, which began in Paris in 1968 and, after five years of turbulence, in January 1973 produced a cease-fire between the United States and North Vietnam to end the VIETNAM WAR. Under the agreement, the United States would withdraw its forces, leaving the fate of South Vietnam to be settled by a tripartite commission. This outcome had become possible because the NIXON administration wanted to get out of a war that had grown into a disaster at home in the United States, though in fact various U.S. forces remained in the country until 1975. For their work as negotiators, Le Duc Tho and U.S. secretary of state Henry KISSINGER won the 1973 Nobel Peace Prize; Tho, however, refused to accept the award, since the war dragged on in South Vietnam.

LeMay, Curtis Emerson (1906–1990) Although his stocky (5′8″) figure and his downturned mouth with a cigar usually clamped between his teeth made him appear the stereotypical no-nonsense military commander, General LeMay was one of the leading innovators in U.S. Air Force history and was the principal creator of the STRATEGIC AIR COMMAND.

A native of Columbus, Ohio, LeMay entered Ohio State University after failing to receive an appointment to West Point and joined the Reserve Officers' Training Corps while working his way through school. In 1930, having enlisted in the regular army, he became a second lieutenant in the air corps. Two years later he collected an engineering degree from Ohio State. During the 1930s his interest in technical matters led to his becoming an expert in a navigation over water, a new field at that time; in 1938 he won acclaim for locating an Italian liner 600 miles at sea.

In 1942 LeMay as a colonel led his bomb group into the air campaign against Germany. He quickly demonstrated his tactical resourcefulness by forbidding crews to attempt to avoid enemy fire on the final bombing run by zigzagging. This move was criticized as a prescription for air-crew suicide but immediately proved its soundness and became standard procedure; LeMay had not reached his decision casually but had decided on it after his mathematical analysis showed that evasive maneuvers gave the bombers no additional protection but merely scattered bombs all over the landscape. He also instituted the wedge-shaped "box formation" for air groups, which enabled his B-17s to make maximum use of their firepower and at the same time, LeMay said, "wasn't too hideously difficult for non-veteran pilots to manage in their positioning and spacing and speed." In 1945 LeMay, directing the air campaign against Japan, evolved a new set of tactics for that situation, dispensing with formations and even guns, and concentrating on the use of incendiary bombs.

After duty in the Pentagon, LeMay, now a lieutenant general, went to Germany in 1947 to take command of U.S. Air Forces in Europe. Thus, in 1948, during the BERLIN BLOCKADE AND AIRLIFT, it

Le Duc Tho *(l.)*, chief North Vietnamese negotiator, shakes hands with the head of the U.S. delegation, Henry Kissinger, at the conclusion of the January 1973 peace talks in Paris.

was his aircraft that played the principal part in this unprecedented operation; to keep his hand in, the general flew on several missions. He left Germany at the end of September to become commanding general of the Strategic Air Command, which he worked to build up and render ready for combat operations. During his time as its head, the command acquired the B-52 bomber—which has remained in service throughout the ensuing decades—and the first missiles. LeMay held the position until 1957, leaving to become air force vice chief of staff; in 1961 he moved up to the chief's chair, which he held until his retirement in 1965.

During his career, LeMay once calculated, he had been checked out in exactly 75 different kinds of military aircraft, from tiny trainers to the B-52 and various giant cargo planes. The idea was, he said, "You just got in and flew."

Leningrad case From the late 1940s, after the defection of TITO and the failure of the Berlin blockade, to his death in 1953, Soviet dictator Joseph STALIN became increasingly possessed by egomania, nationalism, xenophobia, and anti-Semitism. Terror against supposed domestic opponents returned, a specially notable manifestation

183

being the mass arrests and executions carried out in Leningrad in February and October of 1950. A strong force behind this purge was said to have been Georgi MALENKOV, who used it to dispose of supporters of his rival, Andrei ZHDANOV, who had died in 1948. *See also* BERLIN BLOCKADE AND AIRLIFT.

Liberation theology   At a conference in Medellín, Colombia, in 1968, Latin American Roman Catholic bishops began something of a transformation in the outlook and behavior of the church. They urged an end to "institutionalized violence" through breaking the long-established alliance between church and conservative oligarchy in many countries. They also moved away from a traditional concern with conversion to focus on social and economic reforms. The bishops and their followers aimed at the creation of a movement among the poor that would rely on Christian kindness, caring, and sharing. Many members of the clergy directed their attention to the exploitation of the area by foreign countries and their local surrogates and established "base communities" in which they discussed political, social, and economic issues with the peasants. This grassroots movement alarmed many of the wealthier people in the Latin American countries and led to charges that the priests were Communists because of their attacks on capitalism and pro-American regimes. This reaction led, in turn, to widespread condemnations of the priests by U.S. officials, especially strongly conservative anti-Communists. *See also* ROMERO, Oscar.

Lie, Trygve (1896–1968)   Norwegian political figure who played a special part in history by becoming the first secretary-general of the UNITED NATIONS. A member of his country's Labor Party, Lie entered Parliament in 1935, serving as minister of justice and minister of trade. When the Germans invaded in April 1940, he fled to England along with other officials; he served throughout the war as foreign minister of the government-in-exile. In April 1945 he went to San Francisco as head of the Norwegian delegation to the founding conference of the UN, in which he took an active part. The following year Lie was elected secretary-

Trygve Lie, first United Nations secretary-general

general, in good part because he had no significant opposition, either from the Soviets or from the West. His term of office saw the development of the Cold War, with all the challenges it presented for the UN, culminating in the establishment of the UN force that helped defend South Korea in the KOREAN WAR. At the emergency session of the Security Council called to discuss the North Korean invasion, Lie called the situation "a threat to international peace" and declared that the council should "take the steps necessary to reestablish peace." Though Lie won reelection for a three-year term in 1951, Soviet objections to the leading role he had played in organizing the UN action drove him to resign in 1952. He was succeeded by Dag HAMMARSKJÖLD.

Ligachev, Yegor Kuzmich (1920–) COMMUNIST PARTY OF THE SOVIET UNION official who came to prominence at the same time as Mikhail GORBACHEV, with whom he was allied but with whom he soon began to disagree. After receiving engineering training in Moscow, Ligachev rose slowly in the Soviet Communist Party hierarchy in Novosibirsk, his native region, far away from the capital. In 1966 he became a candidate (nonvoting) member of the CENTRAL COMMITTEE of the Soviet Communist Party and in 1976 a full member. During the early 1960s he held a bureaucratic party position in Moscow, but in 1965 he was again sent away to Siberia, remaining there as party head in Tomsk until 1983, when he was given a Central Committee position, in charge of party organization, by GENERAL SECRETARY Yuri ANDROPOV, who needed new blood and apparently respected Ligachev's reputation for honesty. In March 1985, when Gorbachev won election as general secretary, the earnest and methodical Ligachev rose with him, becoming a full member of the POLITBURO, and he appeared to be destined to serve as the new leader's right-hand man. In particular, Ligachev proposed and became identified with the antialcohol crusade, which represented a response to the great rise in drinking characterizing the BREZHNEV era. Unfortunately, the effort proved no more successful than Prohibition in the United States; Boris YELTSIN, later the Russian president, said, "People were soon beginning to drink anything that was liquid and contained alcohol." Gorbachev dropped the crusade in 1989.

Overall, it soon became clear that Ligachev held views far more conservative than Gorbachev's. Resentment of what he considered unjust criticisms of the Soviet regime tempered Ligachev's enthusiasm for PERESTROIKA and GLASNOST. The USSR, he declared in a 1987 speech, would never leave the path of Leninism. A year later he was attacking multiparty politics, strikes, and other kinds of "antisocialist" behavior. In July 1990 the party congress responded to his negativism by rejecting his bid for deputy leadership of the Communist Party. In thus losing his political influence, to be sure, Ligachev underwent a fate his associates would soon meet.

Lilienthal, David Eli (1899–1981) U.S. lawyer specializing in utilities litigation who served as chairman of the Tennessee Valley Authority from 1941 to 1946, when President TRUMAN nominated him to be the first chairman of the Atomic Energy Commission, which was established to control nuclear development for both military and civilian purposes. Before receiving confirmation from the Senate, Lilienthal (and his sponsor, Truman) had to overcome fierce opposition from anti–New Deal senators who equated the TVA with socialism or worse and purported to believe that Lilienthal might somehow turn the AEC into something similar. After resigning in 1950, Lilienthal was active in private business concerned with energy and in international consulting concerning energy and resources.

Lin Biao (Lin Piao) (1907–1971) Leading Chinese Communist military commander and onetime designated successor to MAO ZEDONG, who molded his revolutionary forces to fight a "people's war"—by which he meant a struggle fought with the "national liberation" theme uniting various groups in a broad-based front against a foreign enemy. After victory was achieved with the aid of temporary allies, these allies would then be discarded, having served their purpose. Lin Biao, who edited Mao's famous "little red book" *Quotations from Chairman Mao Tse-tung,* commanded Chinese forces in the Korean War (1950–51), became Chinese minister of defense in 1959, and reorganized the People's Liberation Army in 1965 to prepare for the CULTURAL REVOLUTION. During this period he published an influential essay on the people's war idea, "Long Live the Victory of the People's War" *(Peking Review,* September 3, 1965).

In August 1966, when he was named vice chairman of the Central Committee of the Chinese Communist Party, his career reached its peak—this position made him Mao's second in command and official successor. But by the formal conclusion of the Cultural Revolution, at the Ninth Congress of the Communist Party in April 1969, Lin Biao's day had passed. Seeking to reduce the role of the military in the political system, Mao criticized Lin in front of regional commanders. Hearing of Mao's intention to remove him, Lin joined his son in a plot to overthrow the chairman (possibly to assassinate him) and take power. When Mao learned of the planned coup, according to reports, Lin and his wife tried to escape to the Soviet Union. Shot down by Mao's forces, their aircraft crashed in rural Mongolia on September 13, 1971.

Liu Shaoqi (1898–1969)   Veteran Chinese Communist, a member of the party from 1922, who in the 1950s was allied with DENG XIAOPING in favor of modernizing the nation's economy on Western lines. He served as head of the government (1959–68), being dismissed in the wake of the CULTURAL REVOLUTION. He died in prison.

Lloyd, (John) Selwyn (Baron Selwyn-Lloyd) (1904–1978)   British Conservative Party figure who held high office as minister of defense and chancellor of the exchequer. Taking office as foreign secretary in December 1955, Lloyd served until July 1960—which meant that he survived the 1956 SUEZ CRISIS, in which he was heavily involved as a close colleague of Prime Minister Anthony EDEN, while the fiasco caused Eden's resignation.

Lodge, Henry Cabot (1902–1985)   U.S. political figure and diplomat who served during the EISENHOWER administration as ambassador to the UNITED NATIONS and, although a Republican, represented Presidents KENNEDY and JOHNSON as ambassador to South Vietnam during the VIETNAM WAR era (1963–64 and 1965–67).

Grandson of the famous Massachusetts senator Henry Cabot Lodge who fought and defeated Woodrow Wilson over the Treaty of Versailles and the League of Nations, Lodge, after 13 years, lost his own Senate seat in a historically fascinating turn of events. In 1952 he devoted most of his energies to managing Eisenhower's presidential campaign rather than to securing his own reelection, a circumstance that at least in part accounted for his defeat by Representative John F. KENNEDY.

In 1960 Lodge ran for vice president with Richard M. NIXON. By 1963, missing involvement in government and wanting to go to Vietnam, he had made his wish known to Secretary of State Dean RUSK and others; Kennedy accepted Rusk's nomination of Lodge. Having served as a liaison officer with the French army during World War II, Lodge

spoke French fluently, and he brought a wealth of political experience to this unpromising task. Once in Vietnam, he ended the U.S. tradition of passively accepting the autocratic actions of President NGO DINH DIEM, urging and supporting the November coup, in which Diem was killed. In 1969 President Nixon sent Lodge to Paris to represent the United States in the peace talks with North Vietnam.

London Declaration   On July 6, 1990, leaders of the countries in the NORTH ATLANTIC TREATY ORGANIZATION, meeting in London, issued a statement asking the Soviet Union and the other WARSAW PACT members to join with them in making a "commitment to nonaggression," now that the Cold War between East and West had ended. "Our alliance will do its share to overcome the legacy of decades of suspicion," the NATO leaders declared. "The walls that once confined people and ideas are collapsing. As a consequence, this alliance must and will adapt." More than simply an exercise in rhetoric, the declaration was intended to strengthen President Mikhail GORBACHEV's position with his Soviet critics by demonstrating the effectiveness of his policy of developing friendly relations with the West.

Lon Nol (1913–)   Cambodian political figure, appointed premier in 1966, who in 1970 led a U.S.-supported coup against Prince Norodom SIHANOUK and in 1972 became head of state. Educated in French colonial schools, Lon Nol held various positions in the French colonial administration. In 1954, when Cambodia won its independence from France, Sihanouk appointed Lon Nol, an old friend, as minister of national defense.

Beginning in 1967, Lon Nol protested Sihanouk's allowing the North Vietnamese to use Cambodia as a haven from the fighting across the border during the VIETNAM WAR. It was when Sihanouk was meeting with Soviet leaders in Moscow that Lon Nol staged his coup. He then invited U.S. forces to bomb Vietnamese supply bases and trails inside Cambodia, a move that led to disruption in the country and the ultimate defeat of Lon Nol's government by the KHMER ROUGE. Lon Nol fled to Hawaii.

Depicting the result of the overthrow of Sihanouk, an American cartoonist showed Henry KIS-SINGER, then President NIXON's security adviser, telling the president: "All we know about Lon Nol is that his name spelled backward is Lon Nol."

Lonsdale, Gordon (1922–1970) Soviet agent whose real name was Konon Trofimovich Molody. One of the most effective of all KGB "illegals"—agents living in foreign countries with false identities—Molody borrowed the name Lonsdale from a dead Canadian citizen. A native of the Soviet Union who spent part of his childhood with relatives in California, Molody returned to the USSR, worked for Soviet intelligence during World War II, and in 1955 went to London, where he ran various agents who supplied him with secret defense information. Caught and convicted in 1961, Lonsdale returned to the Soviet Union in 1964 in an exchange for Greville Wynne, a businessman who had served British intelligence as a courier for information supplied by Colonel Oleg PENKOVSKY.

In 1967 Lonsdale figured in an oddly comic exchange with Wynne. When Lonsdale's memoirs appeared in England, the British, who took some offense at the author's deriding of their ability to ferret out spies, retaliated by having Wynne broadcast an account of his own varied espionage activities inside the Soviet bloc; Wynne's memoirs appeared later in the same year. Some of the tone of Lonsdale's book no doubt came from his famous editorial associate, Kim PHILBY. Asked once whether he had ghostwritten the book, Philby said: "I did polish the stuff up a bit. Gordon is a wonderful fellow, but he isn't really a literary man." Actually, staff writers in the offices of the KGB had produced the basic manuscript.

Lovett, Robert Abercrombie (1895–1986) U.S. secretary of defense in the latter years of the TRUMAN administration (1951–53), Lovett was one of the many Wall Street figures who came to Washington as part of the defense effort in World War II.

The son of a prosperous Texas lawyer who became chief counsel to the financial and railroad tycoon E. H. Harriman and was later chairman of the Union Pacific Railroad, Lovett interrupted his schooling at Yale during World War I to take the leadership in forming the famous Yale flying unit that went to fight in Europe. Demobilized as a lieutenant commander, Lovett received his degree and went to Harvard, trying both the law school and the business school, before leaving the academic world altogether and heading for Wall Street. A brilliant student, he had simply found both kinds of graduate school boring.

From 1926 until Undersecretary of War Robert Patterson summoned him to Washington in December 1940 to become a special assistant, Lovett was a partner first in Brown Brothers and then in the merged Brown Brothers, Harriman & Co., a position in which he acquired considerable international experience. Always interested in flying, Lovett made a personal tour of U.S. aircraft plants in 1940. His report on his observations led to a call to Washington in December. Shortly after coming to the War Department, he became assistant secretary for air (April 1941), the post he held throughout World War II. He helped the air force acquire the semi-independent status it possessed during the war, and, a strong advocate of strategic bombing, he pushed the production of the B-17 and the B-24. Patterson, Lovett's immediate boss, said that the large and rapid expansion of the air force "was due more to Bob Lovett than to any other man."

Although he resumed his Wall Street partnership after the war, Lovett again answered the call of duty in 1947, when the new secretary of state, General George C. MARSHALL, with whom he had worked closely during the war, called on him to succeed Dean ACHESON as undersecretary. Taking over in the second half of the year, Lovett, a tactful and low-keyed negotiator, had much of the responsibility for shepherding through Congress the enabling legislation for the MARSHALL PLAN. In 1948 he also had an important hand in the creation of the airlift that supported Berlin during the Soviet blockade and in the early development of the NORTH ATLANTIC TREATY ORGANIZATION. Overall, he became known as Marshall's "ace troubleshooter."

Once more, after the outbreak of the KOREAN WAR, duty summoned Lovett to Washington. General Marshall had agreed to come out of his own second retirement and take over the strife-torn Department of Defense on the condition that Lovett agree to serve as his deputy. After restoring the situation at the Pentagon, Marshall in 1951 entered his final retirement and, to general acclaim, Lovett succeeded to the number-one position (September 1951). He proved to be an able secretary of defense, keeping a working balance among the services, and, forward-looking as usual, promoted the development of missiles over long-range bombers.

Despite a career-long problem with hypochondria—a concern that often amused his friends—and a series of real health problems, Lovett lived to be 90 and was for years one of the chief mandarins of the eastern establishment. After leaving the Defense Department and returning to the business world, he came back to Washington periodically to provide advice on various foreign-policy and military issues, notably during the CUBAN MISSILE CRISIS. Although he had voted for NIXON in the 1960 election, he also served President-elect KENNEDY as a recruiter of talent for the new administration; one of his strongest recommendations was given to Dean RUSK for secretary of state. Lovett himself declined to accept any of the portfolios offered to him. His bleeding ulcers, he said, made it impossible for him to take such positions. *See also* BERLIN BLOCKADE AND AIRLIFT; JOHNSON, Louis Arthur.

Loyalty and Security Program   Following the end of World War II and the beginning of open difficulties with the Soviet Union, a series of disclosures of Soviet espionage activities led to congressional pressure on U.S. president TRUMAN to take action against what seemed to many citizens a potentially overwhelming wave of subversive activity. Some administration officials likewise advocated the institution of a program to screen government employees for loyalty to the United States; Democratic Party leaders feared Republican accusations that the administration was "soft on Communism"—fighting words in those days. In November 1946 (just after the Democratic Party had suffered losses in congressional elections), the president ordered the establishment of the Temporary Commission on Employee Loyalty, with the assignment of examining the problem and producing recommendations for action. On March 21, 1947, the president embodied the commission's recommendations in Executive Order 9835, which outlined procedures for a loyalty program. (It might be noted that loyalty and security are differ-

Robert A. Lovett, U.S. undersecretary of state and secretary of defense

ent, if related, concepts; a wholly loyal employee might, for example, suffer from an addiction or be involved in a sexual situation that could render him subject to blackmail and hence a possible security risk. But if the security program kept the employee out of a sensitive position, no security problem could arise. A person would thus not have to be perfect to hold a government job. The loyalty-security distinction did not, however, survive in practice.)

After announcing the program, the Truman administration found itself in the middle between civil libertarians, who feared it represented an abandonment of due process, and administration foes, who proclaimed it inadequate in the face of the Communist menace. As a key part of the program, the federal government (followed by local governments and other institutions) began requiring job applicants to take an oath of loyalty to the United States, as evidence of their non-Communist status; a 1967 Supreme Court decision ruled some loyalty oaths unconstitutional. As Professor Alan Harper commented some years ago, the president had to deal both with the potential Communist threat and with the politically exploitable fears caused by the threat. Truman also had "to balance the essential claims of liberty with the legitimate requirements of security." Always controversial during the 1950s, the program satisfied nobody.

Luce, Henry Robinson (1898–1967)   Probably the most influential American magazine publisher of the 20th century, Luce was born in Tengchow, China, the son of a Presbyterian missionary. After graduating from Yale (1920), Luce studied at Oxford and in 1923, with his friend and classmate Briton Hadden, founded *Time,* which would become famous as the "weekly newsmagazine." Hadden, an iconoclast and waggish spirit who (with the aid of a little borrowing from Homer) developed the involuted and adjective-studded prose called Timestyle, died in 1929, leaving the flourishing business in Luce's hands. Luce launched *Fortune* in 1930 and the company's most famous publication, the picture magazine *Life,* in 1936. A prominent East Coast conservative and Republican Party figure, Luce believed in mixing his opinions with the facts in the columns of his magazines, and became particularly involved in the cause of CHIANG KAI-SHEK and the Chinese Nationalists, giving readers what seemed to many observers to be a rosy view of Chiang's government as a flourishing democracy. His publications played an important part in shaping American attitudes toward China during World War II and in the early years of the Cold War. *See also* CHINA LOBBY.

Lumumba, Patrice (1925–1961)   In 1960, when the Republic of the Congo (now Zaire) won its independence from Belgium, Patrice Lumumba (whose original name was Katako Kombe) became its first prime minister. Previously employed in sales by a Belgian-owned brewery, Lumumba, an

able speaker, founded the National Congolese Movement (Mouvement National Congolais, or MNC) in 1958. After being accused of stirring up riots, he went to prison in 1959 but was released so that he could attend the 1960 Brussels conference that led to Congolese independence. The MNC's success in the May 1960 election gave Lumumba the premiership, but in a chaotic and violent situation, with contending forces struggling for power in the new country. Though Lumumba resisted dismissal by President Joseph Kasavubu, he was overthrown in September by Colonel Joseph Mobutu (MOBUTU Sese Seko). After spending more than two months in his house under the surveillance of UNITED NATIONS troops sent to attempt to restore order in the country, Lumumba fled but was caught by soldiers of Mobutu's forces. Taken to the secessionist province of Katanga in January 1961, he was apparently murdered on the orders of the president of Katanga, Moise Tshombe. Having favored Lumumba, supporting him with advisers and supplies—in opposition to UN policy—the Soviets made him a symbol of the oppression of Africans by the colonialist West, naming a Moscow university for him. *See also* HAMMARSKJÖLD, Dag.

Lysenko, Trofim (1898–1976)   Soviet biologist and agronomist who played one of the most prominent roles in the scientific side of the Cold War. In 1948 Lysenko's views on genetics, though he had held them for many years, suddenly caused a worldwide stir when, with Premier Joseph STALIN's full support, they became expressions of official Soviet scientific policy. On August 26, 1948, the Presidium of the Soviet Academy of Sciences, praising Lysenko's work, declared traditional Mendelian genetics to be "reactionary" and "antinational," nothing but a "reactionary bourgeois" movement in biological science and a "formal-genetic pseudoscience," because it held that characteristics are transmitted through heredity and failed to acknowledge that through intervention a plant could be changed and its acquired characteristics passed on to its progeny. Lysenko and the Soviet academy were thus, in effect, declaring themselves for environment rather than heredity—a view eminently suited to Stalin's own version of Marxism-Leninism. Indeed, said the academy, the Soviet people owed their enjoyment of the blessings of these truths to the discovery of the work of Lysenko's intellectual mentor, a biologist named Ivan Michurin, "through the genius of Lenin and Stalin." Lysenko based his work on the arrestingly simple declaration that genes do not exist.

Even while receiving Stalin's endorsement, Lysenko himself was listed in a secret-police report as a person who "does not enjoy respect." Nevertheless, the endorsement produced a hot war in Soviet biology, with ideology triumphing over scientific investigation. The party instructed all biologists and related scientists to fight against "toadyism and servility to foreign pseudoscience." Those who failed to measure up were purged.

The practical problem with Lysenko's theories was that, since they failed to accord with reality, they inevitably produced disasters when applied to Soviet agricultural programs, such as the reforestation campaign of the early 1950s. Even so, Lysenko arose again under Nikita KHRUSHCHEV, who desperately sought to raise agricultural production, but his dismissal as director of the Institute of Genetics followed Khrushchev's own removal from office.

Lysenko had one notable accomplishment—political rather than scientific—to his credit. When he became president of the Lenin All-Union Academy of Agricultural Sciences in 1938, he was taking a notably shaky position: his two immediate predecessors had been shot. Lysenko, however, held the post until 1956 and then returned for a short stay (1961–62). Though he produced some creditable research in the earliest years of his career, he has gone down as one of the greatest scientific quacks of the 20th century.

M-4 Essentially the Soviet counterpart of the U.S. B-52, this four-engine strategic bomber entered service in 1956. With a top speed of 560 mph and a range, when fully loaded, of about 5,000 miles, the Myasishchyev M-4 (or Mya-4; NATO code name: Bison) could carry four hydrogen bombs or more than 16 tons of conventional bombs. When the Soviets began developing INTERCONTINENTAL BALLISTIC MISSILES, they turned away from strategic bombers. One problem with the M-4, as Soviet leader Nikita KHRUSHCHEV saw it, was simply that the bomber could reach the United States but lacked the range to return home. The Soviets converted many M-4s into reconnaissance aircraft or tankers.

MacArthur, Douglas (1880–1964) One of the most eminent military leaders in U.S. history, General MacArthur played an important role during the Cold War as Allied supreme commander in Japan and as commander in chief of UNITED NATIONS forces in the KOREAN WAR. A man of remarkable complexity, the general attracted large numbers of both disciples and detractors, and his long career ended in a major political controversy.

As the son of an officer who became a senior general, MacArthur grew up on army posts and attended West Point, where he established one of the best scholastic records in the history of the academy and in his final year became first captain, as had Robert E. Lee and John J. Pershing before him.

On U.S. entry into World War I, MacArthur, then 37 and serving as assistant to Secretary of War Newton D. Baker, made a unique contribution to political-military relations by supporting the use of the National Guard in combat and proposing the creation of a National Guard division made up of contingents from various states. When this "Rainbow" division was established, MacArthur became its chief of staff, and in France, a flamboyant soldier twice wounded, he achieved the rank of brigadier general and ended the war as division commander.

During the ensuing years, MacArthur made a notable mark as a modernizing superintendent of West Point, held commands in the Philippines and in the United States, and in 1930 became army chief of staff, just in time to deal with budget cutting caused by the Great Depression. In July 1932 the general involved himself in an ugly episode that many observers would never forget. Exceeding President Herbert Hoover's orders, MacArthur (acting against the advice of an assistant, Major Dwight D. EISENHOWER) took personal charge of the expulsion of a group of unemployed veterans—the Bonus Army—from Washington, D.C., and the demolition of their shantytown camp. Newsreels captured the general in full uniform, hands on hips, medals dangling, surveying the scene with a self-satisfied air suggesting that he had just led troops to a well-earned victory over a formidable foe. MacArthur's defenders later maintained that, in taking direct command of the operation, he did the dirty work himself instead of handing it on to a subordinate. But this explanation hardly accounts for his brushing the president's orders aside and sending troops into the veterans' camp to set it on fire. His pleasure in the operation seemed to speak for itself.

Having told a friend that MacArthur was "one of the two most dangerous men in the country" (the other honoree being Huey Long, the populist Louisiana senator-dictator), President Hoover's Democratic successor, Franklin D. ROOSEVELT, nevertheless extended the general's tenure as chief of staff an extra year, until 1935. In that year, with the Philippines now a commonwealth on its way to independence, MacArthur returned to the islands as military adviser to the local government, a phase of his career that saw him become the first and only field marshal in American history.

In July 1941, as war tensions increased in the Pacific, MacArthur was recalled to active duty in the U.S. Army, with command of forces in the Far East. After the Japanese attack on Pearl Harbor in December, it quickly became evident that local forces could not fight off the invaders, although the Americans and Filipinos kept up a stirring resistance until May. By this time MacArthur had been evacuated to Australia, where he assumed command of the Allied Southwest Pacific Area. From then on, he led an amphibious "island-hopping" war that found him back in the Philippines in October 1944, when, as shown in a famous photograph, the general waded ashore on the island of Leyte. The imaginative and man-power-conserving conduct of this long campaign won him wide praise.

Arriving in Japan to take charge after the war, MacArthur displayed a firmness and deftness of touch that won over the Japanese, who had no idea what to expect from occupation by an enemy army. Often thought of as a political conservative, the general, although acting in an authoritarian fashion, instituted liberal programs, all based on the establishment of constitutional authority. When the occupation ended, Japan had a functioning, democratic government and a rapidly recovering economy; this phase of MacArthur's career, in the view of many commentators, showed him at his best. Indeed, history may well have no matching example of an enlightened and successful military occupation.

Then came the fateful Sunday in June 1950 when Premier KIM IL SUNG's North Korean troops crossed the 38TH PARALLEL into South Korea. Named to command the outnumbered United Nations forces, MacArthur yielded ground to the in-

vaders until his troops could stop them on the Naktong River, above the town of Pusan, on the southeast Korean coast. As a veteran practitioner of amphibious warfare, the general, in launching a counteroffensive, not only struck back directly but preceded this effort on September 15 with an amphibious attack on Inchon, a port high up on the west coast a few miles from Seoul, the capital, also an important transportation hub. Although the JOINT CHIEFS OF STAFF attempted to dissuade MacArthur from the landing, on the grounds of both geography and weather, the operation enjoyed striking success, producing the demoralization and near disintegration of the North Korean army. Within two weeks United Nations troops had taken control of most of South Korea, and on October 8, with President TRUMAN's approval, the troops crossed into North Korea and continued a march northward toward the Yalu River, which flows between North Korea and China.

A week later, at Truman's behest, the president and the general had a meeting at Wake Island that, for a one-day affair, has produced a remarkable amount of discussion and debate as to its purposes and results. In any case, a true meeting of the minds did not occur. Dismissing talk of possible Chinese intervention and forecasting victory, MacArthur later in the month blundered into a crisis when Chinese poured across the Yalu to take part in the war. Instead of going "home by Christmas," as the general had promised, the outnumbered, hard-pressed, battered UN forces retreated back across the 38th parallel. At the end of December the commander of the U.S. Eighth Army, Lieutenant General Walton Walker, was killed in a car crash and was succeeded by Lieutenant General Matthew B. RIDGWAY, an outstanding officer. While MacArthur presided over his Far Eastern command from Tokyo, Ridgway rebuilt the Eighth Army into a strong fighting force, and by the middle of March his troops had reoccupied Seoul. Meanwhile MacArthur was making public statements in opposition to U.S. policy—advocating the defeat of the Chinese by bombing Manchuria and by helping the Chinese Nationalists on TAIWAN attack the mainland. Having allowed MacArthur to flout their wishes by dispersing his ground forces across Korea, by conducting military affairs in the newspapers, and by ordering the disastrous advance to the Yalu, the members of the JCS—all junior to the general—finally recommended to Truman that MacArthur be removed from his command. The president, taking the action on April 11, 1951, met a firestorm of conservative opposition. Unable to concede that he had acted improperly, the general ascribed the dismissal exclusively to Truman, who, he had heard, was "suffering from malignant hypertension," which had produced "bewilderment and confusion of thought." General Ridgway succeeded MacArthur.

Returning to the United States for the first time since the mid-1930s, MacArthur moved from city to city at the head of triumphal processions. These spectacles had a political as well as a personal nature; in the Chicago parade, for instance, a motorcyclist strapped two effigies to his bike labeled, respectively, "HISS" and "ACHESON"—a succinct way of equating the Democratic secretary of state, and presumed underminer of MacArthur, with convicted perjurer Alger Hiss. Although now 71 years old, MacArthur, as he had done previously, entertained presidential ambitions, which Eisenhower's candidacy rendered moot. But on April 19, 1951, the general enjoyed his great moment in the political sun with an address to a joint session of Congress—a dramatically delivered apologia that ended with a line, which would be much quoted, from an old army ballad: "Old soldiers

General Douglas MacArthur, U.S. commander in the Far East

never die; they just fade away." Though MacArthur continued to appear in headlines, a seven-week senatorial hearing on the whole Korean affair dissipated his political force.

With his imperiousness and towering ego, his bravery and his brilliance, General MacArthur has remained a controversial figure in history. Much of his behavior paralleled, to a striking degree, the conduct of his father, the first General MacArthur, whose arrogance ruffled his superiors, who was recalled from an Asian command, who testified in a Senate investigation, and who made a memorable farewell address—unenviably so, since, when he reached his peroration, he fell dead at the lectern. He was his son's great hero. Half a century later the general wrote of his father's death, "Never have I been able to heal the wound in my heart."

McCarran Act   Named for its principal architect, a Democratic U.S. senator from Nevada, this 1951 legislative act contained restrictions on U.S. Communists, who were required to register (both organizations and individuals) and were forbidden employment in defense industries. In addition, foreigners who had been members of Communist (or Fascist) organizations were prohibited from entering the United States. The McCarran Act, passed during the KOREAN WAR and in the heyday of Senator Joseph MCCARTHY (as well as of McCarran himself), was very much a product of its time and, as the result of a tortuous passage through Congress, contained elements contributed by both Democrats and Republicans. (Some of its provisions came from the similarly intended Mundt-NIXON bill, which the House of Representatives had passed in 1948 but which had languished in the Senate.) It did not, however, make membership in the Communist Party illegal, which provided the basis for later legal challenges. President TRUMAN vetoed the act but saw his veto overwhelmingly overridden (286 to 46 in the House and 57 to 10 in the Senate).

In the following year the McCarran-Walter Act extended the original legislation by prohibiting admission to the United States not simply to Communists but to anyone declared subversive by the attorney general (Francis Walter was a representative from Pennsylvania); in a similar vein, members of "Communist-front" as well as Communist

organizations became subject to deportation. This act also became law over Truman's veto.

McCarthy, Joseph Raymond (1908–1957)   One of the few U.S. senators to give his name to a mode of behavior, MCCARTHYISM, Joe McCarthy, for a four-year period in the 1950s, wielded great political power while lacking a program or any other set of discernible views except what his critics regarded as an opportunistic anti-Communism.

Born in a farm village near Appleton, Wis., McCarthy grew up the kind of overall-wearing country boy who in those days came into town primarily to sell eggs and run other errands. Leaving school at 14, he went back to finish several years later, then attended law school at Marquette University, acquiring his degree in 1935. Bright and gifted with a retentive memory, he became known in college as a poker-playing, party-loving young man who depended largely on cramming and a certain amount of bluff to get through his courses. After practicing law on his own for the better part of a year with meager results, he went to work for an established lawyer in a nearby town, and in the following year ran for district attorney; his losing campaign drew critical comments about the harshness of his rhetoric. In 1939 McCarthy succeeded in becoming the youngest person ever elected circuit judge in Wisconsin; he based much of this campaign on making his opponent, who was 66, out to be 73. A local political observer called the newly elected judge "tricky, very tricky."

In 1942, a few months after the attack on Pearl Harbor, McCarthy resigned from the bench to join the Marine Corps. Assigned as intelligence officer for a dive-bomber squadron in the Pacific, he made a few flights as an observer, but in later years he built himself into "Tailgunner Joe," alleged holder of the Distinguished Flying Cross and possessor of a citation—based on forged testimony—from Admiral Chester Nimitz, the theater commander. A shipboard hazing in which McCarthy had injured his foot transformed itself into enemy gunfire that had left him with ten pounds of shrapnel in his leg. In later years, when campaigning, he would sometimes commemorate the supposed event with a limp.

Reelected judge in 1945, McCarthy began working the state in preparation for a 1946 race for the Senate seat of the well-known Robert La-Follette, Jr., whom, to general surprise, he defeated in the Republican primary, a victory followed by an overwhelming win over the Democratic candidate in the general election. By the beginning of 1950, however, McCarthy had little to show for his three years in Washington. (In one poll, in fact, Washington reporters had voted him the remarkable distinction of being the worst senator.) One evening when he was casting about for an issue with which he could make a name and on which he could base his reelection campaign in 1952, a dinner companion, Father Edmund Walsh, head of the Georgetown University School of Foreign Service, suggested that the senator might consider the issue of Communism—taking care, the priest added, to employ a careful and reasonable approach. McCarthy had already made minor use of the Communist question in various statements and speeches, but in this respect he did not stand out from the crowd; indeed, senators like Pat McCarran and representatives like Richard NIXON were well ahead of him. But the perjury conviction of Alger HISS, coming just two weeks after McCarthy's dinner with Father Walsh, and Secretary of State Dean ACHESON's gentlemanly declaration on January 25—"I do not intend to turn my back on Alger Hiss"—together with the ensuing uproar, apparently set McCarthy to thinking deeply. Already an issue permanently floating in the air, the Communist question had become a hot and inviting topic.

Just over two weeks later, on February 9, McCarthy delivered a fateful address to the Ohio County Women's Republican Club in Wheeling, W.Va. As Edwin R. Bayley later wrote in his book *Joe McCarthy and the Press,* this speech "has been the subject of more speculation, argument and investigation than almost anything he said in the next five years." In the key sentence, as reported in the next day's local Wheeling newspaper, McCarthy declared: "While I cannot take the time to name all the men in the State Department who have been named as members of the Communist Party and members of a spy ring, I have here in my hand a list of 205 that were known to the Secretary of State as being members of the Communist Party and who nevertheless are still working and shaping the policy of the State Department." From

then on, the press, though paying increasing attention to the story, could never pin down either precise charges or precise numbers. The senator spoke of 207, 57, 81, and "over 200," but he continually redefined them, sometimes calling them "card-carrying Communists," sometimes merely "bad risks."

Whatever he said or denied he had said, McCarthy had found his issue. From then on, he ruled as Washington's number-one Communist hunter, though in all his career he was never to catch a single one. (Indeed, through his headline-oriented and unsubstantiated charges, he tended to discredit serious and responsible investigations of espionage.) But he displayed a remarkable ability to capitalize on popular worries about U.S. security in the nuclear age and on the widespread conviction that if things go wrong, someone has deliberately made them go wrong. In the 1952 presidential campaign, McCarthy wielded so much influence that General EISENHOWER even altered a speech to delete a defense of General George C. MARSHALL, the man to whom he owed his great career; in an attack extreme even by his own standards, McCarthy had called the father of the MARSHALL PLAN a traitor and "part of a conspiracy so immense, an infamy so black, as to dwarf any in the history of man." Commenting on the low level of public discussion in the campaign, the *New York Herald Tribune* television critic John Crosby observed that Senator McCarthy was "being used on any program that deals in controversy—not to shed enlightenment, which doesn't command much interest—but to throw mud, which does."

The Republican victory in November did not, as some had hoped and expected, end McCarthy's assaults on the executive branch of the government. The State Department, under John Foster DULLES, trimmed its sails to the prevailing McCarthyite wind, and, abetted by his adviser, Roy COHN, the senator went on to attack the army, ostensibly for such lapses of security as promoting a "Fifth Amendment dentist"—an army dentist who declined to testify in a hearing—but actually for refusing to give preferential treatment to G. David Schine, a McCarthy aide who had been drafted. What resulted was the extraordinary 35-day 1954 television spectacle called the Army-McCarthy hearings.

McCarthy's assault on the army proved to be a major miscalculation and a major misreading of the political situation. Simply because he had no positive program or ideas of his own, the senator, performing as a sort of attack dog, had served Republicans of all varieties as a useful tool for bringing down or cowing opponents and winning elections. When the general public saw him in action on television, his hectoring, abusive tactics alienated many who had previously supported him; and by trying to discredit the leadership of the army, he alienated the influential eastern wing of his party—the core of the Republican establishment. After its own investigation, not of the army but of the senator, the Senate voted 67 to 22 to "condemn" him—not, literally, for his conduct in the hearings but for various offenses against the Senate and the investigating panel itself.

The loss of the battle with the army represented not only the end of McCarthy's influence but the end of any visible political activity on the senator's part (for one thing, to be sure, Republican loss of control of the Senate in the 1954 elections took away McCarthy's committee chairmanship). Suffering from apparent alcoholic liver damage, he died only three years later, just 48 years old.

McCarthyism Named for Senator Joseph R. MC-CARTHY, whose activities and style it is supposed to reflect, McCarthyism has been characterized as the use for political purposes of sensationalized attacks on individuals by means of unsubstantiated accusations, particularly involving alleged disloyalty, and using evidence that is questionable or irrelevant; sometimes, more generally, as the use of unfair techniques in the conduct of investigations. *See also* LOYALTY AND SECURITY PROGRAM.

McCloy, John Jay (1895–1989) A self-made man whose mother had supported the family as a hairdresser after the death of his father, John J. McCloy rose to such prominence that a political writer, Richard H. Rovere, declared him the "chairman of the Establishment." But McCloy himself took a different view—"I was just a leg man," he once declared. Adviser to U.S. presidents, Democratic and Republican, from ROOSEVELT to REAGAN, McCloy as U.S. high commissioner played a central role in the birth and development of the FEDERAL REPUBLIC OF GERMANY, guiding the transition from military occupation to civilian rule and supervising the rebuilding of the country and its economy.

Born in Philadelphia, McCloy graduated from Amherst in 1916 and briefly attended the Harvard Law School before entering the army. After returning from France, where he served as a captain in the field artillery, he finished his law studies and entered on a career as a New York lawyer. In spite of his original plan to return home to practice, McCloy did not become a Philadelphia lawyer, because a prominent citizen told him that since he was born, literally, on the wrong side of the tracks, he would never be taken seriously there; McCloy took the man's advice and went to Manhattan. But after 1940 he was to spend much of his time in government service, working first with Secretary of War Henry L. Stimson as adviser on security and then as assistant secretary of war (1941–45); Stimson called him "the man who handled everything that no one else happened to be handling." McCloy put in two years as president of the WORLD BANK before going to Germany in 1949. As high commissioner, McCloy said, he had "the powers of a dictator," but "I think I was a benevolent dictator. I think the rebuilding came off very well, with no significant problems."

Back in the private sector as chairman of the Chase National Bank and its successor, the Chase Manhattan Bank, McCloy continued his involvement in public affairs, advising President EISENHOWER on arms control. He coordinated disarmament activities for President KENNEDY and later served on the Warren Commission, which investigated Kennedy's assassination. An energetic figure with an informal manner, McCloy held board chairmanships of business and philanthropic enterprises ranging from the Ford Foundation and the Salk Institute to E. R. Squibb and Sons. At the Ford Foundation he worked with the CENTRAL INTELLIGENCE AGENCY to use the foundation as a means of funding projects such as the CONGRESS FOR CULTURAL FREEDOM.

Maclean, Donald (1913–1983) One of the famous CAMBRIDGE FIVE Soviet agents, Maclean, the son of a cabinet minister, made no secret of his Communist leanings. As an undergraduate he devoted con-

John J. McCloy, U.S. high commissioner in Germany—"the man who handled everything"

siderable time to work in party activities and displayed his convictions in the student magazine *Granta*. He also declared his intention to go to Russia as a teacher, although he sometimes talked about the possibility of staying on at Cambridge to produce a doctoral analysis of John Calvin from a Marxist perspective.

When, already recruited for the KGB by other members of the group, Maclean came down from the university in 1934, however, he sought a position in the Foreign Office. Now, as a Soviet mole, he made light of his Communist convictions, and after performing satisfactorily during the required lengthy probationary period, found himself in 1938 assigned to the embassy in Paris as an established civil servant. In this key spot in the prelude to World War II, Maclean had access to a variety of correspondence and documents worthy of being forwarded to Moscow. In June 1940, with German guns sounding in the distance, he fled the French capital, taking with him the American bride he had dramatically acquired as the enemy approached the city. Like other members of the Cambridge spy ring, he was already nurturing a serious drinking problem—due partly, perhaps, to the strain of leading a double life.

Later in the war his fellow agent, Kim PHILBY, who had picked up knowledge of British and U.S. nuclear research, prompted Maclean to seek a posting to Washington, which he received in 1944. Here, as first secretary in the embassy, he saw the flow of secret papers relating to atomic affairs and found himself in a perfect spot to serve as a contact person between the British and the U.S. branches of the Soviet espionage effort. In addition, he had access to all the codes and ciphers in use. To crown the affair, he received an appointment as a British member of the Combined Policy Committee on Atomic Energy, a situation that truly gave him the keys to the storehouse. Although an acquaintance commented that Maclean didn't know a cyclotron from a hair dryer, he had the aid of what literally amounted to a consulting physicist. He regularly visited laboratories and manufacturing plants operated by the ATOMIC ENERGY COMMISSION. In 1947, in still another development in the whole remarkable story, Maclean and another KGB agent, Klaus FUCHS, served as British delegates to a conference concerned with the declassification of scientific secrets.

Like Guy BURGESS, however, Maclean as a practicing alcoholic continually found himself in trouble caused by episodes during his drinking bouts; whereas Burgess was sloppily indiscreet and given to such endearing stunts as urinating in the fireplace, Maclean would smash furniture. Recalled home from the United States, he was posted to Cairo. During this period of his life, he took to muttering, when in his cups, lines like "I'm working for Uncle Joe," but no one paid attention—spies, after all, do not normally proclaim their true affiliations. Even though his behavior showed no improvement in Cairo, Maclean, quite incredibly, found himself back in London in charge of the American desk at the Foreign Office. This assignment put him in a position to pass on to his KGB case officer information about U.S. and UNITED NATIONS efforts and actions during the KOREAN WAR.

By late 1950 information developed from the VENONA transcripts of Soviet cipher messages came closer and closer to identifying Maclean as a Soviet mole. In April 1951 the evidence clearly pointed to him, but Philby, as British intelligence representative in Washington, had kept himself fully informed. Apparently Burgess served as the messenger between Philby and Maclean, briefing the latter also on an escape plan contrived with the Soviets. On the evening of May 25, 1951, Maclean sailed across the Channel to St. Malo, and from there disappeared behind the IRON CURTAIN. With him—whether on impulse or as part of the plan remains a question—went the messenger, Guy Burgess. *See also* LILIENTHAL, David Eli; ORLOV, Alexander.

McMahon Act   On October 16, 1945, in the aftermath of the nuclear bombing of Japan, the U.S. Senate chose Senator Brien McMahon, a Connecticut Democrat (1903–1952), to chair a special committee to study and make recommendations concerning the problems presented by the awesome new phenomenon of the ATOMIC BOMB. How should nuclear energy be controlled? What level of secrecy was necessary or desirable? What should be the role of the new UNITED NATIONS organization? As chairman of what became the Joint Committee on Atomic Energy, McMahon oversaw the framing of the McMahon Act, which established the principles for control of atomic energy and under which the ATOMIC ENERGY COMMISSION was created. The heavy restrictions placed on the sharing of nuclear information dismayed the British, who felt excluded from what had been a combined effort. *See also* BARUCH PLAN.

Macmillan, (Maurice) Harold (1894–1986)   Selected as British prime minister by Queen ELIZABETH II in the aftermath of the 1956 SUEZ CRISIS, Macmillan, who was not then the leader of his party, proved a notable success until economic problems and a sex-and-spy scandal (the PROFUMO AFFAIR) brought about his resignation in October 1963. As prime minister he played a leading part in the development of the NUCLEAR TEST BAN TREATY and had to face the frustration caused by General DE GAULLE's veto of the British attempt to enter the EUROPEAN ECONOMIC COMMUNITY (the Common Market).

A member of the family that created the famous Macmillan publishing house and, like Winston CHURCHILL, American on his mother's side, Macmillan was a graduate of Oxford and a World War I veteran who entered the House of Commons in 1924 and, except for two years following the loss of his seat in 1929, remained a member until retiring in 1964. During World War II he served at General EISENHOWER's Allied headquarters in North Africa as British political adviser, an experience that would prove particularly useful later, when he and Eisenhower had become heads of their respective governments; in Algiers, Macmillan also had his first dealings with the leader of the Free French, General de Gaulle.

During the Conservative administrations of

Churchill and Anthony EDEN (1951–57), Macmillan held the three leading portfolios, as minister of defense, foreign secretary, and chancellor of the exchequer. Taking office as prime minister in January 1957, after illness and the Suez Crisis had forced Eden from office, Macmillan worked to reunite his divided party and mend fences with Eisenhower, who had violently opposed the Suez operation. He fulfilled these tasks so well that he earned the nickname Supermac, and in 1959, campaigning with the slogan "You've never had it so good," he led the Conservatives to victory over the Labour Party by more than 100 seats. In general, Macmillan exuded and inspired confidence, as when he returned from a visit to the Soviet Union with the declaration that "there ain't going to be any war." This colloquialism took on a particularly striking quality as delivered by Macmillan, who in speech and personal style—enhanced by his pouchy eyes and drooping mustache—seemed almost a stage 19th-century English aristocrat. Cartoonists loved him, but, as a biographer wrote, "instead of the languid, over-tired, detached scholar whose first love was history and Trollope, Virgil and Homer—and this was the outward pose —he turned out to be the shrewdest party boss for generations." What the public did not know, as well, was that the prime minister had lived for four decades in deep personal unhappiness, as part of a triangle that saw his wife in love with a parliamentary colleague and friend—an affair that ended only with his wife's death. Macmillan was succeeded by Sir Alec DOUGLAS-HOME.

McNamara, Robert Strange (1916–)   U.S. business executive who had held the presidency of the Ford Motor Company for only a few days when President-elect KENNEDY asked him to become secretary of defense. Renowned as a management and budget specialist, a planner and a cost cutter with the brain of a computer, McNamara became in many ways a highly effective secretary of defense but, like the United States as a whole, became enmired in the VIETNAM WAR. Kept in his position by President JOHNSON after Kennedy's assassination, McNamara served until 1968.

Born in San Francisco, McNamara graduated from the University of California in 1937 and in 1939 received an M.B.A. from the Harvard Business School, at which he subsequently taught. During World War II he served in the air force, in which he and associates pioneered in applying the principle of statistical control to operations. (Application of the principle showed, for instance, the B-17 to be a more effective performer than the B-24.) Afterward, McNamara took his methods to Ford under the new regime of Henry Ford II, who oversaw the modernization of the company.

As secretary of defense, McNamara brought with him a group of "whiz kids," young managers and specialists who made great efforts to introduce their leader's attitudes and techniques throughout the world of Pentagon bureaucracy. "McNamarization," as the new cost-effectiveness approach was dubbed, evoked the hostility that might have been expected from service traditionalists. McNamara won enthusiastic presidential approval, however; indeed, President Johnson ordered the heads of other agencies to emulate the McNamara model.

Fearlessly, the secretary hunted down cows long sacred on Capitol Hill, announcing in late 1964 a plan to close a number of unneeded military bases, and topping this unpopular gesture by declaring his intention to merge the army's active reserve and the National Guard. McNamara then presented a proposal to phase out the STRATEGIC AIR COMMAND's B-52 and B-58 bombers. Though the B-52s continued to fly for decades, the B-58 had been phased out by 1970; Congress blocked the reserve–National Guard merger. "Running a large organization is the same, whether it is the Ford Motor Company, the Catholic Church, or the Department of Defense," McNamara observed. "Once you get a certain scale, they're all the same." Even so, the Department of Defense proved to possess notable differences from Ford. Anything but a tight ship, it resembled a loose confederation of diverse interests, with each of the armed services, as George BALL later commented, having its own "passionate constituency." Each service was "a separate barony with its own history, hagiography, ballads, and legends."

By late 1965 McNamara found himself presiding over a gigantic, worldwide operation, as his department sent troops to the Dominican Republic, in the Caribbean; to Europe and Korea as part of continuing commitments; and, ominously, in

Robert S. McNamara *(l.)*, U.S. secretary of defense during the Vietnam War, confers with Secretary of State Dean Rusk.

swelling numbers to Vietnam, in this pivotal year of U.S. involvement in Southeast Asia. Indeed, the secretary became almost as closely identified with the escalation in Vietnam as was President Johnson himself—to the point that "McNamara's War" was the label many critics gave the whole effort. For some time McNamara, like his generals, spoke cheerily of the prospects for victory, producing precise estimates of progress and probabilities in a field less amenable than budgeting and procurement to such quantification. But in 1968, disillusioned, the secretary resigned to become president of the WORLD BANK.

In 1995, three decades after the escalation in Vietnam, McNamara surprised the world with the book he "planned never to write," *In Retrospect*, a mea culpa for his actions and those of the presidents he served. "We were wrong, totally wrong," he said in admitting that U.S. leaders acted out of ignorance of the Vietnamese land and people and of the true interests of the United States, notably in placing misguided reliance on the DOMINO THEORY as a guide to national strategy. In May 1967, despite his public identification with the war, McNamara wrote Johnson that "the war in Vietnam is acquiring a momentum of its own that must be stopped"; later in the year the secretary, though still not questioning the soundness of the basic U.S. aims in the war, told the president that "we could not achieve our objective in Vietnam through any reasonable military means, and we therefore should seek a lesser political objective through negotiations."

Far from winning universal praise, McNamara's

apology rekindled much of the old debate about the war, although, as Max Frankel commented, the secretary made his own case difficult to plead by waiting so long, because "no one under the age of 50 can be expected to fathom the fears and phobias of the 1960s." Many commentators criticized McNamara for not having spoken out in 1967, when his authoritative voice might have helped bring the end of the war. He maintained, however, that his power came solely from the president who appointed him and that he was therefore not entitled to attack that president from outside the cabinet. Not all of his readers agreed with this argument.

MAD   Acronym for the strategic principle called MUTUAL ASSURED DESTRUCTION. Pronounced "mad," the term became popular with political satirists, though students of strategy gamely pointed out that "MAD" could also stand for the somewhat more reassuring "mutual assured deterrence."

Main Adversary   From the end of World War II through the next four decades, Soviet intelligence communications referred to the United States as the "Main Adversary" *(Glavny Protivnik)*. This usage represented something of a demotion for Great Britain, which until then had held first place in the USSR's adversarial esteem. It is noteworthy that the United States acquired this status well before any of the confrontations that marked the start of the Cold War.

Makins, Sir Roger (1904–)   British career diplomat who succeeded Sir Oliver FRANKS as ambassador to the United States in 1952. The son of a general who became a longtime member of Parliament, Makins was a graduate of Oxford (1925) and a barrister, with a special background in economics. Before coming to Washington, he served as a deputy undersecretary in the Foreign Office. As British ambassador, Makins worked hard, but with only limited success, to develop a working partnership with Secretary of State John Foster DULLES, who, the British believed, tended to act without due consultation with his British allies.

Malayan War   In fighting that lasted overall from 1948 to 1957, the British defeated a Communist-led insurgency in Malaya, then a British colony. Their success came partly from the able leadership of General Sir Gerald TEMPLER, the commander in chief from 1952 to 1954, and also from the employment of a variety of counterinsurgency techniques developed by Sir Robert Thompson. In September 1963 the former colony became the independent Republic of Malaysia.

Aside from its intrinsic importance, the war in Malaya took on particular significance from the belief, on the part of many U.S. military planners, that Thompson's techniques—especially his STRATEGIC HAMLET program—could be borrowed for use in the VIETNAM WAR. But, although the United States made heavy use of a Templer saying—"This is a struggle for the hearts and minds of the people"—the techniques did not travel well. For one thing, in Malaya the insurgents had been exclusively Chinese, already hated by the native Malays; no such opposition of groups existed in Vietnam. In addition, the Communists had won the war in the Vietnamese villages long before the Americans arrived in force.

Malenkov, Georgi Maximilianovich (1902–1988)   Joseph STALIN's successor as leader of the Soviet Union, Georgi Malenkov became premier (chairman of the Council of Ministers) and Communist Party first secretary in March 1953, following Stalin's death. Though spoken of as the head of a collective leadership (originally together with Lavrenty BERIA and Vyacheslav MOLOTOV), Malenkov clearly held the number-one position, but within little more than a week he had been forced to give up his party secretaryship to a lesser-known but tough and highly capable politician, Nikita KHRUSHCHEV.

A native of Orenburg, Russia, Malenkov entered the Red Army at the age of 17, taking part in the civil war against the White Russian forces; he joined the Bolshevik Party in 1920. Like many other Communist officials, he attended engineering school, graduating in 1925, and then became a party administrator. This work in due course brought him into close contact with Stalin; the association led to Malenkov's active involvement in the Great Purge (1936–38), when many Communist Party officials, army officers, and others were tried and executed. Continuing as a protégé of Stalin, Malenkov became a candidate (nonvoting) member of the Politburo in 1941. During World War II, as a member of the high-level State Defense Committee, he took charge of aircraft production.

In 1946, Malenkov's future seemed assured when he was named a full member of the Politburo, second secretary of the party Central Committee, and deputy premier. But his rise to prominence drew the fire of a rival, Andrei ZHDANOV, a top Communist Party official who had been party boss of Leningrad during the 900-day German siege of the city and was generally regarded as Stalin's probable successor. Zhdanov's attacks resulted in some loss of influence by Malenkov, but the rivalry ended abruptly with Zhdanov's death in 1948.

Restored to Stalin's full favor, Malenkov within a few years had succeeded to Zhdanov's place as the dictator's heir presumptive. He delivered major party pronouncements, such as his November 1949 declaration concerning the importance of the Chinese Communist victory over the Nationalists. The significance here lay in the change this acknowledgment represented from the aloofness with which Moscow had previously treated MAO ZEDONG. In 1952, at the 19th Congress of the COMMUNIST PARTY OF THE SOVIET UNION, Malenkov was the speaker who suggested a shift in Stalin's thinking toward the possibility of PEACEFUL COEXISTENCE between the Communist and capitalist worlds.

Once in power, Malenkov, a large, pudgy man whom a Czech diplomat described as looking "exactly like a Turkish eunuch," overcame his normal reserve to demonstrate something of a democratic personal style. He won a measure of public favor by focusing on raising living standards instead of emphasizing the development of heavy industry; he also put through cuts in military spending (moves opposed by Khrushchev, who later, however, would follow the same course). Under Malenkov's leadership, some governmental restrictions were relaxed and a number of political prisoners released. Partly as a result of these measures, Malenkov and his colleagues had to face and put down riots in East BERLIN and East Germany in the June 1953 EAST BERLIN UPRISING—the first popular discord since the Soviets had established control of Eastern Europe in the late 1940s.

By February 1955 the tenacious Khrushchev, in his drive for power, had acquired enough support from politicians and the army to force Malenkov's resignation; the premiership went to Khrushchev's nominee, Marshal Nikolai BULGANIN. Still a member of the party Presidium (as the Politburo was called for some years), Malenkov in 1957 joined with Molotov, Lazar KAGANOVICH, and Dmitri Shepilov in an attempt to overthrow Khrushchev. Successful in the Presidium, the ANTIPARTY group lost the battle in the full CENTRAL COMMITTEE. Malenkov was expelled from the Presidium, the Central Committee, and the party itself, but instead of having to face imprisonment or worse—as would unquestionably have been his fate in the Stalin era —he was dispatched to Kazakhstan, far from Moscow, as manager of a hydroelectric plant, a position he held for 30 long years, until he reached his mid-80s.

Malik, Yakov (1906–1980) Veteran Soviet diplomat who held leading ambassadorial posts, including Tokyo during World War II (1942–45) and London (1953–60). He became best known as the Soviet permanent representative to the UNITED NATIONS (1948–52 and 1968–76). By a singular turn of fate, however, the USSR boycotted the UN Security Council in 1950—to protest the continued seating of the Nationalist Chinese (TAIWAN) government instead of the People's Republic of China. Thus Malik was not in his chair at the outbreak of the KOREAN WAR in June to cast a veto against UN action to stem the North Korean invasion. A prominent demarche with which Malik was identified during the war was his accusation before the UN, in February 1952, that the United States had engaged in GERM WARFARE in Korea; this piece of DISINFORMATION had a strong impact around the world, especially when it received support from supposed confessions wrung from U.S. prisoners in Communist hands.

Malinovsky, Rodion Yakovlevich (1898–1967) Soviet marshal, a veteran professional soldier who looked the part, with his beetling eyebrows and burly build. Malinovsky served in the old imperial Russian army and then in the Red Army, rising to high rank during World War II, notably at Stalingrad, where he commanded an army, and during the Soviet advance westward in the later years of the war. In the summer of 1945 he went to the Far East, where, after the war, he became commander in chief of Soviet forces. Returning to Moscow in 1956, he became first deputy minister of defense and commander in chief of Soviet ground forces and, in 1957, minister of defense. In this position he replaced the greatest Soviet military hero, Marshal Georgi ZHUKOV, who had helped Nikita KHRUSHCHEV beat back a challenge to his leadership from the ANTIPARTY GROUP and then, because of his own eminence and popularity, seemed to be looked on as a threat by the man he had helped to stay in power.

Thus Malinovsky was the chief soldier of the USSR during the Sputnik era, the development of new missiles, and the CUBAN MISSILE CRISIS. By Khrushchev's own account, Malinovsky directed the operation for installing missiles in Cuba. When asked by Premier Khrushchev how long, in case war came, it would take the United States to crush Cuba's forces, Malinovsky replied without equivocation, "Something on the order of two days," an opinion that did not please Cuba's Fidel CASTRO when Khrushchev relayed it to him. Malinovsky remained in office after the overthrow of Khrushchev in 1964. After a long struggle with cancer, the marshal died on March 31, 1967, thus giving General Secretary Leonid BREZHNEV the opportunity to appoint his own longtime ally, Marshal Andrei GRECHKO, to the position.

Malraux, André (-Georges) (1901–1976) Eminent French novelist, art critic, and archaeologist, Malraux was a man of many sides. A committed antifascist in the 1930s, he organized an air squadron for the Republican army in the Spanish Civil War. In 1940 he commanded a tank company in the fight against Germany; after three years of silence he emerged as a leader of the Resistance, and he spent part of 1944 as a prisoner of the Germans. In 1945, having returned to Paris, he moved to the political right in protest against the prevailing leftist sentiment of Jean-Paul SARTRE and his followers, and he served as minister of the interior in Charles DE GAULLE's first postwar provisional government.

In the Fifth Republic, Malraux held the portfolio of minister of state responsible for culture throughout de Gaulle's presidency. "The presence

at my side of this inspired friend, this devotee of lofty destinies," said the general, with his own kind of loftiness, "gave me a sense of being insured against the commonplace." As minister in charge of culture, Malraux made reforms on various levels; his most noticeable move was probably his policy of brightening Paris by having all the public monuments cleaned. Malraux's experiences in China in his earlier years led U.S. president NIXON to seek him out in 1972, before going to Beijing, to ask his impressions of MAO ZEDONG and ZHOU ENLAI. Malraux won the Prix Goncourt for *La condition humaine (Man's Fate)* in 1934.

Mao Tse-tung *See* MAO ZEDONG.

Mao Zedong (Mao Tse-tung) (1893–1976) One of the foremost political figures of the 20th century, Mao was leader of the Chinese Communist Party, victor in the civil war (1946–49), and chief creator of the People's Republic of China. Born in Hunan Province to an upwardly mobile peasant family, he rejected the rural life and marriage his parents had planned for him and, after serving briefly in an army fighting the Qing (Manchu) government, studied political philosophy and ethics at the First Normal School in Changsha, reading not only Chinese philosophers but Montesquieu, Rousseau, Mill, Spencer, and other Western thinkers.

Particularly concerned with identifying the cultural and political factors that could account for China's weakness in the modern world, Mao concluded that the country was weak because the people were weak. Hence he dedicated his studies and his writing to strengthening his people. In his essay "A Study of Physical Education," published in 1917, he declared that "physical education not only harmonizes the emotions, it also strengthens the will." In 1919 he moved to Peking (Beijing), supporting himself by a clerical job in the university library, so that he could be near the ethics teacher he had admired in Changsha. This move also put him near the teacher's daughter, Yang Kaihui, whom he married the next year.

An even more profound result of Mao's stay in Peking was his attendance at Marxist study groups organized by the head librarian, Li Dazhao, one of the founders of the Chinese Communist Party. These sessions brought about Mao's conversion to

Communism, and when he took a job as director of a primary school in Changsha, he established a party cell in the city. In 1921 he attended the first plenary meeting of the Chinese Communist Party, held in Shanghai, as the delegate from Hunan. Having become a member of the party Central Committee, he led the 1927 "Autumn Harvest Uprising"—a series of attacks on villages in the Hunan countryside—which ended in complete disaster, forcing Mao to flee to Jinggang Mountain with the remnants of his 2,000-man army. This led the party to censure Mao and expel him from the Central Committee. At Jinggang he entered on his first experience of a strategic withdrawal in the face of superior force: under constant attack by units of CHIANG KAI-SHEK'S GUOMINDANG, he led his small force to the mountains between Jiangxi and Fujian Provinces.

Mao's famous major withdrawal—the celebrated "Long March"—came in 1934 and 1935, when he led his Communist force in a 6,000-mile retreat from the Guomindang to the caves of northern Shaanxi (Shensi). Here, at Yanan, having become head of the Chinese Communist Party, he established the base from which he directed operations against the Guomindang and against the Japanese in World War II. In 1946, despite the arguments of Soviet Premier Joseph STALIN and President TRUMAN's personal representative, George MARSHALL—each of whom, for different reasons, advised him to make peace with Chiang—he took the offensive against the Guomindang. On October 1, 1949, he proclaimed victory, and the establishment of the People's Republic of China followed. Mao later said, perhaps with some pique, that "the Chinese revolution won victory by acting contrary to Stalin's will."

As chairman of the Central Committee of the Chinese Communist Party, Mao led the nation from 1949 until his death in 1976. In 1959, however, he was compelled to retire from the position of chairman of the Central Government Council as the result of the failure of his GREAT LEAP FORWARD program, aimed at increasing production through the establishment of local, peasant-operated (backyard) industries. During his rule of China, in fact, he consistently tended to glorify the peasants (whose revolutionary potential he had discovered at the outset of his career) and to adopt various utopian plans such as the Great Leap Forward and the CULTURAL REVOLUTION of the 1960s. He seemed concerned about keeping the spirit of revolution alive, regardless of the immediate cost in people, money, and even the well-being of the regime.

In a telling comment, Soviet premier Nikita KHRUSHCHEV once observed that Stalin often found himself bewildered by Mao, a bafflement shared by Khrushchev. According to Khrushchev, Mao maintained that, regardless of the West's economic and technical advantages, the balance of forces favored the East, since with its great population China could easily afford to lose 300 million people in a nuclear attack; Mao spoke of this as the "balance of forces according to population." The Sino-Soviet split of the 1960s and the 1970s Chinese-U.S. rapprochement launched by President NIXON were two of the major foreign-policy events of Mao's rule.

In *The Private Life of Chairman Mao* (1994), Li Zhisui, Mao's personal physician for the last 21 years of his life, provides an extraordinary closeup view of the chairman—"eccentric, demanding, suspicious," said the historian Ross Terrill, and also "unregretful, lascivious, and unfailingly fascinating." Henry KISSINGER, Nixon's adviser, spoke of Mao's "raw, concentrated willpower."

Many people around the world knew Mao for his "Little Red Book," *Quotations from Chairman Mao Tse-tung,* which contained the leader's distilled wisdom, tinged with a suggestion of infallibility, on a variety of subjects. Mao encouraged the development of a cult of personality at home, partly, at least, to win support for his ideas as those of a great and inspired leader. (It is possible, as well, that like many other leaders before him, he found the role of icon not altogether disagreeable.) The process produced a bizarre result, however—Mao became a cult hero of the New Left in the West in the 1960s, with his sayings being chanted at public meetings by crowds of young people, as marijuana smoke scented the air above them. Hua Kuo-feng succeeded Mao as head of the Chinese Communist Party. *See also* JIANG QING.

Marcuse, Herbert (1898–1979) A native of Germany, a specialist on the German philosopher Hegel, Marcuse was one of the founders of the Frankfurt Institute of Social Research. During the

1960s he became a hero of young American New Left radicals—despite being almost four decades past 30, the age beyond which people supposedly did not deserve the trust of the young. A refugee from the Nazi regime, Marcuse came to the United States in 1936, became a lecturer at Columbia University, and during World War II worked for the Office of Strategic Services as an intelligence analyst. He later taught at Brandeis University (1954–65) and the University of California at San Diego (1965–70). As a Marxist philosopher, Marcuse dismissed the democratic process as a way of dealing with political and social problems, although, like many of the young people who looked to him as an intellectual mentor, he suggested no alternative to the system he attacked. "It's not up to me," he declared, "to hand down a blueprint." Marcuse's emergence as a prophet of U.S. student revolutionaries when he was a sexagenarian, said Roland Stromberg of the University of Wisconsin, was "as startling as anything in the annals of intellectual history." In supporting such actions as the 1968 student uprising at Columbia, Marcuse uttered deliverances that could be taken as either Delphic or obvious; for instance, "Theory must have something to do with truth if it is to be in any way relevant to conditions."

By favoring the denial of free speech to persons having opinions of which he did not approve, Marcuse seemed to some observers to present a remarkable example of a person who had survived the Nazi dictatorship but failed to learn some essential lessons from the experience. As the holder of such views, Marcuse inspired little admiration in the American press; however, the Soviet media had little use for his antigovernment ideas either, frequently condemning him as a counterrevolutionary (he was even called a CENTRAL INTELLIGENCE AGENCY operative). In seeing industrial society as antidemocratic and irrational, Marcuse, of course, had much company. It was the use he made of these ideas that alienated him from many of his contemporaries, while his advocacy of anarchy during the turbulent 1960s endeared him to the young.

Markov affair   One day in September 1978, Georgi Markov, an émigré Bulgarian writer who lived in London and worked for the BBC World Service,

stood quietly waiting for a bus. Suddenly bumped by a stranger, who apologized for jabbing him with his umbrella, Markov felt a sting in his leg. Mysteriously taken ill, he described the incident to his doctors as he lay dying in a hospital. Four days after the incident, Markov was dead. Examination of his thigh revealed a tiny puncture and the remains of a pellet that had been filled with ricin, a deadly poison derived from the castor bean. The umbrella had literally fired the pellet into Markov's body.

In a 1993 interview, Oleg Kalugin, a former KGB officer, revealed that he had been ordered by his superiors to provide technical assistance to the Bulgarian secret police for the killing. Other information has suggested that this assignment, along with other aid sent by the KGB, came in response to a request by Todor ZHIVKOV, the head of the Bulgarian Communist Party, who wished to get rid of Markov and other dissident émigrés who were criticizing him in the West. The umbrella used on Markov had reached London after a long journey. It was one of several bought by KGB agents in Washington, D.C., and sent to Moscow to be adapted for service. *See* DISINFORMATION.

Marshall, George Catlett (1880–1959)   Rarely in history has anyone received from his thoughtful contemporaries the degree of admiration that came to General Marshall during the last two decades of his life. To the generation of World War II, Marshall was the leading U.S. military figure—army chief of staff and, in British prime minister Winston CHURCHILL's phrase, the "true organizer of victory." Those who came later knew Marshall's name best from the pioneering program for European recovery developed under his leadership as secretary of state. In 1947, presenting the general with an honorary degree, President James B. Conant of Harvard called him "a soldier and statesman whose ability and character brook only one comparison in the history of the nation."

No one could have imagined, when George Marshall was a youthful prankster in Uniontown, Pa., that in later years Harvard's president would place him on an exclusive national pedestal, side by side with George Washington. As an adolescent, however, Marshall developed a serious interest in a career as a soldier and went off to the

Virginia Military Institute. In going to Virginia, he actually moved closer to his family's roots; originally of Tidewater origin, the Marshalls had come to Pennsylvania in the 1870s by way of Kentucky, to which George's great-great-grandfather had moved in 1780. The young man did well at VMI, revealing a gift for leadership that enabled him to become first captain, the top cadet post, in his third year. Marshall later finished first in his class at the Fort Leavenworth infantry and cavalry school and gave outstanding performances with National Guard units in New England and as a young officer in the Philippines. In 1916, as a captain, he received possibly the most remarkable efficiency report in the history of the army. In answer to a form question whether he would desire to have this officer under his command, Marshall's superior commented, "Yes, but I would prefer to serve under his command" (underscoring in original). The colonel declared that Marshall was "a military genius" and should be made a brigadier general immediately.

In fact, however, Marshall would serve for 20 more years before winning his first star. In the interim he would establish an outstanding record as a staff officer in France in World War I, serve as aide to General John J. Pershing—the top U.S. commander in World War I and later chief of staff—and hold the very important position of director of the academic department of the Infantry School at Fort Benning, Ga., a position that allowed him to spot promising young officers; those who trained under him and rose to high positions in World War II came to be known as "Marshall men."

Chosen in 1939 as chief of staff by President ROOSEVELT, with the support of Pershing and of FDR's close adviser, Harry Hopkins, Marshall took over as acting chief on July 1 and began his official term on September 1, the first day of World War II. The general assumed awesome responsibilities, since the United States had only a tiny and poorly equipped army with which to meet the challenges of the time. Thanks in good part to Marshall's standing with Congress, the first peacetime draft in U.S. history was passed in 1940. By the end of World War II, Marshall had taken the army from a strength of only 174,000 troops and 1,000 aircraft in 1939 to the mighty force of 8.3 million and 64,000 airplanes that participated in the victory in 1945.

Recognized for his integrity, military knowledge, gift for seeing situations as they would appear to civilians, and ability to get the best out of his subordinates, Marshall also had a certain special quality that won him the admiration of all who knew him. He never did realize his postwar dream of retirement. Hardly had he turned over the office of chief of staff to his successor, General EISENHOWER, when President TRUMAN called on him to undertake a singularly unpromising task—mediating the conflict in China between the Nationalist government of CHIANG KAI-SHEK and the Chinese Communists.

In essence, the general had to play the part of impartial referee and at the same time support Chiang in order to limit Communist—including Soviet—influence in China. At the time, U.S. policy makers tended to lump all Communists together rather than to pay attention to the differences and even hostilities between MAO ZEDONG and Moscow.

Remarkably, Marshall, with his prestige and ability as a negotiator, managed to secure a truce within a few weeks of his arrival in Nanking; however, it could not hold. In January 1947, after a year of effort, the general requested his recall. In a final statement he blamed his failure to bring peace to China on militarists and extremists on both sides, but the mission had been impossible from the moment of its conception. Undertaken with the aim of creating a strong China friendly toward the United States, the mission instead contributed heavily to the creation of a hostile Communist China. Several years later, Senator Joseph MCCARTHY, in a demagogic Senate speech, asserted that Marshall had gone to China in order to "conclude and perfect the surrender of Yalta."

Even after the conclusion of this taxing and frustrating mission, retirement still eluded the general. Venerated by Truman, who considered him the greatest living American, Marshall returned from China only to find himself becoming secretary of state. Taking office at a pivotal time in postwar history, he presided during his two years in Foggy Bottom (as the department is revealingly known from its location in Washington) over the best-

The father of the Marshall Plan, U.S. secretary of state George C. Marshall *(l.)*, talks with one of his greatest admirers, President Harry S. Truman.

known and most important U.S. initiatives and actions of the Cold War era: the MARSHALL PLAN, the CONTAINMENT policy, and the creation of the NORTH ATLANTIC TREATY ORGANIZATION. Bringing his own outlook to the world situation and drawing on the work of an outstanding group of subordinates, including Dean ACHESON, George KENNAN, and Charles E. BOHLEN, Marshall set out with Truman to put the country on a course it would follow for the next 40 years. Once again, as during his time as chief of staff, his prestige with Congress, Republicans and Democrats alike, won the needed votes for the enabling legislation.

The outbreak of the KOREAN WAR, which came after a period of near chaos in the newly created Department of Defense, caused Truman once again to call on Marshall, who had retired from the State Department in 1949. Appointed secretary of defense, Marshall during his year of service had to bring a degree of order and harmony to the department and to create the fighting force required for the new situation. He also shared in the delicate task of dealing with General Douglas MACARTHUR and in the outburst of partisan anger that followed the general's dismissal from his Far Eastern command. The language several conservative

Republican senators used in speaking of Marshall would have seemed incredible a few years earlier. Blamed during his confirmation hearings for the "loss" of China and later for removing MacArthur, Marshall was called a "front man for traitors" and a "living lie"; Senator McCarthy described him, extraordinarily enough, as "completely incompetent." Such an opinion must be considered highly idiosyncratic.

The country was moving into the fevered anti-Communism that characterized the 1950s, and Marshall, who had undergone an operation for the removal of a kidney, no doubt welcomed his final retirement. In restoring—or, actually, in creating—a working Defense Department, he had accomplished his final mission. In 1953 Marshall's work for European recovery was recognized with the Nobel Peace Prize.

"The moment General Marshall entered a room," wrote Dean Acheson, "everyone in it felt his presence. It was a striking and communicated force." The general, Acheson said, had "no military glamour about him and nothing of the martinet. Yet to all of us he was always 'General Marshall.' The title fitted him as though he had been baptized with it."

Marshall Plan (European Recovery Program)   An unusually distinguished group of visitors—literary, scientific, political, military—came to Cambridge, Mass., on June 5, 1947, to receive honorary degrees from Harvard University. The guests included the semanticist and co-inventor of Basic English I. A. Richards; the liberal Southern editor Hodding Carter; the president of the University of Chicago, Ernest C. Colwell; the "GIs' general," Omar N. Bradley; the nuclear physicist and scientific director of the atomic-bomb project J. Robert OPPENHEIMER; the world's most eminent poet, T. S. Eliot; and the U.S. secretary of state, General George C. MARSHALL.

President James B. Conant of Harvard had asked Marshall to come to Cambridge both in 1945 and in 1946, but the general had begged off, pleading the pressure of his obligations, first as army chief of staff and then as special presidential envoy to China. In 1947, as well, Marshall had first declined Conant's renewed invitation, but in May the general changed his mind and not only agreed to come to Cambridge but told Conant that, as the university president wished, he would make a speech, although only a brief one.

Marshall's change of mind came from no caprice but was the consequence of intensive thought and discussion in the State Department and the TRUMAN administration generally about the economic, political, and social plight of Europe in the continuing aftermath of World War II. President Truman, many years later, gave an effective summary of the picture: "People were starving, and they were cold because there wasn't enough coal, and tuberculosis was breaking out. There had been food riots in France and Italy, everywhere." In addition, the winter of 1946–47 had been unusually harsh. In response to pleas from European leaders, the United States had taken some stopgap measures—loans and shipments of supplies. But in the early months of 1947 U.S. leaders began developing a consensus that the desperate situation in Europe required U.S. action on a much larger scale. The list of those besides Marshall most involved in the discussions included (but was certainly not limited to) Undersecretary of State Dean ACHESON, Navy Secretary James V. FORRESTAL, State Department Counselor Charles E. BOHLEN, and Assistant Secretary of State William CLAYTON. An ad hoc

State Department group assembled under the direction of the head of the new Policy Planning Staff, George F. KENNAN, whose ideas on the CONTAINMENT of Soviet expansionism were increasingly becoming the guides for U.S. policy.

Though given little time to develop a plan (Kennan did not assume his position until May 5), the ad hoc group produced a report calling for U.S. help in the restoration of Europe's economic health not by a kind of welfare program created in Washington but through plans made by the Europeans themselves: "the program must be evolved in Europe," and "the Europeans must bear the basic responsibility for it." The report also contained the specific point that U.S. aid under the proposed program should not be directed at the combating of Communism as such, even though Communists were seeking to turn the European economic crisis to their own ends. Hence Soviet-controlled countries should be regarded as eligible for participation, though to do so they would naturally have to loosen up their economic systems.

Sensing the rapid deterioration of the situation in Europe, Marshall and his advisers decided to use the Harvard commencement as the platform from which to present these ideas to the world. In a quiet speech, mostly drafted by Bohlen, Marshall described the administration's analysis of the European crisis, declared that the Europeans needed help from outside and that the United States ought to supply it, and then delivered a description that was to be widely quoted: "Our policy is directed not against any country or doctrine but against hunger, poverty, desperation and chaos."

British foreign secretary Ernest BEVIN became the first European leader to seize on Marshall's words, and in just over three weeks he and the French and Soviet foreign ministers were meeting in Paris to discuss possible action; soon, however, V. M. MOLOTOV, the Soviet representative, walked out of the meetings, and in July the Soviet Union forbade Poland and Czechoslovakia to join the talks. During the next months, Western European countries formulated a response to Marshall's invitation.

To propose such a plan was one thing; to secure its passage by the U.S. Congress was something else. On December 17 the president signed legislation providing short-term aid. For passage of the Marshall Plan itself, the secretary and his team carefully cultivated opposition leaders in the Senate, notably Michigan's Arthur VANDENBERG, and engaged in a public-relations campaign. Then the Communists gave the Marshall Plan an inadvertent boost. In February Czech Communists took over the government of the country, and a few weeks later Jan MASARYK, the popular and widely known Czech foreign minister, was found dead beneath a window from which he had jumped, fallen, or been pushed. The Communist coup and Masaryk's mysterious death were followed in three weeks by congressional passage of the European Recovery Act. The name "Marshall Plan" came from Truman himself. Venerating Marshall, the president liked to say, humorously but seriously, that a Republican Congress was hardly likely to pass such a program if it bore the name "Truman Plan." Most subsequent commentators have seen the Marshall Plan as the vital step in Europe's recovery from World War II.

Speaking at Harvard on the 40th anniversary of Marshall's speech, West German president Richard von Weizsäcker declared that in 1947 the general had touched deep feelings in Europe. After the horrors of the war, the Continent had most needed "fundamental ethics," and Marshall had not called for an anti-Communist crusade but had spoken as a realist, rather than an ideologist. "He knew," said Weizsäcker, "that prejudice generates violent emotion"—something, the president emphasized, that Europe could not afford in the years following World War II.

Masaryk, Jan (1886–1948)   Son of Tomáš Masaryk, founding president of Czechoslovakia, Jan Masaryk grew up in the old Austro-Hungarian Empire and spent more than ten years in the United States. Coming home at the end of World War I, he became assistant to Eduard BENEŠ, foreign minister of the new Czechoslovak republic, and with Beneš he was to experience the complex tragedies that would afflict his country over the next 30 years. For most of the time between the world wars Masaryk served as ambassador in London but could not bring himself to continue in this position after Britain and France betrayed Czechoslovakia in 1938 at the Munich conference with Adolf Hitler. During World War II Masaryk was foreign minister of the Czech government-in-exile in London, of which Beneš was president, and worked to build up amicable relations with the Soviet Union.

After the war Beneš and Masaryk held the same positions in Czechoslovakia, though Communist members of the government arranged for the appointment of a Slovak Communist as a sort of watchdog in the Foreign Ministry. In 1947, wishing for Czech participation in the MARSHALL PLAN, Masaryk sought Soviet approval, which was withheld after he had accepted the invitation to take part in the planning. He was, as the Czech-American historian Radomír Luža expressed it, "crushed by the humiliation." Masaryk remained at the Foreign Ministry after the Communist coup in February 1948, but only briefly. In one of the early dramatic events of the Cold War, this liberal Czech statesman plunged to his death from his window, an oddly symbolic reminder of the 17th-century defenestration of Prague, when Czech nobles hurled three imperial representatives out of a window of the Hradčany Castle (though those worthies escaped injury). The Czech government maintained that Masaryk had committed suicide. Many in the West refused to believe this assertion. The issue has never been resolved.

massive retaliation   During 1953, in framing its Cold War strategy, the new U.S. EISENHOWER administration began to consider the idea of meeting Soviet challenges at points of U.S. choosing, not necessarily where the actions deemed provocations had occurred. In a speech to the Council on Foreign Relations on January 12, 1954, Secretary of State John Foster DULLES declared that this "new look" concept could succeed because the United States possessed the "deterrent of massive retaliatory power." Press and public immediately transformed this phrase into "massive retaliation," thus giving it a prominent place among the many expressions that have become famous in a form different from the original.

Dulles's speech ignited a firestorm of criticism on both sides of the Atlantic, the Europeans being particularly upset by a sentence in which the secretary spoke of retaliation coming "instantly, by means and at places of our choosing." Did this mean that, without even bothering to consult its allies, the United States would "instantly" transform any confrontation into all-out war? Georges BIDAULT, the French foreign minister, characterized the new policy as "Americans flying and Frenchmen dying." President Eisenhower, though defending Dulles, denied any such implications, and Dulles defended himself in a magazine article intended to achieve what would later be called damage control, declaring that he had in mind not an attack on Moscow but instead the kind of retaliation that would discourage any Communist military adventure. As was subsequently discovered, Dulles had written his speech without the help of any of his professional State Department associates, although Eisenhower had read it and had not called for any changes. Actually, no U.S. administration ever adopted a policy that could properly be described as based on massive retaliation. The term served as shorthand for reliance on airpower as a DETERRENT and, along with that, the general cost-cutting dear to Eisenhower.

Matsu. *See* QUEMOY AND MATSU.

May, Alan Nunn (1911–) British physicist, a Communist from his student days at Cambridge, who became involved in nuclear research in Canada during World War II and volunteered his services to the GRU (Soviet military intelligence), an arrangement that proved remarkably profitable for the Soviets: within a few days of the bombing of Hiroshima, May was able to give his case officer not only technical information but actual samples of U-233 and U-235, the key ingredients of the ATOMIC BOMB. May's activities came to light when the defection of the Soviet spy Igor Gouzenko broke up the GRU network in Canada. Not naturally given to intrigue, May later described his espionage activities as comparable to "being a lavatory attendant; it stinks, but someone has to do it." *See also* FUCHS, Klaus.

Mayaguez **incident** On May 12, 1975, patrol boats operated by Cambodians of the Communist revolutionary government seized a U.S. freighter bound from Hong Kong to Thailand. After some initial confusion, during which the *Mayaguez* was mistakenly identified as a Philippine ship, U.S. forces, acting on orders from President FORD, produced a quick response. Airlifted to a Thai base, U.S. ma-

rines freed the 39 captive sailors in a fierce battle on Koh Tang Island on May 14, but at a high cost—15 battle deaths and 23 killed in the crash of a helicopter; three Cambodian gunboats were sunk, and a Cambodian airbase and oil-storage facility were bombed. Despite the casualties, the American public seemed generally to approve the action. Since it came only two weeks after the fall of Saigon to the North Vietnamese, which represented the final bankruptcy of the U.S. effort in Vietnam, it perhaps gave the public a measure of satisfaction by demonstrating that the United States could still inflict punishment on an enemy.

Mazowiecki, Tadeusz (1927–) Prominent Polish Catholic editor and writer who became one of the leading figures in the SOLIDARITY trade-union coalition and served as premier of the country (1989–90). Having run afoul of the authorities earlier in his career because of his attachment to his religious beliefs, Mazowiecki cofounded the Warsaw Catholic magazine *Wiez* (in English, *Bond*, or *Link)* in 1968. Along with the archbishop of Kraków, Karol Wojtyla (later Pope JOHN PAUL II), and other intellectuals, he worked toward the formulation of a Catholic social philosophy and political strategy that could apply to the conditions of the time. Serving in Parliament from 1961 to 1972, as a leader of the beleaguered opposition to the Polish government, he advocated democracy and pluralism.

During the strikes of 1980, when the Solidarity union was formed, Mazowiecki played a key role as an intellectual who not only went to Gdansk as the representative of a group of 64 distinguished intellectuals who sympathized with the strikers but stayed to help form a "commission of experts" that would help the workers in negotiations with government representatives. He quickly became one of the closest advisers of Lech WAŁESA, the Solidarity leader. Like Wałesa, Mazowiecki operated with the awareness that at any time Moscow deemed the Polish Communist government to be in real danger, Soviet troops could descend upon the country—as on Hungary in 1956 (the HUNGARIAN REVOLUTION) and Czechoslovakia in 1968 (the PRAGUE SPRING)—to stamp out all progress toward democracy. Also, like Wałesa, he received criticism from some circles both within Poland and in the West for his caution—the latter, of course, not being in any danger of facing Soviet tanks. In December 1981, however, Solidarity found itself facing not Soviet but Polish tanks and the imposition of martial law, which for the time being ended all movement toward democracy.

In 1989, when change had come to Eastern Europe, Solidarity regained its legal status, and free elections established its standing in Parliament. President Wojciech JARUZELSKI appointed Mazowiecki prime minister, thus putting a non-Communist at the head of an Eastern European government for the first time since the late 1940s. In 1990 Wałesa, who now considered Mazowiecki too cautious for the new circumstances that prevailed, defeated his adviser for the presidency; although Wałesa did not win a majority in the first round of the elections, Mazowiecki declined to compete in the runoff, thus leaving the prize to his rival.

Medvedev, Roy Alexandrovich (1925–) Soviet historian, a native of Georgia, who achieved worldwide recognition for his studies of the Soviet past—most notably in the book *Let History Judge* (translated into English in 1971)—bravely carrying out his research and writing in the Soviet Union even though he was expelled from the Communist Party and prohibited from teaching. As a freelance operator in acute disfavor with the BREZHNEV regime, Medvedev had to do his work in his apartment, with the help of documents and other materials given him by silent dissenters who held jobs in government and party offices. In *Let History Judge*, subtitled *The Origins and Consequences of Stalinism*, Medvedev maintained that the oppressiveness and excesses of the Soviet regime were essentially the work of Joseph STALIN rather than inadequacies in Communist doctrine itself. Medvedev had lost his youthful belief in Stalin when the dictator ordered the execution of his father. But, ever the disappointed idealist, Medvedev once regretfully observed of Brezhnev that "power was more important to him than ideals." Writing in the Brezhnev era, he argued against "neo-Stalinism" and called for a democratic movement not in the Western sense but involving "the creation of new political doctrines on

the basis of Marxism-Leninism which will analyze our changed political circumstances."

As events in the early 1990s were to make painfully clear, Medvedev's ideas about Marxism-Leninism came close to those held by the man who became the leader of the nation in 1985, Mikhail GORBACHEV, who until almost the last minutes of his tenure in office attempted to defend basic Communist doctrine and the COMMUNIST PARTY OF THE SOVIET UNION. Gorbachev had been in office just three months when Medvedev declared the new leader had met with "goodwill and hope in almost all circles of Soviet society." To give Gorbachev a boost, Medvedev even glossed over the inescapable fact that the political careers of the new leader and everybody else of his political generation had begun when Stalin was in power; their "political pasts," Medvedev said in an interview with *Newsweek,* "are free of ties to the black times of Stalinism." Under Gorbachev, Medvedev won readmission to the Communist Party in 1989 and went on to become a prominent political figure, being elected to the CONGRESS OF PEOPLE'S DEPUTIES and then to the party CENTRAL COMMITTEE in 1990; he later became a member of the SUPREME SOVIET. In 1991, following the unsuccessful coup against Gorbachev, Medvedev—true to his basic ideas—argued in a parliamentary debate against the "liquidation" of the Communist Party. "In people's minds," he declared, "the word liquidation is associated with such facts as liquidation of the Cossacks . . . kulaks. It meant either arrest or murder or deportation." He won the argument, since the Parliament voted to "suspend" the party's activities but not to liquidate it, but this victory, of course, had only ephemeral significance.

Medvedev, Zhores Alexandrovich (1925–) Identical twin of Roy MEDVEDEV. A leading Soviet geneticist, Zhores Medvedev took the lead, through SAMIZDAT publication, in attacking the official Soviet environment-over-heredity doctrine advanced by the agronomist Trofim LYSENKO. In 1963, having read a copy of this typescript, Nikita KHRUSHCHEV's son Sergei attempted, unsuccessfully, to convince his father that Lysenko's ideas had caused the "destruction of biology" in the Soviet Union.

For this and other activities during the BREZHNEV era, Medvedev found himself clapped into a psychiatric hospital, from which he won release after scientists around the world, and inside the USSR as well, made strong public protests. While Medvedev was visiting Britain, the Soviet government removed his citizenship; he took up residence in England in 1973. *See also* PSYKHUSHKA.

Mendès-France, Pierre (1907–1982)   French political leader who, as premier in 1954, negotiated an end to the French war in Vietnam.

A lawyer, Mendès-France fled imprisonment by the Vichy French government after the German victory in 1940 and joined General DE GAULLE's Free French headquarters in London, becoming a flying officer. After the liberation of France in

French premier Pierre Mendès-France

1944, Mendès-France served for a short time as de Gaulle's economics minister and later represented France on the United Nations Economic and Social Council (UNESCO). The disaster of the French surrender at DIEN BIEN PHU and the cost of the war in Vietnam led him to pledge that, as premier, he would end the war, though he wished to maintain the French economic position in the country. Like other French premiers of the time, he held office only briefly, being forced to resign in February 1955. Though the French constitution under which he had served failed to provide the needed degree of governmental stability, Mendès-France opposed the de Gaulle constitution of the new Fifth Republic, drawn up in 1958. At de Gaulle's investiture by the National Assembly, the general said in his memoirs, Mendès-France, no longer an admirer, delivered an "acrimonious" speech.

For some years Mendès-France, who seemed by nature to be something of a controversialist, remained most prominently in the public mind as the statesman who, concerned about French rates of alcoholism, extolled the virtues of milk. His attempts to wean the nation from wine, however, ended, predictably, in complete failure.

MI5   Though MI5 is no longer the official designation of the British Security Service, which is responsible for counterespionage operations, the name has continued in wide use. The organization traces its direct lineage back to 1909, during the Anglo-German "cold war" in the years immediately before the outbreak of World War I. In its spy-hunting duties, MI5 performs tasks similar to the counterspy work of the FBI in the United States.

MI5 had numerous routine successes during the Cold War in its counterespionage activities, but the department suffered notable institutional embarrassment as well. In 1963 a commission investigating the PROFUMO AFFAIR suggested that the security service had reacted with insufficient concern to the discovery that Profumo, the war minister, was sharing a mistress with a Soviet officer (who was later discovered to be a KGB agent). Further discomfiture was produced in 1979, when Prime Minister Margaret THATCHER revealed that a former operative, Anthony BLUNT, had been a member of the CAMBRIDGE FIVE spy ring.

More remarkably, perhaps, Harold WILSON, after his retirement as prime minister in 1976, declared his belief that officials of MI5 had tried to undermine him and thus topple the Labour government, believed insufficiently anti-Communist. Though a former assistant director of MI5, Peter Wright, declared this to be true in his 1987 book *Spycatcher*, MI5, in the best British tradition, did not debate the question.

During the 1980s, British intelligence specialists together with London investigative reporters, led by Chapman Pincher, were preoccupied with a question that had troubled the security authorities a decade earlier: whether Sir Roger Hollis, director-general of MI5 from 1956 to 1965, had been a Soviet mole. Called out of retirement in 1970, Hollis was interrogated by government investigators. No charge was ever proved, at least publicly, and Ivan Shiskin, a KGB agent in London during the 1960s, later said that the charge against Hollis was groundless. Hollis died in 1978, perhaps the blameless victim of defamation. The whole affair has remained an intelligence mystery.

MI6 The original designation of the British intelligence department known as the Secret Intelligence Service (sometimes the Special Intelligence Service) and commonly called the SIS. Since the British government does not acknowledge the existence of the SIS, the department has no formal public name. The counterpart of MI5, the SIS is the agency charged with placing and controlling British agents in foreign countries and thus is in general analogous to the U.S. CENTRAL INTELLIGENCE AGENCY.

The origins of MI6 can be traced back to the Elizabethan era, when the queen acquired the services of an extraordinarily valuable pioneering agent, Sir Francis Walsingham, who possessed, as the historian Richard Deacon said, "a talent for smelling out Protestants and Protestant sympathizers" in the Catholic countries of continental Europe and hence could make use of these persons as informers concerning plots against the Anglican queen. An ideal public servant, Walsingham paid for his operations out of his own pocket—though his dedication to duty bankrupted him.

The SIS in its modern form took shape, like MI5, in the years immediately before the outbreak of World War I, under the direction of the celebrated Captain Mansfield Cumming, who bequeathed to his successors not only the directorship but the use of his initial *C* as the code designation for the director. In the World War I era British intelligence acquired an enormous—if exaggerated—worldwide reputation for almost diabolical cleverness and ruthless efficiency, employed in making and overthrowing governments and changing the course of world events. This mystique found capsule expression in the title of a 1918 collection of stories by Clarence Herbert New: *The Unseen Hand*. The novelist Somerset Maugham served the agency in Russia in 1917, though he could not prevent the overthrow of Britain's ally, Czar Nicholas II. Another British operative of the period, the later-famous Sidney Reilly—a man much given to fanciful schemes—once attempted to steal Lenin's and Trotsky's trousers (a plan perhaps constituting a forerunner of CIA attempts in the early 1960s to discredit Cuban premier Fidel CASTRO by causing his beard to fall out). Reilly later became delusional and was lured into a trap by Soviet agents; the Soviet government executed him.

In the late 1930s the SIS acquired a recruit, Kim PHILBY, whose employment would have fateful consequences during World War II and the Cold War. Despite his heavy drinking, of which he made no secret, Philby, who was in reality a member of the CAMBRIDGE FIVE Soviet spy ring, rose in the service and in 1944 received a remarkably convenient assignment as head of the new SIS anti-Soviet section, a position in which he could protect the Soviet agents he was officially out to get. In 1949 another plum came his way—he became the British intelligence liaison officer with the CIA. In Washington he performed one of his most striking acts of treachery by informing the Soviets of a plan to land a group of anti-Communist exiles on the coast of Albania, thus dooming the operation and the men who attempted to carry it out. In 1951 Philby informed his fellow Cantabrigian spy, Guy BURGESS, that MI5 was investigating him; Burgess and their fellow conspirator, Donald MACLEAN, then escaped from England and went behind the IRON CURTAIN.

In 1956 the SIS became involved in an absurd fiasco when it sent a semiretired diver, Commander Lionel Crabb, to Portsmouth to carry out a never-explained mission around the hull of the Soviet ship *Ordzhonikidze,* which had brought Premier BULGANIN and First Secretary KHRUSHCHEV of the Soviet Union to Britain for an official visit. Crabb never returned home, and his disappearance caused a public uproar and consequent questions in Parliament. This wildly indiscreet project created great diplomatic embarrassment for the prime minister, Sir Anthony EDEN, and convinced left-wing MPs that the SIS wished to torpedo the Soviet visit. The incident led to the dismissal of SIS employees and the improvement of liaison between the agency and its superiors in the Foreign Office, to which it is administratively attached, although, like all intelligence agencies, the SIS continued to have its problems with double agents, defectors, and imperfect coordination with policy makers.

Midway   Class of U.S. attack aircraft carriers that came into service in the middle 1940s. Besides *Midway,* the class included *Franklin D. Roosevelt* and *Coral Sea.* These ships were of about 51,000 tons standard displacement and carried a crew of 4,000.

MiG-15   Soviet single-seat jet fighter that entered service in 1949 and for several years beginning in 1951 served as the standard fighter for WARSAW PACT countries, and from November 1950 saw much action in the KOREAN WAR. An outstanding aircraft, the MiG-15 had a 6,000-pound-thrust power plant modeled on a Rolls-Royce engine that gave it a maximum speed of about 670 mph; its range was 500 miles. Armed with one 37-mm cannon and two 23-mm cannons, it could carry rockets or 2,000 pounds of bombs. The "MiG" designation (frequently given as "MIG") came from the names of the designers, the eminent Artem Mikoyan (brother of the Soviet politician Anastas MIKOYAN, he worked for a time during the 1930s in the United States at the Douglas aircraft plant) and M. I. Gurevich. Mikoyan acquired numerous Soviet honors and for many years sat in the SUPREME SOVIET. Like all Soviet-bloc military aircraft, the MiG-15 received a code name from the NORTH ATLANTIC TREATY ORGANIZATION for purposes of ready identification; the West called it Fagot.

MiG-17   Code-named Fresco by the NORTH ATLANTIC TREATY ORGANIZATION, this single-seat single-engine jet fighter first flew in January 1950 and entered Soviet air service in 1952. Essentially a longer, sleeker, more powerful development of the MIG-15, the MiG-17 had an engine with almost 1,500 more pounds of thrust and was equipped with an afterburner. Top speed: 711 mph. From the middle 1950s the USSR supplied the MiG-17 to WARSAW PACT air forces; the D version gave these forces their first all-weather fighter capacity, since it was equipped with the RP-1 *Izumrud* airborne intercept radar.

MiG-21   Produced in a great variety of versions, the MiG-21 (code-named Fishbed by the NORTH ATLANTIC TREATY ORGANIZATION) first flew in 1955 and from 1962 went on to become the most widely used fighter by WARSAW PACT countries, remaining in service for at least the next three decades; the MiG-21MF was the version most used by pact nations. Versions of the MiG-21 also flew for countries outside the Soviet bloc. Altogether, some 8,000 MiG-21s were built—the largest production total for any jet airplane anywhere. Widely used during the VIETNAM WAR, MiG-21s suffered 68 losses to the fire of U.S. aircraft. A single-seat short-range fighter, the MiG-21 had a maximum speed of about Mach 2 and a range of about 400 miles.

MiG-23   More a family of aircraft than a single type, the Soviet swing-wing single-seat MiG-23 (code-named Flogger by the NORTH ATLANTIC TREATY ORGANIZATION) began development in 1967 as an interceptor, a design followed by a trainer version and the attack version designated MiG-27. The MiG-23MF attained a maximum speed of about Mach 2.3 and had a combat radius of about 530 miles. (The *M* in the designation meant that modifications—in this case, chiefly a new engine—had been introduced; the *F* stood for *forsirovanni,* meaning that engine output had been boosted over that of the previous model). Produced during the 1970s in greater quantities than any other combat

Soviet MiG-21, the fighter aircraft most widely used by Warsaw Pact air forces

aircraft, the members of this MiG family constituted key elements of WARSAW PACT air forces.

MiG-25R High-altitude Soviet reconnaissance aircraft capable of photographing all of Great Britain on one flight. The MiG-25R could attain speeds above Mach 2.5.

MiG-29 Code-named Fulcrum by the NORTH ATLANTIC TREATY ORGANIZATION, this Soviet fighter first flew in 1977 and entered service with WARSAW PACT air forces in the late 1980s. After the reunification of Germany, East German MiG-29s entered the service of the new German air force.

MiG Alley Nickname given during the KOREAN WAR to the air over North Korea because, after November 1950, Soviet-built MiG-15 jet aircraft played an active part in its defense.

Mikolajczyk, Stanislaw (1901–1966) Premier of the World War II Polish government-in-exile in London (July 1943 until November 1944), succeeding General Wladyslaw Sikorski, who was killed in an airplane crash. In the late phases of the war, Mikolajczyk clashed with Britain and the United States over various issues involving the Soviets: the postwar boundaries of Poland, the KATYN FOREST MASSACRE of Polish officers (later proved to have been committed by Soviet forces, not, as said at the time, by the Germans), and the refusal of the Red Army to help the Poles during the August 1944 Warsaw uprising. Though Western statesmen sympathized with Mikolajczyk, they were also concerned with other issues, and the facts of power militated against the London Poles—the Red Army physically controlled the country from which they were exiles. The boundaries of Poland and the makeup of its postwar government proved to be the most contentious issues between the West and the USSR.

After the war Mikolajczyk returned to Poland under an Allied agreement that was supposed to provide for broadening the Soviet-installed government. Appointed vice premier and minister of agriculture, he managed to keep these posts only until 1947, when a rigged election resulted in his defeat. He went into exile again, taking up residence in the United States.

Mikoyan, Anastas Ivanovich (1895–1978)   Born in an Armenian village (and many years later often spoken of by Nikita KHRUSHCHEV as "my Armenian rug dealer"), Mikoyan played a prominent part in Soviet political life for more than 40 years—largely owing to his almost Houdinilike ability to escape unscathed from purges and other perilous situations that in one way or another brought down most of his prominent contemporaries.

As a Bolshevik organizer in his native Caucasus region at the end of World War I, Mikoyan narrowly avoided execution at the hands of a British occupying force, and by 1922, as an associate of both Lenin and Joseph STALIN, he had become a candidate (nonvoting) member of the Communist Party CENTRAL COMMITTEE. He became a full member the following year and a candidate member of the POLITBURO in 1926, with full membership in 1935. As a friend of Stalin's during the 1920s, he, with other old Bolshevik comrades, would attend informal Sunday parties at the secretary-general's dacha. Mikoyan thus became a member of Stalin's small inner circle. Remaining in the Politburo until 1966, he held a variety of cabinet-level posts, most of them relating to economic affairs, through all the Soviet regimes from Lenin to Leonid BREZHNEV. Widely known in the West, he served as minister of foreign trade and was called the Soviet Union's best traveling salesman. In 1936 and 1959 he toured the United States studying food production. Deputy and then first deputy premier during the years 1937 to 1964, he served during 1964 and 1965 as Soviet president (chairman of the Presidium of the SUPREME SOVIET).

Mikoyan performed probably his greatest feat of survival simply by living through the Stalin purges of the late 1930s, when most of his peers met premature ends—neither he nor any other survivors made any recorded efforts to save those who were executed—but by the early 1950s even Mikoyan and other old-Bolshevik stalwarts faced the ultimate danger, which Stalin's death in March 1953 enabled them to escape. Mikoyan developed a particularly effective working relationship with First Secretary Khrushchev, whom he supported in 1956 in investigating Stalin's abuses of power and again in 1957 when the so-called ANTIPARTY GROUP attempted to overthrow him. "I considered him an experienced colleague and very sensible," Khrushchev commented about Mikoyan in a memoir. "I enjoyed discussing international issues as well as domestic problems with him." Thus Khrushchev made considerable use of Mikoyan's bargaining and other diplomatic talents as a foreign-affairs troubleshooter.

On one issue, however, Khrushchev and Mikoyan strongly disagreed. By Khrushchev's own account, Mikoyan violently objected to the decision to send in Soviet troops to put down the 1956 HUNGARIAN REVOLUTION. But the dispute did not appear to affect Mikoyan's relationship with Khrushchev. In 1962 the veteran salesman received a specially delicate mission—to explain to Cuba's Fidel CASTRO the Soviet decision to with-

Anastas Mikoyan (l.), the USSR's widely known "traveling salesman," meets with U.S. president Lyndon B. Johnson.

draw missiles from Cuba. The Armenian, Khrushchev said, was "irreplaceable for such missions," because he could "repeat the general line over and over again without giving an inch and without losing his temper," and after a break could "pick up the argument again without missing a beat." With the removal of Khrushchev in October 1964, Mikoyan's political influence came to an end, although he continued as president until December 1965 and, prosaically enough, kept his Politburo seat until he reached the official retirement age of 70.

Military Council for National Salvation On December 13, 1981, when he moved with troops and tanks against the SOLIDARITY union and other dissidents, Poland's General Wojciech JARUZELSKI proclaimed the establishment of the Military Council of National Salvation, which would serve as "the highest political authority under martial law in Poland." Jaruzelski lifted martial law in 1983.

Mindszenty, József (1892–1975) The strongly anti-Nazi Cardinal Mindszenty (originally named József Pehm) became the Roman Catholic primate of Hungary in 1945, after being freed from his German captors who had briefly taken over the country in the last phase of World War II. But the bishop was not to enjoy liberty for long. Viewing him as a force they wished to neutralize, the Communist leadership placed him on trial in 1948, charging him with treason and also with illegal currency dealings. Remarkably, Mindszenty declared before the proceedings began that any confession he might make should be disregarded, because the authorities would have obtained it by drugging him. He then duly confessed his guilt on most of the charges. These proceedings attracted wide attention; certainly they suggested that the concept of "show trial" pioneered by Joseph STALIN in the Soviet Union in the 1930s still flourished.

Transferred from prison to house arrest in 1955, the cardinal won freedom again during the 1956 HUNGARIAN REVOLUTION, only to be forced to flee to the U.S. embassy when Soviet tanks moved into Budapest. To First Secretary Nikita KHRUSHCHEV, who visited Hungary a number of times in the year after the suppression of the revolution, Mind-

szenty, watching events from the balcony of the embassy, represented "the most reactionary wing of the counterrevolutionary forces which had struck against the . . . building of socialism in Hungary in 1956." For the next 15 years the cardinal lived in his extraterritorial lodging as a symbol of resistance to the government imposed on his country. In 1971, the Vatican, wishing to improve relations with the Hungarian government, negotiated an agreement under which Mindszenty left Hungary. After a brief stay in Rome, he settled in Vienna.

Minuteman U.S. Air Force INTERCONTINENTAL BALLISTIC MISSILE that first appeared in 1961. Made by Boeing, it used solid propellant (three-stage) and could deliver a one-megaton payload (thermonuclear—hydrogen bomb) onto a target 8,000 miles from its launch site.

Mirage III Delta-wing star of the Mirage family of fighters, fighter-bombers, and bombers produced by Marcel Dassault for the French air force and for export sales, the Mirage III won fame (and eager customers for its makers) through its performance for the Israeli air force in the 1967 Six-Day War. First flown in 1956, it entered production as the Mirage IIIC in October 1960. With a top speed of Mach 2.2, it had a combat radius of 745 miles and could carry bombs or missiles.

Mirage IV Looking very much like its Dassault cousin, the MIRAGE III, the Mirage IV played an important part in General DE GAULLE's air strategy as the bomber element of the French nuclear deterrent. With a range of about 2,500 miles, it could carry one 60-kiloton nuclear bomb; it attained a maximum speed at high altitude of about 1,450 mph. The Mirage IV entered production in December 1963.

MIRV *See* MULTIPLE INDEPENDENTLY TARGETABLE REENTRY VEHICLE.

missile gap During the 1960 presidential campaign, the Democrats frequently claimed that the EISENHOWER administration had allowed the United States to fall behind the Soviet Union in the development and deployment of strategic missiles, the

French president François Mitterrand

Mitterrand, François Maurice (1916–) Elected president of France in 1981 and reelected in 1988, Mitterrand had held numerous cabinet posts under the Fourth Republic, succeeded by General DE GAULLE's Fifth Republic in 1958. A native of Bordeaux, Mitterrand had a notable career in World War II. He was taken prisoner by the Germans in 1940, but escaped in late 1941 and became an important leader in the Resistance.

In the presidential election of 1965, Mitterrand, a Socialist, seemed to come out of nowhere to challenge de Gaulle and succeeded in forcing a runoff by capturing almost all of the leftist vote. Mitterrand was defeated again in 1974, this time by Valéry GISCARD D'ESTAING, but by 1981 he had built the Socialists into a powerful force. As president, Mitterrand supported a self-reliance in foreign affairs that stemmed from de Gaulle, though he placed more emphasis on harmonious relations with the United States and other countries in the NORTH ATLANTIC TREATY ORGANIZATION.

Succeeded in 1995 by Jacques Chirac, Mitterrand was the longest-serving president in French history.

Mobutu Sese Seko (1930–) Known in the earlier part of his career as Joseph Mobutu, this soldier and politician became the leading figure in Zaire during the 1960s. Mobutu gave the former Congo this name in 1971 in his quest for "national authenticity." A supporter of Patrice LUMUMBA, Mobutu became chief of staff of the Congolese army when the country won its independence from Belgium in 1960. Within three months, however, his loyalty to Lumumba, the premier and national leader, had worn thin in the face of chaotic conditions in the country. He staged a coup in which both Lumumba and President Joseph Kasavubu lost their posts. Although Mobutu reinstalled Kasavubu as president early in the following year, the arrangement proved merely temporary. In November 1965 Mobutu assumed the presidency himself and went on to ban all political opposition; he also added to his responsibilities by taking on the posts of president of the cabinet, minister of foreign affairs, minister for territorial security, minister of national defense, and minister for veterans' affairs. In effect, as a dictator he had become president for life, or at least for the

awesome new delivery systems for nuclear bombs. This "missile gap" charge gained credibility from the worldwide sensation created by the USSR's launching of *SPUTNIK I* in 1957. But as Robert S. MCNAMARA, President KENNEDY's secretary of defense, later commented, once the new administration had access to all the facts, "it took only three weeks to determine that there was no missile gap." Instead, McNamara said, the United States and its allies actually held a long lead over the Soviets. The secretary maintained, however, that the missile gap "was not a fabrication"; the Democrats had sincerely believed what they said, because they shared an American obsession with "overestimating the strength of our opponents and underestimating our own."

foreseeable future, though anyone in such circumstances must anticipate the possibility of removal from office through the very means by which it was acquired. All these developments had their influence in the world beyond Zaire, because of the enormous mineral wealth—copper, cobalt, uranium, tin, diamonds—found in Shaba (Katanga) Province in the southeastern part of the country. In 1966 Mobutu nationalized the properties of the Belgian syndicate that had controlled the bulk of the minerals.

In 1970, somewhat curiously, Duquesne University granted Mobutu an honorary doctorate.

Moch, Jules (1893–1985) An associate during World War II of General Charles DE GAULLE, Moch held various important positions in postwar French cabinets, including minister of the interior in the government of Robert SCHUMAN. As a native of Lorraine, Schuman was shouted at by Communist deputies as if he were a *Boche* (German); the deputies carried this kind of tactic to the bizarre extreme of shouting "Heil Hitler!" at Moch, who in actuality was a Jew whose son had died in the Resistance at the hands of the Nazi Gestapo. This Communist behavior occurred in late 1947, as Europe was well on its way to splitting into the two blocs that characterized it for more than four decades. In 1950, having now become minister of defense under René Pleven, Moch found himself in a delicate position when the United States pushed France to acquiesce in a plan for German participation in European defense. The complex issue was sensitively and successfully handled by U.S. secretary of state Dean ACHESON. Some years later, after the Soviet Union had test-exploded an awesome-sized HYDROGEN BOMB, Moch commented wryly that within 20 years the target of the bomber had gone from the single point to the city, from the city to the region, from the province to the entire country.

Mollet, Guy (1905–1975) French politician who held the premiership at the time of the SUEZ CRISIS in October 1956. A teacher of English and a leading official of the teachers' union, Mollet joined the French Resistance during World War II and three times was captured and tortured by the Nazi Gestapo. Secretary-general of the Socialist Party

(1946–69), he also served as deputy premier (1951) and premier (1956–57). His premiership foundered not only on the Suez fiasco, which he concocted in collaboration with British prime minister Anthony EDEN, but also on his dispatch of troop reinforcements to Algeria to put down a revolt by settlers. This action created such problems that when he visited Algiers shortly after sending in a new commander, a barrage of threats from the local French-descended population forced him to recall the general. Although General DE GAULLE chose him as one of the drafters of the constitution of the new Fifth Republic, Mollet later denounced the general's decision to withdraw France from the military organization of the Atlantic alliance (NORTH ATLANTIC TREATY ORGANIZATION).

Molody, Konon Trofimovich *See* LONSDALE, Gordon.

Molotov, Vyacheslav Mikhailovich (1890–1986) One of the legendary "old Bolsheviks" from the days before World War I (he was editor of *PRAVDA* at the time of the revolution) and for many years probably Joseph STALIN's closest—and certainly most faithful—associate, V. M. Molotov (unlike many of his fellow Soviet Communist peers) remained to the end of his long life a pure and unrepentant Stalinist. Originally bearing the surname Skriabin, Molotov in 1912, with what seems inspired foresight, adopted the revolutionary alias by which he became known *(molot* is Russian for "hammer"). Tireless and unyielding in negotiations, this solemn, slab-faced Bolshevik won from U.S. president ROOSEVELT the nickname Stone Ass. British prime minister Winston CHURCHILL said that Molotov's smile made him think of a Siberian winter, and U.S. secretary of state John Foster DULLES once commented that he had never encountered comparable diplomatic cunning.

Soviet premier during the 1930s, Molotov in 1939 became commissar for foreign affairs and took in hand negotiations with Germany that led to the conclusion of the Soviet-German Nonaggression Pact and, a few days later, to the outbreak of war and the partition of Poland between Germany and the USSR. During World War II Molotov held a position in the Soviet Union second only to Stalin's. As Soviet foreign minister and Stalin's

Vyacheslav M. Molotov *(l.),* Joseph Stalin's foreign minister and long-time colleague, talks with Stalin. In the background is U.S. diplomat Averell Harriman.

faithful agent in the early days of the Cold War, Molotov, with his rhetorical hammer blows, clashed repeatedly with Western negotiators. Interviewed in 140 sessions during the last decade of his life, Molotov commented that he had considered it his chief duty as foreign minister "to extend the frontier of our Fatherland to the maximum."

One writer concluded from Molotov's own comments to the interviewer that the old Bolshevik was "an amoral, intellectually limited bureaucrat" whose "instinctual devotion to Stalin was that of a robot to its creator." Though diplomatic opponents—Nazi officials, U.S. presidents and secretaries of state, British prime ministers and foreign secretaries—might find this judgment somewhat inadequate, no one could question Molotov's subservience to Stalin, which even extended to divorcing his Jewish wife at the dictator's suggestion and later willingly acquiescing in her imprisonment on absurdly trumped-up charges. His loyalty to Stalin seemed unaffected even by his own demotion to deputy foreign minister in 1949. After Stalin's

death Molotov served again as foreign minister (1953–56); in 1957, after supporting the losing side in the ANTIPARTY GROUP's power struggle with First Secretary Nikita KHRUSHCHEV, Molotov was not shot, as presumably would have been his fate under Stalin, but merely dispatched to Outer Mongolia as ambassador. Near the end of his life, with Stalin decades out of political fashion in the Soviet Union as well as in the rest of the world, Molotov declared, "I have defended Stalin and defend him today, including the terror." Throughout his career Molotov saw a complete division between the Soviet and capitalist worlds and believed that the issue between them could be settled only by violence.

Molotov Plan　A series of trade agreements negotiated during the summer (July to September) of 1947 between the Soviet Union and Eastern European countries. These steps followed the withdrawal of V. M. MOLOTOV, then Soviet foreign minister, from a meeting convened in Paris to discuss the U.S. offer of economic assistance that developed into the MARSHALL PLAN (the European Recovery Program). As a riposte to developments in Western Europe, however, the Molotov Plan represented little more than a feeble effort.

Mongoose, Operation   Code name of the U.S. KENNEDY administration effort to dispose of Cuban leader Fidel CASTRO, following the failure of the BAY OF PIGS OPERATION in April 1961. Mongoose involved a variety of departments and agencies, whose representatives met regularly under the lash of Attorney General Robert KENNEDY. *See also* CENTRAL INTELLIGENCE AGENCY.

Monnet, Jean (1888–1979)   French economist and financial specialist who in the post–World War II

French statesman Jean Monnet, leader in the movement toward European unity

years came to symbolize the idea of Western European unity. In earlier times Monnet had acquired a background in supranational organization through his work with the old League of Nations. Placed in charge of French economic planning in 1945, Monnet saw the opportunity for building up French trade through cooperation with Germany, an approach that led to the EUROPEAN COAL AND STEEL COMMUNITY, which, like any solid arrangement, offered advantages to all participants; for Germany, the plan and the organization that followed opened the way back to international respectability after World War II. As Monnet had foreseen, this practical, step-by-step approach led to further supranational developments, crowned by the EUROPEAN ECONOMIC COMMUNITY (the Common Market) and the EUROPEAN COMMUNITY. Monnet earned great credit for his combination of imaginative boldness and practical wisdom.

Some years earlier, in June 1940, as France fell before German invaders, Monnet had shown his supranational range through his involvement in a plan to stiffen French resolution by proclaiming an indissoluble Franco-British union. Though the plan was not adopted, and it presented a variety of obvious problems, it was, as Prime Minister Winston CHURCHILL observed, no time to "be accused of lack of imagination." Nor could Monnet have been so accused in the 1950s when he developed the SCHUMAN PLAN, the basis of the European Coal and Steel Community.

Montgomery, Bernard Law (Viscount Montgomery of Alamein) (1887–1976)   The best-known British general of World War II, in which he was the victorious commander at the Battle of El Alamein (October to November 1942) and later led armies in Italy and Western Europe, Field Marshal Montgomery served after the war in command of Britain's Army of the Rhine in Germany and as chief of the Imperial General Staff (1946–48). From 1951 to 1958 he was deputy supreme commander of Allied forces in Europe.

Though he affected a dashing personal style, with a uniform of his own devising, Montgomery was an extremely cautious general who perhaps shone to best advantage as a trainer of troops and a morale builder. In a world in which alliances predominated, Montgomery frequently caused stresses and strains through an unfortunate gift for tactlessness and condescension. A national hero to the British, he was generally detested by Americans. U.S. General EISENHOWER's success at surviving a necessarily close World War II command relationship with Montgomery probably represented the future president's greatest diplomatic triumph.

Moro, Aldo (1916–1978) Longtime Italian statesman who was the victim in one of the most sensational crimes of the Cold War era. Kidnapped in March 1978 by members of a terrorist group called the Red Brigades, Moro was held for ransom—not cash but the release by the Italian government of terrorists then in prison. Fifty-four days after his abduction, with the government refusing to negotiate with the kidnappers, Moro was found murdered in Rome. Curiously, he was not an all-out opponent of the Communists but had developed a plan to make cooperation possible between them and his own party, the Christian Democrats, of which he had been chairman since 1976.

A veteran of some 30 years in politics and holder of various cabinet offices, Moro twice served as premier (1963–68 and 1974–76). Possibly, of course, the radical element represented by the Red Brigades did not wish to see any cooperation between the Communists and another political party. Some observers have also maintained that the tragedy was compounded because of Moro's willingness to reach an agreement with the Communist Party; some "elements of the authorities," as one writer put it, "had an interest in Moro not returning, and acted in that interest"— by ineffectual handling of the search for the kidnappers and by refusing to negotiate with them. The U.S. CENTRAL INTELLIGENCE AGENCY has likewise been accused of failing to help. One of the Red Brigades' leaders later saw the whole affair as a curious paradox. "We were acting to bring about change," he said, "and those who used us did so to prevent change."

Moscow Center The name used in the intelligence world for the Moscow headquarters of the KGB. The main offices were located in a gray stone building, with annexes, at 2 Dzerzhinsky Square, two blocks from the KREMLIN. The branch that controlled agents in foreign countries was called the FIRST CHIEF DIRECTORATE.

Moscow News (Moskovskiye Novosti) Prior to the advent of GLASNOST, *Moscow News* was an innocuous weekly newspaper designed for the edification of tourists, but in 1986 it acquired a glasnost-oriented editor, Yegor YAKOVLEV, and became one of the most liberal Soviet periodicals, competing in this respect with *OGONYOK*. Like other voices of glasnost, *Moscow News* came under heavy attack from Communist Party conservatives, notably in 1987 when rightists launched a "new Battle of Stalingrad" against liberal Moscow editors. The unprecedented candor that characterized *Moscow News* stories is well indicated by the headline accompanying a report on the government cover-up of the facts about the nuclear disaster at CHERNOBYL in 1986: "THE BIG LIE."

Moskva Class of Soviet helicopter-carrying cruisers of about 19,000 tons displacement (*Leningrad* was the other ship in the class), which entered service in the late 1960s. Each ship carried 14 anti-submarine-warfare helicopters and was fitted with rocket and missile launchers, depth-charge mortars, and torpedo tubes. The Soviet navy created these cruisers as hunters, their intended wartime prey being U.S. nuclear-powered ballistic-missile submarines (SSBNs). *See also* INVINCIBLE.

Mossadegh, Mohammed (1880–1967) Premier of Iran who nationalized the Anglo-Iranian Oil Company in 1951. This move, which led to a major international dispute, followed unsuccessful Iranian attempts to negotiate improved financial terms with the British, who had opened up the oil fields many years earlier. Seeking payment for their expropriated property, the British attempted to draw the United States into the imbroglio, but the TRUMAN administration, though making an unsuccessful attempt to mediate, not only declined the invitation but declared that it would not tolerate the use of force (and apparently opposed covert action as well). Mossadegh (also known as Mossadeq) appeared to believe that if he refused to compromise, the British would ultimately come to terms. A theatrical figure in striped pajamas who attracted a great deal of attention by his public, and seemingly self-willed, fainting spells, Mossadegh, in the words of Scott Breckinridge, a former CENTRAL INTELLIGENCE AGENCY official, "operated with a mixture of shrewdness and emotional nationalism" that made him a difficult negotiating partner.

In 1953, with the EISENHOWER administration in power in Washington, the State Department took the view that Mossadegh had moved too close to the Tudeh Party, the Iranian Communists, and seemed to be conniving at the removal of the shah, whom the West regarded as a stabilizing force in the entire region. At the same time, the premier was pressing the United States for economic aid, which his country may well have needed to make up for the revenue lost because of a British-led boycott of Iranian oil. This would have led to an unlikely situation in which, as Breckinridge pointed out, the United States would have found itself financing Mossadegh's quarrel with the British. During this period Iran experienced frequent riots, believed by some to have been encouraged by the premier to frighten the United States into supporting him.

In June 1953, after being told that the United States could offer Iran no economic assistance until the oil dispute was settled, Mossadegh turned to Moscow, which reportedly responded with the offer of a loan. Pursuant to presidential order, Allen DULLES, director of the CIA, dispatched agents—including two with well-known names, Kermit Roosevelt (grandson of U.S. president Theodore Roosevelt) and H. Norman Schwarzkopf (father of the 1991 Persian Gulf War commander)—to Tehran, granting them funding to sponsor opposition protests against Mossadegh's administration. Then, with U.S. approval and British support, supporters of Mohammed Reza Shah Pahlavi staged a coup that overthrew Mossadegh, who was put into prison and later exiled.

The U.S. and British intelligence services each claimed that it played a more important role than its counterpart, and in any event Mossadegh's shaky government might have toppled even without foreign involvement. However that may be, Roosevelt later wrote proudly of the whole affair.

The shah's new government signed an arrangement on oil production that made the United States a major player in Iran: 40 percent of production to the United States and 40 percent to Britain, with France and the Netherlands picking up the balance. The shah remained on his throne until the revolution of 1979.

Multilateral Force (MLF)   A KENNEDY administration plan for involving European allies of the United States in their own nuclear defense by equipping surface ships having crews of mixed nationalities with POLARIS missiles. The purpose of mixed crews was to prevent individual nationalistic use of the weapons. The political and practical problems presented by the MLF kept it from finding adherents, however, aside from the West Germans.

multiple independently targetable reentry vehicle (MIRV)   A single missile carrying a number of warheads aimed at different targets. The U.S. deployment of such weapons in 1968 came as a response to the Soviet deployment of very large strategic missiles—the SS-9. The Soviets introduced their own MIRV in 1973. *See also* STRATEGIC ARMS LIMITATION TALKS.

Murphy, Robert (1894–1978)   Veteran U.S. diplomat who first came to prominence as General EISENHOWER's political adviser during the 1942 Northwest African campaign in World War II. Murphy later served as American political adviser in Germany, ambassador to Belgium (1949–52), and ambassador to Japan (1952). Later he was undersecretary of state for political affairs (1959).

mutual and balanced force reduction   In October 1973, during the NIXON-BREZHNEV era of DÉTENTE, the United States and the Soviet Union began a series of talks concerned with establishing limits for conventional arms. Held in Vienna, these discussions, said American historian R. Craig Nation, were "the epitome of the futility of arms control as practiced by both East and West during the Brezhnev era"; the two sides could never establish any basis for accepting estimates of the existing strength of the NORTH ATLANTIC TREATY ORGANIZATION and WARSAW PACT forces in Europe. The talks dragged on for more than 15 years. One staff member of the U.S. team believed that the Soviet representatives found this situation quite agreeable, since they clearly preferred an assignment in Vienna to life back home.

Rather than quietly expiring, however, the subject of conventional-arms control survived to be taken up in new Conventional Forces in Europe talks between NATO and Warsaw Pact delegates. These talks began in March 1989 and, amid circumstances unimaginable just a few years earlier, led to the CONVENTIONAL FORCES IN EUROPE TREATY (CFE-I), signed on November 19, 1990. But within a few months the Warsaw Pact, itself, had vanished.

mutual assured destruction   Widely known by its acronym, MAD, this concept provided one definition of DETERRENCE: the superpowers would not attack each other if each possessed the power to destroy its adversary. In practice, destruction did not have to be "assured" in some objective sense; the strong likelihood of it was enough to carry conviction for most strategists as well as ordinary citizens. For instance, even a country with overwhelming first-strike power would have to fear a retaliatory attack by nuclear missiles launched from submarines.

My Lai   Coastal hamlet in central Vietnam that came to international attention in 1969 as the result of a search-and-destroy mission earlier carried out by elements of the U.S. Americal Division. In My Lai, on March 16, 1968, Lieutenant William Calley ordered the men of his platoon to gather all the residents in the center of the village. Then, on Calley's orders, the soldiers opened fire, killing more than 200 people. During the massacre, Calley's unit was in contact with combat pilots flying over the area. Superior officers, including Major General Samuel Koster and Colonel O. H. Henderson, monitored messages describing the events on the ground; neither of these officers intervened. Calley and 12 of his men were later indicted for murder. In 1971, after a highly publicized trial, Calley was found guilty on 22 counts. None of the others, however, had to face punishment—the charges against them were dismissed, or they won acquittal. Color photographs of the massacre in *Life* magazine helped establish My Lai in the minds of many Americans as a symbol of what they saw as the immorality of the country's VIETNAM WAR policy. *See also* IA DRANG.

N

Nagorno-Karabakh   *See* AZERBAIJAN.

Naguib, Muhammad (1901–1984)   In October 1951, after the Egyptian prime minister, Nahas Pasha, denounced a 1936 treaty giving Britain the right to maintain troops in the Suez Canal zone, strong anti-British demonstrations broke out in Cairo. Scattered fighting followed between British troops and armed bands of Egyptians; finally King Farouk dismissed the prime minister. This move proved to be the king's undoing. On July 21, 1952, a group of army officers under General Naguib (also called Neguib) staged a coup, overthrowing the corrupt and unpopular monarchy. Though Naguib, a soldierly figure who had comanded forces in the fighting in Palestine, officially chaired the junta, the real leader, Colonel Gamal NASSER, soon appeared. Naguib was declared president of the new Republic of Egypt in June 1953, but in November 1954 Nasser emerged from behind the republican throne to take power himself and place the general under house arrest, from which he was released only in 1960. *See also* SUEZ CRISIS.

Nagy, Ferenc (1903–1979)   Hungarian political leader, an agrarian antifascist whom the Germans imprisoned in the latter part of World War II and who in 1946 became premier of a coalition government. In 1947, as part of its drive to eliminate agrarian parties—the principal non-Communist forces in Eastern Europe—the Soviets supplied Hungarian authorities with alleged evidence that Nagy had taken part in a plot against the state. Ordered to return home, Nagy, vacationing in Switzerland, decided he preferred to announce his resignation. He later became a permanent resident of the United States.

Nagy, Imre (1896–1958)   Hungarian political leader who became the symbol of the 1956 HUNGARIAN REVOLUTION. Taken prisoner in Russia during World War I, Nagy joined the Bolsheviks and fought in the Red Army. Back home in Hungary after the war, he was active in the underground Communist Party, and from 1929 until 1944 he lived in the Soviet Union. Returning home after the Germans were driven out, Nagy became minister of agriculture in the new Soviet-supported government and acquired the important portfolio of minister of the interior.

As a man of peasant background, Nagy, who tended to have an independent point of view, paid continuing attention to the concerns of agricultural workers. His opposition to the forced collectivization of agriculture caused the Communist hierarchy to dismiss him from the government in the wave of purges that followed the split between Moscow and TITO's Yugoslavia in 1948. But in 1953, after the death of Soviet premier Joseph STALIN and the June EAST BERLIN UPRISING, the Soviet government of Premier MALENKOV and Communist Party Secretary KHRUSHCHEV demanded that the Stalinist Hungarian dictator, Mátyás RÁKOSI, divest himself of some of his duties and name the relatively liberal Nagy as premier. Though the USSR itself shared the blame for Hungary's economic problems, Rákosi had made his sizable contribution to them. Nagy announced a program that included the balanced development of industry and agriculture, the dissolution of collectives if their members so chose, religious tolerance, and an end to illegal detention.

Nagy's career took its second major downward turn in 1955 when Rákosi caused his expulsion from the Hungarian Communist Party on the grounds of Titoism. But Hungarian intellectuals and others had tasted a measure of independence (though Nagy remained a believer in "scientific socialism"), and Rákosi continued to be despised by the people. When dissent boiled up in October 1956, Nagy, by popular demand, became premier again. As the dissent turned into revolution, Nagy embraced it—in fact, was swept away by it—accepting the idea of a multiparty state and announcing Hungary's withdrawal from the WARSAW PACT. The Soviet army attacked in force. After calling in vain for Western help, Nagy and his associates took refuge in the Yugoslav embassy. Granted a safe-conduct pledge, Nagy went to Romania but was seized by police and returned to Hungary. His execution was announced in 1958. On June 16, 1989, in the wake of change in Eastern Europe, the Hungarian government gave Nagy what amounted to a state funeral, 31 years after his death.

Nam Il (1913?–1976)   Soldier and politician who led the North Korean team that met with UNITED NATIONS negotiators at PANMUNJOM to discuss a cease-fire in the KOREAN WAR. Describing the boring and repetitious nature of the dealings, General William K. Harrison, the UN counterpart of Nam Il, said that when the Korean had something to say, "he just pulled one of his ancient speeches out of his briefcase and read it again."

The truce signed on July 27, 1953, ended the war, not in a peace but in a continuing, and often tenuous, cease-fire.

Nasser, Gamal Abdel (1918–1970)   Egyptian army officer who led a 1952 coup that deposed King Farouk and, first as minister of the interior for two years and then as president from 1954 until his death, became the most prominent leader in the Arab world. Nasser launched a variety of programs designed to reduce unwanted foreign influence, build national spirit, and improve the economic condition of the Egyptian people.

In 1955, moving away from alignment with the West, Nasser signed an arms agreement with Czechoslovakia. U.S. president EISENHOWER and Secretary of State John Foster DULLES attempted to draw him westward again by promising financial support for a cherished Nasser project, the ASWAN HIGH DAM. But in the spring of 1956 the United States reacted to Nasser's withdrawal of Egyptian recognition from CHIANG KAI-SHEK's Nationalist China (a move that was itself part of a diplomatic game) by canceling this promise. The action not only embarrassed Nasser but pushed him into the arms of the Soviets, who offered to sponsor the Aswan Dam. Nasser also nationalized the Suez Canal. What followed was the 1956 SUEZ CRISIS, an ill-judged attempt by the British, the French, and the Israelis to overthrow Nasser's government. Although the United States sponsored UNITED NATIONS resolutions to call off the attackers, its overall policies won no support from Nasser, who welcomed the new Soviet presence in the Middle East.

Nasser's successful resistance to the Western powers established him as a hero in the Arab world, but he found himself in increasing political and economic difficulties in the 1960s, to which he responded by planning an attack on the Israelis—who, however, moved first and in the Six-Day War won a smashing victory over Egypt and its allies. The war had deep and lasting consequences, for it cost Egypt the Sinai peninsula and Syria the Golan Heights and exacerbated the Palestinian problem.

In the wake of the war Nasser proffered his resignation as Egyptian president but recanted the following day. He lived three more years and was succeeded by a remarkable but then little-known statesman, Anwar el-SADAT. Nasser's actions and the U.S. responses to them had opened up channels into the Middle East for the Soviets and in consequence moved U.S. leaders closer to Israel and to dictatorial Asian allies such as the shah of Iran. The 1970s oil embargoes and the Iranian revolutionary hatred of the United States were to follow.

National Liberation Front (NLF)   On December 20, 1960, members of the Saigon Peace Committee and other South Vietnamese dissidents met at Xom Giua, near the Vietnam-Cambodia border, to form a broad-based alliance opposed to the U.S.-

supported South Vietnam government. Though it claimed to be autonomous and independent of the Communist government in Hanoi, the new body—named the National Liberation Front (NLF)—was actually a classic Communist-front organization (as could readily be inferred from its name, a standard form for such groups in THIRD WORLD countries); it also, however, represented the aspirations of many non-Communist South Vietnamese. In January 1959 the 15th Plenum of the Lao Dong (the Vietnamese Communist Party) in Hanoi had adopted a change to combined military and political struggle to overthrow the South Vietnamese government; the consequent decision to form the NLF came at the party's Third National Congress in September 1960.

By conservative U.S. estimates, the NLF held more than 40 percent of the southern countryside during the early days of the VIETNAM WAR, increasing the amount as the war dragged on, and continually harassed the ARMY OF THE REPUBLIC OF VIETNAM in urban areas. On January 30, 1968, the NLF launched the first phase of the TET OFFENSIVE, occupying the courtyard of the U.S. embassy in SAIGON, said to be the most secure building in South Vietnam. Through most of the war the NLF had great success in convincing people around the world that it was independent of Hanoi. At antiwar demonstrations in Europe and America, protesters waved the NLF flag while chanting, "Ho, Ho, HO CHI MINH . . . the NLF is going to win." In May 1969 the NLF was dismantled, allowing the Provisional Revolutionary Government to take over political leadership of the struggle in South Vietnam.

The relationship between the NLF (derogatorily called the VIETCONG by its enemies) and Ho Chi Minh in Hanoi has remained one of the most controversial questions of the war. In contrast to the NLF's claim to be independent, U.S. officials maintained that it was little more than a puppet of Hanoi. Ironically, study of archives in Hanoi during the 1990s has indicated the correctness of the U.S. view, whereas South Vietnamese materials made available during the same period indicate that conflicts between Northerners and Southerners existed in the Communist Party and that the NLF was both Communist and Southern.

National Security Agency (NSA) With headquarters occupying a 1,000-acre tract at Fort George G. Meade, Md., and personnel numbering at times more than 80,000, the NSA during the Cold War was clearly the largest intelligence body in the non-Communist world. It was also by far the most secret U.S. intelligence agency. Established not by legislation (as was the CENTRAL INTELLIGENCE AGENCY) but under an order signed by President TRUMAN on October 24, 1952, the NSA quietly came into being on November 4, 1952, a day when the attention of the news media was focused on the presidential election. The level of secrecy was so high that Truman's order not only carried the Top Secret classification but was labeled with a code name that was also secret.

Charged with the responsibility for all Department of Defense activities relating to communications intelligence, the NSA operated an array of listening posts around the world, decrypted and analyzed the intercepted messages, and created U.S. signal intelligence capacities—codes and ciphers, together with transmission methods and devices, with heavy emphasis on the development of computerization. In addition, the agency held the responsibility for preserving the security of its operations.

National Security Council (NSC) U.S. agency that gained notoriety in the mid-1980s when staff members became identified as the central actors in what the press called the IRAN-CONTRA AFFAIR. Actually, the NSC had long served as the top presidential advisory agency in national security matters, and its executive head—the president's special assistant for national security affairs—had become under different administrations a leading figure in the development of policy; outstanding examples were McGeorge BUNDY under Presidents KENNEDY and JOHNSON, and Henry KISSINGER under President NIXON. A later security adviser who rose to prominence as chairman of the JOINT CHIEFS OF STAFF was General Colin Powell, who served as adviser to President REAGAN.

Established under provisions of the National Security Act of 1947, the NSC consisted of the president as chairman, the vice president, the secretaries of state and defense, and the director of the Office of Emergency Planning (a position since abolished), with (after 1949) the chairman of the JCS and the director of the CENTRAL INTELLIGENCE AGENCY as advisers. In its first years, the NSC was overshadowed by two strong secretaries of state, Dean ACHESON and his successor, John Foster DULLES, but, beginning with President Kennedy, the agency took on great importance. A major politico-military change came in 1986, when the Goldwater-Nichols Defense Reorganization Act gave the chairman of the JCS a seat on the NSC, thus elevating him from advisory status to that of full member. *See also* NSC-68.

National Security Council Paper 68 *See* NSC-68.

NATO *See* NORTH ATLANTIC TREATY ORGANIZATION.

NATO caliber Commonly used term first for the standardized 7.62-mm caliber (as in the U.S. M-14 rifle), and later for the 5.56-mm caliber (as in the M-16). *See also* NORTH ATLANTIC TREATY ORGANIZATION.

Nautilus U.S. submarine, the world's first nuclear-powered ship, that entered service in 1954 and won particular fame four years later by becoming the first vessel not only to reach the North Pole but to sail under the polar ice cap from the Pacific Ocean to the Atlantic. Endowed with the name of the underwater vessel that performed this interoceanic feat in Jules Verne's novel *Twenty Thousand Leagues Under the Sea* (1870), the U.S.S. *Nautilus* seemed destined from its first moments to attempt the long-dreamed-of passage. The submarine itself had been the dream of a naval engineering officer, Rear Admiral Hyman RICKOVER, who fought to achieve it against strong opposition.

On entering service, *Nautilus* immediately became the world's fastest (more than 20 knots) submarine, and the cruising range its nuclear plant allowed completely transformed existing ideas of undersea capabilities. The captain, Commander William R. Anderson, kept the polar mission (code-named Operation Sunshine) a secret even from the crew until the vessel was well out to sea. It succeeded only after previous forays had been rebuffed by ice. On August 1, 1958, Anderson found the Barrow Sea valley, a deep passage off Point Barrow, Alaska, and 62 hours later *Nautilus* had reached the North Pole. Anderson's message to the chief of naval operations at the Pentagon declared simply, "NAUTILUS 90 DEGREES N." Reaching the open water of the Atlantic two days later, skipper and crew had demonstrated that the Northwest Passage long sought by mariners really existed, though in a form far different from anything contemplated by the early explorers of the American continent.

Nehru, Jawaharlal (1889–1964) Prime minister of India from 1947, when the country became independent of Britain, until his death, Nehru was involved in Indian nationalism from his early 20s. A graduate of Cambridge, he returned to India in 1912 and in 1929 succeeded his father as head of the Congress Party. Like other party leaders, he went to prison a number of times through the next two decades; during this period he was the leading associate of Mahatma Gandhi.

An elegant and dignified figure, Nehru devoted much of his energy during the Cold War to keeping India out of entanglement with either East or West, playing an important role as a leader of the nonaligned nations. His neutralism disturbed some American leaders, especially John Foster DULLES, who called it immoral; others regarded it as neutralism with a tilt toward the Soviet Union. But the USSR's Joseph STALIN did not consider it satisfactory, either.

Nehru was followed as prime minister by Lal Bahadur Shastri, who died after only two years in office. This opened the way to power for his minister of information, Indira GANDHI, Nehru's daughter. *See also* NONALIGNMENT.

neutron bomb During the middle 1970s the allies in the NORTH ATLANTIC TREATY ORGANIZATION considered the development and deployment of an enhanced-radiation weapon, commonly called the neutron bomb. The power of this weapon would primarily come not from the force of its explosion but from intense radiation. In the public mind this quality gave the weapon a particularly sinister aspect, so that it became known as the bomb that would kill people while leaving buildings undisturbed. NATO military leaders believed that this precise quality would make the bomb a valuable

At a diplomatic party, Prime Minister Jawaharlal Nehru of India *(l.)* chats with the U.S. ambassador, John Sherman Cooper, and his wife.

weapon for defense against a WARSAW PACT invasion of Western Europe, but the politicians and the public did not agree. In April 1978, U.S. president Jimmy CARTER responded to this opposition by suspending the development of the neutron bomb.

Never Again Club   Informal overall term for the U.S. military officers whose abhorrence of the political, strategic, and logistical problems presented by the KOREAN WAR led them to declare that the United States should "never again" fight another such war. Within little more than a decade, however, U.S. forces found themselves involved in an

analogous, if different, situation in the VIETNAM WAR.

New Course   The series of reforms associated with the Soviet leadership of Georgi MALENKOV during 1953 and 1954, the period immediately following the death of Premier Joseph STALIN. In general, Malenkov paid more attention than had his predecessor to the wants of consumers, and in foreign policy he displayed a markedly different outlook from Stalin. The New Course featured less emphasis on confrontation with the West and introduced marked reductions in military spending. Its author also loosened, to some extent, the Soviet grip on the satellite countries in Eastern Europe, with political prisoners receiving amnesties and some Stalinist leaders being removed from their posts. In March 1954 Malenkov declared the Cold War a "policy for the preparation of a new world holocaust." Perhaps unfortunately, however, Malenkov's New Course did not have long to run. During 1954 he was outmaneuvered by Nikita KHRUSHCHEV in the contest for power; in February 1955 he resigned the premiership. In practice, however, Khrushchev took the nation along the general path Malenkov had favored, though his explosive personal style often obscured this reality —and, indeed, his actions were sometimes, as in the 1956 HUNGARIAN REVOLUTION, as harsh as those of Stalin.

New People's Army   Since World War II the Philippines have seen a continuing Communist insurgency; probably the best-known group was the HUKBALAHAP movement (the "Huks"), which was put down in the 1950s by Ramon Magsaysay. In the 1980s the insurgents took the name New People's Army. Although it signed a truce in 1986 with the new Philippine president, Corazón Aquino, the two sides could not reach any lasting accommodation. In its varying makeup since the end of the war, the Philippine government has been too strong to be overthrown by the insurgents but not strong enough to defeat them.

new thinking   This phrase characterized the approach General Secretary Mikhail GORBACHEV brought to Soviet foreign relations. It amounted to a political and diplomatic PERESTROIKA, a restructuring in which the old hostilities of the Cold War were to be exchanged for international cooperation for mutual security. The term was put into currency in 1984 by two Soviet foreign policy specialists during a low point in relations with the United States and the West in general; it traced its ancestry to a 1954 peace manifesto promoted by Bertrand RUSSELL and Albert Einstein. Thus it sat ready and waiting for Gorbachev when he came to power in 1985 and sought to create a new kind of PEACEFUL COEXISTENCE. The old confrontational formulas not only threatened life on the planet, Gorbachev held, but also hindered the development of necessary internal Soviet reforms. Speaking realistically, Gorbachev declared that "the foreign policy of any government is determined first of all by internal demands." Even so, the new thinking had as a central point the interdependent nature of contemporary international life.

At the same time, new thinking did not exist in a rosy ideal world. Power considerations continued to influence Soviet policy. As the historian Denise Artaud pointed out, while the USSR reduced some of its foreign activities, "the Soviets managed to maintain their economic aid to Cuba, sent spare parts to the Sandinista-controlled Nicaraguan army, and continued to prop up Afghanistan's Communist government—all this during the last year of the Soviet Union's existence."

Ngo Dinh Diem (1901–1963)   President of South Vietnam (the Republic of Vietnam) from 1955 until his death, Diem was a conservative politician who had in turn opposed the French, the Japanese, and the Vietnamese Communists. Exiled by the French but favored by the United States, he returned to Vietnam in 1954 to become prime minister; he assumed the presidency during the following year.

Mandarin and scholar, a devout Roman Catholic who disdained and suppressed the Buddhists (representing the great majority of his country's population), Diem advocated "personalism," a philosophy of his own (with some French roots) that held individual freedom as sacred but maintained that people should not have political freedom until they had acquired enough moral education to handle it properly. His authoritarian rule increasingly concerned some of his U.S. advisers, particularly after he responded to Buddhist demonstrations with violence, accusing the demonstrators of doing the will of the Communists (and many of the *bonzes* were, indeed, not passive priests but militant opponents of the politicians).

On November 1, 1963—with the tacit complicity of U.S. officials in Vietnam—a group of South Vietnamese army officers staged a coup to remove Diem from office. But the Americans had not really faced up to one of the likely consequences of the coup: on the next day Diem and his brother NHU were shot by the forces that had overthrown them. U.S. president John F. KENNEDY received the news of these deaths with shock. The death of

Diem opened a roughly two-year period during which no South Vietnamese government managed to stay in power more than a few months.

Ngo Dinh Nhu (1910–1963) Younger brother of NGO DINH DIEM, Nhu worked for the French colonial administration in Vietnam during his early years and, like his older brother, advocated a third force between French colonialism and the Communist VIETMINH. After the rigged election of 1955 brought his brother to power, Nhu organized the secret Can Lao Party, a Catholic group that held complete political and military control of South Vietnam. As head of the secret police, Nhu also controlled the Special Forces, which he used to crush all opposition to the Diem regime. Nhu likewise supervised the STRATEGIC HAMLET program, a complicated effort to restructure rural areas into "safe villages."

In a November 1, 1963, coup, Nhu and his brother, President Diem, were both assassinated. Of the drug-addicted (opium and perhaps heroin) Nhu the journalist Robert Shaplen wrote: "You could see the madness in his face, a sort of somnambulistic stare, always with that cold smile . . . ; it was as if the devil had taken possession of him."

Ngo Dinh Nhu, Mme. (1924–) Born Tran Le Xuan, Mme. Nhu became the de facto first lady of South Vietnam in 1955 when her bachelor brother-in-law, NGO DINH DIEM, became president of the country. Describing herself as a strong feminist and exercising substantial political power, she drew up many of the country's social laws, including those banning divorce, adultery, prostitution, dancing, boxing, beauty contests, fortune-telling, and public displays of affection. She gave frequent lectures on the role of women in Vietnam and directed the Women's Solidarity Movement, a paramilitary organization that taught urban women how to use weapons.

In 1963, when her husband was attacking Vietnamese Buddhists, Mme. Nhu won wide notoriety for a comment she made concerning Buddhist monks who were protesting the actions of the regime by burning themselves. Mme. Nhu invited them to the presidential palace for a barbecue, saying, "I will supply the gasoline and the matches for the biggest barbecue in SAIGON." A reporter once commented that "Machiavelli would have envied her."

After the November 1, 1963, coup in which her husband and brother-in-law were both murdered, she escaped to Europe and took up residence in Rome.

Nguyen Cao Ky (1930–) South Vietnamese military and political figure who in 1965 became a member of a triumvirate of generals that controlled the government of the country and in 1967 was elected vice president. When General Nguyen Khanh came to power after the overthrow of President NGO DINH DIEM (November 1, 1963), Ky, an air force officer, was one of the young colonels promoted to the newly created rank of "aspirant brigadier general"; by February 1964 he had become head of the South Vietnamese air force. After the removal of Khanh in February 1965, Ky and the other members of the triumvirate, one of whom was General NGUYEN VAN THIEU, took control.

In 1966, despite attacks by terrorists and a boycott by Buddhists, Ky and his associates managed to conduct elections, as he had pledged to do. Some 81 percent of the eligible voters turned out to choose the members of a constituent assembly, though some U.S. observers claimed that they came almost exclusively from areas under military control. At a 1966 conference in Hawaii, after Ky had delivered a speech full of Great Society thoughts to an audience including Lyndon JOHNSON, the U.S. president declared enthusiastically, "Boy, you speak great American!"

General Thieu was chosen as president in the 1967 election that saw Ky become vice president. In the 1971 presidential election, however, Thieu declared Ky ineligible to run against him. Ky fled South Vietnam shortly before the final victorious Communist offensive in the spring of 1975. Moving to the United States, he became a successful businessman.

In an interview almost 20 years later, Ky observed that, in the long run, the South and not the North had won the VIETNAM WAR. SAIGON, he said, was now a flourishing, Western-style city, full of successful private enterprises.

231

Nguyen Thi Binh (1927–) Mme. Nguyen represented North Vietnam as one of the leading negotiators in the Paris peace talks that began in 1968. A member of the Central Command of the NATIONAL LIBERATION FRONT beginning in 1962, she was minister of education of Vietnam after the defeat of the SAIGON government.

Nguyen Van Hieu (1922–1991) A native of southern Vietnam who received his education in Hanoi and then returned south to run VIETMINH propaganda activities against the French. After the North Vietnamese victory at DIEN BIEN PHU in 1954, he began writing for several SAIGON newspapers under the pseudonym Khai Minh (in English, to state clearly). In later years he was one of the NATIONAL LIBERATION FRONT's leading policy makers and diplomats, and became the best-known NLF member abroad.

Nguyen Van Thieu (1923–) President of South Vietnam from 1967 to 1975, General Thieu was a veteran soldier who earlier had held important commands, including that of the Fifth Infantry Division, which provided much of the military backing for the November 1963 coup in which President NGO DINH DIEM was overthrown.

After the removal of General Nguyen Khanh from the presidency, in February 1965, Thieu became chief of state in a power-sharing arrangement that included NGUYEN CAO KY as premier. Establishing themselves through their direction of the National Leadership Committee, Thieu and Ky were elected, respectively, president and vice president in 1967; Thieu succeeded in outmaneuvering Ky to win the top spot for himself. For the 1971 election, Thieu peremptorily declared Ky disqualified and thus ensured his own victory, though his actions profoundly disturbed U.S. ambassador Ellsworth BUNKER, who urged President NIXON to disavow Thieu. Since negotiations to end the VIETNAM WAR stood at a critical point, however, Nixon did not feel able to accept Bunker's recommendation. (On the whole, Thieu for the moment could consider himself most fortunate. He won reelection to the presidency instead of meeting the fate advocated for him by some of the North Vietnamese negotiators, who suggested that the United

States further the cause of peace by having the general assassinated.)

Bitterly opposing the 1973 peace agreement signed in Paris, Thieu agreed to it only on receiving Nixon's guarantee that the United States would intervene if the South Vietnamese government should later face a direct threat from the North. After the Communists swept into SAIGON just two years later, Thieu called the U.S. "desertion" of South Vietnam "an inhumane act by an inhumane ally."

Nike-Zeus This U.S. Army surface-to-air antimissile missile (a defensive weapon against incoming enemy missiles) had a range of more than 220 miles and a speed of Mach 4.

Nimitz Class of five nuclear-powered aircraft carriers that began joining the U.S. fleet in 1975 and continued through the 1980s, the group including, besides *Nimitz, Dwight D. Eisenhower, Carl Vinson, Theodore Roosevelt,* and *Abraham Lincoln.* The production of these huge and very expensive ships encountered strong political resistance from those who believed that a giant carrier essentially constituted a giant target. With a full-load displacement of 94,000 tons, the Nimitz-class carriers house about 80 fixed-wing aircraft of various types and six helicopters; the crew numbers more than 6,000. These carriers played prominent parts in the 1991 Persian Gulf War.

Nineteen Eighty-four Of the many 20th-century writers who have sought to explain and dramatize the nature of life under a totalitarian regime, the most famous was the British essayist and novelist George Orwell (1903–1950; original name, Eric Blair). Though Orwell's essays present his best writing, the book with which he is most identified, and which made people around the world look on the approach of the 1980s with some trepidation, is *Nineteen Eighty-four* (1949), wherein he presents a people governed by Big Brother, assaulted by slogans like "war is peace" and "freedom is slavery," and deprived of all privacy and dignity. The book is to be taken as a warning about the dangers of totalitarianism generally; Orwell knew enough of it from Germany and the Soviet Union to fear it for the Western democratic world as well. In describing the Ministry of Truth, he even had as a partial source his own World War II experience in the British Ministry of Information.

The distinguished critic Denis Donoghue described *Nineteen Eighty-four* as "a political fable, projected into a near future in a mood variously to be described as one of threat, warning, despair, or rage." For another leading critic, Lionel Trilling, *Nineteen Eighty-four* showed us "the danger of the ultimate and absolute power which mind can develop when it frees itself from conditions, from the bondage of things and history." The Soviet historian Alexander Nekrich commented that "George Orwell is perhaps the *only* Western author to understand the deepest essence of the Soviet world."

Nitze, Paul (1907–) One of the most important designers of U.S. policy in the early years of the Cold War, Paul Nitze was the son of a professor of Romance languages at the University of Chicago and came to government service from an establishment background—he was educated at Hotchkiss and Harvard (1928, cum laude), and worked at the Wall Street investment-banking firm of Dillon, Read & Co. In a memorable message, James FOR-RESTAL, his superior at Dillon, Read, summoned him to Washington in 1940 to work on drafting the first U.S. peacetime selective-service act. The operative telegram said simply: "BE IN WASH-INGTON MONDAY MORNING. FORRES-TAL."

Nitze did various jobs during World War II, including, at the end, serving as vice chairman of the Strategic Bombing Survey. After the war, working on economic matters for the State Department, he suggested that the United States create a large-scale aid program for Europe, several months before the idea became common in the department. In 1949 Nitze joined the Policy Planning Staff as deputy to his good friend George KENNAN, whom he succeeded as director of the staff in November 1949, though he did not officially take over until January 1, 1950. Much more attuned to Nitze's views than to those of Kennan, Secretary of State Dean ACHESON gave the new director the assignment of producing the basic TRUMAN administration Cold War blueprint that would become

known as NSC-68; this document called for the United States to build up the military in order to "check and roll back the Kremlin's drive for world domination." Nitze, who, unlike Kennan, believed that the United States should develop the HYDRO-GEN BOMB, also chaired the committee that made such a recommendation to Truman. Acheson called Nitze "a joy to work with because of his clear, incisive mind."

After leaving the State Department at the end of the Truman administration, Nitze continued through the years to figure prominently in the development of U.S. Cold War policy, serving as assistant secretary of defense for international security affairs during the KENNEDY administration and secretary of the navy (1963–67) and deputy secretary of defense (1967–69) under Lyndon JOHNSON. A member of the U.S. delegation to the STRATEGIC ARMS LIMITATION TALKS and chairman of the U.S. negotiating team in arms-control talks in Geneva (1981–84), Nitze was principally responsible for the INTERMEDIATE-RANGE NUCLEAR FORCES TREATY (INF); he also frequently acted as a governmental adviser without portfolio. In the 1970s Nitze played a leading part in the organization of the COMMITTEE ON THE PRESENT DANGER, which took a dubious view of DÉTENTE and opposed SALT II. Overall, Nitze served over the years as the very model of the modern Cold War statesman and technocrat.

Nixon, Richard Milhous (1913–1994) Elected 37th president of the United States in 1968, Richard Nixon seemed in many ways to embody the ideas and passions of the Cold War. One of the first American politicians to discover the electoral usefulness of anti-Communism, Nixon employed this device in his first congressional race, in 1946, to defeat a liberal Democrat. He won national prominence as a member of the U.S. House of Representatives' Un-American Activities Committee, through his leading role in revealing the Communist past of a former State Department official, Alger HISS. He rode the same issue in his successful campaign for the Senate in 1950. Though not notably right-wing in most of his views, as vice president under EISENHOWER (1953–61), Nixon served as the warrior in the political trenches while the president took a higher, less partisan stance.

After becoming president, Nixon showed himself to be a pragmatist capable of adapting to changing realities. Instead of continuing with 1950s-style Cold War rhetoric, he moved to develop a relationship with Communist China—making a historic trip to Beijing in 1972 to meet with MAO ZEDONG and ZHOU ENLAI—and to establish DÉTENTE and an arms agreement with the Soviet Union; each of these moves drew applause from around the world. Nixon won a huge reelection victory in 1972 over the Democratic George McGovern. And then, in August 1974, facing impeachment, he became the first U.S. president in history to resign the office.

During the days of Nixon's funeral and its attendant ceremonies in April 1994, politicians and other commentators revealed doubts about how to characterize his life and career. No precedent existed for dealing with an ex-president who had resigned the office and received an unconditional pardon from his successor for any crimes he might have committed while president. Generally, however, with the passions of the 1970s having grown cold over the ensuing two decades, Nixon was praised for his achievements and for the dogged way in which, through his books and memoirs, travel, and personal appearances, he had built himself into an elder statesman widely honored abroad and increasingly respected in his own country. In his eulogy, U.S. president Bill Clinton called Nixon "a fierce advocate for freedom and democracy around the world." But as a man who had aroused some of the fiercest political hatreds of his time, Nixon left behind many opponents who would never take a warm view of him.

The son of a Southern California family of modest means, Nixon was brought up as a Quaker. He hoped to attend a leading university but had to settle for Whittier College, from which he graduated in 1934. He flourished at Whittier, winning student offices, shining in debates, playing football, and finishing second in his class. He later credited his football coach at Whittier with having been a great teacher—one of his prime lessons is embodied in the sentence "Show me a good loser and I'll show you a loser." Whether from nature or nurture, this fighting attitude would characterize Nixon throughout his political career. Many years later the speaker of the U.S. House of Repre-

sentatives, Sam Rayburn, would characterize him as "all knees and elbows."

After graduating from college, Nixon attended Duke University Law School on a scholarship. Awarded his law degree in 1937, he unsuccessfully sought a job with a Wall Street law firm and then returned to California to practice in Whittier. He joined a little-theater group, in which he met a local teacher, Thelma Ryan (known as Pat), whom he married in 1940. (He had proposed immediately; her impression, as she later remembered it, was, "I thought he was nuts or something.") After Pearl Harbor, Nixon worked briefly in Washington for the Office of Price Administration (an experience that left him with an abiding distaste for bureaucracy) and then joined the navy, serving in the Pacific as an operations officer with an air-transport command.

Even before he came back home after the war, a group of influential Southern California Republicans asked him to consider running for Congress. These men wanted to unseat Jerry Voorhis, a strongly New Deal Democrat who had been in Washington since the mid-1930s and had supported public power and other programs looked on with loathing by rich conservatives. A shy, introverted man, Nixon nevertheless eagerly accepted this offer to go into the glad-handing world of elective politics and entered on a campaign that would serve as a template for the first long phase of his political career. Despite being the hand-picked candidate of persons with almost unlimited wealth, Nixon attacked Voorhis as the beneficiary of a labor political action committee "slush fund" (even though the PAC had not endorsed him) and declared, as though it were a well-known fact, that the PAC operated on Communist principles. Voorhis's denials did him little good; Nixon was on his way.

When he arrived in Washington, Nixon wasted no time in involving himself in anti-Communist activities. In February 1947, having drawn an assignment to the House Un-American Activities Committee, he figured in the contempt citation of one Gerhard Eisler, who refused to appear before the committee and whom Nixon called the "key man" of the Communist Party in the United States. In the autumn of 1947 Nixon and the other committee members launched an inquiry into Communist influence in the movie business, which attracted wide attention and led to the indictments of the so-called HOLLYWOOD TEN.

In making Nixon nationally famous, the Alger Hiss case, which broke in 1948, also did much to make him hated by liberals, who saw Hiss as an innocent public servant sandbagged for purely political reasons by an unprincipled alley fighter. Unfortunately for the liberals, however, a jury convicted Hiss of perjury and all subsequent investigation and evidence confirmed the correctness of the verdict. In 1950, moving on to run for the Senate against a former actress, Congresswoman Helen Gahagan Douglas, Nixon made heavy use of his now-familiar Communist charge; a flood of Nixon handbills printed on pink paper called Mrs. Douglas "the pink lady" who as a representative in Congress had followed the Communist line. With the coming of the KOREAN WAR in the summer preceding the election, alleged pink ladies did not find themselves well situated to attract votes; Nixon won the seat by a margin of almost 700,000. This campaign, however, produced Nixon's enduring nickname, Tricky Dick.

A young and rising Republican star, a Westerner and a man who "was willing to engage in all-out combat and who was good at it" (as Nixon later described himself), the senator became Eisenhower's choice as his running mate in 1952, in a campaign heavy with talk of "20 years of treason" and similar accusations of Democratic disloyalty. Nixon almost lost his place on the ticket, however, when reporters discovered that some of his California supporters had put together a private fund to help pay his expenses. Fighting back, Nixon demonstrated his grasp of the power of TV in a direct, personal, and highly effective broadcast speech in which he presented himself as a hardworking, honest family man who, whatever might come, would not force his two little daughters to return their cocker spaniel, Checkers, to its donor.

A diligent vice president through the eight years of Ike's two terms, Nixon represented the president and the country in numerous trips abroad; the 1958 NIXON TRIP TO SOUTH AMERICA provided a particularly noteworthy example, as did the 1959 KITCHEN DEBATE in Moscow, where Nixon "stood up to KHRUSHCHEV" in front of the television cameras. Although ample evidence indicates that Ike

Who's he voting for? Playing a game with the press in one of his early campaigns, Richard M. Nixon asks for secrecy concerning his choice.

did not have a personal liking for Nixon, *Time* magazine knowingly presented the vice president as a favored colleague. "When the press of other business calls Ike away in mid-meeting," said one story, "Ike turns to Nixon and says, 'Dick, you take over.'" Nominated for president by the Republicans in 1960, Nixon lost to John F. KENNEDY in the closest election, in percentage terms, in American history. This time TV, Nixon's ally in 1952, turned against him, as he was outshone by Kennedy in the first-ever televised debates between presidential candidates. Despite the urging of supporters who wanted him to challenge the election results because of claimed vote fraud, Nixon refused. Among his reasons for declining was surely the idea that if he should lose the recount, as might well happen, he would have shown himself to be not only a loser but a sore loser. In 1962, in a televised press conference he held after his defeat in the California gubernatorial election, Nixon allowed the resentment that always seemed to burn inside him to come to the surface: he declared to the reporters who had covered his campaign, "You won't have Nixon to kick around any more, because, gentlemen, this is my last press conference."

It was not, however. Six years later, Nixon, having taken on the chore of mending the Republican Party after its overwhelming defeat in the 1964 presidential election, demonstrated that in the age of television one did not have to hold political office to have stature with the voters. Although he had been a private citizen since leaving the vice presidency, he won the presidential nomination in the troubled summer of 1968 and went on to defeat Vice President Hubert Humphrey and independent candidate George Wallace in November. Having campaigned on a plan to end the VIETNAM WAR, he proved to have devised nothing more complex than the withdrawal of U.S. troops from the area while making South Vietnam increasingly responsible for its own defense. Instead of ending the war in a short time, as he, as well as the public, hoped, Nixon saw it continue until a truce was signed in 1973, even though the new ties with China removed any strategic purpose from the war; the truce agreement proved to be little more than a cover for U.S. abandonment of the war and of the South Vietnamese state the Americans had created. Meanwhile, often besieged by ANTIWAR PROTESTERS and desperately wanting to end the conflict, Nixon appealed to the "silent majority" for support and resorted in vain to the "madman theory," as he called it in conversation with aides—threatening even the use of nuclear weapons. In addition, he and his national security adviser, Henry KISSINGER, had extended the war to CAMBODIA.

Nixon's relationships with the two great Communist powers, China and the Soviet Union, represented happier chapters of his presidency. As observers often said, the opening of a relationship with China (1971–72) could probably have been attempted only by a president with Nixon's degree of immunity to charges of being soft on Communism. (On his ceremonial visit to the Great Wall, Nixon told the accompanying reporters, "This is a great wall.") Not only did the new relationship with China change the balance of power in the world, it did not interfere with the achievement of détente with Soviet general secretary Leonid BREZHNEV and the USSR, which led to the SALT I (arms-limitation agreement) in May 1972. These major diplomatic moves presented a Nixon who appeared to be much more the craftsman, devising policy according to a plan, than the ideologue in international affairs. William G. Hyland, an associate of Kissinger, wrote that Nixon "had long experience in dealing with the Soviet Union and had developed a good feel for Soviet attitudes and reactions; he had a natural instinct for manipulation."

Years earlier, in 1958, Nixon had delivered an interesting insight into his thinking about the relationship between public statements and policy. In a conversation with British reporters, he had offered a surprising endorsement of the fiery left-wing Labourite Aneurin BEVAN, with whom he had very little political common ground. Speaking of the difference between Bevan's responsible conduct at a recent Labour Party conference and the exaggerated rhetoric Bevan often displayed at political rallies, Nixon said that "a politician ought to be permitted a bit of leeway [for] a certain amount of demagoguery and a certain amount of appeal to the galleries, as long as he acts responsibly when it comes to actual policy decisions." After Nixon's death, his former chief of staff, Alexander HAIG, called him "the most competent and capable president in foreign policy in the post–World War II era."

Reelected in 1972 in one of the greatest landslides in American history, Nixon quickly demonstrated how closely tragedy can follow triumph. Obsessed by leaks of government secrets, the administration had engaged in various acts of illegal surveillance and breaking and entering, leading to the WATERGATE AFFAIR—a 1972 burglary that by 1974 had produced the indictment of several of Nixon's closest associates and aides. Finally, in August, the president admitted, after many months of evasion and denial—"I am not a crook," Nixon declared in November 1973—that he had approved and participated in attempts to cover up the facts of the Watergate burglary, including interfering with the FBI investigation of the case. Already, in late July, the House of Representatives' Judiciary Committee had voted articles of impeachment; action by the full House seemed certain to follow. The vital evidence was contained in tape recordings made of all conversations in the Oval Office; Nixon's long struggle to keep control of the tapes constituted a central part of the Watergate drama. Besides detailing his actions to suppress the investigation, they revealed his view of the whole affair. On a tape not released until 1993, Nixon declared to aides, four days after the break-in, that "the reaction is going to be primarily in Washington and not in the country, because I think the country doesn't give much of a shit about bugging." In a televised speech on the evening of August 9, Nixon announced his resignation, effective at noon the following day. In September his successor, Gerald FORD, granted him an unconditional pardon.

For the next two decades, with extraordinary single-mindedness, the ex-president devoted himself to reversing the tide of his personal history. Articles, books, foreign trips, TV interviews—a variety of continuing activities presented Nixon to the public as an experienced and thoughtful statesman who admitted to mistakes but went no further toward confession and apology. The whole Watergate drama baffled many Europeans on both sides of the IRON CURTAIN—to the West the American reaction to the scandal appeared excessive, and to the East it appeared incredible. High-ranking Soviets could not be persuaded that so trifling a matter had led to such profound consequences; détente itself, they believed, must be the real target of American forces that did not desire a working relationship with the USSR.

In a 1990 interview, Nixon made a highly revealing observation about himself. "No one," he said, "had ever been so high and fallen so low." What seemed to be bound up with that fall was the view he unvaryingly displayed of a world made up of friends and enemies; "they," the enemies, were always there. Perhaps the truth was simply that Nixon could never genuinely believe in the reality of the heights to which he had risen and, at the same time, always actively feared that the great fall lay waiting just ahead.

See also JACKSON-VANIK AMENDMENT.

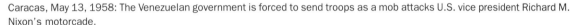

Caracas, May 13, 1958: The Venezuelan government is forced to send troops as a mob attacks U.S. vice president Richard M. Nixon's motorcade.

Nixon trip to South America During its first five years the U.S. EISENHOWER administration displayed little interest in Latin American matters, aside from involvement in the 1954 plot that overthrew the government of Guatemala's President Jacobo ARBENZ. But people in the region demonstrated powerful anti-American feeling in 1958 when Vice President NIXON made what was intended to be a goodwill trip to South America. Arriving in Peru after uneventful stops in several other countries, Nixon encountered angry students at San Marcos University, even though the rector had withdrawn his invitation for a vice presidential speech. Emerging from his car after it had received a barrage of fruit and stones, Nixon stood on the trunk and, blaming the riot on Communist agitators, fired angry words back at the students. "Cowards!" he shouted. "Are you afraid of the truth?" At another university he encountered more hecklers and more violence.

On May 13, after a peaceful stop in Ecuador, Nixon moved on to unquestionably the most dangerous country in the region, Venezuela, whose people resented the support the United States had long given the recently overthrown dictator Marcos Pérez Jiménez. A mob met Nixon at the gates of the Caracas airport, dumping garbage on his car and spitting on it. Lining the 12-mile route into the city, Venezuelans attacked the motorcade with rocks and dung and smashed the glass of the vice president's limousine. The arrival of soldiers saved Nixon and his wife, Pat, from worse violence, but his security remained doubtful. (A concerned President Eisenhower ordered a standby rescue operation, which someone could not resist code-naming Operation Poor Richard.)

The whole episode showed how strongly many Latin Americans blamed their political and economic woes on their powerful northern neighbor. The Eisenhower administration took action in response, formulating new aid programs that led to the KENNEDY administration's ALLIANCE FOR PROGRESS.

Nkrumah, Kwame (1910?–1972) In assuming office as prime minister of the republic of Ghana in February 1957, Nkrumah thereby became the leader of the first British African colony (the former Gold Coast) to win its independence. Born into a middle-class family (he was not sure of the correct date), he studied in the United States and Britain and was influenced in his thinking by the Jamaican-born black leader Marcus Garvey (who had wanted to establish an African state for U.S. blacks) and the anthropologist M. J. Herzkovits.

Seeing imperialism as an aberration in a long African history of peace, Nkrumah held a vision of continental unity produced through socialism. His biographer, Genovera Marais, depicts him as haunted by time—his worry that he would not survive long enough in power to see the development of Pan-Africanism (the unifying of Africans and the elimination of colonialism) or the maturing of his socialist economic program. His fear proved well-founded, as officials of his Convention People's Party mismanaged the national economy, producing rising popular discontent, even as Nkrumah was declared president for life in 1964. He survived several assassination attempts but in 1966, while he was out of the country, army officers staged a successful coup, forcing him to take up residence in Guinea, where he was welcomed by President Sékou TOURÉ and stayed on as a permanent guest. "Even if they succeed in destroying me," Nkrumah once declared, "my writings will survive."

NLF *See* NATIONAL LIBERATION FRONT.

nomenklatura A vital, pervasive, and complex part of the Soviet system, *nomenklatura* was often spoken of as the list of positions under the control of the Communist Party but is more fully defined as the apparatus by which the party assigned jobs and distributed privileges (cars, apartments, travel, access to elite stores). Nomenklatura lists existed on the local as well as the republic and national levels and within individual organizations, such as the KGB and the Academy of Sciences, but the most significant list was that of the CENTRAL COMMITTEE of the COMMUNIST PARTY OF THE SOVIET UNION. Actually, three lists were involved, all of them secret: one of jobs, one of candidates for jobs, and one of "reserve" candidates—those who, if lucky, would in due course be moved up to the candidate list.

Every sort of position, from ambassador to Great Britain to metropolitan of the Orthodox Church to coach of a soccer team appeared on some nomenklatura listing. Essentially, the system was designed to enable the Communist Party to keep tight control over Soviet society by centering the dispensing of positions and privilege in party headquarters in Moscow. Inevitably, such a system encouraged bureaucratic conservatism and gave rewards to mediocrity.

A striking Russian precedent for the nomenklatura system existed in the table of ranks established by Peter the Great in 1722; this listing set up 14 levels for military officers and civil servants, all of them under central control—in this case, the will of the czar. As the historian B. H. Sumner commented, the table of ranks "set the stamp on the hierarchical, bureaucratic ordering of the upper class in military and state service, which during the next two centuries became so prominent a feature of the social structure of Russia."

nonalignment   In the years following World War II when many former African and Asian colonial possessions of the European powers achieved political independence, the new governments frequently tended to avoid falling under the sway of either East or West, though they often seemed ideologically susceptible to Communist influence. Conferences of nonaligned nations would frequently pass resolutions favoring the Communist viewpoint in major international disputes, one reason being obvious: they had never been colonized by Communists. Sometimes, as frequently happened with India, a country seemed to practice nonalignment, or neutralism, with a tilt toward Moscow or Peking. In any case, in practice many nonaligned nations dealt with both SUPERPOWERS, seeking, as would be expected, their own advantage. This refusal to take sides sometimes irked the leaders of both blocs. Once, in a notable statement, U.S. secretary of state John Foster DULLES declared bluntly, "Neutralism is immoral." For his part, the USSR's Joseph STALIN, as a French historian observed, "detested the idea of neutralism." It had been his ideological spokesman, Andrei ZHDANOV, who in 1947 proclaimed the division of the world into two camps. If a country was not "socialist," it belonged ipso facto to the "imperialist" side. *See also* BANDUNG CONFERENCE.

NORAD   *See* NORTH AMERICAN AIR DEFENSE COMMAND.

Norstad, Lauris (1907–1988)   Supreme commander of the NORTH ATLANTIC TREATY ORGANIZATION from 1956 to 1962, Norstad was a U.S. Air Force general who began his military career in the cavalry. A West Pointer in the class of 1930, he graduated from primary and advanced flying schools within a year and a half of entering active duty and was transferred from the cavalry to the air corps.

Primarily an air staff officer during World War II, Norstad ended the war as director of plans and operations for the War Department. In 1947 he was a leading negotiator for the army in working out the agreement with the navy that underlay the unification, limited as it was, of the armed forces. In 1951 he became commander of NATO air forces in Central Europe; he followed this appointment with the command of all NATO air forces. In 1952 the boyish-looking Norstad became the youngest four-star general in American history. His appointment as NATO supreme commander in 1956 represented an acknowledgment of his outstanding ability.

North American Aerospace Defense Command   *See* NORTH AMERICAN AIR DEFENSE COMMAND.

North American Air Defense Command (NORAD)   Integrated U.S.-Canadian system, established in May 1958, to detect and respond to possible attack by the Soviet Union. Coordinated from the command center near Colorado Springs, Colo., it incorporated the existing stations of the Distant Early Warning (DEW) Line stretching from Greenland to Alaska. In 1981 NORAD became the North American Aerospace Defense Command. When President REAGAN paid a visit to the center, one of his aides asked the general in command what would happen if a Soviet nuclear warhead were to hit nearby. "It would blow us away," the general replied simply. Asked what could be done about it, the general said, "Nothing." Reagan concluded, according to former secretary of state George SHULTZ, "that was a hell of a state of affairs." The result was Reagan's interest in the STRATEGIC DEFENSE INITIATIVE.

North Atlantic Treaty Organization (NATO)   The third of the three prime U.S. foreign-policy legacies of the TRUMAN administration (along with the TRUMAN DOCTRINE and the MARSHALL PLAN), NATO came into being in 1949—after the signing of the North Atlantic Treaty on April 4—as a Western response to fears inspired by the BERLIN BLOCKADE (1948–49). Signing the treaty as original members were the United States, Canada, Iceland, Britain, France, Belgium, the Netherlands, Denmark, Norway, Italy, and Portugal. Greece and Turkey joined in 1952, West Germany in 1955, Spain in 1982.

For the United States, NATO as a peacetime formal military alliance represented a new departure in foreign affairs; the idea did not find immediate universal approval, especially on Capitol Hill, where it encountered opposition not only from traditionalists but also from those who favored greater U.S. involvement in Asia and less in Europe. Where, formerly, the Atlantic Ocean had been regarded as a barrier setting off the New World from the Old, now the concept of the Atlantic community began to win prominence.

Though for many Europeans NATO primarily possessed conceptual importance—as a guarantee that the United States would not abandon them—the alliance began to develop a genuine military organization after the outbreak of the KOREAN WAR, particularly when, on January 1, 1951, U.S. general Dwight D. EISENHOWER became the supreme commander.

In 1966, General DE GAULLE took France out of the Military Committee of NATO, though it remained on the North Atlantic Council, the highest body of the alliance. *See also* ACHESON, Dean; BEVIN, Ernest; PEARSON, Lester Bowles; WARSAW PACT.

Novotný, Antonín (1904–1975)   First secretary of the Czech Communist Party (1953–68) and president of Czechoslovakia (1957–68). Novotný, a hard-core Soviet-oriented Communist who un-

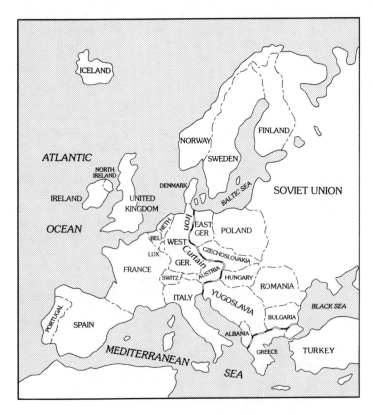

Divided Europe

waveringly followed the line set by the Kremlin, was memorably described by Cuba's Fidel CASTRO as "a clinical case of mediocrity." Novotný was forced to give up his posts during the PRAGUE SPRING of 1968.

NSA   *See* NATIONAL SECURITY AGENCY.

NSC   *See* NATIONAL SECURITY COUNCIL.

NSC-68 (National Security Council Paper 68)
This document, completed in April 1950, was created as a blueprint for U.S. Cold War strategy following the Chinese Communist victory over the Nationalists in 1949 and, more specifically, following the first Soviet nuclear detonation in August 1949. In essence, NSC-68, drafted primarily by Paul NITZE, who had succeeded George F. KENNAN as head of the State Department Policy Planning Staff, gave global scope to the CONTAINMENT policy and also militarized it. To prevent a Soviet-initiated war, the document said, the United States must undertake a massive rearmament program. (In fact, even without NSC-68 a rearmament program was clearly necessary, since the services had greatly deteriorated after World War II, as the beginning phase of the KOREAN WAR would show only two months after the presentation of NSC-68.) The new rearmament program should prepare the country for any kind of war that might develop, conventional or nuclear, the document declared, and expense could not be a prime consideration—as much as 20 percent of the Gross National Product (GNP) should be devoted to it, if necessary, the increase to be achieved through deficit spending. The outbreak of the Korean War in June 1950 ensured the adoption of NSC-68 by the TRUMAN administration and its support in Congress.

Nuclear Nonproliferation Treaty   In July 1963, shortly before the signing of the NUCLEAR TEST BAN TREATY, U.S. president John F. KENNEDY declared that, while time remained, the existing nuclear powers ought to move toward preventing the spread of nuclear weapons to other countries. The great powers feared the consequences if such weapons should fall into the hands of small countries or factions and volatile leaders. Kennedy's as-

sassination came before any progress could be made toward framing the treaty, but his successor, Lyndon B. JOHNSON, took up the cause. After lengthy and complex negotiations, the United States and the Soviet Union reached agreement on the text of a treaty submitted to the UNITED NATIONS General Assembly on June 12, 1968; these two countries and Britain signed the document on July 1. The treaty required countries possessing nuclear arms to refrain from helping other countries acquire them, and it also required nonnuclear countries to make no such attempts. Though declining to sign the treaty, France declared that in the future it would conduct itself "exactly like the signatory states." Cuba's UN representative complained that the treaty "legalized the difference between the strong and the weak."

The treaty had to be regarded as only a beginning. No one was surprised that a variety of countries that had or hoped to acquire nuclear weapons refused to sign it; the list included China, Israel, South Africa, India, and Pakistan. Nevertheless, over a period of some years, the Nonproliferation Treaty succeeded in winning ratification from more than 100 countries. A particularly important signature, which came in 1969, was that of West Germany's Chancellor Willy BRANDT. By this act the chancellor alleviated Soviet fears that the FEDERAL REPUBLIC OF GERMANY might seek to build its own bomb and thus threaten the status quo in Central Europe. Critics of the treaty commented that by giving the illusion that safeguards existed, it tended to diminish international vigilance concerning the spread of weapons technology and material.

Nuclear Test Ban Treaty   On August 5, 1963, three nuclear powers—the United States, the Soviet Union, and Great Britain—signed a treaty requiring them to relinquish the testing of nuclear weapons in the atmosphere, in outer space, and under water. (The treaty is known as the Limited Test Ban Treaty because it did not include underground testing.) This achievement, the first agreement ever created to impose a curb on nuclear development, followed some years of discussion and negotiation, going back to the Geneva SUMMIT conference in 1955; matters moved at a quicker pace after the

CUBAN MISSILE CRISIS of 1962. Behind the agreement lay the scientifically attested poisoning of the atmosphere by radioactive fallout, though the treaty also represented a step in the direction of arms control.

Seeking to find a modus vivendi with the Soviets, and concerned because he had recently felt it necessary to call an end to an informal moratorium on testing, U.S. president KENNEDY increasingly embraced the idea of the treaty, which was also energetically advocated by British prime minister Harold MACMILLAN. On June 10, 1963, Kennedy made the test-ban idea the theme of his commencement speech at American University in Washington, D.C. In calling for peace, the president said, he did not mean "a Pax Americana enforced on the world by weapons." With Soviet premier KHRUSHCHEV already having agreed to hold discussions, Kennedy dispatched to Moscow the veteran diplomatic troubleshooter Averell HARRI-MAN, who deftly negotiated the agreement; a Soviet diplomat said that when he heard Harriman was going to Moscow, he knew Kennedy was serious about the treaty.

The Nuclear Test Ban Treaty excluded underground testing because reliable verification methods did not exist (except for on-site inspections not acceptable to the Soviets)—and agreements between East and West always had to be built on objective fact, not on trust. Within two years, more than 90 other countries also ratified the treaty. Charles DE GAULLE's France, however, took an aloof stance, as had become customary in its international dealings, and the Chinese derided the whole concept of the treaty. They exploded their first atomic bomb on October 16, 1964.

Under the provisions of a second treaty (January 21, 1967), the United States and the Soviet Union pledged themselves not to place nuclear weapons in space.

O

OECD *See* ORGANIZATION FOR EUROPEAN ECONOMIC COOPERATION.

OEEC *See* ORGANIZATION FOR EUROPEAN ECONOMIC COOPERATION.

Ogonyok Soviet weekly picture magazine (in English, *Little Flame*) that played an important part in the GORBACHEV era as an organ of reform, presenting details of Joseph STALIN's misdeeds and reporting on previously taboo subjects like street crime. It featured such novelties as public-opinion polls and candid war reporting (notably, dispatches describing the horrors of the fighting in AFGHANISTAN). This liberal approach irritated conservative Communists who preferred the magazine as it had been in its previous, party-line days. Writing in *PRAVDA*, a group of these conservatives accused *Ogonyok* of slandering members of the party, calling it (as reported by Robert G. Kaiser of the *Washington Post*) a "dirty foam on the new wave" of GLASNOST. The existence of such controversies illustrates the significant fact that Mikhail Gorbachev, on taking power, did not automatically acquire control of the media and numerous other aspects of Soviet life.

Ohio The U.S. Navy developed this large class of nuclear-powered submarines in the 1970s to serve as launching platforms for the new Trident missile—first the Trident I and, from 1989, the Trident II. The *Ohio* became operational in 1982, and by the end of the Cold War 11 sister ships had joined the class. Plans called for the earlier Ohios to be retrofitted with the newer missile. Each submarine carried 24 Tridents and could stay on patrol for 70 days.

Olympic boycott From the American point of view, the 1980 Olympic Games in Moscow became "the Olympics that never were." In December 1979 the Soviet Union sent troops into AFGHANISTAN to intervene in the murderous and complex local politics of the country. This seeming application of the BREZHNEV DOCTRINE to a state that, unlike the countries of Eastern Europe, had never been occupied by Soviet forces evoked an angry and worried response from U.S. president Jimmy CARTER, whose countermeasures included an embargo on grain shipments to the USSR and a boycott, voted by the U.S. Olympic committee, of the 1980 games to be held in Moscow; 61 countries—Canada, West Germany, and Japan among them—joined the United States in the boycott. In 1984 the Soviets and most other EASTERN BLOC members reciprocated by refusing to take part in the Los Angeles games.

Oppenheimer, J(ulius) Robert (1904–1967) American nuclear physicist who during World War II directed the Los Alamos Laboratory, where the first ATOMIC BOMBS were fabricated. In 1953, however, Oppenheimer was declared a security risk because of his objections to escalating potential nuclear destructiveness through development of the HYDROGEN BOMB (and alleged attempts to hinder its production) and also because earlier, in the 1930s, he had associated with known Communists. After the war he became director of the Institute for Advanced Study at Princeton, N.J., and from 1947 to 1952 he served as chairman of the General Advisory Committee of the U.S. ATOMIC ENERGY COMMISSION. In June 1954 the commission permanently removed Oppenheimer's security clearance. In December 1963, however, as a gesture of recompense, the commission honored him with its Fermi Award, presented by President Lyndon B. JOHNSON.

Grappling with the moral responsibility of involvement in scientific research to unleash nuclear power, Oppenheimer once stated, "In some sort of crude sense which no vulgarity, no humor, no overstatement can quite extinguish, the physicists have known sin: and this is a knowledge which they cannot lose."

In 1994, as if to demonstrate that in the world of espionage the last word can be almost impossibly hard to come by, a retired KGB officer, Pavel Sudoplatov, declared that Oppenheimer, Enrico Fermi, and other scientists had willingly made information available to the Soviet Union. Most observers believe these accusations remain to be substantiated. *See also* SAKHAROV, Andrei Dmitrievich; TELLER, Edward.

Orange Alternative   As the Communist governments in Eastern Europe lost their grip on their respective states during the 1980s, various nongovernmental, grassroots political groups began to appear. The emerging of such a "civil society," said the historian Moshe Lewin—one that can affect public opinion and stage independent actions—"marks the start of a new age, from which there is no turning back." Such a group in Poland was the semianarchist Orange Alternative.

Organization for Economic Cooperation and Development (OECD)   *See* ORGANIZATION FOR EUROPEAN ECONOMIC COOPERATION.

Organization for European Economic Cooperation (OEEC)   Body established by West European countries to administer aid received under the MARSHALL PLAN. Having remained in operation after Marshall aid was completed, the OEEC later enlarged itself in December 1960 by including the United States, Canada, and Japan and renamed itself the Organization for Economic Cooperation

and Development (OECD), devoted to the furtherance of free trade.

Orlov, Alexander (1895–1973)   Described by a counterintelligence specialist of the CENTRAL INTELLIGENCE AGENCY as the most "versatile, powerful and productive officer in the 73-year history of the Soviet intelligence services," Alexander Orlov (born Leiba Lazarevich Feldbin) also had perhaps the most unusual career of any Soviet agent. He spent much of his life dodging and deceiving the services both of his own country and of the United States. He had a prominent hand in a variety of operations and countries—notably in Spain, where during the Civil War he was the chief Soviet security representative with the Loyalists and numbered among his accomplishments the training of the agent who murdered Leon Trotsky in Mexico in 1940. Orlov's significance for the Cold War comes from his work in 1934 to recruit and train members of the CAMBRIDGE FIVE spy ring.

"In common with many Jews who were to play a leading role in the birth of the Soviet state," say Orlov's biographers, John Costello and Oleg Tsarev, Orlov reacted instinctively "to the Tsarist pogroms." He believed, he said, "in the program and the promises of Lenin." Becoming a Communist in the revolutionary year of 1917, he worked with the first Bolshevik secret police, the Cheka, and then with its successor, the OPGPU, stationed in Paris and Berlin.

After his accomplishments in London in setting up what became the most notorious and one of the most effective of all spy operations, and his successes in Spain during the Civil War, Orlov in 1938 fled Joseph STALIN's attempt to purge him and launched a second career in the United States as a supposed defector from Communism instead of, as was actually the case, a man trying to preserve his own life. Although taken as a legitimate defector by U.S. intelligence and by numerous politicians who hailed him as a hero, Orlov kept his own counsel about his greatest secrets; in particular, he held to the proposition he had made in a coded letter to Stalin that, if left unmolested, he would not betray Kim PHILBY and the other agents he had recruited years earlier. Nor did any of his recruits reveal his involvement with them; Orlov plays no role in any of the many studies of the

Cambridge ring that appeared before Costello and Tsarev's *Deadly Illusions* (1993), based on newly released KGB files.

Ostpolitik   After becoming, in 1969, the first Social Democratic chancellor of the FEDERAL REPUBLIC OF GERMANY, Willy BRANDT devoted special attention to relations with the GERMAN DEMOCRATIC REPUBLIC and with the Soviet bloc in general. Declaring that "governments have to proceed from the facts as they find them; they have to look ahead and study how today's conditions can be developed into a better future," he launched his *Ostpolitik* (Eastern policy), which led to normalized relations with East Germany, a 1970 renunciation-of-force treaty with the Soviet Union, and a treaty with Poland recognizing the controversial Oder-Neisse Line, originally drawn at the 1945 POTSDAM CONFERENCE, as that country's western boundary. These arrangements came only after considerable discussion and bargaining. The boundary agreement, although it acknowledged an existing fact and thereby relaxed some tensions, did not win universal acclaim from Brandt's constituents, some of whom saw it as the formal renunciation of land that should remain at least potentially German. The efforts Brandt put into carrying out his conciliatory policy toward the East won him the 1971 Nobel Peace Prize.

Eighteen years later, on being awarded the Peace Prize of the German book trade, Václav HAVEL (who had not yet become the Czech president) commented that Ostpolitik "signified, of course, the first glimmer of hope for a Europe without cold war and IRON CURTAIN; yet at the same time—alas—it more than once signified the renunciation of freedom, and hence of a basic condition for any real peace." Whether Ostpolitik and DÉTENTE delayed or accelerated the collapse of Communism in Eastern Europe would remain a complex and much-debated question. In any case, of course, neither Brandt nor anyone else in the world could foresee in 1970 the amazing events that would take place two decades later, best symbolized by the fall of the BERLIN WALL. *See also* CURZON LINE; HALLSTEIN DOCTRINE.

P

Pankow District in northeastern Berlin on the Panke River. When the city was divided into East and West, Pankow (pronounced *Pongko*) fell in East Berlin, bordering the boundary with West Berlin. Because the East German government buildings were situated in the Pankow district, political commentators and reporters often referred to the regime as the Pankow government.

Panmunjom Village in South Korea situated 35 miles north of Seoul on the North Korean border near the city of Kaesong, just south of the 38TH PARALLEL—the line that by Allied agreement in 1945 separated Soviet and U.S. occupation forces. Negotiations for a truce in the KOREAN WAR opened in Kaesong but switched in October 1951 to Panmunjom, where they dragged on until an agreed-upon text was signed on July 27, 1953. The boundary between North and South Korea is marked in Panmunjom, the "truce village," by a foot-wide painted strip of concrete.

Pasternak, Boris (1890–1960) Soviet writer who won worldwide fame in the late 1950s both for his epic novel *Doctor Zhivago* (translated into Italian, 1957; English, 1958) and for the Soviet government's forcing him to decline the 1958 Nobel Prize for literature. Chiefly known earlier in his career as a lyric poet, Pasternak succeeded during the STALIN era in surviving accusations of "formalism" (one of the standard criticisms directed against artists deemed to be lacking in socialist realism), but with *Doctor Zhivago* he drew "thunder and lightning," as Premier Nikita KHRUSHCHEV's son Sergei later wrote, "for giving his manuscript to an Italian publisher"—a move that apparently scandalized everybody. Soviet ideologists pilloried Pasternak, feeding Khrushchev himself with carefully picked-out pages of quotations from the book. Describing what sounds like a typical governmental procedure in the East or West, Khrushchev in retirement commented that probably nobody in the Soviet leadership except the ideological chief, Mikhail SUSLOV, actually read *Doctor Zhivago*, and that probably Suslov was simply briefed by an aide and saw only a one-page reader's summary. Banning *Doctor Zhivago* was a mistake, Khrushchev said— "there's nothing anti-Soviet in it." Because of this move, "the intelligentsia abroad rose up against the Soviet Union, including those members of the intelligentsia who were not against socialism." Despite the fame won by *Doctor Zhivago*, literary critics worldwide generally consider Pasternak's poetry to have been his best and most influential work.

Pathet Lao The principal Communist organization in Laos; the name literally means "Land of the Lao." The origins of the Pathet Lao go back to the early Indochinese Communist Party in the 1920s. During the First Indochina War (against the French), the Pathet Lao worked closely with the VIETMINH, led by HO CHI MINH. In the 1960s, during the VIETNAM WAR, the United States opposed any grant to the Pathet Lao of a share in the government of Laos; the organization's forces withdrew under U.S. attacks to the two northernmost provinces of Laos. After the U.S. departure from Indochina in 1975, however, the Lao People's

Democratic Republic, a Communist-dominated government, was established.

Pauker, Ana (1894–1960) Foreign minister and virtual dictator of Romania for a time in the late 1940s, Ana Pauker (née Rabinsohn) was a veteran Communist, having joined the Romanian party in 1921 and become a member of the Central Committee the following year. As a Communist, she spent much of the 1920s and 1930s in prison, underground, or in exile, and early in World War II went to Moscow as part of an exchange of political prisoners between the USSR and Romania, which then supported Germany. She returned to Romania with the Red Army in 1944 as a major in the KGB (then the NKGB) and became cosecretary of the Communist Party of Romania. After 1948 Pauker and her allies in government lost out in a power struggle with Gheorghe GHEORGHIU-DEJ, although she held her foreign-affairs portfolio until 1952.

Peace Corps U.S. service organization established by executive order of President KENNEDY in March 1961 to send volunteers to THIRD WORLD countries as teachers, health workers, agriculturalists, and the like. This program, observed Andrew M. Scott of the University of North Carolina in its early days, "is a cross between technical assistance and cultural exchange." In return for dedication and willingness to relate closely to the people of the host country, the administrators of the Peace Corps accepted "a fairly low level of technical competence, measured by normal technical assistance standards."

The first Peace Corps volunteer, Tom Livingston of suburban Chicago, went on duty as an English teacher in Ghana in September 1961. Although often attacked by Communists as an agency of imperialism, especially of the CENTRAL INTELLIGENCE AGENCY, the Peace Corps won worldwide admiration and demonstrated its staying power through political changes overseas as well as in the United States. In the first three decades, more than 130,000 Peace Corps volunteers served in more than 100 countries. A notable event occurred in 1978, when a Peace Corps alumnus, Paul Tsongas (1962–64), won election to the U.S. Senate.

peaceful coexistence Expression often identified with Soviet premier Nikita KHRUSHCHEV, who discarded the idea that war between the "capitalist" and the "socialist" camps was inevitable and often declared, in various ways, that the Soviet Union and its system would achieve supremacy over the West by outcompeting it. The concept actually goes back to Lenin, however. By the early 1920s it had become clear both that the Bolshevik Revolution would not be followed by similar revolutions in other countries and that the fledgling Bolshevik state desperately needed to establish trade relations with the West. Lenin made the concession to the need for "accommodation and retreat," which he saw as opening a period of "peaceful coexistence." After World War II Premier Joseph STALIN and his ideological specialist, Andrei ZHDANOV, looked on the world as the two hostile and inevitably warring camps of the original Bolshevik formulation; even so, say some scholars, the concept of peaceful coexistence still had a theoretical place in Soviet doctrine. Addressing the 1952 congress of the Communist Party of the Soviet Union, Stalin's spokesman, Georgi MALENKOV, indicated that the leader himself had given some thought to the concept. Many years later, in 1985, Mikhail GORBACHEV declared to the French Parliament on his first trip to the West as GENERAL SECRETARY that civilization could survive only by "learning to live together, to cohabit side by side on this small planet, mastering the difficult art of taking into account each other's mutual interests. This we call the policy of peaceful coexistence."

Pearson, Lester Bowles (1897–1972) One of the leading advocates and promoters of the Atlantic idea and the NORTH ATLANTIC TREATY ORGANIZATION, Lester Pearson was Canada's most prominent diplomat during the Cold War and held political office as secretary for external affairs and prime minister. For his efforts to mend the situation in the Middle East after the 1956 SUEZ CRISIS—he proposed the creation of the UNITED NATIONS emergency force for the area—Pearson received the 1957 Nobel Peace Prize.

A native of the Toronto area and son of a Methodist minister, Pearson, whose nickname was Mike, saw duty in World War I in Greece in a hospital unit and then switched to the Royal Flying Corps, where his career came to an abrupt end after he crashed on his first solo flight. After returning to the University of Toronto, Pearson went to Oxford, winning his degree in 1923. In 1928, following several years as a history teacher and football and hockey coach, he entered the Canadian diplomatic service; an important aspect of his work during the ensuing period was his attendance at League of Nations meetings. After a brief time back in Ottawa, he went to Washington in 1942 and in January 1945 became Canada's ambassador to the United States. Heavily involved in the planning of the United Nations, the successor to the League of Nations, he found himself attracted to the possibility of becoming the new organization's first secretary-general; Soviet insistence on a European in the job, however, rendered the question moot.

In 1948 Pearson switched from professional diplomacy to political office, becoming secretary of state for external affairs (a seat in Parliament had to be found for him) in the cabinet of Louis ST. LAURENT. In this position he played a large part in the design of the North Atlantic Treaty, signed on April 4, 1949. In January 1958, after the Liberal Party lost a general election, Pearson succeeded St. Laurent as party leader. In 1963 the Pearson-led Liberals defeated John Diefenbaker's Conservatives in a tight campaign in which one of the issues concerned the placing of U.S. nuclear missiles in Canada; some Americans accused Diefenbaker of retreating from an agreed arrangement. While saying he would be ashamed to see Canada go back on its word, Pearson shrewdly pitched his campaign on bread-and-butter issues—the kind Bill Clinton's U.S. presidential campaign three decades later would reduce to the simple formula "It's the economy, stupid!" After five years as prime minister, with his well-earned diplomatic luster dimmed by his inability to quash the corruption of government ministers, Pearson retired. Partisan politics had simply not been his game.

Peng Dehuai (1898–1974) Veteran Chinese Communist general who in April 1951 succeeded LIN BIAO in command of Chinese forces during the KOREAN WAR. In 1954 he became Chinese minister of defense, serving until 1959, when he was removed because of disagreements with MAO ZEDONG.

Penkovsky, Oleg Vladimirovich (1919–1963) Regarded by many Western commentators as the greatest spy of the Cold War on either side, Penkovsky was a GRU (Soviet military intelligence agency) colonel who was recruited in 1961 by the British Secret Intelligence Service, or MI-6, and run jointly with the U.S. CENTRAL INTELLIGENCE AGENCY (the Americans having previously rejected as a provocation his offer to work with them). What led this Soviet intelligence officer to become a double agent? The Soviets later claimed that thoughts of wine, women, and song lured him to the Western side, but former CIA director Allen DULLES dismissed this as "the usual method of discrediting an individual whose motives may, in fact, have been far worthier than they are willing to admit"; Penkovsky, Dulles believed, "had lost faith in the system that employed him."

During a period of about 18 months in 1961 and 1962, Penkovsky turned over some 10,000 pages of Soviet documents to Britain and the United States, a feat of espionage that established him as the most important agent ever operated by the West against the USSR. His material included information about Soviet air defenses, nuclear-battlefield doctrine, and weaknesses in the Soviet missile forces; the last-named knowledge strengthened U.S. president John F. KENNEDY's hand during the CUBAN MISSILE CRISIS. Of particular use in the missile crisis were details of missile-site construction (including the kinds of trucks and tents used) supplied by Penkovsky; this material enabled the Americans to identify the construction in Cuba as sites for ballistic missiles—"offensive missiles," as they were called during the diplomatic discussions. (In the world of intelligence, where little information can categorically be declared final, some held the view that Penkovsky's purpose, either consciously or as an unwitting tool of the Soviet government, was to help bring about the result that actually occurred—the missiles would be withdrawn from Cuba in exchange for a U.S. pledge not to invade the island.)

After Penkovsky came under suspicion, the KGB photographed him in his apartment and followed his trail as he continued to deliver documents, and Soviet agents monitored radio messages to Penkovsky from Allied controls in West Germany. During the missile crisis, on October 22, 1962, as he apparently was leaving Moscow on a vacation trip, Penkovsky was seized by KGB agents. At his public trial, which followed intense interrogation including torture, his connection with the British businessman and agent Greville Wynne, who had been his contact in the USSR, was used as evidence against him; Penkovsky made an unsuccessful effort to protect Wynne before finally confessing. He was executed five days after the trial. Wynne was convicted and imprisoned in 1963 but in 1964 was exchanged for the Soviet spy Gordon LONSDALE (Konon Trofimovich Molody), convicted of espionage in England in 1961.

Pentagon   Imposing both as a building and as a symbol, the Pentagon has served since the 1940s as the headquarters of the U.S. defense effort and as a synonym for the Defense Department, just as *White House* has long stood for the president and his administration. Lying across the Potomac from Washington (in what was previously a wasteland of dumps and shacks called Hell's Bottom) and originally built to bring together army workers scattered throughout the city, the huge building— the largest in the world at the time—was begun in the summer of 1941 and took in its first tenants within a year. Newspaper and magazine stories described the Pentagon with awe, and legends quickly arose, the most famous telling of a Western Union telegraph messenger who innocently wandered into the endless maze of corridors and emerged three days later as a lieutenant colonel. Though General MARSHALL, the army chief of staff, offered to share the Pentagon with the navy, the sailors stayed aloof until a unified Department of Defense came into being in the late 1940s. More than half a century after it was built, the Pentagon continued to have impressive statistics; its telephone switchboard, for instance, remained the largest in the world. During the Cold War and beyond, the very massiveness of the Pentagon led opponents of the United States to employ it as a symbol of the U.S. power and influence they deplored.

Pentagon Papers   In June 1971 the *New York Times* created a sensation by beginning the publication of a mass of classified documents taken from Defense Department files on Southeast Asia.

The papers, which amounted to a history of U.S. decision making during the VIETNAM WAR, had been leaked to Neil Sheehan of the *Times* by Daniel Ellsberg, a former Pentagon official and analyst for the Rand Corporation. Since the documents had not all received presidential approval, they could not be considered as necessarily embodying official U.S. policy. Nevertheless, the documents revealed that the JOHNSON administration had purposefully misled the American public about the conduct and progress of the war. Though all of the material had been produced before he took office, President NIXON reacted violently to the leak of the Pentagon Papers, which he regarded as a highly serious breach of national security. When the administration failed to persuade the courts to forbid the papers' publication ("prior restraint" became a much-discussed phrase), Nixon and his staff established a special, extralegal unit to sniff out the trail of the Pentagon Papers and find the culprit who had leaked them to the press. Called the "plumbers" because their purpose was to plug such leaks, members of the unit broke into a psychiatrist's office looking for information about Ellsberg, one of the doctor's patients, who was rightly suspected as the source of the leaks. Once in action, the plumbers went on to gain unwanted fame in the WATERGATE AFFAIR after they were caught burglarizing the headquarters of the Democratic National Committee in the Washington Watergate complex.

people's democracies   After the end of World War II, as the countries formerly occupied by the Soviet army began to become Communist states making up the EASTERN BLOC, the Soviet Union sought to give them rhetorical appeal for their own populations, and also throughout the world, by characterizing the states as people's democracies. Since the essence of democracy (and the literal meaning of the word) is the vesting of political power in the people, the term *people's democracies* is obviously a tautology. The creators of the term, however, appear to have preferred the resonance of the phrase, as they saw it, to any semantic precision. The term also has a certain appropriateness to the 20th century, during which the world's media have promoted a continual linguistic inflation. What was once a *star* is now a *superstar*, or— more modestly—a *gift* is now a *free gift* and a *friend,* a *personal friend.* So, perhaps *people's democracies* should merely be taken as a symptom of its era.

People's Democratic Party of Afghanistan   Pro-Soviet Afghan Communist party, led by Noor Mohammed Taraki, that staged the April 1978 coup in which the republican government of President Mohammed Daoud was overthrown and he and his whole family murdered. The coup also assured Taraki's ascendancy over a party rival who was actually a KGB agent. Whether or not the Soviet government had a hand in the coup, it signed a treaty of cooperation with the new regime and thereby found itself in a position to be lured into its disastrous AFGHANISTAN adventure.

peredyshka   Russian for "breathing space," this term was sometimes applied to a theory held by Western analysts that Soviet leader Mikhail GORBACHEV, in his early years in power, used talk of reform and freedom to lull the West into an unjustified sense of security, to buy time to build up the Soviet Union after the stagnation of the late 1970s and early 1980s.

perestroika   This term, together with its frequent companion, GLASNOST, came to symbolize around the world the change brought to the Soviet Union by Mikhail GORBACHEV. Where *glasnost,* usually translated as "openness," related to the ability of the people to discuss problems, *perestroika*—"restructuring"—had to do with the nature of the problems themselves.

In addressing a session of the COMMUNIST PARTY OF THE SOVIET UNION CENTRAL COMMITTEE on April 23, 1985, Gorbachev, who had been in office as GENERAL SECRETARY only six weeks, declared, after making a ritual bow to the "major successes" of the Soviet system in the past, that the country must "achieve a substantial acceleration of social and economic progress," which could be reached through "restructuring of the economic mechanism." This development, he went on to say, would involve the loosening of central control and the creating of economic incentives. Perestroika remained a prime theme throughout Gorbachev's time in power, although he later conceded that

even restructuring was not strong enough medicine for the ills of the Soviet economy.

The term *perestroika,* as Archie Brown of Oxford University observed, could be translated in various ways and even in the Soviet Union had various meanings, from economic modernization to bureaucratic restructuring to a more fundamental rebuilding of the system, and it generally took on political as well as economic significance. In any case, Gorbachev, in his efforts at perestroika, found himself opposed by the massive inertia of the long-established bureaucracy and also by some of the party leaders, who took doctrinal exception to his strictures. At one point, in September 1987, a later strong Gorbachev critic, Boris YELTSIN, wrote that perestroika thus far had amounted to "a lot of inflated language for public consumption, while in reality the implementation has been self-serving and bureaucratic."

It was to help him in his campaign for perestroika that Gorbachev summoned the aid of glasnost—"openness and discussion," or, in short, "publicity." Gorbachev offered no precise definition of the new policy—he was feeling his way—and for a time neither the people of his own country nor those in the West could be sure that change had really come to the Soviet government.

Pérez de Cuéllar, Javier (1920–   )   Peruvian public official who succeeded Kurt WALDHEIM as secretary-general of the UNITED NATIONS at the beginning of 1982 and served until 1992. Pérez de Cuéllar had previously represented his country in diplomatic posts in Europe and the Soviet Union and at the United Nations. During his term of office he succeeded in building up the UN as an international stabilizing force and keeper of the peace with a concern for human rights. He guided the organization into the post–Cold War era, in which it assumed greater importance than it had previously possessed.

Pershing   Medium-range missile installed in Europe by the United States in the 1960s. The Pershing had a range of about 450 miles. In the early 1980s a NORTH ATLANTIC TREATY ORGANIZATION plan to deploy Pershing II missiles in Western Europe, as a counter to new Soviet SS-20 missiles, stirred up a wave of protest in Britain and West Germany. The

Javier Pérez de Cuéllar, fifth United Nations secretary-general

Pershing II had a range of 1,560 miles. Although the missiles were installed in the mid-1980s, they had a short active life; they were removed under the 1987 INTERMEDIATE-RANGE NUCLEAR FORCES TREATY (commonly known as the INF Treaty).

Petrov affair   In April 1954 two KGB agents in Australia, Vladimir and Evdokia Petrov, requested political asylum; Mrs. Petrov was literally wrested from the custody of two Soviet agents who were conveying her home to Moscow. Though the Petrovs produced no great revelations about Soviet spying activities in Australia, they did furnish the useful information that, as had been suspected, the missing CAMBRIDGE FIVE spies Guy BURGESS and Donald MACLEAN were in Moscow. They also provided some details about Soviet penetration of French intelligence.

The Petrov case had particular repercussions in Australian politics, since it broke just before the 1954 election. After the expected victors, the Australian Labour Party, turned out the losers, some of its supporters declared that the entire Petrov affair had been staged by the Liberal-Country Party coalition government in collusion with the security service in a dramatic bid to keep the Labour Party out of office. Australian government documents released in the 1980s, however, suggest that the timing of the Petrovs' defection bore no relation to Australian party politics.

"Vladimir Petrov" is said to have been an alias for Afansy M. Shorokhov.

Philby, Harold Adrian Russell (Kim) (1912–1988)
One of the most successful spies of all time, Philby (born in India and always called Kim, after the boy-spy hero of the Rudyard Kipling novel) was a member of the famous CAMBRIDGE FIVE, the group of young agents recruited at the university by the KGB in the 1930s.

After a period of public left-wing display, including marriage to an Austrian Communist, Philby, on the instruction of his Soviet case officer, established himself as a right-wing journalist with a degree of sympathy for the Nazi cause. This successful cover operation led, after his reporting from Spain during the Civil War, to his employment by the British intelligence service (MI6), an arrangement made by Guy BURGESS, another member of the Cambridge Five. Despite his heavy drinking, of which he made no secret, Philby was considered "sound" by his establishment superiors and rose in rank. In 1944 he took on an espionage dream assignment as head of the new anti-Soviet section of MI6, a position in which he could protect the persons he was officially out to get. In 1949 another plum came his way—he became the British intelligence liaison officer with the U.S. CENTRAL INTELLIGENCE AGENCY. In Washington he performed one of his most striking acts of treachery by informing the Soviets of a plan to land a group of anti-Communist exiles on the coast of Albania, thus dooming the operation and the men who attempted to carry it out.

After the disappearance behind the IRON CURTAIN of his friends and fellow agents Burgess and Donald MACLEAN in 1951, U.S. suspicions of Philby—particularly on the part of the CIA's

James J. Angleton, who earlier had defended him—forced Philby's dismissal. In 1956, publicly exonerated but still under heavy suspicion, he was sent to Beirut as, of all things, an MI6 agent, his cover being an assignment as a stringer for the *Observer* and the *Economist*. If the move had a logical basis at all, it was apparently the idea that he would either give himself away as a Soviet agent or prove to be a useful British agent. In January 1963 he disappeared from Beirut, evading a not notably energetic official British attempt to stop him and surfacing publicly six months later at a press conference in Moscow. Nicholas Elliott, the British agent sent to Beirut to confront Philby with evidence of his spying, had previously defended him and helped him make the connection with the *Observer*. But on seeing his old friend, Elliott declared: "I once looked up to you. My God, how I despise you now." (Philby later claimed that the British intelligence service warned him he was under suspicion because it preferred to see him escape rather than find itself the central figure in a security scandal. If so, the service made its last colossal miscalculation concerning Philby.)

Given officer's rank in the KGB (to visitors he claimed, probably falsely, to be a general), Philby married a Russian woman and was set up in a comfortable apartment. In Moscow he produced a memoir, *My Silent War* (1968), in which he seemed to derive great pleasure from taunting former colleagues who had liked and admired him.

Although fully accepted by the British establishment, which had entrusted him with important duties and secrets, Philby declared he had not been a traitor because "to betray, you must first belong. I never belonged."

Phoenix, Operation U.S. Vietnam program, begun in 1968, to stabilize the countryside and reduce the number of VIETCONG (VC) attacks by coordinating intelligence and paramilitary efforts against the Communist organization called the Vietcong Infrastructure (VCI); the South Vietnamese operated a similar program, *Phung Hoang*. Attacked by antiwar critics as an assassination program, Phoenix was defended by its sponsors as including capture, conversion of the enemy to the government side, and inflicting of casualties in combat. After the

VIETNAM WAR, North Vietnamese officials declared Phoenix to have been highly effective.

Picasso, Pablo (1881–1973) For many years during the Cold War, Picasso's drawing of a white dove served Communist and Communist-influenced groups around the world as their official peace symbol. Active in the Communist Party in the late 1940s and early 1950s, Picasso attended party-sponsored "peace conferences" in Wrocław, Paris, Sheffield, and Rome. Asked to design a poster for the Paris conference in 1949, the artist drew inspiration from his pet white pigeon to produce the dove that would become world famous.

Until the Germans bombed the Basque city of Guernica in 1937, Picasso had always refused to ally himself with any political movement, but his outrage over the destruction of the city drove him to paint the great antiwar mural *Guernica* for the Spanish pavilion at the 1937 Paris World's Fair.

Having been persuaded to join the French Communist Party in 1944 as a gesture against Hitler and Franco, Picasso declared: "Until Spain can welcome me back, the French Communist Party has opened its arms to me. I have found there all those whom I esteem the most—the greatest scientists, the greatest poets." Certainly, in Picasso, who for the next three decades would continue to reign as the world's leading artist, the party had acquired one of its most notable and most influential ornaments. But Picasso was hardly a leader of the party; in fact, his commitment to artistic freedom clearly put him in opposition to Soviet cultural requirements and policies. A sort of pragmatic bargain seemed to have been struck. As one critic put it, it "seemed understood" that the artist would "contribute a drawing or a signature to a manifesto," and "in return the party never tried to tell Picasso what to make."

Pieck, Wilhelm (1876–1960) First president of the GERMAN DEMOCRATIC REPUBLIC (East Germany), Pieck was a veteran international Communist who left Germany after the arrival of the Nazis in power in 1933 and became secretary of the Comintern. After World War II he took over the leadership of the German Communist Party and presided over its merger with the Social Democratic Party (creating the Socialist Unity Party) in the Eastern zone of occupied Germany. Elected president of the new East German state by the legislature in October 1949, he won reelection in 1953 and 1957.

ping-pong diplomacy In its careful progress toward the development of normal relations with the People's Republic of China (Communist China), the U.S. NIXON administration decided in March 1971 to remove passport restrictions on American citizens wishing to travel to China. The Chinese responded on April 6 by inviting the U.S. table-tennis team, traveling in Japan, to pay a visit to China, where the game enjoyed great popularity. With the approval of the administration, the team accepted the invitation and, with a full retinue of coaches and reporters, arrived in China on April 10. This piece of "ping-pong diplomacy" represented the first symbolic act on the way toward a new U.S.-Chinese relationship.

Pleven Plan Proposal developed by French economist and planner Jean MONNET and made public on October 24, 1950, by French premier René Pleven (1901–1993) to create an all-European army as a way of involving West Germany in the defense of Western Europe without creating a separate German army. Pleven served twice as premier—1950–51 and again 1951–52. *See also* EUROPEAN DEFENSE COMMUNITY.

Podgorny, Nikolai Viktorovich (1903–1983) Leading Soviet politician in the 1960s and chairman of the Presidium of the SUPREME SOVIET (Soviet president) from 1965 until being removed from office in 1977 by Leonid BREZHNEV, who wished to be the ceremonial head of the government as well as GENERAL SECRETARY of the COMMUNIST PARTY OF THE SOVIET UNION. A native of the Ukraine, a factory worker in his youth, and later an engineer, Podgorny during World War II held Ukrainian and national offices relating to food production. In the following years he became a strong supporter of his fellow Ukrainian political figure Nikita KHRUSHCHEV, rising to full membership of the party Presidium (the POLITBURO) in 1960 and becoming a secretary of the CENTRAL COMMITTEE, and thus a prominent political figure, in 1963. It was apparently at this time that he developed a close rela-

tionship with another Ukrainian and possible rival for power, Leonid Brezhnev. More than a year later, these two, with others, brought down Khrushchev, whose position had actually been shaky for several years. But when Podgorny was named chairman of the Presidium of the Supreme Soviet, on December 9, 1965, in succession to Anastas MIKOYAN, this move indicated he had been outmaneuvered for real power by Brezhnev, who himself had once held this almost purely honorific position. Podgorny nevertheless proved useful in the job, undertaking challenging diplomatic missions such as his 1971 trip to Egypt to try to repair the damage after President SADAT had uncovered a KGB plot to stage a coup against his government and had arrested some 90 conspirators. In 1977, however, when Brezhnev decided that he wanted the presidency again, this unwelcome move meant Podgorny's permanent retirement.

Point Four Often used as a general term for U.S. aid or proposed aid to THIRD WORLD countries, *Point Four* came from U.S. president TRUMAN's 1949 inaugural address. Outlining the four main points of U.S. foreign policy, the president listed: support for the UNITED NATIONS, helping European economic recovery through the MARSHALL PLAN, and military assistance to "freedom-loving" countries. The fourth point, said Truman, should be "a bold new program for making the benefits of our scientific advances and industrial progress available for the improvement and growth of underdeveloped areas." The program, which sent Americans abroad to work in practical ways with local people in such activities as disease prevention, agriculture, and public works, was a forerunner of the PEACE CORPS, created during the KENNEDY administration. Point Four began in 1950 with an appropriation of $34.5 million; within a year Americans were working in more than 30 countries.

Polaris U.S. submarine-launched nuclear-tipped missile developed in the late 1950s. Built by Lockheed, it had a range of some 2,800 miles. Because it could be launched not only from a submarine but from a submerged submarine, the Polaris gave U.S. nuclear forces a far greater flexibility than they had possessed previously when totally dependent on land-based missiles. *See also* SKYBOLT.

Polish uprising, 1956   On the morning of June 28, 1956, shouting "We want bread" and "Down with Communism," workers in a locomotive factory in Poznan erupted into rioting, which brought harsh repression from the Polish army, commanded by the Soviet-appointed Marshal Konstantin ROKOSSOVSKY. But the discontent spread across the country, finally, in October, bringing a visit to Warsaw by Soviet first secretary Nikita KHRUSHCHEV. Fortunately for the Poles, they—unlike the Hungarians during the same period—did not push matters far enough to induce Khrushchev to employ the Soviet army. Instead, Rokossovsky was dismissed, and a former prominent Polish Communist, Władysław GOMUŁKA, was not only reinstated but became premier. He stopped the collectivization of agriculture and allowed increased contacts with Western countries. These moves, however, did not prove to be lasting. *See also* HUNGARIAN REVOLUTION.

Politburo   Literally the "political bureau" of the COMMUNIST PARTY OF THE SOVIET UNION, the Politburo served organizationally as the executive committee or board of directors of the party CENTRAL COMMITTEE, a group of several hundred persons chosen (in theory) by the party congress. This three-tiered hierarchy, with its attached Secretariat, was standard for the party at all levels from the national down to that of the individual factory.

In practice, and certainly during the STALIN era, the GENERAL SECRETARY rather than the Central Committee selected the members of the Politburo, which as a body traced its origin back to October 23, 1917, the date on which Lenin decided to call for a Bolshevik seizure of power in Russia. From the middle 1920s until 1952, the Politburo consisted of 12–13 members; Stalin then raised the membership to 25 and changed the name to Presidium of the Central Committee of the Communist Party. But in 1966 the name reverted to Politburo.

From an actuarial point of view, membership in the Politburo proved during the Stalin era to be decidedly unhealthful: of the 25 persons who served on it, 11 were shot and 3 died either as suicides or under suspicious circumstances. Thus, clearly, the overwhelmingly predominant and continuing influence on the USSR was that of Stalin himself.

Like other Communist Party organizations, the Politburo lost its power in the sweeping political changes of 1990.

Pol Pot (1928–)   Dictator of CAMBODIA (Kampuchea) in the late 1970s, Pol Pot was the head of a movement that professed belief in a utopian society peopled by peasants, but in practice he proved to be, in percentage terms, one of history's greatest mass murderers.

Born to well-off peasant parents and originally named Saloth Sar, Pol Pot was educated in Cambodia and in Paris, where he became involved with the French Communist Party. Back home after 1953, he rose rapidly through the ranks of the Khmer People's Revolutionary Party, becoming, in 1963, its secretary-general. He also developed his own guerrilla organization, the KHMER ROUGE, which he led against the Cambodian governments of Norodom SIHANOUK and LON NOL. After defeating Lon Nol's forces in 1975, Pol Pot and the Khmer Rouge—proclaiming their hostility to Western influences, which they saw as the enemies of the revolution—entered on the most ruthless forced movement of populations in modern history, driving people from the cities of Cambodia into rural work camps. Some two million Cambodians (out of a population of perhaps seven million) are estimated to have perished in Pol Pot's "killing fields" and torture chambers. Like both the USSR's STALIN and China's MAO ZEDONG, Pol Pot established impossible economic goals and then disposed of the "saboteurs" who failed to reach them. His officials were so lacking in practical knowledge that when trouble arose with the water supply in Phnom Penh, they realized that none of them knew where the water in the faucets came from.

Considering the Vietnamese his chief enemies, Pol Pot harassed his neighbors with a series of 1978 border raids, hoping to regain territory lost by Cambodia through the years. But in January 1979, Hanoi, far more powerful, fought back with an invasion that drove the Khmer Rouge out of power and into the countryside. For the next 14 years Pol Pot waged a campaign of terror in the rural areas, until a peace agreement in 1993 officially established a coalition government. Observers, however, did not necessarily conclude that this agreement ensured continuing peace in Cambodia.

Pompidou, Georges (1911–1974) President of France for the last five years of his life, Pompidou had been a World War II associate of General DE GAULLE, whom he served as an aide from 1944 to 1946. A schoolteacher before the war, Pompidou held governmental administrative positions afterward, until joining the Rothschild Frères investment bank in 1955; within four years he had become its administrative head. In 1958, when de Gaulle returned to power, he called on Pompidou to become his personal chief of staff, and in 1962, though Pompidou had no political standing, the general, having become president of France, appointed this faithful associate as premier. Seeing Pompidou as a practical man, who "tended towards cautious attitudes and a circumspect approach," de Gaulle expected to make use of the premier's administrative talents to put the Fifth Republic on a firm footing after the resolution of the crisis in Algeria, but maintained the younger man in office far longer than planned. Though Pompidou lost an early vote in the National Assembly, de Gaulle reappointed him after winning a national plebiscite.

In 1968 Pompidou's resourceful handling of the students and workers who led the May revolt against the government showed that his six years in office had given him considerable political skill. Two months later, however, de Gaulle dismissed his right-hand man. In 1969, after the general resigned the presidency, Pompidou ran for the office and won a solid victory. Though a Gaullist, as president he—as was hardly surprising—proved more flexible than the general in his dealings with other countries; in particular, he canceled de Gaulle's veto of British membership in the EUROPEAN ECONOMIC COMMUNITY (the Common Market).

Popular Movement for the Liberation of Angola Marxist faction in the 1970s Angolan civil war. Aided by more than 15,000 Cuban troops sent by Fidel CASTRO and supplies furnished by the Soviet Union, the Popular Movement took control of Angola in 1976. Unita rebels, however, backed by the United States and South Africa, battled on in this proxy Cold War struggle until the signing of an armistice in May 1991. In October, after contesting the results of an election, the Unita forces resumed fighting.

Poseidon U.S. submarine-launched nuclear-tipped missile, similar to, but newer and larger than, the POLARIS. Built by Lockheed, it had a range of some 2,800 miles.

Potsdam Conference Sometimes called the BERLIN Conference, this meeting—held from July 17 to August 2, 1945—was the last Allied Big Three conference of World War II. For the first time, Harry S. TRUMAN, who succeeded President ROOSEVELT upon the latter's death on April 12, represented the United States. Winston CHURCHILL began the conference as head of the British delegation, but on July 28, after the results of a general election were determined, he was replaced by the Labour Party leader, Clement ATTLEE. Thus, at the end, only Soviet premier Joseph STALIN remained of the original Big Three who first met at Tehran in November 1943.

From a Cold War perspective, of particular significance at Potsdam were discussions devoted to the administrative, economic, and political questions concerning control of Germany. To coordinate occupation policies, the leaders established the Allied Control Council, but this body had no authority over developments within each individual zone, and since council actions would require unanimity, each member could veto any proposal it disliked. Thus overall occupation policies would depend not on any structural arrangement but solely on voluntary agreement among the occupying powers. For Berlin, which all regarded as a special case, the Big Three created the Allied Kommandatura to exercise joint control of the city (which also would have its separate zones) and to supervise the municipal government that was supposed to be elected in due course.

Economic matters created a number of vexing questions. Demanding, with understandable insistence, that Germany make reparation for the dam-

A famous photo from the Potsdam Conference *(l. to r.):* British prime minister Winston Churchill, U.S. president Harry S. Truman, and Soviet marshal Joseph Stalin display three-way friendship.

age wreaked by the armies that had invaded the USSR, the Soviets obtained the assent of the United States and Britain; the reparations would come not from current German production but from the removal of factories and other facilities and equipment from Germany to the Soviet Union. Since, as a popular joke put it, the zonal division of Germany had given the Russians the farms, the British the factories, and the Americans the scenery, one of the Potsdam provisions called for the Soviets to supply the other zones with agricultural products in exchange for the industrial equipment they were to receive. The occupying powers were supposed to treat Germany as "one economic whole," but in practice this agreement produced endless wrangling, with the Soviets failing to deliver the farm products it called for. In consequence, the Western powers suspended the delivery of factories and equipment in the spring of 1946.

In territorial matters, the conference gave specific shape to agreements reached by the Big Three a few months earlier at the YALTA CONFERENCE. East Prussia was partitioned between the USSR and Poland. The area of Germany east of the Oder and Neisse Rivers was transferred to Poland—an arrangement supposedly for administrative purposes and subject to final action by the anticipated peace conference, but which, with its expulsion of millions of Germans from the area, would prove to be permanent. (The boundary would be confirmed in a 1970 treaty as a result of West German chancellor Willy BRANDT's OSTPOLITIK policy.)

The Allied leaders also established the Council of Foreign Ministers, which received the assignment of preparing peace treaties for the defeated members of the Axis: Bulgaria, Hungary, Finland, Italy, and Romania. Despite all the problems that arose between East and West in the next 18 months, by February 1947, following a series of meetings in Paris, the mission had been fulfilled; the treaties were signed on February 10.

During the Potsdam Conference, President Truman received word that far away in New Mexico the first test of an ATOMIC BOMB had been "successful beyond the optimistic expectations of anyone." After talking the matter over with Churchill, the president quietly informed Stalin that the United States had a new weapon "of unusual destructive force." Stalin took this good news in stride, remarking only that he hoped the Americans would "make good use of it against the Japanese." As later revelations would show, until quite recently Stalin had known far more about the A-bomb than had Truman himself, thanks to the espionage activities of Klaus FUCHS and other Soviet agents (Truman had not been told about the bomb before assuming the presidency); however, information about the successful test could not yet have reached Stalin through his clandestine channels.

Some commentators have held that the news made Truman cocky and disinclined to deal fairly with Stalin. But one of the most striking facts about the diplomacy of the era was that during the very month of the Potsdam Conference, the U.S. State Department warned the president not to allow the British to lure him into supporting any settlement in Europe based on spheres of influence. Such a policy, the president's advisers said in essence, would not be well received either in the Soviet Union or in the United States.

POWs *See* PRISONERS OF WAR.

Prague Spring In 1968 the Czechoslovak Communist Party leader Alexander DUBČEK presided over an effort to create a democratic socialist regime—"socialism with a human face." This "Prague Spring," as it became known, followed several years of lively cultural activity that had existed independent of the Communist Party, with prominent contributions coming from the novelist Milan Kundera and the playwright Václav HAVEL. Having become party first secretary in January 1968, Dubček, who advocated the separation of govern-

mental and party functions, began to loosen the prevailing tight controls on the press and on foreign travel and generally to advocate governmental support of human rights. He aimed, more or less, at leading Marxism-Leninism along a democratic and reformist path, but also sought freedom for Czechoslovakia to develop its own domestic and foreign policies independent of Soviet dictation. Neither he nor Havel and the other liberal writers believed, however, that Czechoslovakia could go so far as to declare full independence without risking the whole reform effort. But control proved difficult to exercise. A manifesto drawn up by a group of intellectuals, the "TWO THOUSAND WORDS," which called for thoroughgoing democracy, proved so reflective of popular sentiment that citizens of all backgrounds flocked to sign it.

These attitudes and events concerned not only the Kremlin but also the leaders of Czechoslovakia's neighboring WARSAW PACT states, who denounced them. Moreover, the course of the Prague Spring deeply threatened leading Czech officials in the antireform camp; they secretly sent the Soviet authorities two letters pointing to "an anti-Communist and anti-Soviet psychosis" and urging them to intervene with military force to put down "the imminent danger of counterrevolution." Russian president Boris YELTSIN turned over these letters, contained in a file marked "NEVER TO BE OPENED," to the Czech government in July 1992.

During the night of August 20–21, 1968, troops of the Warsaw Pact states invaded Czechoslovakia. Czechs reacted by removing street signs so that the invaders would not know where they were and by putting up posters depicting the Russians, in Kundera's words, as "a circus of illiterates"; people in the streets jeered at the invading troops. Interviewed in the 1990s, senior Polish and Hungarian commanders acknowledged that after entering Czechoslovakia and seeing the existing situation, their troops were both confused and dismayed—they had been told they were coming to the defense of an ally threatened by American "imperialists" and West German "revanchists." After being hauled away to the USSR, Dubček and his colleagues underwent pressure strong enough to cause them to give their approval to the invasion. When Dubček returned to Prague, wrote Kundera, "he was so devastated after his six-day detention he could hardly talk; he kept stuttering and gasping for breath."

Although the invasion resulted from a complex play of forces within the Kremlin and the EASTERN BLOC, Leonid BREZHNEV, the Soviet leader, declared several weeks later that the USSR had the duty to intervene, without regard to national boundaries, anywhere "socialism" was threatened by moves toward "the restoration of capitalism." In the West this declaration was dubbed the BREZHNEV DOCTRINE. But for once, wrote Kundera, the Russians had committed their crimes in the open, with the evidence preserved in stills and motion pictures "stored in archives throughout the world." *See also* VELVET REVOLUTION.

Pravda   The best-known Soviet newspaper, *Pravda* (in English, *Truth*) was established by the Bolsheviks in St. Petersburg in 1912, under the aegis of Lenin and with the involvement of Joseph STALIN, though the latter did not play the major role he subsequently ascribed to himself; he did, however, serve for a time as editor, until removed on Lenin's orders. During World War I, under the czarist regime, publication of *Pravda* was forbidden, but it resumed at the time of the February revolution in 1917. An early editor was the leading Communist intellectual Nikolai Bukharin (1888–1938), who later briefly edited the government newspaper *IZVESTIA. Pravda* served as the chief Communist Party organ until August 1991, when its editors made the mistake of supporting the attempted coup against Soviet president Mikhail GORBACHEV. Publication was suspended following this severe miscalculation; after the dispossession of the COMMUNIST PARTY OF THE SOVIET UNION, *Pravda* reappeared as an independent newspaper.

Prevention of Nuclear War, Agreement on the   Accord designed to ensure the avoidance of misunderstandings in international crisis situations. Reached during Soviet leader Leonid BREZHNEV's visit to Washington in June 1973, this agreement was one of a series of arrangements made between the United States and the Soviet Union during the first half of the 1970s, going back to the beginning of STRATEGIC ARMS LIMITATION TALKS (SALT) in 1969 and favored by both Brezhnev and President NIXON.

Prime case   In July 1982 British prime minister Margaret THATCHER confirmed reports that a Russian-language translator, Geoffrey Arthur Prime (1938?–   ), had been arrested on a charge of violating the Official Secrets Act. Though the prime minister gave few details, her statement followed widespread rumors about a major espionage case involving poor security at the British signal-intelligence nerve center, the GOVERNMENT COMMUNICATIONS HEADQUARTERS (GCHQ) at Cheltenham.

The rumors did not prove to be exaggerations. As later became evident, Prime ranked with John Anthony Walker, Jr., of the WALKER SPY RING in the United States as one of the most important of all KGB Cold War agents. By a remarkable coincidence, Prime and Walker offered their services to the KGB at the same time—January 1968—and both had access to high-level communications.

Prime, in 1968 a British army corporal working in signal intelligence in Germany, simply gave a Soviet officer a note indicating his willingness to spy for the KGB, and a series of meetings ensued; although professing admiration for the Soviet Union, Prime also took payments of about £40 a session. Back in England after being discharged in late summer, Prime, having been trained by his spymasters in the use of DUBOKs and other trappings of espionage, succeeded in getting himself hired as a translator at Government Communications Headquarters, first in London and later at the Cheltenham center. In this work he acquired and passed on thorough intelligence concerning GCHQ operations and personnel, including information about U.S. procedures. Officials in Washington said that the quantity and quality of the material Prime supplied his Soviet controllers about American and British interception of Soviet communications made his case one of the most damaging Soviet penetrations of Western intelligence since World War II. Precise assessment of the damage remained difficult, said a U.S. intelligence official, because "you never can tell for sure what led the Russians to change encryption systems or switch to different channels. It's what you don't know in a case like this that scares you most."

Unlike other prominent British KGB agents such as the CAMBRIDGE FIVE, Prime was not a university graduate but attended a small technical college. "There's no doubt he is highly intelligent," said the head of a local taxi company where Prime worked after wearying of his government job and drifting away from it in 1977. "Anyone who can do the *Times* or the *Daily Telegraph* crossword puzzles in 40 minutes must be."

In the pattern of many underground agents, Prime was a loner with a troubled private life. In his case, his particular problems manifested themselves in child molestation, beginning in the early 1960s with obscene telephone calls. His spying activities came to light only after his arrest in 1982 on three charges of assaulting young girls.

Prime's unsociable nature had attracted little attention at GCHQ; as an official report said, the nature of the work caused it to attract "many odd and eccentric characters." Prime's boss at the taxi company professed a similar outlook. Expressing no surprise on hearing that his former driver had worked in intelligence, he observed that "taxi drivers come in all kinds."

prisoners of war (POWs)   Had a large number of U.S. servicemen taken prisoner during the KOREAN WAR and the VIETNAM WAR been kept as prisoners despite official denials? And, in the case of those captured in Korea, had any of them been transferred to the Soviet Union, as had often been rumored since the war ended? Americans could not let these questions go unanswered.

In 1993 American researchers working in Russian intelligence archives discovered documents indicating that North Vietnam had held far more prisoners of war than it acknowledged having at the end of the war; since 1973 the fate of some 2,200 U.S. servicemen had remained in question. Until 1995, this issue prevented the establishment of normal diplomatic relations between the United States and Vietnam.

In 1954 and again in 1956 the U.S. government had received Soviet denials when questions were raised about U.S. prisoners unaccounted for in Korea. Many years later, in 1992, Russian president Boris YELTSIN stated that, according to Soviet records, 59 U.S. servicemen captured in Korea had been interrogated by Soviet officials and 12 crew members of U.S. aircraft shot down on reconnaissance missions not related to the Korean conflict were taken to the USSR. Then, in 1993, after piecing together information from various American

and Russian sources, the U.S. government handed the Russian government a report titled "The Transfer of U.S. Korean War POWs to the Soviet Union." This transfer, said the report, "was mainly politically motivated with the intent of holding them as political hostages, subjects for intelligence exploitation and skilled labor within the camp system"; the United States believed that the Soviets had hunted for American pilots who could provide information about U.S. Air Force operations and aircraft. One instance of this had been reported in 1992, when a former Marine Corps corporal whose story seemed to have been ignored since the 1950s told how he had been interrogated, probably in China, by Soviet officers for two days and then returned to a POW camp in Korea, apparently because his questioners realized that he was not a pilot. The new U.S. conclusions amounted to a complete reversal of previous statements that the government had no evidence of such transfers. The news drew bitter accusations from POW activist groups. One officer said flatly that "the U.S. government lied and deceived families by saying their family members were dead when the government knew there were live POWs from the Korean War in Russia."

Profumo affair   On June 4, 1963, the British secretary of state for war, John Profumo (1915–), resigned his office, thus admitting the truth of accusations regarding his involvement in a sex-and-security scandal that had claimed the attention of newspaper readers around the world. Earlier, in March, Profumo had told the House of Commons that his friendship with a 21-year-old call girl named Christine Keeler had "no impropriety whatsoever" about it. Actually, however, Keeler had served as Profumo's sometime mistress since the summer of 1961, when the two met by the swimming pool at Cliveden, the famous country house of the Astor family, in an encounter stage-managed by a London society osteopath and procurer, Stephen Ward.

The security aspect of the affair arose when Keeler told reporters that, besides Profumo, her clients and lovers included one Captain Yevgeny Ivanov, an attaché at the Soviet embassy who was actually a GRU—military intelligence—officer for whom the ensnaring of the British war minister could represent a considerable coup. When, after Profumo's original denial, Ward told officials the war minister was lying, Prime Minister Harold MACMILLAN put fresh pressure on Profumo, who then admitted the truth. A government investigation concluded at the time, gently, that the whole matter amounted essentially to a case of moral misbehavior, for which Her Majesty's Government could hardly take responsibility.

In fact, however, as soon as the Profumo-Keeler relationship had been established, Ivanov had wasted no time in trying to acquire, through Ward, information about U.S. plans to place nuclear weapons in West Germany. A heavily compromised war minister could obviously have been of considerable potential use to Soviet intelligence; Profumo's resignation, of course, removed the grounds for these hopes. From another point of view, though, Ivanov may well have achieved his purpose by causing Profumo's disgrace and thus bringing down a Tory government. Lord Denning, the government's investigator, also suggested that Ivanov and his masters may have aimed at dividing Britain from the United States by shaking American confidence in the reliability of British government ministers.

The British newspaper mogul and Conservative politician Lord Beaverbrook professed astonishment at the whole business. "Why in God's name," he cried, "should a great political party tear itself to rags and tatters just because a minister's fucked a woman?" But despite Beaverbrook's bafflement, the Profumo scandal did, in fact, play a large part in bringing about Macmillan's resignation later in 1963, and to some extent it affected the outcome of the general election of October 1964, when the Conservatives lost control of the House of Commons by just four seats.

Project K Code name for the location and building of U.S. NATIONAL SECURITY AGENCY headquarters at Fort Meade, Md. (1954–57).

psykhushka Russian term for the psychiatric ward of a hospital. This word took on political significance when, particularly during the BREZHNEV era, the Soviet government, instead of shooting certain dissidents or even confining them in conventional prisons, sent them on open-ended sentences to "special" psychiatric hospitals, publicly treating these dissenters as though their dissidence indicated insanity instead of conventional criminality. *See also* MEDVEDEV, Zhores.

Public Against Violence One of the two citizen coalitions, along with Václav HAVEL's CIVIC FORUM, that took the lead in the Czechoslovak 1989 VELVET REVOLUTION. Public Against Violence was the Slovak counterpart of the Czech Civic Forum.

Pueblo **incident** The North Korean capture, on January 23, 1968, of an essentially unarmed U.S. electronic-surveillance ship, the *Pueblo,* caused an uproar in the United States. Concentrating on recovering the crewmen, however, President JOHNSON resisted demands for military action against North Korea ("I do not want to win the argument," he told his advisers, "and lose the sale"). After almost a year of effort, U.S. representatives succeeded in negotiating the release of the 82 crewmen (one had been killed in the capture), though the whole affair was tainted by crew members' supposed confession that the *Pueblo* was in North Korean territorial waters when its captors, a submarine chaser and three patrol boats, seized it. Since such intelligence-gathering activities had been practiced for years by both the United States and the Soviet Union, the basic question had to do with the motives and timing of the seizure. Johnson later decided that the operation represented an attempt to distract U.S. attention and perhaps divert U.S. strength from South Vietnam, where (unbeknownst to him at the time, of course) the TET OFFENSIVE would be unleashed in just eight more days.

Pugwash conferences International meetings held in the 1950s and 1960s, officially unofficial, to discuss disarmament. Inspired by the British philosopher and mathematician Bertrand RUSSELL, the first such meeting, convened in July 1957 by Cyrus Eaton, a Cleveland financier and industrialist, was held at his summer home in Pugwash, Nova Scotia. Scientists and others, sometimes quite high-level persons, from East and West attended Pugwash conferences, which were held in the United States, the Soviet Union, and other countries.

Q

Q-5 Twin-engine turbojet attack aircraft designed in the People's Republic of China and built at the Nanchang state factory; first flown in 1972. The Q-5 (designated A-5 in the export model) had a maximum speed of about 750 mph and could carry more than 4,000 pounds of bombs.

Quemoy and Matsu Small coastal islands that remained in the possession of the Nationalist Chinese government after it migrated to TAIWAN in 1949. Though belonging to the Taiwan government, the islands (Quemoy is actually a group of four tiny islands) lie only a few miles from the mainland; the Quemoy group screens the harbor of Amoy, and Matsu is just east of Foochow. Since the islands are located about 100 miles from Taiwan but right on the mainland's doorstep, they served as advance bases for Nationalist raids on the coast and continuing irritants to the Chinese Communist government. On September 3, 1954, Communist artillery began pouring heavy fire on the islands—an action that immediately put the United States in a delicate and, in some respects, absurd position. CHIANG KAI-SHEK's Nationalists obviously could not hold Quemoy and Matsu without U.S. support, but the islands actually had no sort of strategic value worth running the risk of war. To abandon the Nationalists, however, would, in the view of Secretary of State John Foster DULLES, cause the United States to lose credibility with its allies in Southeast Asia. On the other hand,

Americans not enamored of Chiang feared that the Nationalists might use the crisis to involve the United States in a war with the Chinese Communists to try to reestablish themselves on the mainland.

In December 1954 the United States signed a treaty of mutual assistance with the Taiwan government. A very interesting letter supplemented this document. It declared that only by mutual agreement could force be used to defend the islands; thus the United States simultaneously reaffirmed its support for Taiwan and ensured that Chiang would take no offensive action without the approval of Washington. Shortly afterward, Congress passed the Formosa Resolution, empowering the president to use force, if necessary, to defend Taiwan (then called Formosa). (Among senators who tried, unsuccessfully, to have Quemoy and Matsu excluded from this umbrella of protection was John F. KENNEDY.) In the spring the crisis heated up for a time, but it soon became a side issue because of diplomatic events elsewhere in the world. Yet in 1958 the Chinese Communists again began putting pressure on the islands, and U.S. president EISENHOWER ordered the U.S. Seventh Fleet into the Taiwan Strait; the Communists eased the pressure by bombarding the islands only on alternate days and taking care not to hit U.S. facilities. Backstage diplomatic efforts then succeeded in defusing this crisis.

Overall, Quemoy and Matsu had taught the participants two lessons: Chiang would get no support in any attempt to attack the mainland, and the Communist Chinese could expect no support from the Soviets in their attempt to assert their sovereignty; KHRUSHCHEV had made his disapproval plain. Concerning the entire Quemoy-Matsu affair, MAO ZEDONG once commented, "Who would have thought, when we fired a few shots at Quemoy and Matsu, that it would stir up such an earth-shattering storm?" And indeed, for a time it had appeared that a major war might explode from those shots fired at a few small and inconsequential islands.

R

RA-5C U.S. Navy supersonic twin-engine attack aircraft, operated from carriers. Named the Vigilante, the RA-5C was built by North American, first flew in 1958, and served through the following two decades. Planning for the RA-5C began even before the airplane it was to replace, the Douglas A3D Skywarrior, had entered service. Though intended to carry nuclear weapons, the Vigilante found its real role, beginning in 1964, in reconnaissance and performed heavy duty during the VIETNAM WAR as a reconnaissance/attack aircraft. Its two General Electric engines, with afterburners, gave the plane a top speed of Mach 2.1; it cruised at 560 mph with a range of 2,650 miles.

Radford, Arthur William (1896–1973) Second chairman of the U.S. JOINT CHIEFS OF STAFF, succeeding General Omar N. Bradley in August 1953, Admiral Radford was a naval aviator who won his wings in 1920. A native of Chicago, he graduated from the U.S. Naval Academy in 1916. In World War II Radford commanded a carrier task force in the Pacific; later he was commander in chief of the Pacific Fleet. In this capacity he played an important part in the conference leading to the signing of the ANZUS PACT in the summer of 1951.

As chairman of the Joint Chiefs, the admiral proved to be a strong and consistent hawk, beginning in March and April 1954 with his advocacy of a plan to assist the French in Vietnam by sending aircraft from Philippine bases to bomb VIETMINH forces besieging DIEN BIEN PHU (Operation VULTURE). President EISENHOWER, however, did not authorize the operation.

After serving as chairman of the Joint Chiefs until 1957, Radford retired from the navy.

Radio Free Europe With operating headquarters in Munich, the Radio Free Europe organization, established in 1950, maintained a five-station network, with (in the 1960s) 32 transmitters located in West Germany and Portugal broadcasting to the countries of the EASTERN BLOC, except the Soviet Union, in their native languages. According to surveys, Radio Free Europe's more than 500 hours a week of programming—political commentary, entertainment, sports, religious features—regularly reached more than 25 million people. Ostensibly a private endeavor maintained by Radio Free Europe, Inc., in New York, RFE was actually operated by the International Organizations Division of the CENTRAL INTELLIGENCE AGENCY. In 1973, as the result of publicity given to the CIA's involvement in this and other "counter-Communist" programs, the management of Radio Free Europe and RADIO LIBERTY was transferred to a new entity, chartered by Congress, called the Board of International Broadcasting. Radio Free Europe continued to enjoy great popularity in Central and Eastern Europe after the lifting of the IRON CURTAIN. *See also* CONGRESS FOR CULTURAL FREEDOM.

Radio Liberty Similar in concept to RADIO FREE EUROPE, Radio Liberty, established in 1951, broadcast programming to the Soviet Union 24 hours a day, in 17 languages, from 14 transmitters in Spain and West Germany and 3 on Taiwan. Officially sponsored by the Radio Liberty Committee, Inc., the network was, like Radio Free Europe, a project of the International Organizations Division of the CENTRAL INTELLIGENCE AGENCY, and control of it was also transferred in 1973 to the Board of International Broadcasting. Like Radio Free Europe, it kept its popularity after the lifting of the IRON CURTAIN.

Rákosi, Mátyás (1892–1971) The strongly Stalinist premier (1952–53) and Communist Party leader of Hungary (1944–56), Rákosi ranked among the most detested of all EASTERN BLOC political figures. A native of Budapest (né Róth) and a Communist as a young man, he spent 13 years in the prisons of the fascist-oriented Horthy regime before being released in 1940. Having spent most of World War II in Moscow, he returned home with the Red Army to take charge of the Hungarian Communist Party.

In 1949 Rákosi ordered the arrest of László Rajk, the foreign minister, on the grounds of Rajk's having maintained connections with Marshal TITO, at the time a treasonable course of action for a Stalinist. When Rajk refused to confess to the fabricated crimes of which he was accused, Rákosi ordered Rajk's close friend János KÁDÁR to promise the prisoner a safe-conduct out of the country in exchange for an admission of guilt. Kádár did as he was told and Rajk dutifully confessed, as his part of the bargain, but Rákosi failed to make good on his promise; instead, he ordered Rajk hanged.

After Soviet premier Joseph STALIN's death in March 1953, Rákosi found little favor with the new masters of the Kremlin, Georgi MALENKOV and then Nikita KHRUSHCHEV. The latter ordered Rákosi removed as party first secretary in July 1956, but by then Rákosi's harshly repressive rule had created the conditions that exploded in the October HUNGARIAN REVOLUTION. The fallen dictator did, however, leave the world a verbal legacy. He originated the term *SALAMI TACTICS* to describe the technique for taking over a non-Communist government in the aftermath of World War II.

Rapacki Plan Proposal presented to the UNITED NATIONS General Assembly in October 1957 by the foreign minister of Poland, Adam Rapacki (1909–1970), to establish a nuclear-free zone in Central Europe including East and West Germany, Poland,

and Czechoslovakia. This development was to be followed by negotiations for German reunification. The plan, which represented Soviet first secretary Nikita KHRUSHCHEV's emphasis on competition and PEACEFUL COEXISTENCE rather than confrontation—and also, presumably, his acknowledgment of the USSR's nuclear inferiority to the United States—found little favor with the countries in the NORTH ATLANTIC TREATY ORGANIZATION because they viewed nuclear weapons as a counterweight to WARSAW PACT superiority in conventional weapons and troop strength. Although NATO members would hardly have agreed with the proposals in any case, Khrushchev did not help his cause by such public comments as his boasting about the missile might with which the USSR could attack the United States.

Reagan, Ronald Wilson (1911–) In 1966, Ronald Reagan gave up his job as host of the television program *Death Valley Days* to seek the biggest role of his life—governor of California. Drawing on his experience as a movie actor to make effective use of his easy, confidence-inspiring manner, Reagan defeated the incumbent governor, Edmund "Pat" Brown, by almost one million votes. But, as it turned out, this triumph was merely a beginning. Fourteen years later, as the Republican nominee for president of the United States, Reagan defeated the incumbent president, Jimmy CARTER, by more than 8 million votes (and by a margin of 489 to 49 in the Electoral College), thus becoming the first self-acknowledged actor to win the White House. Running for reelection four years later, with a larger popular vote cast on both sides, the Reagan/BUSH ticket outpolled Democrats Walter Mondale and Geraldine Ferraro by almost 17 million votes.

Having grown up in small towns in northern Illinois, Reagan graduated from Eureka College in 1932 with a degree in economics and sociology but, following the advice of his high school drama teacher, decided to seek a career in communications. Before long his broadcasts of Chicago Cubs baseball games over station WHO in Des Moines made his warm, friendly voice familiar in households across the Middle West. Reagan dreamed, however, of becoming a movie actor, and in 1937, while he was in California with the Cubs during spring training, an episode occurred that could have come directly from a movie script. Seeking an actor to play a radio announcer, a talent scout for Warner Brothers spotted him, and a new career began. Reagan's most famous movie role came in 1940, when he played the part of a Notre Dame football player, George Gipp—the Gipper—in *Knute Rockne, All American.* Contrary to what has often been said, Reagan displayed considerable talent as an actor, most notably in the 1942 film *King's Row.*

A Democrat for most of his career in Hollywood, Reagan involved himself actively in union affairs, but by the early 1950s he had moved to the right. A speech in support of Barry GOLDWATER delivered at various times through the 1964 campaign turned Reagan from a media star campaigning on behalf of a candidate into a political figure in his own right. The impact of "the speech," as it became known, propelled him into candidacy for the governorship of California in 1966. (Reagan's administration opened with a scene that could have been snipped from one of the famous Hollywood screwball comedies of his early acting days. He took the oath of office and began signing documents six days before his term began, thinking he was simply subscribing to a loyalty oath and notarizing standard forms.)

On assuming office in 1981 as the 40th president of the United States, Reagan, fulfilling campaign pledges, took various economic steps to combat the existing 11.2 percent inflation and 20 percent interest rates. After weathering a severe recession, he went into the late stages of the 1984 presidential campaign with inflation reduced to 4.3 percent, incomes going up, and the stock market on a prolonged rise. By the end of his time in office, inflation stood at 4.4 percent and unemployment at 5.3 percent, the lowest level since the 1974 oil crisis. In counterbalance, Reagan's policies had produced enormous budget deficits, turning the United States from the world's largest creditor into one of its biggest debtors. In his characteristically insouciant way, Reagan liked to hold Congress responsible for the red ink, although almost all of it was contained in the budgets he sent up to Capitol Hill.

In foreign affairs, Reagan quickly established himself as the West's most vocal anti-Communist, and along with his words he produced action, presiding over an enormous military buildup that would ultimately cost more than two trillion dollars. In 1983, the year in which he proposed the development and deployment of an antimissile system called the STRATEGIC DEFENSE INITIATIVE (SDI), he castigated the Soviet Union as the "EVIL EMPIRE." But in his second term the picture evolved, in step with changes in the world brought about by Mikhail GORBACHEV's ascent in the USSR. British prime minister Margaret THATCHER, an ideological near-twin of Reagan, perceived that Gorbachev represented something new in Soviet politics and hastened to Washington to bring the message. Economic problems in the USSR, important among them the pressures resulting from the U.S. defense buildup (including SDI), played their part in producing Soviet liberalization and a nonconfrontational stance toward the West to which Reagan proved responsive. According to his secretary of state, George SHULTZ, the president "was a leader in saying the United States must be strong, but he parted company with . . . [many of his conservative supporters] in saying we must negotiate with the Soviets on the basis of that strength." In December 1987 Reagan and Gorbachev signed a new kind of arms agreement, the INTERMEDIATE-RANGE NUCLEAR FORCES TREATY, which instead of merely limiting growth in stocks of weapons actually called for the destruction of medium-range missiles. Overall, the two men held four SUMMIT meetings, at one of which they were seen walking arm in arm across Red Square.

The great scandal of the Reagan years, the IRAN-CONTRA AFFAIR, resulted from the president's strong and consistent desire to liberate Americans held hostage in Lebanon. In late 1986 the nation learned that, despite Reagan's often-proclaimed policy of refusing to make concessions to terrorists, his administration had sent weapons to the radical government of Iran in an attempt to induce the Iranians to put pressure on terrorists in Lebanon to release the Americans held in captivity. Although it had its obvious negative aspects (including the misleading of U.S. allies), this effort at least showed the administration's determination to win freedom for the hostages. But very soon an additional aspect of the arrangement came to light: officials of the NATIONAL SECURITY COUNCIL, including the president's national security adviser, Admiral John Poindexter, and Marine Lieutenant Colonel Oliver North, had taken some of the profits resulting from the arms deals and used them to support the CONTRAS operating against the SANDINISTAS in Nicaragua. Professing not to know about this aspect of the affair, Reagan—dubbed "the Teflon president" by Colorado congresswoman Patricia Schroeder—emerged from the situation somewhat damaged, but less criticism stuck to his "Teflon" surface than might have been expected. A special investigating commission determined that part of the problem lay in Reagan's loose management style—hardly a surprising conclusion in view of the president's well-known aversion to detail.

In summing up the Reagan administration, a British correspondent, Henry Brandon, observed that "Americans and the world at large will look back to the Reagan years wondering what was real and what was make-believe, uncertain what was conjured up by his news and image managers and by Mr. Reagan's own magical appeal to a predominantly middle-class public." Yet Reagan had shown himself flexible enough to move from sermons about the "evil empire" to a genuine cooperative relationship with his Soviet opposite number.

On March 30, 1981, just over two months after taking office as president, Reagan was shot by a disturbed young man, John Hinckley, who seemed to believe that such an action would win him the favor of a Hollywood actress, Jodie Foster. Wounded in the chest by a bullet that almost reached his heart, the president won universal admiration for the gallantry and even humor with which he reacted to the assassination attempt.

Reagan Doctrine   The principle, enunciated early in the presidency of Ronald REAGAN, that the United States would employ military force to oppose Soviet influence in THIRD WORLD countries. In practice, this meant sending military aid to such anti-Communist insurgents as those in Nicaragua.

Recovery, Operation   A large-scale crash program mounted by the government of South Vietnam to repair damage caused to cities by the 1968 North Vietnamese TET OFFENSIVE. The success of these and related efforts led some observers to conclude that the government had achieved a measure of stability, but these hopes did not prove to be justified. "Divisiveness," wrote the American correspondent Robert Shaplen, "is still endemic."

Red Guards   Created in 1966, these formations made up of high school and university students served Chinese Communist leader MAO ZEDONG as shock troops in his struggle for power with Liu Shaoqi, one of the leaders, with DENG XIAOPING, of a faction less strongly ideological and more pragmatic than Mao's followers (for example, the group favored conventional industrialization). The Red Guards served Mao as a kind of personal legion, quickly becoming powerful enough to force the formidable Liu from public life.

Red Star (Krasnaya Zvezda)   The chief newspaper of the Soviet military establishment, with a peak circulation of about 1.6 million. Though the editors of *Red Star* somewhat liberalized their published outlook during the GLASNOST era, the newspaper remained essentially a voice of the old order and found little favor with the wide reading public created by the new openness.

Reuter, Ernst (1889–1953)   This German Social Democratic politician, who took office in 1948 as the first mayor of the postwar city of West Berlin, had an extraordinary history. As a young Social Democrat, Reuter opposed the kaiser's policies at the outbreak of World War I, but these views did not keep him from being drafted into the German army. The Bolshevik Revolution of 1917 found him in Russia as a wounded prisoner of war. Heartily approving of the revolution, he organized fellow prisoners into a soviet and was later appointed by Lenin as commissar of the Russian Volga German colony, an assignment that put him under the immediate supervision of Joseph STALIN. In 1921 Reuter was elected general secretary of the German Communist Party, but in the following year, too independent to submit to dictation from Moscow, he not only resigned his office but left the party, returning to the Social Democrats. His advocacy of independence of action for Communist parties outside the USSR marked him as a perpetual enemy in Soviet eyes.

Before the coming of the Nazis, Reuter served as

an official of the BERLIN city government, specializing in transportation and utilities. During the 1930s the Nazis imprisoned him three times; he spent the World War II years in Turkey as a professor and also, drawing on his municipal-government experience, worked with the Turkish government. After the division of the former German capital into East and West Berlin, Reuter became mayor of the latter, his election, on December 5, 1948, coming during the great crisis of the era, the BERLIN BLOCKADE AND AIRLIFT. His background in the Berlin city government helped him make an important contribution to the success of the airlift.

Revolt of the Admirals   During the late 1940s the U.S. Navy and Air Force engaged in a bitter struggle over control of the nation's nuclear weapons. The symbols of this interservice battle, which grew into one of the greatest of modern turf wars and claimed a chief of naval operations as its hapless victim, became the air force's B-36 bomber and the navy's proposed supercarrier *United States*. Haunted by a sense of insecurity in the new nuclear world, the navy maintained that it should be given the means to build up a carrier force, crowned by a supercarrier, that could operate anywhere in the world to deliver nuclear attacks on an enemy. In addition, navy officials declared that only carrier-based aircraft could provide tactical support for operations in Europe against invading Soviet armies. In December 1947 a naval air admiral advised his superiors to "start an aggressive campaign aimed at proving the navy can deliver the atom bomb more effectively than the air force can." The air force, on the other hand, declared that its strategic bomber force should be the country's primary nuclear-weapons delivery arm.

Amid confusing and contradictory claims about the efficacy of each approach and dubious statements about Soviet defensive strength and air capabilities (greatly exaggerated by navy representatives), the new secretary of defense, Louis JOHNSON, appointed by President TRUMAN in March 1949 with orders to cut defense spending, decided to scuttle the supercarrier. In response, the admirals trained their big guns on the air force's new, propeller-driven B-36, the largest warplane ever

built, which began service in June 1948. The ensuing brawl became a public affair of press leaks and near slander. Though the huge B-36 was not unreservedly admired even within the air force, the admirals helped ruin their own case by circulating unsubstantiated rumors about a conflict of interest involving Secretary Johnson. Despite testimony by a galaxy of the navy's World War II stars—Admirals King, Nimitz, Halsey, and Spruance—the air force won the battle, and the proposed supercarrier *United States* permanently disappeared from the navy estimates. Having lost the loyalty of his admirals, who believed that he had not represented the navy's cause with appropriate zeal and vigor, Admiral Louis Denfeld, chief of naval operations, soon found himself put out to pasture.

Reykjavík Summit   October 11–12, 1986, meeting between U.S. president REAGAN and Soviet general secretary GORBACHEV (originally billed as a kind of mini-SUMMIT to prepare for a later conference). It produced surprises and excitement, suggesting new possibilities in East-West summitry, but yielded no concrete results. Going beyond any anticipated positions (at least on the part of the United States), Reagan and Gorbachev agreed to eliminate intermediate-range ballistic missiles in Europe, and as the discussions were proceeding, press reports suggested to the world that this summit meeting had a new atmosphere, a feeling of momentous events taking place. But, since Reagan would not go so far as to pledge not to develop and test the STRATEGIC DEFENSE INITIATIVE, the meeting, for all its wide-ranging discussion, ended with no new agreement. In Gorbachev, however, the Reykjavík summit showed the world a new kind of Soviet leader at work. It also showed that the West did not quite know what to make of him.

Ten days later, however, back in Moscow, Gorbachev indulged in some old-time talk at a meeting of the POLITBURO. Angry at a U.S. order to reduce the number of Soviet personnel in the United States, the Soviet general secretary declared that since Reykjavík "our 'friends' in the U.S.A." were doing "everything to inflame the atmosphere," acting "extremely crudely—they behave like bandits." The Soviet Union, he said, could not

U.S. president Ronald Reagan (l.) and Soviet general secretary Mikhail Gorbachev are somber as they prepare to leave the 1986 Reykjavík summit meeting, after earlier sessions raised hopes for an arms-control breakthrough.

"expect any constructive actions or proposals from the U.S.A. administration."

RF-101 *See* F-101.

Rhee, Syngman (1875–1965) Widely respected Korean nationalist who spent most of his political life in the struggle for Korean independence. From 1919, with Korea under Japanese occupation, Rhee, living in the United States, served as president of the provisional Korean republic, lobbying for his cause. After World War II and the establishment of South Korea (the Republic of Korea) in 1948, the American-educated Rhee (A.B., George Washington University; M.A., Harvard; Ph.D., Princeton) was elected the country's first president by the National Assembly. To many conservatives in the United States he was "the George Washington of Korea." But General John R. HODGE, the U.S. postwar occupation commander in Korea, found Rhee dishonest and brutal.

In 1953, as the KOREAN WAR dragged on while armistice negotiators haggled toward a workable result, Rhee, who violently opposed any arrange-ment that would leave two Koreas instead of a unified republic and who also felt himself a relatively powerless pawn in U.S. hands, tried to sabotage the truce talks by threatening to remove his army from UNITED NATIONS control and continue the war on his own. He then released some 25,000 North Korean prisoners of war, whose objection to being repatriated formed one of the issues in contention. U.S. president EISENHOWER dispatched a mission to Korea with instructions either to win Rhee over with promises of cash grants and military supports or to threaten a withdrawal or to stage a coup to replace Rhee with a more amenable figure. The combination of offers and threats, abetted by a heavy Chinese attack, brought Rhee to heel. (The U.S. problem with Rhee evoked a notable and widely applicable dictum from the University of Chicago political scientist Hans J. Morgenthau: "You should never allow yourself to be dictated to by a small ally.") After the war, Rhee gradually lost popularity as his government faced charges of vote fraud and corruption. A civilian revolt forced him from office in 1960. He lived the remainder of his life in Hawaii.

Rickover, Hyman George (1900–1986) U.S. naval officer who pioneered the development of nuclear-powered engines for the navy. Rickover supervised the design and building of the world's first nuclear-powered submarine, the U.S.S. *NAUTILUS*. A U.S. Naval Academy graduate (1922), Admiral Rickover was a controversial figure whose confrontational personality and disdain for conventional administrative procedures kept him in bad odor with navy seniors, but he won such support in Congress that, by special legislation, he remained on active duty until the age of 82—an all-time record. "Everything is special in Rickover's world," said Edward N. Luttwak of Georgetown University, "meeting unheard-of standards of precision and reliability in men and machines." Like many such single-minded innovators, Rickover attracted both disciples and detractors; the former group included, prominently, the young naval officer who became President Jimmy CARTER.

Ridgway, Matthew Bunker (1895–1993) One of the finest combat commanders in American history, General Ridgway pioneered U.S. airborne tactics and held the army's highest positions: commander in the Far East (during the KOREAN WAR), supreme commander in Europe, and chief of staff.

A genuine "army brat," Ridgway graduated from West Point in 1917 but saw no overseas service in World War I. Later, like many other officers destined for high command, he studied at the Infantry School at Fort Benning under the watchful eye of George MARSHALL, whom he came to know well on subsequent peacetime assignments. Shortly after the Pearl Harbor attack, Ridgway took command of the 82nd Infantry Division, which soon, under his supervision, found itself transformed into the 82nd Airborne Division (his chief of staff was Maxwell TAYLOR). The division saw its first action in the invasion of Sicily on July 10, 1943, when it made a night jump that did not go according to plan but still proved extremely effective. A strong advocate of airborne operations, Ridgway jumped with his troops on the eve of the Normandy invasion and led them in the capture of the town of Ste.-Mère-Église—an action vividly shown in the motion picture *The Longest Day*. Ridgway, who according to an official army history "displayed an uncanny ability for appearing at the

General Matthew B. Ridgway, UN commander in Korea, NATO supreme commander, and U.S. Army chief of staff

right place at the right time," then took command of the newly created XVIII Airborne Corps, which he led through the rest of the campaign; these troops won special fame for the part they played in the relief of Bastogne, in the Battle of the Bulge.

At the end of 1950, Ridgway participated in relief of another kind when he went to Korea to take command of the Eighth Army after the death of its commander, General Walton H. Walker, which had occurred following the great blows struck against this force in northern Korea in November by Chinese Communist troops. Ridgway's performance in infusing his battered army with his own aggressive spirit was called by the military historian Brigadier General S. L. A. Marshall "one of the greatest achievements ever by an American general." On the day after he arrived, Ridgway is said to have interrupted a British staff officer's briefing on withdrawal plans by declaring, "I'm more interested in your plans for attack." Far exceeding the expectations of his superior in Tokyo, General Douglas MACARTHUR, the tough and charismatic Ridgway led his forces in carefully managed battles that not only ended the American retreat but won back the 38TH PARALLEL, the division between North and South Korea. (As a battlefield trademark, Ridgway wore a grenade clipped to the strap of a parachute chest harness; he balanced the picture with a first-aid kit on the other strap. Since when seen from any distance, he appeared to be wearing two grenades, troops dubbed him Old Iron Tits.) When President TRUMAN cashiered MacArthur for his indiscretions and insubordination, Ridgway replaced him as U.S. and UNITED NATIONS commander in the Far East. In 1952, after General EISENHOWER left his NORTH ATLANTIC TREATY ORGANIZATION command to campaign for the presidency, Ridgway replaced him.

In October 1953 Ridgway came home to become army chief of staff, but this phase of his career did not prove to be a happy one; he called it his "toughest, most frustrating job." Opposing the administration's emphasis on the doctrine of MASSIVE RETALIATION, Ridgway, in his desire to maintain army troop levels and hence the ability to fight wars other than nuclear ones, ran into direct conflict with the economy-minded Eisenhower, who called the chief of staff's views "parochial." But Ridgway also performed a great service for Ike and for the United States by convincing the president that U.S. intervention in Vietnam in support of the French forces besieged in DIEN BIEN PHU would be an act of utter folly. The proposed air strikes, said Ridgway, represented the old and delusive U.S. faith in "the cheap and easy way" of dealing with military problems. Eisenhower accepted Ridgway's advice not to authorize Operation VULTURE, which perhaps differed from the views of some other presidential advisers not so much in its content as in its thorough detailing of the possible consequences of intervention—and in its forcefulness; Ridgway was not known for trimming his views to please his audience. One result of his candor was that after serving one two-year term as chief of staff, he was not reappointed by the president. Ridgway retired and went into private business.

Rio Treaty   At the 1947 inter-American conference in Rio de Janeiro, the United States advocated and promoted the creation of a regional mutual-security pact under Articles 51 and 52 of the UNITED NATIONS charter, which provided for the establishment and functioning of such pacts until the UN itself could take needed action. The conference opened on a disappointing note for the Latin American representatives, who hoped for promises of U.S. economic aid. The U.S. secretary of state, George C. MARSHALL, grappling at the time with all the problems associated with U.S. aid to Europe, had the unpleasant task of informing his fellow delegates that economic discussions must be deferred. Later in the conference, however, he expressed his interest in developing long-range plans for Latin American economic development. After some wrangling with Latin American nationalists, U.S. negotiators succeeded in pushing through a final document that called for mutual defense if an attack should occur on any signatory nation; when a two-thirds majority agreed on the nature of the assault, the others must come to the aid of the nonaggressor. Thus, in its own immediate region, the United States assured itself of support against the Soviet Union. The treaty, also known as the Pact of Petropolis, was signed on September 2, 1947.

Rogers, William Pierce (1913–)   As U.S. secretary of state under his close friend President NIXON (1969–73), Rogers occupied a curious position. Though he administered the affairs of the State Department, his role in forming and executing foreign policy was distinctly secondary to that of the national security adviser, Henry KISSINGER, who with the president formed a very close two-man team.

A native of upstate New York, Rogers was a graduate of Colgate University (1934) and held a law degree from Cornell (1937). During World War II he served in the navy, attaining the rank of lieutenant commander. Appointed deputy attorney general by President EISENHOWER in 1953, he served as attorney general during Ike's second term. A strong civil-rights supporter, Rogers established the Civil Rights Division of the Justice Department.

A gentlemanly person, Rogers, who had no

background in international affairs, seemed to accept the role given him by Nixon, which, as summed up by a British correspondent, Henry Brandon, was "to keep the State Department at bay, while the president and Henry went about making foreign policy."

Rokossovsky, Konstantin (1896–1968) Soviet marshal, an outstanding commander in World War II who later served as defense minister of Poland, while retaining his Soviet citizenship and rank.

After spending three years in the imperial Russian army during World War I, Rokossovsky joined the Red Army, rising through the 1920s and 1930s to divisional and then corps commands. In 1937, however, his military career came to a sudden halt, when Joseph STALIN's Great Purge of Soviet officialdom, civilian and military, swept him up and, sparing him the firing squad, sent him to prison. Released because of the need for his services in World War II, Rokossovsky commanded a series of fronts (army groups), including the Don Front, which played the largest part in the defeat of the Germans at Stalingrad. In August 1944, Rokossovsky's First Belorussian Front figured in one of the war's bitterest controversies, when it stopped its advance at the Vistula River while the Germans slaughtered the Polish underground forces in Warsaw. Whatever Rokossovsky's forces might or might not have been able to do in this circumstance (the Soviets by way of explanation adduced numerous logistical problems), and whatever the Poles may have intended to accomplish by trying to liberate Warsaw themselves, Rokossovsky was following Stalin's orders, and it certainly suited Stalin for the Germans to destroy a large force of non-Communist Poles.

After the war, Rokossovsky served as commander of Soviet forces in Poland. In 1949, in a notably unusual move, Stalin arranged for Rokossovsky to become minister of defense of Poland and commander in chief of Polish forces, positions the marshal held until 1956; he also played an unofficial but quite real role as the symbol of Stalin's domination of Poland. According to Nikita KHRUSHCHEV's later account, Rokossovsky had no desire for the assignment; he "literally fell on his knees and begged Stalin not to send him to Poland," saying that he "couldn't bear to leave" the Soviet

Union. Finally accepting (since, in reality, he had little choice), he induced Stalin to allow him to retain his Soviet citizenship and marshal's rank. In 1952 Rokossovsky added the portfolio of deputy premier of Poland.

In 1956 Rokossovsky used up his credit in Poland by ordering troops to fire on Poznan workers involved in the anti-Soviet demonstrations that sparked the POLISH UPRISING. The new Polish premier, Władysław GOMUŁKA, was said to have urged the Kremlin to recall the marshal, which was done. As Khrushchev said later, although Rokossovsky was a Pole, "he was not a Polish Pole but a Soviet Pole." Back in his true home, Rokossovsky served for a time as deputy minister of defense.

Rolling Thunder, Operation Code name for U.S. bombing attacks on targets in North Vietnam, authorized during the VIETNAM WAR in 1965 and continued, with interruptions, until 1968. Admiral U. S. Grant Sharp, the U.S. commander in the Pacific, described Rolling Thunder as action intended to be a "decisive step in the right direction"—that is, to lead HO CHI MINH's North Vietnamese government toward negotiations by convincing it that U.S. attacks could destroy its military capacity. The hope proved ill-founded.

Rome, Treaty of The document, signed in 1957, that established the EUROPEAN ECONOMIC COMMUNITY—the Common Market.

Romero, Oscar (1917–1980) Archbishop of El Salvador, a leading critic of the ruling U.S.-supported El Salvador junta who was shot dead by an assassin as he said Mass in a hospital chapel in March 1980. Though numerous human-rights organizations condemned the murder, the U.S. government—especially the REAGAN administration, which took office in January 1981—imposed no sanctions, choosing instead to emphasize the anti-Communist nature of the government, which had begun as a moderate military-civilian coalition but quickly became exclusively military, with a heavy reliance on violence. *See also* LIBERATION THEOLOGY.

Roosevelt, (Anna) Eleanor (1884–1962) Widow of U.S. president Franklin D. ROOSEVELT, Mrs. Roosevelt, who had earlier created an independent career as a newspaper columnist and author, became a world figure in her own right after she accepted President TRUMAN's request to serve as a U.S. representative to the UNITED NATIONS.

Shortly after succeeding President Roosevelt in 1945, Truman wrote Mrs. Roosevelt a lengthy handwritten letter asking her advice about managing the presidency. The former first lady wrote back suggesting, characteristically, that Truman not waste his time writing longhand letters. She also offered him shrewd advice about developing a personal relationship with Winston CHURCHILL, then British prime minister and the closest international associate of the United States. "If you talk to him about books," she said, "and let him quote to you from his marvelous memory, everything on earth from Barbara Frietchie to the Nonsense Rhymes and Greek tragedy, you will find him easier to deal with on political subjects. He is a gentleman to whom the personal element means a great deal." Essentially, however, Mrs. Roosevelt gave Truman the message that his conduct of the presidency would depend entirely on himself.

From 1946 to 1951 Mrs. Roosevelt chaired the UN Commission on Human Rights and, against heavy odds, succeeded through lengthy and patient negotiations in winning the adoption of the Universal Declaration of Human Rights. This declaration not only endorsed the kinds of political rights embodied in the founding documents of the United States but added later ideas such as the right to marriage and the right to receive education. Through the years numerous public-opinion polls declared Mrs. Roosevelt to be the most admired woman in the world.

Roosevelt, Franklin Delano (1882–1945) President of the United States during the Great Depression and through World War II, Franklin D. Roosevelt died on April 12, 1945, less than a month before the great Allied coalition achieved total victory over Germany. His long time in the office (he was the only president to win reelection three times) was marked, as the historian Martha H. Byrd said, "by innovation, determination and great faith in the world's future." Despite his clear and profound faith in democracy, Roosevelt was often accused of seeking to become a dictator—a

charge he seemed to regard as too absurd for comment.

Though the Cold War would not be openly declared for a year or more after his death, frictions between the Soviets and the Anglo-Americans had already sprung up during the weeks following the YALTA CONFERENCE—the meeting in the Crimea that had concluded in warmth and Allied amity. Recognizing the new realities of power, however, Roosevelt made no euphoric statements about the results of the conference to his personal chief of staff, Admiral William D. LEAHY, but simply said, "It was the best I could do." With British prime minister Winston CHURCHILL, Roosevelt had counseled firmness and patience in dealing with Soviet premier Joseph STALIN, and in one of his last messages had told the prime minister, "Our course thus far is correct."

In general an opponent of colonialism—notably in Vietnam—Roosevelt favored the concept of international trusteeship as a halfway house toward independence, but nevertheless, under pressure, retreated from this position with respect to Vietnam in early 1945. Though he saw that colonialism was in its last stages, the British and others had not yet come to this realization. During the war Roosevelt consistently irritated Churchill and other British leaders by urging moves toward independence for India, and he was not likely to have encouraged France or any other colonial power to have continued in its colonial ways.

On receiving the news of Roosevelt's death, the army newspaper *Yank* included him in its list of the latest military casualties. Around the world people heard the bulletins with shock and sorrow. Black-bordered flags flew at half-staff in Moscow. At home, tearful crowds lined the railroad tracks to see the funeral train pass by. Everywhere, said Anne O'Hare McCormick of the *New York Times,* a single sentiment prevailed: "We have lost a friend."

Rosenberg case In April 1951, a little more than six months after U.S. president TRUMAN had shocked Americans by announcing that the Soviet Union had exploded its first ATOMIC BOMB—an event most people did not expect to happen for years to come—a U.S. district court in New York sentenced a married couple, Julius (b. 1918) and

Ethel (b. 1915) Rosenberg, to death for having delivered nuclear secrets to the Soviets. The accused parties in the trial, which began on March 6, included, besides the Rosenbergs, David Greenglass (Ethel Rosenberg's brother) and Morton Sobell, all of whom were charged with spying for the Soviet Union in 1944 and 1945. Greenglass, who confessed, declared he had regularly given the Rosenbergs secret data for delivery to their Soviet case officer. A soldier assigned to the Los Alamos, N.Mex., laboratory, where the first atomic bombs were assembled and the first detonation carried out, Greenglass had been a machinist working on the bomb. The kind of naive idealist who could say of the Soviet dictator Joseph STALIN and his colleagues that they were men who hated to use force and did so "with pain in their hearts," Greenglass had been recruited by his wife, Ruth, on the instigation of Julius Rosenberg, his brother-in-law. Though Greenglass was sympathetic to Communism, his idealism did not keep him from taking money from the Soviets for the data he provided.

On March 29 the jury found all the accused guilty. Sobell, who had fled to Mexico but was returned for the trial, drew (as a lesser offender) a 30-year prison sentence; Greenglass (because of his testifying for the prosecution), 15 years; and the Rosenbergs, the death penalty. In sentencing the Rosenbergs, Judge Irving R. Kaufman declared, "Plain, deliberate murder is dwarfed in magnitude by comparison with the crime you have committed."

Because these were technically the first peacetime death sentences for espionage in U.S. history—though the trial took place during the undeclared KOREAN WAR, in which Communist China had become a combatant—and the Rosenbergs denied their guilt, the case caused an enormous worldwide stir; to many observers it looked like a particularly horrendous product of MCCARTHYISM. It also became what was called the most appealed federal trial in recent history, with 16 appeals being heard by federal district court, 7 by the Second Circuit Court of Appeals, and 9 by the U.S. Supreme Court. President TRUMAN left appeals for clemency to be acted on by his successor, President EISENHOWER, who found no grounds for granting

it. The Rosenbergs were executed at Sing Sing prison on June 19, 1953.

By imposing the unprecedented death sentence, the court inadvertently confused two questions—that of guilt and that of appropriate punishment. Since the punishment was extreme, it followed, in some minds, that the charges themselves were probably unfounded, the entire affair being regarded simply as a product of hysterical anti-Communism. In fact, however, the basic evidence against the accused parties came from signal intelligence—decrypts of Soviet cipher messages concerning espionage operations in the West. For obvious reasons, this evidence played no part in the trial itself. In later years, Soviet leader Nikita KHRUSHCHEV put an interesting cap on the affair: "I heard from both Stalin and MOLOTOV," he said, "that the Rosenbergs provided very significant help in accelerating the production of our atomic bomb." *See also* FUCHS, Klaus; VENONA.

Rostow, Walt Whitman (1916–   )   U.S. economist and historian who served as national security adviser to President JOHNSON (1966–69) but is perhaps best remembered as the coauthor (with General Maxwell TAYLOR) of a 1961 report advocating an increased U.S. military commitment to South Vietnam.

A native of New York City, the son of Russian Jewish immigrants, Rostow graduated from Yale in 1936 and acquired his doctorate in 1940; in between, he attended Oxford as a Rhodes scholar. During World War II he served as a strategic-bombing planner, and in the 1950s he taught at the Massachusetts Institute of Technology. In Cambridge he became acquainted with Senator John F. KENNEDY (Dem.-Mass.), for whom he became a close adviser, and in 1961 he followed the new president to Washington as deputy to McGeorge BUNDY, who raised the position of presidential national security adviser to a level of great influence. Known for the numerous lengthy memorandums he turned out, Rostow once evoked from Kennedy the comment: "Walt Rostow can write faster than I can read."

One of the most important documents of the VIETNAM WAR era, the report produced by Taylor and Rostow after they returned from their fact-finding trip changed the face of the war, most particularly by calling for the dispatch of an 8,000-man "logistic task force"; by the time of Kennedy's death, the United States had 20,000 advisers and troops in Southeast Asia. Staying on with President Johnson, Rostow, a true believer in the DOMINO THEORY, stood out as one of the leading war hawks. Succeeding Bundy in 1966 as national security adviser, he held the post until the end of Johnson's presidency.

Rusk, (David) Dean (1909–1994) Chosen in 1960 by U.S. president-elect KENNEDY as his secretary of state, Dean Rusk continued to hold the office throughout the presidency of Kennedy's successor, Lyndon JOHNSON, and as an enunciator of administration policy became almost as closely identified with the VIETNAM WAR as Johnson himself.

A native of north Georgia, the son of a postal worker, Rusk graduated from Davidson College in 1931 and went off to Oxford as a Rhodes scholar; he spent most of his last year in BERLIN, however, just as Adolf Hitler and the Nazis consolidated their power. (Surrounded by symptoms of the new German nationalism, Rusk, in one of his university classes, found himself explaining the absurdity of the lecturer's belief that Germany should demand territorial enclaves in such heavily Teutonic American cities as Milwaukee and St. Louis. On another occasion, however, he was unable to convince a pair of linguistically challenged storm troopers that his dark-skinned friend from India was the purest Aryan in Berlin.) In 1934, back in the United States with his Oxford degree, he went to Mills College, a women's school in Oakland, Calif., to teach government and within a year had become dean of the faculty of the small college.

As the holder of a reserve commission acquired from his ROTC training at Davidson, Rusk was called to active duty in December 1940. Ten months later he was sent to Washington to set up a military intelligence section on British colonies in Asia—an amusing assignment since he had spent considerable time in Europe but knew nothing at all about Asia. During much of World War II, however, Rusk would serve in Asia as General "Vinegar Joe" Stilwell's deputy chief of staff, a post in which he acquired valuable diplomatic experience as a liaison between Stilwell and Lord Louis Mountbatten, the Allied supreme commander in Southeast Asia.

After the war Rusk worked briefly as a special assistant to the secretary of war and held various State Department positions, including deputy undersecretary (1949) and assistant secretary for Far Eastern affairs (1950). Even before leaving the army, however, he put his mark on Asia by suggesting the 38TH PARALLEL as the dividing line between North and South in Korea. In 1951 he played a major part in negotiating the Japanese Peace Treaty in association with John Foster DULLES. After concluding this task, he resigned from the State Department to become president of the Rockefeller Foundation, where he remained until coming to Washington as secretary of state.

At the State Department, Rusk found himself in something of a peculiar position, both because he was working for a president who had a strong interest in foreign affairs and a desire to involve himself in every detail of policy, and also because he brought no great reputation with him while having such eminent subordinates as Adlai STEVENSON and Averell HARRIMAN. A strong organization man, Rusk was also a skillful negotiator and won considerable popularity on Capitol Hill. But as an executive he adopted an inscrutable style that sometimes left even President Kennedy saying, "You never know what he is thinking." Rusk also had to share the presidential foreign-policy ear with a strong-minded national security adviser, McGeorge BUNDY. Rusk won Kennedy's favor by his loyalty and discretion, however, as when he strongly advised the president not to engage in the BAY OF PIGS OPERATION, which his military experience told him had no chance of success, but afterward engaged in no public (or, apparently, even private) I-told-you-so's.

Continuing as secretary of state under Johnson —a fellow poor Southerner who had risen to the top—Rusk, with his lingering dry, schoolmasterly style, became a familiar figure before congressional committees and on news programs. As a charter member of Johnson's TUESDAY LUNCH CLUB, Rusk played a leading part in making the administration's Vietnam policy, and overall, in the new administration, the State Department played a more central role in policy making than it had done under JFK.

U.S. secretary of state Dean Rusk

Jobless after leaving the State Department in January 1969, Rusk found that his leading role in Vietnam policy had blotted his résumé. Hearing that the Johns Hopkins School of International Studies had offered him office space, students in that era of ANTIWAR PROTESTS threatened to burn down the building. Finally, however, the University of Georgia offered Rusk a professorship in international law, the subject he had wished to teach more than 30 years earlier.

Russell, Bertrand Arthur William, 3rd Earl Russell (1872–1970) British philosopher, mathematician, and author who spent much of his life campaigning for pacifist causes. Russell first went to prison for his activities in 1918, during World War I, when he defended conscientious objectors. Forty-three years later, in 1961, he was jailed again, this time for his part in a sit-down demonstration staged in Whitehall by the CAMPAIGN FOR NUCLEAR DISARMAMENT, which he had founded. Russell also set up an International War Crimes Tribunal to prosecute the United States for the VIETNAM WAR with Yugoslav politician and writer Vladimir DEDIJER as its president and French philosopher Jean-Paul SARTRE as chair.

Russell could hardly claim perfect consistency, however. In 1947 he declared that if the Soviets refused to internationalize nuclear weapons, along the lines proposed by the United States, they should be forced to do so by being threatened with nuclear attack. In 1953 Russell angrily denied he had ever advocated any kind of preventive war (calling the story, interestingly, "a Communist invention"). Six years later, however, he disavowed his denial, declaring that in 1953 he had simply forgotten what he had said in 1947.

RYAN, Operation (Raketno Yadernoye Napadenie—in English, Nuclear Missile Attack) Soviet intelligence operation in the early 1980s, intended to discover details about a supposed Western plan to attack the USSR in a nuclear first strike. Described by Oleg Gordievsky, a former KGB officer, as the largest intelligence operation ever undertaken by the Soviets, RYAN involved an unprecedented collaboration between the KGB and the GRU, the military-intelligence agency. Proposed in 1981, partly, at least, in response to the bristling anti-Soviet rhetoric of U.S. president REAGAN, RYAN had as its leading advocate Yuri ANDROPOV, the director of the KGB, who within a year would head his nation as GENERAL SECRETARY of the COMMUNIST PARTY OF THE SOVIET UNION. Maneuvers in Europe by the NORTH ATLANTIC TREATY ORGANIZATION added to Soviet fears. However, since no such Western plan existed, RYAN failed to confirm the fears and suspicions held by its creators.

Ryzhkov, Nikolai (1929–) Soviet politician who became premier (chairman of the Council of Ministers) in September 1985, as Mikhail GORBACHEV, the new GENERAL SECRETARY, moved to install persons of his own choice in key positions. An engineer and factory manager, Ryzhkov had held economics positions in previous governments and became a secretary of the Communist Party CENTRAL COMMITTEE in 1982, under Yuri ANDROPOV.

Though an ally of Gorbachev and a presumed supporter of PERESTROIKA, Ryzhkov, perhaps because of his technical background, tended to move cautiously with respect to reforming the Soviet economic system. Increasing economic problems led to frequent calls for his resignation, though for Gorbachev he performed the useful function of drawing the fire of critics, enabling the leader to appear more progressive. In 1990 Ryzhkov went to the hospital with a heart attack, but he ran for the presidency of the Russian republic in June 1991 with the strong backing of the Communist Party. The election, however, proved a triumph for Boris YELTSIN, and, inferentially, a setback for Gorbachev, although he made no personal endorsement of any candidate. Ryzhkov ran poorly, failing to win in any large city and taking less than 11 percent of the votes in Moscow or Leningrad.

S

SAC *See* STRATEGIC AIR COMMAND.

Sacred Cow Douglas C-54 four-engine transport —the C-54C—used as his official aircraft by U.S. president Franklin D. ROOSEVELT and, for a time, by President Harry S. TRUMAN. Though the window behind which the president sat was furnished with a pane of bulletproof glass, the aircraft did not have armor plating. Called the Skymaster by the military, the C-54 in its commercial version was designated the DC-4A. The *Sacred Cow* carried President Roosevelt on the 1,375-mile flight from Malta to Saki in the Crimea for the YALTA CONFERENCE in February 1945.

Sadat, Anwar el- (1918–1981) President of Egypt who, under the close supervision of U.S. president CARTER, negotiated the September 1978 CAMP DAVID ACCORDS ("Framework for Peace in the Middle East") with Israeli prime minister Menachem BEGIN.

A member of the group of army officers led by Colonel Gamal NASSER that overthrew King Farouk in 1952, Sadat held various positions under Nasser during the 1950s and 1960s and, as vice president, succeeded Nasser on the latter's death in 1970; he later won election in his own right. Though few knew what to expect from the new president, he quickly proved to be forceful and imaginative and, to the West, signaled a welcome change from Nasser, who had brought Soviet advisers to Egypt and armed himself with Soviet weapons. In July 1971 Sadat helped the government of Sudan put down an attempted coup staged by army officers with the support of the Commu-

nists. In 1972 he expelled the Soviet advisers from Egypt, and in 1976 he denounced the Soviet-Egyptian Treaty of Friendship and Cooperation he himself had signed, apparently for tactical reasons, not long after taking office. Sadat made his most dramatic move—one that led straight to Camp David—when, on November 20, 1977, he flew to Tel Aviv to meet with Begin and other Israeli officials. All these actions, crowned by the Camp David Accords—despite the disappointing practical results of the agreements—demonstrated the end of Soviet influence in the politically most important Arab state and tied Sadat and Egypt firmly to the West. Sadat and Begin jointly won the 1978 Nobel Peace Prize, the somewhat surprising award casting the Nobel committee as cheerleaders for peace in the Middle East.

"By one of the miracles of creation," said former U.S. secretary of state Henry KISSINGER, Sadat, this "peasant's son, the originally underestimated politician, had the wisdom and courage of the statesman and occasionally the insight of a prophet. Yet nourishing all these qualities was a pervasive humanity."

On October 6, 1981, while reviewing a military parade, Sadat was shot dead by a group of extremist conservative soldiers. Observers reported that he refused to give the assassins the satisfaction of seeing him try to duck their fire.

Saigon City in far southern Vietnam along the Ben Nghe (Saigon) River, just above the 10th parallel, chosen by President NGO DINH DIEM as the capital of the Republic of Vietnam and so serving from 1955 to 1975; it was also the U.S. military head-

Egyptian president Anwar el-Sadat *(r.)* relaxes with U.S. president Jimmy Carter at Camp David, September 1978

quarters during the VIETNAM WAR. In 1968 the city saw fierce street fighting during the TET OFFENSIVE, when NATIONAL LIBERATION FRONT guerrillas besieged the city and invaded the courtyard of the U.S. embassy. During the 1960s and early 1970s the population of Saigon, swollen by floods of refugees from rural areas of the country, reached almost two million. On April 30, 1975, tanks of HO CHI MINH's North Vietnamese army rolled into the city and crashed through the gates of the presidential palace, thus providing a symbolic end to the 20-year war. After reunification of the two Vietnams was completed in 1976, the Communists in Hanoi officially changed the name of Saigon to Ho Chi Minh City; however, most people, even in Vietnam (North and South), continue to call the city Saigon.

St. Laurent, Louis (1882–1973) Influential Canadian advocate of the North Atlantic alliance as minister of external affairs (1946–48) and prime minister (1948–57). A native of Quebec and mem-

ber of the Liberal Party, St. Laurent succeeded the veteran statesman W. L. Mackenzie King as prime minister. *See also* NORTH ATLANTIC TREATY ORGANIZATION.

Sakharov, Andrei Dmitrievich (1921–1989) "Father of the Soviet H-bomb," as he became known, the Soviet nuclear physicist Sakharov gained greater world renown as a human-rights advocate. In 1948 he joined a Soviet thermonuclear-weapons research program, to which he made contributions said to have been vitally important. He worked, as well, on controlled fusion reactions. For his remarkable accomplishments, Sakharov was made a full member of the Academy of Sciences at the age of 32. Then, beginning in the late 1950s, though not advocating disarmament, he became a pioneer in pointing to the dangers of radioactive fallout and arguing for a halt to nuclear tests. His efforts, at first not appreciated by the Soviet government, helped bring about the NUCLEAR TEST BAN TREATY of

1963, signed by U.S. president KENNEDY and Soviet premier KHRUSHCHEV.

From these political activities Sakharov went on to express his concern about a range of scientific issues, including pollution of the environment, and to advocate Soviet-American cooperation and even a "convergence" of the two systems (notably in *Progress, Coexistence, and Intellectual Freedom,* a 10,000-word essay that circulated in the Soviet Union as a SAMIZDAT manifesto and on July 22, 1968, was published in the *New York Times*). Declaring that "the exposure of STALIN must be carried through to the end," he characterized Stalinism in a telling sentence as resembling fascism but exhibiting "a much more subtle kind of hypocrisy and demagogy, with reliance not on an openly cannibalistic program like Hitler's but on a progressive, scientific, and popular socialist ideology" that "served as a convenient screen for deceiving the working class" and caused other evils. His strictures against "neo-Stalinists" could hardly endear him to the BREZHNEV regime, which banned him from classified research and in 1980 sentenced him as a dissident to internal exile at Gorky. Meanwhile, in 1975, his passionate defense of human rights brought him the Nobel Peace Prize. During the 1970s, anticipating the kind of point Mikhail GORBACHEV would make in the next decade, Sakharov argued that Soviet industry had come to a dead end from which it could escape only if the people had greater freedom.

In December 1986, Gorbachev entered Sakharov's life directly. Sakharov had written the new leader a letter at the beginning of July 1985, after coming off a hunger strike undertaken on behalf of political prisoners, but Gorbachev offered no response. Earlier in 1986, Gorbachev described Sakharov as a justly convicted lawbreaker. Now, on December 16, he telephoned Sakharov in Gorky to tell him that he could return to Moscow, a free man. Whether this was simply a tactical move by Gorbachev, as it surely was at least in part, or whether it resulted from deep conviction, or both —as was most likely the case—this call constituted a sensational event, for Sakharov, for Gorbachev, and for the Soviet policies of PERESTROIKA and GLASNOST. Sakharov returned to active political life, this time as a member of the new CONGRESS OF PEOPLE'S DEPUTIES, in which he spoke with great moral

authority. His death came unexpectedly. *See also* HYDROGEN BOMB.

salami tactics   Expression used to describe the standard Communist method of taking over European governments. The Hungarian Communist leader, Mátyás RÁKOSI, claimed that he had destroyed his country's post–World War II coalition government by slicing off the non-Communist parties "like pieces of salami." (In Rákosi's particular case, one of the slices, the Smallholders' Party, amounted to more than half of the whole salami, since it had won 57 percent of the vote in the 1945 election. Rákosi dealt with the problem by slicing this chunk into smaller pieces.)

SALT   Acronym used for both the STRATEGIC ARMS LIMITATION TALKS and the Strategic Arms Limitation Treaty.

samizdat   As dissidence developed during the 1970s in Eastern European countries and within the Soviet Union itself, the growth and circulation of underground—*samizdat* (in English, "self-published," formed by analogy with *gosizdat,* "state-published")—political statements increased. An important stimulus came from the USSR's snuffing out of the Czech PRAGUE SPRING in 1968, a development that convinced some Soviet intellectuals the problem resulted not from the "excess of STALIN," as one writer commented, but from the system itself. These publications, usually typewritten, achieved wide circulation, even though the KGB controlled all copying machines and no one could legally make a copy of any document without special permission. A further difficulty in the way of the brave and enterprising self-publishers came from the fact that every typewriter was registered with the police, who were supposed to maintain files containing typing samples from each machine.

Sandinistas   In the early 1960s a guerrilla movement developed in Nicaragua in resistance to the long-established dictatorship of the Somoza family; various non-Marxist and Marxist groups joined together to form the Sandinista National Liberation Front, named for a popular leader of the 1920s and 1930s who opposed U.S. Marine occupiers of Nicaragua and was murdered on the orders of the original Somoza, Anastasio. With U.S. military and economic aid and the support of the Nicaraguan National Guard, the Somozas held on to their power until 1979, when, after a series of setbacks and under pressure from the U.S. CARTER administration, the last Somoza fled.

Though the U.S. administration attempted to work with the Sandinistas and their leader, Daniel Ortega (1945–), problems arose as Fidel CASTRO sent 2,500 Cubans to aid his "revolutionary son"; the newcomers battled former members of the Somoza National Guard. Ortega also began instituting programs viewed by some North Americans as dangerously socialistic. These developments led to the statement in the 1980 Republican Party platform criticizing the "Marxist takeover of Nicaragua" and then to REAGAN administration efforts to overthrow the Sandinistas through a trade embargo and, more importantly, through arming the CONTRAS in Honduras and Costa Rica. There followed a ten-year civil war, which became a focal point of the Reagan administration's anti-Communist effort in the THIRD WORLD. In 1990, after revelation of the IRAN-CONTRA AFFAIR and peacebrokering efforts by President Oscar Arias Sánchez of Costa Rica, elections were held in which the Sandinistas lost to a coalition led by Violeta de Chamorro.

Sapphire Ring   The code name of a KGB network that was said to have penetrated the SDECE (Service de Documentation Extérieure et de Contre-Espionage), the French foreign-intelligence agency, in the 1950s. The information came from a Soviet defector, Anatoli Golitsyn, who provided other valuable information to Western intelligence agencies, though no cases growing out of the Sapphire affair ever came to trial.

Sartre, Jean-Paul (1905–1980)   The most prominent philosophical and literary figure in post-World War II France, Sartre until his death remained an emblem of the French intellectual left. His philosophy of EXISTENTIALISM insisted on the individual's "freedom and responsibility to choose to act and thus to define his being." His lifelong companion, Simone de Beauvoir, said that Sartre, who demonstrated little interest in politics before the war came in 1939, then developed a "new

moral attitude based on the notion of authenticity" that "demanded that man 'assume' his situation . . . by engaging in action."

Captured by the Germans during the 1940 fighting, Sartre after his release wrote for the underground press and for a time took an active part in the Resistance. After the war, together with his friend Albert CAMUS, he attempted to create a political movement (the Rassemblement démocratique et révolutionnaire) that could freely criticize both the U.S. and Soviet governments and would ally itself with the non-Communist left. As it turned out, however, Sartre, though frequently inconsistent and self-contradictory, never favored U.S. policy during the Cold War and blamed the United States for the KOREAN WAR. In 1967 he chaired the war-crimes tribunal organized by Bertrand RUSSELL "to judge American military conduct in Indochina." Sartre supported the French Communist Party, without joining it, but on the other hand in 1948 published an anti-Stalinist play, *Les Mains salés (Dirty Hands),* and as editor of the review *Les Temps modernes* he exposed the GULAG—Soviet forced-labor camps. Yet, in 1954, he returned from a trip to the USSR with praise for the "beauty" of the Soviet government. He broke permanently with Camus over the latter's rejection of Communism. Sartre exemplified in many ways what the historian Paul Johnson has called the "almost compulsory French intellectual adherence to the traditions of the extreme left." His best-known writings include *Being and Nothingness* (English translation, 1956) and the novel *Nausea* (English translation, 1949).

SCAP   Initials standing for Supreme Commander, Allied Powers, the title borne by General Douglas MACARTHUR during the occupation of Japan after World War II.

Schlesinger, James Rodney (1929–)   U.S. public official, an economist, who became notable as a sort of high-level utility player, serving both Presidents Richard NIXON and Jimmy CARTER (a Republican and a Democrat) in various roles. Coming to Washington at the beginning of the Nixon administration as assistant director of the budget, Schlesinger moved to the ATOMIC ENERGY COMMISSION in 1971 as chairman; this change grew partly out of

Schlesinger's work on energy policy while at the Bureau of the Budget. In late December 1972, with the Nixon administration moving deeper into the WATERGATE AFFAIR, the president called on Schlesinger to direct the CENTRAL INTELLIGENCE AGENCY, some of whose former operatives had been involved in the Watergate burglary and related operations; at the CIA Schlesinger succeeded Richard Helms.

In 1973 Schlesinger became secretary of defense. Here he worked to build up conventional Allied forces in Europe, but after his whirlwind six years in office, Schlesinger's criticism of the U.S. policy of DÉTENTE with the Soviet Union brought his dismissal by President Gerald FORD. William G. Hyland, a member of the White House national security staff during the Nixon and Ford administrations, paid tribute to Schlesinger's accomplishments at the Department of Defense; the secretary, Hyland said, began "to break out of the strategic straitjacket of the 1960s, which had dictated the strategy of threatening to retaliate against the Soviet population and cities." Shifting part of U.S. missile targeting away from cities to cover some of the Soviet military installations "would give any future president the chance to avoid the agonizing decision of whether to retaliate against the people of the Soviet Union, killing perhaps a hundred million and ensuring a similar retaliation against the United States."

After assuming the presidency in 1977, Ford's successor, Jimmy Carter, turned to Schlesinger for advice on energy policy, and later in 1977 the president named Schlesinger secretary of energy—a thankless job in that era of energy crisis. Wearied from incessant struggles with Congress over administration energy-conservation policies, Schlesinger resigned in 1979 and joined the Center for Strategic and International Studies at Georgetown University.

A native of New York City, Schlesinger earned bachelor's, master's, and doctoral degrees from Harvard. A pipe-puffing man of portentous mien, Schlesinger taught economics at the University of Virginia (1955–63) and worked in strategic studies for the Rand Corporation (1963–69).

Schmidt, Helmut (1918–) When West Germany's Chancellor Willy BRANDT was forced to re-

sign in May 1974 after one of his closest associates was unmasked as an East German spy, the Social Democratic Party chose Finance Minister Helmut Schmidt to succeed him; the Bundestag ratified the nomination on May 16. A natural choice, with his reputation as a man who could get things done, the self-assured Schmidt served as chancellor until October 1, 1982, when the Christian Democratic leader, Helmut KOHL, replaced him.

An organizer and leader of the Socialist Students' League following World War II, Schmidt first won election to the Bundestag in 1953 and, except for a three-year period in the 1960s, served

West German chancellor Helmut Schmidt

continuously. He became defense minister in 1969, when Brandt became chancellor, and finance minister in 1972. As chancellor, Schmidt tried to continue Brandt's policies, including the search for rapprochement with the EASTERN BLOC called OSTPOLITIK. After a close 1976 election that left Schmidt's parliamentary coalition with a majority of only ten, he was reelected chancellor by the Bundestag by only one vote.

U.S. president Jimmy CARTER found dealing with the chancellor something of a trial, partly because he "seemed reluctant to do anything which might be interpreted as anti-Soviet" and also because he "drones on, giving economic lectures."

In 1980 elections, Schmidt's coalition and the chancellor himself did better than in 1976, but by 1982 he had lost strength in the Bundestag and in October was turned out in a no-confidence vote. Kohl then began his long stay in office.

Schumacher, Kurt (1895–1952)   German political leader whose life story embodies the central tragedies of 20th-century European history. A native of East Prussia, Schumacher fought in battles on the eastern front in the early days of World War I, losing his right arm to a savage burst of machine-gun fire in a December 1914 battle against Russian forces. Active in politics as a Social Democrat in the 1920s, he publicly defied the Nazis on their arrival in power in 1933 and then went into hiding, but his missing arm made him easily traced; he spent the next ten years in concentration camps, being released in 1943 so broken in health—able to walk only with support—that his captors no longer considered him any kind of menace to the Nazi state.

A Socialist during his entire career, Schumacher became chairman of the German Social Democratic Party after World War II; resisting efforts to combine the Social Democratic and Communist parties, he was successful in the west but saw the fusion take place in eastern Germany, producing the Socialist Unity Party. As the head of the Social Democrats in West Germany, he became leader of the opposition to Chancellor Konrad ADENAUER's Christian Democrats. Schumacher had strong reservations about the free-trade policies involved in postwar programs like the MARSHALL PLAN, but with the labor movement squeezed between Mar-

German Socialist leader Kurt Schumacher

shall aid and the Communists, he declared to a 1947 party congress, *"Primum vivere, deinde philosophari."* Live first; practice philosophy later.

Described by a *Newsweek* interviewer as an "emaciated skeleton," Schumacher, whose tribulations had ruined his digestive system, lived on a regimen that could hardly have helped matters— "nerves and zeal," it was called by one observer, "plus codeine, cigarettes, bismuth and 15 cups of jet-black tea a day."

Schuman, Robert (1886–1963)   French statesman who served as premier from November 1947 to July 1948 but is most remembered for his achievement as foreign minister (1948–53) in advancing the cause of Franco-German reconciliation and European unity. In 1950 Schuman proposed what became labeled the SCHUMAN PLAN, the creation of a EUROPEAN COAL AND STEEL COMMUNITY.

A native of Luxembourg, Schuman, whose family came from Lorraine, went to prison during World War I rather than serve in the German army. A lawyer and longtime member of the French Parliament, he was arrested by the German Gestapo in 1940; he escaped in 1942 and spent the rest of World War II in the Resistance. After the war he served as finance minister before becoming premier and then foreign minister. Continuing his efforts for European unity, he served as the first president of the European Parliamentary Assembly (1958–60).

A formal and dignified man, Schuman often spoke, said U.S. secretary of state Dean ACHESON, "in the abstract generalizations natural to lawyers trained in the civil law," but he possessed a keen if quiet sense of humor. His legacy from his early years in Lorraine when it was part of the German Empire gave him both French and German as native languages and provided the foundation of his devotion to the creation of genuine friendship and cooperation between France and Germany.

Schuman Plan Post–World War II U.S. policy toward Europe, particularly the MARSHALL PLAN, did much to promote a sense of European unity. It also helped the former Allies in Western Europe acknowledge the potential importance of the German economy for European recovery. The statesman who most prominently grasped and made use of these realities was the French foreign minister, Robert SCHUMAN, who in 1950 proposed a move that seemed wildly radical to many at the time, the pooling of French and German iron and steel production under the control of a single authority. The organization that resulted was the EUROPEAN COAL AND STEEL COMMUNITY. The plan was drafted by one of the outstanding European public servants of the era, Jean MONNET of France, but Schuman embraced it and gave it the political support necessary to bring it to reality.

French premier and foreign minister Robert Schuman

Scorpion, **U.S.S.** In May 1968, near the end of a three-month mission, the U.S. nuclear submarine *Scorpion* was diverted from its homeward course to Norfolk, Va., to take a look at Soviet naval vessels near the Canary Islands. Nothing was subsequently heard from the *Scorpion*, which in any case would have observed a period of radio silence before its expected arrival at Norfolk on May 27. When the submarine failed to appear—and no later word ever came from it—much speculation suggested it might have been involved in some unheralded Cold War clash with the Soviet ships. But naval records released in 1993 show that the *Scorpion* was actually more than 200 miles away from the Soviet vessels when it sank. The documents indicate that the "most probable" cause of the disappearance was not hostile action but the explosion of one of the submarine's own torpedoes, which in some fashion became armed and was then jettisoned by the crew. Instead of streaking away from the *Scorpion*, runs the navy reasoning, the torpedo must have veered around and homed in on the hull of the submarine and thus have hit it and exploded. The *Scorpion* sank in 11,000 feet of water, a depth almost as great as that of the final resting place of the *Titanic.* So ended a mystery—a Cold War incident that never was.

SDI   *See* STRATEGIC DEFENSE INITIATIVE.

SEATO   *See* SOUTHEAST ASIA TREATY.

Second World   Like FIRST WORLD and THIRD WORLD, this label was applied to one of the three "worlds" into which popular opinion divided the nations during the later Cold War. The Second World comprised the Soviet Union, China, and other Communist countries. *See also* NONALIGNMENT.

Secret Intelligence Service   *See* MI6.

Semipalatinsk   City in Kazakhstan, on the edge of the southern desert belt that stretches across the Asian part of the former Soviet Union; site of the USSR's nuclear testing center. During the four decades from 1949, when the Soviets exploded their first nuclear device, until 1989, when President Mikhail GORBACHEV ordered the end of testing in the area, Semipalatinsk was the scene of some 500 tests, 100 of them in the atmosphere (before the signing of the NUCLEAR TEST BAN TREATY in 1963). Investigation since the end of the Cold War has revealed that these tests produced the world's most extensive case of environmental nuclear poisoning, with not only the ground but also the people being affected. As one local physician declared, the government "deliberately exposed people to radiation" in order to study its effects. Numerous unusual birth defects have been reported through the years, and many people in the area suffer from immune-system disorders similar to those produced by the Acquired Immune Deficiency Syndrome (AIDS).

SHAPE   The acronym for Supreme Headquarters, Allied Powers in Europe, the name of General Dwight D. EISENHOWER's headquarters as supreme commander of NORTH ATLANTIC TREATY ORGANIZATION forces.

Shining Path (El Sendero Luminoso)   This "deliriously Maoist guerrilla group," as the writer Alma Guillermoprieto called it, began operating in the mountainous Ayacucho Province of Peru in the early 1980s, working in Indian and peasant communities. With violence as its weapon, it issued vague promises of destroying the Peruvian state and creating a utopian, egalitarian society. Shining Path, led by a former college professor named Abimael Guzmán, concerned U.S. officials because of its violence (which, said Guillermoprieto, "rampaged through the countryside, bringing the art of murder to new levels of senselessness and gore"), its ties to Communists, and its reliance on the drug trade as a source of funds. The United States helped the Peruvian government in its war against Shining Path and likewise gave aid to the Colombian government as it battled a similar group, the M-19. In the 1990s, with the end of the Cold War and the use of effective tactics against Shining Path by the administration of Peruvian president Alberto Fujimoro, the group's influence declined.

Sholokhov, Mikhail Alexandrovich (1905–1984)   Soviet novelist, winner of the 1965 Nobel Prize for literature (and the first Soviet writer allowed to accept the prize), who as a very young man took an active part in the Russian civil war and became an enthusiastic Bolshevik. A lean, muscular man who looked like a middleweight fighter, Sholokhov was considered by many critics to have been the USSR's greatest epic novelist, something of a modern Tolstoy; he managed, remarkably, to combine strong Soviet patriotism with a reputation for some degree of independent thinking. Born in the Don Cossack region, he told the story of the people of that area during World War I, the Russian Revolution, and the civil war in his four-volume novel *The Quiet Don* (1928–40), published in English as *And Quiet Flows the Don* (1934) and *The Don Flows Home to the Sea* (1940). In 1959 he accompanied Soviet premier Nikita KHRUSHCHEV on his tour of the United States. In 1966, after the conviction of the writers Andrei SINYAVSKY and Yuli DANIEL for publishing abroad without permission, Sholokhov showed himself to be no liberal. A number of intellectuals had spoken out at the trial for the freedom to publish, earning themselves nothing but the loss of their jobs. But this failed to satisfy Sholokhov, who called for the execution of the accused writers in the name of the revolution.

Sholokhov lived for some time at 19 Starokomyushenny Lane in Moscow, in the apartment to which Khrushchev was later assigned, after his removal from office in 1964.

Shostakovich, Dmitri Dmitriyevich (1906–1975)

To Westerners in the 1930s and 1940s, unaccustomed to the idea of linking art directly to the demands of programmatic politics, the ups and downs that characterized the career of Dmitri Shostakovich often seemed to sum up the alien and inexplicable side of Soviet Communist life. Shostakovich did not choose the path of aesthetic dissent, however, but strove to accommodate himself to the official requirements as embodied in the doctrine of socialist realism, which, as explained by Maxim Gorky in 1934, called for literary artists (and, by extension, all artists) to become "engineers of the soul" and to devote themselves not to "criticizing everything" but to celebrating man's "deeds, creativeness." As a young composer Shostakovich displayed a witty and satirical touch (as in *The Nose* and *The Golden Age*), and in the middle 1930s his opera *Lady Macbeth of the District of Mzensk* received criticism from the COMMUNIST PARTY OF THE SOVIET UNION as lacking in the qualities demanded by socialist realism. (Joseph STALIN, the Soviet dictator and number-one aesthetic specialist, reportedly arose from his balcony seat over the brasses and stamped out of the premiere performance. Next day the reviewer in *Pravda* duly described himself as "flabbergasted by a deliberately disjointed, confused torrent of sound"; the whole thing, he declared, was "some sort of leftist confusion instead of natural human music.") This development caused the composer to lay aside temporarily his introspective Fourth Symphony and, in 1937, to give the USSR and the world the Fifth, which he described as an answer to his critics. His Seventh (Leningrad) Symphony became popular in the West during World War II as a symbol of the Soviet struggle against the invading Germans. Even Stalin's death, however, did not end Shostakovich's in-and-out conflict with party authorities; his Thirteenth Symphony, which premiered in the relatively, if intermittently, relaxed KHRUSHCHEV era, earned him official censure.

Shultz, George Pratt (1920–   )

Holder of a variety of high-level posts under Presidents NIXON and REAGAN, Shultz succeeded Alexander HAIG as U.S. sec-retary of state in June 1982 and served until the end of Reagan's tenure in January 1989.

A native of New York City, Shultz graduated from Princeton in 1942 and acquired his doctorate in industrial economics from the Massachusetts Institute of Technology in 1949, having taken time out to serve in the Marine Corps in World War II. After teaching at MIT, he moved to the University of Chicago Graduate School of Business, at which he taught industrial relations (1957–68) and served as dean (1962–68). Having acquired an outstanding reputation as a labor mediator, he was chosen by Nixon as secretary of labor, serving from 1969 until 1970. The president then appointed him director of the newly created Office of Management and Budget, and from there Shultz moved to the Treasury. He resigned as secretary of the treasury in 1974 to enter private business as executive vice president of a San Francisco–based international construction firm, the Bechtel Corporation, and became president the following year. While holding high positions at Bechtel, he also taught management and public policy at Stanford.

In 1981 Shultz agreed to serve as chairman of Reagan's Economic Policy Advisory Board, and in 1982 the president chose him to replace Haig at the State Department. Shultz presided over the department during one of the most remarkable eras in the history of U.S. foreign relations. In 1983 his chief, President Reagan, denounced the Soviet Union as the "EVIL EMPIRE," but at the end of his term six years later the president had developed a genuinely friendly relationship with Soviet leader Mikhail GORBACHEV, who came to power in 1985; the two had four SUMMIT meetings, during one of which they were seen strolling arm in arm across Red Square. In 1987 the United States and the USSR agreed to destroy their stocks of intermediate-range missiles. Generally open to Soviet initiatives, Shultz also attempted to further peace in the Middle East by meeting with officials of the Palestine Liberation Organization.

The nightmare of Shultz's time in office, as of the Reagan administration generally, was the IRAN-CONTRA AFFAIR, which saw the United States acting in a clandestine fashion both in Iran and in Nicaragua. This activity, with its headquarters in the White House, bypassed the State Department. When administration leaders discussed it in late

1985 and early 1986, Shultz raised strong objections, maintaining that trading arms for hostages, directly or indirectly, would violate U.S. policy and would put the administration in the position of doing what it "preached to and pressured" other governments not to do. In November 1986 the secretary declared to Reagan, "I can't exist as secretary of state in this environment," but he continued to try to convince the president that his subordinates were deceiving him. One of the few high officials to resist the arms-for-hostages arrangement, Shultz failed to win his running argument with Reagan.

Sidewinder   U.S. air-to-air missile first produced in 1953 and used by the United States (air force and navy) and by the air services of many allied countries. Designated the AIM-9, this solid-fuel missile had a range of two miles, homing on its target through an infrared guidance system.

Sihanouk, Norodom (1922–)   One of the 20th century's most remarkable survivors, Sihanouk first assumed the throne of CAMBODIA in 1941, following the death of his grandfather. During World War II he cooperated with the invading Japanese because he made winning Cambodia's independence from France his overriding aim; his efforts were finally successful in 1953. In 1955 he renounced the throne to become prime minister, and in 1960 became head of state as Prince Sihanouk. At the end of the 1960s Cambodia became the target of U.S. bombing attacks directed against KHMER ROUGE (Red Cambodian) forces during the VIETNAM WAR. In 1970 Sihanouk was overthrown by a military coup in which LON NOL was abetted by the U.S. CENTRAL INTELLIGENCE AGENCY. In the latter 1970s, after spending more than two years under house arrest, Sihanouk allied himself with the now-triumphant Khmer Rouge government led by the infamously murderous POL POT, whose regime was crushed in 1979 by the Vietnamese army. After becoming the head of a government-in-exile, Sihanouk bided his time so effectively that on September 24, 1993, having returned home in triumph, he was for the second time in his adventurous life crowned king of Cambodia. Khmer Rouge forces, however, refused to recognize the new constitution and continued guerrilla operations against the government.

Sinyavsky, Andrei Donatovich (1925–)   Soviet writer tried in February 1966 along with Yuli DANIEL for publishing "subversive" stories in the West. The two were accused by *IZVESTIA* of "secretly sending foreign publishing houses dirty libels against their country, against the Party and against the Soviet system." Symptomatic of General Secretary BREZHNEV's return to strong literary controls after the relatively loose supervision writers had enjoyed during the KHRUSHCHEV decade, the arrest and trial of these two writers aroused a stir not only in the Soviet Union but in the West. For *Izvestia,* foreign concern meant simply that "when a pair of turncoats turn up in their trenches, they hasten to heroize them." Apparently considered the more dangerous of the pair (he had taught at Moscow University) or the more effectively satirical, Sinyavsky—who used the pseudonym Abram Tertz—drew a seven-year sentence (to Daniel's five). Expelled from the USSR after his release, he settled in Paris and became a lecturer at the Sorbonne.

Skybolt   This U.S. Air Force two-stage ballistic missile (with a range of 1,000 nautical miles), designed to be launched from a bomber at surface targets, became the center of an international political controversy in November 1962, when the U.S. KENNEDY administration canceled an agreement made by President EISENHOWER with British prime minister Harold MACMILLAN to provide Britain with Skybolts. Technical problems had persuaded Secretary of Defense Robert MCNAMARA to recommend that the United States abandon the missile, a recommendation approved by the president. Unfortunately, this decision left Britain without the weapon on which its nuclear defense would be based. The British felt the United States owed them either Skybolt or a comparable weapon (namely, the POLARIS missile) in exchange for the use of the Holy Loch naval base by U.S. submarines. The U.S. decision also confirmed a shift in policy toward a Britain removed from the independent-deterrent game in favor of an all-European effort. The British Conservative government, however, was determined to preserve its deterrent independence. After much recrimination and real bitterness, Kennedy finally solved the problem by agreeing to give Britain Polaris missiles under a formula whereby both countries pledged themselves to use their "best endeavors" to work toward a multilateral European deterrent force.

Slansky, Rudolf (1901–1952)   Czech Communist politician, general secretary of the party and deputy prime minister, who was arrested in November 1951 for alleged dealings with Marshal TITO, tried in a proceeding suffused with anti-Semitic utterances by the prosecution, and hanged. The case of Slansky and other officials arrested with him arose in Joseph STALIN's last and increasingly paranoid years, when he instigated purges throughout Eastern Europe that included Communists, especially Jews, who in fact were, like Slansky, loyally subservient to the Soviet Union. In 1947 Slansky took the lead in working toward the 1948 Communist takeover of the Czech government by calling for the expulsion of non-Communist parties from the National Front—using Hungarian Communist Party leader Mátyás RÁKOSI's tried-and-true SALAMI TACTICS. The elimination of Slansky not only met Stalin's requirements but marked a factional victory for Czech president Klement GOTTWALD. Slansky was rehabilitated in 1963.

Smith, Walter Bedell (1895–1961)   On November 1, 1950, just over three months after the outbreak of the KOREAN WAR, General Smith took office as the second director of the U.S. CENTRAL INTELLIGENCE AGENCY. This appointment by President TRUMAN signaled the importance the administration attached to the still-new agency as a prime instrument in waging the Cold War. Smith came to the position with impressive credentials, having served during World War II as General EISENHOWER's chief of staff (Ike liked to call him "the general manager

General Walter Bedell Smith, U.S. ambassador to the USSR and CIA director

of the war") and later as ambassador to the Soviet Union (1946–49).

A native of Indianapolis, Smith left college shortly after enrolling because of his father's illness; he entered the army from the National Guard during World War I. Later, attending the Infantry School at Fort Benning, Ga., he became one of the many future stars of the army who caught the eye of then-colonel George MARSHALL, who early in World War II made him secretary of the General Staff and then U.S. secretary of the Combined (Anglo-American) Chiefs of Staff.

Known as Beetle (a nickname he liked so well that he had his personal stationery engraved with a small black beetle), Smith had the countenance and something of the manner of a bulldog. Ike characterized him as "strong in character and abrupt by instinct"; some acquaintances ascribed part, at least, of Smith's famous irascibility to the ravages of ulcers.

In General Smith, with his high-level political and military experience, said the British historian John Ranelagh, the CIA acquired a director who "put it unmistakably at the top table and gave it the force to fend off State and the Pentagon." In 1953, however, President Eisenhower brought Smith into the State Department as undersecretary and later in the year appointed him chairman of the new Operations Coordinating Board—an organization intended to combine the conceiving, developing, and implementation of high national strategy. After serving as chairman of the U.S. delegation to the 1954 Geneva Conference on Indochina that produced the GENEVA ACCORDS, Smith retired; he had been made a full general in 1951.

Solidarity In August 1980 Polish workers struck for higher wages to help them meet rising prices. Lech WAŁESA, a former worker in the Lenin Shipyard at Gdansk, urged workers to demand not only better pay but the right to form independent unions. As the strike spread along the Baltic coast, Wałesa, who had become the leader, entered negotiations with the government that ended with concessions won. Soon, in a development without precedent in a Communist-controlled country, some ten million workers had enrolled in new unions to form a coalition named the National Coordinating Committee of Independent Autono-

mous Trade Unions, or more simply Solidarity (Solidarnosc), with Wałesa as chairman.

On February 11, 1981, after a year of continuing turbulence, General Wojciech JARUZELSKI became premier of Poland, but even with a degree of cooperation from Solidarity (which feared Soviet intervention if the Communist Polish government appeared to be in danger of being overthrown), the new premier faced continuing dissidence. On December 13, 1981, Jaruzelski—acting partly under pressure from BREZHNEV's regime in Moscow—brought in troops and tanks, instituted martial law, and rounded up and interned thousands of Solidarity members, thus for the time being putting an end to the Polish revolution. Jaruzelski's coup shocked Solidarity leaders, who had not believed that he would use violence against them. Wałesa spent most of 1982 in prison.

Solidarity did not regain its legal standing until April 1989, when the GORBACHEV era of PERESTROIKA and GLASNOST transformed the situation in Eastern Europe, with the former Soviet satellites now allowed to follow their own paths. Although Solidarity professed to be nonpolitical in nature, it had become recognized as a national movement with perhaps the central responsibility for Poland's future. In the June 1989 elections, the first free elections since the establishment of the EASTERN BLOC, anti-Communist candidates won 99 of the 100 seats in the upper house of the Polish Parliament. Elected president in 1989, Jaruzelski appointed Tadeusz MAZOWIECKI as prime minister, the first non-Communist head of government in Eastern Europe since the 1940s. In 1990 the voters chose Wałesa over Mazowiecki as president of Poland. *See also* JOHN PAUL II.

Solzhenitsyn, Alexander (1918–) Story writer, novelist, and essayist Solzhenitsyn is one of the most celebrated modern Russian writers. He is the author of three famous works about the Soviet GULAG, the system of prison camps: *The First Circle* (first English translation, 1968), *One Day in the Life of Ivan Denisovich* (first English translation, 1963), and the nonfiction *Gulag Archipelago* (first English translation, 1974–78). He received the 1970 Nobel Prize for literature.

A physics and mathematics honors graduate of the University of Rostov, Solzhenitsyn saw combat as an artillery officer in World War II and before the war was over underwent the experience that shaped much of his future life and writing. Arrested in 1945 for having made unfavorable comments about Joseph STALIN in a private letter, he spent the ensuing eight years in the gulag, where he began writing—secretly—and three more years in exile in Kazakhstan. During the 1950s he underwent treatment for cancer, which led ultimately to his novel *Cancer Ward* (first English translation, 1968).

Premier Nikita KHRUSHCHEV himself later commented on the circumstances surrounding the publication of *One Day in the Life of Ivan Denisovich.* Having succeeded a few years earlier in banning Boris PASTERNAK's famous novel *Doctor Zhivago,* Mikhail SUSLOV, the Communist Party's veteran ideological chief, opposed the publication of *Ivan Denisovich.* "How will the people perceive this?" Suslov asked Khrushchev, according to the latter's account. "How will they understand?" This time, however, Khrushchev—who had been concerned at the unfavorable publicity the USSR received worldwide for suppressing Pasternak's novel and forbidding him to accept the 1958 Nobel Prize for literature, and who also wished to loosen the literary strings somewhat—approved publication of *Ivan Denisovich* in the Soviet literary magazine *Novy Mir,* a decision that angered conservative Communists. This and several succeeding stories made Solzhenitsyn famous in Europe and America.

But now his fortunes began to change. The departure of Khrushchev in 1964 and the accession of Leonid BREZHNEV produced something of a neo-Stalinist political and intellectual climate in the USSR. Solzhenitsyn's succeeding works were banned, and he was vilified in the press (though the bitterness of his public attacks on the Communist Party for its many misdeeds very likely would not have been stomached by Khrushchev either). After the publication in the West of the first volume of *The Gulag Archipelago,* Solzhenitsyn was expelled from the Soviet Union in February 1974 —being too eminent, it seems, for the Brezhnev regime to apply to him its current practice of *PSYKHUSHKA,* confinement to a psychiatric hospital as a victim of some ailment such as "paranoid reformist delusions." In 1976 Solzhenitsyn took up

residence in the small town of Cavendish, Windsor County, Vt.

Solzhenitsyn was a dissenter of a special type— not a liberal like Andrei SAKHAROV or a Marxist-Leninist who simply wanted to make the system work better (as to some extent were both Roy MEDVEDEV and, even more so, Mikhail GORBACHEV himself) but a foe of "progressive ideology" wherever he saw it, East or West; in 1974, in fact, Solzhenitsyn considered the West as essentially "in an even worse and more perilous predicament than we are" because it had experienced two or three more decades of progressive experience. He accompanied this lament for the contemporary world with a succinct, brilliant, and blistering critique of Marxism and Communism—not only "decrepit and hopelessly antiquated" but "primitive," "superficial," "totally mistaken in its predictions," and "never a science." He underlined these assertions with a series of factual points describing the course of events in Russia, and presented telling complaints that still sounded contemporary, East or West, decades later—about the dangers of dependence on chemical fertilizers, the destruction of soil, the bulldozing of a tree-lined street to replace it with a "poisoned zone of asphalt and gasoline." Solzhenitsyn saw Christianity as "the only living spiritual force capable of undertaking the spiritual healing of Russia." But neither Christianity nor any other institution should have special privileges: freedom was Solzhenitsyn's dream.

To many Westerners, Solzhenitsyn as a Soviet exile proved something of a disappointment with his criticisms that seemed to apply as much to his new hosts as to his old opponents. He performed more as a scold and scourge than as a celebrated and duly grateful refugee novelist. Part of Solzhenitsyn's problem in the West—as KGB director Yuri ANDROPOV delightedly reported in a 1976 memorandum to his fellow ministers in the Kremlin— resulted from DISINFORMATION spread by KGB agents, some of it making Solzhenitsyn out to be an old-style Russian anti-Semite.

By 1991 one of Solzhenitsyn's themes—that the West was failing to put up an effective fight against Communism—had lost its point. But, unfortunately for him, the Holy Russia of which he dreamed seemed unlikely to take the place of the dismantled Communist state. In 1994, announcing his intention to return to Russia, as he had always planned, Solzhenitsyn said, "I know that I will be torn apart by people's tragedies and the events of the time." On his arrival back home, in May, he declared that he would do no more writing—he would be too busy.

Soong Qingling (1895–1981)   One of the famous Chinese Soong sisters (daughters of the wealthy Shanghai businessman Charlie Soong), Qingling married Sun Yat-sen, the founder of the Republic of China, in 1914. She was 16 years younger than her husband, who had two grown children by an earlier marriage. Her sister Meiling became the wife of CHIANG KAI-SHEK, and as Mme. Chiang had considerable international influence in her own right. Though not a member of the Chinese Communist Party, Soong Qingling supported MAO ZEDONG against the Nationalist government of her sister's husband, and in 1949, the year of victory over Chiang, she became a vice chairman (an honorific position) of the Communist Party's Central People's Government Council. In later life she several times rejected invitations to take up party membership and expressed severe criticism of the CULTURAL REVOLUTION.

Southeast Asia Treaty   Agreement signed in Manila on September 8, 1954, by representatives of the United States, Britain, France, Australia, New Zealand, the Philippines, Pakistan, and Thailand. Considered to be in many ways an analogue to the North Atlantic Treaty, which had created the NORTH ATLANTIC TREATY ORGANIZATION, the Pacific treaty was commonly known as SEATO; its principal negotiator, U.S. secretary of state John Foster DULLES, had originally thought of it as MANPAC, for Manila Pact.

Souvanna Phouma (1901–1984)   A French-trained civil engineer, Prince Souvanna Phouma with his half-brother, Prince Souphanouvong, led a coalition government in Laos during most of the 1950s. Overall, he served as prime minister four times, in short bursts, during that decade, then held the office for 13 years (1962–75). The brotherly duumvirate had a markedly unusual aspect: whereas Souvanna Phouma was non-Communist, Souphanouvong was head of the Communist PATHET LAO.

When the United States asked Souvanna Phouma to rid the government of Communists, the two princes instead joined forces to defeat General Phoumi Nosovan, whom the Americans had commissioned to destroy the Pathet Lao. After 1962, Souvanna Phouma shared power for a time with the Pathet Lao, until the United States harassed the organization forcibly enough during the VIETNAM WAR to drive it into the two northernmost provinces of Laos. But after U.S. withdrawal from Indochina in 1975, the Pathet Lao came to power and deposed Souvanna Phouma, converting the monarchy into the People's Democratic Republic of Laos.

Soviet coup, 1991   *See* STATE COMMITTEE FOR THE STATE OF EMERGENCY IN THE USSR.

Sovietology   Name often applied to the systematic study of the origins, nature, and behavior of the Soviet Union. The earliest American Sovietologists were diplomats, such as George KENNAN and Charles BOHLEN, who in the early 1930s were stationed in Baltic capitals preparing themselves for service when the United States and the Soviet Union should establish diplomatic relations, which happened in 1933. In Riga, Kennan wrote in a memoir, the Russian Section was a small unit that received Soviet magazines and other publications, studied them—statistics, propaganda, and all—and reported to the U.S. government on conditions in the USSR. "The suspicious Soviet mind," Kennan commented, "at once stamped this little research bureau as a sinister espionage center." However, "incredible as this must have appeared to people schooled in the habits of the locale, we who worked in the Russian Section were exactly what we purported to be. We had no secret agents, and wanted none." But Kennan did make one particular point about these activities, which concerned the value to be derived from the study of propaganda. "The prevarications of the propagandist," he said, "can be as revealing to the thoughtful student as the evasive answers of the patient to the psychiatrist." From such beginnings came the huge field of study and analysis of the Soviet Union prominent in the years following World War II. Observers of political maneuverings and the changes in the hierarchy of the Communist Party were often called Kremlinologists.

Spaak, Paul-Henri (1899–1972) Belgian statesman, premier both before and after World War II, who played a leading part in the development of the UNITED NATIONS and in the movement toward European unity. In 1957 he succeeded Lord ISMAY as secretary-general of the NORTH ATLANTIC TREATY ORGANIZATION, serving until 1961.

As foreign minister as well as prime minister, Spaak promoted the establishment of the BENELUX customs union and, in the period before the creation of NATO, strongly advocated U.S. participation in European defense. His supranational devotion won him the first presidency of the UN General Assembly (1946), the presidency of the Consultative Assembly of the COUNCIL OF EUROPE (1949–51), the presidency of the EUROPEAN COAL AND STEEL COMMUNITY (1952), and the chairmanship of the committee that drew up the Treaty of Rome to establish the EUROPEAN ECONOMIC COMMUNITY (1957).

Special Operations Aircraft During the VIETNAM WAR era, the United States developed a variety of low-tech aircraft, both fixed-wing and rotary, suitable for carrying out missions and providing operational support in limited wars fought in a variety of terrains and conditions. Early in the period, older aircraft such as B-26s from World War II proved to be useful in instances in which later high-speed jet aircraft showed limited value.

Sputnik I The first artificial earth-orbiting satellite, launched by the Soviet Union under General Secretary KHRUSHCHEV on October 4, 1957. The *beep-beep* that *Sputnik* emitted as it passed overhead became for a time a symbol of Soviet prowess in rocketry. Although Charles E. Wilson, the U.S. secretary of defense, dismissed the *Sputnik* launching as a "neat technical trick," the feat attracted worldwide acclaim and spurred the United States into a supercharged effort to catch up with its rival. *Sputnik* even caused an examination of the state of U.S. education. Contrary to a common belief, however, President EISENHOWER was already

advocating the development of a coordinated missile program. On January 31, 1958, a U.S. Army team led by Wernher von BRAUN, using a Jupiter-C rocket, launched the first U.S. satellite, called *Explorer I*. The space race had begun.

SR-71 After a Soviet missile brought down an American U-2 reconnaissance aircraft in 1960, U.S. intelligence turned again to the creators of the U-2, Lockheed's famous design team, headed by Clarence "Kelly" Johnson, for a replacement immune to ground fire. The result was the SR-71—the Blackbird. Proclaiming the prototype to the world on February 27, 1964, President Lyndon B. JOHNSON called it an interceptor; the design evolved into the SR-71. Since the CENTRAL INTELLIGENCE AGENCY knew that sooner or later the Soviets would succeed in downing a U-2, the decision to create a successor had been made in 1959. The great heat that super speeds would generate called for titanium, which through a series of fronts and subterfuges the CIA had managed to obtain from the USSR.

Powered by twin Pratt & Whitney jets that gulped up to 8,000 gallons of fuel an hour, the SR-71—which was, so far as is publicly known, the fastest, highest-flying aircraft ever built—made its first flight on December 23, 1964. The aircraft could exceed Mach 3 speeds and is known to have achieved altitudes of 100,000 feet. It had a wingspan of 55 feet 7 inches and length of 107 feet 7 inches. Although SR-71s were shot at perhaps thousands of times in reconnaissance flights over Soviet, Chinese, and other territory, none was ever hit. From its aerie 16 miles up, the SR-71's cameras in one hour's time could take note of every garbage can in an area the size of New York, New Jersey, and Pennsylvania combined.

Retired from service in 1989 in favor of satellites—partly because keeping one of these airplanes in the air cost $250,000 an hour—the SR-71s went out with a flourish, one of them setting a Los Angeles–to–Washington speed record of 68 minutes 17 seconds, the average speed being 2,112.5 mph. With its heat-resistant titanium skin, radar-deflecting curved surfaces, and special radar-absorbing paint, the SR-71 was an extraordinary

SR-71, U.S. photoreconnaissance aircraft, reached record speeds and altitudes.

achievement in itself and a precursor of the Stealth bomber (F-117A).

SS-20   *See* INTERCONTINENTAL BALLISTIC MISSILE.

Stalin, Joseph (1879–1953)   Born Iosif Vissario-novich Dzhugashvili in Gori, a town in Russian Georgia, Stalin was a true proletarian—the son of an alcoholic cobbler and an illiterate laundress—who rose from these obscure and unpromising provincial origins to become a far mightier auto-crat than any of the czars who ever sat on the throne of imperial Russia. Absolute master of the Soviet Union from the late 1920s until his death, and after World War II dictator of one of the world's two SUPERPOWERS, Stalin became one of the most important figures of the 20th century and—considering the size and power of his country and the unrivaled scope of his personal authority—per-haps the most powerful person who has ever lived. As the leader of an international political faith, he governed the minds of people around the world.

Born on December 21, 1879, the future "man of steel" (*stalin* means "steel-like" in English) en-dured a troubled childhood, with beatings by his drunken father and a series of serious illnesses, in-cluding smallpox. His father died when Joseph was ten, leaving his hardworking mother to sup-port four children by washing, sewing, and per-forming other household tasks for better-off families. After finishing at the local church school, Joseph went off on scholarship to the Orthodox seminary at Tiflis. By training to become a priest, he followed one of the few avenues of advance-ment open to someone of his nationality and sta-tion and at the same time lived his devout mother's cherished dream. Unfortunately for her hopes, however, her son was expelled in 1899—according to Communist legend, for revolutionary activity.

Within a year or two (the dates vary), young Dzhugashvili had unquestionably become engaged in revolutionary activities; he specialized in or-ganizing strikes and demonstrations. Soon there began the pattern of arrests standard among Russian revolutionaries. But for Dzhugashvili the pattern bore some distinctive markings: along with the frequent arrests (seven from 1902 to 1913) came light sentences and frequent escapes. Did this easy treatment by the authorities mean, as some observers have thought, that Dzhugashvili had inside connections with the police? Such an arrangement has never been proved, but it would have had nothing odd about it in the Russia of that day, when revolutionaries and secret police operated in a bewildering tangle of loyalties, so that an agent's primary fealty sometimes simply could not be determined. (The U.S. diplomat and expert in SOVIETOLOGY George KENNAN was told by various veteran Communists with whom he raised the question that Stalin was certainly capable of betraying comrades to the police out of jealousy or to avenge some injury, but probably not for money or from political conviction.)

In any case, though by 1903 Dzhugashvili had become a Bolshevik, he played only a minor role in revolutionary affairs until 1912, when Lenin (from Switzerland) lifted him from obscurity to make him a member of the CENTRAL COMMITTEE of what had now become the independent Bolshevik Party. The following year, now using the name Stalin, after finally becoming a respected revolutionary and briefly editing the just-founded *PRAVDA,* he found his days of lenient police treatment at an end. Arrested and exiled to Siberia, he returned only in March 1917, after the abdication of Czar Nicholas II and in time for the Bolshevik seizure of power in November (called the October Revolution because Russians still followed the Julian calendar).

Though chosen as one of the nine members of the party Central Committee and, in 1919, one of the five members of the POLITBURO, Stalin found himself in a peculiar position as a peasant, at least figuratively—untraveled and with limited education, surrounded by Lenin and other cosmopolitan figures to whom discussion and disputation had always been meat and drink. Curiously, however, this inferiority would quickly begin to work to his advantage. Respecting the Georgian's organizational ability and realizing he showed no promise as an ornament of the salon or the platform, Lenin and his colleagues gave Stalin various posts concerned with party business, which assumed growing importance as the early revolutionary state became increasingly centralized, bureaucratic, and repressive. The only member of the ruling circle who was not an intellectual, Stalin advanced in 1922 to the post of GENERAL SECRETARY—a position that held no appeal for Leon Trotsky, Lev Kamenev, and other party luminaries. "Comrade Card-Index," as Stalin was called by those who myopically failed to see the potential importance of this kind of activity, took full advantage of this opportunity not simply to manage party affairs but, building on work begun by Yakov Sverdlov (1885–1919), to create a nationwide organization staffed by persons loyal directly to him. Too late, the dying Lenin realized his error. "Comrade Stalin," he said in his testament (as foreign observers later called notes Lenin wrote at the time), "has concentrated an enormous power in his hand; and I am not sure that he always knows how to use that power with sufficient caution." Besides, Lenin said, Stalin was "too rude." He should be removed from his position in favor of someone else "more patient, more loyal, more polite and more attentive to comrades, less capriciousness, etc."

After Lenin's death in January 1924, however, nobody proved able to stop Stalin's rise. Besides his great personal drive and his organizational ability, he could draw on traits of character said to be typical of Georgian mountaineers—great patience (if not of the bureaucratic kind) while waiting for his strategic moment to come and great ability to hide his thoughts and motives—these characteristics serving a profound vindictiveness with its attendant skill at exacting revenge for any sort of insult or injury. With his gift for political intrigue and an inbred ruthlessness to add to these qualities, Stalin was well equipped to make himself absolute master of the Soviet Union. His moves during the next few years resembled the maneuvers that characterized the struggles for power within the ancient Roman triumvirates. Allying himself with Kamenev and Grigory Zinoviev to dispose of Trotsky, Stalin then formed a second triumvirate with Nikolai Bukharin and Alexei Rykov that drove his former allies from office. The disgrace of Bukharin and Rykov came later. Ultimately, during the Great Purge of the 1930s, all four of these ex-triumvirs faced firing squads.

Besides his skill in political maneuvering and his

Joseph Stalin, ruler of the Soviet Union for almost three decades

reliance on force, Stalin built his success on a talent for propaganda and self-promotion. In particular, he became perhaps the first of the great modern media politicians with his use of radio—brand-new in the 1920s—to reach directly from the Kremlin into cities and farms across the USSR. The most remote village in Siberia had its radio loudspeaker mounted in the town square, from which would issue, as if by magic, the voice of Comrade Stalin, coming all the way from Moscow to reach the ears of his people.

By 1928 Stalin had driven all his peers and rivals from the field. He had already promulgated a major change in Communist ideology with his doctrine of "socialism in one country," de-emphasizing the old aim of world revolution in favor of building up the USSR as a bastion of socialism. This pronouncement also served as a tactic against Trotsky, whose continuing belief in "permanent revolution" was said to imply, wrongly, that, without outside support from the European proletariat, the Soviet Union would lose its socialist qualities.

At the end of 1928 Stalin set out on an extraor-

dinary course of action aimed at transforming the Soviet Union into a modern state with a great industrial base and a flourishing agricultural sector. The most vividly remembered aspect of this period was the forced collectivization of agriculture, with its liquidation of reluctant peasants—the kulaks—who were driven into concentration camps or shot in enormous numbers. During this era, bullets and famine together may have caused as many as ten million deaths.

Whether or not his ruthless actions had actually created any effective threats to his supremacy, Stalin turned the second half of the 1930s into the Great Purge of alleged saboteurs and traitors in all parts of Soviet society—political figures, soldiers, technocrats, police officials, writers, teachers. The consequent weakening of the armed forces, which lost a high proportion of senior and field-grade officers, led other countries to write off the USSR as a potentially strong factor in diplomacy and war. World War II would show that this judgment, though perfectly reasonable, was totally wrong. Initially, however, Stalin's own conduct in 1941 contributed to the success of the invading German forces. Having made a tactical alliance with Adolf Hitler in 1939, the Soviet dictator—terrified of giving his new friend any pretext for making war on the USSR—ignored all the abundant signs and warnings of Hitler's intentions and allowed Soviet forces to be overwhelmed in the first days of the German invasion.

After emerging from an initial period of shock, when for two weeks the nation heard nothing from its chief, Stalin went on to prove himself an effective war leader, displaying a good grasp of strategy and a mastery of detail. But, though he increasingly chose able commanders, he disliked delegating authority and tended to meddle in operations. Not surprisingly, high officers who had been fortunate enough to escape the Great Purge had little desire to question his orders.

As a wartime negotiator with his eminent Allied colleagues, British prime minister Winston CHURCHILL and U.S. president Franklin D. ROOSEVELT, Stalin enjoyed striking success—not because he outwitted them, as has sometimes been said, but because Churchill and Roosevelt for much of the war feared the making of a second Hitler-Stalin deal and were willing to go a long way to prevent it; because Stalin took full advantage of the Red Army's situation as the force that was necessarily bearing the heaviest load of the fighting; and because of Stalin's readiness and ability to lie on a truly grand scale. In addition, it must be said, neither of the Western leaders had an adequate understanding of Russia and Communism, or of the true extent of Stalin's power. But in the latter stages of the war, it was not Western woolly-mindedness but the Red Army's advance into Central Europe that put Stalin in a position to impose his will on the countries of the region. Notably, the Western Allies (especially Churchill) argued desperately for a Poland free and friendly to the USSR, not quite realizing the deeply incompatible nature of these objectives. Nor did any terms agreed upon at the YALTA CONFERENCE sanction the division of Europe, though a case has been made that at the World War II Tehran Conference in 1943, Roosevelt had given inferential approval to Stalin's designs on Poland.

Throughout the war, Stalin appears to have anticipated the postwar conflict with the Western powers that became institutionalized as the Cold War. This expectation went back at least as far as his efforts in 1941 to reach territorial agreements on Eastern Europe with Britain and the United States—agreements that would have sanctioned Soviet control of the Baltic states and eastern Poland and thus were unacceptable to Churchill and Roosevelt. Speaking to V. M. MOLOTOV in 1945, Stalin said (according to interviews with Molotov recorded in the 1980s by a young Soviet scholar) that "now was the time to grab everything we could." Stalin told Marshal TITO in April 1945: "This war is not like those of the past; whoever occupies a territory imposes his own social system on it. Everybody imposes his own system as far as his army can advance. It could not be otherwise."

Many years later, Nikita KHRUSHCHEV observed: "After the defeat of Hitler, Stalin believed that he was in the same position as Alexander I after the defeat of Napoleon—that he could dictate the rules for all of Europe. Stalin even started believing that he could dictate new rules to the whole world. Part of his mistake was to exaggerate our capabilities and ride roughshod over the interests of our friends." Wanting U.S. and British troops to move into Austria, Yugoslavia, and Czechoslovakia and

to block off Denmark, Churchill telegraphed U.S. president Harry TRUMAN on May 12, 1945—just four days after the declaration of victory over Germany—that "an IRON CURTAIN is drawn down upon their [Soviet] front. We know nothing of what is happening behind it."

As Stalin had told Tito, the Soviet Union proceeded to impose its "social system" on the countries that had been occupied by the Red Army. Though the Cold War was a complex phenomenon, the division of Europe signaled and symbolized its beginning. In practice, the establishment of the EASTERN BLOC meant the extension of Stalin's rule across Eastern and parts of Central Europe. His intelligence service lost no time in declaring that the United States had replaced Britain as the MAIN ADVERSARY of the Soviet Union.

In the USSR itself, Stalin presided over a strange phase of national self-consciousness and xenophobia in which party spokesmen made extravagant and sometimes absurd claims concerning Soviet achievements in invention, science, and other activities. So remarkable had the leader's ego become that he even allowed the state cosmetic trust to flatter him by producing and selling a perfume called Stalin's Breath. In his final years, matters turned grimmer, when his personal paranoia led to rising persecutions, climaxing in the DOCTORS' PLOT —accusations that Kremlin doctors, most of them Jewish, had planned to murder various Soviet leaders.

Before the hapless doctors could be executed, however, dramatic events were to intervene. In the evening of March 2, 1953, a worker from the Kremlin hospital appeared at the apartment of a Moscow physician, A. L. Miasnikov, saying, "I have come to get you to come to the ill master."

"I quickly took leave of my wife (it was not clear where you might end up from there)," Miasnikov observed tellingly, and with two other physicians he drove to Stalin's summer house in Kuntsevo, a western suburb of the city. There they found a group of medical members of the state bureaucracy, all conscious of the fact that treating Stalin was a dangerous business—after all, other Kremlin doctors at that very moment sat in prison waiting for the executioners' summons. Stalin lay breathing heavily; an examination produced clear evidence of a cerebral hemorrhage "against a background of hypertension and atherosclerosis."

Miasnikov and his colleagues spent the night on watch, always in the company of a member of the CENTRAL COMMITTEE. Taking no chances, the politicians solicited advice from a variety of doctors belonging to different Soviet institutes and councils. Young officers offered their blood for transfusions, and one wrote, "Let the surgeons tear out my young heart and insert it in Comrade Stalin." As time passed, "it occurred to someone that perhaps he had had a mild heart attack on top of everything else." When, after taking electrocardiograms, a young woman physician declared that Stalin had indeed suffered a heart attack, the doctors shivered: failure to diagnose myocardial infarction in another case had been one of the charges against the imprisoned Kremlin doctors. But Miasnikov took the lead in declaring the electrocardiogram changes merely "cerebral pseudoinfarct" readings. As the days dragged on, the comatose Stalin began vomiting blood. Marshal Nikolai BULGANIN sarcastically wanted to know how the doctors accounted for that.

Finally, at 9:50 P.M. on March 5, Stalin's breathing stopped and his pulse failed. "The great dictator," wrote Miasnikov, "until just a short while ago omnipotent and untouchable, had been transformed into a pitiful, miserable corpse, which tomorrow pathologists would carve up into bits." When the autopsy showed extensive sclerosis of cerebral arteries, Miasnikov speculated that the weakening of inhibition to be expected in such cases had manifested itself with Stalin as "a loss of orientation concerning what was good and what was bad . . . who was a friend and who was an enemy." Also characteristic of such cases, said the doctor, is an exaggeration of character traits, so that a person of suspicious temperament becomes pathologically suspicious. Thus one could perhaps account, in Stalin's case, for "the loss of the ingredient of appropriateness in the analysis of people and events." Miasnikov's thorough and circumstantial account, which appeared in *Literaturnaia gazeta* in 1989, appears to remove any grounds for believing the long-circulated rumor that Stalin was murdered by Politburo colleagues.

Though strongly clashing opinions were held about this man who wielded unprecedented and unrivaled power, no one could doubt that a giant had passed. While he ruled the Soviet Union, the country had survived terror, famine, and invasion to become one of the two leading states of the world.

Long years later, on the 40th anniversary of Stalin's death and more than a year after the USSR itself had disappeared, a small band of the elderly faithful appeared at the Kremlin with carnations and tulips for the dictator's grave. "People remember how well we lived under Stalin," declared an old woman. "Everything was for the people. Now everything is for the rich." On that same day, in Stalin's home village in Georgia, hundreds of people, accompanied by funeral music, marched into the town square, where they could contemplate the statue of the man of steel still standing in its center.

START *See* STRATEGIC ARMS REDUCTION TALKS.

Star Wars *See* STRATEGIC DEFENSE INITIATIVE.

State Committee for the State of Emergency in the USSR The self-bestowed title of the members of the group that staged an attempted coup or putsch against Soviet president Mikhail GORBACHEV in August 1991. Calling themselves the "Soviet leadership," this group of Communist hard-liners, fidgeting before the TV cameras in their initial press conference, made plain their objections to reform and to the general mood in the country of continuing crisis. The members of the committee—a substantial group that looked initially as if it might carry the day—included (in alphabetical order, as they listed themselves in their original proclamation) O. D. Baklanov, first vice chairman of the USSR Defense Council; V. A. KRYUCHKOV, chairman of the KGB; V. S. Pavlov, prime minister of the USSR; B. K. Pugo, USSR minister of internal affairs; V. A. Starodubtsev, chairman of the USSR Peasants' Union; A. I. Tizyakov, president of the Association of State Enterprises and Industrial, Construction, Transportation, and Communications Facilities; D. T. Yazov, USSR minister of defense; and G. I. Yanayev, acting president of the USSR. Last on the list but not least in importance, Yanayev was the leader of the group. After the failure of the coup, Alexander YAKOVLEV, one of its strongest opponents and a close associate of Gorbachev in the creation of PERESTROIKA, characterized the plotters as "fools" who did not understand the feelings of the Soviet people. *See also* YELTSIN, Boris Nikolaevich.

Stealth *See* F-117A.

Stevenson, Adlai Ewing (1900–1965)   One of the most dramatic personal confrontations of the Cold War took place during the CUBAN MISSILE CRISIS in October 1962, when Adlai Stevenson, the U.S. ambassador to the UNITED NATIONS, asked the Soviet representative whether the USSR would deny having placed offensive missiles in Cuba. Sounding like a district attorney, leaning forward, staring at his Soviet counterpart, Stevenson posed his question and then rapped out: "Yes or no? Don't wait for the translation. Yes or no?" Declaring he was not in a U.S. court of law, Ambassador Valerian ZORIN refused to reply, thus, as it turned out, saving himself from committing international perjury.

The grandson of Grover Cleveland's vice president, Stevenson came from a well-off Illinois family. After graduating from Princeton (1922), he attended the Harvard Law School for two years (where he did poorly), worked for a time for the family newspaper in Bloomington, Ill., and then acquired his law degree from Northwestern University. In 1933 he entered on two straight decades of government service, going to Washington as special counsel for the new Agricultural Adjustment Administration. From 1941 to 1944, during World War II, he served as an assistant to the secretary of the navy and in 1945 as an assistant to the secretary of state. He participated as an adviser in the founding conference of the UN in 1945 and the 1946 General Assembly session in London.

In 1948 Stevenson won the governorship of Illinois and in this far-from-gentle sphere of political activity quickly showed a grasp of practical realities that later observers, who often criticized him for a hesitancy reminiscent of Shakespeare's Hamlet, might have been surprised to see. On one occasion, for instance, it took him only a few minutes to end a prison riot that had baffled the warden and guards.

Nominated for president in 1952 by the Democrats, Stevenson had the misfortune to oppose one of the all-time greatest and most popular American heroes, Dwight D. EISENHOWER, and to be supported by an administration that had become generally unpopular and presided over what seemed an endless KOREAN WAR. Though the campaign was spirited, the outcome, seen in retrospect, was foreordained. Yet Stevenson's grace and wit had wide appeal, and his effort to "talk sense to the American people" won him many admirers at home and abroad—so much so that on the morrow of the election a British commentator would say, "His was the boldest attempt in our time to become a philosopher king." In defeat Stevenson had become a world figure.

In 1956 Stevenson had no choice but to accept the Democratic nomination again, though he was to lose to Ike this time by a slighter larger margin than in 1952. In 1960, with Richard M. NIXON at the head of the Republican ticket, John F. KENNEDY claimed the Democratic nomination. The hopes of some Stevenson supporters, however, including Eleanor ROOSEVELT, died only with reluctance. On December 12, 1960, President-elect Kennedy announced the appointment of Stevenson as U.S. ambassador to the UN.

Stikker, Dirk (1897–)   Dutch statesman who served as secretary-general of the NORTH ATLANTIC TREATY ORGANIZATION (1961–64). A strong supporter of NATO, Stikker had previously been foreign minister (1949–53); later he served as the Netherlands' ambassador to Britain.

Straight, Michael (1916–)   Well-known American editor and writer who played an important part in the espionage case of the CAMBRIDGE FIVE by identifying Anthony BLUNT as one of the Soviet agents. The son of wealthy American parents, Straight grew up in England and in the 1930s attended Cambridge, where he was active in Communist organizations and developed friendships with Blunt, a teaching fellow, and Guy BURGESS, a recent graduate—both of whom were involved with Soviet intelligence and engaged in recruiting students to become future moles, or underground agents. Though rejecting a specific assignment, Straight acceded to Blunt's order to go to the

United States after graduating and await further, undefined instructions.

During the ensuing years Straight worked in various Washington offices and with the liberal *New Republic* (founded by his parents), of which he was later editor and publisher; during World War II he served in the U.S. Army Air Forces. So far as is known, he performed no missions for the KGB and last met with a Soviet contact in 1942. Although aware of the continuing espionage of his friends, Straight kept silent until 1963, when he told his story to the FBI after declining U.S. president John F. KENNEDY's invitation to become chairman of a new agency, the National Endowment for the Arts. A British interrogator later told Straight that his information had provided "the first hard evidence" against Burgess and Blunt.

From 1969 to 1977, Straight served Presidents NIXON and FORD as deputy chairman of the National Endowment for the Arts.

Strategic Air Command (SAC) Generally regarded during the Cold War as the key element of the U.S. armed forces, the Strategic Air Command, with its long-range bombers and later its INTERCONTINENTAL BALLISTIC MISSILES, constituted the principal delivery agency for nuclear bombs and hence was considered the custodian of U.S. DETERRENCE. Its special significance was acknowledged by the command arrangement, which called on SAC, headquartered in Omaha, Neb., to report directly to the JOINT CHIEFS OF STAFF rather than to the command of the air force. Under the EISENHOWER administration in particular, with its cost-cutting approach to conventional weapons, SAC clearly figured as the centerpiece of the U.S. military.

Strategic, in this context, refers to organized attack on the war-making capacity of the enemy, normally involving the bombing of targets in the enemy homeland: missile launch sites, factories, communications facilities, and the like. The Tactical Air Command, in contrast, was created as a mobile strike force for use in support of military operations in "brushfire" wars. *See also* LEMAY, Curtis Emerson.

Strategic Arms Limitation Talks (SALT) In 1972, U.S.-Soviet arms-limitation discussions begun in 1969 bore fruit in the treaty known as SALT I, which established limits on various kinds of nuclear delivery systems. U.S. president NIXON and Soviet premier KOSYGIN signed the agreement in the Kremlin on May 26, 1972. The leaders also agreed to place limits on the deployment of ANTIBALLISTIC MISSILES (ABMs), which, in the labyrinthine world of nuclear strategy, were regarded by some authorities as offensive rather than defensive weapons because, if they proved truly capable of serving their defensive purpose, ABMs would free their possessor for offensive action. (In the 1980s, similar arguments would greet the REAGAN administration's proposed STRATEGIC DEFENSIVE INITIATIVE.)

The signatories of SALT I regarded the treaty, which was to run for five years, as a first step toward future negotiations. Somewhat surprisingly, in view of earlier U.S. views, SALT I permitted the Soviets to increase the lead they already held in the number of INTERCONTINENTAL BALLISTIC MISSILES (ICBMs) and to keep their superiority in submarine-launched ballistic missiles (SLBMs). The USSR would be allowed 2,358 ICBMs, the United States 1,710; for SLBMs, the Soviet Union 62, and the United States 44. This arrangement was satisfactory only because of the U.S. lead in MIRVs (MULTIPLE INDEPENDENTLY TARGETABLE REENTRY VEHICLES; that is, missiles carrying multiple warheads). The agreement established a kind of parity between the two powers. But a U.S. expert on international relations, Zbigniew BRZEZINSKI, pointed out a problem: What would happen when Soviet technology caught up with American? Would the Soviets willingly reduce this asymmetry?

The superiority-vs.-parity question continued to shadow arms discussions between the SUPERPOWERS. In 1974, meeting at Vladivostok, General Secretary BREZHNEV and U.S. president FORD reached a working understanding that, however, did not become SALT II until June 1979, when Brezhnev signed along with Jimmy CARTER, the third president to represent the United States in the talks. This agreement called for equality—2,250 vehicles each, including MIRVs—but Congress rejected the treaty, which became a victim of the Soviet invasion of AFGHANISTAN and the consequent end of DÉTENTE. The United States declared, however, that it would nevertheless respect the terms of the treaty.

In May 1972, Soviet premier Alexei Kosygin *(l.)* and U.S. president Richard M. Nixon sign the SALT I agreement in Moscow.

Strategic Arms Reduction Talks (START)   U.S.-Soviet meetings that led to the signing of the Strategic Arms Reduction Treaty, signed in the Kremlin by U.S. president BUSH and Soviet president GORBACHEV on July 31, 1991. The proclaimed purpose of the treaty was to produce a 50 percent reduction in each side's strategic weapons. Less than three weeks later came the putsch by the STATE COMMITTEE FOR THE STATE OF EMERGENCY IN THE USSR that attempted to overthrow Gorbachev. In 1992, after the breakup of the USSR, the Russian Supreme Soviet ratified the treaty.

Strategic Defense Initiative (SDI)   A program proposed in 1983, particularly favored and eloquently advocated by U.S. president REAGAN, under which the United States would create a great defensive shield that could destroy incoming enemy missiles. The administration put considerable funds into furthering the project, which won the name Star Wars from skeptical observers. Proponents of the program included physicist Edward TELLER, a fierce anti-Communist who is often called the father of

the HYDROGEN BOMB. Though Reagan declared publicly that SDI constituted a force for peace and that once it was achieved the United States would share it with the Soviet Union, thus supposedly freeing each SUPERPOWER from the fear of nuclear annihilation, the Soviets did not accept the concept (which, they maintained, contravened the ANTIBALLISTIC MISSILE provisions of SALT I), and many Americans considered the project so loaded with uncertainties that, as a gambling proposition, it amounted to a colossally expensive long shot.

Nevertheless, considerable evidence exists that SDI was taken far more seriously in the Kremlin than it was in the U.S. Congress and that its potential existence helped convince Soviet leaders they could not hope to continue the costly arms competition with the United States. In a 1993 meeting of former U.S. and Soviet officials, a former Soviet foreign minister, Alexander Bessmertnykh, declared that the prospect of SDI had led Soviet military officials to demand better missiles but had enabled those in the government opposed to the Cold War to promote agreements on arms limita-

U.S. president Ronald Reagan *(r.)* and his secretary of state, George Shultz, with a mysterious component of "Star Wars"—the proposed Strategic Defense Initiative

tions. Thus, from this point of view, the often-derided SDI (a "very personal" matter to Reagan, according to former Secretary of State George SHULTZ) played a part in ending the Cold War. Shultz said, however, that Reagan supported SDI as a mechanism of defense, not as part of any deliberate plan to lead the Soviets to bankrupt themselves through spending on defense. In any case, the project faded away after Reagan left office and the Cold War wound down. Secretary of Defense Les Aspin declared the "end of the Star Wars era" on May 13, 1993, saying that henceforth weapons in space would be the subject of only small-scale research.

strategic hamlet In March and April 1962 the Americans and the South Vietnamese launched a major effort against the insurgent VIETCONG. The plan called for bringing peasants from the countryside into villages surrounded by moats and walled off by fences of bamboo stakes. In these villages the people would be protected against Vietcong attacks, and the Vietcong would at the same time be cut off from its source of supplies and recruits. Once in the villages the people would, according to the plan, be won for the government of South Vietnam through participation in free elections and through land reform, the availability of medical care, and the creation of schools. The strategic-hamlet idea was developed by Sir Robert Thompson and was based on British counterinsurgency experience during the MALAYAN WAR. Within a year the South Vietnamese claimed great success for the program, with seven million people supposedly having been gathered into 7,000 hamlets. American reporters expressed doubts about this optimism. Some of them reported on visits made to stockades into which peasants had been driven at bayonet point to engage in forced labor. This reaction offered an early instance of the long disillusionment that was to characterize press reactions to official Vietnamese and U.S. statements about the VIETNAM WAR.

Success Notably optimistic code name given by the CENTRAL INTELLIGENCE AGENCY to the June 1954 operation in Guatemala that caused President Jacobo ARBENZ to flee the country. The ease with which the coup produced the desired result seemed to justify the designation.

Suez crisis In July 1956 Secretary of State John Foster DULLES announced that the United States would withdraw the financial support it had promised to Egypt for the building of the ASWAN HIGH DAM. Embarrassed both personally and financially by this reversal, Egyptian president NASSER proceeded to nationalize the canal (most of the shares of which were held in Britain and France), declaring that this step would give him the income he needed to replace the withdrawn U.S. loan.

Stung, in turn, by their loss of control of the canal, the British and French together with Israel, then Egypt's bitter enemy, contrived an elaborate riposte. The Israeli army would invade Egypt, thus —if all went well—freeing the canal and also enabling Israel to deepen its border by taking control of the Sinai peninsula. With these objectives accomplished, Britain and France would then appear with troops in the guise of peacemakers.

On October 29, 1956, the Israelis attacked with tanks, crossing the Sinai and moving toward the canal. The British and French entered the action by bombing Egyptian airfields, which, as a British official conceded, was a strange move for peacemakers to make, since the Egyptians were the victims of aggression and had attacked nobody. The slipshod venture even included a British and French ultimatum issued to both sides—withdraw ten miles from the canal on either side—although the Israelis were still 70 miles away. "The whole thing was so cocked up," said Sir Anthony Nutting of the British Foreign Office, "as well as being grossly dishonest."

On November 5, after what seemed endless delay, with hostile opinion building around the world, British and French forces began landing at Port Said and elsewhere. But the game was up. The

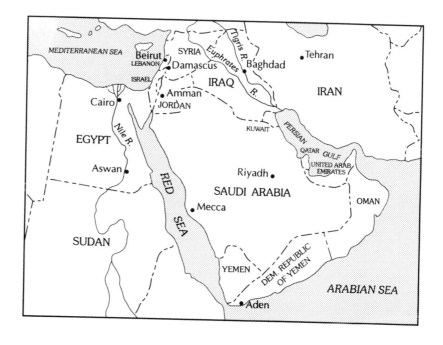

The Middle East

U.S. EISENHOWER administration, furious at this attempt to present it with a fait accompli, joined with the Soviet Union in opposing the venture (the Soviets threatened to send "volunteers" to the canal) and pressed the members of the ad hoc coalition to abandon their attacks. Tellingly, the U.S. government refused to lend Britain the money to replace oil supplies lost when Nasser ordered the canal blocked. Particularly distressing for the West, from a Cold War perspective, was the timing of the invasion. The attack on Egypt occurred while the Soviets were crushing the HUNGARIAN REVOLUTION and thus directed some of the world's attention and energies away from the freedom fighters battling Soviet tanks in the streets of Budapest.

The Suez plan, an attempt at a sort of imperialistic last hurrah by Britain and France, marked the end of the political career of the British prime minister, Sir Anthony EDEN, although he stayed on in office until the following January. For the Soviets, however, it was the beginning of an opportunity to influence events in the Middle East.

Sukarno (Kusno Sosro) (1901–1970) Indonesian political activist who joined other nationalists during World War II to plan for independence from the Netherlands after the war and on August 17, 1945, was chosen president of the new country as it proclaimed its independence. But the Dutch, who spent the war under German occupation, returned to Indonesia, which they still regarded as their colony, in the autumn of 1945, and a four-year war ensued. Finally, facing UNITED NATIONS sanctions and a U.S. economic boycott, the Dutch agreed to grant Indonesia its independence. In 1950, under the new constitution, Sukarno officially took office as the country's president.

The son of a schoolteacher, Sukarno graduated in 1926 from the technical college at Bandung and opened an engineering firm. But he quickly demonstrated his overriding interest in politics, becoming involved with several groups that sought a form of political order between radical Marxism and Islam. During the war for independence (1945–49), he made skillful use of the Indonesian Communists against the Dutch.

As president, Sukarno with his gift for oratory attempted to unite the various ethnic and cultural groups of his 3,000-mile-long country's distinct islands and populations. In 1955, as host of the BANDUNG CONFERENCE, he became a spokesperson for African and Asian nationalists who rejected the more theoretical and ideological concerns of the Marxists and the members of radical Islamic groups, and a proponent of the NONALIGNMENT concept for the THIRD WORLD. But he could never free himself of the need for Communist political support, and his balancing of cabinets between anti-Communist army officers and politicians with Communist sympathies proved ultimately to be an impossible task.

By 1965 Sukarno had succumbed to what one writer called "an obsession with the external signs of national greatness as expressed in wasteful monuments and empty slogans." On September 30, 1965, rebellious army officers attempted a coup, and the Indonesian Communist Party tried to take advantage of the confusion by launching its own offensive against the government. Army leaders not involved in the coup, however, put down the rebellion, leaving Sukarno in office but only as a figurehead. The army, under General Suharto, also launched a counteroffensive that literally wiped out the Indonesian Communist Party, officially banned in 1966. By March 1967 Sukarno had lost all of his political power; he lived on, under house arrest in Djakarta, until July 1970.

summit In the early years of the Cold War, as nuclear weapons increased in destructive force and diplomats seemed powerless to affect events, former British prime minister Winston CHURCHILL began to advocate a "conference at the summit," in which the leaders of the great powers would come together and confront the fundamental issue of war or peace. Just two months after the death of Soviet premier Joseph STALIN in March 1953, Churchill gave the House of Commons a description of such a meeting as he envisioned it (although, curiously, he did not use his own word *summit* in this particular speech): "The conference should not be overhung by a ponderous or rigid agenda, or led into mazes of technical details. The conference should be confined to the smallest number of Powers and persons possible. It should meet with a measure of informality and a still greater measure of privacy and seclusion." Even if it produced no firm and specific agreement, Churchill said, the conference could lead the participants to decide that "they might do something better than tear the human race, including themselves, into bits." Though no meeting followed immediately, in the ensuing years, beginning with a 1955 four-power conference in Geneva, numerous heads-of-government meetings took place—not often, however, with the seclusion and the air of Olympian purpose Churchill had prescribed.

Among notable summit meetings: Paris, May 1960, the summit that never was—Soviet premier KHRUSHCHEV walked out after U.S. president EISENHOWER refused to apologize for a U-2 reconnaissance flight over the Soviet Union; Vienna, June 1961, U.S. president KENNEDY and Khrushchev debated the status of BERLIN; GLASSBORO, N.J., June 1967, U.S. president JOHNSON and Soviet premier KOSYGIN discussed the VIETNAM WAR and other issues; Moscow, May 1972, U.S. president NIXON and Soviet general secretary BREZHNEV signed the ABM (ANTIBALLISTIC MISSILE) Treaty and SALT I; Vladivostok, November 1974, Brezhnev and U.S. president FORD developed principles for SALT II; Vienna, June 1979, U.S. president CARTER and Brezhnev signed SALT II; Reykjavík, October 1986, U.S. president REAGAN saw Soviet leader Mikhail GORBACHEV demonstrate the style of a new kind of Soviet leader; Malta, December 1989, U.S. president BUSH and Gorbachev declared the Cold War over.

As time went on, Churchill's coinage, intended to apply only to the highest-level meetings, became widely used and progressively debased. The press came to apply *summit* to almost any kind of important conference.

superpower　At the end of World War II, it became plain that a new kind of world order had emerged. Just two countries, the United States and the Soviet Union, could now realistically be considered great powers, capable of acting independently in world affairs. Germany and Japan lay devastated, and the traditional Western European powers, Britain and France, were sapped by the war (France, in addition, had to combat the social and other effects of a four-year German occupation). The term *great powers* would probably have described the two giants accurately enough, but in an era of hyperbole, *superpower* seems an inevitable coinage, and its use certainly avoids ambiguity. Holding the status of superpower, however, did not carry with it, for either the United States or the USSR, the ability to have everything its way, even within its own sphere of influence, East or West—a point commentators on both sides often seemed to overlook. In addition, many countries of the THIRD WORLD sought to remain outside either bloc in a stance of NONALIGNMENT, though often coyly allowing themselves to be courted by both superpowers.

Supreme Soviet　Literally, the "supreme council," established under the 1936 constitution of the Soviet Union as the national legislative body, with two houses, the Council of the Union (elected on the basis of population) and the Council of Nationalities (elected territorially, by republics, regions, and area). The first Supreme Soviet, numbering 1,143 deputies, was convoked on January 12, 1938. At the head of the Supreme Soviet stood the Presidium, a group originally of 37 members serving as a collective president, as Soviet premier Joseph STALIN called it. As titular head of the Soviet state, the chairman of the Presidium received ambassadors and performed other such ritual duties and was frequently spoken of as the president of the Soviet Union.

Though the members of the Supreme Soviet constituted an elite group made up of Soviet achievers, this body in practice served, as one scholar described it, merely as a "ratifying and propagating body." Under the Soviet system the COMMUNIST PARTY OF THE SOVIET UNION and its leaders, not the government, held the real power; the Supreme Soviet, whose members were chosen in uncontested elections, was a legislature in form, not in substance. But even though deputies had no function except to applaud decisions already taken by the party, these jobs were highly desirable; a deputy received two free trips to Moscow every year, the privilege of shopping in elite stores, and inclusion on priority lists for obtaining a desirable apartment and a private car.

Under constitutional changes adopted in 1990, deputies to the Supreme Soviet were to be elected by the new CONGRESS OF PEOPLE'S DEPUTIES from its own membership.

Suslov, Mikhail Andreyevich (1902–1982) One of the least known but most influential of all party leaders, Suslov became a member of the COMMUNIST PARTY OF THE SOVIET UNION's CENTRAL COMMITTEE in 1941, and through the four ensuing decades of his life—as head of Agitprop (Propaganda and Agitation Department), editor of *PRAVDA,* Central Committee secretary, and member of the Politburo (from 1955)—he acted as the ideological chief of the Communist Party. Suslov showed himself to be one of history's most notable éminences grises, not only surviving but as a behind-the-scenes operator supervising changes in the Soviet hierarchy. Unwaveringly conservative, he could justly be called the last Stalinist. Already the party's chief ideologue in 1948, he led the Soviet campaign to ostracize Yugoslavia and its leader, Marshal TITO. In the KHRUSHCHEV era he was the official who caused the banning of Boris PASTERNAK's famous novel *Doctor Zhivago,* a decision Khrushchev later regretted; Suslov probably made the decision, Khrushchev concluded, simply on the basis of an unfavorable brief report given him by an aide. Suslov also opposed the publication of *One Day in the Life of Ivan Denisovich,* Alexander SOLZHENITSYN's famous story about existence in the Soviet GULAG. "How will the people perceive this?" Suslov asked Khrushchev, according to the latter's account. "How will they understand?" This time, however, Khrushchev approved publication in the Soviet literary magazine *Novy Mir,* a decision that left conservative Communists unhappy and angry.

After Khrushchev's 1959 trip to the United States and his seeming rapprochement with President EISENHOWER, followed in 1960 by the shooting down of a U.S. U-2 spy plane on the eve of a SUMMIT conference in Paris, Suslov pressed for a harder line toward the United States and the West. At the fateful meeting of the Communist Party Presidium on October 14, 1964, which followed months of anti-Khrushchev plotting led by Suslov, it was he who read off the lengthy bill of particulars against Khrushchev, while the head of the party sat listening with reddening face. Suslov charged the accused with a range of offenses running from playing "organizational leap-frog," to using "dirty language" in speaking to the presumably sensitive members of the party Presidium, to practicing "great-power chauvinism" in dealing with smaller Eastern European countries. For the first time in history, the leader of the Soviet Union and the Communist Party was removed from office in accordance with party rules and allowed simply to fade into retirement. Suslov, it appears, rejected the opportunity to succeed Khrushchev himself; instead he gave his support to Leonid BREZHNEV.

Almost a decade later, however, the long-surviving Suslov appeared to disavow Washington summitry as practiced by Brezhnev. In the early 1980s, even at the age of 80, Suslov still wielded enough influence to exert an adverse effect on the career of KGB director Yuri ANDROPOV, who had to wait for Suslov's death to achieve a position of power; he succeeded Suslov as Central Committee secretary in charge of ideological matters and became Brezhnev's successor later that year.

Suslov "is an honest man and undoubtedly loyal to Communist ideals," Khrushchev charitably observed several years into his forced retirement, "but his limitations are very harmful."

symmetrical response The doctrine, developed during the TRUMAN administration, that the West—certainly the United States—must take action in response to any Soviet challenge to Western interests, wherever the perceived provocation might arise. This was not, however, a formula for nuclear or other large-scale war; an action would be calibrated to the need, which under the doctrine could include general war but might merely call for some kind of local action. Looking back to the early days of the United States, the authors of the basic document quoted the *Federalist:* "The means to be employed must be proportioned to the extent of the mischief." The doctrine, based on a theory of MASSIVE RETALIATION, raised very serious questions, because it would leave the initiative to the adversary and, by requiring action anywhere at any time, could constitute an enormous drain on U.S. financial and material resources. *See also* ASYMMETRICAL RESPONSE; NSC-68.

T

T-10   Soviet 50-ton heavy tank that entered service in the 1950s. The T-10 carried a 122 mm gun and two 12.7-mm machine guns and cruised at about 30 mph.

T-54   Designation of two Soviet tanks: (1) 35-ton battle tank produced in huge quantities for the USSR and other WARSAW PACT countries. It entered service in 1948, with some 30,000 of this tank and a variant, the T-55, coming off the lines before production ceased in 1963. It was armed with a 100-mm gun and two 7.62-mm machine guns. (2) Medium (40-ton) tank that first appeared in 1954.

T-62   Soviet battle tank that entered service in about 1963 as the successor to the T-54 and T-55. It carried a 115-mm gun and reached a road speed of about 30 mph.

Tactical Air Command   *See* STRATEGIC AIR COMMAND.

Taiwan   In 1949, after their defeat by MAO ZEDONG and the Chinese Communists, the Chinese Nationalist army of CHIANG KAI-SHEK and hundreds of thousands of refugees fled to offshore islands, principally Taiwan (then known as Formosa). Here, declaring themselves the legitimate government of China, the newcomers took over the island government, suppressing all independent political activity by native Taiwanese. The Nationalists put restrictions on speech and the press and punished dissenters with imprisonment and sometimes execution. Teachers were forbidden to teach Taiwanese history, and use of the local Taiwanese dialect was prohibited in schools and public affairs. Something of a historical precedent existed for this incursion: in the 17th century a Chinese general fleeing the Manchus set up an independent kingdom on the island, displaying no more interest than did his 20th-century successors in the wishes of the local population. During the succeeding centuries, the proportion of the population having Chinese origin increased and the native aborigines were pressed into the interior of the island. In 1895, following a war with China, Japan took possession of Taiwan; it was returned to China after World War II.

Whatever its political problems, Taiwan in the decades following the war rose from poverty to striking prosperity, with the help in the 1950s of U.S. aid. Concentrating on geopolitical concerns, the U.S. EISENHOWER administration, recognizing that in Taiwan it had an "unsinkable aircraft carrier" with which to curb Communist China, gave Chiang strong support while declining to recognize the government of mainland China. By 1965 Taiwan found itself able to take a noteworthy step—it became the first country receiving U.S. aid to inform the donor that it no longer needed help. In 1978, after the U.S. CARTER administration formalized relations with the People's Republic of China (Communist China), the United States—amid much political controversy and bitterness—ended its formal diplomatic relations with the Republic of China, as the Taiwan government was called. *See also* CHINA LOBBY; QUEMOY AND MATSU.

Taiwan Straits Crises   *See* QUEMOY AND MATSU.

TASS Universally used acronym for Telegraph Agency of the Soviet Union, the title of the office that had the responsibility of distributing foreign news (carefully selected and heavily censored) inside the USSR and of sending abroad news from within the country. First known as ROSTA (for Rossiskoye Telegrafnoye Agentsvo), it was a branch of Agitprop, an abbreviation of "Agitation and Propaganda Department," the original title of a Communist Party branch that, like other Soviet organizations, underwent periodic changes of name. The role of such agencies in Soviet life was clearly stated in an Agitprop publication declaring that "the press, propaganda, agitation, science, the movies, literature, art, the radio, museums, libraries, and other cultural and educational institutions are all means for political education of the masses." As described by a *New York Times* correspondent, David K. Shipler, the Soviet media projected "a mirror image of Soviet defects onto the United States, making Soviet problems into American ones." For high Soviet officials Tass provided a special service—a daily secret memorandum containing uncensored foreign news. The organization also acted through radio broadcasts as the official voice of the Kremlin.

Taylor, Maxwell Davenport (1901–) One of the most prominent U.S. military officers of the Cold War era, Taylor served as chief of staff of the army from 1955 to 1959 and in 1961, under President KENNEDY, came out of retirement to assume a brand-new position, military representative of the president. From 1962 to 1964 he was chairman of the Joint Chiefs of Staff. Heavily involved in decisions concerning the VIETNAM WAR, in 1964 he succeeded Henry Cabot LODGE as ambassador in SAIGON.

A native of a small town in Missouri, Taylor took the entrance examinations for both West Point and Annapolis but failed the latter. Years later he observed, "If the Strait of Malacca had been in Europe, I might have been an admiral instead of a general"—a comment reminiscent of the 19th-century painter James A. McNeill Whistler, who once said, looking back at his dismissal from West Point, "If silicon were a gas, I might be a major general." Taylor graduated from the military academy in 1922.

General Maxwell Taylor, U.S. Army chief of staff, chairman of the Joint Chiefs

In 1942, after working as one of the secretaries of the General Staff, Taylor became chief of staff of the 82nd Infantry Division, commanded by Major General Matthew B. RIDGWAY; the division was transforming itself into the 82nd Airborne, which led Taylor to make the later comment that he became a paratrooper "entirely by accident." In the 1944 Normandy invasion and the ensuing fight across Europe, he commanded the 101st Airborne Division. After the war Taylor served as superintendent at West Point and as U.S. military commander in BERLIN before going to Korea in 1953 to command the Eighth Army during the KOREAN WAR; the next year he became commander of U.S. forces in the Far East, and in 1955 he was briefly UNITED NATIONS supreme commander in Korea.

As chief of staff, Taylor, who wished to increase the flexibility of the army by building up conventional forces, clashed with the chairman of the JOINT CHIEFS OF STAFF, Admiral Arthur W. RADFORD, who favored the doctrine of MASSIVE RETALIATION, and with President EISENHOWER, who supported reliance on the nuclear threat on both strategic and fiscal grounds. Taylor, like his predecessor as chief of staff, General Ridgway, resigned over his differences with the administration. As expressed in his 1959 book, *An Uncertain Trumpet,* Taylor's ideas, offering the possibility of graduated response and limited war, appealed to the incoming President Kennedy. Dispatched by Kennedy to Vietnam on a fact-finding mission in 1961, Taylor and Walt ROSTOW, a presidential adviser, returned with the recommendation that the United States make a sizable increase in support to the government of South Vietnam. Appointed chairman of the Joint Chiefs in 1962, Taylor served until the summer of 1964, when President JOHNSON named him ambassador to South Vietnam. Continuing as a hawk on the Vietnam War, Taylor advocated increased U.S. support of the Saigon government. Taylor resigned as ambassador in 1965. *See also* ASYMMETRICAL RESPONSE; NSC-68; SYMMETRICAL RESPONSE.

Teller, Edward (1908–) Hungarian-born physicist, working in the United States since 1935, sometimes called the father of the HYDROGEN BOMB. Teller attended the universities of Karlsruhe, Munich, Göttingen, and Leipzig, receiving his doctorate from the last-named, where his dissertation director was Werner Heisenberg. In the United States, Teller was professor of physics at George Washington University, Columbia, the University of Chicago, and the University of California (Berkeley). He began working on the ATOMIC BOMB in 1941 and in 1942 joined J. Robert OPPENHEIMER in establishing the Los Alamos laboratory, where the first bombs were designed and made. From these fission bombs Teller's interest progressed to the development of a superbomb that would work by nuclear fusion.

In the late 1940s Teller, a strong proponent of the fusion, or hydrogen, bomb and a fierce anti-Communist, engaged in bitter battles with Oppenheimer and associates who opposed development of the new weapon. In January 1950, however, after the Soviets exploded their first atomic bomb,

U.S. president TRUMAN ordered the scientists to move forward on the H-bomb; the USSR had won Teller's case for him, and he soon had (with Ernest O. Lawrence) a new laboratory, at Livermore, Calif. The first test of the fusion bomb came in November 1952, at Eniwetok, in the western Pacific.

In 1954, when Oppenheimer appealed the loss of his security clearance from the U.S. ATOMIC ENERGY COMMISSION, revoked because of his objections to the H-bomb and his association with known Communists in the 1930s, Teller was the only scientist to testify against his former colleague, declaring that it would be "wiser" not to grant clearance to Oppenheimer. In the public arena, Teller became an outspoken opponent of moves toward banning nuclear testing. Some months before the adoption of the 1963 NUCLEAR TEST BAN TREATY, president KENNEDY commented dryly in a press conference: "I understand Dr. Teller is opposed to it. Every day he is opposed to it." In the 1980s Teller was among the scientists who supported president REAGAN's concept of the STRATEGIC DEFENSE INITIATIVE—the "shield" in space.

In 1960 Teller resigned as Livermore laboratory director to concentrate on teaching and research. An important theoretical physicist, Teller worked in many areas of the field. For his contributions to the development of nuclear energy, he received the 1962 Enrico Fermi Award. *See also* SAKHAROV, Andrei Dmitrievich.

Templer, Sir Gerald (1898–1980) British general who won renown when, as high commissioner for Malaya (1952–54), he put down a Communist guerrilla insurrection. A corps and division commander in Italy in World War II, Templer served for a time as director of military government in the British sector of occupied Germany and was later director of British military intelligence (1946–48). He received the appointment to Malaya after giving a command performance for Winston CHURCHILL. In January 1952, newly returned to office as prime minister, Churchill made a trip to America, and, meeting in Ottawa, he and the governor-general, Field Marshal Alexander, agreed on the need for a determined and resourceful commander in

Malaya. Recommended by Alexander, Templer was flown to Ottawa, where he so impressed Churchill that the prime minister offered him the appointment on the spot. In Malaya, Templer, with the advice of Sir Robert Thompson, confronted the guerrillas, largely ethnic Chinese, with a systematic antiterrorism campaign. An unforeseen by-product of Templer's Malaya operations was the belief held by many U.S. observers that these successful techniques could be used to equal effect elsewhere, as in Vietnam. After returning home from his victory in Malaya, Templer crowned his career with a term as chief of the Imperial General Staff (1955–58). *See also* STRATEGIC HAMLET.

Tet Offensive   On January 30, 1968, during the New Year celebrations called Tet, forces of the NATIONAL LIBERATION FRONT and HO CHI MINH's North Vietnamese army attacked 36 of 44 provincial capitals, 5 of the 6 chief cities of South Vietnam, 64 district capitals, and 50 hamlets. These forces also invaded the U.S. embassy in SAIGON, a facility that just a few weeks earlier had been proclaimed the most secure building in the world.

The Central Committee of the Lao Dong, the Vietnamese Communist Party, had begun planning the Tet Offensive in October 1967 with the passage of Resolution 114, also called the Quang Trung Resolution, after the emperor who had defeated invading Chinese forces during the Tet of 1789. The planners saw three possible outcomes: (1) their forces would win a victory that would force the United States to enter into negotiations to end the war; (2) they would experience partial success that nevertheless would allow the U.S. and South Vietnamese forces to retake important areas and carry on the war; (3) they would fail completely, thus encouraging the United States to bring more troops to Vietnam and extend the war to the North.

The carefully prepared offensive caught the United States and South Vietnam off guard. As the key element of a strategic deception plan, the North Vietnamese in the autumn of 1967 carried out a series of raids in the countryside, especially along the border with Laos, to lure U.S. forces away from the cities. In particular, two North

Vietnamese divisions attacked the U.S. Marine outpost at KHE SANH, near the Laotian border, producing a battle that became known as the American DIEN BIEN PHU. While the Americans were concentrating on the countryside, the Communists opened their offensive.

Like many other aspects of the VIETNAM WAR, Tet cannot easily be evaluated. The Communist planners would probably have called the result a "2." The North did not defeat the South or cause a revolution there, and it suffered enormous losses, perhaps as many as 40,000, with the VIETCONG experiencing particularly heavy damage. In view of these results, U.S. military leaders labeled Tet a Communist defeat. But the offensive—particularly the assault on the embassy, which news reports presented in overheated fashion—had an enormous impact in the United States, amounting, in fact, to a psychological victory for Hanoi. What had happened at the embassy was that an old taxi and a truck pulled up outside it; 19 or 20 Vietcong jumped out, blew a hole in the wall with explosives, and dashed into the compound, shooting five U.S. guards. The ability of the North Vietnamese and the Vietcong to reach into the cities shook whatever U.S. complacency existed. The optimistic reports on the war sent back to Washington by General WESTMORELAND's staff met open challenges from such prominent moderates as the leading television news broadcaster, Walter Cronkite, who reportedly burst out: "What the hell is going on? I thought we were winning the war."

The administration of U.S. president Lyndon JOHNSON never recovered from the shock of the Tet attacks. Though the president believed, he later wrote, that "the military and political defeat of the Communists in the Tet offensive would stand as a major favorable turning point in the war," subsequent developments did not bear out this doggedly cheerful judgment. The impression of Tet that lasted came from the early reports of Communist victory, even though they were later shown to be exaggerated. Besides, the political situation did not justify U.S. optimism.

Thant, U (1909–1974)   Burmese educator, government official, and author who served as his country's permanent representative to the UNITED

U Thant, third United Nations secretary-general

NATIONS from 1957 until his election on November 3, 1961, to succeed Dag HAMMARSKJÖLD as UN secretary-general after the latter's death in an airplane crash in Africa. As an Asian rather than a Westerner, Thant won the approval of Soviet premier Nikita KHRUSHCHEV, who had clashed with Hammarskjöld and attempted to have him removed from office. "We knew we could count on him to be more flexible than Hammarskjöld," Khrushchev said of Thant later, and even though "from a strictly proletarian, Communist point of view" he failed to satisfy all Soviet desires, "he didn't let himself be led around on a leash by the United States." Like Hammarskjöld, Thant found himself intervening in a variety of crises, from the CUBAN MISSILE CRISIS of 1962 to the Six-Day War between Israel and the Arab states in 1967. Though he also strove to end the VIETNAM WAR, Thant met scant success in these efforts. He retired in 1972. Kurt WALDHEIM, an Austrian, became the new UN secretary-general that year.

Thatcher, Margaret (1925–　)　The first woman to serve as prime minister of any European country,

Margaret Thatcher (original surname, Roberts) also holds the 20th-century British record for longevity in office (1979–90). "Thatcherism," as the blend of her style and actions was known, represented a marked turn away from the collectivist mentality that had essentially dominated British political life since 1945 and featured a new vigor that ensured strong feelings about the prime minister—she was admired or loathed, but few people were neutral about her. Carefully coiffed and tailored, precisely spoken, she perhaps inevitably won the nickname Attila the Hen.

The daughter of a grocer in Grantham, Lincolnshire, she studied chemistry and X-ray crystallography at Oxford and took part in politics as president of the University Conservative Association. After working in industry as a research chemist, she later became a lawyer. She married Denis Thatcher, a very wealthy businessman. Elected to the House of Commons from a suburban London district, Margaret Thatcher held a junior position in Prime Minister Harold MACMILLAN's government. After the Conservatives won the election of 1970, Edward HEATH sent her to the Ministry of Education. Following the loss of the two 1974 elections to Harold WILSON, however, Thatcher criticized Heath's economic policies, ran for the party leadership, and won.

The continuing great domestic issue in British politics during that era was the power of the labor unions, which had driven Heath from office and five years later administered the same treatment to the Labour prime minister, James CALLAGHAN. Succeeding Callaghan, Thatcher pushed through legislation to curb the unions and moved away from the welfare state supposedly cherished by all Britons. She even received the support of some Labourites who wanted to see her cow the unions enough to make them cooperate with any future Labour government rather than destroy it. Though the Falkland Islands war in 1982 did not present Cold War issues, it aroused a wave of patriotism that restored the popularity Thatcher had lost through her economic-austerity measures. In 1983 she defeated Labour in a landslide and went on to smash the militant coal miners' union. An upturn in the economy gave her a third victory at the polls in 1987, making her the first prime minister ever to win three straight elections. Weary of its contin-

British prime minister Margaret Thatcher

ual defeats, the Labour Party, in a tribute to its opponent, began to make public declarations in favor of the market economy.

Devoted in strong principle to British friendship with the United States, Thatcher found that the inauguration of the conservative President REAGAN in January 1981 had given her something of an ideological soul mate in Washington. Both dedicated Cold Warriors, they faced a need for readjustment with the arrival on the Soviet scene of Mikhail GORBACHEV. In December 1984, when Gorbachev visited London a few months before his election as GENERAL SECRETARY of the COMMUNIST PARTY OF THE SOVIET UNION, Thatcher came away from a lengthy talk with the visitor believing him to represent something new. She declared, "I like Mr. Gorbachev—we can do business with him." Her next task was to carry the message to Reagan, the president who had called the USSR "the EVIL EMPIRE."

By 1990 various developments, including national resentment of a poll tax imposed in 1989, had aroused dissent and division within the Thatcher government. Avoiding defeat in an election for the leadership of the Conservative Party, Thatcher resigned on November 22. She was succeeded by John Major.

Thaw, The   Name often given to the period following then First Secretary Nikita KHRUSHCHEV's famous 1956 "secret speech" to the 20th Congress of the COMMUNIST PARTY OF THE SOVIET UNION, in which he listed and denounced the crimes of the late dictator Joseph STALIN. During the Thaw, artists and writers experienced some relief from the previous rigid state control and censorship. The term *Thaw* came from the title of a novel by the Soviet writer Ilya EHRENBURG (first English translation, 1955), which reflected the beginnings of relaxation following Stalin's death in 1953. Much of the credit for these beginnings was owed to G. F. Alexandrov, minister of culture (1954–55). *See also* PASTERNAK, Boris.

There Is No Alternative   One of the notable fruits of Soviet leader Mikhail GORBACHEV's policy of GLASNOST, this book appeared in the summer of 1988. A collection of articles by various advocates of change in the Soviet Union, including the Nobel laureate physicist and human-rights activist Andrei SAKHAROV, the book surprised the people with a new brand of candor. Yet, remarkably, it had been issued by an official publisher. In his chapter, for example, Sakharov boldly denounced the 1968 Soviet invasion of Czechoslovakia to crush the PRAGUE SPRING as an interference in another country's attempt at PERESTROIKA. He also called for an investigation of the KGB.

Third World   Like FIRST WORLD and SECOND WORLD, this label was applied to one of the three "worlds" into which popular opinion divided the nations in the years during the Cold War. The first of the three terms to come into use, *Third World* appeared first in French *(Tiers Monde)* in 1963. By

far the most widely used of the three, Third World pertained to underdeveloped or undeveloped countries, mostly in Africa and Asia, many of them having newly won independence from European colonial empires. Latin American countries came to be classed in the Third World, as did some European countries, such as Greece, with low levels of productivity. In an important sense, *Third World* is most accurately described as a negative term; that is, it referred to countries that were neither industrialized and prosperous nor Communist. *See also* BANDUNG CONFERENCE; FIRST WORLD; SECOND WORLD; NONALIGNMENT; POINT FOUR.

38th Parallel   In September 1945 U.S. planners in the State and War Departments disagreed about the desirability of maintaining a U.S. presence on the Korean peninsula, State favoring it and War disinclined to become involved in occupying territory on the Asian continent. In either case, U.S. forces would be required to accept the surrender of Japanese troops in Korea, a need that called for a decision about the location of the ceremonies. With Soviet forces already in position in the northern part of Korea, and likely to occupy the entire peninsula if the United States did nothing, a committee—on the suggestion of Colonel Dean RUSK—hastily decided on the 38th parallel as the line of demarcation. This conceptual line was chosen because no suitable natural line of any kind—river, mountains—existed. Those making the decision did not know, however, that half a century earlier the Japanese and the Russians had agreed on the 38th parallel as the boundary between their Korean zones of influence. Perhaps this seeming acknowledgment of their former position in Korea accounted for the readiness with which the Soviets accepted the decision. The crossing of the 38th parallel on June 25, 1950, by North Korean troops with Soviet-made tanks signaled the beginning of the KOREAN WAR.

Thor   U.S. medium-range ballistic missile installed in Western Europe and Turkey in the late 1950s. The Thor had a range of about 300 miles.

Thorez, Maurice (1900–1964)   Veteran French Communist leader, a coal miner who joined the

Socialist Party as a young man and became one of early members of the French Communist Party. In 1930 Thorez became secretary of the French section of the Comintern and secretary of the political department of the French party; from 1935 to 1963 he was the party's secretary-general. Condemned to death for desertion from the army at the beginning of World War II, he spent most of the war years in Moscow, returning to France after the liberation under an amnesty granted by General DE GAULLE, the head of the provisional government. Shortly thereafter, when de Gaulle went to Moscow for a meeting with Joseph STALIN, the Soviet dictator delivered a joke of his own special kind: "Don't put Thorez in prison," he said— "at least, not right away." De Gaulle did not do so. Instead, Thorez, who was elected to Parliament, served as vice premier (1946–47) when the Communists enjoyed influence in the French government.

Tiananmen Square   The "Gate of Heavenly Peace" and the main entrance to the Forbidden City in Beijing, this square has been the site of a number of protests and uprisings under the Communist regime in China. On April 5, 1976, large crowds of demonstrators expressed grief over the death of Premier ZHOU ENLAI; most observers interpreted this outpouring of sentiment as criticism of MAO ZEDONG and the CULTURAL REVOLUTION, because Zhou, as a moderate, had undergone attacks for not supporting this Maoist idea.

On December 17, 1978, 28 young people staged a Tiananmen Square protest against living and working conditions in rural southwest China; this action has been viewed as the first rumblings of a movement for democracy. Eight years later, in early January 1987, students held a massive pro-democracy rally in Tiananmen. Communist Party hard-liners retaliated with attacks on the students and the teachers who had inspired them; a number of university professors lost their jobs, and the authorities arrested hundreds of students.

Then, in the spring of 1989, came the most famous of the Tiananmen Square uprisings. Following the death of Hu Yaobang, a reformer expelled from the Communist Party for sympathizing with earlier pro-democracy activities, students orga-

nized a pro-Hu demonstration to remind the government that the democracy movement existed; the idea probably originated in the history department of the People's University in Beijing. The demonstration began on April 17 with a sit-in near the Great Hall of the People. Ordered by Chairman DENG XIAOPING and Premier Li Peng to leave the square, the students refused and a siege ensued. In mid-May, Soviet president Mikhail GORBACHEV, arriving on an official visit, found himself in a delicate position: he was acclaimed for his reforms by the demonstrators, who were acting in opposition to the conservative hosts with whom he wished to establish good relations. On May 17 the number of demonstrators reached one million.

Three days later Li Peng declared martial law and ordered units of the army to clear the square. For two weeks the students—who had been joined by workers, storekeepers, clerks, peasants, and others—held off the troops, but on June 3 units of the 27th Army arrived; the next day these forces attacked with tanks and a massacre followed, while the world watched on television. Thousands of demonstrators were killed—shot and crushed under the treads of the tanks—and thousands of survivors arrested, some of them later to be executed. This handling of the uprising, which marked a victory for the hard-liners Deng Xiaoping and Li Peng, aroused worldwide horror and led many in the West to oppose economic and other arrangements with China.

Ticonderoga   Class of U.S. Navy 7,000-ton guided-missile cruisers that entered service during the 1980s, their primary purpose being to defend carrier battle groups against both air and underwater attack. A Ticonderoga carried an array of missiles for use against land, surface, and airborne targets. An important feature of the Ticonderogas was the AEGIS missile-tracking system, which represented a great advance on previous radar. It was a ship of this class, the U.S.S. *Vincennes,* that brought down an Iranian passenger aircraft over the Persian Gulf in 1988.

Tito, Josip Broz (1892–1980)   One of the most important Cold War figures as the European Communist national leader who declared independence from Soviet control, Tito was originally named Josip Broz but became widely known during World War II by his Communist alias when he led Yugoslav resistance to the Germans.

The son of a Croatian father and a Slovene mother, young Broz underwent a transformational experience during World War I when, as a prisoner of war, he spent five years in Russia (1915–20), seeing the Bolshevik Revolution close up and taking part in the civil war that followed it. Back home in the new Balkan state that would become Yugoslavia, he joined the Communist Party and, like many another revolutionary, found himself in and out of prison. After he spent some time in Moscow, the Comintern sent him back to Yugoslavia in 1937 as secretary-general of the Yugoslav Communist Party, with the mission of reorganizing it.

When the German army swept through the Balkans in 1941, Tito fought back at the invaders as the head of a Serbian-based guerrilla group called the Partisans. By his effectiveness, and perhaps also because some key British intelligence officials supported him as a Communist, he won British and U.S. support in his rivalry with the Serb leader, Draža Mihajlovič, who with his Chetniks was loyal to the government-in-exile, headed by King Peter II. So effective were the Partisans that before the war ended, they held control of most of the country.

During the years between the world wars, Yugoslavia—the "southern Slav" state assembled from distinct and often bitterly hostile national groups (Serbs, Croats, and Slovenes) that had been part of Austria-Hungary—was held together by the will of a king who acted as dictator, Alexander I, who fell victim to an assassin in Marseilles in 1934. After the war Tito filled Alexander's role. In 1945 the monarchy was abolished and Tito, as head of the Communist-dominated National Liberation Front, won the presidency in an election that could hardly be called a contest, since no other party or group had the right to field a candidate.

Though Tito proceeded to establish a thoroughly Communistic regime, with a powerful secret police and purges of dissidents, within a few years he demonstrated that he was a national Communist rather than a vassal of the Soviet Union. Tito and his followers had won power primarily through their own efforts, not because the Red Army had given it to them, as had been the case in other EASTERN BLOC countries; nor did Yugoslavia have a common boundary with the USSR. As a self-made and self-confident leader, Tito, like Joseph STALIN in the USSR, allowed scant criticism of his ideas and actions. According to Nikita KHRUSHCHEV, Stalin declared that all he had to do was "shake his little finger and Tito would disappear." This forecast proved inaccurate. After refusing to confess his alleged sins of deviationism, Tito was expelled from the COMINFORM in 1948 and from that point on followed his own path, playing a prominent part among nonaligned nations, though he remained a Communist ruler and in Cold War disputes his support generally went to the East rather than the West. On November 29, 1949, the Cominform members called for his overthrow. Recognizing the value of his independence, the United States gave Tito's Yugoslavia financial support. In 1968 Tito aroused fresh hostility toward himself in the Kremlin by condemning the Soviet invasion of Czechoslovakia and Soviet leader BREZHNEV's move to crush the PRAGUE SPRING.

Increasingly, observers speculated about the succession in Yugoslavia: Who could take Tito's place? The answer, it appeared, was nobody. Preparing for his death, Tito set up a collective presidency, with representatives from the country's six constituent republics. The arrangement was not destined to endure. In the 1990s the tragic events in the former Yugoslavia served to highlight Tito's political achievement. *See also* DEDIJER, Vladimir; DJILAS, Milovan; TOGLIATTI, Palmiro; YUGOSLAV-SOVIET CONFLICT OF 1948.

Togliatti, Palmiro (1893–1964)   Head of the Italian Communist Party from 1944 until his death, Togliatti had been one of the founders of the party in 1921. Most of the intervening years, however, he had spent in exile, as a refugee from the Fascist regime of Benito Mussolini. In the 1930s he served as the chief Comintern representative in the Spanish Civil War. As leader of the Italian party, Togliatti enjoyed considerable success, seeing it become the largest Communist Party in Western Europe. In the post-STALIN 1950s he advocated a degree of ideological independence from Moscow, developing his own direct relationship with Marshal TITO of Yugoslavia, who had been expelled from the COMINFORM in 1948. "The Soviet model," Togliatti declared in 1956, "can and must no longer be considered obligatory." Instead, each national party should develop its own means of protection against "stagnation and bureaucratization."

Touré, (Ahmed) Sékou (1922–1984) In 1958, as head of the Democratic Party of Guinea, Touré became president of the country when it declared its independence from France. His leadership was marked by his "personalism"—the use of his charismatic personality to give his party complete control of Guinean political and social life. A strong supporter of the Soviet Union during the 1960s, Touré strove to build up a local form of socialist government but insisted on his independence in foreign affairs; during the CUBAN MISSILE CRISIS in 1962, for example, he refused to allow Soviet aircraft to refuel in Guinea on their way to Cuba. During the 1970s he moved toward a moderate overall foreign policy. Assassination attempts in June 1969 and April 1971 weakened his control over the country and affected his ability to unite political and military leaders behind his programs. Touré survived for 13 years, however, dying of a heart attack in 1984; his choosing to go to the United States for medical treatment suggested the degree to which his earlier pro-Soviet leanings had moderated.

Trieste crisis At the end of World War II, both Yugoslavia and Italy claimed the city of Trieste, at the head of the Adriatic Sea, and its surrounding area. Trieste, mostly Italian speaking, had belonged to Italy since 1919, but the population of its hinterland was largely Slovenian. In May 1945 British and Yugoslav troops almost clashed in the city, the British being supported by the United States and the Yugoslavs by the Soviets. In 1947 the UNITED NATIONS, led by Secretary-General Trygve LIE, created a compromise entity called the Free Territory of Trieste, divided into two zones, one of which was soon occupied by Anglo-American forces, the other by the Yugoslavs. On June 12, 1949, the people of Trieste voted to return to Italy. Finally, in 1954, the Free Territory was officially divided between Italy and Yugoslavia and ceased to exist.

trip-wire principle Often used with respect to U.S. forces stationed in Europe, this phrase conveyed the idea that U.S. forces were there not primarily to repel a Soviet invasion themselves but to make it plain that if such an invasion were to occur, the United States would come to the aid of the victim and a general conflict would ensue.

Trudeau, Pierre Elliott (1919–) Prime minister of Canada in four different terms amounting to almost all of the time between 1968 and 1984. A lawyer and editor in Montreal, Trudeau, a Liberal, became prime minister while still a relative newcomer to electoral politics, having entered the House of Commons in 1965 and the cabinet (as minister of justice) in 1967. Wealthy, an intellectual and a sportsman with touches of a jet-set lifestyle, Trudeau appealed to young people in the late 1960s heyday of political youth, so much so that his political activity touched off a phenomenon the press labeled "Trudeaumania." In dealing with Quebec separatists who resorted to violence, however, Trudeau acted with such vigor and determination against the "bandits" that some civil libertarians accused him of misusing his power.

Truman, Harry S. (1884–1972) President of the United States during the formative years of the Cold War, Harry Truman had the distinction of being the only president to serve in the White House during two major hot wars. Having taken office as 33rd president on the death of President ROOSEVELT on April 12, 1945, four months before the Japanese surrender that brought World War II to its end, Truman was also president during the bulk of the KOREAN WAR (1950–53).

As a young man in Missouri, Truman wanted to attend West Point but could not do so because of his nearsightedness, and his family lacked the means to send him to any other college; hence he became the only 20th-century president who lacked a college degree. He worked as a bank clerk, a road overseer, and a postmaster before taking over the operation of the family farm in 1906. As a member of the Missouri National Guard, he served in France in World War I as a field-artillery captain, an experience that gave him a group of comrades for life and also lent a realistic dimension to his reading of military history, a favorite pursuit.

After the war, having married his childhood sweetheart, Bess Wallace, Truman went into a haberdashery partnership in Kansas City but was forced into bankruptcy by the 1921 recession—though he saw to it in future years that every creditor received full payment. Then, backed by the Kansas City Democratic Party boss, Tom Pendergast, Truman entered politics, winning election as county judge, an administrative position; in office he acquired a reputation for honesty and efficiency. With the exception of the years 1924 and 1925, he held the judgeship until his election to the U.S. Senate in 1934. A supporter of FDR's New Deal, Truman attracted little attention in Washington until he had to make a fight for his reelection in 1940, with Pendergast convicted for income-tax evasion and Roosevelt seeming to favor a rival candidate, the well-heeled apple grower Lloyd Stark. Drawing comfort from his reading of Plutarch, who described how the Emperor Nero "began to take his friends for granted," as Truman later put it, "and started to buy his enemies," Truman saw Nero-like traits in Stark and decided, rightly, that he could win despite the odds.

Truman came to national prominence during World War II for his effectiveness as chairman of the Special Committee Investigating National Defense, known universally as the Truman Committee, which served as the public watchdog over the great national industrial expansion and won general admiration for avoiding partisanship while resisting any temptation to dabble in military affairs. In 1944 Roosevelt, having agreed to drop Vice President Henry WALLACE from the Democratic ticket, accepted suggestions that Truman replace him, though Truman had not waged any campaign to win the position.

Having seen very little of FDR after the election, Truman in April 1945 entered on the presidency remarkably unprepared. He had to face problems arising from Soviet actions in Eastern Europe, the end of the war with Germany, and East-West conflicts in the establishment of the UNITED NATIONS.

He also had to learn about the development of the ATOMIC BOMB and deal with issues it raised.

At the POTSDAM CONFERENCE in July, Truman met for the first time with British prime minister Winston CHURCHILL and for the only time with Soviet premier Joseph STALIN. Describing the impression made on him by the new president, Churchill later spoke of his "gay, precise, sparkling manner and obvious power of decision." At Potsdam, having been informed that the atomic bomb had been successfully tested, Truman told Stalin the United States had a new weapon "of unusual destructive force." Stalin took this good news quietly, remarking only that he hoped the Americans would "make good use of it against the Japanese." At the time, though Western leaders had no way of knowing it, Soviet spy networks had kept Stalin up to date on progress on the bomb (but news of the successful test could not yet have reached him through these channels). Churchill warned Truman of a Soviet IRON CURTAIN falling across Eastern Europe (though he called it an "iron fence").

Adopting the recommendation of a political-scientific group called the Interim Committee, created to advise him on the use of the atomic bomb, Truman approved an operation to drop the bomb on a joint civilian-military target in Japan. This decision (or, to put it more precisely, the decision not to overrule his scientific and military advisers) would lead to unending controversy, but Truman never wavered in his conviction that he had acted correctly. Aside from his "reasonable belief that use of the bomb could in the long run save the hundreds of thousands of Japanese and American lives that would have been lost in an invasion, and also would shorten the war," as the U.S. historian Daniel J. Boorstin has observed, the president, and with him the government, were caught up in the momentum of events. "Billions of dollars had gone into the making of it," Boorstin said. "People were organized all over the country in various ways. It was impossible to stop." And, indeed, shortly after the dropping of the second bomb, the Japanese surrendered, ending World War II.

During the next two years, Truman had to deal with demobilization and reconversion of the economy to civilian purposes. After the 1946 elections he had to face a Republican-controlled Congress

During his 1948 whistle-stop train campaign, U.S. president Harry S. Truman made a point of introducing his daughter, Margaret, and his wife, Bess, to the crowd.

hostile to many of his proposals, essentially continuations of New Deal ideas. In foreign affairs, the administration hoped to avoid a division of Europe into East and West by working with the Soviets on an overall settlement, but at the same time Washington began to prepare for such a division if it should come. The year 1947 proved to be pivotal. Opposition to perceived Soviet expansionism led to the TRUMAN DOCTRINE. The need to take a major hand in European recovery from the war caused the creation of the MARSHALL PLAN. The establishment of the NORTH ATLANTIC TREATY ORGANIZATION, in 1949, represented the institutionaliza-

tion of the CONTAINMENT policy, designed to hold the Soviet Union in check.

Meanwhile, in the dramatic November 1948 election, Truman, universally regarded as a certain loser, conducted a fiery campaign to defeat New York's Republican governor, Thomas E. Dewey, and win the White House—a feat accomplished despite the defection of leftist Democrats who supported Henry Wallace and Southern Democrats who backed Strom Thurmond. Seeking, like everyone else, to explain this remarkable upset, a British newspaper, with considerable insight, headed its leading article "Roosevelt's Fifth Term."

When Truman left Washington in 1953, following the inauguration of President EISENHOWER, he enjoyed very limited public esteem. He had led the country into the unpopular and seemingly unending KOREAN WAR. His administration had been marked by various financial scandals and, despite its landmark foreign-policy initiatives (often not supported by many Republicans), was widely considered soft on Communism. Over the years, however, though scholars have debated the necessity for and the wisdom of many of Truman's actions, he has come to be remembered by most people as the straight-talking, issue-confronting president whose desk bore the sign: THE BUCK STOPS HERE. *See also* POINT FOUR.

Truman Doctrine   In early 1947 the British government, led by Prime Minister Clement ATTLEE, informed Washington that it could no longer support the 40,000 troops it maintained in Greece or continue its aid to the Greek government, which was battling a guerrilla army; in only six weeks, its forces would pull out. Turkey, at the same time, staggered under the weight of the army it felt it had to maintain to resist external pressure from the Soviet Union. The British decision meant that if the United States wished to resist Soviet expansionism, it must move rapidly to replace the British in the eastern Mediterranean. On March 12, 1947, President TRUMAN, asking Congress for $400 million, declared that "it must be the policy of the United States to support free peoples who are resisting attempted subjugation by armed minorities or outside pressures." Thus, while the president made a specific request, he was actually enunciating a sweeping U.S. commitment with no limitations of time or place; U.S. diplomat George KENNAN later criticized the message for this "universalistic and pretentious" note. Ironically, Kennan's own writings would provide much of the basis for the Truman administration's CONTAINMENT policy.

Congressional approval of even the limited Greek-Turkish aid bill did not come automatically, since no true U.S. foreign-policy consensus yet existed; however, after considerable foot-dragging by senators and representatives, the aid bill emerged from Congress in May. One reason Truman pitched his case so high had to do not with exter-

nal considerations but came from his conviction, as the Republican senator Arthur VANDENBERG from Michigan put it, that he had to "scare hell out of the country" to get action from Congress. Concerned about the "flamboyant anti-Communism" in a speech draft sent to them at a foreign ministers' conference, Secretary of State MARSHALL and Charles BOHLEN cabled back to Washington asking that the message be toned down. Truman declined, saying that without the rhetoric he would not get the money. Thus was taken the first great step in the epochal 1947 U.S. policy parade. *See also* MARSHALL PLAN; POINT FOUR.

Tu-16   Soviet strategic bomber, a swept-wing design created by Andrei Tupolev, that entered service in 1955. Powered by two large turbojet engines, it had a maximum speed of about 580 mph and a range, fully loaded, of about 3,000 miles; the maximum range was 3,975 miles. Armed with seven 23-mm cannons, the Tu-16 could carry two nuclear bombs or more than nine tons of conventional bombs. The NORTH ATLANTIC TREATY ORGANIZATION gave this widely used aircraft the code name Badger. As time passed, the Tu-16 appeared in a variety of versions, as tankers, reconnaissance aircraft, and airborne launching platforms for missiles.

Tu-20   A swept-wing design from Andrei Tupolev, the large Tu-20, which first flew in 1954 and entered service in 1956, drew much comment because it was powered by turboprop engines. Code-named Bear by the NORTH ATLANTIC TREATY ORGANIZATION, the Tu-20 began life as a strategic bomber, with a top speed of 575 mph and a range of 7,800 miles. It could carry four HYDROGEN BOMBS or more than 20 tons of conventional bombs and was armed with 23-mm cannons. Like other bombers, the Tu-20 has been modified for various roles. One day, in a U.S.-Soviet negotiating session, Soviet leader Leonid BREZHNEV complained about NATO's use of code names, saying they tended to disparage Soviet weapons; he particularly objected to the labeling of the Soviet ANTIBALLISTIC MISSILE as the Galosh. One of his U.S. interlocutors managed to mollify him, however, by pointing out that Soviet bombers had received names like Bear and Bison.

Soviet Tu-20 is tracked by a U.S. Air Force F-102 during 1968 NATO exercises.

Tu-22   Soviet twin-jet supersonic bomber (Mach 1.5) first observed by the NORTH ATLANTIC TREATY ORGANIZATION in 1961. Used by both the air force and the navy, it bore the NATO code name Blinder.

Tu-26   Code-named Backfire by the NORTH ATLANTIC TREATY ORGANIZATION, the Tu-26 was the last Soviet bomber to come from the Tupolev design bureau during the lifetime of its founder, who died in 1972. A twin-jet, swept-wing aircraft, the supersonic Tu-26 had a top speed of 1,260 mph at high altitude. For defensive purposes it carried two 23-mm guns; its offensive armament varied depending on the mission, but it had the capability of delivering at least four nuclear bombs or six tons of conventional bombs, with further bombs carried externally. It also could carry cruise and other missiles.

Tuesday Lunch Club   Nickname for the informal group of high officials, including Secretary of State Dean RUSK, who met frequently—though not every Tuesday—with U.S. president Lyndon JOHNSON during the VIETNAM WAR to supply information and discuss ideas and proposals concerning the war. Consisting of four or five or more, the club suited Johnson's conversational approach to decision making far more than did the more formal NATIONAL SECURITY COUNCIL. Because of its influence it was often called the Tuesday Cabinet.

Twining, Nathan Farragut (1897–1982)   Appointed chief of staff of the U.S. Air Force by President EISENHOWER in June 1953, in succession to General Hoyt S. VANDENBERG, General Twining moved up in August 1957 to succeed Admiral Arthur W. RADFORD as chairman of the JOINT CHIEFS OF STAFF.

A Wisconsin native who grew up in Portland, Ore., Twining graduated from the U.S. Military Academy in 1919 and, to the unquestioned surprise of colleagues, switched to the air corps, which, as everyone knew in those days, had no respectable future; he won his wings in 1923. During World War II, when commanding in the Solomon Islands, Twining, after his airplane was forced down in a tropical storm in the Coral Sea, drifted on a raft for six days; the general proved his marksmanship by shooting down an albatross

The Tuesday Lunch Club—U.S. president Lyndon B. Johnson's foreign-policy advisers—meets on January 23, 1968, the day North Koreans seize the U.S.S. *Pueblo*. Secretary of State Dean Rusk sits at the president's right, Secretary of Defense Robert McNamara at his left. Diagonally across the table, facing the camera, is Clark M. Clifford, soon to succeed McNamara.

that helped provide the group with food. (After being rescued, Twining recommended that rafts be equipped with smoke pots and that fliers be given waterproof watches.) In December 1943 Twining went to the Mediterranean to succeed Jimmy Doolittle as commander of the 15th Air Force. In August 1945 it was a B-29 of his command, the 20th Air Force, that dropped the ATOMIC BOMB on Hiroshima.

As air force chief of staff, Twining proved to be a quietly effective military politician who supported the Eisenhower administration's emphasis on MASSIVE RETALIATION and budgetary restraint, though he once pointedly commented that the United States should not build first-class combat aircraft without making sure there were enough trained crews to fly them. He won appointment as chairman of the Joint Chiefs in 1957, being suc-

ceeded as air force chief of staff by one of the U.S. military's sharpest intellects, General Thomas D. White. Twining's conciliatory style could not keep him from conflict with Eisenhower, who was frequently reduced to red-faced rage by the willful parochialism of the armed services—as, for example, when, after the Soviets stunned the world by launching *SPUTNIK I* in 1957, the U.S. services continued squabbling over who should control missile development, with Twining claiming primacy for the air force and insisting that the army have no missile with a range greater than 200 miles. Twining retired shortly before the 1960 presidential election.

"Two Thousand Words" A prodemocratic manifesto created by writers and other intellectuals and published in Czech newspapers during the PRAGUE

SPRING of 1968. Foreseeing the possibility of Soviet armed intervention, the document pledged the group's support to the DUBČEK government.

Typhoon   Class of Soviet nuclear-powered ballistic-missile submarines that well demonstrated the Soviet fondness for size, these bulky boats being by far the largest of all such craft in the world, with a displacement of more than 21,000 tons and a 75-foot beam. Entering service through the 1980s, the Typhoons were formidable craft that would have been difficult to damage and could reach any target on any continent with their solid-fuel SS-N-20 missiles, each carrying six or more MIRV warheads.

U-2 U.S. reconnaissance airplane that holds a unique place in history because of its role in disrupting an East-West SUMMIT conference. In early 1954 a governmental technological-advisory panel recommended the creation of a high-altitude photoreconnaissance aircraft, and in only 18 months (and just eight months after the signing of the contract) the WU/2A made its first flight (August 4, 1955). Created at Lockheed in the famous "Skunk Works" presided over by the great designer Clarence "Kelly" Johnson (1910–1990), the craft had a wingspan of 80 feet and an overall length of 49.6 feet, was powered by a single jet engine, and carried a crew of one or two; the maximum listed speed was 494 mph, and the range in later models reached 3,000 miles.

The United States deployed a total of 22 U-2s, their primary mission being to fly over the Soviet Union at heights (well above 70,000 feet for later models) beyond the range of Soviet ground fire. Such a reconnaissance tool was much desired by U.S. intelligence officers, who had concluded that the closed nature of the Soviet Union made the development of accurate intelligence estimates almost impossible; the officers felt the need for information that might bear on a possible surprise attack on the United States. (An internal CENTRAL INTELLIGENCE AGENCY history made available in 1994 revealed, rather surprisingly, that despite the continuing fears of air force leaders, U-2 flights never discovered any Soviet missiles.) The U-2 was produced under the aegis of the Central Intelligence Agency, which operated it with the support of the STRATEGIC AIR COMMAND; the CIA official most involved in the development of the aircraft was Richard BISSELL.

The shooting down of a U-2 in May 1960 and the capture of its pilot, Francis Gary Powers, led to the breaking up of a summit conference in Paris. When U.S. president EISENHOWER departed from long-honored diplomatic custom by refusing to deny personal knowledge of an intelligence opera-

The airplane that disrupted a summit conference—the U.S. U-2.

tion, Soviet premier KHRUSHCHEV walked out of the meeting. This incident also showed that U-2s could no longer overfly hostile territory with impunity.

U-2s played a key part, as well, in the greatest Cold War confrontation, the 1962 CUBAN MISSILE CRISIS. On October 14, 1962, Major Richard S. Heyser, piloting a U-2, took the first photographs over Cuba of what proved to be Soviet-built sites for offensive missiles; later in the month, flying one of many follow-up missions, Major Rudolph Anderson, Jr., was killed when his U-2 was shot down.

With its mystique enhanced by its memorable rhyming name, sounding like an ironic joke or pun, the wide-winged, long-nosed, top-secret U-2 quickly achieved almost legendary status. *See also* NATIONAL SECURITY AGENCY.

ugly American   After the appearance of the novel with this title (written by William J. Lederer and Eugene Burdick, published in 1958), the term *ugly American* came into wide use to characterize U.S. citizens working overseas. Whether representing government or business, the ugly American was supposed to be arrogant, ostentatious, and contemptuous of the surrounding alien culture. Foreign critics of U.S. policies made great play with the term, and American commentators deplored the behavior it allegedly epitomized because it was believed to create resentment of the United States and thus foster the spread of Communism in the THIRD WORLD. Many such people certainly existed, as *The Ugly American* takes great pains to demonstrate, but, as often happens when a concept is dropped into the stream of popular culture, the media and the public distorted the story. The novel's fictional character called the "ugly American" was actually a hero of the story—a person who lived and worked sympathetically and effectively with the natives of a Southeast Asian country; he was described as ugly simply because he was not considered handsome; he was, in fact, a "good" American. The behaviorally ugly Americans were the slick political, diplomatic, and military types who appeared in the novel and, no doubt, in many real-life contexts and settings.

Ulbricht, Walter (1893–1973)   East German Communist who, as general secretary of the party (called the Socialist Unity Party) led the country from 1950 until 1971; during the last 11 years he was also head of state (chairman of the Council of State), a position he held until his death.

An early member of the German Communist Party, Ulbricht served five years in the Reichstag, the lower house of the federal Parliament, and left the country with the coming of the Nazis in 1933. Having fled to the USSR, where he became a Soviet citizen, he returned from Moscow with the Red Army at the end of World War II. When the GERMAN DEMOCRATIC REPUBLIC (East Germany) came into being in 1949, Ulbricht was named deputy premier, becoming general secretary (the real

Walter Ulbricht, East German head of state and Communist Party leader

position of power in the state) the following year. A thorough believer in the ideas and methods of Soviet premier Joseph STALIN, Ulbricht, who bore a striking resemblance to the hapless Professor Unrath in the famous German movie *The Blue Angel,* found himself out of sympathy with Stalin's successors in 1953 when they moved to ease some of the repressions fastened on Eastern and Central Europe under Stalin. In June 1953, as a result of Ulbricht's policies—particularly his order calling for increased industrial output without accompanying increases in pay—workers in East Berlin rose in spontaneous riots against the East German government and the Soviet occupying forces. The next day the EAST BERLIN UPRISING exploded into mass demonstrations against the regime. As Soviet troops put down the disturbances, 25 demonstrators were killed and 378 injured.

During the late 1950s Ulbricht survived various tensions and crises in BERLIN, and in 1961 he claimed an unusual place in history as the man behind the building of the BERLIN WALL. In 1968, when the USSR moved to crush the PRAGUE SPRING movement toward liberalization in Czechoslovakia, Ulbricht sent East German forces to support the Soviet action. During the period of West German chancellor Willy BRANDT's OSTPOLITIK, however, Ulbricht, with his unyielding hostility to any normalization of relations with West Germany, found himself in opposition to Soviet policy and was forced to resign.

Underwater Sound Surveillance System (SOSUS)

Also called Project Caesar, SOSUS is a system of cables with hydrophones, some 30,000 miles long, stretching across the ocean floors of the Atlantic, the Pacific, and the Caribbean. Created to detect the movements of Soviet submarines, the top-secret system went into operation in 1954. Despite its secret status, SOSUS began to receive public attention in 1984 from the references made to it by Tom Clancy in his novel *The Hunt for Red October.*

United Fruit Company

In 1899 the Tropical Trading Company merged with Boston Fruit to create the United Fruit Company, the firm that would become known in Latin America as el Pulpo (the Octopus), because of the way its operations reached like tentacles into all areas of the local economies. United Fruit held special sway in such Caribbean-basin countries as Honduras and Guatemala. The company played a special Cold War role in 1954, when company officials protesting the Guatemalan government's expropriation of company lands drew attention to the government's ties to Communists in the labor unions, leading to the coup, sponsored by the CENTRAL INTELLIGENCE AGENCY, that overthrew President ARBENZ's government. U.S. secretary of state John Foster DULLES declared that, although nationalization did not necessarily equal Communism, it happened to do so in this case. Nationalists in other Latin American countries seized on these actions as ultimate instances of Yankee imperialism, a point much employed by Cold War opponents of the United States.

United Nations

Originally spoken of as the United Nations Organization, or UNO, the UN, as it is commonly called, grew out of discussions during World War II, particularly those held in the summer of 1944 at Dumbarton Oaks, an estate in Washington, D.C., at which representatives of the United States, Britain, the Soviet Union, and China drew up a concrete plan for a new international organization. At the time, "United Nations" was the designation of the powers fighting the Axis; thus the wartime coalition bequeathed its name to the new body that was intended to keep the peace in the world after the war. The founding conference of the UN convened in San Francisco in April 1945, with representatives of 50 countries present. This conference produced the enabling document of the UN, the United Nations Charter, signed on June 26, 1945. It went into effect, after receiving a sufficient number of ratifications, on October 24, which became United Nations Day. The preamble to the charter declared that the peoples of the United Nations were "determined to save succeeding generations from the scourge of war, which twice in our lifetime has brought untold sorrow to mankind" and that, to accomplish this and other high purposes, they would "practice tolerance and live together in peace with one another as good neighbors."

The designers of the UN created a structure like that of a bicameral legislature, with a Security

United Nations: President Lyndon B. Johnson of the United States addresses the General Assembly, December 17, 1963.

Council and a General Assembly. The Security Council, consisting originally of 11 members, was expanded to 15 in 1965. Five of these members—the chief wartime allies: the United States, Britain, the Soviet Union, China, and France—hold permanent seats; the other members serve two-year terms. The distinctive feature of the Security Council is that each of the permanent members has the right of veto, so that no action can take place without the unanimous consent of these five countries; U.S. president ROOSEVELT, British prime minister CHURCHILL, and Soviet premier STALIN adopted this arrangement at the YALTA CONFERENCE in February 1945. (The creation of the UN force in 1950, at the beginning of the KOREAN WAR, was possible only because at that time the Soviet representative was protesting the continued participation of the Nationalist Chinese government—which continued to hold its seat after its defeat by the Chinese Communists—by boycotting the Security Council.)

The General Assembly includes representatives of all the member countries, with each having one vote. Though this body was intended less for action than was the Security Council, it adopted, on November 3, 1950, the U.S.-backed "Uniting for Peace" resolution, intended to allow action against aggression when the Security Council found itself deadlocked by veto.

The practical work of the UN is carried on by the Secretariat, headed by the organization's chief executive, the secretary-general, who is supported by a kind of international civil service, though national sentiments and rivalries persist. The UN also operates a number of specialized groups, such as the Economic and Social Council (UNESCO) and the Food and Agriculture Organization, and it took over other bodies already in existence, such as the International Labor Organization. The UN also maintains the International Court of Justice, which succeeded the Permanent Court of International Justice (the World Court) established under the League of Nations.

To bring the UN to the United States, the Rockefeller interests spent $8.5 million buying land on the East River in midtown Manhattan and presented it to the organization as the site of a permanent home.

The UN did not, of course, emerge from a vacuum but was conceived as a successor to—and improvement on—the old League of Nations, which, lacking real power, had been unable to prevent the coming of World War II and had functioned in a certain unrealism because neither the United States nor the Soviet Union belonged to it. Certainly one of the most familiar UN activities since the 1950s has been the appearance at various points of crisis of UN peacekeeping forces—the famous "blue helmets."

The UN was born amid the most remarkable paradox. Conceived to work for peace in the kind of world that had just fought World War II, the organization would, within six weeks, find itself catapulted into the nuclear age; yet none of the persons who created the UN knew they were designing an organization for a world that no longer existed. International relations—certainly international psychology—would take on a new shape. Within a handful of years the two SUPERPOWERS would possess HYDROGEN BOMBS. How the planners would have altered their design had they known about the ATOMIC BOMB must, of course, remain a matter of conjecture. *See also* HAMMARSKJÖLD, Dag; LIE, Trygve; PÉREZ DE CUÉLLAR, Javier; THANT, U; WALDHEIM, Kurt.

Ussuri River   In November 1860, when the Russians, as part of their eastward expansion, estab-

lished outposts in Manchuria, they succeeded after some difficulty in negotiating a treaty with China giving them control of an area between the Ussuri River and the Sea of Japan, near Vladivostok. More than a century later, however, this region—like a number of other spots along the 4,000-mile Soviet-Chinese boundary—had become a scene of confrontation. Throughout the 1960s relations between the USSR and China had steadily worsened (the result of the much-discussed Sino-Soviet "split" and of Chinese apprehensions over the BREZHNEV DOCTRINE). On March 2, 1969, relations reached a dramatic low point on tiny Damansky (Chenpao) Island in the Ussuri River, when shooting broke out, with many casualties; it was followed two weeks later by a full-scale battle on the frozen river with big guns and tanks. For the Soviet Union, this flare-up in a distant corner of the empire with a former ally and client possessed significance far beyond its scope; it dramatized the plight of the USSR as friendless on the great-power level—in confrontation with the United States and the other Western powers, with Japan, and now with its neighboring Asian Communist giant. Almost immediately Leonid BREZHNEV, the Soviet leader, began to move toward DÉTENTE with the West, the achievement of which would offer something of a challenge in view of the USSR's continuing suppression under the Brezhnev Doctrine of any manifestation of Czech independence. As time would show, the situation also offered opportunities to the new U.S. president, Richard M. NIXON.

V

Valiant   British Royal Air Force strategic bomber, built by Vickers-Armstrong and first flown in May 1951; production began in December 1953 and continued until August 1957. Powered by four Rolls-Royce turbojet engines, the Valiant had a high-altitude top speed of about 550 mph and a range, with auxiliary tanks, of 4,500 miles. It could carry up to 21,000 pounds of conventional bombs. During the abortive SUEZ CRISIS of November 1956, Valiants bombed targets in Egypt. In January 1965 evidence of metal fatigue in Valiant airframes forced the grounding of the entire fleet.

Vance, Cyrus Roberts (1917–   )   U.S. secretary of state during the CARTER administration (1977–81), Vance, a quiet man of widely admired character, previously served the federal government in various offices and assignments and went on to develop a reputation as an international troubleshooter, particularly in the continuing Balkan crisis of the 1990s.

A native of Clarksburg, W.Va. (his mother was a cousin of the eminent lawyer and ambassador John W. Davis, the Democratic presidential candidate in 1924, once described by King George V as the most perfect gentleman he had ever known), Vance had an outstanding record at Yale, being particularly noted for a remarkable memory. He spent World War II as a destroyer gunnery officer, taking part in the landings on Tarawa, Saipan, and other Pacific islands.

After graduating from the Yale Law School, Vance went into a New York firm and, on the recommendation of Lyndon JOHNSON, was selected in 1961 by President KENNEDY as general counsel of the Defense Department, a job that called for him to work closely with Secretary Robert MCNAMARA. In July 1962 Vance became secretary of the army, and in 1964 McNamara's deputy. Chronic back trouble caused him to resign in 1967, but he made himself available, at President Johnson's request, to investigate the 1967 riots that ravaged Detroit; his subsequent report constituted an outstanding discussion of contemporary urban problems. In 1968 and 1969, Vance was a U.S. negotiator in the Paris peace talks with North Vietnamese representatives.

As Jimmy Carter's secretary of state, Vance favored the policy of DÉTENTE with the Soviet Union nurtured by President NIXON. As a result, he found himself in continuing conflict with Carter's national-security adviser, Zbigniew BRZEZINSKI. The president himself seemed to move back and forth between his two subordinates, but by the end of the 1970s, even before the Soviet invasion of AFGHANISTAN, détente had faded. Vance played a key part in negotiation of the 1978 CAMP DAVID ACCORDS between Egypt and Israel.

Having opposed the failed April 1980 attempt to rescue the U.S. hostages in Tehran, Vance resigned as secretary of state. Though resuming the practice of law, he continued to make himself available for public-service assignments and in the early 1990s spent a great deal of time and effort attempting to bring peace to the former Yugoslavia.

Vandenberg, Arthur Hendrick (1884–1951)   A Republican U.S. senator from Michigan from 1928 until his death, Vandenberg became a key figure in the development of bipartisan U.S. post–World War II foreign policy. Originally an isolationist, opposed to U.S. overseas commitments, he underwent a political conversion during the war, as he explained in a Senate speech on January 10, 1945; subsequently, Vandenberg attended the founding conference of the UNITED NATIONS, and in 1946 he served as a delegate to the UN General Assembly. Assiduously wooed by Dean ACHESON and other TRUMAN State Department officials, Vandenberg, as chairman of the Senate Foreign Relations Committee, gave vital support to major administration proposals: the TRUMAN DOCTRINE, the MARSHALL PLAN, and the NORTH ATLANTIC TREATY ORGANIZATION. In 1948 the senator's Vandenberg Resolution supported U.S. participation in regional security arrangements, as in Western Europe.

Before coming to the Senate, Vandenberg had been editor and publisher of the *Grand Rapids Herald;* in 1940 he was considered as a possible presidential nominee by his party. He had a special scholarly interest in Alexander Hamilton, about whom he wrote several books.

Vandenberg, Hoyt Sanford (1899–1954) Chief of staff of the U.S. Air Force from 1948 to 1953, General Vandenberg took office in the middle of the great interservice war that divided the JOINT CHIEFS OF STAFF over U.S. defense strategy and control of nuclear weapons.

The Milwaukee-born Vandenberg, a nephew of Michigan senator Arthur VANDENBERG, graduated from West Point in 1923 and entered the air corps. During World War II he served in staff positions until receiving command of the Ninth Air Force in France in 1944. After the war he held the position of assistant chief of staff for intelligence of the General Staff; then, in June 1946, he took command of an interim organization called the Central Intelligence Group, which in the following year would grow into the statutory body called the CENTRAL INTELLIGENCE AGENCY. A knowledgeable man in the world of bureaucracy, Vandenberg increased the staff of the group from about 100 to 400, commenting that "if I didn't fill all the slots, I knew I'd lose them."

In May 1947 Vandenberg left the Central Intelligence Group to become chief of the air staff, and in October he became vice chief of staff of the newly independent U.S. Air Force. The next year he succeeded General Carl Spaatz as chief of staff and found himself hurled head-on into the doctrinal and power battle called the REVOLT OF THE ADMIRALS. Though he served until 1953, Vandenberg suffered from ill health during the last year of his term, with much of the work performed by the officer who was to succeed him, General Nathan F. TWINING.

Van Fleet, James Alward (1892–1992) U.S. general who took command of the Eighth Army in Korea on April 14, 1951, succeeding Lieutenant General Matthew RIDGWAY, who had moved up to the position of supreme commander in the Far East after the relief of General Douglas MACARTHUR.

Born in New Jersey, Van Fleet grew up in central Florida. At West Point he was a member of the famous class of 1915 that also produced Dwight EISENHOWER and Omar Bradley. In World War I, proving to be an outstanding combat soldier, Van Fleet commanded a machine-gun battalion, winning a Silver Star. In World War II he led an infantry regiment at Utah Beach in the Normandy invasion and received a Distinguished Service Cross for "extraordinary heroism" in the fighting at Ste.-Mère-Église. He became a division commander in the autumn of 1944, spearheading the relief of Bastogne at the Battle of the Bulge, and ended the war in command of a corps. Although a reporter spoke of Van Fleet's "spectacular rise," the general might well have achieved greater responsibilities and higher rank had his name been anything except Van Fleet; it appears that the army chief of staff, General George C. MARSHALL (who suffered from a notoriously poor memory for names), habitually confused Van Fleet with a similarly named officer who was afflicted with a drinking problem, and for some time resisted suggestions that Van Fleet receive promotion.

After the war Van Fleet went to Greece in charge of the U.S. mission sent under the TRUMAN DOCTRINE to advise the government in training and organizing Greek forces to suppress the Communist revolution. General Marshall, now secretary of state, had come to regard Van Fleet as having been "one of the aggressive fighting corps commanders in Europe." Despite an array of morale and other problems, Van Fleet, aided by favorable political developments, did his job so well that within a year the Greek army won a total victory. Though Van Fleet and Ridgway were not friends, it was Van Fleet's performance in the mountains of Greece that led the JOINT CHIEFS OF STAFF to call on him for the KOREAN WAR.

Velvet Revolution   Name given to the events in November and December 1989 in Czechoslovakia, when large-scale antigovernment protests caused the Communist-dominated cabinet to resign; it was succeeded on December 10 by the first government in 41 years without a Communist majority. Then, in due course, came the election of a non-Communist president of the republic. The association with velvet derives from the remarkable smoothness with which this great change was accomplished.

The year 1989 opened in Czechoslovakia with a police onslaught on demonstrators who were commemorating the self-immolation 20 years earlier of a student protesting the Soviet suppression of Czech independence. Strikingly enough, the Prague police brought in their dogs and water cannons just one hour after the government signed a new international human-rights agreement. Among those arrested in the demonstrations was playwright and leading dissident Václav HAVEL, who had spent several of the preceding 12 years in prison (he was released four months later).

As the year proceeded, protesters defied the prohibition on demonstrations to express their memory of the Soviet invasion in 1968 that crushed the PRAGUE SPRING. The government declared that, despite the waves of change sweeping across Eastern Europe, "no dramatic change in the situation in Czechoslovakia can be expected." Some Western diplomatic observers seemed to agree; the Czech dissidents, they said, were out-of-the-mainstream intellectuals indulging themselves in nostalgic dreams of a Prague Spring that would not come again. On October 27 the government asserted itself with the rearrest of Havel and other leading democratic activists, but in Prague the next day thousands of people staged a demonstration calling for an end to Communist control of the country, in line with the liberalization taking place in other EASTERN BLOC countries. The government,

however, flung in heavily armed policemen to crush this demonstration and any attempts to rekindle it in following days.

In November the picture changed. The Velvet Revolution itself began on the 17th with a large-scale, student-organized demonstration that drew the attack of riot police, who beat men, women, and children with their truncheons. The protests continued, and on November 20 a crowd of more than 200,000 in Wenceslas Square demanded freedom. The next day shaken government officials began talks with representatives of opposition groups, including CIVIC FORUM, the brand-new coalition headed by Václav Havel. With the demonstrations spreading across the country, Soviet leader Mikhail GORBACHEV declared his support for the changes taking place across Eastern Europe; this time no Soviet-sponsored WARSAW PACT tanks would come to put down the people. Although the Czech Communist Party hierarchy desperately reshuffled itself, opposition leaders declared these changes could not serve as a substitute for democracy. On November 27 a nationwide general strike dramatized popular support for the drive toward genuine freedom. The world began to see that, lacking Soviet support, the Eastern European governments had no strength of their own to sustain themselves. An attempt by the government to create a new cabinet with limited non-Communist representation was rebuffed by the opposition, which declared itself ready for another general strike if necessary.

Finally, President Gustáv HUSÁK, the hard-line head of state since 1975, announced his decision to resign after a new government was formed. Declaring himself a writer with no political ambitions, Havel said that if necessary he would be willing to take the office. The new, non-Communist cabinet took the oath on December 10, Husák turned in his resignation, and on December 29, 1989—though still having its large Communist membership—Parliament elected Havel as his successor, little more than a month after the fall of the BERLIN WALL. Alexander DUBČEK, the tragic hero of the 1968 Prague Spring, was chosen chairman of Parliament. The government that controlled Czechoslovakia for 41 years had departed—not so much overturned, perhaps, as simply dissolved.

Venona In 1944 the U.S. Office of Strategic Services obtained a Soviet intelligence code book, which, by order of President Franklin D. ROOSEVELT, was later returned to the then-U.S. ally. Despite the president's wish, however, the OSS kept a copy of the book, an act that led to fateful consequences in the Cold War. The code book, when combined with other information—some of it cryptological, some of it supplied by a Soviet defector named Igor Gouzenko—proved to be the key unlocking the secrets contained in thousands of messages sent between Soviet agents in the West and headquarters in Moscow during the last year of the war. This brilliant feat of cryptanalysis was performed by a U.S. Army code breaker named Meredith Gardner; the material his work produced received the code name Venona. Consequences of Venona included the unmasking of the atomic spies Klaus FUCHS, Bruno Pontecorvo, David Greenglass, and Julius and Ethel Rosenberg. (The last three, along with Morton Sobell, were defendants in the ROSENBERG CASE.) Venona also brought about, either directly or ultimately, the destruction of the KGB spy ring known as the CAMBRIDGE FIVE. Though a U.S. traitor, William Weisband, told the KGB about the Venona secret in 1948, U.S. and British intelligence already had decrypted a huge mass of cipher messages concerning Soviet secret operations in the West.

Vietcong This term, a shortened version of *Vietnam Cong-san* (Vietnamese Communist), was a derogatory name for the military forces of the NATIONAL LIBERATION FRONT, which controlled the insurgency in South Vietnam against the U.S.-backed government in SAIGON. The abbreviation VC was commonly used. *See also* VIETNAM WAR.

Vietminh In May 1941 the Indochinese Communist leader HO CHI MINH supervised the creation of the Vietnam Doc Lap Dong Minh Hoi (in English, League for the Independence of Vietnam). Commonly called the Vietminh, this organization provided the Communists with a force to mobilize against the French and also against the occupying forces of the Japanese. The purpose of the front was tactical, hence limited, never strategic. Its flexibility allowed the Communist Party to make quick changes in course to meet current conditions, but the party never modified the strategic goals.

The Vietminh also fielded an army, commanded by VO NGUYEN GIAP, which seized power in August 1945 after the Japanese surrendered. In 1946, when negotiations with the French broke down and French troops returned to Vietnam in force, armed hostilities between the French and the Vietminh resumed.

From 1946 until the French defeat at DIEN BIEN PHU in 1954, the National United Front, of which the Vietminh had been the first component, was known as the Lien Viet Front. Since 1954 it has been called the Fatherland Front. The Communists abandoned the term *Vietminh* in 1951, but many Vietnamese in the South continued to use it.

Vietnamization The process, adopted as U.S. policy by the NIXON administration in April 1969, of turning the control and conduct of the VIETNAM WAR over to the ARMY OF THE REPUBLIC OF VIETNAM (ARVN), led by General NGUYEN VAN THIEU. The term appears to have been first used in 1968 by General Creighton ABRAMS.

Vietnam War The conflict between the United States and the Vietnamese government in SAIGON on one side, and the Communists of northern and southern Vietnam on the other. Some historians call the war the Second Indochina War (the first being the earlier conflict between the Vietnamese and the French); to the Vietnamese, it is the American War.

The longest war in which the United States has ever fought, Vietnam had origins going back to 1950, when the TRUMAN administration began to give heavy support to the French effort during the First Indochina War. By the time the fortress of DIEN BIEN PHU had surrendered in 1954, U.S. contributions amounted to more than 80 percent of the French military budget.

After the GENEVA ACCORDS produced a cease-fire agreement to end the First Indochina War in 1954, the EISENHOWER administration chose to support the creation of an independent republic in southern Vietnam rather than face the possibility that HO CHI MINH's Communists would win the national elections called for in the accords. Indeed, Ike himself later admitted his belief that Ho would

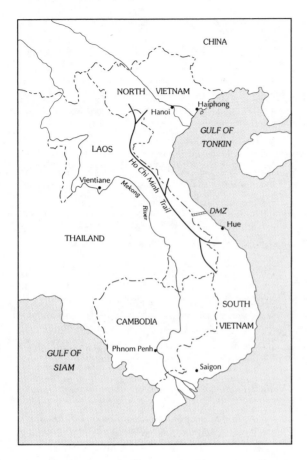

Southeast Asia

tional Front for the Liberation of South Vietnam, or NATIONAL LIBERATION FRONT (NLF), which its enemies called the VIETCONG. The U.S. government asserted that the North created the NLF to help the Communists in their effort to overthrow the Diem regime, since they had failed to unify the country through political means. The war, in what was to live as a famous phrase (originated by Sir Gerald TEMPLER), became a contest for the "hearts and minds" of the South Vietnamese peasants, who made up some 80 percent of the population. It was not a battle in which the government in Saigon scored many victories. Diem himself was overthrown and killed in a November 1963 coup.

With direct U.S. involvement lasting until 1973, the war cost the United States almost two billion dollars a month and a total of more than 58,000 lives. The social and psychological costs were likewise enormous, as the war became the most divisive issue in modern U.S. history. Every day, for the first time in history, TV news programs brought the horrors of war into American living rooms. Increasingly, the venture in Vietnam appeared to have no understandable purpose. It had no front lines and no apparent strategic aims but seemed more and more a real-life imitation of the endless conflicts described in George Orwell's *NINETEEN EIGHTY-FOUR.* ANTIWAR PROTESTS spread across the country and, indeed, around the world. The antipathy between reporters in Saigon and the U.S. command—whose daily briefing for the press came to be called the "five o'clock follies"—produced a "poisonous atmosphere," as a *New York Times* correspondent, Malcolm W. Browne, described it. This whole process led to changed public perceptions of government and politicians and, together with the revelations from the WATERGATE AFFAIR of the 1970s, produced a new kind of confrontational journalism, in which public figures would no longer enjoy immunity from any kinds of questions and accusations.

A wholly unanticipated tragic aspect of the war was the widespread use of drugs by soldiers in Vietnam. "It seemed like we were encouraged to drink alcohol," one veteran said later, "and pot was everywhere." One former infantry rifleman remembered the great logistical effort made by the army to ferry beer to troops on line. "But we

have won. American energies went into a nation-building project in the South with NGO DINH DIEM at the helm. Diem created the Republic of Vietnam (South Vietnam) and through an arranged election became president of the new country.

As early as 1956, Diem declared that his government faced attack from Communist North Vietnam. Actually, the nature of the insurgency has remained one of the most controversial questions of the war. Washington saw it as a war of aggression waged by North Vietnam against South Vietnam; those who opposed U.S. intervention claimed that the opposition to Diem arose within the South in response to the perceptions of the people.

In 1960 the Communists established the Na-

didn't like hot beer," he said, "so we swapped it to the local Vietnamese for cold Coke." Beyond the use of alcohol and marijuana was what *Newsweek*, in May 1971, called the epidemic of heroin addiction, said to involve some 30,000 to 40,000 service personnel in Vietnam—10 to 15 percent of all GIs in the country—and to pose a greater threat to the soldiers than came from Communist firepower. When these men returned to civilian life, the army provost marshal in Saigon reported to Connecticut congressman Robert Steele, they would find themselves "condemned to a life of crime and an early death." The columnist Stewart Alsop called this "the worst horror to emerge from the war—worse even than MY LAI." Iowa senator Harold Hughes, himself a former practicing alcoholic, agreed, calling for the armed services to provide treatment for addicted GIs instead of releasing them to bring "a horrifying addition to what is already the main source of crime in our cities." Belatedly acknowledging the problem, the services mounted antidrug information and treatment programs, as did the Veterans Administration. General Creighton ABRAMS and Admiral Elmo Zumwalt gave strong support to these efforts, but the treatment efforts were hampered by the high rate of relapse among all treated drug addicts everywhere; VA clinics reported that about half of their "graduates" returned to their drug habit almost immediately, and this was merely a preliminary figure. The drug problem, Vietnam-based or otherwise, found no quick fix, nor did it do so during the ensuing decades.

Though President NIXON and Secretary of State KISSINGER promised South Vietnamese president NGUYEN VAN THIEU they would send American help if the North Vietnamese carried on the war after the signing of the peace agreement in January 1973, these officials lacked the authority to back up such a commitment and, indeed, had no reason to suppose that Congress would agree to it. Essentially, the United States resigned from the Vietnam War.

Overall, the Vietnamese death toll in the war reached almost two million. The fighting came to its end in April 1975, with remaining U.S. troops escaping as fast as possible from the foundered South Vietnamese ship of state. After 50 years of continuous struggle, the Lao Dong—the Viet-

namese Communist Party—had finally won the victory. *See also* BUNDY, McGeorge; JOHNSON, Lyndon Baines; KENNEDY, John Fitzgerald; ROSTOW, Walt Whitman.

Vittles, Operation   U.S. code name for the U.S.-British BERLIN airlift (1948–49), which fed and warmed a city larger than Los Angeles. Though the authorities originally baptized the effort Operation Manna, the participating GIs popularized the name Operation Vittles. The British called their airlift effort Operation Plainfare.

Voice of America (VOA)   Division of the United States Information Agency that since the 1940s has broadcast news, analysis, and features all over the world. During the 1960s, midway in the Cold War era, the VOA produced about 800 hours of programming a week, in 36 languages, broadcast to over 102 transmitters in the United States and overseas. About 40 percent of the broadcasts were aimed at Communist countries. *See also* RADIO FREE EUROPE; RADIO LIBERTY.

Vo Nguyen Giap (1912–)   North Vietnamese general who put together the 300,000-man army that defeated the French in the First Indochina War (1946–54), his crowning victory coming at the siege of DIEN BIEN PHU. Continuing as commander in chief during the Second Indochina War against the South Vietnamese and the United States—the VIETNAM WAR—Giap gained further fame for his planning and direction of the TET OFFENSIVE, launched on January 30, 1968.

As a university student in Hanoi in the 1930s, Giap met two men with whom, in widely contrasting ways, his destiny would be connected: Truong Chinh, the future chief ideologue of the Communist Party of Vietnam, and NGO DINH DIEM, the future president of the Republic of Vietnam (South Vietnam). In 1938 Giap and Truong Chinh collaborated on a book, *The Peasant Question,* that advocated a peasant-led Marxist revolution. The next year, fearing arrest by the French, Giap fled to China, where he met HO CHI MINH, with whom he developed the People's Army of Vietnam.

Giap's pivotal 1954 victory over the French came in large part from his unparalleled ability to move men and supplies. The U.S. commander in

Vietnam, General William C. WESTMORELAND, said of Giap that "he was very determined, was a great general."

Voroshilov, Kliment (1881–1969) One of the earliest Bolsheviks, Voroshilov survived a long career of ups and downs as a political general to become, in 1953, Soviet president (the term by which the chairman of the Presidium of the SUPREME SOVIET was often known). A veteran of the civil war (1918–20)—where, by serving with Joseph STALIN, he made the most fortunate friendship of his life—and of the subsequent fighting against Poland, Voroshilov became people's commissar of military and naval affairs in 1925; the portfolio was re-labeled defense commissar in 1934. Voroshilov held the position until Stalin dismissed him in 1940 for leaving the Red Army ill prepared even for operations against Finland. Though Voroshilov was generally considered ineffectual, Stalin's purges of the army had worked ample damage on their own. Despite his previous failure, Voroshilov served during World War II as chairman of the State Defense Committee, attending important inter-Allied conferences and somehow staying in Stalin's good graces (KHRUSHCHEV saw him as a "whipping boy"). In later years, Voroshilov vacationed with Stalin in the Crimea. Though Khrushchev accused him of being an idler, spending his time attending the opera and posing for pictures with all his medals (some 15), Voroshilov seemed to have the knack of keeping friends, or at least of not making enemies. He held the largely honorific presidency of the USSR until 1960, when he resigned on the grounds of ill health. He was succeeded by Leonid BREZHNEV.

Belatedly, in 1961, Khrushchev denounced Voroshilov as a supporter of the ANTIPARTY GROUP, which had attempted to remove him as GENERAL SECRETARY of the COMMUNIST PARTY OF THE SOVIET UNION in 1957. When the marshal acknowledged the truth of the accusation, Khrushchev urged that he be given clemency—which, not surprisingly, was done. Once again, Voroshilov had escaped real trouble. In April 1962 he won reelection to the Presidium of the Supreme Soviet.

Vulture, Operation A proposed plan, particularly advocated in March and April 1954 by Admiral Arthur W. RADFORD, chairman of the U.S. JOINT CHIEFS OF STAFF, to assist the French garrison of DIEN BIEN PHU during the First Indochina War by sending some 60 B-29s from Philippine bases to bomb the besieging VIETMINH forces. The French government apparently believed that Radford, who regularly took hawkish positions, could persuade President EISENHOWER to authorize the operation. When Premier Joseph Laniel made such a request, however, he received a bleakly negative answer. Although, as subsequent events would show, the U.S. government attached great significance to the fate of Vietnam, it was not at this point prepared to take any unilateral action, and certainly not without congressional approval. The army chief of staff, General Matthew RIDGWAY, expressed the strongest opposition to Radford's plan.

Vyshinsky, Andrei Yanuaryevich (1883–1954) Soviet lawyer who held various party and government positions but will always be first remembered as the chief prosecutor in the trials of the Great Purge (1936–38). During the Cold War, Vyshinsky served as foreign minister (1949–53) and chief delegate to the UNITED NATIONS (1945–49 and again during the year following the death of Premier Joseph STALIN in 1953).

A professor of law and then rector of Moscow State University, Vyshinsky also practiced as a state prosecutor, gaining a reputation as a penetrating and relentless questioner. After becoming the chief Soviet prosecutor in 1935, he had the opportunity to put his ferocity (it is not too strong a word) to work during the Great Purge trials, in which a remarkable variety of officials and party members amazed the world by confessing to treasonable activities. The trials, however, did not exist to uncover guilt, which had already been established by torture and other extralegal means, but to exhibit this guilt to the public; the accused, like actors on stage, delivered lines written for them (though much of the time the confusing drama seemed the work of amateur playwrights delivered by amateur performers). Summing up at the conclusion of one group trial, Vyshinsky demanded that the group's members be shot like mad dogs. One of the defendants hastened to concur, saying that he and his fellows were all "bandits, assassins, Fascists, agents of the Gestapo" and thanking the prosecutor for "having demanded for us the only penalty we deserve." Interestingly, Vyshinsky once published a book on the theory of evidence; his view of evidence possessed an essential simplicity: the best evidence in any case, he said, is a confession, which establishes absolute guilt. As Soviet UN representative, Vyshinsky brought his intransigent, prosecutorial style to the international arena.

Vysotsky, Vladimir (1938–1980)   Soviet actor, also a composer and singer. During the BREZHNEV era, Vysotsky became the poet of moral crisis, expressing the general alienation from the corruption and drift of the time and the popular rejection of officialdom and its slogans. By the end of his life, which came prematurely because of his abuse of alcohol and drugs, Vysotsky had become the most popular poet in the USSR.

W

Waldheim, Kurt (1918–) Secretary-general of the UNITED NATIONS from 1972 to 1982, elected president of Austria in 1986. The son of a civil servant, Waldheim studied law at the University of Vienna and early in World War II was drafted into the German army. Wounded in fighting on the Eastern Front, he was discharged in 1942. He won his law degree in 1944, and in 1945, after Austria was separated from Germany, entered diplomatic service. In 1955 and 1956 he was Austrian observer at the United Nations. After serving as ambassador to Canada (1956–60), Waldheim went home to Austria for four years and then returned to the United Nations, this time as Austrian ambassador, a post he briefly lost as the result of a change of cabinets in 1970. In 1972 he was elected secretary-general, to succeed Burma's U THANT. During his 1986 campaign for the Austrian presidency, Waldheim came under an international cloud when accused of involvement in the summary shooting of Yugoslav partisans and the deportation of Jewish prisoners during World War II. Whatever the degree of his involvement, the attacks from outside seemed to strengthen him with Austrian voters. Waldheim was succeeded at the UN by Peruvian Javier PÉREZ DE CUÉLLAR.

Kurt Waldheim, fourth United Nations secretary-general

Wałesa, Lech (1943–) Leading figure of the Polish revolution of the 1980s as head of the labor coalition called SOLIDARITY; elected president of Poland in 1990. The son of a carpenter, Wałesa went to work in Gdansk in 1966 as an electrician in the Lenin Shipyard. Just ten years later he was dismissed for his activity as spokesman in a demonstration against the "erosion" of agreements made by the Polish government after the violent smashing of food riots in 1970. Though unemployed for the next four years, Wałesa edited an underground newspaper and took a leading part in the activities of the Workers' Self-Defense Committee.

In August 1980 came the event that changed Wałesa's life and, ultimately, that of his country.

With workers striking across Poland for higher wages to help them meet rising prices, Wałesa climbed over the fence at the Lenin Shipyard to urge workers to strike until the government gave them the right to form an independent union. Taking charge of the situation, as the strike shut down yards along the Baltic coast, he entered negotiations with the government that ended in the concessions sought by workers. Soon some ten million workers had enrolled in new unions, which grouped themselves under the National Coordinating Committee of Independent Autonomous Trade Unions, known more simply as Solidarity (Solidarnosc), with Wałesa as chairman.

In December 1981, however, the Polish government—acting out of its own desperation and also under pressure from the BREZHNEV government of the USSR—responded to the continuing militancy of the people by imposing martial law. This move marked the failure (or the essential futility) of negotiations between the government and Solidarity, in which Wałesa—who at the time believed in the "self-limitation of the revolution"—had sought some sort of effective compromise. Poland, Wałesa wrote, was not an independent country, and its government had to be acceptable to the leaders of the USSR. In the early morning of December 13, Polish troops and tanks took over the country as if it were an enemy power. The government declared Solidarity illegal and interned thousands of its members. Refusing now to negotiate with the authorities, Wałesa went to prison for almost a year.

It was not until the great changes began in Eastern Europe in 1989 that Solidarity won back its legal status, with Wałesa returning as chairman (on a festive day during which he was presented with a gigantic white cake). Deciding at first to stay out of elective politics, Wałesa changed his mind in 1990 because he saw that in the new situation the Communists could be totally driven from government; the time of compromise was long gone. In November he defeated his adviser from 1980, Tadeusz MAZOWIECKI, for the presidency of Poland.

Earlier, in 1983, Wałesa had received the Nobel Peace Prize for his militant advocacy of workers' rights. But Westerners, particularly those on the political left, sometimes found him a disconcerting revolutionary leader, a hard man to understand, and not simply because of his relative conservatism. A leading Polish reporter wrote of him: "When he says that Solidarity is neither left-wing nor right-wing, he speaks primarily about himself. He is not interested in formulas or concepts." On seeing a picture of Wałesa with a rosary, the Spanish film director Luis Buñuel observed: "How can a workers' leader be religious? This is a contradiction in terms." But the Poles, who were as attached to the church as they were to the changes they had sought and won, with the assistance of three papal visits from Pope JOHN PAUL II, saw the matter quite differently.

Walker spy ring   One day in January 1968 a U.S. Navy chief warrant officer named John Anthony Walker, Jr., presented himself at the Soviet embassy in Washington, like anybody applying for an ordinary job, and came away with an arrangement to act as a spy for the KGB. Over the next two decades, Walker, with the assistance of his brother, his son Michael, and his friend Jerry Whitworth (his daughter declined to join the family firm), turned over to his controllers top-secret cipher keys and thousands of secret cipher messages; his first offering was a month's worth of settings for the KL-47 cipher machine. Walker acted not from ideological conviction of any kind but simply on the idea that the confidential information to which he had access could readily be turned into cash. Overall, the Soviets paid him more than a million dollars—the most any spy had ever received up to that time; son Michael, however, later said that his father, whom he appeared to revere, had passed on to him only a thousand dollars.

Walker's chronically troubled marriage ended in divorce and finally, in 1985, his ex-wife told the FBI about his espionage activities. Making a deal for himself and his son—though each faced considerable time in prison—Walker fully implicated Whitworth, who did not have the benefit of any plea bargain. With the Walker spy ring, the KGB scored its greatest American success.

Wallace, Henry Agard (1888–1965)   Secretary of agriculture (1933–40) and vice president of the United States (1941–45), Henry Wallace was nominated by President ROOSEVELT as secretary of commerce at the beginning of the president's fourth term and, after some debate in the Senate, was confirmed as secretary but not as head of the Reconstruction Finance Corporation and other government lending agencies. Not in any respect a typical politician, Wallace was an agricultural scientist and something of a visionary in government, a trait creating deep distrust on the part of many conservative senators and other officials. He continued as secretary of commerce under President TRUMAN but, after colliding with the president on foreign-policy questions—not his official area of responsibility—resigned from the cabinet in 1946. (Wallace's approach to dealing with the Soviets was characterized at the time by diplomat and U.S. Soviet expert George F. KENNAN as "the glad hand and the winning smile"—an approach, Kennan said, that could not work.) In 1948, as the nominee of the leftist Progressive Party, Wallace ran for the presidency in that year's unusual four-candidate campaign. Though siphoning more than one million votes away from the Democrats, Wallace's candidacy did not keep Truman from winning his dramatic victory.

Warnke, Paul Culliton (1920–)   One of the many U.S. officials who have moved between the government and major law firms, Warnke served in 1977 and 1978, during the CARTER administration, as director of the Arms Control and Disarmament Agency, a position that made him the chief U.S. representative at the STRATEGIC ARMS LIMITATION TALKS with the Soviet Union.

A native of Webster, Mass., Warnke graduated from Yale in 1941 and enlisted in the Coast Guard; he spent the World War II years on support and assault craft in both the Atlantic and the Pacific. Following the war he attended Columbia Law School, graduating in 1948, and after practicing in Washington (with Covington & Burling, the firm with which Dean ACHESON was identified) went to the Defense Department in 1966 as general counsel. Having developed anti–VIETNAM WAR sentiments, he acted as an adviser to the 1972 Democratic antiwar presidential nominee, George McGovern. Warnke then joined the well-established Washington law firm headed by Clark CLIFFORD.

As the nominee to direct the arms-control agency, Warnke faced a great deal of wary questioning by senators. Was he so tainted by McGovernism that he would fail to protect U.S. defense interests? Was he covering up his real views in order to win confirmation (not, indeed, the rarest phenomenon in such situations)? After the inquest, Warnke won approval from the committee and from the full Senate, though he had to endure a parting blast from one of the most hawkish senators, the Democratic Henry "Scoop" Jackson of Washington.

As arms negotiator, Warnke displayed a willingness to take into account the differing geographical and strategic situations of the United States and the Soviet Union. This approach upset those who saw that the Soviets would be left with greater numbers and weight of land-based missiles; however, Warnke said, "the Soviet Union does not have the option of going to sea to the extent that we do." During the SALT negotiations, Warnke and his associates managed, after seemingly endless discussion and delay, to persuade the Soviets to abandon their secrecy sufficiently to exchange lists of categories of strategic weapons. "You realize," said the Soviet representative, "that you've just repealed about four hundred years of Russian history. And maybe that's not a bad idea."

Warsaw Pact   Called the East European Mutual Assistance Treaty and the Treaty of Friendship, Cooperation, and Mutual Assistance, this document signed in May 1955 established the Warsaw Treaty Organization, an alliance of the eight EASTERN BLOC countries: Albania, Bulgaria, Czechoslovakia, East Germany (the GERMAN DEMOCRATIC REPUBLIC), Hungary, Poland, Romania, and the Soviet Union. Though the Soviets already maintained military forces in several of the countries, the alliance created a legal basis for the existence of these forces, and it represented a formal (and hastily organized) response to the integration of West Germany into the NORTH ATLANTIC TREATY ORGANIZATION, which took place officially on May 9, 1955. The official headquarters of the Warsaw Pact alliance was located in Moscow. To ensure a uniformity of military doctrine among the members of the alliance, selected officers from all countries attended the Soviet Voroshilov (General Staff) Academy, where they were taught by leading theoreticians and had the benefit of lectures by outstanding soldiers, including chiefs of staff. The students then took the approved doctrine back to their own staffs and academies. An important book, *Soviet Military Strategy*, edited by Marshal V. D. Sokolovskii, published in the USSR in 1962, discussed the importance of unifying the "political, economic and military forces of all the socialist countries" to "repel an attack and completely break up the aggressive plans of the imperialists"; the "highest political agency for coordinating all the efforts of the socialist countries during war," declared this authoritative work, "may be the Political Advisory Committee created according to the Warsaw Pact."

Documents from the files of the former East German National People's Army (NVA) reveal that Warsaw Pact planning, drawn up under Soviet direction, envisioned an attack by five fronts (army groups) against NATO forces in Northern and Central Europe; the Soviet Baltic Fleet, the Polish navy, the People's Navy of East Germany, and various air forces also had roles in the plan. If the Warsaw Pact countries should undertake a nuclear offensive, the primary targets would be NATO nuclear installations and equipment, air force and air defense facilities, command posts, troops, and West German ships and naval bases.

As the Albanian government of Enver HOXHA distanced itself from the policies of the USSR under Nikita KHRUSHCHEV, the country ceased its participation in Warsaw Pact activities; it formally left the alliance in 1968. In the same year, the mutual-assistance concept embodied in the language of the treaty was employed by Leonid BREZHNEV as the formal basis for intervention by Warsaw Pact forces in Czechoslovakia to quell the PRAGUE SPRING.

The withdrawal of Soviet support, under the leadership of Mikhail GORBACHEV, for the governments of the PEOPLE'S DEMOCRACIES of Eastern Europe and their consequent collapse in 1989 and 1990, the changes within the Soviet Union itself, and the consequent end of the Cold War brought the end of the Warsaw Pact alliance; it was formally dissolved in May 1991.

Warsaw Treaty Organization   *See* WARSAW PACT.

Watergate affair   What U.S. president NIXON's press secretary, Ron Ziegler, described as a "third-rate burglary" of the Democratic National Committee headquarters (located in the Watergate office-and-apartment complex in Washington) on June 17, 1972, led, tortuously and painfully, to an event unprecedented in U.S. history: the resignation of a president, which came more than two years later, in August 1974. Part of an effort to help ensure Nixon's reelection—though its precise purpose has been much debated—the break-in, it became clear, was authorized by members of the staffs of the White House and the Committee to Reelect the President (known, inevitably, as CREEP); finally the president as well as his subordinates became implicated, not in the burglary but in the subsequent attempt to cover up White House involvement in it. Investigation also showed that the perpetrators of Watergate had engaged in other illegal activities, such as faking diplomatic cables to implicate the KENNEDY administration in the assassination of South Vietnam's President NGO DINH DIEM in 1963 and breaking into a psychiatrist's office to obtain the medical records of Daniel Ellsberg, a defendant in the PENTAGON PAPERS case. Facing impeachment, Nixon, in a televised speech on August 8, 1974, announced his resignation.

Seeing President Nixon as the statesman who had removed U.S. forces from Vietnam to end the VIETNAM WAR, opened relations with China, and nurtured DÉTENTE with the Soviet Union, many Europeans expressed incredulity that what they considered such a minor affair had driven him from office. General Alexander HAIG, Nixon's former chief of staff who had become the NORTH ATLANTIC TREATY ORGANIZATION commander in chief, reported that "almost every head of state" asked him, "What in God's name have you American people done to one of the most effective leaders of this generation?" Though Nixon had his negative side, said the British chancellor of the exchequer, Denis HEALEY, much of the world was grateful to him for "a serious attempt both to control the arms race and to reach an understanding with the Soviet Union."

One important group of international spectators looked at Watergate with deep skepticism. To officers of the KGB and a number of other Soviets, already disturbed over Soviet-American tensions produced by the JACKSON-VANIK AMENDMENT to the Trade Reform Act, U.S. ruling circles opposed to détente—Zionists, the military-industrial complex —were the real culprits. Certainly the publicly stated reasons for Nixon's fall could hardly be taken seriously. After all, wrote Soviet defector Arkady Shevchenko in 1985, "Watergates are routine and permanent features of life in the Soviet Union from top to bottom." Hence the incident that toppled Nixon could in itself only appear "trivial."

Americans generally held an opposing view. The revelation of Nixon's opinions and conduct strengthened a disillusion with politics and politicians that had developed during the Vietnam War.

Wedemeyer, Albert Coady (1897–1989) U.S. Army officer who commanded U.S. forces in the China Theater during the last year of World War II (1944–45) and served as chief of staff to Generalissimo CHIANG KAI-SHEK. An extremely able planner and commander, Wedemeyer in the late 1930s attended the German Kriegsakademie (where he became a close friend of Count Claus von Stauffenberg, the man who planted the bomb in Adolf Hitler's headquarters in 1944). With his great personal charm, Wedemeyer got on well with Chiang and produced improvements in the Chinese army. In the chaotic situation prevailing after World War II ended, Wedemeyer saw to it that U.S. forces did not become involved in any conflict with Chinese Communist forces.

In July and August 1947, at the request of President TRUMAN, Wedemeyer carried out a fact-finding mission to China. Though his report laid bare the corruption and incompetence of the Chinese government, he did not advocate a hands-off U.S. policy, thus differing with Truman and with his own mentor, General George C. MARSHALL. His highly controversial report did not appear until 1951. Asked by Senator William E. Jenner why he had joined in the suppression of the report, Marshall replied: "I did not join in the suppression of the report. I personally suppressed it." He had sent Wedemeyer to China to "find out something" for him, he said, "not for a public speech."

Weinberger, Caspar Willard (1917–) Chosen as secretary of defense by U.S. president-elect Ronald REAGAN in December 1980, Weinberger supervised the buildup of the U.S. armed forces that characterized the Reagan administration. He served as secretary until November 1987, when, with the administration in some disarray over the IRAN-CONTRA AFFAIR, he resigned; Weinberger had opposed the providing of arms to the Iranian revolutionary government but did not resign over that issue. Later he expressed discontent with decreases in defense funding in the immediately preceding years, though he gave the state of his wife's health as the reason for his retirement.

Born in San Francisco, Weinberger was the son of a lawyer and took his own law degree at Harvard, after graduating from Harvard College. During World War II he served in the infantry, rising to the rank of captain, and afterward he practiced law in San Francisco and also took an active part in state politics, serving in the legislature and holding Republican Party offices, one of his posts being Governor Reagan's director of finance. Moving to Washington in 1970, he held high-level positions in the NIXON and FORD administrations, including secretary of health, education, and welfare (1973–75).

As Reagan's secretary of defense, Weinberger regularly supported the budget requests of the armed services and proved to be a resolute Cold Warrior whose hostility to the Soviet Union sometimes seemed to exceed even that of the president. Before Reagan left Washington for the 1985 SUMMIT meeting in Geneva, Weinberger cautioned him not only against making any agreement with the Soviets but even against moving in such a direction. A notable legacy of Weinberger's tenure at the Department of Defense was the rise of General Colin Powell, whose career was supported by the secretary and who later became chairman of the JOINT CHIEFS OF STAFF.

West Germany See FEDERAL REPUBLIC OF GERMANY.

Westmoreland, William Childs (1914–) U.S. general who as commander in Vietnam from 1964 to 1968 became identified with the massive troop buildup and the general escalation of the VIETNAM WAR.

A native of Spartanburg County, S.C., Westmoreland attended The Citadel in Charleston be-

General William C. Westmoreland, U.S. commander in Vietnam and army chief of staff

Vietnam, Westmoreland regularly produced optimistic reports for Washington, but by 1968 the administration's frustration had become too great and the political price too high for the management of the war to continue on the same course. Westmoreland was brought back to the United States as chief of staff, and soon, under President NIXON, different policies were at work in Vietnam.

Described by a distinguished military historian who worked with him as "a real Boy Scout," Westmoreland was a pleasant, silver-haired man who, if such things existed, could have been featured on a recruiting poster for generals.

Wheeler, Earle Gilmore (1908–1975) The highest U.S. officer during the VIETNAM WAR as army chief of staff (1962–64) and chairman of the JOINT CHIEFS OF STAFF (1964–70). Under General Wheeler the armed forces were expanded and brought up to date to fight the war in Asia.

Born in Washington, D.C., Wheeler was a 1932 graduate of West Point and during World War II served as an infantry-division chief of staff, training troops and seeing no combat. Posted to the NORTH ATLANTIC TREATY ORGANIZATION in the early 1950s, he returned to the United States in 1955 as a major general to take a high-level planning position at the PENTAGON. For two years (1958–60) he had his only direct command experience as commander of the Second Armored Division. He next became Joint Staff director for the Joint Chiefs of Staff and then, after a brief return to Europe, came the appointment as army chief of staff.

Though Wheeler's lack of combat experience made some of his JCS colleagues view him lightly, as a desk-bound bureaucrat, he proved to be an able, highly professional chairman. Presiding over the JCS during a period of extreme stress, Wheeler had to contend with civilian policies in Vietnam of which the military strongly disapproved; the soldiers, in brief, wanted all-out war or nothing. Though arguing against the JOHNSON administration's gradual-escalation approach to the war, Wheeler in August 1967 is said to have managed to keep the chiefs from submitting a group resignation—"mutiny," the JCS chairman called it. The discontent of the generals and admirals ultimately found its reflection in provisions of the 1986 military-reform act giving the chairman of the JCS a

fore going to West Point, from which he graduated in 1936. Commissioned in the field artillery, he became an infantry battalion commander in World War II in North Africa and Sicily and then a division executive officer in France. During the KOREAN WAR, having taken paratroop training, he commanded the 187th Airborne Regimental Combat Team. In 1958 he became commanding general of the famous 101st Airborne Division. By the time he moved to West Point as superintendent of the academy in 1960 (the second youngest officer, after Douglas MACARTHUR, to hold this post), he had made 115 jumps.

It was on February 22, 1965, that General Westmoreland made a fateful request of President JOHNSON, asking for troops to be sent to Vietnam to protect the U.S. air base at Da Nang. Just two weeks later units began arriving—the first wave of a force that in the next three years would grow to more than half a million. During his command in

General Earle Wheeler, chairman of the U.S. Joint Chiefs of Staff

seat on the NATIONAL SECURITY COUNCIL. Despite Wheeler's disagreement with U.S. limited-war policies in Vietnam, President Johnson developed such respect for the general that he caused his term of office to be extended by a year. Wheeler, though suffering from heart disease, stayed on for yet another year under President NIXON before retiring as a full general in 1970.

White, Harry Dexter (1892–1948)   U.S. economist (professor at Lawrence College) who, as a Treasury Department official, played a prominent part at the 1944 Bretton Woods conference, which drew up the plans for the INTERNATIONAL MONETARY FUND (IMF) and the WORLD BANK. In 1945 White became the IMF's first director. Evidence secured after World War II, however, revealed White as a Communist agent, member of the network, controlled by Whittaker CHAMBERS, that included Alger HISS. White died of a heart attack shortly after testifying to a congressional committee.

Williams, G(erhard) Mennen (1911–)   During the presidential campaign of 1960, John F. KENNEDY made Africa something of an issue, declaring that the United States had lost ground there because "we have neglected and ignored the needs and aspirations of the African people." Soon after he took office in January 1961, he acted on his statement by filling a newly created position, assistant secretary of state for African affairs. The position went to the former governor (1948–60) of Michigan, G. Mennen Williams, the scion of a wealthy family—known as Soapy because his grandfather had founded the Mennen company—and strong supporter of the civil rights movement.

During his first trip to Africa, Williams stirred up something of a hornets' nest in London by observing that he believed in Africa for the Africans —at a time when Britain still held colonies in the continent. Kennedy, questioned about the statement, defended his traveling subordinate by commenting crisply, "I don't know who else Africa should be for." U.S. aid to Africa rose briskly (though still only a small part of total aid to all developing countries) but went into a decline after Kennedy was assassinated. The country in general did not share the president's sensitivity to Africa's needs or his hopes for its future. *See also* THIRD WORLD.

Wilson, (James) Harold (1916–1995) Always seeming to be the proverbial young man in a hurry, Harold Wilson became the youngest British prime minister of the 20th century when the Labour Party won a narrow victory over the Conservatives in 1964. Earlier, after an outstanding career at Jesus College, Oxford, Wilson had become a lecturer at New College when he was only 21.

A Yorkshire native, Wilson, sometimes called Little Harold, entered Parliament in the Labour year of 1945, and at the age of 31 was a member of the cabinet as president of the Board of Trade. Elected party leader after the death of Hugh Gaitskell in 1963, Wilson followed up his 1964 victory by calling another election in 1966 and came away with a majority that had gone from 3 to 97.

Though earlier identified with the left wing of the Labour Party, Wilson proved to be a pragmatist in office. He supported U.S. president JOHNSON's policies on the VIETNAM WAR, a stance that drew much criticism, and he also encountered increasing fiscal problems; Wilson lost the 1970 election to Edward HEATH and the Conservatives. Returning to office in 1974, he stayed for two years before surprising the nation by resigning.

Wolf, Markus (1923–) Founder and longtime head of the East German foreign-intelligence agency, the Main Department of Reconnaissance, known as HVA from the initials of its name in German, Hauptverwaltung Aufklärung. Wolf came from a Communist background, his father having been a German Communist writer who fled to the Soviet Union when the Nazis came to power. During his career as director of the HVA, which lasted from its establishment (under a different name) in 1952 until his retirement in 1987, Wolf built up a reputation that put him among the

Prime Minister Harold Wilson of Great Britain

341

great spy masters of modern times. In his best-known and most successful coup, he installed an East German agent, Günther Guillaume, as confidential secretary to West Germany's Chancellor Willy BRANDT; when the scandal broke in 1974, Brandt had to resign.

Since Germany was one nation with two governments, the infiltration of agents into the opposing camp presented a lesser problem than planting agents in a foreign country. Even so, Wolf performed impressively in releasing thousands of moles to tunnel under West Germany. Though he operated effectively at high levels—as his success with Guillaume demonstrated—Wolf made a specialty of acquiring information from well-placed female secretaries. HVA agents seduced, and sometimes even married, the women.

In 1993 Wolf figured in an unusual trial. Its verdict was based on the principle that Germany had indeed been one country during the Cold War, even if divided in two. The veteran espionage chief's activities brought him a six-year sentence for treason, though he had never been a citizen of West Germany, the country he was convicted of betraying. In 1995 an appeals court overturned the verdict.

World Bank   Properly the International Bank for Reconstruction and Development, the World Bank (along with the INTERNATIONAL MONETARY FUND) was a result of the July 1944 UNITED NATIONS Monetary and Financial Conference, held at Bretton Woods, N.H. This meeting, in which the eminent British economist John Maynard Keynes played the most important part, led the way to much of the relative postwar stability, when the world, after some problem years, enjoyed an era of great economic growth.

The bank came into formal existence in 1945, with a membership of 28 countries. It lends money to member countries and to private businesses, to encourage investment and international trade. The World Bank provided beginning funding for the postwar reconstruction of Europe and later furnished capital to THIRD WORLD countries. The United States provided $3 billion of its $4.9 billion initial capital.

World Peace Congress   Meetings organized by the COMINFORM as part of the so-called world peace movement and held concurrently in Paris and Prague on April 20–25, 1949. Attended by representatives from 72 countries, the congress produced a declaration advocating the abolition of nuclear weapons and the reduction of conventional forces. One year later, March 15 to 19, 1950, a second congress, convened in Stockholm, adopted the Stockholm Appeal, again calling for an end to nuclear armaments. The appeal was circulated throughout the world and gained 560 million signatures. Subsequent congresses produced propaganda but never equaled the impact of Stockholm.

Wörner, Manfred (1934–1994)   Taking office in July 1988 as the seventh secretary-general of the NORTH ATLANTIC TREATY ORGANIZATION, Wörner became the first German to hold the position. An international lawyer with a special interest in defense matters, he had served as West German defense minister for the previous six years.

As secretary-general of NATO, Wörner acted, in effect, as the chief political officer of the alliance. After the lifting of the IRON CURTAIN and the reunification of Germany in 1990, Wörner led efforts to help Eastern Europe move beyond its Communist past by forging close links with NATO. He was one of the first leaders to urge the alliance to develop new roles, such as peacekeeping, with the end of the Soviet military threat.

Named for the famous Red Baron of the German air force in World War I, Manfred von Richthofen, Wörner, a member of the Bundestag since 1965, took flight training in the middle 1960s and qualified as a jet pilot.

"X article" So called because the byline reads simply "By X," this article in the quarterly *Foreign Affairs,* July 1947, attracted so much attention that several years later its author, the U.S. diplomat George F. KENNAN, could still be introduced to a lecture audience as "the famous Mr. X." Titled "The Sources of Soviet Conduct," the article, appearing during the middle of the year that gave rise to momentous U.S. policy decisions and declarations, including the TRUMAN DOCTRINE and the MARSHALL PLAN, created a national sensation.

Originally written as a memorandum on Soviet Communism for Secretary of the Navy (and soon to be Secretary of Defense) James FORRESTAL and revised for publication in *Foreign Affairs,* the article appeared just as Kennan took up his duties as head of the new Policy Planning Staff in the State Department. When the identity of the author became known (Arthur Krock of the *New York Times* revealed it), journalists and public alike saw it as a declaration of official U.S. policy toward the Soviet Union. Though Kennan's thinking certainly exerted great influence on the development of U.S. policy, the article did not have official standing. The State Department cleared it for publication in a routine, bureaucratic manner, with the sole stipulation that Kennan's name not be attached to it. Nevertheless, the article contains many thoughts that in themselves were to become both famous and influential; for example, "the main element of any United States policy toward the Soviet Union must be that of a long-term, patient but firm and vigilant CONTAINMENT of Russian expansive ten-dencies"; Kennan cautioned, however, that "such a policy has nothing to do with outward histrionics: with threats or blustering or superfluous gestures of outward 'toughness.'" Also memorable was the observation: "the Soviet pressure against the free institutions of the western world is something that can be *contained* [italics supplied] by the adroit and vigilant application of counter-force at a series of constantly shifting geographical and political points, corresponding to the shifts and manoeuvres of Soviet policy, but which cannot be charmed or talked out of existence. The Russians look forward to a duel of infinite duration." In translating the article for Soviet premier and general secretary Joseph STALIN, top officials of the KGB, then called the MGB—wishing to give their master what they thought he would expect to hear —rendered *containment* as *strangulation;* subordinate analysts, however, argued for the proper translation and managed to win their point.

The Soviets could not be charmed or talked out of the conflict, Kennan asserted, but if U.S. policy were maintained, it could not only halt Soviet expansion but through its pressure force a change in Soviet attitudes. The United States had the power, said Kennan, "to promote tendencies which must eventually find their outlet in either the break-up or the gradual mellowing of Soviet power." Though the exact nature of the containment policy would always be debated—how much diplomatic? how much economic? how much military?—Kennan's article gave the United States the word itself, the definition, and the grounds for such a strategy.

Y

Yakovlev, Alexander (1923–)   Official of the COMMUNIST PARTY OF THE SOVIET UNION, a close associate of Mikhail GORBACHEV contributing to the adoption of GLASNOST and the evolution of PERESTROIKA and the development of overall policy. Though he did not become well known outside the Soviet Union, Robert Kaiser of the *Washington Post* has called him "the second great personality of the Gorbachev revolution."

The son of a peasant family, Yakovlev served as a young marine company commander during World War II. Left with a limp after suffering a wound, he was discharged. He then studied to be a teacher but spent most of the next 30 years as a party official. In the late 1950s he took time out to acquire a doctorate in history, spending one of these years at Columbia University.

In 1973, during the BREZHNEV era, Yakovlev published a newspaper article that, though not wildly radical, aroused so much conservative ire that it was believed to have caused him to lose his post as head of the Department of Propaganda. Yakovlev later said, however, that his objection to Brezhnev's growing cult of personality caused his dismissal. Instead of being disgraced, he was, in accordance with his wish, dispatched to Canada as ambassador; he remained in the post until summoned back to Moscow in 1983 by Yuri ANDROPOV. This development probably occurred because Yakovlev had begun a friendship with Andropov's protégé Gorbachev when the latter paid a visit to Ottawa.

After Gorbachev came to power in 1985, Yakovlev filled various positions that saw him in charge of propaganda and then of international policy. He became a member of the CENTRAL COMMITTEE in 1986 and of the POLITBURO in 1987. Interestingly, he did not bring to his service any special reputation as a liberal, and had gone on record in describing the United States as "a nation governed more by deception and demagoguery than by conviction." Though he showed no later sign of becoming particularly pro-American, his most important service to Gorbachev came from his support of perestroika and from his resourcefulness as a supplier of ideas. He saw perestroika not simply as a rebuilding of the political and economic system, with an emphasis on the market as a necessary basis of democracy, but as a way of restoring ethical standards in public life. In 1990 he left the Central Committee and thus the Politburo as well. Disapproving of Gorbachev's continuing dependence on conservative party leaders, Yakovlev by his strictures against these men lost some of his influence with his friend.

One special service Yakovlev tried to offer Gorbachev did not accomplish its purpose. Just a few days before the attempted August 1991 coup against Gorbachev by the STATE COMMITTEE FOR THE STATE OF THE EMERGENCY IN THE USSR, Yakovlev declared in *IZVESTIA* that Stalinists in the Communist Party—the very persons he had warned Gorbachev about—were putting together a "party and state coup," but, from all the evidence, when the attempt came it surprised the Soviet president as much as it did the world. During the days of the coup Yakovlev stayed in his office day and night, acting as a collector and disseminator of information for those opposing the junta. Just after the coup collapsed, Yakovlev described the plotters as "fools," persons who failed to understand that even though the Soviet people had expressed various discontents, they had no wish to bring back a repressive government.

Yakovlev, Yegor Vladimirovich (1930–) Soviet writer who played an important role in the GORBACHEV era as editor of *MOSCOW NEWS*, a previously innocuous newspaper that became, under his editorship, an organ and embodiment of GLASNOST. Earlier in his career, Yakovlev, an independent thinker, had worked for, and been dismissed from, a variety of Soviet publications. Offered the post of editor of *Moscow News* in 1985, while living in Prague, he weighed the decision for a year, apparently wishing to see whether the promised glasnost was a reality.

Yalta Conference   A landmark event so frequently spoken of throughout the Cold War and so burdened with the numerous fateful consequences ascribed to it as to have taken on almost mythic significance, the Yalta Conference was in fact the second and final meeting of the Big Three Allied leaders who had held power through most of World War II: U.S. president Franklin D. ROOSEVELT, British prime minister Winston S. CHURCHILL, and Soviet premier Joseph STALIN. (By the time of the final wartime summit conference, at Potsdam, FDR was dead, and during that conference Churchill was replaced by the new British prime minister, Clement ATTLEE.)

Meeting from February 4 to 12, 1945, in villas near the Crimean resort town of Yalta, the Big Three dealt with a broad range of questions. An important military consideration for the United States was the obtaining of Stalin's agreement on the terms and the timing of Soviet entry into the war against Japan following the defeat of Germany. The leaders also took up matters concerning the proposed new UNITED NATIONS organization left unresolved at the planning conference at Dumbarton Oaks in Washington. The question of voting strength in the General Assembly caused particular problems, with Stalin demanding that two Soviet republics, the Ukraine and BYELORUSSIA, receive seats, thus giving the USSR three votes instead of one. Eager to settle the matter, Roosevelt agreed, but—unwisely, as it turned out—asked

that the decision be kept secret, presumably until he could deal with it politically after returning home. Before the end of the month, however, the story leaked to the press. Although the decision had little substantive significance (since the Security Council, not the General Assembly, would be the center of UN action), the fact of the secrecy made a bad impression in some political quarters, and it gave rise to a long-lasting question: If this was a secret agreement from Yalta, what other secret pacts had FDR made? In fact, the president had concluded another series of unpublicized agreements, having to do with concessions China would be asked to make to the Soviet Union in exchange for Soviet help in the war against Japan; the likelihood that Stalin wanted to fight and conquer Japan does not seem to have entered into Western calculations. So, from the beginning, something of a questionable air hung over Yalta. As the historian Herbert Feis wrote, "The secrecy has caused the agreement to be regarded in a sinister light. Undoubtedly this is one of the reasons why . . . its importance has been so exaggerated in public controversy."

Concerning Germany, the Big Three reached agreement on dividing the country into three zones of occupation after victory was won, with BERLIN receiving special status as a jointly controlled zone. After some discussion, Stalin agreed to the Anglo-American request that France be given a zone, stipulating that none of it should come from territory assigned to the USSR for occupation. Other questions, including reparations, were left for later decision at lower levels, since the leaders could not reach agreement on them.

Of particular importance for current and future relations between the Soviets and the Anglo-Americans was the question of Poland's boundaries and the composition of its government. The issue had caused much debate and argument since the preceding summer. The Western Allies recognized the Polish government-in-exile set up in London early in the war; the Soviets had recently recognized the provisional government established at their direction by the Committee of National Liberation, the so-called Lublin Committee, consisting of Communist political figures. Expressing a view that would have appeared most odd in a negotiation involving any other set of parties, the Lublin Poles

On his arrival in the Crimea for the Yalta Conference, U.S. president Franklin D. Roosevelt *(r.)* is greeted by Soviet foreign minister Vyacheslav M. Molotov *(center)*.

insisted that the USSR be given most of the area of Poland assigned to it by the Soviet agreement with Hitler in 1939—the territory east of the Ribbentrop-Molotov Line (in practical effect, the CURZON LINE). The United States and Britain not only accepted this proposal but also agreed that Poland should be compensated for this selflessness at the expense of Germany; the western Polish boundary would be moved to the Oder and Neisse Rivers, though the negotiators at Yalta did not draw the precise line.

Since Poland lay behind Soviet military lines and within the Soviet military sphere, the Western Allies had little leverage. They attempted, however, to pursue what was clearly an impossible dream: to induce Stalin and the people of Poland to agree on a government that would be simultaneously independent, democratic, and friendly to the Soviet Union. Churchill gallantly argued for "an election on the basis of universal suffrage by secret ballot with the participation of all democratic parties and the right to put up their candidates." The Western leaders seemed at moments to believe that if only Stalin would make the attempt, he could see the merit in such ideas. Stalin, however, declared that

his security concerns were a matter of "life and death." The best Churchill and Roosevelt could get was agreement that the Lublin government should be reorganized "on a broader democratic basis," including members of the London Polish government. The exact composition of this new Polish government was left to a three-power committee, headed by Soviet foreign minister V. M. MOLOTOV. After that matter was settled, said Stalin, the kinds of elections advocated by Churchill would surely follow. But in the following months the parties involved made no progress toward the "broader democratic" government, while the Soviets took complete control of Poland. Many subsequent writings refer to this handling of the Polish question as if it represented a settled policy by Churchill and Roosevelt to hand Eastern Europe to Stalin. But it seems clear that these statesmen were moved not by choice but by necessity. Churchill, in particular, fought a hard fight for a genuinely broadened government. He spoke from the continuing awareness that in 1939 Britain had gone to war with Germany as the result of a guarantee given to Poland. Stalin, no doubt, never entertained any idea that Churchill, or Roosevelt, felt concern for the rights of the people of Poland. Roosevelt's chief of staff, Admiral William D. LEAHY, commented that the agreement was so elastic that the Soviets could "stretch it all the way from Yalta to Washington without ever technically breaking it."

"I know, Bill—I know it," FDR answered. "But it's the best I can do for Poland at this time."

During a banquet on February 8 at which he was host, Stalin, in response to a toast, offered the prophetic observation that allies could easily maintain unity during a war but that "the difficult task came after the war when diverse interests tended to divide the allies." He hastened to express his belief that "the present alliance would meet this test." But however many varying interpretations these "diverse interests" were to be subjected to in the ensuing years and decades, they clearly had already become established realities.

The final session of the conference ended on a jocular note. As the statesmen posed for the photographers, Stalin entertained Roosevelt and Churchill by declaiming what were said to be the only English expressions he knew: "You said it!" "So what?" "What the hell goes on around here?" and "The toilet is over there." But the Soviet dictator actually knew at least a little more English than he let on. In a diplomatic negotiation not long afterward, he expressed his disagreement with a statement by brushing aside the translator and saying brusquely, "No! I say no!"

Particularly in the early years of the Cold War, though by no means only during that period, opponents of U.S. Democratic administrations made great political capital of the conference in the Crimea, attempting with considerable success to give the word *Yalta* the negative emotive power of *Munich*. But quite a different view also survived in the popular mind. Forty years after Yalta a British novelist, Fay Weldon, would speak of the "Yalta Treaty" as an agreement whereby Roosevelt and Stalin "divided the world into spheres of influence, without any reference whatsoever to its inhabitants. You take Bulgaria, I'll have Chile. What about AFGHANISTAN? Oh, um, well we'll have that and you take Finland." And so on.

Charles Maier of Harvard University has commented that "the interpretation of Yalta is a revealing litmus." At the end of the war and again,

to the Left, in the 1960s, it represented the peak of Allied harmony; in the 1950s it was seen as a U.S. sellout to the Soviet Union, particularly by U.S. conservatives; or it was "joint condominium over legitimate national aspirations." The end of the Cold War has meant the appearance of new viewpoints, new arguments, and the long-overdue voices of former IRON CURTAIN countries.

Yeltsin, Boris Nikolaevich (1931–) A peasant boy from Sverdlovsk, in western Siberia, Yeltsin—like many other leaders of the COMMUNIST PARTY OF THE SOVIET UNION—studied engineering. After graduating, he applied his specialty, civil engineering, in construction in Sverdlovsk until 1968, when he became a full-time party APPARATCHIK. By 1976 he had become first secretary of the regional party committee. His climb up the party ladder continued; he became a member of the CENTRAL COMMITTEE in 1981 and first secretary of the Moscow party committee in 1985. He, like Yegor LIGACHEV and others, represented some of the new blood brought into the center after the BREZHNEV era.

A tall, strongly built man, popular in his role as party boss of Moscow, with his rough-hewn personal style, his emotionalism, and his democratic ways, Yeltsin figured in one of the striking early scenes of GLASNOST in October 1987. At a session of the Central Committee held in observance of the 70th anniversary of the Bolshevik Revolution—the kind of ceremony that had always run on precisely scripted lines—Yeltsin erupted in a speech critical of Ligachev, previously an ally, and went on to indicate disenchantment with Soviet leader Mikhail GORBACHEV at the slow development of PERESTROIKA. He spoke of the dangers involved in the "adulation of the general secretary" by some members of the Politburo and, adding "I am clearly out of place as a member," expressed his desire to step down. He was given a second-level position in the bureau that supervised building construction.

But Yeltsin's career, which thus seemed to have gone into eclipse, was in fact far from over. In March 1989, running as an independent for a seat in the new CONGRESS OF PEOPLE'S DEPUTIES, he defeated an opponent who had the blessing of party elders. Later that year, the voters of Sverdlovsk elected him to the SUPREME SOVIET of the Russian republic. Having become recognized as a liberal opponent of Gorbachev, Yeltsin moved on to win election in 1990 as chairman of the Russian Supreme Soviet—president of Russia (still, at the time, part of the Soviet Union). Though many still doubted his depth and staying power, and he was looked on by some as a kind of heavy-drinking buffoon, Yeltsin would later win a general election for the presidency of the Russian republic, which would give him the kind of popular mandate never achieved by Gorbachev.

The great moment for which Yeltsin will always be remembered came during the attempted August 1991 coup against Gorbachev by the STATE COMMITTEE FOR THE STATE OF EMERGENCY IN THE USSR. The personal popularity Yeltsin had built up in Moscow helped bring crowds into the streets to defend the "White House," the Russian Federation government building, against expected attack by Soviet troops. Making the White House the headquarters of the opposition to the plotters, Yeltsin became the symbol of freedom as he stood atop a tank in front of the building, proclaiming his defiance of the junta, while television cameras took in the scene for broadcast to the whole world. As Alexander YAKOVLEV commented later that week, Yeltsin had demonstrated true courage—one person with a rifle could have ensured the end of his resistance to the coup. His words and his actions during the week of the coup made him the dominant political figure in the Soviet Union.

Yevtushenko, Yevgeny (1933–) Soviet poet, an animated, winning speaker who, like the late Welsh poet Dylan Thomas (with whom he shared no other traits), won fame not only for his verse but also for his public readings, enormously popular in the West as well as at home. In the KHRUSHCHEV era, Yevtushenko, while still quite young, became well-known for his poems "Zima Station" and "The Heirs of Stalin," and, especially, "Babi Yar," which dealt with anti-Semitism. In 1959, with Andrei Voznesensky and Bella Akhmadulina, he recited his poems to crowds of 10,000 or 20,000 people in Mayakovsky Square. Like other Soviet writers, Yevtushenko found a far colder artistic climate after Khrushchev's removal from office in 1964—the BREZHNEV freeze following the Khrushchev THAW.

Writers in the Soviet Union, facing situations unfamiliar in the West, responded to ideological changes and restrictions in various ways. Although he clearly wished to be regarded as a spokesman for his generation, Yevtushenko censored himself. As Valentina Polukhina has pointed out, he did not touch upon "forbidden themes," and even in "Babi Yar" he was condemning a Nazi crime, not a Soviet one. Another critic, Roland Stromberg, spoke of Yevtushenko as a "kind of tame liberal, exhibited by the Establishment and used to rebuke more extreme recalcitrants." After the coming of Leonid Brezhnev, Yevtushenko wrote poetry about economic matters and, in his political verse, attacked the West. Nevertheless, he ranks overall as a liberal voice and was eager for GLASNOST when the possibility of achieving it arose. In December 1985 he called for it in a speech to the Moscow writers' organization, though the idea was still so new that for the printed version censors edited out many of his observations. In 1989, when conservatives writing in *PRAVDA* attacked the liberal magazine *OGONYOK*, Yevtushenko joined other writers in fighting back (though *Pravda* refused to publish their reply). Elected in 1989 to the new CONGRESS OF PEOPLE'S DEPUTIES, Yevtushenko—clad in a dazzling white suit—demanded in a speech that the Congress strip the COMMUNIST PARTY OF THE SOVIET UNION of its traditional "leading role."

In 1993, when asked by an interviewer for his thoughts on the future of Russia, Yevtushenko replied, "History is a writer who uses blood instead of ink."

Yoshida, Shigeru (1878–1967) Though not the first post–World War II Japanese premier, Yoshida was the leading statesman of the period and, as prime minister almost continuously from 1946 to 1954, presided over the country's recovery from the war. During his administration the United States and Japan signed both a peace treaty and a treaty of alliance (July 8, 1951).

Yugoslav-Soviet Conflict of 1948 In June 1948 the COMINFORM expelled the president of Yugoslavia, Marshal TITO, for refusing to confess his alleged sin of deviationism. This move was actually the result of Tito's refusal to submit to control by Soviet premier Joseph STALIN; despite Stalin's boast that Tito would not be able to resist Soviet pressure, the Yugoslav leader succeeded in following his own path, playing a prominent part among nations practicing a policy of NONALIGNMENT, although he remained a Communist and in Cold War disputes his support generally went to the East rather than the West. Tito's independendent stance caused U.S. officials to overlook ideology in favor of practical strategy and politics; in the face of some dissent, the United States began to give Yugoslavia economic aid. The Yugoslav-Soviet split presented the West with a useful example of an alternative to the USSR. Hence Stalin's preoccupation with "Titoism" as a Communist heresy was not, from his narrow point of view, altogether unjustified.

Z

zakonomernosti   According to Soviet Marxist doctrine, the development of historical events is governed by definite and knowable laws, called *zakonomernosti*, from the Russian *zakonomernost'*; in English, "historical inevitability." This word, in turn, is related to the German *Gesetzmassigkeit*; in English, "conformity to theoretical principles." The belief in *zakonomernosti* meant that history and politics were viewed as exact sciences, like mathematics, in which any problem necessarily has one correct answer—so to speak, the "politically correct" answer. Bernard Lewis of Princeton University called the idea a "delusion" whose "forcible application has brought untold misery to untold millions of people."

Zhdanov, Andrei (1896–1948)   Soviet politician and leader, considered by many observers during the mid-1940s as the probable successor to Joseph STALIN as head of the COMMUNIST PARTY OF THE SOVIET UNION. Having taken part in the October Revolution in 1917, Zhdanov became a party official, serving as party boss in Novgorod and then taking over in Leningrad after the assassination of Sergei Kirov in 1934. Much mystery surrounded Kirov's murder, some commentators viewing it as having taken place at the instigation of Stalin himself (Kirov was said to have a Western orientation and to oppose the use of terror); the dictator, however, used the murder as part of the background for the Great Purge of alleged enemies of the party and the state (1936–38). Having won Stalin's favor and thus survived the purge, Zhdanov became a full member of the POLITBURO in 1939. He remained party boss of Leningrad throughout World War II and the great 900-day German siege of the city. After the war he engaged in a fierce contest for favor with another of Stalin's protégés, Georgi MALENKOV, and for a time outshone his rival. Then, in 1948, came Zhdanov's unexpected death, officially from heart disease. Stalin later used the doctors' supposed handling of the Zhdanov case as one of the rationalizations for his imprisoning of Kremlin doctors in the DOCTORS' PLOT.

During his two-year period of greatest national ascendancy (1946–48), Zhdanov acted as Stalin's herald and spokesman on cultural and intellectual issues, fiercely attacking Western influences in literature, music, and the mass media; this expression of xenophobia, which became known as the Zhdanovshchina, even extended to science, as in the rejection of Mendelian genetics in favor of the groundless theories of Soviet biologist and agronomist Trofim LYSENKO. Western "bourgeois" culture, Zhdanov declared in a 1946 speech, existed "in a state of emaciation and depravity" and was "putrid and baneful in its moral foundations." Unlike Western literature and art, with its "gangsters, chorus girls, praise of adultery," its "adventurers and rogues of every kind," said Zhdanov, Soviet culture must "educate the people and arm them ideologically."

Zhdanov also acted as the keynote speaker at the founding conference of the COMINFORM, held in Poland in 1947 and designed to some extent as the Soviet response to the U.S. MARSHALL PLAN. In his speech he declared that since 1945 the world had become irrevocably divided into an imperialist camp led by the United States and a progressive socialist camp led by the Soviet Union.

Zhivkov, Todor (1911–   )   Head of the Bulgarian Communist Party, with various titles and offices, for 35 years, Zhivkov was born near Sofia and, like a number of other revolutionary leaders in history, worked as a printer. A member of the Communist Party from 1932, he organized partisans during World War II to fight the Germans, with whom the reactionary Bulgarian government was allied. After the war Zhivkov became a candidate (nonvoting) member of the party Central Committee and in 1949 a full member. He won election to the POLITBURO in 1951 and, beginning in 1954, when he became first secretary of the party, he ruled as dictator of Bulgaria until overthrown in the wave of change that swept through Eastern Europe in 1989.

In his early years in power Zhivkov professed anti-Stalinism, in support of Nikita KHRUSHCHEV, but in the 1960s, particularly after Leonid BREZHNEV came to power in Moscow, he reflected hardline Communism in Bulgaria, clamping a repressive regime on his country and developing his own cult of personality, with such Stalinist features as placing his picture on public display. Overall, Zhivkov acted, for perhaps 30 years, as the Soviet Union's most faithful ally, in good part because his own tenure in office depended on Soviet support. The coming of Mikhail GORBACHEV, with PERESTROIKA and GLASNOST, led Zhivkov to pay lip service to these new ideas. He was even forced to de-emphasize his cult of personality by having his picture removed from public buildings.

These moves could not save him, however. In November 1989, following public demonstrations of disaffection with the regime, a group of party officials and military commanders, in an attempt at controlled revolution from the top, forced him to resign. The days when Zhivkov and others like him could call on the Kremlin for help had passed, and the following month Zhivkov was expelled from the Communist Party. As happened elsewhere, the party changed its name, becoming the Bulgarian Socialist Party, and thus distanced itself from the regime of its longtime head. *See also* CLUB FOR THE SUPPORT OF GLASNOST AND PERESTROIKA.

Zhou Enlai (Chou En-lai) (1898–1976)   Chinese Communist leader, widely respected both in China and in other countries, who became premier and foreign minister after the Communist victory in October 1949. Born to a well-known but poor Mandarin family in Jiangsu Province and educated at an American missionary school in Tianjin (Tientsin) and at a university in Japan, Zhou was briefly imprisoned for radical political activities and, on his release, went to Paris, where he studied for two years and in 1922 established a European branch of the Chinese Communist Party.

In 1924 he became political director of the Whampoa Military Academy, which had been established by Sun Yat-sen, founder of the Chinese republic and the GUOMINDANG (Kuomintang), and was directed by CHIANG KAI-SHEK. Originally a rival of MAO ZEDONG, Zhou became the party leader's closest adviser. He spent the war years (1941–45) in Chungking, the Chinese capital, as the link between Mao and Chiang Kai-shek. During the 1950s Zhou crafted a Chinese foreign policy in which the country sought to show itself a responsible member of the international community. At the same time he devoted much of his attention to strengthening relations with other Communist countries; in 1950 he went to see Soviet premier Joseph STALIN with the message that China would intervene in the KOREAN WAR with 500,000 troops to save the desperate North Korean regime. In 1953 Zhou personally took charge of mending the split that threatened to divide China from the Soviet Union when, after the death of Stalin, Georgi MALENKOV began speaking of the horrors of war and of improving relations with the West. Zhou led the Chinese delegation to the 1954 Geneva Conference, which produced the GENEVA ACCORDS ending the First Indochina War between France and Vietnam. He is credited with playing an important part in the development of the U.S.-Chinese rapprochement of the early 1970s.

At the Fourth National People's Congress in January 1975, Zhou presented his "Four Modernizations"—a sweeping plan for advances in agriculture, industry, science and technology, and national defense. The Four Modernizations, he declared, would make China prosperous into the 21st century. After all his long years of surviving as the levelheaded administrator through the twists and turns of Chinese Communist policy, Zhou was attacked by Mao in 1976, shortly before the leader's death on September 9. "It is time," said Mao, "to criticize him." But whatever its political force, the criticism could have no personal effect on Zhou, who had died in January.

Zhu De (Chu Teh) (1886–1976)   One of the earliest and most influential of Chinese Communist military officers, Zhu De, who had studied in Germany, became commander in chief of the People's Liberation Army during the Long March of 1934 and, together with MAO ZEDONG, developed the Communists' strategy of a many-fronted war, with mobile attacks and escapes to the mountains—the approach that ultimately brought the victory over the GUOMINDANG, led by CHIANG KAI-SHEK. Zhu De remained a trusted adviser of Mao throughout his career, although during the CULTURAL REVOLUTION, when no reputation was sacred, he was pilloried as a "black general" who sought to eclipse Mao.

Zhukov, Georgi (1896–1974)   Probably the Soviet Union's most illustrious soldier, Zhukov was born into a peasant family. He served in the imperial Russian army in World War I and then joined the Red Army, becoming a member of the Bolshevik Party in 1919. Until he entered the Soviet high command in 1939, he spent his career in the cavalry and its successor, the armored force.

Used by Premier Joseph STALIN as a high-level troubleshooter during the early part of World War II, Zhukov became deputy supreme commander of the Red Army in August 1942 and retained the position until the end of the war. Prominent in the battles of Moscow and Stalingrad, he led the final Soviet drive across Poland and against Berlin, though he spent much of his time at headquarters as Stalin's adviser. After taking the German surrender on May 8, Zhukov served for a time as Soviet commander in occupied Germany, developing something of a friendship with General Dwight D. EISENHOWER, the U.S. commander.

Liked by Westerners who met him, Zhukov had also become the Soviet public's favorite general, rather like Ike in the United States. Under Stalin, such popularity could hardly last. Bringing the marshal back to the USSR, Stalin put him out to pasture as commander first in Odessa and then in

the Urals and, having the power to make historians write whatever he chose, saw to it that the name of the country's leading general was expunged from accounts of the war. After Nikita KHRUSHCHEV took effective control of the USSR in 1955, however, Zhukov returned to prominence as defense minister.

In June 1957, Zhukov's control of the military proved of vital importance to Khrushchev. Outvoted in the Presidium by supporters of the ANTI-PARTY GROUP, Khrushchev faced removal from office. Rallying, however, the leader decided to take his case to the parent group of the Presidium, the CENTRAL COMMITTEE, many of whose members were rushed to Moscow on aircraft provided by Zhukov; the maneuver proved successful—Khrushchev retained the general secretaryship of the party, and Zhukov became a full member of the party Presidium (as the POLITBURO was called for a time). The leader's gratitude did not turn out to be lasting, however. Only a few months later, in October 1957, the man whose help had saved Khrushchev found himself dismissed for "violating Leninist principles concerning the administration of the armed forces" and engaging in "adventurism" and "Bonapartism." No more than Stalin, it turned out, did Khrushchev want a hero soldier in high office—and certainly not one who could be accused of commissioning a full-size portrait of himself on a white horse, nor one to whom the leader was heavily beholden. Following Khrushchev's overthrow in 1964, the BREZHNEV government restored Zhukov's honors.

Zorin, Valerian (1902–1986)   Soviet political official and diplomat who served as the USSR's permanent representative to the UNITED NATIONS from October 1952 to April 1953 and again in the 1960s. He came to particular notice as the ambassador to the UN at the time of the CUBAN MISSILE CRISIS in 1962, when he engaged in a memorable exchange with the U.S. ambassador, Adlai STEVENSON. Earlier, Zorin had been the first post–World War II Soviet ambassador to Czechoslovakia and, as deputy foreign minister, had been on hand in Prague at the time of the February 1948 Communist coup, which he was widely believed to have directed, though it appears that the Czech Communists required no outside help. One Czech writer declared that Zorin had assured Premier Klement GOTTWALD that the Soviet Union would not allow any Western interference "in the internal affairs of Czechoslovakia"; since no such interference was attempted, Zorin had no need to act.

As a young man, Zorin had been active in the Komsomol, and he had served in the Soviet Foreign Ministry during World War II. In 1947, at a meeting of the United Nations Economic Council for Europe, Zorin spoke in opposition to the MAR-SHALL PLAN. At another 1947 meeting, which was to plan a conference on freedom of information and the press, Zorin advanced an ironic proposal for "worldwide punishment of owners of newspapers that print libelous material about other countries."

In January 1963 Zorin was succeeded as chief Soviet UN delegate by Nikolai Federenko. After a second stint as deputy foreign minister (1963–65), he served as ambassador to France (1965–71).

NARRATIVE CHRONOLOGY: THE COLD WAR YEAR BY YEAR

BACKGROUND:
THE RISE OF THE SOVIET STATE

1917

March 12–15	Revolution in Russia overthrows the imperial government of Czar Nicholas II; a provisional government is established under a moderate, Prince Lvov; Alexander Kerensky soon becomes the leading figure.
April 16	Bolshevik leader Vladimir Ilyich Lenin, long in exile, returns from Zurich to Russia, having crossed Germany in the famous "sealed train" provided by the German government.
November 7	In Petrograd, with few shots being fired, the Bolsheviks take control. In the name of the Revolutionary Military Committee, Lenin proclaims the overthrow of the provisional government; Bolshevik fighters surround the Winter Palace and capture the provisional-government leaders. Kerensky, the premier, flees to Paris. (The revolution occurs on October 25 on the old-style Julian calendar—hence the Soviet designation as the October Revolution.)
November 8	All-Russian Congress of Soviets votes approval of the October Revolution and establishes, as the executive authority of the new government, the Council of People's Commissars, with Lenin as chairman and Leon Trotsky as commissar for foreign affairs. A lesser figure, J. V. Stalin, receives the portfolio of nationality affairs.
November 20	At Brest Litovsk, the Bolshevik government seeks to end Russia's participation in World War I by beginning truce negotiations with Germany and Austria-Hungary.
December 20	Council of People's Commissars decrees the establishment of the Extraordinary Commission to Fight Counter-Revolution (the Cheka), the world's first modern secret-police organization; it will later be known by a variety of designations, the final one being KGB.

1918

January 10	Russian Czarist generals and Cossacks proclaim the anti-Bolshevik Don Republic, which, though short-lived, is the first major development in a continuing Russian civil war.
February 14 (1)	Dates move up by 13 days as the Bolshevik government adopts the Gregorian calendar.
March 3	World War I ends for Russia as the Bolsheviks and the Central Powers sign a peace agreement at Brest Litovsk.
March 11	Bolshevik government establishes Moscow as the national capital.
March–April	Allied forces (British, French, Japanese) land in Murmansk and later in Vladivostok, officially to keep military supplies from falling into German (or German-collaborating Bolshevik) hands, and proceed to become involved in the Russian civil war, giving their backing to various anti-Bolshevik groups.
April 13	Czarist General Anton Denikin takes charge of rebel forces in the Caucasus region; Peter Krasnov heads the Cossacks.
July 16	Czar Nicholas II, his wife, and their children are shot by the Bolsheviks at Ekaterinburg; the next day other family members are murdered at Alapayevsk.
August 11	Lenin reacts to opposition from peasants by telegraphing Bolsheviks in one province to seize hostages and execute them in a way that will make people "for hundreds of miles around . . . see, tremble, know and scream out: *let's choke* and strangle those blood-sucking kulaks" (this document became available only in 1991).
August 16– September 3	U.S. troops arrive in the Russian Far East to join Allied forces.
August 30	Dora Kaplan, an agent of the Social Revolutionary Party, shoots and seriously wounds Lenin.
September	Anti-Bolshevik forces combine in the All-Russian National Conference; Admiral Alexander Kolchak heads the War and Navy Ministry of this shadow government.

1919

March 2	First Congress of the Comintern (Communist International) opens.
March 27	Delegates in Moscow establish the Third International.
November 18	Declaring that the Bolsheviks cannot be defeated by force of arms, British prime minister Lloyd George removes support for White armies.

1920

February 7	Bolshevik collaborators called the People's Army execute Admiral Kolchak, who was turned over to them by the French.
April	General Baron Peter Wrangel takes command of the small anti-Bolshevik force remaining under Denikin's command.
May 7	Invading the Ukraine, the Poles, who have rejected the Curzon Line as their eastern boundary, occupy Kiev.
July 10	As the Russian counteroffensive reaches into Poland, Polish leaders appeal to the Allies for help; the French send General Maxime Weygand and military supplies.
August 14	In the "miracle on the Vistula," Polish forces put the Red Army to rout.
October 12	Poles and Russians sign an armistice, leaving the Poles in possession of large tracts regarded by the Bolsheviks as properly Russian.
November 16	Russian civil war ends in victory for the Bolsheviks' Red army at Kerch and the flight of Baron Wrangel's White army from the Crimea.

1921–25

1921

March 18	Bolsheviks put down a rebellion at the Kronstadt naval base. The radical sailors called for a "third revolution" against the "torture chambers of the Cheka" and the "moral servitude" imposed on the people by the Communists, but they received little outside support.

March 18	Soviet government signs a peace treaty with Poland; under the settlement sizable populations of White Russians and Ukrainians are incorporated into Poland.
April	To stave off economic collapse, Lenin suspends "war communism" in favor of a tactical turn to capitalistic methods; this phase is called the New Economic Policy.
July	Chinese Communist Party holds first plenary meeting in Shanghai—consisting of 12 delegates meeting secretly, first in a girls' school and then, after a police raid, on a houseboat. One of the delegates is a young man named Mao Zedong (Mao Tse-tung).

1922

April 3	Joseph Stalin, "Comrade Card-Index," becomes secretary-general of the Communist Party of the Soviet Union.
April 16	Meeting at Rapallo, in Italy, the Soviet and German foreign ministers surprise the world by concluding an agreement calling for cooperation and the cancellation of debts and indemnities; it also has military significance, with the Soviets exchanging training facilities for German technical expertise.
May 26	Lenin suffers a stroke, which will be followed by a second attack on December 16; he relinquishes active direction of state affairs. Stalin and two other Bolsheviks, Lev Kamenev and Grigory Zinoviev, form a directing triumvirate, excluding Trotsky.
December 14	Lenin drafts a series of notes that later become known as his testament; they include a warning against some of the ideas and habits of "Comrade Stalin."
December 30	Bolshevik state—uniting Russia, the Ukraine, Byelorussia, and Transcaucasia—is officially named the Union of Soviet Socialist Republics.

1923

March 9	Lenin suffers his third stroke.

1924

January 21	Lenin dies. (Stalin misleads the absent Trotsky about the date of the funeral, so that Trotsky is not present for this almost sacramental occasion.)
February 2	British government, under Labour prime minister Ramsay MacDonald, extends diplomatic recognition to the Soviet Union; recognition by other European states quickly follows.

1925

March–April	14th Congress of the Communist Party of the Soviet Union hears Stalin declare the necessity of "socialism in one country," the USSR, as the antecedent to world revolution; Stalin removes Trotsky as war commissar.
April	In a sign of the developing times, the city of Tsaritsyn acquires a new name: Stalingrad.

1926–29

1926

December	At a meeting of the Communist Party of the Soviet Union Central Committee, Stalin savagely attacks the "opposition" leaders—Trotsky, Zinoviev, and Kamenev—in a five-hour speech.

1927

October	Stalin succeeds in causing the expulsion of Trotsky and Zinoviev from the Central Committee.
November	Trotsky, Zinoviev, and Kamenev are expelled from the Communist Party (though the latter two later gain reinstatement).

1928

January 16
Stalin orders Trotsky exiled to Alma-Ata, in the Kazakh Republic.

July–August
Sixth Congress of the Comintern declares that the preservation of the Soviet Union, the world's first socialist state, is the prime task of Communist parties in all countries.

1929

January 18
Stalin directs the Politburo to order Trotsky deported from the Soviet Union.

December 27
Stalin begins his prolonged and violent drive for collectivization of the peasants with a declaration calling for a "determined offensive against the kulaks" to "eliminate them as a class."

THE 1930s AND WORLD WAR II

1930

December 20
V. M. Molotov becomes Soviet premier, i.e., chairman of the Council of People's Commissars.

1933

November 17
U.S. president Franklin D. Roosevelt and Soviet envoy Maxim Litvinov conclude negotiations for U.S. recognition of the Soviet government.

1934

September 19
USSR joins the League of Nations.

1935

May 2 — USSR signs a treaty of alliance with France.

October — Donald Maclean, one of the Cambridge Five, goes to work in the British Foreign Office. The spy ring is made up of men recruited at Cambridge by the KGB in the middle 1930s.

1936

August — Stalin's Great Purge of the Communist Party of the Soviet Union (1936–38) begins; many veteran political and military figures are executed; Zinoviev and Kamenev are among the first casualties.

1937

January 1 — The new and democratically phrased "Stalin constitution" of the Soviet Union officially goes into effect.

June 11–12 — The Soviet military establishment is shaken by the conviction and execution of Marshal Mikhail Tukachevsky and other generals.

1938

September 30 — The sacrifice of Czechoslovakia to Hitler's demands at Munich causes rethinking on foreign policy in all quarters of Europe, not least in Moscow.

1939

May 2 — Molotov becomes Soviet foreign commissar, replacing Maxim Litvinov, identified with a policy of rapprochement with Britain and France.

May 20 — Molotov and the German ambassador, Count von der Schulenburg, begin discussions aimed at improving German-Soviet relations.

| August 12 | Negotiations for a possible alliance begin in Moscow between the USSR and the Western allies Britain and France. Entered on belatedly and proceeding in profound mutual mistrust, these sessions present a model of halfheartedness. |

| August 23 | German foreign minister Joachim von Ribbentrop flies to Moscow. Surprising the world, the two supposed mortal enemies, the USSR and Hitler's Germany, sign a nonaggression pact. |

| September | Guy Burgess, one of the KGB's Cambridge Five spy ring, goes to work on a contract basis for the British intelligence agency, MI6—on loan from the BBC. |

| September 1 | War begins with a German invasion of Poland. |

| September 3 | Britain and France declare war on Hitler's Germany. |

| September 17 | Red Army invades Poland; the country is then divided between Germany and the Soviet Union. |

| November 30 | Soviet forces invade Finland (the war continues until March 12, 1940). |

1940

| June | Soviet Union annexes Estonia, Latvia, and Lithuania. |

| July | With the help of Guy Burgess, H. A. R. "Kim" Philby joins MI6, the British Secret Intelligence Service; Philby will become the most renowned member of the Cambridge Five spy ring. |

| August | Benefiting, like Kim Philby, from his connection with Guy Burgess, Anthony Blunt, another Cambridge Five spy, joins MI5, the British Security Service. |

| August 20 | Using an ice pick, Soviet NKVD agent Ramón Mercader murders Leon Trotsky in Mexico. |

1941

| April 13 | USSR and Japan sign a neutrality pact. |

| May 6 | Stalin takes government (as well as party) office as premier of the USSR. |

June 22	Germany invades the Soviet Union.
July 30	Representing U.S. president Roosevelt, Harry Hopkins arrives in Moscow to assess Soviet capabilities and intentions in the war with Germany.
August 25	British and Soviet troops occupy Iran.
September 15	Germans complete the investment of Leningrad (the siege will last until January 1944).
December 6	Soviet forces launch counteroffensive against the Germans, saving Moscow.

1942

July 5	Germans complete the conquest of the Crimea.
November 19	Soviets open a major counteroffensive at Stalingrad.

1943

February 2	Trapped German forces at Stalingrad surrender to the Red Army.
April 17	Polish government-in-exile in London asks the International Red Cross to investigate the 1939 murders of thousands of Polish officers whose corpses have been discovered buried in the Katyn Forest, near Smolensk.
May 22	In a gesture to opinion in Allied countries, Stalin dissolves the Comintern.
July 5–12	Red Army defeats the Germans at Kursk, in the war's greatest tank battle.
October 19	U.S. secretary of state Cordell Hull and British foreign secretary Anthony Eden meet in Moscow with Soviet foreign minister Molotov; in the future the Council of Foreign Ministers will be assigned many chores left unfinished by the Allied Big Three.
November 28	The Allied Big Three (Stalin, Roosevelt, Churchill) begin a conference at Tehran (the meeting ends on December 2); the world will not learn for many years that Stalin's refusal to come to a more generally suitable

spot probably owes more to his fear of flying than to considerations of policy.

1944

June 6	Western Allies land in France to begin the drive into Germany from the west.
July 23	The Soviet government establishes the Polish Committee of National Liberation (the Lublin Committee), which it controls.
August 1	Polish underground forces and citizens in Warsaw rise against the German occupiers; the struggle lasts more than two months, until October 2. Stalin's refusal to allow anything but late and limited Western aid to reach the rebels engenders considerable Allied bitterness.

1945

January 17	Red Army takes Warsaw.
February 4	The Allied Big Three hold a second meeting, at Yalta in the Crimea (conference ends on February 12).
February 27	Yalta-inspired optimism begins to fade as Andrei Vyshinsky, chief Soviet prosecutor during the Great Purge, ignoring the Allied Control Council in Romania, demands the replacement of the existing government by a "democratic front."
April 12	President Roosevelt dies of a stroke at Warm Springs, Ga.; Harry S. Truman becomes 33rd president of the United States.
April 25	Founding conference of the United Nations organization convenes in San Francisco. On June 26 representatives of the participating countries will sign the United Nations Charter, which will go into effect on October 24.
May 8	V-E Day—the official day of Allied victory over Germany.
May 24	In a victory toast to the Soviet people, Stalin gives a suggestion of things to come by emphasizing Soviet primacy in all matters—apparently as an attempt to insulate soldiers and others from the effects of exposure to the West.

July 16	The world's first explosion of a nuclear device takes place at Alamogordo, N.Mex.
July 17	Allied Big Three hold a third conference, at Potsdam, with Harry Truman having succeeded Roosevelt and Clement Attlee replacing Churchill during the meeting (the conference ends on August 2). The leaders establish the Council of Foreign Ministers to deal with continuing specific problems.
July 28	By an 89–2 vote, the U.S. Senate gives its approval to the charter of the United Nations.
August 8	Soviet Union declares war on Japan.
August 14	Japan surrenders to the Allied powers, ending World War II (the surrender document is signed September 2, on the battleship *Missouri*).

CONFRONTATION

1945

August 17	United States and the USSR agree on the 38th parallel as the boundary between occupation zones in Korea.
September 2	Democratic Republic of Vietnam, proclaimed by Ho Chi Minh, declares its independence from France.
September 11	Having been assigned the task of creating peace treaties with the German satellite states, the Allied Council of Foreign Ministers proves unequal to the task; the meetings end on October 2.
October 21	In the first postwar general election, the French choose a Constituent Assembly.
November 15	Meeting in Washington, Truman, Attlee, and Canadian prime minister Mackenzie King declare their intention to cooperate on nuclear policy.
November 16	In a speech to the Belgian Parliament, former British prime minister Churchill declares that British affairs "are becoming ever more closely interwoven with those of the United States."
November 17	Nationalist Sukarno declares the Netherland East Indies (Indonesia) independent.

November 27   General George C. Marshall begins a mission to China to mediate between Chiang Kai-shek's Guomindang (Kuomintang) government and the Communists.

November 29   Marshal Tito proclaims the People's Republic of Yugoslavia.

December 16   Under Soviet protection, rebels in Iranian Azerbaijan proclaim independence; three days later, Kurds in western Azerbaijan, also supported by the Soviets, proclaim the Kurdish People's Republic.

In Moscow, U.S., British, and Soviet foreign ministers (rather than the five-member Council of Foreign Ministers) begin another attempt to discuss World War II peace treaties; the sessions, which make limited progress, continue for ten days.

1946

January 10   "Committee of Three"—made up of President Truman's representative, General Marshall; a representative of the Nationalist Chinese government; and a representative of the Chinese Communists—reaches agreement on an order for the cessation of hostilities in China.

UN General Assembly holds its first meeting, in London. During this session Trygve Lie of Norway becomes the first secretary-general of the organization.

January 19   Government of Iran complains to the UN Security Council that the Soviet Union is interfering in Iran's internal affairs.

January 31   Representatives of various Chinese groups agree on a new governmental structure for the country.

February 3   Washington columnist Drew Pearson publishes the first account of the Soviet nuclear espionage ring in Canada revealed to the authorities by Igor Gouzenko.

February 9   In a speech just before the Soviet election, Stalin declares that Communism and capitalism are "incompatible"; this is, of course, long-established Marxist-Leninist doctrine.

February 12   Departing from an earlier U.S. position, Secretary of State James F. Byrnes withholds recognition from the Bulgarian Communist regime, declaring that opposition parties must have a fair chance to play a political part; the secretary also complains to the Albanian Communist government about its treatment of U.S. officials.

February 22	George F. Kennan, U.S. chargé d'affaires in Moscow, sends the State Department a five-part analysis of Soviet views and actions that will become famous as the Long Telegram.
	U.S. State Department expresses concern about the situation in Soviet-occupied northern Iran.
February 25	Chinese Nationalists and Communists agree on a program to integrate Communist forces into the national army.
March 2–4	United States accuses the Soviets of hampering the economic rehabilitation of Hungary and Austria.
March 5	At Westminster College, in Fulton, Mo., former British prime minister Winston Churchill delivers what is probably the most famous postwar speech, in which he describes the "iron curtain" that has "descended across the Continent" and emphasizes the "special relationship" between the United States and Britain.
March 25	Following Western diplomatic pressure, the Soviet government announces the withdrawal of its forces from northern Iran; the situation there has become something of a symbolic issue between the West and the USSR, and problems will remain.
April 18	With General Marshall temporarily away in the United States, Chinese Nationalists and Communists clash in Manchuria; the Nationalists capture Changchun, an important city.
April 22	Communist and Socialist parties merge in the Soviet zone of Germany, creating the Socialist Unity Party (which will, in effect, be the Communist Party).
April 25	Conference convenes to draw up peace treaties between Allies and countries cobelligerent with Germany. After making little progress, it will take a recess.
June 9	Fearing the popularity of the USSR's leading World War II general, Marshal Georgi Zhukov, Stalin condemns his "unworthy" attitude and soon sends him off to a provincial command.
June 15	Second conference of foreign ministers opens, with several agreements being reached concerning peace treaties with German World War II satellites.
	United States presents Baruch Plan for atomic energy to the United Nations.
July 12	U.S. House of Representatives concludes congressional action on a much-needed $3.75 billion loan to Britain.

July 29	Building on the progress made in the second foreign ministers' conference, the Allies and the USSR open a World War II peace conference in Paris. After much debate, it will produce treaties for the German satellite countries.
August 14	Central Committee of the Communist Party of the Soviet Union attacks two Soviet literary journals for publishing "hooligan" and "decadent" works; thus begins the repression, administered by Andrei Zhdanov, that will be known as the *Zhdanovshchina*.
August 30	Nationalist-Communist agreements in China have collapsed; Nationalist forces capture Chengde; Nationalists reject peace moves.
September	Civil war begins in Greece between government forces and Communist-led guerrillas.
September 6	In an important speech in Stuttgart, U.S. secretary of state James F. Byrnes declares that U.S. troops will stay in Europe as long as other powers maintain occupying forces.
September 17	Speaking in Zurich, Winston Churchill urges the creation of a "United States of Europe."
October	Peace treaties signed with the allies of Germany.
November 13	General Marshall tells Chiang's Chinese Nationalist government that the United States cannot support civil war in China.
November 25	Following several spy scandals involving U.S. Communists, President Truman responds to congressional pressure by establishing the President's Temporary Commission on Employee Loyalty.
December 3	Government of Greece complains to the UN Security Council that the country's Communist neighbors are furnishing aid to Greek Communist rebels.
December 4	French Fourth Republic officially begins.
December 19	Communist Vietminh forces attack the French in Tonkin, beginning the First Indochina War.

1947

January 1	U.S. and British occupation zones in Germany are combined to create "Bizonia."

January 8	General Marshall leaves China, his impossible mission having failed.
February 10	In the Salon d'Horloges of the French Foreign Office, representatives of German World War II satellites—Italy, Romania, Bulgaria, Hungary, and Finland—sign peace treaties with the Allies.
	Testifying in the U.S. Senate Atomic Energy Committee hearing to confirm David Lilienthal as chairman of the Atomic Energy Commission, Undersecretary of State Dean Acheson concedes, under pressure from Tennessee Democratic senator Kenneth McKellar, that he is "quite aware of the fact that Russian foreign policy is an aggressive and expanding one." Having declared his opposition to "this sort of general talk," Acheson sees his concerns justified on February 14, when the Soviets formally protest his comment.
February 21	British embassy in Washington informs the State Department that in six weeks Britain, hard-pressed financially, will cease providing aid to Greece and Turkey, countries considered possible victims of Soviet expansionism. The British express the hope that the Americans will replace them in the eastern Mediterranean area. The news is unwelcome but not wholly unexpected.
February 25	Secretary of State Marshall and Undersecretary Acheson recommend to President Truman that the United States take "immediate action to extend all possible aid to Greece and, on a lesser scale, to Turkey."
March 4	Assuring the French of their continuing support, the British sign the symbolically named Treaty of Dunkirk, which pledges the two countries to aid each other in case of war with Germany.
March 10	Conference of Allied foreign ministers opens in Moscow, officially to draw up peace treaties for Germany and Austria; it ends in disarray on April 24, with no agreement on the treaties or on other questions between East and West.
March 12	President Truman asks Congress for $400 million in aid to Greece and Turkey—the beginning of the Truman Doctrine; Congress complies on May 1.
March 21	Truman issues Executive Order 9835 calling for investigation of the loyalty of all federal employees.
May 5	Communist ministers are dismissed from the French government by Premier Paul Ramadier and from the Italian government by Premier Alcide de Gasperi.
May 8	Addressing the Delta Cotton Council, a Mississippi organization, U.S. undersecretary of state Acheson discusses the economic plight of Eu-

rope; President Truman will later call the speech, which reflects current thinking in the State Department, "the prologue to the Marshall Plan."

May 30	Hungarian Communists, abetted by the Soviets, force Premier Ferenc Nagy from office.
June 5	At Harvard, General Marshall delivers a speech calling for a program of U.S. aid to Europe; the result will be the Marshall Plan.
July	Quarterly journal *Foreign Affairs* appears with U.S. diplomat and Sovietologist George Kennan's famous article, "by X," titled "The Sources of Soviet Conduct"; it will be influential in forming the Truman administration's containment policy.
	Algerian-born French writer Albert Camus publishes *La Peste (The Plague),* a novel that is also an important existentialist document.
July 2	USSR rejects aid under the Marshall Plan, and in turn, the countries of Eastern Europe do likewise.
July 20	Netherland forces attack nationalist rebels in the East Indies (Indonesia), beginning a two-year war.
July 26	Truman signs the congressional act intended to bring unification of the armed forces and appoints Secretary of the Navy James Forrestal as the first secretary of defense.
August 12	In a letter to Yugoslavia's Marshal Tito, Stalin criticizes a new agreement between Yugoslavia and Bulgaria.
September 2	Western Hemisphere nations sign the Treaty of Rio, intended to ensure inter-American solidarity against aggression.
September 22–27	Communist delegates meeting at Szlarska Poreba in Poland establish the Cominform (Communist Information Bureau). In his keynote speech, "On the International Situation," Andrei Zhdanov, Stalin's spokesman and heir presumptive, declaring that the world is divided into two hostile camps, describes the Cominform as a response to the Marshall Plan.
November 15	Influential supporters of U.S. administration foreign-policy aims announce the formation of the Committee for the Marshall Plan to Aid European Recovery, with former secretary of war Henry L. Stimson as chairman. Two weeks later the committee names Mrs. Wendell L. Willkie (widow of the 1940 Republican presidential nominee) head of the women's division.
November 21	Communist governments of Poland and Hungary dissolve opposition parties.

December	Civil war in China resumes.
December 24	Leftist guerrillas in Greece proclaim a provisional government.
December 31	Romanian monarchy is overthrown by Communists; King Michael abdicates.

1948

February 16	People's Republic of Korea (North Korea) is proclaimed by Kim Il Sung.
February 25	Bowing to Communist pressure, Czechoslovak president Eduard Beneš appoints a Communist-dominated cabinet controlled by Premier Klement Gottwald; the Communists have in the preceding days taken control of the militia, the police, and other vital agencies. Having failed to resist the coup, Beneš retires from active political life, resigning on June 7.
March 10	Authorities in Prague announce the death, allegedly by suicide, of the non-Communist foreign minister, Jan Masaryk.
March 17	Alarmed at the possible implications of the Communist coup in Czechoslovakia, Britain, France, and the Benelux countries sign the Treaty of Brussels, establishing the West European Union.
March 20	After accusing the Western Allies of undermining the four-power control of Germany, Soviet representatives walk out of the Allied Control Council.
March 27	Stalin attacks Yugoslav Marshal Tito's conduct and policies in a letter that leads to a Soviet-Yugoslav split and, on June 28, the expulsion of the Yugoslav Communist Party from the Cominform.
April 1	Soviets impose restrictions on road and rail traffic between Allied zones in Germany and Berlin.
April 2	U.S. congressional action establishes the Economic Cooperation Administration to operate the European Recovery Program—the Marshall Plan—adopted on March 31.
April 30	At a conference in Bogotá, the United States and the Latin American nations establish the Organization of American States.
June 13	U.S. Senate adopts the Vandenberg Resolution (a collaborative effort between Senator Arthur Vandenberg, Republican from Michigan, and

the State Department), which endorses U.S. participation in regional security arrangements and thus represents a step toward the creation of the North Atlantic Treaty Organization.

June 18   Following failure to achieve four-power agreement, Western powers introduce currency reform in the Western zones of Germany (including West Berlin).

June 24   Soviet restrictions on traffic between Allied zones in Germany and Berlin now become a complete land-and-water blockade.

June 28   Western Allies begin airlifting vital supplies into West Berlin.

August 2   Whittaker Chambers tells the U.S. House of Representatives Un-American Activities Committee that ten years earlier Alger Hiss, a former State Department and United Nations official, gave him secret State Department documents to pass on to the Soviet Union.

August 15   Republic of Korea (South Korea) is proclaimed.

August 26   Apparently for doctrinal reasons that appeal to Stalin, the Soviet Academy of Sciences adopts the pseudoscientific views of the geneticist Trofim Lysenko, who holds (in defiance of Mendelian genetics) that acquired characteristics can be inherited.

August 31   Soviet politician Andrei Zhdanov, thought to be Stalin's probable successor, dies unexpectedly of heart disease. His case is used by Stalin to implicate Kremlin doctors in the 1953 Doctors' Plot.

November 2   In perhaps the greatest political upset in U.S. history, President Truman confounds the pollsters by defeating the Republican presidential nominee, New York's Governor Thomas E. Dewey; the winner receives 24.1 million votes to Dewey's 22 million, with other candidates gathering 3 million; Truman wins 303 electoral votes.

November 20   Communist Party of the Soviet Union Politburo orders the disbanding of the Jewish Anti-Fascist Committee; a number of its members are arrested. This development opens an increasing campaign against Jews, which extends to attacks on the cultures of other minority national groups.

December 1   USSR proclaims its "full support" for the new government established in the Soviet sector of Berlin.

December 3   U.S. House Un-American Activities Committee, with Republican representative Richard M. Nixon of California as the key figure, reports significant findings in the Hiss case from the "Pumpkin Papers" produced by Whittaker Chambers.

December 5	Municipal elections are held in the three Western zones of Berlin.
December 10	UN General Assembly adopts the Universal Declaration of Human Rights; Eleanor Roosevelt has been a leader in the drive to create this document.
December 12	UN General Assembly recognizes the South Korean government as the government of all Korea.
December 15	Federal grand jury indicts Alger Hiss on two counts of perjury for lying about his past connection with a Soviet espionage ring.

1949

January 7	Resigning as U.S. secretary of state, General George C. Marshall enters his second retirement from government service. He is succeeded by former undersecretary Dean Acheson, who at his confirmation hearing will tell the senators that he is "no appeaser."
January 14	Mao Zedong demands the unconditional surrender of Chiang Kai-shek's Nationalist Chinese armies.
January 19	Under heavy pressure from Communist Chinese armies, the Nationalist government announces the moving of the capital from Nanking to Canton and calls for a cease-fire; two days later President Chiang Kai-shek will announce his resignation, his declared aim being to ease the path to peace negotiations.
January 20	President Truman begins his second term with an inaugural address in which he calls for a "bold new program" to help underdeveloped countries; this initiative will be known as Point Four.
January 22	Chinese Communist forces take Peiping (Beijing).
January 25	Soviet government announces the creation of Comecon (the Council for Mutual Economic Assistance), one of its efforts—all were of limited effectiveness—to counter the Marshall Plan in Eastern Europe.
January 28	UN Security Council orders the Netherlands to end the war against the Indonesian rebels and grant independence to the country; on February 26 the Dutch government announces its compliance.
February 8	In Hungary, a court sentences Cardinal Mindszenty to life imprisonment; he is accused of plotting against the government and conducting illicit currency transactions.

February 11	As efforts to unite the U.S. armed services continue to encounter problems, President Truman appoints General Dwight D. Eisenhower his chief military adviser and temporary chairman of the Joint Chiefs of Staff (the chairmanship does not yet exist as a statutory office).
March 3	Plagued by mental illness, James Forrestal, the first U.S. secretary of defense, resigns; on May 22 he will commit suicide.
March 4	Having lost Premier Stalin's favor, V. M. Molotov is replaced as foreign minister by the redoubtable chief prosecutor in the 1930s Great Purge, Andrei Vyshinsky.
March 25	Moving his headquarters to Beijing, Mao Zedong declares the city to be the capital of China.
April 4	In Washington, 12 Western nations sign the North Atlantic Treaty.
April 22	Under heavy attack, the Chinese Nationalists abandon Nanking.
May 3	General Lucius D. Clay ends his service as U.S. military governor in Germany; when he returns home, he receives glowing tributes from President Truman and Congress.
May 5	Ten Western European countries sign an agreement creating the Council of Europe, an outgrowth of the Western European Union.
May 8	German Parliamentary Council approves the Basic Law (constitution) for a West German federal republic made up of the 11 states *(Länder)* of the U.S., British, and French occupation zones.
May 9	In Berlin, the Soviet commander, General Vassily Chuikov, announces the lifting of the land blockade, which effectively ends on May 12.
May 18	Marking the transition from military control, President Truman appoints John J. McCloy, president of the World Bank, as U.S. high commissioner for Germany.
May 23	Konrad Adenauer, president of the Parliamentary Council, proclaims the Federal Republic of Germany.
May 25	Chinese Communist forces occupy Shanghai.
June 5	Former emperor Bao Dai, restored to power by the French, returns from exile and once more becomes chief of state of Vietnam.
June 12	In a plebiscite, the people of Trieste vote to rejoin Italy.
June 16	Peering into the clouded future, President Truman foresees an imminent end to the "hysteria" over loyalty issues.

June 29	United States moves to withdraw its troops from Korea.
June 30	Netherlands forces begin a withdrawal from Indonesia.
August 11	Truman appoints General Omar Bradley chairman of the Joint Chiefs of Staff, a position now established by law.
August 16	Speaking perhaps a bit prematurely, UN Secretary-General Trygve Lie expresses the view that the world is moving from "cold war" to "cold peace."
August 24	North Atlantic Treaty goes into effect following its ratification by France.
September 7	West German Parliament begins its first session, thereby bringing into active existence the Federal Republic of Germany; on September 12 Theodor Heuss becomes president, and on September 14 Konrad Adenauer is elected chancellor.
September 17	North Atlantic Treaty foreign ministers agree to improve defenses by establishing military committees.
September 21	Allied High Commission replaces military governments in West Germany.
September 23	U.S. and British governments announce their discovery that the Soviets have exploded a nuclear device.
September 30	After more than 275,000 flights, the Allied airlift to West Berlin is officially ended. The blockade had been lifted on May 12.
October 1	People's Republic of China is established in a proclamation by Mao Zedong.
October 7	Communist leader Wilhelm Pieck proclaims the German Democratic Republic (East Germany); three days later the Soviets transfer all administrative responsibilities to the new government.
October 14	Eleven U.S. Communist Party leaders are convicted of advocating the overthrow of the U.S. government by force and violence.
October 15	Canton falls to Chinese Communist forces without a battle.
October 27	Defeated in the interservice rivalries that characterize attempts to unify the U.S. armed services, Admiral Louis Denfeld, chief of naval operations, tenders his resignation as requested by President Truman.
November 7	Marshal Konstantin Rokossovsky, a Soviet officer, is appointed defense minister of Poland and commander in chief of the Polish army.

November 29	Members of the Cominform call for the overthrow of Marshal Tito's Yugoslav government and of the international "Tito clique."
December	Operation to land Albanian émigrés in their home country to attack the Communist government fails when Kim Philby, a member of the Cambridge Five spy ring, betrays it to the Soviets; two-thirds of the Albanians are killed, the rest later shot or imprisoned; Philby will perform further such services for the KGB.
December 16	Chinese Communist Party chairman Mao Zedong arrives in Moscow for his first visit to Soviet premier Stalin.
December 28	United States grants diplomatic recognition to the new Republic of Indonesia.

1950

January 10	Protesting the continued seating of Nationalist China, Yakov Malik, the Soviet UN ambassador, begins boycott of the Security Council.
January 14	Ho Chi Minh declares the Democratic Republic of Vietnam to be the legal government of the country; the USSR and Communist China grant recognition.
January 21	In the United States, Alger Hiss is convicted of perjury in denying espionage activities; he receives a five-year prison sentence.
January 31	President Truman announces the U.S. decision to proceed with the development of nuclear fusion (the hydrogen bomb).
February 9	In a speech at Wheeling, W.Va., Senator Joseph R. McCarthy (Rep.-Wis.) attacks the State Department for harboring Communists; he professes to have a list of 205 such employees.
March 1	Reestablished on Formosa (now Taiwan), Chiang Kai-shek resumes the presidency of what he and the United States continue to call the Republic of China.
April 25	Truman approves NSC-68, a large-scale blueprint for U.S. defense.
May 9	Robert Schuman, French foreign minister, proposes the creation of a unified European coal-and-steel community.
June 23	University of California at Los Angeles administration dismisses 157 staff members who have refused to say whether or not they are or have

been members of the Communist Party (a court will later order them reinstated).

June 25   In the early morning hours (local time), North Korean troops cross the 38th parallel into South Korea, beginning the Korean War (2:00 P.M. June 24 in Washington, D.C.).

Meeting in an emergency session, the UN Security Council calls on North Korea to withdraw its forces from South Korea.

June 27   Truman announces the sending of U.S. naval and air units to aid in the defense of South Korea. He also declares that the U.S. Seventh Fleet will prevent the outbreak of any hostilities between the two Chinas by neutralizing the Formosa Strait.

United States sponsors a Security Council resolution calling on UN members to help defend South Korea. Adoption of the resolution gives authority, for the first time, to create a UN armed force.

June 30   On the urging of General Douglas MacArthur, the U.S. commander in the Far East, based in Tokyo, Truman approves the sending of U.S. ground forces to Korea. In the ensuing days, however, ill-prepared U.S. and Korean forces are driven south by Kim Il Sung's army.

August 3   U.S. Military Assistance and Advisory Group arrives in Saigon.

August 4   Eighth Army and Republic of Korea forces establish themselves in a defensive area, the Pusan Perimeter in southeastern Korea.

August 11   In a speech to the European Assembly at Strasbourg, former British prime minister Winston Churchill, still a private citizen, calls for a European army, with German participation.

August 15   President Sukarno proclaims the Republic of Indonesia.

September 8   In San Francisco, 49 countries sign the Japanese peace treaty; John Foster Dulles has directed the negotiations for the Allied side.

September 15   Successful UN amphibious landing at Inchon, near Seoul, changes the current of the Korean War; UN forces now move north in two prongs as North Koreans fall back in a rout.

October 26   Wearing Korean uniforms, limited numbers of Chinese troops intervene in fighting in far northern Korea.

November 1   In Washington, Puerto Rican nationalists try to storm Blair House, Truman's temporary residence, in an attempt to assassinate him.

November 3	UN General Assembly adopts the "Uniting for Peace" resolution, sponsored by the United States, to enable the assembly to deal with future questions of aggression.
November 20	UN forces in North Korea reach the Yalu River, the border with China.
November 26	Contrary to General MacArthur's predictions, Chinese units cross into North Korea "in great and ever increasing strength" and attack UN troops.
December 1	In various interviews, General MacArthur publicly accuses the administration of imposing "an enormous handicap" on him by denying him "unlimited attack" on China.
December 15	President Truman declares a national emergency. Eighth Army withdraws below the 38th parallel.
December 26	Lieutenant General Matthew B. Ridgway arrives in Korea to take command of the U.S. Eighth Army, succeeding the late Lieutenant General Walton Walker; MacArthur remains as supreme commander.
December 30	United States, France, Vietnam, Cambodia, and Laos sign a mutual-defense pact.

In North Korean mountains in the autumn of 1950, U.S. Marine tanks find the going difficult on icy roads.

December 31	Chinese Communist forces cross the 38th parallel, invading South Korea.

1951

January 4	Following a breakthrough on the U.S. Eighth Army's front, Chinese Communist troops recapture Seoul.
January 17	Chinese premier Zhou Enlai (Chou En-lai) rejects UN proposal of a cease-fire in Korea.
January 23	President Truman announces the creation of the Commission on Internal Security and Individual Rights; he expresses the hope that the commission will succeed in combating both subversion and conformity. Retired admiral Chester W. Nimitz is appointed chairman.
January 28	General Ridgway's UN forces advance back toward Seoul.
February 1	UN General Assembly adopts a resolution, sponsored by the United States, naming China as an aggressor in Korea.
February 10	UN forces recapture Seoul and Inchon.
March 9	British foreign secretary Ernest Bevin resigns because of ill health (heart disease); he dies on April 14.
March 29	U.S. federal court jury finds Julius and Ethel Rosenberg and Morton Sobell guilty of treason for delivering nuclear secrets to the Soviets. On April 5 the Rosenbergs will receive death sentences.
April 2	The North Atlantic Treaty Organization takes tangible form when Supreme Headquarters, Allied Powers in Europe (SHAPE) is activated as General Eisenhower assumes command.
April 3	In Korea, U.S. troops surge across the 38th parallel.
April 5	House of Representatives leader Joseph W. Martin, Jr. (Rep.-Mass.), makes public a letter in which General MacArthur maintains that "there is no substitute for victory" and—contrary to U.S. policy—advocates an invasion of the Chinese mainland by Nationalists from Taiwan.
April 11	American Legion confers novel respectability on Spain's Generalissimo Francisco Franco by awarding him its Medal of Merit for his "valiant fight against Communism."

On April 18, 1951, French foreign minister Robert Schuman *(center)* and fellow delegates sign the treaty establishing the European Coal and Steel Community.

April 11	President Truman dismisses General MacArthur from all of his positions; General Ridgway succeeds him, thus becoming the top U.S. and UN commander in the Far East. Lieutenant General James A. Van Fleet succeeds Ridgway as Eighth Army commander.
April 18	Delegates in Paris sign the treaty establishing the European Coal and Steel Community.
April 19	After drawing enthusiastic crowds wherever he appears, General MacArthur makes a memorable address to a joint session of Congress, in which he declares, quoting an old ballad, "old soldiers never die . . . they just fade away." Moving on to New York the next day, he receives a triumphal welcome, as he will later in Chicago and Boston.
April 22	Aneurin Bevan, a leading and vocal opponent of increased defense spending, resigns from the British Cabinet.
April 23	Czechoslovak authorities arrest William N. Oatis, Associated Press correspondent in Prague, charging him with espionage; on July 4 he re-

ceives a ten-year prison sentence. The affair creates outrage in the United States, with both houses of Congress voting to cut all ties with Czechoslovakia until Oatis is released.

May 2   Following action by the Iranian Parliament, the shah issues a decree nationalizing the properties of the Anglo-Iranian Oil Company.

May 3   U.S. Senate committees open hearings to investigate the relief of General MacArthur; these activities will continue until June 25 and end in the dissipation of public interest in the subject.

May 23   Chinese Communist government takes control of Tibet.

May 25   British Foreign Office officials Guy Burgess and Donald Maclean, two of the Cambridge Five spy ring, take a Channel boat from England to France and disappear. Some Western observers "fear" (correctly) the two have gone to Russia.

June 13   After the conclusion of U.S. nuclear tests in the Pacific, the task-force commander, General Elwood Quesada, declares that the results show the public's fear of radiation to be exaggerated.

          UN forces in Korea capture Pyongyang, 100 miles above the 38th parallel.

June 23   Yakov Malik, Soviet delegate to the UN, proposes the negotiation of a cease-fire in Korea and the withdrawal of the opposing forces on both sides of the 38th parallel.

June 30   In a radio broadcast, General Ridgway proposes the negotiation of a Korean armistice.

July 1   Chinese and North Korean commanders agree to proposals to meet with UN representatives to discuss a cease-fire.

July 10   UN and Communist negotiators in Korea have their first meeting at Kaesong.

July 16   Large-scale riots, considered to have been inspired by the Communists, bring the imposition of martial law in Tehran.

July 21   Korean truce negotiations go into recess when UN representatives reject the Communist demand to include troop withdrawals on the agenda; the meetings resume within the week, when the two sides agree on an agenda omitting the Communist demand.

September 12   Retiring from U.S. government service for the third time, General Marshall resigns as secretary of defense; he is succeeded by his deputy, Robert A. Lovett.

September 27	Iranian troops take control of the Anglo-Iranian oil refinery at Abadan.
October 8	After much discussion, Korean truce negotiators agree on Panmunjom as the site for the meetings.
October 12	U.S. government establishes the Mutual Security Agency (for military aid to foreign countries), with the diplomat and businessman Averell Harriman nominated as administrator.
October 25	In Britain, Winston Churchill leads the Conservatives to victory in a close general election and returns as prime minister.
November 3	Soviet government expresses strong objections to the admission of Turkey to the North Atlantic Treaty Organization.

1952

January 5	British prime minister Churchill begins a lengthy American tour with meetings in Washington; he expresses particular displeasure with the existing agreement that the NATO Atlantic fleet command is to go to a U.S. officer. The following week, in Ottawa, he appoints General Sir Gerald Templer to command the British effort against guerrillas in Malaya.
January 7	Responding to the news that his backers are entering his name in the New Hampshire primary, General Eisenhower issues a statement from his NATO headquarters saying that he would run for president if drafted by the Republican Party. In his diary he later comments that he will not seek the nomination but adds, "I'm willing to go part way in trying to recognize a 'duty,' but I do not have to seek one, and I will not."
February 7	President Truman nominates George F. Kennan as U.S. ambassador to the Soviet Union.
February 15	Britain's King George VI dies after a long battle with cancer; Elizabeth, the new queen, hears the news while on safari in Africa.
February 23	NATO powers announce a plan to create an army of 50 divisions within the year.
March 12	British general Lord Ismay, a close World War II associate of Churchill's, is appointed the first secretary-general of the North Atlantic Treaty Organization.

March 29	Truman announces that he will not be a candidate for reelection to the presidency of the United States.
April 15	Truman signs the treaty with Japan that officially brings World War II to an end.
April 28	Accepting General Eisenhower's request to be relieved of his NATO command so that he can return to the United States as a political candidate, President Truman appoints General Ridgway to succeed Ike.
May 9	Communist Korean War prisoners on Koje Island stage an insurrection, holding the U.S. commandant prisoner for more than three days. A month later (June 10), U.S. troops will fight a pitched battle with Koje prisoners, who are said to be killing fellow prisoners who will not rebel against their American guards.
May 12	General Ridgway succeeds General Eisenhower, now a presidential candidate, as NATO supreme commander.
May 27	United States, Britain, and West European countries adopt the Pleven Plan (first advanced October 24, 1950) for the European Defense Community, but the agreement is not subsequently ratified by France.
July 3	Soviet Union vetoes a U.S. resolution in the UN Security Council for an impartial inquiry into North Korean and Chinese charges that UN troops have made use of germ warfare.
July 21	Egyptian officers overthrow King Farouk; General Naguib is the head of the junta, but the strong man is Colonel Gamal Abdel Nasser.
July 26	Winning the Republican presidential nomination on the first ballot, Eisenhower promises to lead "a great crusade" against the Democrats.
September 23	In what will be forever known as "the Checkers speech" (after the name of his children's dog), California senator Richard M. Nixon defends himself against charges of improperly using money from a secret fund established by supporters and holds on to the vice presidential spot on the Republican ticket.
October 3	In Australian waters, the British detonate their first atomic bomb.
	In the wake of indiscreet remarks by George Kennan (in which he likens the isolation of Western diplomats in Moscow to his situation as an internee in Berlin early in World War II), the Soviet government demands his recall as U.S. ambassador.
October 22	With the British-Iranian oil conflict still unsettled, Iran breaks diplomatic relations with Britain.

October 24	In a U.S. presidential campaign speech, discussing the delay in ending the Korean War, Ike makes a striking pledge; if elected, he says, "I shall go to Korea."
November 4	Eisenhower defeats the Democratic candidate, Adlai E. Stevenson, for the U.S. presidency by a popular vote of 33.9 million to 27.3 million and an electoral count of 442 to 89.
November 10	Opposed by the USSR for his role in the Korean War, Trygve Lie resigns as UN secretary-general.
November 29	Fulfilling his campaign promise, President-elect Eisenhower departs for Korea.
December 3	Caught up in the purge sweeping through the Eastern Bloc—allegedly for dealings with Yugoslavia's Marshal Tito—Rudolf Slansky, former general secretary of the Czechoslovak Communist Party, and 11 other officials are hanged.

1953

January 5	Hoping to build on their World War II friendship, British prime minister Churchill arrives in the United States for meetings with President-elect Eisenhower.
January 13	Soviet media announce the discovery of the alleged conspiracy against Soviet leaders that will become known as the Doctors' Plot; the death of Stalin will save the lives of most of the accused doctors ("assassins in white coats").
January 20	Dwight D. Eisenhower takes office as 34th president of the United States. Much of the comment at his inaugural ceremony concerns his departure from a century-old tradition by wearing a homburg instead of a top hat.
February 2	President Eisenhower announces that the U.S. Seventh Fleet will no longer neutralize the Formosa Strait.
March 5	Joseph Stalin dies from a cerebral hemorrhage. He is succeeded in the Kremlin by a collective leadership headed by Georgi Malenkov, with Nikita Khrushchev as, first, acting and then, in September, permanent first secretary of the Communist Party of the Soviet Union.
March 14	Stalin's final illness apparently claims a second victim, as Czechoslovak Communist leader Klement Gottwald dies of a respiratory infection he is said to have caught while attending Stalin's funeral.

THE KHRUSHCHEV ERA

1953

March 28	The new Soviet leadership gives an indication of its intention to move in a liberalizing direction by offering amnesty or shortened sentences to most persons held in prisons.
April 7	UN General Assembly chooses Dag Hammarskjöld, Swedish diplomat and civil servant, to succeed Trygve Lie as secretary-general.
April 14	In Southeast Asia, Ho Chi Minh's Vietminh forces invade Laos.
May 2	U.S. Senate subcommittee expresses grave concern about a shortage of ammunition for troops in Korea.
May 8	French government appoints General Henri Navarre commander of forces in Indochina.
June 14	New thinking in the Kremlin leads to an agreement between the new leaders and Yugoslavia's Marshal Tito to exchange ambassadors.
June 16	In East Berlin, workers riot against stepped-up output requirements; the trouble quickly spreads across East Germany.
June 19	Convicted U.S. atomic spies Julius and Ethel Rosenberg are executed at Sing Sing prison.
July 2	Soviet pressure forces the resignation of the Hungarian premier, Mátyás Rákosi, who remains the hard-line Communist Party boss.
July 7	Central Committee of the Communist Party of the Soviet Union charges Lavrenty Beria, minister of internal affairs (and thus head of the secret police), with seeking power and committing other criminal acts.
July 11	U.S. General Alfred M. Gruenther succeeds General Ridgway as NATO supreme commander.
July 27	UN and North Korean negotiators sign agreement for a continuing cease-fire to end the Korean War. It includes a long-argued proviso that prisoners will be repatriated on a voluntary basis (many North Koreans do not wish to return).
August 8	Soviet premier Georgi Malenkov declares that the USSR has broken the U.S. monopoly of the hydrogen bomb; on August 20 the Soviet government announces the completion of an H-bomb test.

August 16	In Iran, Premier Mossadegh reacts to his dismissal by the shah by arresting the shah's leading supporters; the shah is forced to flee. Three days later, however, army units loyal to the shah overpower Mossadegh's supporters.
September 26	United States and Spain sign an agreement under which the Spanish will grant rights for bases in exchange for U.S. military and economic assistance.
October 12	In criticizing the level of security at Fort Monmouth, N.J., Senator Joseph R. McCarthy begins a series of events that will culminate in the 1954 Army-McCarthy hearings.
November 21	On his return from a trip through South America, Milton Eisenhower, the president's brother, recommends greater U.S. aid to Latin American countries.
December 3	U.S., British, and French leaders gather in Bermuda for a Western summit, at which Winston Churchill vainly urges approaches to Soviet premier Malenkov; originally scheduled for June, the meeting was postponed until December owing to Churchill's illness.
December 23	USSR Supreme Court condemns Lavrenty Beria, head of the Soviet secret police then called the NKVD, and associates to death; in one way or another (various accounts exist), he is executed. The government announces the conviction on December 24; actually, Beria is believed to have been executed some months earlier.

1954

January 12	U.S. secretary of state John Foster Dulles propounds the defense doctrine that will become known as massive retaliation.
January 21	*Nautilus,* the world's first nuclear-powered submarine, is launched at Groton, Conn.
February 3	President Eisenhower declares his opposition to the "Bricker amendment," a move by conservative senators to limit the treaty-making power of the president (Ike later notes that Ohio's Republican senator Bricker is "almost psychopathic on the subject"). On February 25 the U.S. Senate, for now, will vote down this proposed constitutional amendment.
March 1	Puerto Rican nationalists in the gallery of the U.S. House of Representatives stage a shooting spree in which five congressmen are wounded.

March 13	In Vietnam, Vietminh forces attack the French at the fortress of Dien Bien Phu.
April 7	In a press conference, Eisenhower presents the "domino theory," a view of the possible progress of world Communist power.
April 9	Western high commissioners in Germany reject a March 26 Soviet declaration that the German Democratic Republic (East Germany) is a sovereign state.
April 13	Australian government reveals the defection of the KGB resident in Australia, Vladimir Petrov, and his wife, Evdokia. The Petrovs provide some information about the British defectors Burgess and Maclean, members of the Cambridge Five spy ring.
April 18	Colonel Nasser, the power behind the throne in the Egyptian junta, becomes premier.
April 22	With a full-scale battle raging between the U.S. Army and Senator McCarthy over the army's alleged tolerance of subversive activities, the Army-McCarthy hearings begin in Washington. They will continue until June 17.
April 26	Geneva Conference on peace in Asia opens.
May 7	Dien Bien Phu falls to the Vietminh after an almost two-month siege.
May 12	Soviets deny that any U.S. soldiers taken prisoner in Korea were sent to the USSR; this issue will be clarified 40 years later.
June 1	Though declaring physicist J. Robert Oppenheimer loyal to the United States, a security board recommends that he not be reinstated as a consultant to the Atomic Energy Commission. The commission later permanently revokes his security clearance.
June 18	Pierre Mendès-France, who has promised to make every effort to end the war in Vietnam, becomes French premier.
	Small band of Guatemalan dissidents, organized and backed by the U.S. Central Intelligence Agency, invades the country from Honduras; President Jacobo Arbenz flees.
July 21	First Indochina War in Vietnam ends with the signing of an agreement in Geneva (to accord with a Mendès-France deadline, the agreement is dated July 20).
August 4	After having disappeared in July, Otto John, head of the West German security service, is granted political asylum in East Germany. (In De-

cember 1955, however, he will reappear in West Germany and receive a four-year prison sentence.)

August 24	U.S. government outlaws the Communist Party as an organization, but the fact of membership in itself will not be considered criminal.
August 30	French National Assembly rejects the European Defense Community treaty.
September 3	Chinese Communists begin intermittent shelling of the offshore islands Quemoy and Matsu held by Chiang's Nationalist forces, leading to a continuing and sometimes heated dispute with the United States, which officially backs Chiang.
September 8	Southeast Asia Treaty (SEATO) is signed in Manila.
September 19	Iranian government and an international oil consortium reach an agreement that will permit the reopening of the troubled Abadan refinery; the consortium will thus operate the Iranian oil fields.
October 3	In London, the Western Allies sign an agreement for the rearmament of West Germany and its integration into the North Atlantic Treaty Organization.
October 5	After years of conflict following World War II, Italy and Yugoslavia—the two directly concerned powers—and the United States and Britain—the two occupying powers—reach what seems an eminently sensible agreement on Trieste, whereby the city, with its Italian majority, goes to Italy and the surrounding area, with its Yugoslav majority, goes to Yugoslavia.
December 2	U.S. Senate votes to condemn Senator Joseph McCarthy for offenses against the Senate.

1955

February 7	U.S. Seventh Fleet assists Chiang Kai-shek's Chinese Nationalist government in evacuation of Tachen Islands, off Taiwan.
February 8	Georgi Malenkov resigns as premier of the USSR. He is replaced by Nikolai Bulganin, but the real power is held by Communist Party first secretary Nikita Khrushchev. Next day, Marshal Georgi Zhukov becomes minister of defense.

February 24	Turkey and Iraq sign the Baghdad Pact. This mutual-security treaty will include a larger group, still identified as the Baghdad Pact, and will give rise to the Central Treaty Organization (CENTO) in August 1959.
April 5	Sir Winston Churchill, 80 years old, tenders his resignation as British prime minister. ("I don't want to go," he says, "but Anthony [Eden] wants it so much.") The next day, indeed, Eden, the longtime heir apparent, succeeds Churchill.
April 16	President Eisenhower establishes the International Cooperation Administration for foreign aid.
April 21	U.S. military occupation of Germany formally ends, though by agreement troops will remain.
May 5	German Federal Republic (West Germany) becomes a sovereign state. ("We are free among the free," declares Chancellor Adenauer.) On May 9 West Germany formally becomes the 15th member of the North Atlantic Treaty Organization.
May 14	Representatives of Soviet-bloc countries sign the treaty of alliance known as the Warsaw Pact.
May 15	Western allies and the USSR sign the Austrian State Treaty, which will end the occupation of Austria.
May 26	Khrushchev and Bulganin arrive in Belgrade for meetings aimed at the resumption of relations between the USSR and Marshal Tito's Yugoslavia.
July 18	Summit meeting marked by the "spirit of Geneva" opens with U.S. president Eisenhower, French premier Edgar Faure, British prime minister Anthony Eden, and Soviet premier Bulganin; the conference continues until the 23rd. During the meeting Ike proposes mutual aerial reconnaissance through "open skies"; the USSR rejects the plan.
August 4	Rapidly produced, the first U.S. U-2 reconnaissance aircraft makes its initial flight.
September 9	West Germany's Chancellor Adenauer arrives in Moscow for discussions on normalizing relations between the Federal Republic and the USSR; agreement is announced on September 13. On the 22nd, speaking in the Bundestag, the chancellor declares that his government's decision to enter into diplomatic relations with the USSR is a practical matter and not an arrangement "to be put on a level with a friendly treaty relationship."
September 20	Pham Van Dong succeeds Ho Chi Minh as North Vietnamese premier; Ho, however, remains as president.

September 23	British Foreign Office admits in a White Paper that the "missing diplomats," Donald Maclean and Guy Burgess, were in reality longtime Soviet agents.
September 24	President Eisenhower suffers a heart attack while vacationing in Colorado. News coverage is brilliantly managed by the president's press secretary, Jim Hagerty, and Ike makes a good recovery.
September 26	Prince Norodom Sihanouk becomes premier of Cambodia.
October 23	*New York Sunday News* names Kim Philby as the "third man" of the Cambridge Five, who warned Burgess and Maclean in 1951 that British and U.S. security services suspected them of espionage for the Soviet Union.
October 26	Having rejected the elections called for by the 1954 Geneva Accords, Premier Ngo Dinh Diem proclaims himself president of the Republic of Vietnam (South Vietnam) and thus chief of state in succession to the deposed former emperor, Bao Dai, for whom a plebiscite led to dismissal from office.
November 7	Speaking on the basis of information supplied by the U.K.'s security services, Foreign Secretary Harold Macmillan tells the House of Commons there is "no reason to conclude that Mr. Philby has at any time betrayed the interests of this country, or to identify him with the so-called 'third man,' if, indeed, there was one."
November 21	Fighting in Malaya continues as the British step up action against the guerrillas.
December 1	Western Allies declare that, despite Soviet contentions, Berlin remains an occupied city.
December 9	West German government announces what will come to be known as the Hallstein Doctrine, under which it will not maintain diplomatic relations with countries that recognize East Germany.

1956

February 11	Missing since 1951, British KGB agents Guy Burgess and Donald Maclean, members of the Cambridge Five, hold a press conference in Moscow, confirming Western speculation that they had fled behind the Iron Curtain.
February 25	In a "secret speech" at the 20th Congress of the Communist Party of the Soviet Union, First Secretary Khrushchev denounces the "cult of

personality" built by Stalin and describes a variety of crimes committed by the late dictator. (Though widely quoted in the Soviet Union, this "de-Stalinization" speech will not be officially published there until 1989.)

May 2	As part of his attempt to shake up his increasingly conservative and bureaucratic comrades in the leadership of the Chinese Communist Party, Mao Zedong delivers a speech in which he revives a Confucian slogan: "Let a hundred flowers bloom, let a hundred schools of thought contend."
June 28	Calling for lower food prices and the end of Communist rule, Polish factory workers in Poznan erupt in riots.
July 19	United States withdraws offer of a loan to Egypt for construction of the Aswan High Dam, a move that leads to Egypt's nationalization of the Suez Canal on July 26.
August	Kim Philby takes up his duties as a British intelligence agent (despite, or perhaps because of, his suspect past) and newspaper correspondent in Beirut.
October 21	Khrushchev allows the appointment of Władysław Gomułka, a former political prisoner, as first secretary of the Polish Communist Party, thus calming the uprising in Poland.
	Speakers in various Hungarian cities call for the removal of Soviet troops from the country.
October 23	Popular demonstrations in Budapest and across Hungary explode into battles with the authorities, as the Hungarian Revolution begins. A group of more than 100,000, celebrating Gomułka's appointment as Polish first secretary, marches to the home of Hungarian party official and former premier Imre Nagy.
October 25	János Kádár becomes first secretary of the Hungarian Communist Party.
October 26	Representatives of 70 countries sign the enabling document of the International Atomic Energy Agency, to promote the peaceful use of nuclear energy.
October 28	Gomułka and other Polish Communist leaders call for the Soviets to withdraw from Hungary.
October 29	As part of a plan concerted with Britain and France, which desire to regain control of the Suez Canal, Israeli forces attack the Egyptians in the Sinai Desert.

UN Security Council refuses to defend the Hungarian Revolution. Yugoslavia's Marshal Tito urges Hungarians to stop the uprising before world peace is imperiled.

October 30   Imre Nagy, the newly appointed Hungarian premier, announces the abolition of one-party government in Hungary; Hungarian rebels storm Communist Party headquarters in Pest and execute the defenders.

October 31   President Eisenhower criticizes the Anglo-French-Israeli combination against Egypt.

November 1   Demanding that the Soviets immediately withdraw troop reinforcements they have sent to Hungary, Premier Nagy denounces the Warsaw Pact and declares Hungary a neutral state.

November 4   Having decided that matters in Hungary are out of hand, the Soviet authorities send tanks into Budapest with First Secretary Kádár at their head; fierce fighting begins.

November 5   Britain and France join in the attack on Egypt; a cease-fire, however, quickly follows.

November 6   President Eisenhower wins a second term with a solid victory over the Democratic nominee, Adlai E. Stevenson, with 35.6 million popular votes to Stevenson's 26 million and an electoral count of 457 to 73.

November 7   Soviet troops gain control of Budapest and other Hungarian cities, though fighting continues.

November 19   Reacting to criticism of his tepid stand on Hungary, India's Prime Minister Nehru criticizes Soviet actions and calls for UN observers.

November 22   Overwhelmed by a flood amounting to perhaps 100,000 refugees from Hungary, the Austrian government asks other Western countries for help.

November 23   Violating a safe-conduct agreement, the Soviets kidnap Imre Nagy and his close associates.

December 2   A small group of revolutionaries, led by Fidel Castro, lands in Cuba, from temporary headquarters in Mexico, and moves into the Sierra Maestra jungle.

December 4   Acting in accordance with UN orders, Britain and France begin to withdraw troops from Egypt. Israeli withdrawal also proceeds, though the Israeli government indicates its intention to retain control of the Gaza Strip. A UN peacekeeping force will take up positions between the two sides.

U.S. Army announces the deactivation of its pigeon-based communications operations; the remaining birds (some 1,000) will be sold, except for 18 which, honored for having saved American lives, will be presented to various zoos.

December 12   UN General Assembly condemns, 55 to 8, Soviet actions in Hungary.

Formerly one of Yugoslav Marshal Tito's closest associates, Milovan Djilas draws a three-year prison sentence for his remarks in Western newspapers critical of Tito's foreign policy.

1957

January 5   U.S. president Eisenhower asks for congressional approval of actions to aid Middle Eastern countries threatened by Communist aggression—the Eisenhower Doctrine.

January 6   New Hungarian premier János Kádár declares that his government depends on Soviet troops to protect "the peaceful life of the Hungarian people."

January 17   Seeming at this point to be firm allies, the Soviets and the Chinese Communists release a joint declaration condemning the Eisenhower Doctrine.

February 1   In a development indicating that for the West, at least, World War II is truly over, Lieutenant General Dr. Hans Speidel, once Field Marshal Erwin Rommel's chief of staff, takes command of NATO Central European ground forces.

February 7   In the department of dubious science, three American physicists report on a study said to show that the testing of nuclear weapons presents no threat to the health of human beings.

February 15   Andrei Gromyko becomes Soviet foreign minister.

March 9   President Eisenhower signs the congressional act authorizing U.S. forces to come to the aid of Middle Eastern countries.

March 17   Ramon Magsaysay, the strongly anti-Communist president of the Philippines, dies in an airplane crash.

March 20–24   President Eisenhower and Harold Macmillan, the new British prime minister, meet to mend political fences after the Anglo-American rift over Suez.

March 25	Delegates of six Western European countries sign the Treaty of Rome, which brings into being the European Economic Community (the Common Market).
May 15	Britain explodes its first hydrogen bomb, thus becoming the third member of the fusion club.
June 21	Canadian Conservative leader John Diefenbaker becomes prime minister following a surprising victory in the general election.
June 29	In a triumph for Nikita Khrushchev, the Central Committee of the Communist Party of the Soviet Union removes Georgi Malenkov, V. M. Molotov, and other members of the "antiparty group" from their offices.
July 14	Revolutionary coup topples the Iraqi monarchy; King Feisal and others are killed.
August 31	Moscow announces the dispatch of antiparty group member V. M. Molotov not to prison but to Outer Mongolia as ambassador.
September 14	In accordance with the report of a special committee, the UN General Assembly condemns the USSR for its actions to crush the Hungarian Revolution and its continuing defiance of UN resolutions.
September 15	A landslide victory for his coalition in general elections returns West German chancellor Konrad Adenauer to office.
October 4	Launching by the USSR of the world's first artificial satellite, *Sputnik I*, creates a shock leading to stepped-up U.S. expenditures on missilery and science education; *Sputnik I* is soon followed by *Sputnik II*.
October 26	Marshal Rodion Malinovsky replaces Marshal Zhukov as Soviet defense minister; Zhukov's dismissal appears to be the thanks he earned from Khrushchev for the vitally important support he gave the first secretary in June to counter the antiparty group.
November 25	Eisenhower suffers a stroke but, as in the case of his other illnesses, makes a quick recovery.

1958

January 1	European Common Market and Atomic Energy Community come into being.

January 13	British government issues a statement declaring that a Soviet attack on the West, whatever the weapons used, will evoke British retaliation with the H-bomb.
January 21	West German chancellor Adenauer rejects a Soviet proposal to establish a nuclear-free zone in Central Europe; the idea was discussed two weeks earlier by the Polish foreign minister, Adam Rapacki, and it will continue to receive mention.
January 31	United States produces a retort to the Sputniks by launching the first U.S. satellite, the army's *Explorer I*.
February 22	United States agrees to supply intermediate-range ballistic missiles (IRBMs) to Britain.
March 17	After various discouragements, the U.S. Navy succeeds in launching its own satellite, *Vanguard I*.
March 26	In accordance with First Secretary Khrushchev's wish, Marshal Bulganin resigns as Soviet premier; Khrushchev takes the post himself, while retaining his party secretaryship.
March 30	Prime Minister John Diefenbaker and the Progressive Conservatives win an impressive victory in Canadian general elections.
April 1	Fidel Castro and his followers step up their attacks on the regime of Cuban president Fulgencio Batista.
April 4	Having declared that the Soviet Union is ceasing its nuclear testing, Premier Khrushchev calls on the United States and Britain to do likewise; unfruitful procedural exchanges will follow. On May 9 Khrushchev announces his acceptance of President Eisenhower's proposal for experts to study the possible working of such an agreement.
May	Chinese government adopts Mao Zedong's complex industrial development plan, the Great Leap Forward.
May 13	U.S. vice president Richard M. Nixon, touring Latin America, is violently attacked by anti-American demonstrators in Caracas.

June 1	French National Assembly votes General de Gaulle's return to power as premier; the Algerian crisis presents his number-one challenge.
July 15	President Chamoun of Lebanon asks for U.S. military assistance under the Eisenhower Doctrine. The administration dispatches troops to Lebanon to ward off a presumed possible assault by the United Arab Republic.
July 29	U.S. government establishes the National Aeronautics and Space Administration (NASA); its founding was stimulated by the Soviets' *Sputnik I*.
August 1	In something of a reprise of his 1953 trip to Latin America, Milton Eisenhower returns from a tour of Central America with similar recommendations for greater U.S. aid to the countries of the region.
August 21	Technical advisers meeting at Geneva agree on the feasibility of a nuclear-test monitoring system; next day, the United States and Britain propose a one-year moratorium on such tests. On August 29 Khrushchev agrees to open negotiations.
August 23	China resumes the long-suspended shelling of Quemoy and Matsu, leading to a new diplomatic crisis with the United States.
October 2	USSR announces the resumption of nuclear testing (already detected and announced by the United States).
October 23	Soviet writer Boris Pasternak receives the Nobel Prize for literature. Premier Khrushchev will not allow him to attend the award ceremony.
November 10	In what amounts to an ultimatum, Khrushchev declares that the Soviet government intends to turn its responsibilities in Berlin over to the East German government.
November 27	Khrushchev steps up the new Berlin crisis by proposing that West Berlin become an independent city—that is, an island in the middle of East Germany.
December 14	Western Allies reject Khrushchev's demand that they withdraw troops from Berlin. The Allies later propose a four-power meeting to discuss the general German situation.
December 17	In a development generally considered the result of the costly failure of the Great Leap Forward, Mao Zedong resigns as chairman of the Chinese Central Government Council (and, thus, chief of state), while retaining his position as head of the Chinese Communist Party.
December 21	General de Gaulle is elected president of the new French Fifth Republic.

1959

January 1	Elements of Fidel Castro's Cuban rebel forces occupy Havana, resulting in the resignation of Cuban president Fulgencio Batista and the beginning of the Castro era.
January 4	Anastas Mikoyan, Soviet minister of foreign trade and a favorite troubleshooter for Premier Khrushchev, arrives for a two-week tour of the United States.
January 8	De Gaulle takes office as president of France.
January 10	USSR proposes a large-scale conference to negotiate a peace treaty for Germany; the suggested Soviet draft does not meet the often-reiterated Western stipulation that unification must come from free elections in all of Germany. On February 16 the West will suggest the convening of a four-power foreign ministers' conference to discuss the German question.
February 11	Receiving a traditional welcome in New York, West Berlin's Mayor Willy Brandt is honored as a symbol of resistance to Soviet demands.
February 20	British prime minister Macmillan arrives in Moscow for a visit that will last until March 3; he and his hosts reach no agreement on any questions of policy.
March 11	USSR and East Germany announce their agreement to conclude a German peace treaty with no delay.
March 17	Amid fighting following a Chinese Communist order for his surrender, the Dalai Lama flees from Tibet to India.
March 24	Iraq withdraws from the Baghdad Pact.
March 30	Admiral Arleigh Burke, U.S. chief of naval operations, indicates the beginning of a change of emphasis in U.S. defense planning (which will develop in the Kennedy administration) by testifying to a congressional committee that, given its great nuclear strength, the United States should now begin to build up its limited-war capability. (The testimony, given earlier, is released this day.)
April 4	NATO Council supports the Allied determination to maintain the existence of West Berlin and the rights of all the occupying powers.
April 15	Fatally ill with cancer, John Foster Dulles resigns as U.S. secretary of state; on April 22, Christian Herter takes office as his successor. Dulles dies on May 24.

April 28	Never noted for his tact, Field Marshal Viscount Montgomery declares on television that the less-than-vigorous current U.S. international leadership (as he regards it) has been the result of the poor health of U.S. leaders—President Eisenhower and Secretaries of State Herter and Dulles. Predictably, Montgomery, seeming surprised that anyone has taken offense, soon issues an apology.
May 11	In Geneva, a foreign ministers' conference opens, with West Berlin and German reunification as the principal topics. The conference will last almost three months and produce no agreement.
July 24	Going almost nose to nose, Vice President Nixon and Premier Khrushchev argue about the comparative merits of U.S. and Soviet life in the Kitchen Debate at a U.S. trade fair in Moscow.
September 15	Khrushchev arrives in New York for a tour of the United States as President Eisenhower's guest; he will travel coast to coast, visit an Iowa farm and a Hollywood studio, and stay until September 27.
October 16	U.S. general George C. Marshall dies after a long illness.

1960

January 11	United States formally protests Cuban seizure of U.S.-owned property.
February 28	Soviet premier Khrushchev promises $250 million aid to President Sukarno of Indonesia.
March 19	Still showing some signs of life, talks on a nuclear test ban receive conditional approval from Khrushchev, who agrees to discuss President Eisenhower's proposal for banning all except small underground tests.
May 5	Khrushchev announces that the USSR has shot down a U.S. U-2 reconnaissance aircraft over Soviet territory on May 1 near Sverdlovsk.
May 6	Leonid Brezhnev replaces the veteran Marshal Voroshilov as chairman of the Presidium of the Supreme Soviet (president); election to this sinecure appears to be a severe setback for Brezhnev.
May 7	United States admits the charge that a U-2 aircraft shot down over the USSR was on a surveillance mission.
May 16	In a belated and point-making response to President Eisenhower's admission that he knew of the May 1 U-2 reconnaissance mission, Khrushchev walks out of a summit meeting in Paris; when he does not return on the 17th, the conference is adjourned.

June 21	Patrice Lumumba becomes the first premier of the Belgian Congo (which nine days later becomes the Republic of the Congo).
June 27	Disarmament talks in Geneva end in disarray.
July 14	UN Security Council moves to intervene with troops in the civil war in the Congo; two weeks later Secretary-General Hammarskjöld will go to the Congo to supervise operations—a mission that produces Soviet objections.
July 20	U.S. Navy accomplishes the first successful underwater launching of a Polaris missile.
August 17	U.S. U-2 pilot Francis Gary Powers goes on trial in Moscow; he will receive a ten-year sentence.
September 23	In New York for the UN General Assembly session, Premier Khrushchev calls for Secretary-General Hammarskjöld's dismissal and his replacement by a troika—a three-person executive. During his stay Khrushchev will hammer on the desk to disrupt a speech by British prime minister Macmillan, and on October 12 he will display one of his most colorful sides by twice taking off his shoe and banging it on the table, as the presiding officer breaks his gavel vainly trying to control the behavior of Eastern Bloc delegates before adjourning the "most disorderly meeting in UN history."
September 26	U.S. vice president Richard M. Nixon and Massachusetts senator John F. Kennedy meet on a historic occasion—the first televised debate between U.S. presidential candidates. Radio listeners generally give first place to Nixon, but Kennedy wins television viewers.
October 19	After mounting quarrels with Cuba, the United States announces restrictions on all trade with the country except food and medical supplies.
November 8	John F. Kennedy, the Democratic candidate, is elected president of the United States, defeating Richard M. Nixon in an extremely close election (34.2 million to 34.1 million popular votes; 303 to 219 electoral votes).
December 1	Lumumba, now the former premier of the Congo and a fugitive, is captured by Congo army troops.
December 14	United States, Canada, and Western European countries agree to establish the Organization for Economic Cooperation and Development (OECD).
December 20	National Liberation Front is established in South Vietnam.

1961

January 3	United States breaks diplomatic relations with Castro's Cuba.
January 8	French president de Gaulle wins referendum on granting self-determination to Algeria.
January 17	In his "farewell address," President Eisenhower makes what will become perhaps his best-known pronouncement as he tells the American people to "guard against the acquisition of unwarranted influence, whether sought or unsought, by the military-industrial complex." Contrary to many comments, the warning expresses Ike's long-held awareness that "the potential for the disastrous rise of misplaced power exists and will persist."
January 20	John F. Kennedy assumes office as the 35th president of the United States with the call "Ask not what your country can do for you—ask what you can do for your country."
March 1	President Kennedy issues an executive order establishing the Peace Corps.
March 13	Kennedy proposes the Alliance for Progress, an endeavor to involve the United States in social and economic development in Latin America.
April 12	Major Yuri Gagarin of the Soviet Union becomes the first human being to orbit the earth.
April 17	Cuban exiles backed by the U.S. Central Intelligence Agency stage a disastrously unsuccessful landing at the Bay of Pigs on the Cuban south coast.
May 5	Successfully completing his suborbital mission, Commander Alan Shepard becomes the first American in space.
May 9	U.S. vice president Lyndon Johnson begins a visit to Vietnam as the president's representative; in his report he will advocate substantial U.S. support for South Vietnam.
May 25	In a speech to Congress, President Kennedy proposes that the United States achieve a manned flight to the moon "before the decade is out," thus launching an unprecedented and successful scientific-industrial endeavor.
June 3–4	President Kennedy and Premier Khrushchev meet in Vienna; the conference ends in acrimony, with Khrushchev insisting that he will sign a separate peace treaty with the German Democratic Republic.

In the days following August 12, 1961, East German workers put up the barrier of barbed wire and concrete blocks the world will soon call the Berlin Wall.

July 1	General Maxwell Taylor becomes special military adviser to President Kennedy.
July 24	Kennedy administration warns the Soviets not to interfere with Western access to West Berlin.
August 12	East Germans close the border between East and West Berlin and begin building the Berlin Wall.
September 4	United States establishes the Agency for International Development (AID).
September 18	UN secretary-general Hammerskjöld dies in an air crash while on his mission to negotiate a cease-fire in the Congo. He will be succeeded at the United Nations by Burma's U Thant.

October 26–27	U.S. and Soviet tanks confront each other at Checkpoint Charlie in Berlin.
October 31	Joseph Stalin's body is removed from its resting place in the Lenin mausoleum and reburied by the Kremlin wall. "He pressed himself against the chinks," says Soviet poet Yevgeny Yevtushenko, "pretending to be dead."
November 3	Returning from a fact-finding trip to Vietnam for President Kennedy, General Taylor and administration adviser Walt Rostow, in the Taylor Report, call for the dispatch of an 8,000-man "logistic task force" to support South Vietnam.

1962

February 6	United States establishes the Military Assistance Command, Vietnam (MACV) in Saigon; it is to include some 1,000 advisers.
February 7	U.S. embargo is imposed on all trade with Cuba.
February 10	In a swap with the Soviet Union, the United States trades convicted spy Rudolf Abel for Francis Gary Powers, the U-2 pilot shot down in May 1960 over the USSR.
February 20	Lieutenant Colonel John H. Glenn, Jr., becomes the first American to orbit the earth.
March 22	In South Vietnam, U.S. officers launch the strategic-hamlet program to combat Vietcong insurgency in the countryside.
May 12	United States dispatches marines and aircraft to Laos.
July 1	French control officially ends in Algeria after the country votes for independence.
July 23	Western powers, the Soviet Union, and China sign the Geneva Accords on Laos.
October 14	U.S. U-2 reconnaissance flight discovers the construction of Soviet missile bases in Cuba.
October 22	In an address to the American people, President Kennedy announces the discovery of the missile bases and declares that the United States is imposing a "quarantine" on the shipment to Cuba of offensive weapons.

On August 18, 1962, Peter Fechter, an 18-year-old construction worker, is shot and fatally wounded by East German border guards for trying to cross the Berlin Wall.

October 23   Premier Castro calls the U.S. blockade an act of piracy and denies receiving offensive missiles. The Soviet Union warns the United States it is risking nuclear war.

British foreign secretary Lord Home promises British support for the U.S. position in the Cuban Missile Crisis.

October 24   UN secretary-general U Thant offers to act as mediator in the Cuban crisis and asks the superpowers to suspend action.

October 25   President Kennedy and Premier Khrushchev welcome Secretary-General Thant's offer of mediation, but Kennedy declares that the blockade will continue.

October 26   Under questioning by U.S. ambassador to the UN Adlai Stevenson, Soviet UN ambassador Zorin refuses to deny that the missiles are offensive. In a letter to President Kennedy, Premier Khrushchev offers to remove the missiles in exchange for a U.S. pledge not to invade Cuba.

October 27   In a new message broadcast by Radio Moscow, Khrushchev now calls for the removal of U.S. missiles from Turkey in exchange for the removal of Soviet missiles from Cuba. Kennedy rejects any discussion of Turkish missiles and accepts Khrushchev's October 26 letter as a basis for settlement of the crisis.

October 28   Khrushchev announces his decision to withdraw Soviet missiles from Cuba, while Kennedy agrees to lift the blockade and not to invade Cuba.

October 31   Khrushchev sends Deputy Premier Mikoyan to Cuba to win Premier Castro's acceptance of the U.S.-USSR agreement.

November 1   Castro refuses to allow any international inspection of Cuban sites, even by the Red Cross.

November 2   USSR accepts the proposal for the Red Cross to inspect freighters bound for Cuba to verify their cargoes.

November 8   United States announces that all known offensive-missile sites in Cuba have been dismantled.

U.S. Kennedy administration informs the British government that, for technical reasons, it is canceling a planned arrangement to supply Britain with the Skybolt, an aircraft-launched ballistic missile (ABM).

November 16   U.S. administration declares that surveillance flights will continue until Cuba agrees to a satisfactory method of inspection.

November 20   Kennedy announces the lifting of the Cuban blockade but declares that a no-invasion pledge will be withheld until Soviet pledges are carried out.

December 1   After meetings with U.S. officials, Soviet deputy premier Mikoyan expresses his belief in the U.S. desire to resolve the Cuban situation.

December 18   In a conference with British Prime Minister Macmillan at Nassau (which continues until the 21st), U.S. president Kennedy agrees to substitute the Polaris missile for the canceled Skybolt, thus averting domestic political disaster for Macmillan.

December 23   After extensive negotiations in which the United States agrees to send medical supplies and food to Cuba, the Castro government releases 107 Cuban exiles captured in the Bay of Pigs landing; more than 1,100 will follow shortly.

| December 26 | In a move that creates considerable trouble for himself with Communist Party officials, Premier Khrushchev establishes a new, complex, and quickly unpopular system of party organization. |

1963

January 7	United States and the Soviet Union jointly inform UN secretary-general U Thant that the Cuban Missile Crisis is over.
January 20	Letters between President Kennedy and Premier Khrushchev suggest that a nuclear test-ban treaty could be within reach, since the Soviet premier expresses willingness to allow inspections in the USSR; on January 26 Kennedy will advance the process by suspending U.S. underground testing.
January 23	Kim Philby disappears from Beirut; on January 27 he arrives in the USSR. In his memoirs he will taunt his former Western colleagues.
January 29	French president de Gaulle's government vetoes British entry into the European Economic Community; the action draws an angry public reply from Prime Minister Macmillan. One important factor appears to be the general's resentment of what he regards as the close U.S.-U.K. relationship regarding missiles.
January 31	In a reversal, the Soviets abandon talks about a nuclear test ban; the United States resumes underground testing.
March 22	Macmillan's secretary of state for war, John Profumo, denies in the House of Commons that there is any truth to rumors of his involvement with a call girl named Christine Keeler, also involved with a Soviet officer.
April 5	Physicist J. Robert Oppenheimer, whose security clearance was removed in 1954, wins the 1963 Enrico Fermi Award, given by the Atomic Energy Commission.
April 9	Declaring that "he mobilized the English language and sent it into battle," President Kennedy confers honorary U.S. citizenship on Sir Winston Churchill.
April 22	Lester Pearson, Liberal Party leader and an important figure in the development of the North Atlantic Treaty Organization, becomes prime minister of Canada.
May 8	Seven persons die in Buddhist antigovernment protests in Hue, South Vietnam.

May 11	Soviet court issues a death sentence to Oleg Penkovsky, a Western mole in the KGB considered by some the greatest Western agent of the Cold War.
June 4	John Profumo admits his involvement with Christine Keeler and hands in his resignation.
June 10	In a commencement address at American University in Washington, President Kennedy accelerates movement toward a nuclear test-ban treaty when he declares that "a fresh start is needed" for "a treaty to outlaw nuclear tests."
June 11	In Saigon, a Buddhist monk burns himself alive as an act of protest against the government. At one point, Mme. Nhu, President Diem's sister-in-law, speaks airily of "the biggest barbecue in Saigon."
June 20	U.S. and Soviet representatives sign an agreement to establish the "hot line" between Washington and Moscow. It becomes operational in August.
June 26	In expressing U.S. support for the people of Berlin, President Kennedy visits the city two years after the building of the Berlin Wall and tells a huge crowd of citizens: "Today, in the world of freedom, the proudest boast is *Ich bin ein Berliner!*"
July 1	Prime Minister Macmillan admits to the House of Commons that Kim Philby was the much-discussed "third man" involved in the escape behind the Iron Curtain of Donald Maclean and Guy Burgess in 1951.
July 14	Communist Party of the Soviet Union rejects criticism from the Chinese Communist Party, thus formalizing the break between the two parties.
July 16	In Saigon, militant Buddhists hold further anti-Diem demonstrations.
July 25	United States, Britain, and the Soviet Union agree on the terms of the Nuclear Test Ban Treaty.
August 3	In the running battle of the two giant Communist powers, the Soviet government attacks the Chinese for opposing the Test Ban Treaty.
August 5	United States, Britain, and the USSR sign the Nuclear Test Ban Treaty in Moscow.
August 21	Continuing its conflict with the Buddhists, the South Vietnamese government arrests some 100 monks.
August 22	Henry Cabot Lodge succeeds Frederick Nolting as U.S. ambassador to South Vietnam.

On November 22, 1963, aboard *Air Force One*, Lyndon B. Johnson takes the presidential oath of office from Dallas judge Sarah T. Hughes. Flanking the new president are his wife, Lady Bird *(l.)*, and Jacqueline Kennedy.

October 16	Ludwig Erhard, the central figure in the West German "economic miracle," succeeds Konrad Adenauer as chancellor.
October 18	Weakened by the Profumo scandal and ill health, Harold Macmillan resigns as British prime minister; his successor is Lord Home (soon to become Sir Alec Douglas-Home).
November 1	South Vietnamese officers overthrow, then murder (November 2) President Ngo Dinh Diem and Special Forces head Ngo Dinh Nhu, his younger brother. Mme. Nhu escapes to Rome.
November 12	Arrest in Moscow of a Yale professor, Frederick Barghoorn, on allegations of spying, evokes a strong reaction from President Kennedy; on the 16th the Soviet government releases him.
November 22	President Kennedy is assassinated in Dallas; Vice President Lyndon B. Johnson succeeds to the presidency.
November 24	Lee Harvey Oswald, the assassin of President Kennedy, is himself murdered by Jack Ruby, a small-time nightclub proprietor with some mob connections. Ruby's involvement gives the tragedy perhaps its most bizarre angle.

1964

February 4	Chinese government launches a sharp attack on Soviet premier Khrushchev, accusing him of working in association with the United States to achieve world domination.
February 22	United States and the USSR agree to expand scientific, cultural, and other exchanges.
February 27	President Johnson announces that the United States has a new high-performance aircraft, the A-11, which he calls an interceptor; actually it will develop into the SR-71, the successor to the U-2 for reconnaissance duty; the SR-71 will prove to be one of the most remarkable aircraft ever built.
April 3	Communist Party of the Soviet Union announces the expulsion of three veteran and formerly high-placed members: Georgi Malenkov, V. M. Molotov, and Lazar Kaganovich.
April 20	U.S., British, and Soviet negotiators agree to reduce the production of fissionable materials for military purposes.
May 19	U.S. State Department describes the discovery of numerous microphones that Soviet workers installed in the walls of the U.S. embassy in Moscow.
May 27	Jawaharlal Nehru dies; he has been prime minister of India since 1947, when the country acquired its independence.
June 20	General William C. Westmoreland assumes command of U.S. forces in Vietnam; three days later General Maxwell Taylor succeeds Lodge as ambassador.
July 15	Anastas Mikoyan succeeds Leonid Brezhnev as chairman of the Presidium of the Supreme Soviet (president); the change actually represents a return by Brezhnev to a more active political arena.
August 2/4	U.S. destroyers *Maddox* and *C. Turner Joy* report attacks by North Vietnamese patrol boats in the Gulf of Tonkin; navy investigators later conclude that the second attack did not actually take place.
August 7	U.S. Congress passes the Gulf of Tonkin Resolution, endorsing armed resistance to attack in Vietnamese waters.
September 27	Warren Commission (so called after its chairman, Chief Justice Earl Warren), appointed by President Johnson to investigate the assassination of President Kennedy, releases its report, which finds no evidence

of a conspiracy and concludes that Lee Harvey Oswald, acting alone, committed the murder.

October 14	Communist Party of the Soviet Union Central Committee accuses Khrushchev of various offenses; he is forced from all his offices; Leonid Brezhnev succeeds him as first secretary, Alexei Kosygin as premier.
October 16	Communist Chinese produce their first nuclear test explosion.
	Harold Wilson becomes British prime minister after leading the Labour Party to an election victory over Douglas-Home's Conservatives.
November 3	President Johnson overwhelms Republican senator Barry Goldwater of Arizona in the U.S. presidential election, winning 43.1 million popular votes to Goldwater's 27.1 million; the electoral count is 486 to 52.
December 30	UN Security Council votes for an end to foreign intervention in the Congo.

DÉTENTE AND DECLINE

1965

January 24	Sir Winston Churchill dies in London. At the funeral, former U.S. president Eisenhower in his eulogy moves his audience with the simple statement: "Farewell, old friend."
February 6	With the new Soviet leadership showing more interest in Vietnam than former premier Khrushchev displayed, Premier Alexei Kosygin arrives in Hanoi for talks with North Vietnamese leaders.
February 7	Vietcong open a general attack on U.S. military installations in South Vietnam—notably, at Pleiku—and U.S. bombers carry out first missions against North Vietnam. These become Operation Rolling Thunder, intended to interdict supply lines from the North to the South.
February 25	After incessant changes of government in South Vietnam, Major General Nguyen Van Thieu and Air Vice Marshal Nguyen Cao Ky take charge; their control will be solidified on June 13.
March 8	U.S. Third Marine Regiment arrives in Vietnam. The first U.S. combat troops sent to Southeast Asia, they have the specific mission of defending the U.S. base at Da Nang.

March 22	Nicolae Ceauşescu becomes first secretary of the Romanian Communist Party; in relation to Moscow, he will pursue what often seems a daringly independent course.
April 28	President Johnson dispatches U.S. marines to the Dominican Republic following a political coup; the action draws much criticism, particularly (but not only) because it is taken without consultation with the Organization of American States. A week later the council of the OAS will vote to establish an inter-American peacekeeping force in the Dominican Republic.
July 8	Henry Cabot Lodge returns to Saigon as U.S. ambassador.
July 26	As the escalation in Vietnam continues, President Johnson declares that the United States will soon have 125,000 troops there.
September 30–October 1	Indonesian army units crush a coup attempt launched by army officers and joined by Communists; the countercoup develops into a massacre of the Communists.
November 7	U.S. secretary of defense Robert McNamara recommends to the president that the United States declare a bombing pause in Vietnam, in order to offer an opening for diplomatic activity.
November 11	Government newspapers in China strike up a familiar theme: the Soviet Union is working with the United States to achieve world domination.
December 19	In a runoff election against François Mitterrand, General de Gaulle wins reelection as president of France.

At his Texas ranch, President Lyndon B. Johnson *(l., out of his chair)* discusses the Vietnam situation with military and civilian advisers, including Secretary of Defense Robert McNamara *(to Johnson's l.)* and General Earle Wheeler *(directly facing the president).*

| December 25 | Announcing the suspension of Operation Rolling Thunder, President Johnson calls on North Vietnam to enter into peace negotiations. During this year of escalation of the war, the number of U.S. military personnel in Vietnam has grown from about 23,000 to some 184,000; U.S. allies have sent 22,000 troops. |

1966

January 19	Indira Gandhi, daughter of the late Jawaharlal Nehru, becomes prime minister of India.
January 31	Bombing pause ends in Vietnam; U.S. forces resume Operation Rolling Thunder.
February 6	In Honolulu, President Johnson and South Vietnamese premier Ky, accompanied by large staffs, begin three days of conferences; at the conclusion of the meetings they issue a joint statement called the Honolulu Declaration, in which the South Vietnamese outline their goals—defeating the Vietcong, "constitutional democracy . . . dignity, freedom and peace"—and the United States pledges to support them. Johnson declares that he wants "coonskins on the wall."
February 14	Soviet writers Andrei Sinyavsky and Yuli Daniel, accused of having published anti-Soviet writings in the West (and thus of being "turncoats"), draw prison sentences.
February 19	In a press conference, U.S. Democratic senator from New York Robert Kennedy suggests that in a Vietnam peace settlement the National Liberation Front might be given a share in the government of South Vietnam.
March 9	France declares its intention to withdraw from the NATO military structure—which means that NATO's headquarters and installations will have to move elsewhere; a site near Brussels becomes the new location of the headquarters.
April 1	Walt Rostow succeeds McGeorge Bundy (who has resigned) as the president's national security adviser.
May 1	Placing heavy reliance on bombing, the U.S. command in Vietnam launches attacks on oil tanks at Haiphong and Hanoi.
May 23	Buddhist-led rebellion in Da Nang ends as 1,000 South Vietnamese marines take the city.

June 1	After many weeks of dissidence and open fighting, South Vietnamese Buddhist leaders and the government agree to participate in an expanded National Leadership Committee.
June 29	Australian prime minister Harold Holt arrives in Washington; during his visit he will declare that his country will go "all the way with LBJ."
August 8	Central Committee of the Chinese Communist Party adopts a resolution establishing the Cultural Revolution, favored by Mao Zedong and bitterly opposed by P'eng Chen and other influential leaders.
August 31	French president de Gaulle calls on the United States to agree to withdraw its forces from Vietnam.
September 11	South Vietnamese voters choose 117 members of a constituent assembly. Despite Vietcong attempts to disrupt the voting, more than 80 percent of those registered go to the polls.

In October 1966, at Cam Ranh Bay, Vietnam, President Lyndon B. Johnson *(r.)* and the U.S. commander, General William C. Westmoreland, visit wounded soldiers.

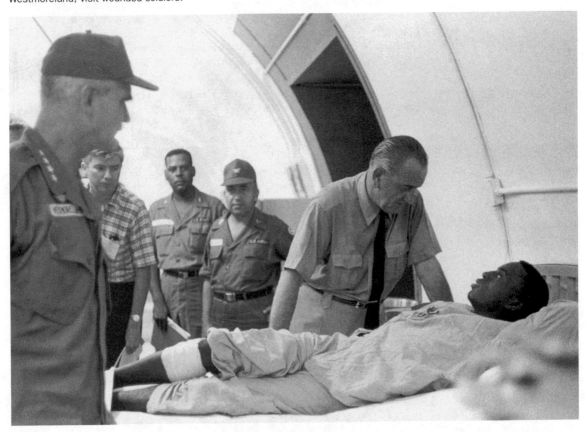

October 1	In its continuing detachment from the military aspects of the North Atlantic Treaty Organization, France ceases to be a member of the NATO Military Committee.
October 22	Convicted double agent George Blake makes a daring escape from Britain's Wormwood Scrubs prison; Blake is believed to have been responsible for divulging to the KGB the identities of more than 40 Western agents.
October 26	On an extensive Asian tour, President Johnson flies into Cam Ranh Bay, Vietnam, to visit U.S. troops.
November 10	British prime minister Wilson announces Britain's intention to try again to enter the European Economic Community.
December 1	"Grand Coalition" of Christian Democrats and Social Democrats takes office in West Germany.
December 6	Anticipated secret peace discussions in Warsaw between U.S. and North Vietnamese negotiators fail to take place when the North Vietnamese representatives do not appear.
December 13	Communist Party of the Soviet Union Central Committee denounces Mao Zedong, accusing him of following an "anti-Leninist" policy.

1967

January 27	In Washington, the United States, the USSR, and 58 other countries sign a treaty prohibiting nuclear weapons in space.
April 21	Right-wing "colonels" take power in a military coup in Greece.
May 1	Veteran U.S. diplomat Ellsworth Bunker succeeds Henry Cabot Lodge as ambassador in Saigon.
May 18	In response to a request by Egypt's President Nasser, UN secretary-general U Thant orders the UN peacekeeping force out of the Sinai.
May 22	President Johnson orders a halt to U.S. air attacks within ten miles of Hanoi.
June 5	Six-Day War between Israel and Arab countries begins; it ends on June 10.
June 17	Chinese Communist government detonates its first hydrogen bomb.

June 23	President Johnson and Soviet premier Kosygin meet at Glassboro, N.J., with a second session following on June 25.
July 13	U.S. secretary of defense McNamara and military commanders ask for the raising of troop strength in South Vietnam to 525,000 (less than the generals originally wanted); after consideration, President Johnson approves.
July 24	French president de Gaulle creates an uproar by declaring *"Vive le Québec libre!"* in Montreal, thus appearing to endorse the Quebec separatist movement.
August 24	U.S. air attacks cease in the Hanoi area.
September 3	In voting considered neither totally honest nor totally corrupt, Nguyen Van Thieu is elected president of a newly re-created South Vietnamese government, with Nguyen Cao Ky as vice president.
September 5	Attempting to restore order in China after the excesses of the Cultural Revolution, the Communist Party Central Committee and other leadership organizations order the masses to turn in their arms.
September 29	In a speech in San Antonio, President Johnson offers to stop the bombing of North Vietnam "when this will lead promptly to productive discussions"—a somewhat looser formula than any previously presented by the administration.
October 8	International revolutionary known as Che Guevara dies in a reported encounter between Bolivian army troops and guerrillas.
October 21	In the United States, the Pentagon building and environs are the scene of a huge Vietnam War protest demonstration.
November 27	President de Gaulle rejects a new British attempt to join the European Economic Community (the Common Market).
December 17	Harold Holt, the Australian prime minister, disappears while skin-diving off the coast of the state of Victoria.

1968

January 3	Minnesota senator Eugene McCarthy, an opponent of the war in Vietnam, announces his candidacy for the Democratic U.S. presidential nomination.

January 5	Alexander Dubček is elected first secretary of the Czechoslovak Communist Party; observers expect him to move in the direction of liberalization.
January 21	North Vietnamese forces attack the U.S. Marine base and airfield at Khe Sanh, beginning a siege.
January 23	North Korean patrol boats board and seize a U.S. intelligence ship, the *Pueblo,* in the Sea of Japan.
January 30	North Vietnamese and Vietcong forces launch the strong and widespread Tet Offensive in South Vietnam.
February 27	The Johnson administration, which has just received a request for more troops for Vietnam, suffers a severe blow when the revered news broadcaster Walter Cronkite declares that the United States and South Vietnam cannot win the war.
March 1	Clark M. Clifford, a veteran Washington figure and one of President Johnson's trusted advisers, succeeds Robert McNamara as U.S. secretary of defense.
March 8	In Warsaw, university students, battling police, shout their support of the liberalizing Prague Spring in Czechoslovakia.
March 16	Senator Robert F. Kennedy of New York announces his candidacy for the Democratic presidential nomination.
	U.S. troops are involved in a massacre of civilians in My Lai, a Vietnamese hamlet.
March 22	Liberalizing Czech leaders compel discredited Stalinist president Antonín Novotný to resign; the Czech party Presidium adopts a program to rehabilitate some 3,000 victims of Stalinism.
March 23	In an attempt to allay the concerns of Czechoslovakia's Warsaw Pact neighbors, Czech first secretary Dubček, at a meeting in Dresden, assures General Secretary Brezhnev and Premier Kosygin of the Soviet Union, and other pact leaders, that Prague Spring liberalization moves do not threaten Czech adherence to Eastern Bloc policies.
March 30	In something of a tactical concession to Brezhnev, the Czechs choose one of his World War II associates, General Ludvík Svoboda, as president.
March 31	Ordering a partial halt to the bombing of North Vietnam, U.S. president Johnson at the same time announces that he will not run for reelection. Asked afterward how he feels about this momentous decision, he replies, "I think I feel pretty good."

April 5	U.S. and South Vietnamese army troops drive to Khe Sanh and lift the siege.
April 20	Minister of Justice Pierre Elliott Trudeau, newly elected leader of the Liberal Party, succeeds Lester Pearson, who is retiring, as prime minister of Canada.
May 3	So-called May Crisis begins in France with riots by discontented left-wing students at the Sorbonne; a general strike follows later in the month.
May 5	North Vietnamese and Vietcong forces open the second phase of their general Tet Offensive, with Saigon as the principal target; the attacks are largely overcome within a week.
May 10	Preliminary peace talks on Vietnam open in Paris. Formal conference sessions begin May 13; they will make little progress.
June 5	Missing for a week, the U.S. nuclear submarine *Scorpion* is declared lost; despite much speculation at the time, analysis 25 years later will show that hostile action was not involved.
	After winning the California Democratic presidential primary, Robert Kennedy is shot by an assassin and dies in the early morning hours of June 6.
June 23–30	Drawing strength from popular discontent with left-wing rioting, General de Gaulle wins reelection as French president by a huge majority; Gaullist candidates win a clear legislative majority, the first such for any party since the era of Napoleon III.
June 25	Trudeau leads the Liberals to a strong victory in Canadian parliamentary elections (155 House of Commons seats to 109 for other parties).
June 30	Soviet fighters force a U.S. troop–carrying airliner to land on an island north of Japan; the pilot later recants his admission of having strayed into Soviet air space, declaring that he agreed to the statement simply to obtain the release of aircraft, crew, and passengers.
July 1	The United States, the Soviet Union, and Britain sign the Nuclear Nonproliferation Treaty; West Germany will sign in 1969. President Johnson also announces plans for U.S.-Soviet discussions that will become known as SALT (Strategic Arms Limitation Talks).
	General Creighton Abrams replaces General Westmoreland as U.S. Army commander in Vietnam.

July 10	To general surprise, de Gaulle follows his victory in the French elections by replacing Premier Georges Pompidou with a longtime associate, Maurice Couve de Murville.
July 12	Czech foreign minister expresses apprehension over an ominous article in *Pravda* (Moscow) likening Czechoslovak democratization to the events in Hungary in 1956 that led to revolution and bloody repression.
July 14–15	Leaders of the USSR and four other Warsaw Pact states confer on Czech liberalization; Dubček declines to take part.
July 23	Putting pressure on the liberal Czech government, the Soviets announce large-scale military maneuvers in territory near Czechoslovakia.
July 29– August 1	In the sort of move never seen before, 9 of the 11 members of the Communist Party of the Soviet Union Politburo travel to Cierna-nad-Tissou, Czechoslavakia, to meet with the Czech party Presidium; this step represents Soviet general secretary Brezhnev's last major attempt to control the Dubček government without resorting to military means.
August 20–21	Warsaw Pact troops invade Czechoslovakia in force—22 divisions—to crush the Prague Spring and compel compliance with the Soviet view of "socialism"; marchers in Prague confront Soviet troops with cries of "Russian murderers, go home!"
August 24	France detonates its first hydrogen bomb.
August 28	In the United States, riots by Vietnam War protestors and police mark the Democratic Party convention in Chicago, at which Vice President Hubert Humphrey is nominated for president.
August 29	Czechoslovak government announces the removal of such recently granted freedoms as the right to form political parties.
September 12	In line with its Maoist orientation, Albania withdraws from the Warsaw Pact.
October 31	President Johnson suspends all aerial and other bombardment of North Vietnam; such a development has been the unwavering demand of North Vietnamese negotiators in Paris.
November 5	In a very close election, Republican Richard M. Nixon defeats Vice President Hubert Humphrey for the U.S. presidency (popular vote: 31.8 million to 31.3 million; electoral vote: 301 to 191).
December 2	At a press conference, President-elect Nixon introduces Henry A. Kissinger as his national security adviser.

1969

January 5	President-elect Nixon appoints Henry Cabot Lodge head of the U.S. delegation to the Vietnam peace talks in Paris; Lodge replaces Averell Harriman.
January 16	The now-vanished Prague Spring acquires a martyr when a Czech student, Jan Palach, publicly burns himself to death to protest the Soviet suppression of the movement for liberalization; Palach will be remembered in the Prague Autumn—the Velvet Revolution—20 years hence.
January 20	Nixon, committed to ending U.S. involvement in the Vietnam War, assumes office as the 37th president of the United States.
January 25	New Vietnam peace conference opens in Paris.
February 17	President de Gaulle announces French withdrawal from participation in activities of the Western European Union.
March 2	Fighting between Soviet and Chinese forces breaks out in the Ussuri River area near Vladivostok.
March 13	U.S. Senate ratifies the Nuclear Nonproliferation Treaty.
March 28	Having long suffered from heart disease, former president Dwight D. Eisenhower dies.
April 17	Alexander Dubček is forced out as first secretary of the Czechoslovak Communist Party; he is succeeded by party hard-liner Gustav Husák.
April 28	After losing the April 27 national referendum on procedural matters, General de Gaulle (as he said he would do) resigns as president of France.
May 14	President Nixon proposes mutual troop withdrawals from South Vietnam.
June 8	After meeting at Midway Island with South Vietnamese president Thieu, President Nixon announces that 25,000 U.S. troops will be brought home from Vietnam.
June 15	Georges Pompidou wins a runoff election to become president of France.
July 20	Fulfilling the hope expressed by President Kennedy in 1961, U.S. astronauts land on the moon. Astronaut Neil A. Armstrong is the first human being to walk on its surface; he says, "One small step for a man, one giant leap for mankind."

July 25	In an interview with reporters on Guam, Nixon declares that in future wars in Asia, Asians rather than Americans must bear the primary responsibility; this view is termed the Nixon Doctrine.
September 2	Ho Chi Minh dies on this day, according to North Vietnamese announcements.
September 27	Though President Nixon will carry out the withdrawal of U.S. troops from South Vietnam, he is met with skepticism by President Thieu, who declares that the process will take years, and by the North Vietnamese, who have already professed to see the entire operation as a trick.
October 21	Social Democrat Willy Brandt becomes chancellor of West Germany; he will soon launch his policy of improved relations with the Eastern Bloc (Ostpolitik).
November 15	Vietnam War protest demonstration in Washington, D.C., draws a crowd estimated at 250,000.
November 17	United States and Soviet representatives, meeting in Helsinki, begin the series of arms-limitation talks that will lead to the treaty called SALT I.
November 20	Nixon administration announces the resignation of Henry Cabot Lodge as head of the U.S. delegation to the Vietnam peace talks.

1970

January 20	As a suggestion of what the Nixon administration is going to do later, the United States and China take up behind-the-scenes diplomatic talks in Warsaw suspended two years earlier.
February 27	Western Allies accept a Soviet proposal for negotiations about the future status of Berlin; the first meeting will take place on March 26.
March 18	U.S.-supported forces of Lon Nol overthrow Prince Norodom Sihanouk in Cambodia (while the prince is meeting with Soviet leaders in Moscow).
April 30	President Nixon announces that U.S. and South Vietnamese forces are invading Cambodia to attack "sanctuaries" used by Communist forces.
May 4	At Kent State University in Ohio, panicking National Guardsmen kill four students during a demonstration to protest the U.S. invasion of Cambodia.

May 17	Though U.S. Army spokesmen assert that the incursion into Cambodia has resulted in the capture of the Communists' so-called Central Office for South Vietnam (COSVN), the claim will prove exaggerated.
June 19	Edward Heath becomes British prime minister as Conservatives defeat Labour in the June 18 general election.
June 29	Last U.S. ground troops leave Cambodia; next day the Senate passes the Cooper-Church Amendment, which cuts off funds for all operations in Cambodia after June 30; however, the amendment fails in the House of Representatives (until the end of the year, when it turns up attached to another bill and is passed).
August 12	As part of his policy of Ostpolitik, West German chancellor Brandt signs a renunciation-of-force treaty with Soviet premier Kosygin.
September 28	President Nasser of Egypt dies of a heart attack.
October 8	Eminent Soviet writer and leading dissident Alexander Solzhenitsyn is awarded the Nobel Prize for literature.
October 14	North Vietnamese reject President Nixon's peace plan, offered a week earlier, which calls for a cease-fire in place.
October 15	Anwar el-Sadat wins popular election as president of Egypt.
November 9	Charles de Gaulle dies. In announcing the news, President Pompidou makes the memorable observation: "France is a widow."
December 7	In a continuing program of Ostpolitik, Willi Brandt signs a renunciation-of-force treaty with Poland.
December 14	After the Polish government announces basic price increases, workers in Gdansk riot and the outbreak spreads to other cities.
December 20	Władysław Gomułka is forced to resign as Polish first secretary; Edward Gierek succeeds him.

1971

February 8	With U.S. approval and support, South Vietnamese forces invade Laos to disrupt North Vietnamese supply lines.
April 6	In ping-pong diplomacy, the U.S. table-tennis team is invited to visit China, thus demonstrating the arrival of a possible new turn in U.S.-Chinese relations.

April 9	Soviet leadership calls for a "scientific-technical revolution" to produce higher educational levels, better economic performance, and greater preparedness in the armed forces.
May 3	Erich Honecker succeeds Walter Ulbricht as East German party general secretary.
May 27	USSR and Egypt sign a treaty proclaiming their friendship.
June 10	United States lifts its embargo on trade with China.
June 13	*New York Times* begins publication of the Pentagon Papers, containing secret details of the U.S. involvement in Vietnam.
July 15	President Nixon discloses the startling news that his security adviser, Henry Kissinger, has been negotiating in Beijing, preparing the way for a presidential visit in 1972.
September 3	The four occupying powers sign an agreement on Berlin.
September 13	Lin Biao, formerly designated successor to Mao Zedong and then opponent of Mao, is said to have died in an airplane crash while trying to flee China.
November 12	President Nixon announces a new cut of 45,000 U.S. troops in Vietnam, to be achieved by next February 1.
November 15	In his maiden speech to the General Assembly following the admission to the United Nations of the People's Republic of China, the chief of the Chinese delegation, Huang Hua, launches a ferocious attack on the United States, declares that his country will "liberate" Taiwan, and also makes general criticisms of Soviet policy.
December 17	Representatives of East and West Germany sign an accord guaranteeing West Germany free access to West Berlin by highway, rail, and canal.
December 26	United States resumes the bombing of North Vietnam.

1972

January 1	Kurt Waldheim of Austria succeeds U Thant as United Nations secretary-general.
January 22	In a meeting at Brussels, representatives of Western European countries sign an agreement increasing the membership of the European Economic Community from six to ten (the potential new members being

Britain, Denmark, Ireland, and Norway). In a referendum, however, Norwegian voters will turn down membership.

January 25	President Nixon introduces a Vietnam peace proposal that includes the withdrawal of all U.S. troops within six months in exchange for a cease-fire across Indochina and the release of all U.S. prisoners.
February 3	Communist representatives reply to Nixon's offer on Vietnam with a demand for complete withdrawal of all U.S. and UN forces by a date to be set.
February 21	Nixon arrives in China for a weeklong visit, ending 23 years' estrangement between the United States and the Communist government; leaders of the two countries pledge to work for the normalization of relations.
March 10	Lon Nol becomes head of state in Cambodia.
March 23	The on-and-off Vietnam peace talks in Paris take a new turn when the United States declares them suspended until Communist representatives are ready for what are called serious discussions.
March 30	North Vietnamese forces strike through the Demilitarized Zone in a major attack against the South; U.S. commanders retaliate by bombing supply facilities in the Hanoi and Haiphong areas.
April 4	In Stockholm, the perseverance of the Swedish Academy, which tries to send a representative to Moscow to present the 1970 Nobel Prize for literature to Alexander Solzhenitsyn, is frustrated by Soviet officials, who refuse to issue a visa for entry.
May 8	U.S. naval forces mine North Vietnamese ports and impose a blockade.
May 22	President Nixon arrives in Moscow for meetings with General Secretary Brezhnev; the visit will last until May 26, when Nixon and Soviet premier Kosygin sign the treaty known as SALT I, limiting various kinds of nuclear delivery systems.
June 17	In the early-morning hours, Washington police arrest a group of burglars who have broken into the headquarters of the Democratic National Committee in the Watergate complex.
July 18	President Sadat orders some 17,000 Soviet advisers to leave Egypt.
July 28	Returning to the United States from a trip to Hanoi, actress Jane Fonda declares that U.S. opponents of the war are "the real patriots."
August 12	Nixon announces the withdrawal of the last U.S. ground forces in Vietnam.

October 23	Americans suspend raids against North Vietnam.
October 26	North Vietnamese release a peace agreement drafted by their chief negotiator, Le Duc Tho, and U.S. national security adviser Henry Kissinger.
November 7	President Nixon defeats Democratic senator George McGovern of North Dakota in the U.S. presidential election, carrying every state except Massachusetts; the popular-vote count is 47.2 million to 29.1 million—the largest margin in history.
November 19	In West German elections, Social Democrat Willy Brandt, benefiting from the popularity of his Ostpolitik, returns to office as chancellor with an increased margin over the opposition Christian Democrats–Christian Socialists.
November 22	Preliminary conference on European security opens in Helsinki; this idea is strongly advocated by Soviet leader Leonid Brezhnev.
December 12	South Vietnamese president Thieu rejects the revised Kissinger–Le Duc Tho peace proposals.
December 18	U.S. bombers begin "Christmas raids" on Hanoi and Haiphong.
December 21	East and West Germany sign the Basic Treaty, establishing principles that are to govern relations between the two states.

1973

January 27	In Paris, the United States, South Vietnam, North Vietnam, and the National Liberation Front sign a peace agreement that is supposed to put an end to the Vietnam War.
January 30	Trial of the Watergate burglars concludes when final two defendants, G. Gordon Liddy and James McCord, are found guilty on all counts; the other five defendants had previously pled guilty.
January 31	Mutual and Balanced Forces Reduction talks between the United States and the Soviet Union open in Vienna; they will last for more than 15 years.
February 20	Cease-fire agreement is signed in Laos by its government and the Communist Pathet Lao.

February 22	Moving toward the normalization of diplomatic relations, the U.S. and Chinese governments announce plans to establish liaison offices in Washington and Beijing.
March 26	In the United States, Watergate conspirator James McCord implicates two important officials, John W. Dean and Jeb Stuart Magruder, in the Watergate affair, and two days later tells a U.S. Senate committee that former attorney general John Mitchell also had advance knowledge of the planned break-in.
March 29	The last detachment of U.S. troops leaves South Vietnam.
April 3	In a meeting at the Western White House in San Clemente, Calif., President Nixon promises South Vietnamese president Nguyen Van Thieu that the United States will continue to supply economic aid to South Vietnam.
April 27	In a renovation of the Soviet Communist Politburo, two conservatives are retired and Andrei Gromyko, Marshal Andrei Grechko, and Yuri Andropov become full members.
April 30	Following declarations by Nixon that any government employees indicted in connection with the Watergate affair will be discharged, Press Secretary Ron Ziegler announces that earlier presidential statements denying the involvement of any White House staff members are "inoperative." On this day three of the president's top aides resign: H. R. Haldeman, chief of staff; John Ehrlichman, assistant for domestic affairs; and John Dean, presidential counsel.
May 1	U.S. federal investigators announce the discovery of evidence linking Haldeman, Ehrlichman, Mitchell, and other White House and Republican officials to cover-up activities related to the Watergate burglary.
May 11	Federal judge dismisses all charges against Daniel Ellsberg and Anthony Russo, the defendants in the Pentagon Papers case.
	As an expression of Chancellor Willy Brandt's Ostpolitik, the West German Bundestag ratifies the treaty that establishes relations with East Germany (though it does not grant full recognition).
May 17	Chaired by Senator Sam J. Ervin, Jr. (Dem.-N.C.), the U.S. Senate Watergate Committee opens hearings.
May 19	West German chancellor Brandt and Soviet general secretary Brezhnev sign a series of agreements that provide for technical, cultural, and other forms of cooperation between West Germany and the USSR.

June 13	Negotiators for the United States, North Vietnam, South Vietnam, and the Vietcong agree to stop all violations of the Vietnam cease-fire accord.
June 16	Brezhnev arrives in Washington for a week long visit, during which he and President Nixon sign a pact on the prevention of nuclear war and agree to speed up the SALT II negotiations.
June 25	In testimony to the U.S. Senate Watergate Committee, John Dean declares that President Nixon has taken part in the Watergate cover-up since shortly after the break-in occurred.
July 16	In Watergate testimony, a former White House aide, Alexander Butterfield, creates a sensation by revealing that for more than two years President Nixon has recorded conversations in the Oval Office and his Executive Office Building quarters; thus begins a lengthy battle for control of these tapes.
	U.S. secretary of defense James Schlesinger confirms reports that in 1969 and 1970 the U.S. Air Force conducted secret bombing attacks on Cambodian targets.
July 17	In Afghanistan, Prime Minister Mohammed Daoud overthrows the monarchy and proclaims a republic.
July 21	France faces down worldwide protests to conduct a series of nuclear tests over a South Pacific atoll.
August 14	As required by Congress, U.S. bombing in Cambodia ends.
August 22	Nixon announces his nomination of Henry Kissinger as secretary of state; Kissinger's confirmation follows on September 21.
September 11	Chilean military junta leads a coup that overthrows the Marxist government of President Salvador Allende; Allende himself dies in the fighting, apparently by suicide.
September 18	UN General Assembly admits East and West Germany.
October 10	Implicated in financial scandals, U.S. vice president Spiro Agnew resigns his office.
October 12	President Nixon announces his nomination of Representative Gerald R. Ford (Rep.-Mich.) as the new vice president.
October 20	In the "Saturday Night Massacre," U.S. attorney general Elliot Richardson resigns after refusing to fire Watergate special prosecutor Archibald Cox; President Nixon fires Richardson's deputy, William

	Ruckelshaus; Solicitor General Robert H. Bork then fires Cox. Subsequently, Leon Jaworski becomes special prosecutor.
October 23	Having fought a long delaying action, Nixon through his attorney tells a federal judge he will release his office tapes to the court; later, however, the judge is told that two key tapes do not exist.
November 7	Both houses of the U.S. Congress override Nixon's veto of the War Powers Act, which puts limits on the president's ability to commit U.S. forces to combat without prior congressional authorization.
November 21	White House reveals the existence of an 18½-minute gap in an important Watergate tape—that of a conversation between the president and Haldeman three days after the break-in. In January 1974 a group of court-appointed technical experts will report that the gap is the product of repeated erasures and rerecordings and could hardly be the result of accident.

1974

January 19	People's Republic of China expels three Soviet diplomats accused of espionage.
February 7	Frustrated by a prolonged deadlock with the coal miners' union, British prime minister Edward Heath calls for a general election on February 28.
February 13	Soviet government reacts to the publication in the West of Alexander Solzhenitsyn's study of the prison-camp system, *The Gulag Archipelago,* by depriving him of his citizenship and exiling him.
March 4	Despite having failed to win a majority in the general election, the British Labour Party under Harold Wilson returns to power.
March 7	In the Watergate affair, a Washington, D.C., grand jury indicts a group of former top officials and presidential aides.
April 2	President Georges Pompidou of France dies after a long illness; he has served since June 1969.
April 25	Günther Guillaume, one of West German chancellor Willy Brandt's closest aides, is arrested after being revealed as an East German mole. West German security officers declare that, having discovered Guillaume's treachery, for the past year they have been feeding false information through him to his masters. Brandt resigns as West German

chancellor on May 6. Helmut Schmidt, a Social Democratic associate of Brandt, succeeds him on May 16.

May 19	Narrowly outpolling François Mitterrand in the voting, Valéry Giscard d'Estaing wins the runoff election to become president of France.
June 12–19	President Nixon tours the Middle East.
June 28–July 3	Nixon and Soviet general secretary Brezhnev meet in a Moscow summit marked by little progress in arms matters.
July 8	Prime Minister Pierre Elliott Trudeau's Liberal Party wins a majority in Canadian general election; for the previous two years Trudeau has governed at the head of a minority government.
July 24	U.S. Supreme Court rules that Watergate special prosecutor Leon Jaworski must have access to tapes and documents held by President Nixon.
July 27–30	House of Representatives Judiciary Committee votes articles of impeachment of President Nixon.
August 9	Richard M. Nixon becomes the first president of the United States to resign; Vice President Gerald Ford succeeds to the office.
August 15	Assassin fails to kill Park Chung Hee, the president of South Korea, but fatally wounds Park's wife.
September 4	President Ford appoints George H. W. Bush, chairman of the Republican National Committee, as U.S. liaison representative in China. United States opens diplomatic relations with the German Democratic Republic (East Germany); Ford appoints former senator from Kentucky and ambassador to India John Sherman Cooper to the new diplomatic post in East Berlin.
September 8	Saying that he wishes to avoid lengthy litigation and the national trauma that would accompany it, Ford issues an unconditional pardon to former president Nixon for any federal crimes he "committed or may have committed or taken part in"; the announcement creates widespread surprise and dismays Nixon's opponents.
October 10	Having gone to the country only eight months after the previous general election, Harold Wilson this time leads the British Labourites to a slim majority in the House of Commons.
November 23–24	Meeting at Vladivostok, President Ford and Soviet general secretary Brezhnev approve a draft agreement calling for the limitation of offensive nuclear weapons—SALT II.

1975

| January 7 | Beginning a victory campaign, the North Vietnamese easily defeat the South Vietnamese in Phuoc Long Province, some 75 miles from Saigon. |

| January 14 | With the USSR having rejected the tying of trade to emigration policy (a concept embodied in the Jackson-Vanik Amendment), the long-planned trading relationship between the United States and the Soviet Union is voided. |

| March 10 | North Vietnamese forces move south in a major invasion, capturing Ban Me Thuot in the Central Highlands in two days. The South Vietnamese retreat turns into a rout. |

| March 30 | North Vietnamese take Da Nang. |

| April 1 | President Lon Nol of Cambodia flees the country as Khmer Rouge forces move in. |

| April 5 | Chiang Kai-shek, the longtime Nationalist Chinese generalissimo, dies. |

| April 17 | Cambodian government surrenders to the Khmer Rouge. |

| April 21 | South Vietnamese president Nguyen Van Thieu resigns his office. |

| April 29–30 | In a frantically assembled operation, U.S. citizens and a limited number of Vietnamese are evacuated from Saigon. North Vietnamese tanks batter down the gates of the presidential palace in Saigon, putting both a literal and a symbolic end to the Vietnam War. |

| May 12 | Cambodian Communist gunboats seize a U.S. freighter, the *Mayaguez*. |

| May 14 | In a fierce battle, U.S. Marines free *Mayaguez* sailors captured by the Cambodians. |

| June 10 | Commission chaired by U.S. vice president Nelson Rockefeller reports that the Central Intelligence Agency has conducted a variety of illegal clandestine operations. The commission recommends that Congress create a joint "oversight" committee for intelligence. |

| August 1 | Representatives of 35 countries—Europe, East and West, Canada, and the United States—gather in Helsinki to sign the Helsinki Final Act of the Conference on Security and Cooperation in Europe, which had its first session in 1972; the agreement is widely regarded as a de facto World War II peace treaty. |

September 5	Lynette "Squeaky" Fromme, a bizarre follower of the convicted murderer Charles Manson, makes an apparent attempt to assassinate U.S. president Ford.
September 22	In San Francisco, President Ford escapes safely from a second assassination attempt when a bystander hits the arm of Sara Jane Moore as she fires at the president.
October 9	Andrei Sakharov, Soviet nuclear physicist and political activist, is awarded the Nobel Peace Prize.
November 1	In the "Halloween massacre," President Ford dismisses Secretary of Defense James Schlesinger and CIA director William Colby and replaces Henry Kissinger with Lieutenant General Brent Scowcroft as national security adviser; Kissinger remains as secretary of state. Ford also nominates former Republican national chairman George Bush as director of the Central Intelligence Agency; Donald Rumsfeld will become secretary of defense. Vice President Rockefeller declares, at Ford's request, that he will not be a candidate for vice president in the 1976 election.
November 12	Soviet authorities refuse to grant Andrei Sakharov a visa for travel to Oslo to receive the Nobel Peace Prize. Unlike Solzhenitsyn in 1972, however, Sakharov possesses classified information the Soviets want to protect.
November 20	Generalissimo Francisco Franco, ruler of Spain since the civil war of the 1930s, dies in Madrid.
November 21	U.S. Senate committee investigating the CIA (Church Committee) reports that the agency was involved in a variety of assassination plots against foreign leaders, notably Cuba's Fidel Castro; the source of the orders for these attempts, however, remains unclear.
November 26	Portuguese government forces put down an uprising by left-oriented paratroopers and other soldiers that began the previous day.
December 4	U.S. Senate intelligence committee reports that, though not having evidence of direct CIA participation in the coup against President Allende of Chile, it believes that the agency created the "atmosphere" that made it possible.
December 10	In Oslo, Elena Bonner, wife of Andrei Sakharov, receives the Nobel Peace Prize for her husband.
December 19	U.S. Senate votes to cease the funding of support for the Unita group in the Angolan civil war.

1976

January 8	Chinese premier Zhou Enlai dies.
January 20	In the United States, newspaper accounts based on a leaked House of Representatives intelligence-committee report declare that the secrecy with which intelligence agencies operate removes them from congressional scrutiny.
January 27	Concerned about politicization of the Central Intelligence Agency in light of the 1975 investigations, the U.S. Senate confirms George Bush as director of the agency after he promises not to become a vice presidential candidate.
February 17	Following review of the CIA investigations, President Ford announces a large-scale reorganization of the agency, including new operating guidelines and the establishment of an independent supervisory board.
March 15	Egyptian government cancels the 1971 friendship treaty with the Soviet Union.
March 16	Harold Wilson surprises supporters and opponents alike by resigning as British prime minister.
April 5	James Callaghan, foreign secretary in the Wilson cabinet, wins in Labour Party balloting to choose a new party leader and thus succeeds Wilson as British prime minister.
April 26–28	U.S. Senate intelligence committee reports on foreign, military, and domestic intelligence operations call for fundamental reforms and new charters for U.S. agencies. On May 19 the Senate will vote to establish a permanent "oversight" committee.
May 28	In Moscow, President Ford and General Secretary Brezhnev sign a treaty imposing limits on the size of underground nuclear explosions used for peaceful purposes, despite criticism of such agreements from Ford's rival in the presidential primaries, California's Republican former governor Ronald Reagan.
June 24	Polish government plan for major increases in food prices sets off riots; next day, behind a screen of equivocation, the government cancels the increases.
July 2	Former separate states of North and South Vietnam are officially reunited, with Hanoi as the capital.

September 9	Mao Zedong dies. "In homes all over China," writes a Western historian, "the ancestral tablets . . . had been removed from their places of honor and replaced by images or portraits of Mao Tse-tung."
October 3	In a close election, Helmut Schmidt's coalition retains power in West Germany.
October 12	Chinese reports, later confirmed, describe the arrest of the Gang of Four, including Mao's widow, Jian Qing; the Chinese Communist Party is now headed by Hua Kuo-feng.
November 2	In the U.S. presidential election, Georgia's Democratic former governor Jimmy Carter, a newcomer to national politics, defeats President Ford by 40.1 million popular votes to 39.1 million; the electoral race is close, 297 to 240 (one staunch elector casts his ballot for Ronald Reagan).

1977

January 1	Czechoslovak dissenters issue human rights and freedoms manifesto, Charter 77; it is smuggled into West Germany on January 6.
January 21	On his first full day in office, President Jimmy Carter pardons all Vietnam War draft resisters.
February 17	Letter of encouragement from President Carter is delivered to Soviet dissident Andrei Sakharov.
March 17	Having previously spoken of his concern for human rights, Carter, in an address to the United Nations, declares that such considerations will play an important part in the formulation of U.S. policy.
March 24	United States and Cuba have governmental contact for the first time since the suspension of diplomatic relations.
	General Secretary Brezhnev becomes president of the USSR, in succession to Nikolai Podgorny; Brezhnev remains general secretary of the Communist Party of the Soviet Union.
April 9	Spanish government of King Juan Carlos legalizes the Communist Party.
May 25	Chinese Communist government repeals its ban on performances of Shakespearean plays.
June 30	U.S. president Carter, stating his preference for cruise missiles, declares his opposition to production of the controversial B-1 bomber.

August 18	Chinese Communist Party adopts a new constitution.
September 1	World Psychiatric Association censures *psykhushka*, the Soviet practice popular in the Brezhnev era of imprisoning dissidents in psychiatric hospitals.
September 12	United Nations awards a peace medal to Soviet president Leonid Brezhnev.
September 25	Pol Pot, a possible all-time champion in the field of violence administered per capita, is proclaimed head of Cambodia's revolutionary government.
September 27	Picking up negotiations toward SALT II, President Carter and Soviet foreign minister Gromyko outline a basis for a treaty.
October 9	Negotiators for the USSR and China agree on terms for navigation in the contested Ussuri River area.
November 19	Egypt's President Sadat begins his historic visit to Israel to meet with Prime Minister Menachem Begin; Sadat calls for "peace with justice" between the two countries.

1978

January 6	President Carter returns from an Asian and European trip marked by a translator's bungle in Warsaw, when Carter was mistakenly said to speak of the "lusts" rather than the "desires" of the Polish people.
March 5	China adopts a new constitution, replacing the 1975 constitution, that seems to lessen the previous emphasis on ideology; the same meeting of the People's Congress dissolves the revolutionary committees established in the 1960s by Chairman Mao.
March 16	Members of the Italian Red Brigades kidnap Aldo Moro, chairman of the Christian Democrats and former premier.
April 7	President Carter orders suspension of the development of the neutron (enhanced-radiation) bomb, which has not found favor with the NATO countries in which it would be deployed.
April 10	United Nations announces that Undersecretary-General for Political and Security Council Affairs Arkady Shevchenko has defected from the Soviet Union. In actuality, weary of being "as obedient to the system as a robot to its master," Shevchenko has for some years worked with

U.S. intelligence agencies. Understandably, the Soviets insist that he be replaced as undersecretary-general.

April 27 — Afghan leftists led by Noor Mohammed Taraki overthrow and then murder President Mohammed Daoud.

May 9 — Italian security forces find Aldo Moro's body in a parked car in Rome; he and his bodyguards have all been shot.

June 7 — Discussing the unsatisfactory state of Soviet-U.S. relations and its negative effect on arms-limitation negotiations, President Carter declares in a major speech at the Naval Academy commencement ceremonies that "détente must be broadly defined and truly reciprocal," with both countries exercising restraint in trouble spots.

June 8–9 — Admiral Stansfield Turner, director of the Central Intelligence Agency, tells congressional committees that rebels invading the Shaba Province of Zaire were trained and equipped by Cuba; Cuban leader Fidel Castro later denies any involvement.

July 13 — The weakened association of China and Albania, earlier united in their opposition to Soviet policies, comes to an end as the Chinese announce the halting of aid. Unlike China, Albania, led by First Secretary Enver Hoxha, continues a policy of unrelenting hostility to the USSR. Curiously, Albania, though the recipient of aid, seems at least partially to have taken the initiative to cut it off.

September 5 — President Carter, Israeli prime minister Menachem Begin, and Egyptian president Anwar el-Sadat meet at Camp David in Maryland to discuss peace between the two Middle Eastern countries.

September 7 — In London, a Bulgarian secret-police agent shoots Georgi Markov, a defector from Bulgaria, with a pellet from what is ostensibly an ordinary umbrella; four days later Markov, a Bulgarian defector and broadcaster for Radio Free Europe, dies. Similar incidents follow with other Bulgarian exiles.

September 17 — Begin and Sadat sign the Camp David Accords, intended to establish a framework for peace.

October 16 — Roman Catholic College of Cardinals elects a Polish cardinal, Karol Wojtyla, to succeed Pope John Paul I, who died unexpectedly on September 28. The new pope, who takes the name John Paul II, is the first non-Italian to hold the papacy since the 16th century.

November 6 — Increasing violence leads the shah of Iran to institute martial law.

December 15 — President Carter announces the institution of normal diplomatic relations between the United States and the People's Republic of China.

| December 25 | Vietnamese forces invade Cambodia with the aim of destroying the Khmer Rouge regime and creating a "friendly" government for the country. |

1979

January 1	United States and the People's Republic of China establish normal diplomatic relations. On January 31 President Carter and the Chinese deputy premier (but chief figure), Deng Xiaoping, will sign agreements for scientific and cultural exchanges.
January 7	Phnom Penh, capital of Cambodia, is taken by Vietnamese forces, supported by Cambodian exiles.
January 16	After weeks of upheaval, the shah flees Iran; his chief opponent, the Ayatollah Khomeini, returns home to assume the spiritual and political direction of the country.
February 27	Heavy border fighting breaks out between Vietnam and China.
March 13	In a move that will have international repercussions more than four years later, Maurice Bishop stages a coup in Grenada.
March 26	Israel and Egypt sign a peace treaty.
March 28	Seemingly endless strikes undermine British prime minister James Callaghan, whose government loses a vote of confidence in the House of Commons.
	In the United States, an accident occurs at the nuclear power plant at Three Mile Island, Pa.
May 3	Conservatives, led by Margaret Thatcher, win an impressive victory in the British general election; she becomes the first woman prime minister of any European country.
June 2	Pope John Paul II receives a thunderous welcome on the first of his papal visits to Poland, his homeland.
June 7	President Carter approves the development of the MX missile.
June 18	Carter and Soviet president Leonid Brezhnev sign the SALT II treaty in a meeting at Vienna.
July 17	Sandinista guerrilla forces take control of Nicaragua; President Somoza resigns and flees the country.

August 15	Reprimanded for having met with a member of the Palestine Liberation Organization, the U.S. ambassador to the United Nations, Andrew Young, resigns.
October 6	Speaking in East Berlin, President Brezhnev announces a Soviet plan to withdraw some 20,000 troops from East Germany during the coming year.
October 26	South Korea's President Park Chung Hee is assassinated.
November 4	Iranian crowds seize the U.S. embassy in Tehran and make hostages of the staff and families.
November 15	Prime Minister Margaret Thatcher tells the House of Commons that in 1964, after being given immunity from prosecution, Anthony Blunt, Surveyor of the Queen's Pictures, confessed to having been a KGB agent.
December 12	In one of the more strenuous Western defense debates in some years, France and Greece refuse to accept the installation of U.S. cruise missiles, while the other NATO members agree to their deployment.
December 27	President Hafizullah Amin of Afghanistan is overthrown in a coup and murdered; invading Soviet forces support the new government. This development marks the definitive end of U.S.-Soviet détente. The Chinese government issues its own demand for Soviet withdrawal from Afghanistan.

1980

January 4	In response to the Soviet invasion of Afghanistan, President Carter declares a U.S. embargo on sales of technology to the USSR and sharply cuts grain sales; the day before, he asked Congress to put aside for the present the ratification of SALT II.
January 24	In another response to matters in Afghanistan, Carter expresses interest in selling arms to China.
February 4	Turning his hostility for the moment away from the United States, the Ayatollah Khomeini condemns the Soviet invasion of Afghanistan.
March 24	Archbishop Oscar Romero is assassinated in San Salvador as he says mass at a hospital chapel. In violence that breaks out at his funeral, 26 people will be killed and many more wounded.

Chronology 1980

April 7	United States breaks diplomatic relations with the revolutionary government of Iran, where militants have held hostages in the U.S. embassy since November 4, 1979.
April 22	In accordance with President Carter's wish (as originally expressed on January 20), the U.S. Olympic Committee protests the Soviet invasion of Afghanistan by voting a boycott of the forthcoming Olympic Games in Moscow; 61 other countries will join the boycott.
April 24	Ill-conceived U.S. attempt to rescue the hostages in the Tehran embassy is aborted because of equipment failure and the collision of aircraft.
April 28	U.S. secretary of state Cyrus Vance resigns in protest of the failed rescue raid in Iran (he submitted his resignation before the launching of the operation).
May 4	Yugoslavia's President Tito dies. Without his strong dictatorial hand at the helm, Yugoslavia in the following years will see disintegration and continuing war.
August 14	Beginning in Gdansk, workers in Poland go on strike, demanding the right to create independent labor unions. With Lech Wałesa, a shipyard worker, playing a leading part, the trade union Solidarity is born.
August 30	Polish government's agreement to allow the creation of independent unions leads Solidarity to call an end to the strike.
September 6	In Poland, Stanislaw Kania becomes Communist Party first secretary, replacing Edward Gierek, who came to the position during labor strife a decade earlier.
October 5	West German general elections continue Helmut Schmidt in power as chancellor.
October 20	After six years outside the military framework of the North Atlantic Treaty Organization, Greece returns.
October 23	Long ailing, Soviet premier Kosygin retires; Nicolai Tikhonov succeeds him.
November 4	Ronald Reagan, the Republican challenger of Jimmy Carter, wins election as president of the United States, with a popular vote of 43.9 million to Carter's 35.5 million; the electoral count is 489 to 49. An independent candidate, John Anderson, receives 5.7 million votes.
December 13	José Napoleon Duarte, civilian—and thus a rarity in power in El Salvador—becomes president.

| December 14 | Mindful of the Warsaw Pact invasion of Czechoslovakia in 1968 to crush the Prague Spring, NATO members warn the Soviet government that intervention in Poland would "fundamentally alter the entire international situation." |

1981

January 18	U.S. and Iranian negotiators sign agreement to exchange U.S. hostages in Tehran for Iranian assets frozen in the United States.
January 20	Ronald Reagan takes office as the 40th president of the United States.
January 24	Obeying the call of Solidarity, millions of Polish workers go on strike again, with the goal of obtaining a five-day workweek.
February 11	General Wojciech Jaruzelski becomes premier of Poland. Next day, desperately needing labor peace to shore up the economy and fend off Soviet intervention, he asks workers not to strike for three months.
March 2	President Reagan announces his support (accompanied by military supplies) of the president of El Salvador, José Napoleon Duarte, against leftist guerrillas.
March 30	Reagan is wounded in an assassination attempt by a demented lone gunman (the president will be released from the hospital just 12 days later).
April 1	Reagan administration suspends aid to Nicaraguan Sandinistas, accusing them of supporting rebels in El Salvador.
April 17	Polish farmers now join workers in having the right to form an independent (nongovernmental) union.
May 13	Mehmet Ali Ağca, a Turkish gunman, severely wounds Pope John Paul II, an icon of the Polish Solidarity movement. Later investigation indicates the would-be assassin has ties to the Bulgarian secret police.
June 16	U.S. secretary of state Alexander Haig declares that, in a reversal of existing policy, the United States will now sell arms to China.
August 8	President Reagan orders the production of neutron bombs; the weapons are to be stockpiled in the United States.
September 18	Moscow warns the Polish government to crack down on the Solidarity union for what it calls an anti-Soviet campaign.

October 6	Fundamentalist Muslim Egyptian army officers assassinate President Sadat at a military review; next day Vice President Hosni Mubarak succeeds as president.
October 10	In Bonn, some 250,000 West Germans protest the planned deployment in Europe of U.S. cruise missiles.
October 18	In Poland, General Jaruzelski becomes head of the Communist Party as well as head of the government.
November 30	United States and the USSR begin discussions on a possible treaty to limit intermediate-range nuclear missiles.
December 13	In Poland, Jaruzelski institutes martial law and arrests members of the labor union Solidarity. Several striking coal miners in Silesia are killed. Though the Reagan administration declares that Jaruzelski has the "support of the Soviet Union," many observers will say that he has acted to head off Soviet intervention.

1982

January 1	Javier Pérez de Cuéllar of Peru takes office as secretary-general of the United Nations, in succession to Kurt Waldheim. Like Waldheim, he will serve in the office for ten years.
January 11	North Atlantic Treaty Organization condemns the USSR for its support of Prime Minister Jaruzelski's crackdown in Poland.
January 25	Mikhail Suslov dies; he was a little-known but highly influential ideological arbiter of the Communist Party of the Soviet Union.
January 28	After 42 days in the hands of Italian Red Brigades elements, a U.S. officer, Brigadier General James L. Dozier, is freed when police storm the apartment in Padua where he is being held.
March 8	United States charges that Soviet troops are using poison gas on Afghans; some 3,000 are said to have been killed.
March 25	Declaring that the country faces U.S. aggression, the Sandinista government of Nicaragua suspends civil rights for 30 days.
March 29	In general elections in El Salvador, President José Napoleon Duarte's Christian Democrats win a plurality; the high turnout of voters represents a rebuff of leftist guerrillas, who have sought through violence to keep the people from validating the election by voting in it.

April 28	Polish government announces its relaxation of martial-law restrictions, with the release of 800 persons who were detained.
May 26	Yuri Andropov, director of the KGB since 1967, resigns to move into a politically more promising position as secretary in charge of ideology for the Communist Party of the Soviet Union Central Committee; this move has become possible because of the recent death of Mikhail Suslov, no admirer of Andropov.
May 30	Though the U.S. Senate has never ratified SALT II, the United States, under both Presidents Carter and Reagan, has abided by its terms; Reagan now declares that the United States will continue to do so as long as the Soviet Union does the same.
June 15	Soviet spokesmen tell the United Nations that in a conflict the USSR will not engage in the "first use" of nuclear weapons.
June 29	U.S. and Soviet negotiators resume arms talks in Geneva.
July 21	Polish government frees 1,227 more detainees.
August 13	Though Solidarity is now banned in Poland, it displays strength from underground by staging a large-scale march in Gdansk that is attacked by riot police.
August 31	Commemorating the second anniversary of the 1980 Gdansk strike, Solidarity conducts demonstrations in Warsaw and other Polish cities; riot police are again called into action.
October 1	West German chancellor Helmut Schmidt loses a vote of confidence in the Bundestag. Helmut Kohl succeeds him.
November 10	Soviet president Brezhnev dies after a long illness.
November 12	Central Committee of the Communist Party of the Soviet Union elects Yuri Andropov, until recently chairman of the KGB, as general secretary in succession to Brezhnev.
December 4	Chinese National People's Congress adopts a new constitution for the country; the president will now be elected.
December 7	U.S. House of Representatives votes down one billion dollars sought by the Reagan administration for development of the MX intercontinental ballistic missile (ICBM), originally approved for development by President Carter.
December 9	Foreign ministers of the NATO powers vote support for the installation of cruise and Pershing missiles in Europe during the coming year; the

decision can be reconsidered, however, if the West reaches an arms agreement with Warsaw Pact countries.

December 12   In Poland, Prime Minister Jaruzelski lifts some of the martial-law restrictions imposed in December 1981.

1983

January 20–21   French president Mitterrand and German chancellor Kohl express their agreement for the "zero option" on arms development in Europe.

January 25   Probably wishing to avoid the creation of Maoist martyrs, the Chinese government commutes the death sentences of the Gang of Four to life imprisonment.

February 2   Strategic Arms Reduction Talks (START) between the United States and the USSR resume in Geneva.

February 8   Second so-called follow-up Conference on Security and Cooperation in Europe talks open in Madrid.

March 6   In West German elections, the Christian Democratic Party, with its allied Christian Social Union, wins 244 seats in the Bundestag, defeating the Social Democrats, who take 193 seats; on March 29 Helmut Kohl is formally elected chancellor.

March 7   Summit meeting of nonaligned states, with Indian leader Indira Gandhi presiding, opens in New Delhi.

March 23   U.S. president Reagan announces his support for a new and controversial concept of national defense, the Strategic Defense Initiative.

March 30   Reagan reveals a U.S. proposal to limit the deployment in Europe of cruise and Pershing missiles if the Soviets make reciprocal moves.

April 1   In England, thousands of protesters form a 14-mile human chain between weapons facilities and Greenham Common, where U.S. cruise missiles are to be installed.

April 2   Soviet foreign minister Gromyko rejects President Reagan's March 30 proposal concerning intermediate-range missiles.

April 5   French government expels 47 Soviet officials, ostensibly diplomats, as intelligence agents seeking scientific secrets.

April 7	Chinese government cancels sports and other contacts with the United States to protest the U.S. grant of asylum to a defecting woman tennis player.
April 18	In Beirut, a terrorist bomb explosion at the U.S. embassy kills some 60 persons and wounds twice as many.
May 4	U.S. House of Representatives votes its formal, though nonbinding, support for a nuclear freeze and for reduction in nuclear stockpiles.
	Iranian government outlaws the Tudeh (Communist) Party.
May 28	Heads of the Western "seven" industrialized nations (a group actually including one non-Western country, Japan), meeting at Williamsburg, Va., endorse Intermediate Nuclear Forces (INF) arms-control negotiations.
June 5	Nicaragua expels three U.S. diplomats after accusing them of attempting to murder (by poisoning) the Nicaraguan foreign minister.
June 6	Soviet Union and Finland renew their 1948 friendship treaty for a further 20 years.
June 9	In British general election, Margaret Thatcher's Conservatives win a large majority in the House of Commons (397 seats to Labour's 209).
June 16	Supreme Soviet elects General Secretary Andropov as chairman of the Presidium—president of the USSR.
	Pope John Paul II begins a second visit to Poland; he will meet with and reaffirm support for Solidarity leader Lech Wałesa.
June 18	Chinese National People's Congress elects Li Xianian president of the People's Republic of China. More importantly, Deng Xiaoping becomes chairman of the Central Military Committee.
June 26	Christian Democrats lose ground in Italian elections but remain the largest party in Parliament.
July 17	Contadora group leaders (the presidents of Colombia, Mexico, Panama, and Venezuela) call for the removal of all foreign military advisers and troops from Central America.
July 18	President Reagan appoints former secretary of state Henry Kissinger chairman of a newly established committee on U.S. policy in Central America.

July 20	In a close vote (220 to 217) the U.S. House of Representatives authorizes $2.5 billion for development of the MX ICBM. Six days later the missile has an easier time in the Senate (58 to 41).
July 21	Prime Minister Jaruzelski lifts martial law in Poland.
August 3	U.S. government announces military aid for the Republic of Chad.
August 12	In a Cabinet reorganization, Canadian prime minister Trudeau removes Gilles Lamontagne as defense minister.
August 25	United States and the Soviet Union sign a five-year grain agreement.
September 1	Soviet interceptor shoots down KAL 007, a Korean civilian airliner, in Soviet airspace inland from the Sea of Japan.
September 26	Speaking at the UN General Assembly, President Reagan advances new Intermediate Nuclear Forces (INF) proposals.
October 4	Reagan produces new disarmament proposals under which deployment of new strategic-missile warheads would be more than offset by the scrapping of two existing warheads.
October 17	Robert "Bud" McFarlane becomes Reagan's assistant for national security affairs, in succession to William Clark.
October 22	Crowds in Western European capitals protest the planned installation of U.S. intermediate-range missiles; the total to be deployed is 572.
October 23	Terrorist truck bomb destroys U.S. Marine headquarters in Beirut; another attack destroys barracks occupied by French paratroopers. Deaths total almost 300.
October 25	U.S. forces invade Caribbean republic of Grenada, following the murders on October 19 of the prime minister, Maurice Bishop, and other officials.
October 31	U.S. cruise missiles, the subjects of great controversy, begin arriving in England.
November 2	UN General Assembly votes, 108 to 9 (with 27 abstentions), disapproval of the U.S. invasion of Grenada.
November 4	Declaring North Korea responsible for an explosion in Rangoon that killed four South Korean officials and others, Burma breaks diplomatic relations with North Korea.
November 22	West German government approves the installation of cruise and Pershing II missiles in West Germany.

November 24	Soviet participants in Intermediate Nuclear Forces (INF) negotiations in Geneva walk out of the talks to protest the sending of U.S. missiles to Western Europe.
November 30	By pocket veto, President Reagan rejects legislation linking U.S. military aid to El Salvador to progress concerning human rights.

1984

January 11	U.S. Kissinger Commission calls for a comprehensive approach to economic development in Central America and sees a serious threat to U.S. security in Soviet and Cuban involvement in the region.
January 12	On a visit to Washington, Premier Zhao Ziyang of China signs an agreement with the United States on industrial cooperation.
January 17	Conference on Confidence- and Security-Building Measures in Europe, attended by representatives of 35 countries, opens in Stockholm. The stated objective is to search for ways to reduce the risk of war in Europe.
February 9	Long-ailing Soviet general secretary Yuri Andropov dies.
February 13	In a turn back toward the Brezhnev era, the Communist Party of the Soviet Union Central Committee chooses Konstantin Chernenko, a close Brezhnev associate, as Andropov's successor as general secretary. In his acceptance speech Chernenko, although making conciliatory remarks, declares that no power will be allowed to upset the "military equilibrium" that has been achieved.
February 19	Canadian prime minister Pierre Trudeau announces his intention to retire after 15 years (except for a nine-month interlude) in office.
April 4	President Reagan advocates a "comprehensive worldwide ban" on chemical weapons.
April 10	U.S. Senate adopts (84 to 12) a nonbinding resolution condemning U.S. participation in the mining of Nicaraguan harbors; two days later the House of Representatives joins in the condemnation (281 to 111).
April 11	In Moscow, the Supreme Soviet elects General Secretary Chernenko head of state (chairman of the Presidium).
May 6	José Duarte defeats a right-wing candidate to win reelection as president of El Salvador.

May 8	Retaliating for the 1980 U.S.-led boycott of the Moscow Olympics, the Soviet Union announces its withdrawal from the summer games, to be held in Los Angeles; in the following weeks other Eastern Bloc countries join the boycott.
May 16	U.S. State Department denounces the Soviet government's treatment of Andrei Sakharov, Soviet physicist, longtime dissident, and winner of the 1975 Nobel Peace Prize, who has entered on a hunger strike to publicize his demand for adequate medical treatment for his wife.
June 10	Published report of the Italian state prosecutor declares that the Bulgarian secret service played a part in the 1981 assassination attempt on Pope John Paul II.
July 14	United States and the USSR agree to update the hot line linking Washington and Moscow.
September 4	Led by Brian Mulroney, the Progressive Conservative Party sweeps to an overwhelming victory in the Canadian national election; the winners take 211 seats in the House of Commons to 40 for the Liberals, long the dominant party.
October 20	Chinese government, with Deng Xiaoping as the key figure, announces plans to relax state economic controls and move toward free-market policies.
November 6	Ronald Reagan wins reelection as U.S. president, overwhelming Walter Mondale, a former vice president (1977–81), in both the electoral vote (525 to 13) and the popular vote (54.2 million to 37.4 million); Reagan's popular total is the highest any candidate has ever received. The Democratic ticket has historic significance, however, because of its inclusion of New York representative Geraldine Ferraro, the first woman on a national ticket of any major party.
December 3	Herbert Blaize, regarded as a moderate, is chosen prime minister of Grenada.
December 15	Mikhail Gorbachev, considered by some knowledgeable observers as the probable next leader of the Soviet Union, arrives in Britain for a visit. During his six-day stay he makes a highly favorable impression on his hosts, winning from Prime Minister Margaret Thatcher a judgment that will become famous: "I like Mr. Gorbachev—we can do business together."
December 19	Britain and China sign an agreement transferring Hong Kong to Chinese sovereignty, effective in 1997, thus bringing to an end British control that had been assumed in stages during the 19th century.

December 19   United States announces its withdrawal from the controversial United Nations Educational, Scientific and Cultural Organization (UNESCO), which it accuses of mismanagement and "hostility toward the institutions of a free society."

THE TIME OF RESTRUCTURING

1985

January 7–8   In discussions at Geneva, U.S. and Soviet representatives decide to resume arms-reduction negotiations, even though the United States has not agreed to stop the installation of medium-range missiles in Western Europe.

February 4   U.S. government reveals that, despite the alliance with New Zealand and Australia, the "antinuclear" New Zealand government has refused to allow a U.S. destroyer to visit a New Zealand port.

February 15   In Cambodia, invading Vietnamese troops capture and burn the headquarters of the Khmer Rouge.

February 20   In a speech to a joint session of the U.S. Congress, Margaret Thatcher points to growing Western military strength and declares her support for President Reagan's Strategic Defense Initiative, popularly named "Star Wars."

March 10   After little more than a year in office, Soviet general secretary Chernenko dies.

March 11   In a fateful election, the Communist Party of the Soviet Union Central Committee chooses Mikhail Gorbachev as general secretary; a vigorous 54, he presents a striking contrast with his two immediate predecessors and is the youngest Soviet leader since Joseph Stalin's early days.

March 28   Close vote in the U.S. House of Representatives completes congressional approval of funding for new MX missiles.

April 8   Soviet general secretary Gorbachev announces that the USSR will suspend the deployment of SS-20 (intermediate-range) missiles in Europe and asks the United States to reciprocate.

April 23   Reporting to the Communist Party of the Soviet Union Central Committee, Gorbachev makes the first of his many calls for the restructuring—perestroika—of the Soviet economy. Later, this term will take on wider meanings.

May 16	Reacting to the ravages of alcoholism in the USSR, the Soviet government announces the details of an extensive antialcohol campaign; Gorbachev's associate Yegor Ligachev is the leading sponsor of the endeavor.
May 20	In what proves to be one of the major spy cases of the Cold War, the FBI arrests John Anthony Walker, Jr., a retired navy warrant officer, who since 1968 has delivered top-level cipher secrets to the Soviets. The arrests of Walker's son and brother follow within a few days.
	United States inaugurates Radio Martí, a broadcasting service aimed at Cuba, named for a 19th-century fighter for Cuban independence from Spain.
June 10	President Reagan announces that the United States will continue to respect the provisions of SALT II, even though the Senate has never ratified this treaty.
June 11	In an important speech to a Communist Party of the Soviet Union Central Committee conference, Gorbachev calls for thorough reforms to overhaul the Soviet economy.
July 2	Veteran Soviet foreign minister Andrei Gromyko is moved up to the largely ceremonial presidency of the USSR; Eduard Shevardnadze succeeds him at the Foreign Ministry.
July 13	For eight hours, while U.S. president Reagan is in colon surgery and recovery, Vice President Bush exercises presidential power.
July 19	Eluding surveillance, a top-ranking Soviet KGB officer, Oleg Gordievsky, who has actually worked for British intelligence since 1974, begins an escape from the USSR that within a few days puts him in the West.
August 25	In a growing espionage scandal, West German police arrest one of President Richard von Weizsäcker's secretaries as an East German spy; a month later a secretary to Chancellor Helmut Kohl defects to East Germany.
September 27	Nikolai Ryzhkov succeeds Nikolai Tikhonov as premier (chairman of the Council of Ministers) of the USSR.
October 15	President Daniel Ortega, leader of the Sandinistas, announces the suspension of civil rights in Nicaragua.
November 19	President Reagan and General Secretary Gorbachev begin a three-day summit meeting in Geneva, the first meeting between U.S. and Soviet leaders since 1979. Much of the discussion is devoted to arms limitation.

December 24   Boris Yeltsin becomes first secretary of the Moscow Communist Party
                     Committee.

1986

February 25   In a major speech to the participants in the 27th Congress of the Com-
                     munist Party of the Soviet Union, General Secretary Gorbachev calls
                     for radical economic reforms.

April 26   At a nuclear power station at Chernobyl, in the Ukraine, an explosion
                     and fire in a reactor core create deadly radioactive clouds that spread
                     across Europe.

May 14   Sidestepping his policy of openness—glasnost—Gorbachev attacks
                     Western countries for their criticism of the Soviet Union in the wake
                     of the Chernobyl disaster.

August 23   FBI agents charge Gennadi Zakharov, a Soviet physicist on the staff of
                     the United Nations, with espionage.

August 30   In a riposte to the arrest of Zakharov, KGB operatives in Moscow pick
                     up an American correspondent, Nicholas Daniloff of *U.S. News &
                     World Report,* accusing him of espionage. The arrest arouses a fire-
                     storm of criticism in the United States.

September 21   Representatives of each side at a meeting of NATO and Warsaw Pact
                     powers reach an agreement to give the other notice of important mili-
                     tary maneuvers.

September 26   U.S. government expels 25 Soviet nationals on the UN staff.

September 29   After U.S.-Soviet negotiations, alleged spies Zakharov and Daniloff
                     are, in effect, swapped.

October   Reagan and Gorbachev meet in a summit at Reykjavík. The meetings
10–12   seem marked by a new spirit that arouses great interest and expecta-
                     tions but end with no arms agreements.

November 13   White House officials give congressional leaders the news that Reagan
                     administration representatives have attempted to obtain the release of
                     U.S. hostages in Lebanon by secretly selling arms to the revolutionary
                     government of Iran, believed to control the groups holding the hos-
                     tages.

November 25   White House admits that money received in the arms deal with Iran (perhaps as much as $30 million) has been used to provide military supplies to the Nicaraguan contras.

December 16   Though having expressed no previous sympathy for the imprisoned dissident scientist Andrei Sakharov, Gorbachev causes a sensation by telephoning the prisoner to tell him he is now free.

1987

January 16   Following large pro-democracy demonstrations in major cities, Chinese Communist Party general secretary Hu Yaobang resigns.

January 27   Attacking "inertia" and "social corrosion," Soviet general secretary Gorbachev introduces a plan for political reform, which includes such innovations as competing candidates and the secret ballot.

February 27   Tower Commission (chaired by former Republican senator John G. Tower of Texas), appointed to examine the Iran-contra affair, criticizes President Reagan's "management style," finding that he "did not seem to be aware of the way in which the operation was implemented."

February 28   In a revised approach to arms-control discussions, Gorbachev suggests that negotiators deal with medium-range missiles separately from strategic missiles.

March 6   Politburo member Yegor Ligachev, though considered a close associate of Gorbachev, declares that criticism of the Soviet past must not become excessive.

May 5   U.S. Congress begins hearings on the Iran-Contra affair. The first witness, Major General Richard Secord, declares that CIA director William J. Casey and other high government officials were involved in the arrangement.

May 6   CIA director Casey dies.

May 15   Reagan admits knowledge and support of nongovermental efforts to provide aid to the contras.

May 26   FBI director William H. Webster takes office as director of the Central Intelligence Agency (former senator Tower having declined the White House offer of the post).

May 28   A 19-year-old West German, Mathias Rust, amazes the world and embarrasses Kremlin officials by flying a light single-engine airplane (a

Cessna 172) from Helsinki through Soviet air defenses and into Red Square in Moscow; Gorbachev responds by dismissing various top defense officials.

June 11   Prime Minister Margaret Thatcher leads the Conservatives to a third straight victory in the British general elections, a feat not equaled by such predecessors as Gladstone, Disraeli, and the younger William Pitt.

June 14   Beginning his third papal visit to Poland, John Paul II stirs great popular enthusiasm and expresses strong support for the Solidarity union. Behind-the-scenes Soviet KGB attempts to discredit the pope after his earlier visits have obviously failed.

June 25   At a Communist Party of the Soviet Union Central Committee meeting, Gorbachev presents a program of economic reform, which next day receives the committee's approval.

July 8   Former National Security Council staff member Marine Lieutenant Colonel Oliver L. North tells U.S. congressional Iran-contra investigators that the late CIA director, William J. Casey, helped provide secret military aid to the contras.

July 15   Rear Admiral John M. Poindexter, former chief of the U.S. National Security Council, tells Congress he authorized the use of money from Iran to provide aid to the contras.

July 22   Gorbachev declares Soviet willingness to join in the abolition of all intermediate-range missiles.

August 7   Presidents of Nicaragua, Costa Rica, El Salvador, Honduras, and Guatemala sign a peace agreement for Central America.

September 29   Gorbachev solves a mystery—and settles the nerves of many concerned persons—by reappearing after a prolonged absence from public view. He explains that he was writing a book, *Perestroika*.

October 21   After surprising the participants at the Central Commmittee's celebration of the 70th anniversary of the Bolshevik Revolution by criticizing first Gorbachev, then Gorbachev's associate Ligachev, Boris Yeltsin declares his wish to resign as a candidate (nonvoting) member of the Politburo and as party first secretary in Moscow.

November 2   In attacking the long-prevailing "administrative-command system" by which the Soviet economy has been run, Gorbachev declares that the "enormous and unforgivable" guilt of Stalin provides "a lesson for all generations."

In December 1987 General Secretary Mikhail Gorbachev of the Communist Party of the Soviet Union (l.) and President Ronald Reagan of the United States meet in a Washington summit. During the sessions they sign a treaty eliminating intermediate-range missiles.

November 11	At a meeting of the Moscow Communist Party Committee at which he is denounced by Gorbachev and others, Yeltsin is removed as first secretary of the committee.
November 18	Congressional Iran-Contra Committee criticizes President Reagan for failing to execute the law, as the U.S. Constitution requires.
November 23	U.S. and Soviet negotiators produce an agreement on a treaty to eliminate intermediate-range nuclear missiles, the Intermediate-Range Nuclear Forces (INF) Treaty.
December 7–10	President Reagan and General Secretary Gorbachev meet in a summit in Washington, during which they sign the INF Treaty. Gorbachev is acclaimed by American crowds; this phenomenon becomes known as Gorbymania.

1988

January 9	Backtracking in its antialcohol campaign, the Soviet government announces the opening of 200 new liquor stores in Moscow.
January 22	Conference on Security and Cooperation in Europe opens third follow-up session in Vienna.
February 8	General Secretary Gorbachev announces the planned withdrawal of Soviet troops from Afghanistan, to begin on May 15.
March 13	Opposition to Gorbachev is indicated by the publication in the press of a letter, written by a chemistry professor, Nina Andreyeva, but endorsed by several influential party leaders, that denounces Gorbachev's reformist moves as acts of betrayal of the Soviet heritage and attacks the reformers' "obsession" with Stalin.
March 14	Gorbachev arrives in Yugoslavia for a five-day visit; two days later he calls for an U.S.-Soviet freeze on Mediterranean naval forces.
March 17	United States and the Soviet Union set up a joint group to monitor military incidents to prevent their escalation.
March 31	U.S. Senate approves $47.9 million in aid to Nicaraguan contras, including $17.7 million in humanitarian aid.
April 10	Soviet general secretary Gorbachev proposes limitations on tactical nuclear weapons and pledges the USSR to destroy all chemical weapons.
May 8	François Mitterrand is reelected president of France in second-round balloting.
May 11	In a move emblematic of glasnost, the Soviet journal *Literaturnaya Gazeta* publishes excerpts from *Nineteen Eighty-four,* George Orwell's 1949 fictional depiction of life in a totalitarian state.
	Kim Philby, the most famous spy produced by the Cold War, dies in Moscow.
May 15	Soviet troops begin their withdrawal from Afghanistan, in accordance with an agreement signed in April in Geneva.
May 22	Károly Grósz succeeds János Kádár as general secretary of the Hungarian Communist Party.
May 27	U.S. Senate votes approval of the Intermediate-Range Nuclear Forces (INF) Treaty.

May 29	General Secretary Gorbachev and President Reagan begin a three-day summit meeting in Moscow; INF-treaty ratification is confirmed.
June 3	In a news conference—a rare event in the USSR—Soviet dissident Andrei Sakharov attacks the government's suppression of human rights.
June 9	In Nicaragua, cease-fire negotiations between the government and the contras end in failure.
June 21	Canada announces the expulsion of 17 Soviet diplomatic personnel for industrial espionage; the USSR counters with action against five Canadians.
June 25	Ministers of the European Community and Comecon announce mutual recognition.
June 28	At a Communist Party of the Soviet Union conference in Moscow, General Secretary Gorbachev presents a plan for a new administrative structure of the government. The new system calls for a powerful presidency and a new parliament, the Congress of People's Deputies.
July 1	Communist Party of the Soviet Union conference votes support of perestroika.
July 11	Nicaraguan government expels eight U.S. diplomats, including the ambassador, for alleged incitement of antigovernment acts; U.S. takes reciprocal action the next day.
July 16	Warsaw Pact leaders call for reduction of conventional forces in Europe, to be accomplished in three stages.
July 29	Gorbachev announces the scheduling of elections to the Congress of People's Deputies for March 1989, with election of the president to follow in April.
August 21	Popular demonstrations in Moscow and Prague mark the 20th anniversary of the Warsaw Pact invasion of Czechoslovakia to crush the Prague Spring; police disperse the demonstrators.
August 31	After meeting with the Polish interior minister, Solidarity leader Lech Wałesa calls for workers to end the current wave of industrial strikes.
September 16	Gorbachev proposes a naval freeze in the Pacific area, with Soviets to evacuate Cam Ranh Bay base in Vietnam (built by the United States) and U.S. forces to evacuate the Philippines.
September 26	In the face of continuing economic problems, Mieczyslaw Rakowski becomes prime minister of Poland.

September 30	At a meeting of the Central Committee of the Communist Party of the Soviet Union, the retirement is announced of the veteran diplomat Andrei Gromyko, who has been serving as president; Yegor Ligachev, previously a close Gorbachev adviser, is demoted. The next day Gorbachev is elected president in succession to Gromyko.
October 4	Interesting signal for Kremlin watchers: when Romanian president Ceauşescu arrives in Moscow for an official visit, President Gorbachev is not at the airport to welcome him.
October 11	Ladislav Adamec succeeds Lubomír Strougal as premier of Czechoslovakia.
October 12	Twenty-six members of the Red Brigades are given life sentences for involvement in the 1978 murder of Italian statesman Aldo Moro.
October 20	Soviet dissident Andrei Sakharov is elected to the Presidium of the USSR Academy of Sciences.
November 1	USSR and China announce the conclusion of a boundary agreement.
November 2	British prime minister Margaret Thatcher begins a visit to Poland; she will meet with Solidarity leader Lech Wałesa.
November 7	Visiting the United States, Soviet dissident Andrei Sakharov declares that Western countries should support Soviet president Gorbachev's policy of perestroika.
November 8	U.S. voters choose Republican Vice President George H. W. Bush as president in succession to Reagan over the Democratic governor of Massachusetts, Michael Dukakis. The Democrats make gains in both the Senate and the House of Representatives. Bush defeats Dukakis with 426 electoral votes to 111; the popular vote is 48.8 million to 41.8 million.
November 16	Estonian Soviet republic declares itself sovereign, with the right to veto Soviet laws.
December 7	In a speech to the UN General Assembly, Soviet president Gorbachev announces that the USSR will reduce its armed forces by 500,000 men and will also reduce the numbers of conventional armaments.
December 29	Soviet government orders the names of deceased leaders Brezhnev and Chernenko removed from all towns and other entities. The next day General Yuri Churbanov, Brezhnev's son-in-law, is sentenced to 12 years' imprisonment for corruption; others on trial also go to prison.

1989

January 4	U.S. fighters shoot down two Libyan MiG-23s over the Mediterranean about 70 miles north of the coast. The U.S. pilots say the MiGs had launched a deliberate attack.
January 11	Hungarian study commission reports that the 1956 revolution was a genuine uprising, not a counterrevolution staged by foreign agencies. The Hungarian Parliament passes legislation giving private citizens the right, with some conditions, to form political parties.
	Leaders of the government and Communist Party of Montenegro respond to hostile demonstrations by resigning en masse.
January 15	Using clubs, dogs, and water cannon, Czech police attack Prague demonstrators commemorating the self-immolation 20 years earlier of the student Jan Palach, who was protesting the Soviet invasion. Rallies continue, with crowds calling for free elections and the release from jail of the leading Czech dissident, playwright Václav Havel, arrested during the demonstrations.
January 18	Parliament of Estonia adopts legislation whereby Estonian becomes the official language of this Soviet republic; those who speak other languages must learn Estonian within four years. This move symbolizes local resistance to Russification efforts by the government of the USSR. In the following months other Soviet republics will pass similar laws.
January 19	Prime Minister Jaruzelski's government publishes a Polish Communist Party resolution calling for negotiations leading to the legalization of unions, including Solidarity; the resolution apparently wins adoption only over the strenuous opposition of many Central Committee members. The stimulus for the measure is the desperate state of the Polish economy.
January 20	George Bush takes office as the 41st president of the United States.
January 25	President José Duarte of El Salvador rebuffs an offer by Marxist guerrilla forces to take part in the March presidential election, because of numerous conditions demanded by the guerrillas.
February 3	Government of Czechoslovakia announces that Soviet troops are to leave the country.

February 14	Sandinista government of Nicaragua pledges to hold free elections in February 1990. The presidents of other Central American countries produce a plan for relocating contra forces after their bases are closed.
February 15	Last Soviet troops leave Afghanistan, ending the "Soviet Union's Vietnam."
February 18	In a striking move, a Polish government report blames the Soviets, not the Germans, for the World War II Katyn Forest Massacre of Polish officers in 1939 (a verdict acknowledged in 1992 by the Russian government).
February 21	Instead of releasing him, Czechoslovak government sentences Václav Havel to nine months' imprisonment for inciting illegal popular protests.
February 23	Indonesia and China move to restore diplomatic relations, broken in 1967 when the Indonesians accused the Chinese of involvement in an attempted 1965 coup.
February 26	Chinese police cause an international stir by keeping a leading dissident, Fang Lizhi, an astrophysicist, from attending a banquet at which U.S. president Bush is not only present but is the host. Fang later receives asylum in the U.S. embassy.
February 28	In testimony to the U.S. Senate Intelligence Committee, Richard Kerr, deputy director of the Central Intelligence Agency, says that Gorbachev-led reforms in the USSR may be long-lasting. There follows a public debate between the agency and the Defense Department over the true importance of the reforms.
March 6	In an important sign of the times—and of President Gorbachev's outlook—a spokesman for the Soviet Foreign Ministry repudiates the 1968 Brezhnev Doctrine, declaring that the future of every Eastern European country is "in its own hands."
March 12	Huge crowd in Riga, the capital of Latvia, calls for recognition of Latvian as the leading language of this Soviet republic. Some members of the crowd urge independence from the USSR.
March 15	In another part of the Eastern Bloc, thousands of Hungarians expand ceremonies commemorating the 1848 uprising against Austria into protest marches against the Communist government.
March 17	Richard Cheney receives U.S. Senate confirmation as President Reagan's secretary of defense, ending a political battle that saw the Senate reject Reagan's earlier choice for the post, former senator John Tower.

March 19	Right-wing candidate Alfredo Cristiani wins election as president of El Salvador.
March 26	In a long step toward democracy, Soviet citizens elect the members of the new Congress of People's Deputies. Some expected winners in Moscow, Leningrad, and elsewhere are defeated (a revolutionary development in Soviet history); among the important winners is President Gorbachev's foe Boris Yeltsin, who receives 90 percent of the vote in his Moscow race.
April 2	Visiting Fidel Castro's Havana, Gorbachev limits himself to generalities about Soviet relations with Cuba.
April 5	Government of Vietnam announces plans to end the occupation of Cambodia (Kampuchea), which began in 1979.
	In negotiations between Polish government officials and leaders of the trade union Solidarity headed by Lech Wałesa, participants work out an agreement whereby the union will regain the legal status it lost in 1982 and will be allowed to field candidates for 35 percent of the seats in the lower house of the legislature (the Sejm); the agreement is signed on April 7.
April 6	Soviet government rescinds laws dating from the 1960s that restrict the exercise of religion.
April 9	In dispersing demonstrators in Tbilisi, Georgia, Soviet troops, using poison gas and clubs, kill 19 and wound many more.
April 13	Anticipating the winding down of fighting in Nicaragua, the U.S. Congress votes almost $50 million in nonmilitary aid (food, medicine, and the like) to the contras.
April 17	Expressing approval of the Polish government's decision to allow free elections, President Bush announces a U.S. economic-aid program for Poland.
April 22	Crowds building up for several days in Tiananmen Square in Beijing reach a total of more than 100,000. Honoring the memory of Hu Yaobang, a reformer who sympathized with pro-democracy activities (and who died just a week earlier), the demonstrators also call for increased political freedoms and refuse to leave the square; a siege ensues.
April 25	Soviet president Gorbachev and his Central Committee supporters remove 110 obstructionist "dead souls" from their positions on the committee and the Central Auditing Commission.
	In a symbolic move, the USSR begins making good on its plan to reduce its military presence in Eastern Europe by removing a group of tanks from Hungary.

April 27	Appearing on Hungarian television, Alexander Dubček, who had been Czechoslovak Communist Party head during the 1968 Prague Spring, accuses Leonid Brezhnev of having deceived him before launching the Soviet-led invasion that crushed the movement toward liberalization.
May 2	Hungarian authorities begin dismantling the barbed-wire Iron Curtain along the country's border with Austria.
May 12	U.S. president Bush, who has seemed to act slowly in response to Soviet president Gorbachev's overtures, declares he will move beyond the containment policy instituted during the Truman administration.
May 14	Arriving in Beijing for a visit with Deng Xiaoping, the de facto ruler of China, Soviet president Gorbachev is acclaimed by demonstrators in Tiananmen Square.
May 17	Polish Parliament ends the Communist government's long struggle with the Roman Catholic Church by adopting a law giving legal status to the church.
May 18	Czechoslovak authorities release Václav Havel from prison after he has served four months of his sentence; he declares he will continue to speak out against the government.
May 20	Three days after the crowds in Tiananmen Square reach an estimated one million, Premier Li Peng declares martial law in Beijing. Citizens of the city hamper troops in their move from the outskirts to the square.
May 25	By a large majority, the Congress of People's Deputies elects Mikhail Gorbachev president of the Soviet Union.
May 30	Students in Tiananmen Square set up a statue of the "Goddess of Democracy," 30 feet high; the figure bears a provocative resemblance to the Statue of Liberty in New York harbor.
June 2	President Bush appoints former child movie star Shirley Temple Black U.S. ambassador to Czechoslovakia; she earlier served in the U.S. delegation to the UN General Assembly.
	Sosuke Uno succeeds Noboru Takeshita as Japanese premier; Takeshita resigned in the wake of the so-called Recruit scandal, involving bribery.
June 3	Ayatollah Khomeini, the spiritual and political master of Iran, dies.
June 4	Chinese Communist troops with tanks attack demonstrators in Tiananmen Square. Thousands are shot or crushed to death in the ensuing massacre, which evokes protests from nations around the world.

In Poland, the Solidarity trade union wins a strong majority of the votes in the first round of parliamentary elections. Even though the April agreement limits the number of seats Solidarity representatives can occupy, this victory represents a striking advance toward greater freedom for Poles.

June 15

On a visit to West Germany, Soviet president Gorbachev, in speaking of the Berlin Wall, declares that "nothing is eternal in this world."

During a visit to Warsaw, French president Mitterrand announces a program of debt relief and loans for Poland.

June 16

In Budapest, the disinterred body of Imre Nagy, the premier executed for his role in the 1956 Hungarian Revolution, receives the equivalent of a state funeral. This act of mea culpa by the government is the occasion of strong antigovernment speeches.

June 20

In response to the Tiananmen Square massacre, the U.S. government cancels meetings between U.S. and Chinese officials.

June 22

Cease-fire agreement in Angola offers hope that the civil war, which began in 1975, may come to an end.

July 7

Gorbachev tells participants in a Warsaw Pact summit in Bucharest that pact members have the freedom to choose their own road to socialism.

July 9

U.S. president Bush arrives for a visit in Poland, and on July 10, in a cautious speech to the Polish Parliament, he offers $100 million in direct aid, far short of the hoped-for three-year $10 billion program. Later Bush calls on Solidarity to work with the Communist Party.

July 19

Polish Parliament elects General Jaruzelski president.

July 22

Giulio Andreotti, a Christian Democrat, becomes premier of Italy; this will be his sixth time in office.

July 25

Lech Wałesa declares that Solidarity will not enter a coalition with the Communists.

July 29

President Jaruzelski resigns as Polish Communist Party leader and is succeeded by a close associate, Premier Mieczyslaw Rakowski, who opposes Solidarity.

August 7

United States objects to the declaration by five Central American presidents that the Nicaraguan contras must be disbanded by December 8.

August 12	Chinese government moves toward greater indoctrination of students in Communist principles by declaring that graduates must serve in factories and other nonacademic settings before carrying on further study.
August 18	Czechoslovak government announces its objection to a Polish government statement condemning the Warsaw Pact invasion of Czechoslovakia 20 years earlier; three days later a Soviet spokesman declares the 1968 invasion to quell the Prague Spring must be seen in the context of its time.
August 22	In an important move, Soviet president Gorbachev, in a telephone call, urges the Polish Communist leadership to join a coalition led by Solidarity.
	Lithuanian Parliament declares the country's annexation in 1940 by the USSR to be void.
August 23	People of the Baltic republics—Latvia, Lithuania, and Estonia—observe the 50th anniversary of the 1939 Nazi-Soviet pact and display their continuing nationalism and resentment of the central Soviet government by forming a human chain across the three states.
August 24	Tadeusz Mazowiecki, a close adviser of Lech Wałesa during the formative years of Solidarity, becomes the first non-Communist premier in Eastern Europe since the late 1940s, and the Polish Communist Party also becomes the first Eastern Bloc Communist Party ever voted out of office.
September 2	In Nicaragua, the coalition called the National Opposition Union selects Violeta de Chamorro as its presidential candidate in the campaign against the Sandinistas.
September 4	For a meeting that will be marked by the expression of moderate views, representatives of the nonaligned nations convene in Belgrade.
September 10	Opening the border with Austria, the government of Hungary declares its willingness for the country to serve as a passageway between East and West Germany for East Germans who wish to move to the other Germany.
September 12	In a situation appearing to call for a measure of diplomatic delicacy, U.S. president Bush does not receive the visiting Boris Yeltsin (no admirer of Soviet president Gorbachev) in the Oval Office but meets him elsewhere.
September 25	Speaking before the UN General Assembly, President Bush urges the abandonment of chemical weapons.
September 26	Last Vietnamese troops leave Cambodia.

October 7	Soviet president Gorbachev, visiting East Germany, advises party leader Erich Honecker to move toward reform.
	Renaming itself the Hungarian Socialist Party, the Hungarian Communist Party abandons Leninism.
October 16	Large East German crowds, demonstrating in Leipzig, call for governmental reforms.
October 18	East German Communist Party dismisses Erich Honecker, its general secretary since 1971; Egon Krenz, head of the security police, succeeds him as general secretary and chief of state.
	Hungarian Parliament adopts extensive liberalizing constitutional revisions, including the removal of *People's* from the name of the republic.
October 23	In East Berlin, demonstrators numbering some 300,000 call for greater political freedom, including the right to establish opposition parties.
October 25	Though Yugoslavia is not within the orbit of the Kremlin, its Communist Party follows the liberalizing trend by declaring its support for individual freedoms and other democratic rights.
	A popular singer and song enter the politico-diplomatic lexicon when a Soviet spokesman rephrases a Gorbachev declaration about the satellite states to make it the "Sinatra Doctrine"—they will "do it their way."
October 27	In an attempt to quell spreading unrest, police in Prague arrest Václav Havel and other prominent dissidents.
	Warsaw Pact powers declare that each member state has the right to choose its own course and members may not interfere in each other's internal affairs.
October 28	Taking heart from the liberalization occurring in neighboring countries, thousands of demonstrators in Prague call for an end to Communist rule; heavily armed police crush the demonstrations.
November 1	East German government orders the opening of the country's border with Czechoslovakia, a move that brings an immediate rise in emigration.
	President Ortega of Nicaragua announces the ending of the cease-fire his government earlier ordered against the contras.
November 7	In the quickening pace of events in Central and Eastern Europe, East German premier Willi Stoph and his ministers resign; the next day, a majority of the members of the Communist Party Politburo follow suit.

November 9–10	Berlin Wall falls. Hundreds of thousands of East Germans take advantage of the lifting of restrictions on travel to the West by crossing through the wall to sample life in West Germany. Crowds begin dismantling the wall itself. Cautiously, not wishing to raise any problems for Soviet president Gorbachev, U.S. president Bush says (more than once), "I'm not going to dance on the Berlin Wall."
November 10	Interrupting a visit to Poland because of the "dramatic situation" that has arisen in Berlin, West German chancellor Helmut Kohl takes time to sign an agreement proffering Poland $1.9 billion in aid, the largest amount yet pledged by any Western country. Todor Zhivkov, veteran dictator of Bulgaria, joins the swelling procession of resigned Communist officials by yielding his posts as president and general secretary of the party.
November 15	Speaking before the U.S. Congress, Lech Wałesa asks for more economic aid to help Poland build democracy.
November 16	Although Gorbachev has not resisted the tide of events in Eastern Europe, he declares that the Soviet Union is not ready at home to support the institution of private property or the establishment of rival political parties. In San Salvador, a squad wearing army uniforms shoots six Jesuit priests, bringing expressions of outrage from members of the U.S. Congress together with threats to stop aid to the Salvadoran government.
November 17	In Prague, what will become known as the Velvet Revolution begins with a huge demonstration organized by students; savage police attacks fail to stop the protests, which continue during the following days.
November 19	Participants in a rally in Prague form a new antigovernment coalition called Civic Forum, headed by Václav Havel.
November 21	Czechoslovak government officials are forced to begin talks with opposition leaders, including representatives of Civic Forum.
November 24	In response to the mounting antigovernment pressures, Czechoslovak Communist Party general secretary Miloš Jakeš resigns, as do many of his subordinates. Ignoring developments in the countries around them, delegates to the congress of the Romanian Communist Party unanimously reelect President Nicolae Ceauşescu to the party secretaryship. It will be his last triumph.
November 26	In the first free election since the establishment of the Communist state, Hungarians vote on the date of the next presidential election.

November 28	Czechoslovak Communist Party officials implicitly acknowledge the victory of the opposition by reluctantly pledging to surrender their 41-year monopolistic political control and agreeing to remove Marxism-Leninism as a compulsory course in universities.
December 1	Pope John Paul II, who has exerted great influence on developments in Poland, is host to Soviet president Mikhail Gorbachev in a meeting at the Vatican. During his visit to Italy, Gorbachev declares that the Czechoslovak reform movement was right in 1968 and is right in 1989.
	Somewhat belatedly, the East German government denounces the 1968 Warsaw Pact invasion of Czechoslovakia.
December 2	Presidents Gorbachev and Bush meet (till December 4) in the "seasick summit" on shipboard off Malta. The conference is highlighted by what amounts to the declaration by the two leaders that the Cold War is over.
December 3	After holding his positions only a little more than six weeks, Egon Krenz, together with all other top East German Communist Party officials, resigns. Ready for the end of the regime, crowds call for the abolition of the party.
December 4	Final word on the 1968 invasion of Czechoslovakia is spoken when the Soviet Union and its allies in the Warsaw Pact issue a statement condemning it and pledging noninterference in each other's affairs.
December 5	Erich Honecker and several of his former associates are detained under house arrest.
December 7	Czech premier Ladislav Adamec resigns in response to demands of the anti-Communist coalition called Civic Forum.
December 10	Czech president Gustáv Husák, a veteran Communist hard-liner, swears in the first cabinet since 1948 without a Communist majority and then resigns.
December 18	Many Americans express anger at President Bush in response to news that his emissary, General Brent Scowcroft, engaged in secret negotiations with China only a month after the Tiananmen Square massacre; announced U.S. policy banned all high-level meetings between the two countries.
December 20	In the early-morning hours, U.S. forces invade Panama (Operation Just Cause) in a proclaimed search for dictator Manuel Noriega.
December 25	Romanian firing squad executes hated President Nicolae Ceauşescu and his wife after a popular tribunal convicts them of genocide and

other crimes. The pair fled an uprising on December 22 and are said to have been captured the following day.

December 28   With an eye on history, the Czechoslovak Federal Assembly chooses as its chairman the former party first secretary Alexander Dubček, expelled from the party in 1969 for presiding over the Prague Spring of 1968. In making this choice, the assembly is acting in accordance with an agreement between Dubček and Václav Havel.

December 29   Czechoslovak Federal Assembly tops off this incredible year by choosing the longtime dissident Václav Havel as president of the Republic, pending an election to take place in 1990.

AFTERMATH: THE DISSOLUTION OF THE SOVIET UNION

1990

January 10   Soviet president Gorbachev begins discussions in Vilnius, Lithuania, where the Communist Party has declared itself independent of the Soviet party and the country is moving toward independence.

January 20   Reform groups in the Communist Party of the Soviet Union call for faster progress toward political pluralism.

March 11   Republic of Lithuania, annexed by the USSR in 1940, declares its independence; Gorbachev rejects the move and attempts to retain control of the political situation.

March 15   Central Committee of the Communist Party of the Soviet Union agrees to an amendment to the Soviet constitution whereby the party gives up its long-established "leading role" in the state. At the same session, a new and powerful presidency is established for the USSR, with Mikhail Gorbachev elected to fill it.

May 4   Parliament of Latvia declares independence from the USSR; as he did in the case of Lithuania, Gorbachev denounces the action.

May 29   Boris Yeltsin wins election as chairman of the democratically elected Supreme Soviet of the Russian Republic.

May 30   Gorbachev and U.S. president Bush begin a summit in Washington; during his stay, which will last until June 4, Gorbachev will travel across the country.

June 8	Yeltsin's Russian Parliament declares that Russian law now has primacy over Soviet law.
July 2	During the ten-day 28th Congress of the Communist Party of the Soviet Union, President Gorbachev manages to retain control. On July 12, however, Russian leader Yeltsin, continuing to display what seems to be his accurate sense of the future, resigns from the Soviet Communist Party.
August 8	*Pravda* publishes the draft of a new official and perestroika-oriented program for the Communist Party of the Soviet Union; the program was adopted at the July Central Committee plenum, the last such meeting ever held. On the basis of what they described as the lessons of history, the drafters of the document declared forthrightly that "the tragedy of our society was that the initial work of building socialism was distorted and burdened down to the extreme by mistakes, despotism, and crude perversions of the principles of socialism and popular rule."
October 3	The division of Germany comes to an end as East and West Germany reunite.
November 19	NATO and the Warsaw Pact countries sign the Conventional Forces in Europe (CFE-I) Treaty.
November 23	Attempting to hold the USSR together, President Gorbachev advocates adoption of the new Treaty of the Union, which calls for a federation looser than the existing system.
December 20	Soviet foreign minister Eduard Shevardnadze, a close Gorbachev ally, creates a sensation not only in Moscow but around the world by suddenly announcing his resignation, declaring "a dictatorship is approaching."

1991

January 2–13	Increasing Soviet intervention in Lithuania climaxes in a battle at the Vilnius TV tower in which 13 people are killed.
January 14	Speaking amid contending forces, Soviet president Gorbachev declares he did not know of government intentions to use force in Vilnius.
January 16	In the Persian Gulf area, U.S. troops and allies begin UN-sanctioned Operation Desert Storm against Iraq.
January 20	Soviet troops kill four people in Riga.

February 19	In a televised speech, Russian leader Boris Yeltsin calls for Soviet president Gorbachev's resignation.
March 17	Soviet people vote to adopt President Gorbachev's Union Treaty.
March 31	The Warsaw Pact officially ceases to exist.
June 12	Yeltsin receives a striking mandate by winning popular election as president of the Russian Republic.
July 29	In the Kremlin, Soviet president Gorbachev and U.S. president Bush sign the Strategic Arms Reduction (START) agreement.
August 19	Hard-line members of President Gorbachev's government (calling themselves the State Committee for the State of Emergency in the USSR) stage a putsch, placing the president under house arrest in the Crimea and claiming to establish a temporary regime devoted to national unity and restoration; this move interferes with the signing of the Union Treaty, the mechanism by which Gorbachev has hoped to preserve the Soviet Union. On the same day, Russian president Boris Yeltsin declares the new government illegal and openly defies it. The coup collapses. By August 22, Gorbachev has returned to Moscow, only to resign on August 25 as general secretary of the discredited Communist Party of the Soviet Union.
November 6	President Yeltsin abolishes the Communist Party in Russia and confiscates its property.
December 1	Voters in the Ukraine choose independence from the Soviet Union.
December 3	Soviet president Gorbachev calls for maintenance of the USSR; Russian president Yeltsin recognizes Ukraine as an independent state.
December 8	Russia, Ukraine, and Belarus sign an agreement creating the Commonwealth of Independent States as successor to the Soviet Union.
December 25	Mikhail Gorbachev resigns as president of the now-defunct Soviet Union.

Index

NOTE: Page numbers in boldface indicate main discussion. Page numbers in italics indicate maps or photographs.

Illustration Credits

Pp. xviii–xix: Gyula Pauer; p. 2: U.S. Army Military History Institute; p. 3: U.S. Department of State, courtesy Harry S. Truman Library; p. 4: German Information Center; p. 16: National Park Services—Abbie Rowd, courtesy Harry S. Truman Library; p. 19 (both photos): U.S. Air Force Museum; p. 20: U.S. Air Force Museum; p. 21: U.S. Air Force Museum; p. 26: Gyula Pauer; p. 28: German Information Center; p. 30: Owen Franken—German Information Center; p. 32: George C. Marshall Research Library; p. 33: French Embassy; p. 38: UN Photo 183619 / M. Grant; p. 39: German Information Center; p. 42: National Archives; p. 47: Ronald Reagan Library; p. 49: University of Kentucky Special Collections; p. 52: French Embassy; p. 54: Jimmy Carter Library; p. 60: German Information Center; p. 64: Reprinted by permission of the Winston Churchill Memorial and Library, Westminster College, Fulton, Missouri; p. 66: U.S. Army Military History Institute; p. 69: U.S. Air Force Museum; p. 74: U.S. Air Force Museum; p. 76: Gyula Pauer; p. 80: French Embassy; p. 89: University of Kentucky Special Collections; p. 92: Franklin D. Roosevelt Library; p. 94: University of Kentucky Special Collections; p. 97: German Information Center; p. 101: U.S. Air Force Museum; p. 102: U.S. Air Force Museum; p. 103: U.S. Air Force Museum; p. 104: German Information Center; p. 115: French Embassy; p. 117: Yoichi R. Okamoto, LBJ Library Collection; p. 120: Ronald Reagan Library; p. 124: Yoichi R. Okamoto, LBJ Library Collection; p. 129: U.S. Army Military History Institute; p. 130: United Nations; p. 132: Franklin D. Roosevelt Library; p. 133: Embassy of the Czech Republic; p. 134: British Information Services; p. 139: German Information Center; p. 140: Yoichi R. Okamoto, LBJ Library Collection; p. 146: U.S. Air Force Museum; p. 148: Gyula Pauer; p. 149: Reprinted by permission of the Winston Churchill Memorial and Library, Westminster College, Fulton, Missouri; p. 155: Yoichi R. Okamoto, LBJ Library Collection; p. 162: George C. Marshall Research Library; p. 165: John F. Kennedy Library; p. 173: National Archives; p. 176: Gyula Pauer; p. 177: National Archives; p. 178: Yoichi R. Okamoto, LBJ Library Collection; p. 183: National Archives; p. 184: United Nations; p. 188: George C. Marshall Research Library; p. 193: U.S. Army Military History Institute; p. 197: Yoichi R. Okamoto, LBJ Library Collection; p. 200: Yoichi R. Okamoto, LBJ Library Collection; p. 207: National Park Services—Abbie Rowd, courtesy Harry S. Truman Library; p. 212: French Embassy; p. 215: U.S. Air Force Museum; p. 216: Cecil Stoughton, LBJ Library Collection; p. 218: French Embassy; p. 220: Franklin D. Roosevelt Library; p. 221: French Embassy; p. 229: University of Kentucky Special Collections; p. 235: Hearst Newspaper Collection, Special Collections, University of Southern California Library; p. 237: Richard Nixon Library & Birthplace, Yorba Linda, California 92686; p. 240: Gyula Pauer; p. 251: United Nations; p. 256: U.S. Army, courtesy Harry S. Truman Library; p. 268: Ronald Reagan Library; p. 269: U.S. Army Military History Institute; p. 275: Yoichi R. Okamoto, LBJ Library Collection; p. 278: Jimmy Carter Library; p. 281: German Information Center; p. 282: German Information Center; p. 283: French Embassy; p. 287: U.S. Army Military History Institute; p. 292: U.S. Air Force Museum; p. 294: Franklin D. Roosevelt Library; p. 295: National Archives; p. 300: Ronald Reagan Library; p. 301: Gyula Pauer; p. 306: U.S. Army Military History Institute; p. 309: UN Photo 92603 / Y. Nagata; p. 310: British Information Services; p. 316: National Park Services—Abbie Rowd, courtesy Harry S. Truman Library; p. 318: U.S. Air Force Museum;

Illustration Credits